Restructuring and Privatization in Central Eastern Europe

THE MICROECONOMICS OF TRANSITION ECONOMIES

Series Editor: Josef C. Brada
Arizona State University

The hallmark of this series is its focus not on macroeconomic theory or ideological questions but on financial issues and the behavior of firms and enterprises in economies undergoing transition from socialist to capitalist forms of organization.

FIRMS AFLOAT AND FIRMS ADRIFT
Hungarian Industry and Economic Transition

Josef C. Brada, Inderjit Singh, and Adam Török

RESTRUCTURING AND PRIVATIZATION IN CENTRAL EASTERN EUROPE
Case Studies of Firms in Transition

Edited by
Saul Estrin, Josef C. Brada, Alan Gelb, and Inderjit Singh

RESTRUCTURING AND PRIVATIZATION IN CENTRAL EASTERN EUROPE

Case Studies of Firms in Transition

Saul Estrin
Josef C. Brada
Alan Gelb
Inderjit Singh

M.E. Sharpe
Armonk, New York
London, England

Copyright © 1995 by M. E. Sharpe, Inc.

All rights reserved. No part of this book may be reproduced in any form
without written permission from the publisher, M. E. Sharpe, Inc.,
80 Business Park Drive, Armonk, New York 10504.

Library of Congress Cataloging-in-Publication Data

Restructuring and privatization in Central Eastern Europe :
case studies of firms in transition / edited by Saul Estrin . . . [et al.].
    p. cm. — (Microeconomics of transition economies)
    Includes bibliographical references and index.
    ISBN 1-56324-611-2 (alk. paper)
    1. Privatization—Czechoslovakia—Case studies.
    2. Privatization—Hungary—Case studies.
    3. Privatization—Poland—Case studies.
4. Structural adjustment (Economic policy)—Czechoslovakia—Case studies.
  5. Structural adjustment (Economic policy)—Hungary—Case studies.
   6. Structural adjustment (Economic policy)—Poland—Case studies.
    7. Europe, Eastern—Economic policy—1989–
    8. Industries—Europe, Eastern.
    I. Estrin, Saul.
    II. Series.
    HD4160.3.R47 1995
    338.943—dc20
          95-3493
            CIP

Printed in the United States of America

The paper used in this publication meets the minimum requirements of
American National Standard for Information Sciences—
Permanence of Paper for Printed Library Materials,
ANSI Z 39.48-1984.

| BM (c) | 10 | 9 | 8 | 7 | 6 | 5 | 4 | 3 | 2 | 1 |
| BM (p) | 10 | 9 | 8 | 7 | 6 | 5 | 4 | 3 | 2 | 1 |

Pope, 22, 64
Ptolemäus, 38

Raynaud, 241
Reinhard, A. F., 64, 93
Ritter, P., 38
Riolon, 40
Russel, 24

Saame, 49, 59, 320
Sartre, 12, 14 f.
Scheler, 139, 209
Schelling, 24, 31, 141 f., 267, 349
Schepers, 82
Schiller, 243
Schmitz, G., 260
Schrecker, 144
Sophie Charlotte, 43, 278
Sortais, 140
Sparfvenfelt, v., 20
Specht, R., 246
Spinoza, Spinozisten, 21, 25, 52, 55, 64, 89 f., 98, 129, 207 f., 210 ff., 217, 228, 241, 313 f., 318 f., 356, 371
Stammler, 37
Stein, 24, 41, 43, 64, 180
Stoa, 9, 53
Straton, 55
Suisset, 44

Teilhard de Chardin, 71
Telesio, 55
Thomas von Aquin, 110 ff., 196, 239
Toland, 267
Topitsch, 361 f.
Torricelli, 144
Trendelenburg, 66, 266
Tugendhat, 12
Turenne, 275

Uffenbach, v., 44
Uslar, v., 98

Valerianus Magnus, 44
Vaucanson, 26
Virgil, 286
Voltaire, 22, 41, 62, 69, 270 f., 315

Walch, 280, 295 f.
Wiclef, 89, 119
Wittichius, 333
Wolff, Chr., Wolffianer, 21, 87, 228, 325 f., 334
Wolff, H. M., 29, 370
Wundt, M., 326

Zimmermann, 46
Zocher, 326

Contents

List of Abbreviations	viii
Preface and Acknowledgments	ix
An Introduction to the Case-Study Project *Saul Estrin, Josef C. Brada, Alan Gelb, and Inderjit Singh*	xi

Part I. Case Studies of Czech and Slovak Firms

1. Engineering/Forklift Trucks: Desta
   Jaroslav Jirasek — 3

2. Engineering: PSP
   Jana Matesová — 16

3. Heavy Chemicals: Spolana
   Martin Sauer — 33

4. Textiles/Garments: CS-15
   Jana Matesová — 48

5. Textiles/Cloth: Veba Broumov
   Jana Matesová — 58

6. Electronics: CS-03
   Rudolf Galik — 73

7. Food Processing/Chocolate and Sweets: CS-07
   Rudolf Galik — 88

8. Footwear: Tipa
   Jaroslav Jirasek and Ilja Mracek — 104

9. Plastics: CS-13
   Jan Pavek — 115

10. Pharmaceuticals: CS-12
    Alena Očková — 127

11. Auto Parts: Motorpal
    Jaroslav Jirasek, Vratislav Svoboda, and Tomas Varcop   136

Part II. Case Studies of Hungarian Firms

1. Engineering: DKG
   Judit Zsarnay   155

2. Defense: Theta Works
   Gábor Karsai   164

3. Heavy Chemicals: TVK
   Miklós Szanyi   174

4. Textiles/Garments: Elegant Charm
   László Toth   182

5. Textiles/Cloth: Hungartextile Holding
   Márta Kiefer   191

6. Electronics: Radion Radio and Electrical Works
   Gábor Hoványi   199

7. Glass: Salgglas
   Miklós Somai   212

8. Food Processing/Chocolate and Sweets: Intercsokoládé Kft.
   Lilli Berkó   222

9. Food Processing/Brewing: Kanizsa Brewery Ltd.
   Judit Zsarnay   231

10. Pharmaceuticals: EGIS Pharmaceutical Works Ltd.
    Judit Karsai   241

11. Auto Parts: Bakony Metal and Electrical Appliance Works
    Miklós Somai   252

Part III. Case Studies of Polish Firms

1. Engineering/Railway Rolling Stock: Pafawag Enterprise
   Stefan Krajewski   267

2. Engineering/Machine Tools: PO/5
   Stefan Krajewski   278

3. Textiles/Garments: Wolczanka S.A.
   Marek Belka — 291

4. Textiles/Cloth: Textilpol
   Marek Belka — 303

5. Electronics: Miflex Radio Components Firm S.A.
   Stefan Krajewski — 316

6. Glass: Huta Szkla Hortensja
   Marek Belka — 328

7. Food Processing/Chocolate and Sweets: Drops
   Marek Belka — 344

8. Wood Products: Lodzkie Fabryki Mebli
   Marek Belka — 357

9. Iron/Steel: Czestochowa Steelworks
   Stefan Krajewski — 371

10. White Goods—Refrigerators, Washers, and Dryers: Polar Enterprise
    Stefan Krajewski — 384

11. Footwear: Mokasyn
    Marek Belka — 397

12. Plastics: Boryszew-Erg
    Anna Krajewska — 409

13. Pharmaceuticals: Polfa Enterprise
    Anna Krajewska — 419

14. Auto Parts: Polmo Enterprise
    Anna Krajewska — 431

Index — 445

List of Abbreviations

CAD	Computer assisted/aided design
CAM	Computer assisted/aided manufacturing
CIM	Computer inventory management
CMEA	Council for Mutual Economic Assistance
CNC	Computer numerically controlled
COGS	Cost of goods sold
CSK	Czech and Slovak koruna
EBIT	Earnings before income tax
ESOP	Employee stock ownership plan
HUF	Hungarian forint
ISO	International Standards Office
MBO	Management buyout
PPWW	Excess wage tax
TIM	Total inventory management
TQM	Total quality management
ROA	Return on assets
ROE	Return on equity
SOE	State-owned enterprise
SPA	State property agency

Preface and Acknowledgments

This set of case studies of industrial firms in transition in the Czech and Slovak Republics, Hungary, and Poland is part of a larger World Bank research project entitled "Enterprise Behavior and Economic Reforms: A Comparative Study in Central and Eastern Europe" undertaken in the Transition Economics Division of the Policy Research Department of the World Bank.

The project is being carried out in close collaboration with a number of research institutions in both Eastern and Western Europe. The case studies were carried out by teams led and fielded by local research institutes: the Czech Management Center (CMC) at Čelakovice in the Czech Republic under the leadership of Jana Matesová; the Research Institute for Industrial Economics of the Janus Pannonius University, in Budapest, Hungary, with Adam Török as team leader; and the Department of Economics at the University of Lodz in Poland, with Marek Belka as team leader. In addition, several Western European research institutions, including the London Business School (LBS), the Center for Economic Performance at the London School of Economics (CEP-LSE) in the United Kingdom, Reformes et Ouvertures des Systemes Economiques Socialistes (ROSES) at the University of Paris in France, and Centro de Estudos Aplicados da Universidade Católica Portuguesa (UCP) in Lisbon, Portugal, participated in the planning, review, and write-up of the case studies.

The main funding for the case studies was provided by the Gabinete de Estudos e Planeamento (GEP), Ministerio da Industria e Energia, Lisbon, Portugal. I would like to thank Mr. Alberto Moreno, director of GEP for his support and encouragement for our work throughout and Dr. Jose Amado da Silva and his colleagues at UCP for their participation in the work. Additional support was provided by grants from the Ministry of Higher Education and Research and the Ministry of Industry through ROSES in Paris, France. I would like to thank Professor Xavier Richet (ROSES) and his colleagues for providing their support and for being such wonderful hosts for several meetings in Paris while the work was in progress. We gratefully acknowledge their generous support for the project.

I would like to thank the principal consultants on the project: Josef Brada (Arizona State University), Jan Svejnar (University of Pittsburgh), Mark Schaffer (Heriot-Watt University), and Saul Estrin (London Business School) for their participation in this phase of the research. Saul Estrin took the major role in organizing the write-up and the synthesis of the case-study materials. Robbie Brada assisted us with the thankless task of editing and re-editing the final materials.

Finally, I would like to thank Alan Gelb, chief, Transition Economics, who not only provided valuable guidance in outlining the approach and themes for the studies and participated throughout, but has been a constant source of support and encouragement to our work.

Inderjit Singh
Lead Economist
Transition Economics Division
Policy Research Department
World Bank

An Introduction to the Case-Study Project

Saul Estrin, Josef C. Brada, Alan Gelb, and Inderjit Singh

The growing literature on economic reform in the former socialist bloc highlights macroeconomic stabilization, liberalization, privatization, and institutional reform as the foundations of successful transition to a market economy. Many of the essential institutional reforms have been enacted or are under discussion; Poland, the former Czech and Slovak Federal Republic (CSFR), and especially Hungary, took the lead in this area.[1] While there has been considerable discussion of the mechanics of privatization (Estrin, 1994; Frydman et al., 1993), there is surprisingly little information on how the reforms have impacted on the economic behavior and choices of firms or how firms are responding to the new market environment. Moreover, although many observers accept that the effectiveness of enterprise adjustment holds the key to a successful transition from planning to markets (Kornai, 1990; Lipton and Sachs, 1990), the empirical literature on this subject is small.[2] An important explanation for this lacuna is the difficulty of obtaining reliable or consistent data at the enterprise level.[3] This is the gap that this volume seeks to fill by presenting a large number of cases that examine the behavior of state-owned enterprises (SOEs) in Central and Eastern Europe during the transition.

This volume contains edited versions of all the cases that are in the public domain from a case-study project coordinated by the World Bank and financed by the Portuguese Ministry of Industry and Energy. The project collected detailed qualitative and quantitative information concerning up to fifteen industrial manufacturing firms each in Poland, Hungary, and the former Czech and Slovak Federal Republic (CSFR). The firms were broadly matched by size and sector, and interest was confined to state-owned firms in industrial branches. Readers who study individual cases in detail will see that they contain a wealth of information on key aspects of company behavior as well as on marketing strategy, financial circumstances, organizational structure, governance, and managerial responses to the profound changes in the economic environment. Our purpose in this introductory chapter is to outline the framework behind the project, to explain the methodology, and to provide an interpretation of some key results.

In the absence of reliable panel data on firms in transition, the case-study method is the only one that allows us to analyze systematically the process of enterprise adjustment. However, there are inherent problems with such an exercise. The number of firms that can be covered is limited, so results are not based on a large representative sample. In the case-study project, the choice of firm was made after selecting sectors of industry according to predetermined criteria, and firms in these sectors were selected on the basis of personal contact and willingness to participate. Insofar as managerial willingness to participate in the project or contact with our field participants, who are business economists, reflects more dynamic management, our procedures may have biased the sample toward better firms in each country. Nevertheless, this source of bias should not apply to one country more than another, and our findings highlight differences between rather than within countries as the principal sources of diversity in the pattern of enterprise adjustment.

By its nature, the case-study method does not provide a representative sample, and our findings should not be interpreted as if it did. Instead, the cases provide a detailed snapshot of enterprise adjustment in a selection of firms that we have sought to make typical of their sector and country, and thereby to provide some qualitative and quantitative indicators of the emerging process of company restructuring.[4] Discretion is also required in interpreting the findings because the three countries differed significantly in their institutions, policies, and macroeconomic situations prior to reform.

The intellectual framework behind the project is the subject of the following section of this chapter, while the third section presents the general methodology, including selection criteria for participating firms. An attempt to analyze the major findings from the cases is contained in the fourth section, and conclusions are drawn in the fifth section.

THE FRAMEWORK

The diversity of firms within and between countries implies that a project that proposes to derive comparative results must formulate a common conceptual framework at the outset. This conceptual framework provided the basis for the common questionnaire that was applied in all 43 firms—15 each in Poland and Hungary and 13 in the CSFR.

The framework is summarized in Figure 1,* which starts with the initial conditions facing the firm, categorized according to the sector; the macroeconomic policy environment; and the specifics of microeconomic and institutional reform as it applies to the particular firm, including mode of privatization. Re-

---

*Tables and figures are gathered at the end of each chapter. See p. xxvii et seq.

form itself then entails a number of shocks to the firm's situation, categorized into four groups: managerial and financial autonomy; changes in product markets; the development of factor markets; and changes in ownership and managerial structures. Enterprises' responses to these changing circumstances are calibrated by the firm's financial situation and by the motivation and capabilities of the management. In particular, we are concerned to isolate and explain examples of perverse enterprise behavior, when for example companies react to declines in demand by continuing to produce for inventory or when managers and/or workers consume company assets. We can now consider each potential shock in more detail.

Managerial and Financial Autonomy

Managerial Autonomy

Before reform, enterprises were not really independent in terms of decision-making. Reform greatly widens the range of activities in which the firm is permitted to engage, and in the absence of effective ownership arrangements may greatly increase the autonomy of management or of an employee–manager coalition to make choices.

Financial Independence

The initial increase in managerial autonomy during the early phase of transition may be offset by increased constraints on managers and workers imposed by creditors and, ultimately, by new owners. Financial arrangements were passive under central planning and hardly more demanding under market socialism because *ex-post* subsidies or credits plus automatic cost-plus pricing rules relaxed enterprises' liquidity and solvency constraints. This softness of budget constraints was exacerbated at the macroeconomic level by a chronic tendency to excess demand.

In principle, reform introduces full financial accountability, including accountability to banks and trade creditors, and to owners when these are well defined. By implication, the specter of bankruptcy for insolvent firms is also raised. These factors should partially offset the increase in managerial autonomy or, at least, act to prevent perverse behavior by managers in response to reform initiatives.

Changes in Product Markets

After reforms, prices are freed for both outputs and material inputs, and international competition becomes a reality. In economies that were previously planned, direct horizontal supply relationships between sellers and customers begin to replace the inefficient mix of plan orders for material inputs and the centralized distribution of output and the semilegal or illegal market transactions undertaken to ensure plan fulfillment. In market socialist economies, the array of price regulations, trade and hard currency quotas, and investment credits along with inherent shortages that distort nascent inter-firm supplier relations are eliminated. The opening of markets introduces alternative sources of supply and new marketing opportunities.

The distortion of prices in prereform economies reflected the priorities of the communist regimes (Ellman, 1989). Prices of consumer necessities such as food or rent were kept very low, and prices of luxuries were very high. Within the intermediate sector, inputs such as raw materials and especially energy were cheap, and the resulting final goods were sold at higher prices. Within final goods, engineering, capital equipment manufacture, chemicals, and electronics were kept artificially profitable at the expense of goods for consumers. The reform changed relative prices in the direction of world prices. The opening of product markets also coincided with dramatic shifts in the relative attractiveness of domestic, ex–Council for Mutual Economic Assistance (CMEA), and Western markets. Export markets within the (former) CMEA contracted sharply because of the move to convertible-currency trade, the deteriorating situation in the former USSR, and the loss of most of the former German Democratic Republic's market due to German unification. The relative attractiveness of Western markets also rose because of real devaluations initiated to regain macrobalance and because of the relaxation of trade restrictions by the European Union and the United States.

Development of Factor Markets

In socialist economies, wages were determined centrally and bore little relationship to relative labor scarcities. The emergence of free labor markets, including the development of institutions for bargaining at the level of the plant, industry, and region, was likely to be slower than the emergence of product markets. Markets for financial capital and real capital assets, including land, also developed slowly. Private ownership of productive physical assets has been virtually unknown in these economies and even private ownership of productive land has been rare. The banking system itself has been monopolized in the hands of the central bank, and investment has either been financed directly through the state budget or indirectly via the state-controlled banking system. The locus for important investment decisions has not been either with firms or with specialized financial institutions. Now, enterprises must learn for themselves how to evaluate and finance projects. The relative prices faced in factor markets have also changed considerably. In particular, restrictive macro policies have caused increases in nominal and real interest rates and quantity constraints on the volume of bank credit.

Changes in Ownership and Management Environment

Prior to reform, enterprises were owned by the state, either "strongly" under centralized socialism or "weakly" under market socialism. Weak ownership of firms implied ambiguous property rights, with workers and managers having some rights to surpluses but not the right to realize the value of assets directly. One of the key elements of reform should therefore be to define the concept of ownership and its associated rights and obligations (Estrin, 1991). This will legitimize the varied forms of ownership, in particular private ownership. Because privatization may include the possibility of foreign participation, the process may also have a major impact on management behavior and company performance. The impact on management in any given firm will, of course, depend on the structure of corporate governance that evolves in the course of reforms.

Responses

The firm's responses to its changed circumstances will depend on its initial financial situation, and these responses can be divided into short-run reactions, categorized in principle according to the same structure as shocks, and longer-term responses. It is the latter responses that are associated with restructuring, privatization, and the formation of foreign partnerships.

METHODOLOGY

Choice of Sector

The initial focus of the project was on firms that had been state-owned prior to reform and (partly as a consequence) on manufacturing industry rather than services. This was because it was felt that the problems of transition faced by state-owned firms were in principle quite different from those of emerging private firms in manufacturing industry; a similar argument applied to service activities such as banking or insurance. It was also decided to exclude public utilities, such as power generation and telecommunications, because, once again, these presented very particular and specialized problems deserving separate study.

Finally, we did not seek representativeness of industrial branches across each economy as a whole, but rather selected a range of sectors to illustrate the diversity of enterprise adjustment. The most important consequence of this decision was that the defense sector, which is very large in all the countries, especially in the CSFR, and is typically in very poor shape, is underrepresented in the sample. This leads the study to present a rosier picture of enterprise adjustment than would obtain if more of the defense sector dinosaurs were included. However, such firms have very poor prospects for survival in the medium term. The study therefore provides a snapshot of state-owned enterprise adjustment in the first years of transition in a sample of industries that is somewhat biased toward those firms with some potential to survive and flourish in an internationally competitive market economy.

In choosing particular sectors, it was felt that there should be variation in the following characteristics:

- Stages of production: the principal categories to be covered were raw material and basic industries; intermediate products and goods for final consumption;
- Viability: whether the sector was considered *a priori* likely to be viable in the medium term, given the collapse of the CMEA and changes of relative input and output prices. Also relevant might be the previous share of hard currency exports;
- Market conditions: whether the industry faced competitive, oligopolistic, or monopolistic conditions;
- Size: from small firms, less than 150 workers, through medium, 150 to 1,500 workers, to large ones with more than 1,500 workers;
- Capital intensity: from labor-intensive to capital-intensive activities. Of related significance for capital-intensive sectors was the source of investment funds, ranging from sectors heavily dependent on state munificence to those with large current or potential future foreign investments.

Of course, in practice many of these characteristics were found together in particular firms under the traditional planning system (Ellman, 1989). For example, basic and intermediate sectors were typically large-scale, capital-intensive, monopolistic, and frequently not viable in the new market conditions, at least not without major restructuring.

In addition, the authors of the case studies were advised to seek diversity in the following areas when selecting firms within the predetermined sectors:

- Ownership: ranging from state-owned, or state-owned but being privatized, to those already privately owned;
- Establishment status: whether the firm was a single- or multi-plant operation;
- Organizational status: whether the firm was a holding company or had unified financial status;
- Regional spread: to include the major industrial regions, most significantly Slovakia within the CSFR;
- Where possible to cover interesting constraints or advantages such as environmental or pollution problems, firms affected by an EC quota, or firms heavily R&D, design, or patent dependent.

The five criteria for choice of sector led to the selection of the fifteen sectors outlined in Table 1. The table also summarizes the advice given to the field participants to assist in the selection of firms according to the criteria for selection of enterprises listed above. The actual firms chosen are listed in Table 2. The chosen sectors differ slightly from those proposed in Table 1, because it proved virtually impossible to obtain participation from any firms in the defense sector. Additional firms in food processing or in engineering were substituted. Moreover, because the cases were undertaken during the first wave of the CSFR's mass privatization program, it proved harder to obtain approval for participation in the project there. As a consequence, the project surveyed only thirteen of the proposed fifteen firms in the CSFR.

Timetable

The project was undertaken in four phases during 1992. Between January and April, the fifteen sectors were selected and a common questionnaire to be applied in all three countries was devised and tested in the field. The questionnaire was implemented between April and the summer of 1992, and preliminary drafts of the cases were completed in September. The project team met in September 1992 with the objective of ensuring that the cases were consistent in their coverage of issues and to discuss the emerging findings. The discussion formed the basis for return visits to the firms before Christmas 1992, and the revised cases were completed by February 1993.

It is important to note that the first wave of mass privatization in the CSFR took place during this period, with the result that the cases reflect the impact of this policy on, for example, enterprise governance and ownership. It is likely that the general impression of enterprise adjustment in the CSFR would have been less favorable if the questionnaire had been implemented six or twelve months earlier.

INITIAL CONDITIONS, SHOCKS, AND RESPONSES

Initial Conditions and Shocks

The overall macroeconomic situation, which was similar in all three countries at the time when the cases were being undertaken, was one of recession (Balcerowicz and Gelb, 1994). The case writers' own evaluation of the situation in each sector can be summarized as follows (for more details see Belka et al., 1993; Matesová, 1993; and Török, 1993). The poor macroeconomic situation is evident in most sectors. The most common observations concern the decline in demand, either in the domestic market or associated with the collapse of the CMEA. Also frequently mentioned everywhere are competitive pressures from imports, or, for activities with low sunk costs such as textiles or garments, from the newly emerging private sector. The impact of the disintegration of the wholesale sector on sales is also frequently mentioned in Poland and Czechoslovakia. The effects of the reform on the state-owned sector are not entirely bad, however. In several sectors, improved access to Western markets for selling products and buying higher quality inputs, as well as access to managerial know-how, technology, and finance, is also evident.

For almost every firm, the primary effects of the reform were a decline in demand, an increase in some or all input prices as well as in the cost of borrowing, and the rupturing of domestic and intra-CMEA trade links. Despite careful efforts to discover other unexpected pressures on firms, almost no cases mention changes in managerial or financial autonomy, nor changes in ownership brought about as a consequence of the reform. However, a few cases note some impact from the emergence of factor markets, especially in Poland, which was farthest along the fast-track reform path. One common example is labor market shortages for particular skills, particularly for firms subject to tax-based incomes policies and in direct competition for workers with the private sector.

We use the qualitative and quantitative information collected by the case writers to place the firms into three categories in Table 3:

- category A are good firms whose current and future viability is not considered to be in doubt. Such companies are given a score of 4 or 5 in Table 3;
- category B firms are average in the sense that they are potentially viable, but are currently (1992) making only small profits or modest losses. They are also suffering cash flow problems, and are perhaps increasingly indebted. Such companies are given a score of 3 in Table 3;
- category C firms are doing badly in the sense that they are persistent loss-makers or face apparently insoluble cash-flow problems or have a very large debt, either to banks, to suppliers, or to the government, and are typically unable to meet the interest payments on their borrowing. In economies with clear ownership rights, these firms would be liquidated or financially restructured. Such companies are given a score of 1 or 2 in Table 3.

This classification is the result of detailed analysis of each firm, taking into account the balance sheet and income statement data, the qualitative information about the firms' markets and prospects, and the case writers' own evaluation given their knowledge of the industry, region, and other political and social factors.

The cumulative macroeconomic decline was of a similar order of magnitude in all three countries. However, we find that the Polish firms in our samples are in a markedly worse state than their Czechoslovak and Hungarian counterparts. Thus, only 40 percent of Polish firms are in the good category, as against 60 percent of Hungarian firms. The proportion of good firms in the CSFR (42 percent) is comparable to the Polish figure, but the Czechs and Slovaks have proportionately fewer bad firms—25 percent as against 33 percent. We take this data primarily as indicative of differences between the country samples, rather than as indicating a differential impact of the recession on representative firms in each country.[5] It is significant that the processes of financial decline in Polish firms appear to operate independently of factors associated with the underlying potential profitability or international competitiveness of the sectors in which the enterprises operate. Thus, firms in our sample engaged in activities in which one might expect Poland to be highly competitive on international markets, such as furniture or footwear manufacture, find themselves in a worse state financially than firms in many of what *ex ante* must be considered to be internationally uncompetitive industries, such as steel, plastics, and pharmaceuticals.

The Czech and Slovak firms in the case project were typically in a slightly better financial situation than their Polish counterparts. This seems often to have been because the exchange rate initially was set at a very competitive level in Czechoslovakia, and, although this undervaluation of the koruna, or crown (CSK) eroded somewhat after price liberalization, it still acted as a buffer against international competitive pressure on domestic producers and as a source of profits through exports to the West. Inflation in the CSFR was brought quickly under control, so that the price–quality relationship remained relatively favorable to Czech and Slovak firms. Real interest rates were also somewhat lower in the CSFR. Moreover, wages were prevented from rising so quickly as to either absorb the remaining enterprise profits or rekindle inflationary pressure.

Our Hungarian firms are frequently in better shape than their Polish and Czechoslovak counterparts, and this may reflect either genuine advantages bestowed by the gradual reform process in Hungary or biases in sample selection. However, there are still several nonviable Hungarian cases, and their problems seem to stem mostly from the collapse of CMEA trade and the resulting recession.

Short-Run Responses

One might expect few reactions from state-owned firms to the shocks outlined above, mainly because of the absence of profit motivation. Indeed, some might expect to see only perverse responses, with managers and workers exploiting the possibly temporary vacuum in ownership rights. This could include appropriating the assets. Alternatively, the employees and managers could decapitalize the enterprise and run up debts to maintain or increase employment and to raise wages. Such behavior would be associated with the most minimal short-term responses to the new situation, evident in, for example, continuing to produce at the previous level and accumulating inventories. Such passive responses could be financed by failing to pay suppliers or workers, borrowing from banks, and falling into arrears with social obligations and tax payments. Responses of this sort are given the score of 1 in Table 4.

Managers in the formerly socialist economies are typically engineers; given the appropriate motivation or under pressure from hardening budget constraints, they are well qualified to make short-run adjustments to the production process, for example by closing particular product lines, changing the product mix toward more salable goods, laying off workers, selling machines or even plants, and reorganizing production toward cheaper or higher quality inputs. Short-term responses of this sort are awarded a score of 3 in Table 4. Such reactions are easier and less fundamental for traditional socialist mangers to make than developments in the areas of accountancy, financial control, organizational restructuring, marketing and sales, quality control, information systems, and Western orientation in terms of product outlets, technology, and sources of finance. Firms that responded in these latter areas are awarded a score of 5 in Table 4. Scores of 2 and 4 pick up the intermediate cases.

Table 4, which is based on our reading of the cases, suggests that there were surprisingly few examples of purely passive responses in the state-owned sectors of Central Europe after two years of reform, even in Poland where the sample contains relatively more weak firms. Purely passive responses, with the attendant possibilities of perverse behavior, were only revealed in two firms, one each in Hungary and Poland. Interestingly, both firms are in sectors closely tied to the government. Around 40 percent of the firms displayed active responses and a further 43 percent production responses. Insofar as our sample is representative, and this finding is unlikely to be affected greatly by the slight overrepresentation of both good and bad firms, the cases taken together suggest that managers in state-owned firms did respond in significant ways to the changes in the economic environment brought about by the reforms.

The country dispersion of short-run reactions does not entirely match the distribution according to viability. As expected, passive responses are concentrated in Poland, where 30 percent of firms display scores of 1 or 2 as against 13 percent in Hungary. Surprisingly, although the CSFR sample resembles the Polish more than the Hungarian in viability, there are no examples of passive responses in the CSFR. Czech and Slovak firms actually have the largest proportion in the most active short-run response categories: 50 percent of firms scored 4 or 5 as against 40 percent of Hungarian firms and 30 percent of Polish ones. The story is similar in the middling category, with 50 percent of CSFR firms scoring 3, as against 47 percent of Hungarian firms and 30 percent of Polish ones. Thus, although they are more similar to Polish firms in terms of perceived viability, Czech and Slovak firms are comparable to the better Hungarian firms in terms of their short-run responses. There is also little evidence of a sectoral pattern underlying the degree of short-term responsiveness; the intercountry difference dominates the intersectoral one.

Long-Run Responses

Managerial Motivation

We commence with a discussion of managerial motivation and, in particular, an evaluation of the extent of managerial autonomy and authority. We expect differences according to whether the enterprise is following the objectives of the government or government agencies, of management, or of workers. However, it is surprising to note that the government is almost never cited in the cases as having any direct control or authority over enterprise decision-making.[6] We therefore henceforth restrict our attention to the influence and motives of managers and workers in the enterprise. It is important to know whether managers or workers are associated with proposed or actual ownership changes—for example, whether they stand to gain directly from privatization.

The cases suggest that there are very few problems of managerial control or motivation in either Hungary or the CSFR. Almost every firm in both countries has the highest category of managerial motivation. The picture is much more confused in Poland. Only in a small proportion of state-owned firms do managers have significant motivation or authority. Around one-third of firms appear to have managers who are poorly motivated or have insufficient decision-making authority to implement their plans. The phenomenon that most distinguishes Polish state-owned firms in our sample from their counterparts in Hungary and the CSFR is employee power. One might have expected to see significant workers' power in enterprise decision-making in all three countries. In Czechoslovakia, there was a long tradition of an active and powerful labor movement prior to the communist era; in Poland, the unions were instrumental in bringing down communism. Moreover, in both Poland and Hungary, the institutions for worker power were in place; market socialist reforms in the 1980s had, in principle, given enterprise management to elected committees of managers and workers, although in practice their authority had probably been limited. But only three years after the fall of communism, there is almost no indication from the cases that employees in state-owned firms in the former Czechoslovakia or Hungary have influence in the workplace comparable even to levels evident in unionized firms in Western Europe. The degradation of trade unions under the communists and the threat of unemployment appear to have left workers virtually without a voice in the restructuring and privatization of the state enterprise sector. The situation is markedly different in Poland. Workers are found to dominate decision-making in around one-third of firms in the sample and to have considerable authority in another third. Managers have autonomy comparable to that found in Czechoslovak or Hungarian firms only in the remaining one-third of firms. The cases also provide instances of workers vetoing restructuring or privatization plans, scaring off potential foreign investors, and markedly reducing managerial pay.

Long-Run Strategies

We now turn to the complex issue of long-term strategic thinking in the firm. This topic covers a variety of areas including restructuring, investment plans, refocusing product lines and markets, internal reorganization, and innovation. Long-term strategies in the state-owned sector of transitional economies will also clearly be affected by plans for the clarification of ownership rights and by establishing relationships with foreign enterprises.

It is encouraging to find that a high proportion of firms in the case-study project did appear to have a long-run strategy in place, but here again we find the same pattern of national differences described above. These are clearly related to differences in policies toward reform, and especially toward privatization and foreign direct investment. As we might expect, long-run strategies were in place in the bulk of Hungarian firms from an early stage. Indeed, coherent long-run planning seems to be slightly more common than are very active short-run responses in Hungary. Although our Hungarian sample is perhaps somewhat better than the national firm average, the cases suggest that most firms in Hungary were well advanced in the process of restructuring and finding new products and markets, particularly when viewed alongside the firms from Poland and the CSFR. We find that the long-run plans frequently include privatization, often with the involvement of foreign partners, or entail restructuring with a view to the future sale of the firm.

Although the CSFR sample is less favorable, relative to the national average, than the Hungarian, we find, perhaps somewhat surprisingly, that a majority of firms in the CSFR appear to have developed a long-run strategy by the end of 1992 while another quarter were in the process of doing so. There are a number of important provisos to this finding, however. First, firms in the CSFR may have had long-term plans, but for the most part they had not yet begun to implement them. This is in sharp contrast to Hungary, where restructuring was under way in the majority of enterprises. Moreover, the impact of the first wave of privatization on management thinking is evident in the responses; there were major reevaluations of long-run strategy by enterprises in Czechoslovakia during the study due to the first wave of mass privatization. The cases highlight that proposals to invest, innovate, and restructure in the CSFR were all linked to the privatization process, which encouraged the submission of (often competing) schemes to privatize and restructure and only rarely entailed the involvement of foreigners. The successful implementation of these long-run strategies is therefore intimately connected with the strategy adopted for the Czech and Slovak mass privatization program (see Estrin, 1994).

A significant group of Polish state-owned firms, by contrast, have clearly been suffering from the absence of policy to clarify property rights. Two years into reform, many firms did not have a long-term strategy in place—too many to be explained by the bias in the Polish sample toward weaker firms. The cases suggest that a significant proportion of state-owned firms were slowly drifting into debt and decline with no long-run strategy to address their situation. This is despite the fact that most of the sampled firms had altered their operating practices significantly. In addition to the desperation born of nonviability, this situation was associated with weak managerial authority, significant employee power, and the absence of a sustained strategy to privatize the state-owned sector. Our Hungarian sample is stronger, and managers have far greater authority; also, most of them had some privatization prospect in mind. The most important factors in the CSFR were managerial authority and a clear privatization strategy.

Privatization and the Role of Foreign Partners

The cases taken together highlight the pivotal role of national privatization policies in explaining differences in short- and long-run responses. In Poland, we find only two cases of privatization—one firm that was privatized in the first round of sale by public tender in 1990 and one liquidation. In sharp contrast, every firm in our sample from the CSFR was either already private, being privatized in the first wave of voucher privatization, or preparing plans for the second wave. Although the process of ownership changes was only completed in four of the thirteen firms by January 1993, all the other cases had a timetable .

The Hungarian situation is once again a little more complex. Twenty percent of firms in the Hungarian sample are fully privatized. While this proportion is in fact slightly lower than in the CSFR, the Hungarian cases usually involve more sophisticated forms of corporate governance and often additional finance, new technology, and better managerial structures being transferred to the firm, frequently from majority foreign stakeholders. The Czech and Slovak private firms in the sample are restitutions or management buyouts, in which the ownership change has as yet had much less effect on company resources and behavior. Similarly, the 53 percent of the Hungarian firms in the process of privatization are typically being transferred to known new owners through some sort of market-based procedure. As such, they can have a clearer vision of the likely future forms of corporate governance that will emerge postprivatization than do the 66 percent of Czech and Slovak firms in our sample that were involved in the first privatization wave. The cases from the CSFR make clear that managers were awaiting with some trepidation the outcome of the voucher bidding process, and many were already seeking ways to entrench themselves in their position against what might prove to be highly dispersed outside owners.

The cases also indicate a correlation between viability and privatization, most notably in Hungary. All the viable firms in Hungary are on the path to private ownership; none of the nonviable firms has even started the journey. Since financial status was usually established prior to decisions about ownership changes, this is evidence that, in Hungary at least, viability leads privatization. Hungarian authorities would appear not to be using privatization as way to resolve difficulties in poorly performing firms, but rather as a way to improve the situation in their more successful ones. This is an obvious corollary of a privatization strategy based on sale through public tender. The evidence from the CSFR is also consistent with the interpretation that inclusion in the first privatization wave required reasonable prior financial viability, rather than being a strategy to improve financial performance in the weakest firms.[7] The only Polish firms in the sample to have been privatized were in the high-viability category; the drift to nonviability in Polish firms, however, seems likely to have been both a cause and a consequence of the lack of a sustained privatization strategy.

Finally, it is interesting to explore more carefully the role of Western investors so far in the transformation process. One-third of the Hungarian firms in our sample have significant ownership links (at minimum a joint venture) with Western firms. One firm has even established a hard-currency joint venture with a Russian corporation. No sample firm has been successfully privatized without substantial Western involvement; moreover, there is no case in which there has been significant progress toward ownership changes without foreign involvement. Indeed, the implementation of a long-run response by the firm appears to be contingent on Western involvement.

There was much less Western involvement in Czechoslovakia and Poland than in Hungary. By the end of 1992, there were no firms in the CSFR in our sample with a majority foreign stake, although some joint ventures were beginning to be established. In most sectors where business had been concentrated on either the domestic or the CMEA market there was not even any operational business contact with Western firms. There is no correlation between progress in ownership changes and the extent of foreign involvement because the mass privatization strategy did not rely on foreign investment. At the time of writing, there was even less foreign interest in our sample of Polish firms than in our CSFR ones and only a few cases of even operational business contact.[8]

CONCLUSIONS

The cases taken together suggest that there is no simple relationship between the sharp shocks to the firm's trading environment associated with so-called big-bang stabilization programs and the extent of enterprise restructuring and adjustment. In all three countries, many firms have successfully begun to transform themselves. Low levels of viability act to hinder adjustment and are associated with weak management, although this may be a country- rather than firm-specific phenomenon.

More important for successful microeconomic transition is the speedy establishment of a privatization program. Ownership changes, including in the CSFR, are intimately bound up with long-run strategic thinking more generally. The emphasis on privatization therefore seems to explain much of the considerable and somewhat surprising progress toward enterprise adjustment observed in the CSFR as well as most of the Hungarian cases. Hungarian firms have had more time to restructure and to build Western contacts so as to establish their relatively advanced position. On the basis of our sample, the Czechoslovak record looks good, although it should not be overstated; the cases revealed more progress on paper than in practice at this stage. Nevertheless, it is unlikely that our findings are solely the consequence of sample selection bias. The cases therefore offer a first hint that the CSFR's mass privatization program may have laid the foundations for major progress in restructuring and marketization despite the widely noted deficiencies with regard to corporate governance and the provision of new funds to enterprises. On the other hand, the sustained lack of any effective Polish strategy toward privatization was clearly an important explanatory factor in the failure of much of the state-owned sector to adjust adequately to the new market conditions.

The cases indicate a strong positive correlation between enterprise viability, long-run adjustment, and privatization. Whether the authorities plan to sell firms or to distribute the shares at low or zero prices, ownership changes have been largely restricted to firms that are financially sound. The authorities therefore need another strategy to deal with firms whose economic situation is not sustainable—specifically, either financial restructuring or liquidation. The dangers of allowing the situation to deteriorate further through delay and drift are great. The study has also identified a series of specific factors that have acted to hinder enterprise adjustment in Poland, including poor initial macroeconomic conditions and the power of employees over enterprise decisions. While few if any of these factors obtain in Hungary or the Czech and Slovak republics, they have considerable relevance for the second wave of reforming economies, most notably Russia.

Notes

1. Three of the cases for the CSFR were in what has since become the independent Slovak Republic; the remainder were in the Czech Republic.
2. Exceptions include Gelb, Jorgensen, and Singh (1990); Belka, Pinto, and Krajewski (1992); Estrin, Schaffer, and Singh (1992); and Brada, Singh, and Török (1994).
3. The World Bank project on enterprise adjustment in Poland, Hungary, and the CSFR was developed in part to fill that gap. First analyses using enterprise-level data are now appearing (see, e.g., Estrin and Takla, 1993), but the limitations of the available data leave many questions that can be addressed only within the framework of case studies.
4. The project focused only on the manufacturing sector, and did not cover either the military-industrial complex or service-sector companies such as banks.
5. This view was confirmed by an exercise evaluating the case writers' subjective ranking of the firms in the study relative to the country populations. The rankings were very similar to the categories for viability.
6. In the defense and oil-refining industries, however, management remains closely intertwined with the relevant government department.

7. There are no nonviable or nonprivatizing firms in our Czechoslovak sample, however, so there is no test of the null hypothesis.
8. This seems likely to be in part a consequence of sample selection in Poland; foreign direct investment levels were lower than in Hungary or the CSFR but not negligible at the time when the cases were undertaken. The pace of foreign direct investment into both the Czech Republic and Poland accelerated in 1993.

References

Balcerowicz, L., and Gelb A. *Macro-Policy in Transition: A Three-Year Perspective*, World Bank, 1994.
Belka, M., Pinto, M., and Krajewski, J. "Microeconomics of Transformation in Poland: A Survey of State Enterprise Responses." World Bank Working Paper 983, September 1992.
Belka, M., Krajewska, A., Krajewski, S., and Santos, A. "Country Overview Study: Poland," *Eastern European Economics*, vol. 31, no. 5 (1993): 19–62.
Brada, J., Singh, I., and Török, A. *Firms Afloat and Firms Adrift: Hungarian Industry and Economic Transition*. Armonk, NY: M.E. Sharpe, 1994.
Ellman, M., *Socialist Planning*. Cambridge: Cambridge University Press, 1989.
Estrin, S., *Privatisation in Central and Eastern Europe*. London: Longman, 1994.
Estrin, S., "Privatisation in Central and Eastern Europe: The Lessons for Western Experience." *Annals of Public and Cooperative Economy*, 1991, pp. 159–82.
Estrin S., Schaffer, M., and Singh, I. "Enterprise Adjustment in Transition Economies." World Bank mimeo, 1992.
Estrin, S., and Takla, L., "Competition Policy in Czechoslovakia." In Estrin, S., and Cave, M. (eds.), *Competition and Competition Policy: A Comparative Analysis of Central and Eastern Europe*. London: Pinter Press, 1993.
Frydman, R. et al. (eds.). *Privatization in Central and Eastern Europe*. London: Central European University, 1993.
Gelb, A., Jorgersen, E., and Singh, I. "The Behavior of Polish Firms after the Big Bang," World Bank Research Paper, No. 12, 1990.
Kornai, J. *The Road to a Free Economy*. New York: Norton, 1990.
Lipton, D., and Sachs, J. "Creating a Market Economy in Eastern Europe: The Case of Poland." *Brookings Papers on Economic Activity*, 1990.
Matesová, J. "Will the Manufacturing Heart Beat Again?" *Eastern European Economics*, vol. 31, no. 6 (1993): 3–35.
Török, A. "Hungarian Industry in 1992: An Assessment." World Bank mimeo, 1992.
Török, A. "Hungarian Industry in 1992: An Assessment of Trends and Behaviors." *Eastern European Economics*, vol. 31, no. 6 (1993): 66–80.
Webster, L. "Private Sector Manufacturing in Poland, Czechoslovakia and Hungary." World Bank Industry Development Division, mimeo, 1992.

Table 1

Sectors

Sector/Product group	Firm size (no. of employees)	Criteria for selection
1. Engineering SOE (state-owned enterprise) • machine tools • CAM/CAD	≈ 2,000	heavy, viable, capital-intensive, CMEA-dependent, producer good, monopoly, large, establishment, SOE holding company, heavy reliance on West for R&D, financially constrained, moving from soft to hard budget
2. Defense contractor • military vehicles	≈ 5,000–10,000	heavy, capital-intensive, viable, CMEA-dependent, defense conversion, SOE, medium/large, financially constrained, moving from soft to hard budgets
3. Heavy chemicals • petrochemicals	≈ 10,000	basic, viable, capital-intensive, CMEA-dependent, large, monopoly, energy-intensive, environmental problems, R&D/patent-dependent, financially constrained, technological reconversion, multiplant, changing markets, glutted markets, overcapacity, EC quotas
4. Textiles/garments • private • being privatized	≈ 1,000	small, light, labor-intensive, competitive, Western oriented, viable, single-plant, EC quotas, sensitive to competitive markets, very dependent on working capital/credits, design/market sensitivity
5. Textiles/cloth • being privatized	≈ 500	medium, light, intermediate, competitive, viable, multiplant, EC/MFA-constrained, credit-dependent

Table 1 (cont.)

Sector/Product group	Firm size (no. of employees)	Criteria for selection
6. Electronics • being privatized • military SOE	≈ 2,000	intermediate/final, civil/military, medium/large, CMEA (military), multi-plant, multi-product, viable, financially constrained (bankrupt), knowledge-intensive, reliance on local and Western R&D, foreign investment, design-intensive, capital-intensive, foreign collaboration in investment, competition
7. Glass • table glass • flat glass • industrial glass • private • privatized	≈ 1,000	small/medium, final/intermediate, Western export, viable, multi-product, multi-plant, capital/labor–intensive, design-intensive, foreign investments, competitive, financially constrained
8. Food processing • private • cooperatives • foreign owned	≈ 500–1,000	final, small/medium, viable, potential exports, agriculture-based, foreign investment, competitive, large domestic market, CMEA-dependent, single/multiple plant
9. Wood products • furniture • being privatized	≈ 200–800	final, small/medium, labor-intensive, export potential, foreign investments
10. Iron/steel • integrated mills • SOE	≈ 5,000–10,000	heavy, nonviable, single-town plant, state owned, financially non-viable (bankrupt), large employment, high wage, energy-intensive, capital-intensive, pollution, subsidized, EC quota, single/multiple plant

Table 1 (cont.)

Sector/Product group	Firm size (no. of employees)	Criteria for selection
11. White goods; refrigerators, washers and dryers • being privatized	≈ 2,000–3,000	medium, viable, foreign licensing/ownership, CMEA market, labor-intensive, for re-export to West, credit constraints, competitive, final good
12. Footwear • private • being privatized	≈ 500	light, small/medium, private, CMEA-dependent, labor-intensive, viable, financially constrained, competitive, export potential, foreign investment potential, multi-plant, EC quota, voluntary restraints
13. Plastics • being privatized	≈ 2,000	intermediate, medium/large, capital-intensive, CMEA input–dependent, polluting, energy-intensive, viable, financially constrained, competitive, EC quota
14. Pharmaceutical companies • private • being privatized	≈ 1,000–2,000	knowledge-intensive, medium, patent-dependent, likely to be privatized, foreign direct investment, joint-venture possibilities, capital-intensive, high R&D, final product, potentially viable and exportable, competitive, less financially constrained, long experience of industrial cooperation with the West, CMEA/West exports, environmental problems
15. Auto parts • being privatized	≈ 1,000	intermediate, foreign investment, export potential, large, capital-intensive, strong international competition

Table 2

Firms

Industry	Czechoslovakia	Hungary	Poland
1. Auto parts	Employees: 5,000 Total sales: CSK 1 bil.	Employees: 3,913 Total sales: HUF 3.2 Bil.	Employees: 1,300 Total sales: ca $20 mil.
2. Defense			
3. Electronics/consumer	Employees: 1,200 Total sales: CSK 350 mil.	Employees: 3,000 Total sales: n/a	Employees: 1,540 Total sales: $8 mil.
4. Electronics/industrial machinery		Employees: n/a Total sales: n/a	
5. Engineering/machine tools	Employees: 5,500 Total sales: CSK 2 bil.	Employees: 1,720 Total sales: n/a	Employees: n/a Total sales: n/a
6. Food processing/brewing		Employees: 1,214 Total sales: HUF 5,113.4 bil.	
7. Food processing/chocolate and sweets	Employees: n/a Total sales: n/a	Employees: 2,500 Total sales: HUF 2,766 bil.	Employees: 800 Total sales: $20 mil.
8. Footwear	Employees: n/a Total sales: n/a		Employees: 260 Total sales: $50 mil.
9. Glass	Employees: 3,000 Total sales: CSK 0.8 bil.	Employees: 1,200 Total sales: n/a	Employees: 1,040 Total sales: $5 mil.

10. Heavy chemicals/refinery	Employees: 5,500 Total sales: CSK 4 bil.	Employees: 6,532 Total sales: HUF 33.350 bil.	Employees: 8,200 Total sales: ca $2.0 bil.
11. Iron/steel/metallurgy	Employees: 30,000 Total sales: CSK 4 bil.	Employees: 10,564 Total sales: HUF 33.999 bil.	Employees: 9,000 Total sales: $200 mil.
12. Pharmaceuticals	Employees: 2,500 Total sales: CSK 2 bil.	Employees: 6,182 Total sales: HUF 17.060 bil.	Employees: 1,300 Total sales: $15 mil.
13. Plastics	Employees: 1,500 Total sales: CSK 600 mil.	Employees: 1,500 Total sales: HUF 5,000 bil.	Employees: 740 Total sales: $20 mil.
14. Textile/cloth	Employees: 3,000 Total sales: CSK 1.2 bil.	Employees: 1,752 Total sales: HUF 1,250 bil.	Employees: 652 Total sales: $7 mil.
15. Textile/garments	Employees: 300 Total sales: CSK 50 mil.	Employees: 3,977 Total sales: HUF 6.226 bil.	Employees: 4,100 Total sales: $20 mil.
16. Vehicles		Employees: 12,494 Total sales: HUF 18.176 bil.	Employees: 4,500 Total sales: n/a
17. White goods/refrigerators/washing machines		Employees: 4,704 Total sales: n/a	Employees: 5,500 Total sales: $30 mil.
18. Wood products/furniture	Employees: 1,000 Total sales: n/a		Employees: 1,200 Total sales: $10 mil.

Table 3

Viability by Country and Sector in 1992

	Poland	Czechoslovakia	Hungary
1. Steel	2	—	4
2. Textiles/clothing	2	3	4
3. Pharmaceuticals	4	4	5
4. Car parts	4	1	3
5. White goods	3	—	5
6. Heavy chemicals	4	4	4
7. Vehicles	2	2	3
8. Consumer electronics	3	3	2
9. Machine tools/engineering	1	2	5
10. Furniture	1	3	—
11. Glass	3	—	1
12. Footwear	1	5	—
13. Plastics	4	4	4
14. Textiles/garments	5	3	1
15. Food processing/brewing	—	—	4
16. Food processing/chocolates and sweets	5	5	5
17. Precision tools	—	—	1
Average	2.9	3.25	3.4

Key: 1: nonviable: persistent loss maker or insoluble cash-flow problems; 3: potentially viable: small loss, cash-flow problems, perhaps mounting; 5: viable: profitable firm, short-term future not in doubt.

Table 4

Nature of Responses—Short Run

	Poland	Czechoslovakia	Hungary
1. Steel	3	—	3
2. Textiles/clothing	3	3	5
3. Pharmaceuticals	2	3	5
4. Car parts	4	3	3
5. White goods	5	—	4
6. Heavy chemicals	1	3	3
7. Vehicles	3	4	3
8. Consumer electronics	3	4	3
9. Machine tools/engineering	3	3	4
10. Furniture	2	4	—
11. Glass	2	—	2
12. Footwear	2	5	—
13. Plastics	4	4	3
14. Textiles/garments	4	4	3
15. Food processing/brewing	—	—	5
16. Food processing/chocolate and sweets	4	3	5
17. Precision tools/defense	—	—	1
Average	3	3.6	3.5

Key: 1: denotes passive response only, e.g., accumulation of debt and arrears, nonpayment of suppliers, accumulation of inventories; 3: denotes mainly production responses, e.g., closing production lines, altering product mix, laying off workers, reorganizing production toward cheaper inputs; 5: denotes more active response, e.g., new organization, marketing and sales development, export orientation, quality development, information systems, cost control, etc.

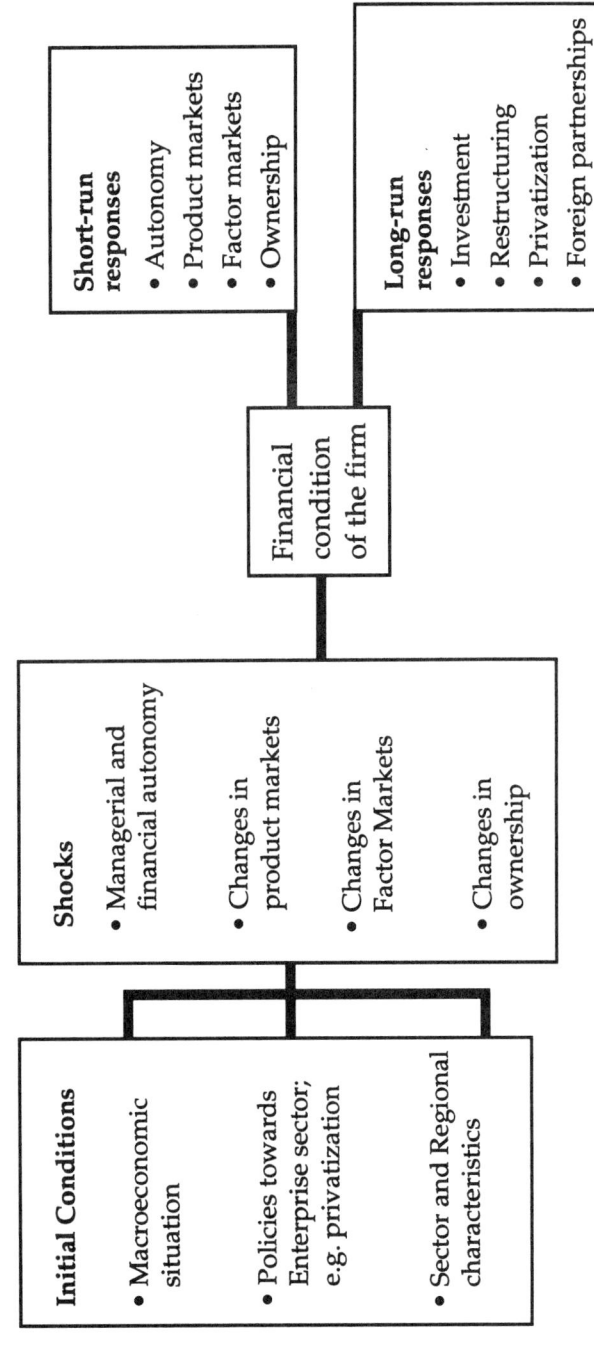

Figure 1. **Shocks and Enterprise Responses.**

Part I

Case Studies of Czech and Slovak Firms

1

Engineering/Forklift Trucks: Desta

Jaroslav Jirasek

THE EUROPEAN INDUSTRIAL SCENE

At the time of this study, Europe was supplied by 40–50 forklift truck manufacturers located worldwide, the leaders being Linde of Germany, Toyota in Japan, and Clark in America. Forklift vehicles are called trucks; however, the dynamic characteristics of their design and market destinations are so closely tied to the materials-handling process that only a few truck makers, such as Toyota, maintain a separate forklift division. Most forklift manufacturers develop, design, and assemble their own models using components that they either manufacture themselves or subcontract. However, there are many manufacturers that supply everything from large components to small specialized parts. Among these was Desta, which ranked approximately 15th–18th. In the Czech and Slovak Republic, this enterprise was almost a monopolist. The other major manufacturer was Zavody tezkeho strojirenstvi, or Heavy Engineering Works (ZTM), in Martin. This Slovak military-vehicle manufacturer was interested in commercial production and created a department to produce forklift trucks based on a British license. Desta was more advanced technically and cheaper, although less reliable. However, after the split of the Czech and Slovak Republic into two sovereign states, an imbalance in foreign trade could cause Desta to lose the Slovak market if that market lacked Czech currency.

DESTA

Desta was a well-known engineering enterprise that flourished in the 1960s when material-transportation vehicles were much in demand. Forklift trucks with the Desta trademark were commonplace and the firm ranked among the top manufacturers worldwide. Now, the same firm was trying to survive. The man who had been in charge twenty years ago was again at the helm; however, he returned after Desta's traditional markets and the products' competitive advantages had been lost. The industry, the business environment, and the firm culture were quite different than they had been and the question was whether Desta would be able to revive its former market position. That is what this study attempts to answer.

The Man at the Top

Desta was a joint-stock firm and a manufacturer of forklift trucks in Decin, a town of 50,000 inhabitants in northern Bohemia near the Czech-German border. The Desta logo was an abbreviation of its former name, Děčínske strojírny, or Decin Engineering Works. In the early 1960s, this traditional engineering firm had been slated to close down and the Ministry of Engineering Industry sent Mr. Grégr (a pseudonym) to administer its dissolution. Contrary to expectations, he found a number of strengths and business opportunities in the firm with which he was able to develop a committed management team. He recommended that they put all their efforts into material-handling equipment, which was in high demand at that time, and he also started vigorous design development and product upgrading.

This man proved to have exceptional leadership ability. After a short time, the firm began to grow and Mr. Grégr raised his expectations even further. He tried to eradicate past provincialism, to arrange study visits and internships for his professional staff, and to attract experienced and knowledgeable individuals. In the second half of the 1960s he even dared to advance the slogan, "To push forward among the best."

At that time, the Institute for Management provided mandatory business management studies for all CEOs and the two to three prospective top managers in all large enterprises. Mr. Grégr completed this six-month program of marketing, accounting and calculation, operations management, computerized information management, research and development management, personnel management, international business negotiations and market penetration, time management, and English. Like all the other top managers, he was then sent to the United States for a four-week study visit.

With his business leadership capabilities strengthened, Mr. Grégr masterminded the exponential growth of the firm so that by the second half of the 1960s, Desta ranked second or third in the forklift trucking industry worldwide. At the International Engineering Trade Fair in Brno, in 1967, all business meetings took place on platforms lifted 2–3 meters above the ground by Desta trucks. It was an inventive and elegant marketing demonstration.

After the Soviet invasion and its political persecutions, Mr. Grégr was removed from his position and put under ideological pressure for his Western inclinations. He was also virtually expelled from the firm by ambitious lower managers who resented his strong-hand style and were eager to use this opportunity for self-promotion. Mr. Grégr then spent most of the next twenty years in Prague as the head of a training center for upgrading welding skills. A number of outstanding welders learned their trade under his tutelage.

In the aftermath of the 1989 revolution and its attendant political upheaval in Czechoslovakia, the revolutionary committee of Desta employees asked Mr. Grégr to return and resume leadership of the firm, which had lost much of its acumen and strength. His return was welcomed and some of his declarations were quoted on the walls of the design room, the computer hall, and management offices.

He was once again able to bring significant changes to Desta and he again drew attention to his personality, not only as the CEO of Desta but also through public activities. He initiated the founding of the Association of Industries, a volunteer group of top managers from leading firms. He supported new professional teaching and training, as well as consulting activities for the management in transition. In 1990, he was appointed Minister of the Engineering Industry of the Czech Republic and, in this capacity, initiated the first important deal involving foreign capital in the new Czechoslovakia, that being the Volkswagen-Škoda joint venture.

His term as a government official only lasted one year. The Ministry of Engineering was dissolved and its responsibilities assumed by the new Ministry of Industry, which is now known as the Ministry of Industry and Trade. Frankly stated, his managing style in a bureaucratic environment was resented by his staff. Once again, he was asked to return to Desta.

This former state firm was converted into a joint-stock firm with a single shareholder, the state. This meant that the firm was detached from the state budget, and it became a self-financed business firm, with Mr. Grégr as CEO.

The regional authorities were promoting a university-level industrial institute and asked him to assist. The initiative did not gain support from the central educational authorities, but Mr. Grégr was awarded a chair at the Czech Institute for Technology in Prague. Professor Ing. Miroslav Grégr, graduate engineer, had developed rare know-how and experience as the top manager of an industrial corporation. Desta's business potential, its strengths, and its weaknesses were all closely associated with the man at the top.

SECTORAL SETTING

The forklift industry is a sector of manufacturing that has probably passed its apex. No principal innovation has occurred for several decades. A forklift is a small truck that loads, lifts, and positions equipment, but all its features are subject to ongoing improvement. Adjustments are made to satisfy new needs, and customizing and improving the safety and comfort of the machines are important. Stiff competition among manufacturers means a constant struggle to increase payloads, to create engines that are environmentally sound, and to im-

6   CASE STUDIES OF CZECH AND SLOVAK FIRMS

prove the external appearance of the equipment. Most firm strategies depend on differentiating their products and lowering the manufacturing costs.

Desta was a multi-plant firm with an ingenious division of production roles. The main plant in Decin was the core of all production activities. Other plants were located in various Czech and Moravian towns, as seen from the following:

Business unit	Location
Headquarters and main plant	Decin
Research and development center	Prague
Destaexport	Prague
Manufacturing plants:	Rumburk, Chlumec, Teplice, Domazlice Vroutek, Bzenec, České Budejovice, Liberec, Humpolec, and Brno.

Seven of the plants were less than 100 km from the headquarters. Bzenec, on the Slovak border, was the farthest. All production plants performed two complementary tasks: each assembled at least one truck model so that the management of each plant had direct access to the market and all employees could see the final outcome of their productive effort; and second, each plant manufactured and delivered parts to other plants. The inter-plant trade was much higher than the gross product of the firm, and 60 percent of the parts were exchangeable among all models. A division of production roles made it possible to achieve a higher economy of scale than most foreign competitors.

It was this interdependence that discouraged a firm split. The firm was able to preserve its maneuvering capability because its production capacities were very flexible, there was mutual assistance between plants in the implementation of new models and follow-up co-production, and the firm tried to enhance worker cooperation in order to upgrade its manufacturing and to develop its management.

DESTA IN THE TURBULENCE OF TRANSITION I: COMPETITIVENESS

Desta was plagued by problems similar to those of most Czechoslovak industrial enterprises including the loss or deterioration of Eastern markets, pressure by restrictive financial policies, and unclear ownership patterns. Previously, Desta had produced 10,000 truck units annually, but in 1993, it planned to manufacture only about 6,000. More than 25 countries in the Western hemisphere, the Middle East, Asia, and Africa were clients of this Czech firm. The current depression affecting the industrially developed countries, however, was depleting various growth markets. For instance, few British customers imported trucks because British industry was in a slump, and this weakened Desta's international competitiveness relative to its past. "Ours is the upper-middle class in forklift trucks, unfortunately no longer the undisputed upper class as it was in the sixties," the CEO admitted. "You cannot simply jump over twenty years during which Desta lived off its former engineering excellence, and was nurtured by past achievements."

The problem could be seen at the first glance: a promotional video tape displayed the post-1989 models, which were excessively robust and lacked modern design. Despite improvements in technical excellence, design, driver comfort, and environmental friendliness, Desta was not among the upper echelon in the world of truck manufacturers.

In the CEO's office, the work flow could be followed on a closed-circuit television, which gave a rather disturbing view of the shop floor. Much work was done by hand. Automation and robotics were sporadic and only a few selected manufacturing cycles were equipped with CNC machinery. All parts, including those subcontracted from outside, and all shop floor operations were subject to total inspection, but neither the operators in the production departments nor the suppliers were expected to guarantee their performance. Quality was a constant source of concern, but improvements still depended almost completely on an inspection group. Even though the total approach had been presented by a foreign consulting firm to all the managers, it had not yet penetrated the firm's industrial culture.

But Desta was trying. In 1992, as many as sixteen new models of forklift trucks were to be introduced to the market. This heroic effort on the part of the development and engineering staff was possible because Desta introduced CAD/CAM practices into both its product design and its manufacturing methods. With so many new models, some capable of high payloads, flaws were apt to occur. Working out these problems of design and manufacturing was to be expected but could also cause unanticipated delays. Many problems were interrelated and Desta badly needed improved design and technology, but these would only be financially viable if production were increased. "Our goal is to produce 20,000 vehicle units per year. Only within such a framework can we afford the sophisticated technology necessary for competitiveness in the international market," said Mr. Grégr.

A typical production robot in Germany would be worthwhile if it replaced three workers, but in the Czechoslovak engineering industry, it would need to replace twenty. "We have to modernize, but we must simultaneously produce capital to pay for the modernization. Any experienced manager would understand the difficulty of the situation. It is not our technological illiteracy, only the strangling pressure of our meager cash flow that dictates a more reserved stance," Mr. Grégr remarked.

Product Innovation

The manufacture of forklifts is a conventional industry. After three decades, the forklift's design is still derived from the first vehicle manufactured for local material-handling, in-plant transportation, storage rationalization, etc. Only a few major changes have been made over the years. Desta's research and development centers, located in Prague and Decin, had plans for the following innovations:

- trucks with augmented functions, such as higher payload, higher lifting capacity, and increased flexibility;
- engines that used a variety of fuels, such as gasoline, motor oil, gas, electric drive;
- engines with significantly lower noise and emission levels;
- catalyzer mufflers;
- self-adjusting brakes;
- healthy and comfortable seats;
- improved steering and switchboard display;
- air-conditioned cabins;
- attractive design;
- electronic control of truck functions;
- remote movement control.

Desta produced variations of the forklift for different market niches, producing, for instance, vehicles specially design to haul steel and wood, and off-road vehicles for use in agriculture and forestry, or construction and earthwork. The enterprise also manufactured smaller vehicles for street cleaning, short-distance traffic, and waste disposal. The general trend was customized trucks with high performance and endurance for specific services. Desta was particularly interested in enhancing the quality of its goods, and was focusing on improving the reliability and endurance of its vehicles, which would result in lower maintenance costs. Environmental concerns were an inseparable feature of this promotion.

DESTA IN THE TURBULENCE OF TRANSITION II: MARKETS

Increased output was a function of increased and solvent demand. Desta had a capable marketing staff cooperating with the research and development team. It had formerly exported through the state trading firm, Motokov, which had an established distribution network and several hundred foreign clients. During the years of Motokov's dominance, Desta's contact with customers was blurred, despite the fact that its experts were invited to participate in business negotiations concerning technically or commercially difficult matters. More recently, the firm organized a mixed distribution network that partly maintained the relationship with Motokov, but also allowed the firm to develop its own channels. As a result, it had established joint ventures in marketing and sales with foreign firms.

Japanese firms still used trading companies, and many Japanese exporters took advantage of the negotiating power of large foreign trade enterprises. Therefore, not all flaws in Desta's foreign trade could be traced back to the use of these firms. Desta's marketing staff had not yet developed competitive commercial skills and this weakness was demonstrated by the drab marketing video and unimaginative commercial brochures that read more like general information pamphlets than invitations to the customer. The brochures were also full of misused terms and misspellings.

Desta had had the advantage of being less dependent on Eastern European markets than other firms, but even so, the disintegration of these traditional markets limited the firm's current ability to expand. As Mr. Grégr put it: "Our present policy is to keep as many former clients as we can. There is interest in the East for our products, and we need those marketplaces in order to increase our production. Most importantly, we must keep our customers in the West, and we are looking for other unexplored markets. Customers' orders are the key to our future. We are aware of this." The CEO added: "We also feel capable of designing a strategy to overcome the existing problems. What we need is about three years and capital support."

DESTA IN THE TURBULENCE OF TRANSITION III: CAPITAL AND TIME CONSTRAINTS

After price liberalization in January 1991, industrial prices increased sharply. Prices for engineering products doubled and this became a heyday for many managers and other employees. Inputs were procured for lower prices than previously but the outputs had higher price tags. This was reflected in higher remuneration for executives and managers and profit-sharing for the employees. This situation showed no signs of changing, but unfortunately, the real economic transformation was to be postponed at least one year.

Then a restrictive financial policy set in that included high interest rates, first at 24 percent, then 17 percent, then 13 percent, with another small reduction expected. This dampened capital investments for large industry and construction and, as a result, the domestic market was reduced by 50 percent.

"When the country is in a depression, rarely does any government adopt a restrictive policy that multiplies the difficulties," several members of the top management team complained. They found the combination of recession and restrictive policies depleting, although they appeared to be more depressed by the government's approach than by the market forces themselves. The firm developed a variety of alternate strategies, although it would welcome a bank that would review its options and provide long-term capital at a reasonable rate. Desta also would not object if the bank were represented on the firm's board and held tight financial control over the firm's activities.

The enterprise was also pressured by indebtedness. The balance of receivables compared to payables was 350 million CSK to 120 million CSK, although this was slowly improving. No goods were shipped unless a bank declaration or letter of credit had been provided, and this was accepted as sound financial practice. As a result, a number of potential clients were turned away.

Desta was looking for more ways to overcome its financial difficulties. In the next year, it planned to introduce Desta-Konto, whereby all employees would be remunerated in a cashless system and there would be limited, regulated, and supervised means of using that money to support the firm's financial plans. A project to establish a Desta-Bank failed, but other options to establish an interfirm banking consortium were being explored.

PRIVATIZATION AND CORPORATE GOVERNANCE

Desta's privatization was almost completed. Its voucher privatization plan had been implemented and, thanks to its well-known trademark, the enterprise was soon entirely bought out. However, no foreign capital had been invested yet and all follow-up procedures still needed to be legally and administratively brought to a close. The enterprise hoped that the ownership would be clarified. There was a rumor that one possible owner might be the Investment Bank, but nothing more was known. The top managers also worried that the attitude of the future owner might reflect their own incertitude.

Labor and Employment

As of June 1992, an individual worker earned about 4,500 CSK per month, which was about the industrial average. Wages and salaries were subject to regulation by means of a progressive taxation. Domestic competition in the labor market was increasing. Retention of skilled operators, technicians, and engineers had become increasingly difficult because these workers could find much higher pay in the private sector. Many small businessmen tried to evade taxes by employing unregistered people, which also allowed them to pay higher wages. Desta could eventually be able to pay higher wages and salaries, making a wider wage and salary differentiation, but not at this time.

In the past two years, employment at Desta had decreased from 4,500 to 3,500. This attrition was divided into two categories: compulsory dismissals and voluntary resignations. The former category included the few foreign workers, those employees who had reached retirement age, which made up the majority, and a few employees with low work morale. Among the voluntary resignations were those who left to start up their own businesses and those who preferred the salaries offered either in the private sector or in Germany. Unwanted leaves amounted to 15 percent.

A skilled operator could earn 30 to 40 CSK per hour, a setter about 25 percent more. Every supervisor had 20 percent of the wages in his department at his disposal, and he could distribute this amount among the best workers as he saw fit. Engineering work paid up to 8,500 CSK monthly, and a good worker could earn around 12,000–15,000 CSK per month in a program such as research and development.

The high wages in Germany were a strong attraction. A skilled operator could easily find employment across the border at half again as much as he earned at Desta. There were, however, certain regulations that had been adopted by both countries.

Despite the workforce reduction, the slump in production was much more severe than the decline in employment. In some ways, overemployment has continued. The remaining workers had some difficulty adjusting to the drop in production. Replacement of experienced employees would be difficult, because training a skilled operator could take five to ten years. Many less-skilled workers were closely tied to firm traditions and enjoyed high esteem among their colleagues; therefore, noneconomic factors sometimes kept employment high. Also, some functions within the firm, such as some tooling and maintenance work, safety services, and janitorial services, had required a certain number of workers, regardless of the volatility in output.

Did the layoffs hurt the employees' morale? Yes and no. Some employees became more job conscious and more attentive to their work performance, others felt uncertain and were looking for other jobs. The unemployment rate in the region was less than 4 percent. When asked how much the firm could gain from improved job definitions, better work supervision, and more active participation among workers, Mr. Grégr said: "Without any sizable capital investment we could increase productivity by some 25 percent, and probably more in several departments."

One issue of increasing importance was wage and salary differentiation. Desta was now a joint stock firm and government regulations, which limited income increases in former state enterprises, would not expire before the end of the year. Thus, the financial situation would not allow for much improvement without a rise in productivity.

PROSPERITY TODAY AND TOMORROW

Mr. Grégr was well aware that Desta would need to adapt to survive. Factors for success had changed and the earlier prosperity could not be regained. Moreover, the efficiency of forklift truck manufacturing had several temporal advantages that disguised certain drawbacks.

The main plant in Decin, which employed approximately 1,000 workers, produced fifteen vehicle units per day. The average price of a Desta truck was 270,000 CSK, almost twice that of an inexpensive car. Therefore, fifteen vehicles amounted to 4.05 million CSK per day. At a profit margin of 17 percent, the daily profit would be 690,000 CSK. The average worker at Decin earned 5,000 CSK a month, which translated into 215 CSK per day per employee, and this in turn, given the labor force at the main plant, equaled 215,000 CSK per day.

Thus, with a labor cost percentage of 6.55 percent, Desta could make a respectable profit, despite its substandard technology and labor behavior.

Inventories contained enough material for fifteen days' worth of inputs, although this was far from the current trend of just-in-time deliveries. At an exchange rate of about U.S.$1 = 30 CSK, a Desta truck could be sold abroad for U.S.$9,000, which made the truck fairly competitive. However, at an exchange rate of U.S.$1 = 15 CSK, as before the 1991 currency devaluation, the same truck cost U.S.$18,000. This excluded Desta from profitable competition because the trucks only sold for about $12,000 in most markets. Thus, the pro-export exchange rate, combined with low labor and land costs, helped promote the export of forklifts.

The 1960s versus the 1990s

"In my view," said Mr. Grégr, "it looks worse now. The general pattern is different and cannot be compared with the past. But the future prospects have a silver lining. Compare: During the 1960s, the firm developed dynamically and we were accepted throughout the world. The general mood among the population was excellent. Everyone was willing to work hard and increase his contribution. In short, the social setting was favorable."

The sixties, however, did not experience two oil shocks, a capital-saving economy, or commonplace programmable automation in production. Terms such as CAD/CAM, CIM, TQM, and TIM, or total maintenance, were hardly known then. These came in the 1970s and 1980s. After twenty years, when the cold war ended, Desta found itself on a lost track, separated from the new competitiveness standards set by the Triad competitive push.

Mr. Grégr continued: "The 1960s were years of alleviated centralism and bureaucracy. I used to be insane in my unyielding drive for excellence. But I acquired most of the needed capital investment, extended research and the development budget, and participated in foreign trade. Now that I am independent, my decision-making is not limited in any formal way. However, the present financial means are considerably less than before."

The general social setting displayed some unfavorable traits. "Many people don't want to work, but they do want to get rich as soon as possible. They see examples around them. Experienced workers and engineers, who worked their profession for years, leave their positions for anything that is better paid. We cannot find any substitute in the free labor market."

Grégr was accustomed to working day and night with his top engineers, but now, three of his leading designers were no longer willing to do this. They had found second jobs, one operating a drivers-training school, the second selling electrical parts, and the third selling ice cream. They were dedicated more to their personal well-being than to the enterprise.

What was important was the continued operation of the enterprise, and problems of performance and efficiency seemed minor in comparison. The idea of developing the firm by shrinking its size sounded strange. It contradicted the managers' past experience and made them anxious. Thus far there had been no institution for teaching the principles of efficiency of shrinkage. However, examples from world enterprises could encourage this idea for the future.

Most executives were young and the 1960s meant little to them. They combined their *élan vital* with the managers' experience, but found the effort too demanding. "I feel the same challenge as in the past," Mr. Grégr concluded. "The difference is a growth strategy then, a restrictive strategy now."

TRANSFORMATION STRATEGY

Many firms of all varieties were exposed to declining market demand, but the majority of executives continued to hope that the recession would pass. Meanwhile, the industrially developed countries were also in a recession caused by overproduction, imbalanced foreign trade and protectionism, and political and social disturbances. Business leaders concluded that there would be no immediate cure for these problems and they fought desperately to trim their firms, to customize their products, and to stay in business. The light at the end of the tunnel could be in rethinking priorities, remaking strategies, and refitting firms not only for the current changes, but also for the future.

Mr. Grégr saw problems in such a way, but had difficulty conveying this to his managers and employees. Because of this, he attempted, however unsuccessfully, to establish a university department called The Institute of Advanced Industrialism. He found the attitude of his employees defensive and felt that they lacked drive. Managers and employees were not used to hard times. Many listened to the information handed down by the top management, but seemed to have little interest in anything other than job security and wages.

Strategic Options

There was no doubt that Desta could survive. The question was how. What options were available? The first course of action would be to continue to trim off production activities with low value added. Next would be an acceleration of the development program with concentration on creative forces and commitment. Because some engineers and technicians were being lured away from the enterprise, a more aggressive expansion policy would be put forth with an emphasis on innovation, quality, and flexibility. On the heels of that, the fact that prices for comparable forklifts were now lower by one-fourth to one-third could be brought to the fore.

At the time of this report, the joint venture with Linde A.G., the strongest European forklift manufacturer, was to begin. Desta would supply the high-quality but lower-priced components, using its own production capacities, and Linde would reinforce its competitive position in the international marketplace.

Exploration of foreign markets would need to be intensified. Some interest had already been indicated, but now Desta needed to respond persuasively. Some markets would depend on possible joint ventures. No possible means of increasing sales could be neglected. The recession had been long and no end was in sight yet. The German recession had been particularly damaging to Desta, on top of which, many other former markets were almost or virtually closed. Lastly, the forklift truck industry would hardly survive intact, and the division of the Czech and Slovak Republic could only increase the risk of a more reduced market for Czech forklift trucks.

Table 1

Financial Outline as of December 31, 1991 (in mil. CSK)

Sales	1,698
Fixed assets	1,232
Capital investment	42
Inventories	354
Accounts receivable	341
Accounts payable	123
Bank credits	253
Cash	35
Profit before taxation	213
Social tax (55%)	119
Disposable profit	91

Note: The auditing report, provided by DRT International, states that:
- the current value of fixed assets was estimated at approximately one-half the nominal value;
- the land recorded in the books was undervalued;
- among firm debtors, around 57 million CSK would probably remain unpaid.

Table 2

Firm Production Costs as of December 31, 1991 (in mil. CSK)

Total costs	1,293
Material costs	943
Depreciation	35
Labor costs	172
Financial expenses	139
Value added	474

Note: Changes in prices as of January 1, 1991, increased the registered value by a factor of 1.95. The average exchange rate for 1991 was U.S.$1 = 29.0 CSK. At the same time, the commercial or PPP exchange rate equaled $1 = 10.2 CSK, or one-third of the official rate. Therefore, statistical sequences before 1991 have to be regarded with care.

Table 3

Organization Chart

	Board of Directors
	Chairman of the Board and CEO
Top managers	• Strategy and Marketing • Economy • Technology (usually with the R&D manager)
Other corporate managers	• Commerce • Production • Quality • Personnel • Ten plant managers

Note: The board had six members; only the chairman was from Desta, others being representatives of the State, i.e., the Ministry of Industry, and of various banks. An autonomous Control Committee, consisting of the Ministry of Industry and two legal and finance experts, supervised the legal and financial activities of the firm governance. The books of the firm were checked annually by an independent international auditing firm.

2

Engineering: PSP

Intelligent Transformation of a Communist Bulwark

Jana Matesová

This case describes the transition of a typical large, heavy industrial firm that, like many others, was a major employer in its region and was previously supported by the communist regime. During 1990–92, this firm was confronted with two major changes that deprived it of most of its markets. First, the political upheaval changed international trade: the USSR's market became illiquid; an embargo on foreign trade with Iraq was announced; the CMEA broke down; and changes in the map of the world disrupted multilateral accords among nations. Second, macro- and microeconomic changes in Czechoslovakia caused a recession on the domestic market.

PSP was the main Czechoslovak subcontractor for an international ironprocessing plant that, in 1986, the communist governments of several East Bloc countries had decided to build in Krivoi Rog, a town in the USSR. But PSP accumulated large inventories of work-in-progress on its balance sheet and its financial position seemed disastrous.

The top management combined a short-term survival strategy with long-term goals, including a reorganization of the firm in order to gain both a good share of the world market and a sound financial position. The management also wanted new viable and liquid markets, and sought to clarify ownership rights of the enterprise. Because PSP's management understood that such a restructuring would be complicated, it decided to do this in a series of steps. The most difficult of PSP's problems, the clarification of ownership rights and the management of its responsibilities to the Krivoi Rog venture, illustrated the political risks that many enterprises must confront.

SECTORAL SETTING

Heavy engineering was a sector of industry in which successful transition would be difficult to achieve without outside help. For forty years, most firms in this sector had not had to fend for themselves. They had been strongly supported by government orders and protected from the competition of the world market. They were large employers with huge fixed assets, many of which were single-purpose devices that would be expensive to liquidate. The firms' production was capital-intensive and energy-consuming; their products often contained too much material; their electronic parts were usually obsolete; and their production was too diversified.[1]

The 1989 revolution brought about major changes for the heavy engineering industry. The Communist Party, with which many of the captains of industry were connected, lost power. The Czechoslovak currency was devalued in two steps in late 1990 and this, combined with the liberalization of prices, caused a sharp increase in the price of inputs in 1991. Also, liquidity in the CMEA market declined during 1990–91. This meant that, although demand for Czechoslovak engineering products was still high, customers were less able to pay. Investment activity on the domestic market also declined. One reason for this was a recession that resulted partly from the political decision to discontinue exports of military equipment and to embargo Iran. Also, external and internal economic factors, such as the breakdown of the CMEA market and a tight monetary policy, contributed to a decrease in investment. And these two factors in turn were not only partly to blame for a liquidity crisis in Czechoslovak enterprises, but also brought about structural changes in domestic industries.

As a result of these changes, heavy engineering experienced both a rapid growth of inventories and a liquidity crisis because banks were less willing than before to provide loans to finance growing assets. Most industries had to cut production significantly. The sharp recession that started in the second quarter of 1991 accelerated in the second half of that year and, as of mid-1992, had not improved. The 1990 total employment in heavy engineering, in the Czech Republic alone, was over 200 thousand, which was about 4 percent of the total labor force. One year later, this figure was 21 percent lower and, in 1992, it decreased by another 13 percent. One of the top managers of PSP described the situation in this way: "After ending the isolation of the past, the Czechoslovak heavy engineering industry is in a sorry plight. We try to understand what we are, where we are dashing, and in which direction we should go."

Substantial restructuring of production and a change in the time horizon of planning would be necessary to find a successful strategy for Czechoslovak investment engineering. The firms needed to develop sound products, become more focused on their major businesses, and increase their market share. Further cuts in employment would be necessary, despite the fact that many firms were major employers in their regions and the income of at least every second household strongly depended on them.

The top management of most enterprises was reluctant to make changes for several reasons. In the first place, in many cases, the managers frequently did not know what to do. They often searched for a foreign strategic partner in the belief that this partner could offer a new strategy, capital, technology and competitive products, managerial know-how, and markets. Many managers were satisfied with what they had already achieved, and wanted to keep their position and social power as long as possible. In the meantime, they often sought to increase their economic power through drifting, fraud, or the underground economy. Many were afraid of the intense conservatism of the firms, especially of the employees, the media, and the local administration, who generally did not want changes. The management argued that, during privatization, the business environment was so uncertain that it was better to postpone any change until the ownership, corporate governance, macroeconomic environment, and, obviously, their own positions became clearer. And lastly, the belief was that as long as the enterprise was producing, it was better to postpone any changes until the recession was over.

PSP IN TRANSITION

PSP had fifteen plants, fourteen of which, along with the headquarters, were located in Prerov, a city of 50,000 in central Moravia. PSP was a major producer of investment engineering products and services and the largest employer in the region, employing more than 5,300 workers at the end of 1991, which represented 10 percent of the total population of the town. The difficulties encountered by the management of other heavy engineering enterprises did not apply to PSP because PSP had successfully maintained its presence in Western markets during the past forty years.

Several years ago, the firm supplied the Brazilian, Iranian, Italian, Egyptian, and Iraqi markets. Because some of its markets were subject to embargo, and most of them had low liquidity, many customers required postponed payment terms. Until recently, all foreign trade had been done through the specialized foreign trade firm, Pragoinvest. PSP was paid in cash on delivery, and the foreign trade firm bore all the risks. Also, one major outlet for PSP's products had been the Soviet market.

HISTORY OF THE FIRM

PSP dates back to 1852. Its predecessors were four private firms: three produced engines, various machines, clutches, gearboxes, and tools and castings, and one was a metal foundry. The government nationalized all four immediately after World War II and incorporated them into a state-owned enterprise. After several reorganizations, in 1951, a state-owned enterprise, Prerovske strojirny Prerov (PSP), comprised of three of these firms, was established. In 1958, PSP merged with several other state-owned engineering enterprises and business units to become one of the leading engineering manufacturers in Czechoslovakia. In 1965, new mergers took place by means of which PSP, together with several smaller engineering firms, joined another large heavy engineering company, CKD Prague. CKD introduced a divisional structure in 1969 and PSP became its own division. This was closed in 1988, and a new enterprise, PSP, which had the legal status of a state enterprise, was simultaneously registered.

PSP's Market Share and Major Competitors

Among the major items manufactured by PSP were finished engineering product lines, castings, industrial gears, and industrial clutches. The top management had built the firm's long-term strategy primarily on engineering, which produces the highest value-added products. The major product lines within engineering were equipment for cement works and/or ceramic works. Table 4 lists total output by major product lines, and Table 5 lists total exports.

According to a market research study done by Stuermer in 1992, PSP's market share for its cement works equipment in major markets was good. The country's cement industry was growing. Large foreign firms such as Heidelberger Zement, Lafarge, Holderbank, Italcementi, and CBR had invested in Czech and Slovak cement works, and they planned more massive investment in the future. Because PSP was a traditional supplier of investment goods for Czechoslovak cement works and it had good reason to believe that this cooperation would continue, the future looked secure.

PSP also maintained a 50–60 percent share in the domestic market for equipment for the ceramic industry, and slightly less than 1 percent of the world market. This share was also growing but, unlike the market for cement works equipment, that for ceramic equipment was highly competitive. PSP had several domestic competitors and, because the quality of the imported products and services provided by foreign competitors was generally higher than PSP's, international competition on the domestic market was growing. Thus far, PSP had managed to maintain competitive prices, but the management realized that this was a short-term advantage. Other PSP products had been produced for domestic engineering and construction firms in the past, but this market was now in a recession and demand had decreased. Moreover, compared to those of foreign competitors, these products were of standard rather than top quality.

CHANGES AND OPPORTUNITIES FOR THE FIRM

Shocks

As mentioned earlier, the entire industry faced major changes during the years 1990–92. Overall, PSP lost as much as 80 percent of its markets, or the markets became highly illiquid. PSP also faced political risk. In addition to the embargo on foreign trade with Iraq in 1990, the government also stopped loans to Cuba and Algeria. The most serious problem, however, was the firm's involvement in a large international venture in Krivoi Rog, and it was this venture that seriously endangered PSP's financial stability.

Several years before, the governments of Czechoslovakia, the German Democratic Republic, Bulgaria, and Romania had contracted with the government of the USSR to construct a large facility for magnetic separation of iron ore in Krivoi Rog, which was located in the Ukraine. Based on this multilateral agreement, each of the four governments assigned a foreign trade firm to contract with the Soviet foreign trade firm, Soiuz Mezhstroiimport, for the construction of the facility, the installation of its equipment, and its operation.

The Czechoslovak foreign trade firm, Pragoinvest, in turn contracted with CKD, an investment engineering group, as the principal contractor. CKD's division, CKD–Principal Contractor, then negotiated a contract with other subcontractors, one of which was PSP. Construction began in 1986 and, when it was completed, the goods were produced and shipped to Krivoi Rog.

The entire investment was financed by long-term, low-interest, government-guaranteed bank loans to be repaid over a number of years. Neither the foreign trade firm nor the contractors and subcontractors were responsible for paying either the interest on the loans or the collateral. Total costs of Czechoslovak deliveries to Krivoi Rog were estimated at more than CSK 11 billion. By financing the deliveries, the Czechoslovak government, like governments of the other countries, would become a shareholder of the facility.

In 1988, the CKD group split into several parts. PSP became an independent state enterprise, and CKD's former division, Principal Contractor, became part of PSP as a separate unit/plant. The political changes during 1989–91 in all participating countries brought about a reassessment of government attitudes toward such large international ventures, and particularly the one at Krivoi Rog.

Another factor that increased the uncertainty of this venture was the question of ownership of the former USSR's share of Krivoi Rog. No one knew who owned the ore or who was responsible for completing the Soviet part of the construction. At the beginning of 1993, neither the Russian nor the Ukrainian government had solved the dilemma, but this needed to be settled before operations could begin. A great deal of work and investment was still required of the former Soviet Union.

Organizational changes in both Czechoslovakia and the USSR also affected the construction of Krivoi Rog. In late 1991, both Soiuz Mezhstroiimport and Pragoinvest ceased to exist. Pragoinvest was liquidated and, because it had been a state-owned firm, the government took over its outstanding obligations and contracts. Many activities at the construction site were discontinued; however, no contracts had yet been repudiated.

In 1991, PSP's management decided to speed up deliveries to the venture, which was a risky decision. On the balance sheet, PSP already had over CSK 8 billion of inventories or work-in-progress in the venture.[2] On the liabilities side, 99 percent of the difference was long-term debt. Compared to the CSK 1.3

billion of PSP's equity, a serious problem seemed to exist (see Tables 8 and 9). In April 1992, the Czechoslovak government decided to stop its involvement in the venture. There was no one in the former USSR with whom the Czechoslovak government could negotiate this decision. The main contractor, PSP's division, continued to buy equipment and services from Czechoslovak subcontractors and to deliver them to Krivoi Rog according to contract. At this point, most of PSP's traditional markets were in recession or were experiencing liquidity crises, and some markets were subject to embargo. Thus, the firm was operating far below capacity and supplying Krivoi Rog seemed to be a good survival strategy.

Late in 1992, the Czechoslovak portion of the deliveries was almost completed. PSP had CSK 10.5 billion (over $350 million) worth of inventories in the project. The Investicni Bank had assumed responsibility for the financing of this venture and was liable for the CSK 10.5 billion in inventories. The bank did not renegotiate the loan, but continued to finance the project during 1992, in spite of the fact that it had not really wanted to provide the loan. During 1990–92, interest rates in Czechoslovakia were between 12 percent and 23 percent, while the loan in question had a fixed interest rate of 6 percent. PSP and the Investicni Bank both repeatedly tried to make the federal government aware of its obligations connected to Krivoi Rog, but the government was busy dealing with both the domestic political situation and the transition.

As the debts accumulated, the firm's management put increasing pressure on the government to decide about the ownership of Krivoi Rog and the government's obligations concerning the loans. PSP participated in a carefully coordinated effort with other Czechoslovak parties involved in this international venture to force the government to decide. In November 1992, the newly formed Czech and Slovak governments were under time constraints because of the January 1, 1993, split of the country into two independent states. Thus, the governments felt it necessary to divide the assets and liabilities of the Federation.

The federal Czech and Slovak governments opened negotiations on the ownership of the former Soviet part of the construction site and facility with the government of Ukraine. Ukraine postponed its decision as to whether or not to bid for the Soviet share of ownership and to assume responsibility for the completion of the construction. The outgoing Czechoslovak government confirmed its decision to stop its investment in the venture and decided to pay the loan collateral, which amounted to more than CSK 10 billion by that time. It also agreed to pay the interest payments on the loan, in yearly installments over a period of ten years, to pay PSP's lost profits from the state budget. Lastly, it decided to transfer the assets from the ownership of the state, and thus from PSP, to a newly established firm. The shareholders of this firm were PSP, which had the largest stake, the other main Czech suppliers of the Krivoi Rog venture, and the large Slovak steel works that intended to use products of the venture, those being iron-ore pellets. All the shareholders were large enterprises that had originally been state-owned but were privatized in 1992.

Opportunities

Despite pressure on the management to make the government decide about the Czechoslovak ownership of the facility, Krivoi Rog also provided a stable market for PSP. In addition to this venture, other opportunities for the firm had arisen. The undervalued currency was supporting PSP's exports. The internal convertibility of the Czechoslovak crown gave PSP a greater variety of opportunities in foreign trade than before. The substantial changes in the business environment necessitated a restructuring of the firm, which, before 1989, had neither been possible nor needed.

THE FIRM'S RESPONSES

The management of PSP was replaced in 1990 for reasons that were partly political and partly professional. Employees were no longer willing to work with managers who had been connected with the former political system. They believed that these managers would be neither able nor willing to transform the enterprise into one able to compete in the new market conditions. PSP's new management hired domestic and foreign consultants to help with market research, to formulate a new strategy, and to improve its managerial expertise. Along with a short-term strategy, the objective of which was to survive without a significant decrease in production, PSP's management defined other short-term goals that had long-term implications.

When PSP's managers realized that they could not immediately find a liquid demand for the firm's products and that financing new markets and renegotiating terms-of-contracts with traditional customers would both take several months, they decided to base the short-term strategy on the riskiest card, the firm's involvement in the Krivoi Rog project. PSP had accelerated deliveries to Krivoi Rog, even though it had no guarantee that the government would repay the loans. These deliveries, however, made it possible for several of PSP's divisions to operate close to capacity.

The mid-range goal was to maintain the firm's market share even if liquidity in the traditional markets was low. However, the firm's financial situation deteriorated rapidly. In 1990 and 1991, PSP accumulated sizable accounts receivable and lost its liquidity. Thus, achieving financial stability took on even greater importance.

Foreign trade became more difficult when Pragoinvest, which had previous handled most of the firm's foreign trade, collapsed. When no satisfactory agency was found, the top management decided that the firm would handle these operations on its own. It did, however, hire specialized firms, particularly Western firms, to do market research and marketing in those sectors it did not know well. In the search for liquid markets, PSP benefited from its network of agents that had been established in some countries for many years. In most cases, the firm did not have to abandon its markets, even though most of them, such as the former USSR, Brazil, Iran, and Egypt, generally had low liquidity. PSP had had excellent experience with a large Brazilian firm and the cooperation between them even became a partnership of sorts.

On the domestic market, most local cement works, which were traditional customers of PSP, acquired foreign private owners in 1991, and their future seemed favorable. When they started to invest in 1992, PSP's management put extraordinary efforts into maintaining good business and social relationships with these firms. Thus, networking and maintaining official and unofficial contacts became an important policy for PSP. The enterprise succeeded in finding another growing market niche in environmental technology on the domestic market. With this technology, the firm was also able to offer a competitive price/quality ratio.

After the 1990–91 accumulation of overdue accounts receivable, particularly in the former USSR, the firm decided to pay more attention to contracts, particularly the terms-of-payment. Detailed knowledge of the markets and the customers and careful negotiation of the contracts helped greatly. In 1992, deliveries to foreign customers were often paid in hard currency prior to delivery, although some trade with the former USSR was in barter.

PSP's relations with other markets were more difficult than those it had with Brazil, Italy, and the former USSR. Customers required renegotiation of terms-of-contracts, which generally meant extending commercial credit by postponing payments. Commercial banks were no longer willing to provide loans to finance increasing accounts receivable. The firm decided to introduce and develop credit management and to improve financial management. The result of these measures was that most overdue receivables were recovered, including those in the former USSR, and those that appeared irretrievable were sold.

In the course of a short-term strategy development, the management also formulated long-term goals for restructuring. PSP concluded that the most important strategic objective was to maintain or increase its share in world markets.

The top managers clearly saw that the restructuring of such a large firm, whose financial stability seemed to be disastrous and whose major markets had lost their liquidity, had to be done in steps. They set their priorities. The primary goal would be solving the liquidity and ownership problem connected to the Krivoi Rog project. The second goal focused on successful privatization. PSP's top management attempted to find a means of privatization that would give the management as much control over the firm as possible. The last goal concentrated on completing the organizational changes, improving the internal organization and communication, and creating a new corporate culture. As part of this goal, the management intended to implement total quality management, to change attitudes, and to harmonize the goals of the laborers, sales people, and managers at all levels. High-quality management and advanced management know-how were stressed.

PRIVATIZATION

PSP was included in the 1992 so-called first wave of privatization in Czechoslovakia. Its management was required to prepare a privatization plan before the end of October 1991. In January 1991, the state enterprise had been transformed into a fully state-owned, joint stock firm. Two months before the transformation, one of the firm's plants broke off and became an independent, but still state-owned, firm.

PSP's management would have preferred a management buyout, but at that time the Ministry for Privatization, which was responsible for selecting the best privatization plans, was not in favor of such buyouts. Thus, the top management proposed a privatization plan that it believed would still provide the managers with effective control of the firm. This plan involved:

- 65 percent voucher privatization;
- 10 percent foreign direct investment in the form of direct sale to the Brazilian customer with which PSP had excellent long-term relations;
- 15 percent transfer to commercial banks;
- 5 percent free transfer of shares to the local administration;
- 3 percent mandatory transfer to the National Restitution Fund;
- 2 percent in restitutions.

The Ministry of Privatization approved this plan in the spring of 1992 and the voucher privatization started the following June. In the first bidding round, the prices of shares in all firms were set at the same level (it was the government that set the prices for each bidding round of the voucher privatization). PSP did not have much success and sold only 6 percent of the shares offered. After the price was cut by two-thirds, an additional 37 percent was sold and it became obvious that investment funds were waiting for a sufficient decrease in the price. In the third bidding round, in which the sale price was reduced by 74 percent of the original level, the demand exceeded the number of shares remaining. Thus, according to rules of voucher privatization, no additional shares were sold and the price was increased again. The price for the fourth bidding round was exactly one-seventh of the price for the first round, and all remaining shares were sold. PSP's voucher privatization, the details of which may be seen in Table 2, was completed in November 1992. However, 30 percent of the firm's ownership still remained in the National Property Fund. This consisted of the 10 percent originally reserved for foreign direct investment, 15 percent for banks, and 5 percent for local administration. Following a precedent set by Skoda Plzen, the management thought that if it submitted a new privatization plan for a management buyout of the last 30 percent of the firm, the new government might accept it.

Changes in Organization of the Firm

In 1990, before the changes were initiated, PSP's 15 plants were based on product lines and were managed from the headquarters as cost-centers. As of

January 1991, the firm became a joint stock firm, and was still fully state-owned. The change in the firm's legal structure was connected to a change in its organization, and therefore, the management introduced a holding structure of fifteen divisions. The main goals of the changes were to decentralize decision-making, to shift more responsibility to lower levels of management, to simulate some features of a market environment within the firm, and to improve the attitudes of lower-level managers and workers.

After the holding structure had become fully implemented, new divisions that develop from the plants would have greater independence. The sales, R&D, and technological departments had already achieved more independence and responsibility, and the overall intention was to transform all divisions into business centers with minimal central control. To this end, internal information systems were being constructed, but it would take some time to achieve the goals of

- making these centers relatively independent;
- building an internal system of incentives and profit sharing that could reflect the performance of divisions before they were responsible for their profits; and
- teaching the divisions how to operate as real entrepreneurs.

In the meantime, PSP's top management planned to introduce an internal bank and to use this bank for clearing among divisions.

Changes in Corporate Governance

Since 1988, when PSP became a state enterprise, the supervisory board had executed corporate governance. The board consisted of both inside and outside directors, and the managing board,[3] whose members were also both inside and outside directors. Members of both boards were selected by PSP and appointed by the Ministry of Industry. Among outside members of the boards, there was a representative of the owner, which was still the state, in the form of the Ministry of Industry. In addition to this representative, there were high-position representatives of the Ministry of Finance, the Commercial Bank (where PSP has its accounts), the Institute of Economic Law, the Institute of State Law, a chartered accountant, and experts from universities and firms. As a fully state-owned joint stock firm, PSP kept its boards. New Czech and Slovak owners who acquired interests in the firm in exchange for vouchers would not be allowed to execute their ownership rights until April 1993, at which point new boards were to be formed. The function of both boards was rather symbolic; the management of the firm did the groundwork; however, the management used the boards as channels of information and as contacts.

The Ministry of Industry appointed the general manager who, at the time of this study, was Mr. Zdenek Muzik, born in 1955, and who had been with the firm since 1979. He was promoted to this position in 1990 and chose his functional managers, all of whom had been promoted from within the firm. The structure of the top management is described in Figure 1.

Building the Common House of PSP: Human Resources

In 1990 and 1991, PSP managers and their consultants worked hard to find the means to achieve the goals described above. The formulation of a mission, of the firm's codex, of social policy guidelines, and of new public relations were important steps in achieving the creation of a new corporate culture. Well-defined labor standards and a change in the system of incentives were also important; however, until the end of 1992, wage regulations prohibited any substantial increase in wages. Even though PSP was a large employer in the region and had social responsibility, it nevertheless had to reduce employment.

What was remarkable and striking about PSP, and distinguished this firm from most others in Czechoslovakia, was its well-organized decision-making process. The responsibilities of all managers were clear, communication between employees seemed to work well, and the top management had the firm under control.

MAJOR FINDINGS

During the period of transition, PSP had operated in a difficult environment. Traditional markets demanding equipment for specific, although mostly obsolete, technology had disintegrated and the entire industry needed restructuring.

PSP's management, unlike managers of many other heavy engineering enterprises, was eager to make the necessary changes. Its professional approach, which was characteristic of the firm, dictated its use of outside experts and professional institutions whenever it could not rely on its own expertise. The transition seemed to have been well-managed and the management had structured the process by dividing it into steps and setting priorities.

PSP's short-term goals, particularly completing production for Krivoi Rog, and its mid-range objectives to maintain high profits/high market share wherever possible, were combined with the long-term objective of increasing its share in liquid markets. PSP competed on a price basis and was able to keep the price/quality ratio at a lower level than most of its competitors. Its strategy for producing was in engineering, particularly designing, building, and equipping large complex facilities for the cement and ceramic industries, and producing ecological technology and equipment for the standard power stations that burned brown coal. The firm had yet to complete its strategies for individual products such as gears and clutches. As a large enterprise with substantial power, especially in its surrounding region, PSP successfully supported its activities through lobbying. The firm's management emphasized networking and maintaining contacts, and had a well-built network of relationships both in Czechoslovakia and in all its strategic markets.

The most interesting aspect of PSP's adaptation during the transition was that of Krivoi Rog. This venture was responsible for the disastrous appearance of the firm's balance sheet and financial ratios; however, it also helped to maintain production during the most difficult period of the transition, 1991 and 1992. In the end, the firm's management succeeded in turning a potential catastrophe into a huge gain for the firm.

Unlike most enterprises in heavy industry, PSP did not just wait for magic assistance. It was a firm with the potential to win new markets and the firm's new top management seemed not only to have no fear of the risks connected with the necessary changes, but also to understand the strategy. The executives tried to manage the firm in a professional manner and hired consultants when needed. SWOT—an analysis of strengths, weaknesses, opportunities, and threats—was one of the major projects on which these consultants worked in 1992. Market research provided information about PSP's market share in strategic markets and its major competitors. Professional firms made industrial forecasts for heavy engineering and its major customers, and also audited and implemented an internal accounting system that matches EC standards.

One striking feature about the firm relative to many others in Czechoslovakia was the organization of the management. The top management of PSP gave the impression of a well-organized team of dedicated, well-balanced managers who knew each other's responsibilities and handled problems well. Communication was quick and reliable, and the employees seemed more dedicated that average. In this turbulent environment, strategy was formulated three years ahead and updated on an annual basis where necessary.

Notes

1. Sometimes, product lines included hundreds of thousands of widgets, from coathangers to nuclear reactors; moreover, the enterprises also provided many services.

2. As of December 31, 1991, total assets of the Principal Contractor division reached CSK 8.300 billion. Total assets of remaining fourteen divisions together accounted for CSK 3.247 billion as of December 31, 1991, of which CSK 8.244 billion were inventories, i.e., the value of the construction site and work-in-progress in Krivoi Rog, compared to inventories of CSK 1.144 billion in remaining divisions. *Source:* PSP's information department.

3. The Czechoslovak legal system as of 1989 to 1992, like that of some West European countries, required corporate governance to be executed by two boards. However, it supplied only vague provisions on the functions and membership of the boards, and no legal requirements at all on the duty of care or the duty of loyalty of the outside directors. Unlike the West European system, Czechoslovak law required that both internal and external directors be on both boards.

Table 1

PSP Market Shares and Main Competitors

Country	Market share	Major competitors	Tendency
Brazil	10%	Polysius, Fuller	0
Italy	4%	Polysius, KHD	growing
Iran	5%	KHD, FLS	rapidly growing
Czechoslovakia	95%	none	growing

Source: Steurmer's market study for PSP, 1992.

Table 2

Privatization of PSP: Bidding Rounds, Prices of Shares, Percentages of the Ownership Sold

Bidding round	Prices of shares per 100 voucher points[1]	Shares sold as a percentage of the total ownership offered for voucher privatization
1st	3	6
2nd	9	37
3rd	38	none[2]
4th	21	100

Source: Center for the Voucher Privatization, Prague.
Notes:
[1] Each holder of the voucher book was allowed to allocate 1,000 voucher points.
[2] More shares were demanded than offered.

Table 3

Changes in Employment

	1988	1989	1990	1991	1st Quarter/92	1st–2nd Quarter/92
Employment	6,078	5,927	5,736	5,056	4,963	4,845
1. Laborers	1,831	1,784	1,709	1,413	1,501	1,469
2. Technicians	717	715	712	708	574	574
3. Managerial staff	1,922	1,884	1,797	1,500	1,482	1,454

Source: PSP's Information Department.

ENGINEERING: PSP 29

Table 4

Total Output by Major Product Lines
(in current prices)

	1988	1989	1990	1991	1st–2nd Quarter/92
Total output Engineering (incl. deliveries of components)	2,018,876	2,011,894	1,925,055	2,439,914	1,037,551
	826,852	838,391	714,939	797,411	486,219
Castings	99,530	99,581	100,414	96,090	135,274
Gears	301,875	300,865	308,491	319,467	149,242

Source: PSP's Information Department.

Table 5

Total Exports and Structure of Exports by Major Product Lines
(thousands of CSK, at current prices and current exchange rate)

	1988	1989	1990	1991	1st–2nd Quarter/92
Total exports Engineering (incl. deliveries of components)	859,388	752,372	762,250	875,628	223,856
	734,314	618,892	624,787	472,554	222,166
Castings	—	—	—	—	—
Gears	122,074	133,480	137,463	403,074	377

Source: PSP's Information Department.

Table 6

Structure of Costs
(1st–3rd Quarter/92)

	Percentage of total costs
Labor	38.0
Material	29.4
Energy	9.0
Depreciation	5.4
Interest payments	5.0
Other overhead	13.2
Total	100.0

Source: PSP's Information Department.

Table 7

Output, Costs, Margin
(1st–3rd Quarter/92)

	Thousand CSK
Total output	1,325,159
Sales	1,267,178
Cost of goods sold	1,152,354
Markup	114,824
Operating profit	(4,511)
Extraordinary profits minus extraordinary losses	167,397
Gross profit/loss	162,886

Source: PSP's Information Department.

Table 8

Financial Ratios
(flows for 1st–3rd Quarter/92 and stocks as of September 30, 1992)

Profitability ratios	
Mark-up/sales	9.06
Gross profit/sales	12.86
Mark-up/cost of goods sold	9.96
Gross profit/cost of goods sold	14.14
Liquidity ratios	
Current ratio	1.85
Quick ratio	0.41
Activity ratios	
Average collection period (days)	146
Average payments period (days)	107
Average inventory turnover/cost of goods sold (days)	331
Leverage	
Debt/equity	8.32
Equity/total assets	0.11
Rate of return	
Return on equity	0.11

Source: PSP's Information Department.
Note: All the data exclude the Principal Contractor division.

Table 9

Balance Sheet Data
(data include the Principal Contractor division, thousands of CSK)

	December 31, 1990	December 31, 1991 (1,000 CSK)
Assets		
Cash	18,290	195,295
Marketable securities	0	12,980
Accounts receivable	550,842	886,238
Inventories	6,505,335	9,387,757
Prepaid expenses	53	0
Total current assets	7,074,447	10,482,270
Fixed assets (total property, plant and equipment)	1,069,047	1,065,522
Total assets	**8,143,547**	**11,547,792**
Liabilities		
Accounts payable	752,499	1,263,656
Accrued expenses payable	27,231	27,868
Total current liabilities	779,730	1,291,524
Long-term debt	1,344,099	564,954
Total liabilities	2,124,629	1,856,478
Retained earnings	24,970	110,530
Common stock	1,249,258	1,252,467
Total owners' equity	**1,274,228**	**1,362,997**

Source: Annual Report of PSP, 1991.

Figure 1. **Structure of Management of PSP**

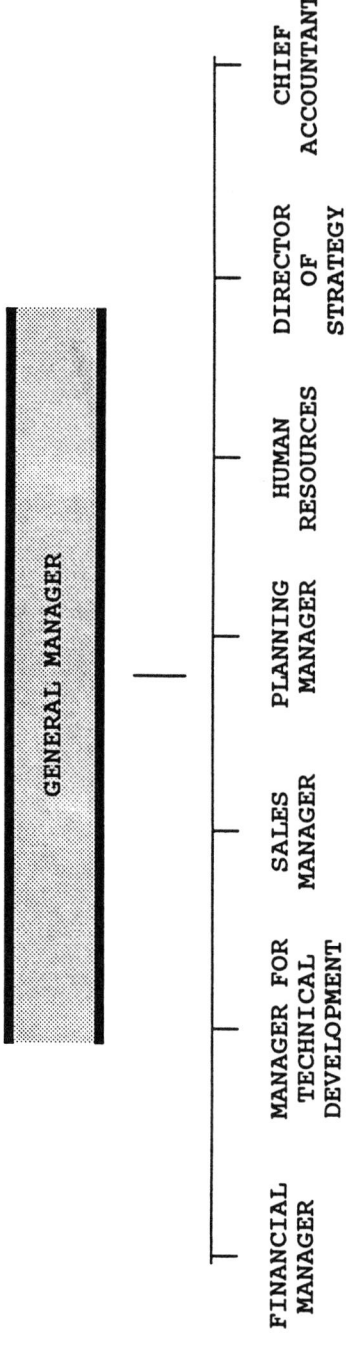

3

Heavy Chemicals: Spolana

Martin Sauer

SECTORAL SETTING

The purpose of the chemical industry of Czechoslovakia was to serve the Czechoslovak economy and supply the widest possible assortment of chemical products. After the postwar period, when coal ceased to be the fundamental basis for the industry, the emphasis shifted gradually to primary processing of crude oil, synthetic rubber, chemical fibers, and heavy organic chemistry and fertilizers, followed by petrochemistry and tar. Spolana used a wide variety of technologies ranging from modern refineries, which were involved in 29 percent of the industry's output, and petrochemical plants to obsolete units, which operated primarily in the fields of inorganic chemistry and fertilizers.

In Czechoslovakia, the most important industries were chemicals, machinery, iron metallurgy, and food. The communists had wanted to make the country the center of heavy industry in the East Bloc, and, by the end of the 1980s, heavy industry contributed almost 60 percent of industrial production and employed one-third of the country's workers. Of a total industrial employment of 2.87 million, over 100,000 worked in the chemical industry. Total industrial output of the CSFR was 1,003 billion in 1990, of which chemical production contributed 114 billion CSK, or about 12 percent.

The volume of this industry, which included about 100 enterprises, equaled the export potential of the textile, clothing, and tannery industries combined. During communist rule, ministries controlled the industry and forced plants to adhere closely to the five-year state plans. Individual firms belonged to large state-owned conglomerates such as Chemopetrol Prague. Firms were assigned the production of specific goods and the state authorities determined prices of inputs and outputs. Thus, there was no competition and the industry was very monopolistic.

The chemical industry was closely connected to the CMEA market and dependent on cheap crude oil from the former USSR. Exports to the ruble zone, especially to the USSR, were comprised mainly of specialty chemicals such as

33

organic dyes, pharmaceuticals, and laboratory chemicals. Prices were rarely those prevailing in the world and trade was generally conducted in transferable rubles. Chemicals, fertilizers, and rubber made up about 5 percent of foreign trade with socialist states, which was carried out through monopolistic state enterprises, the biggest of which was Chemapol Prague.

Since the overthrow of the communist government in Czechoslovakia in November 1989, the industry has been on the move. Direct state control rapidly diminished and the conglomerates were separated into independent state-owned enterprises. Moreover, state ownership decreased as a result of privatization. Many chemical firms were privatized in the first wave at the end of 1992, and the rest were to follow in the second wave in 1993. The state, however, retained a share in enterprises that were considered strategically important, such as refineries.

Even with these changes, the industry's structure did not change much. It remained fairly monopolistic in 1992, with many firms closely connected to one another. The industry was still characterized by heavy investment in production facilities and high fixed costs. Environmental problems connected to production were also common.

SPOLANA NERATOVICE

History of the Firm

Spolana was the fourth largest chemical firm in the country and was built as part of Czechoslovakia's comprehensive industrial network. It was located in Neratovice, a town of 20,000 in central Bohemia on the Labe, or Elbe, river. The chemical industry in Neratovice began in the last years of the nineteenth century when a plant was built to produce carbide. Two other plants were opened in the first years of this century, one to manufacture auxiliary products for the tanning industry and the second, the Sebor firm, to concentrate on processing waste products from gasworks. In 1917, the GEC Cooperative bought Sebor and changed its output to food products. In 1939, the Association for Chemical and Metallurgical Production in Prague, the largest chemical concern in Czechoslovakia at the time, assumed ownership in order to compensate for plants in northern Bohemia that had been lost in the Munich Diktat.

The Association started the electrolytic production of chlorine and dyes as the basis for construction of an inorganic chemical industry, but just before the end of World War II, in March 1945, the plant was damaged by an allied bomb attack. After the war, reconstruction began, but in October 1945, a law was passed nationalizing mines and various industrial enterprises, including the Association and its new Neratovice plant. In 1949, the government ended the Association and created the Spolana Neratovice national enterprise, which became one of the drivers in the chemicalization of the national economy. Its production diversified into such areas as viscose fibers, sulphuric acid, caprolactam, and so on, and sold primarily to domestic and CMEA markets. In 1969, Spolana became a part of the Chemopetrol conglomerate with other major chemical enterprises like Kaucuk Kralupy and CHZ Litvinov, and, as Spolana's growth continued in the 1970s, plastics were added to its production line.

Production Programs

The scope of firm products was wide, ranging from heavy chemicals produced in thousands of tons to specialty chemicals produced in grams. Overall, Spolana had about 300 different products, divided into the areas of industrial chemistry, man-made fibers, plastics, agro- and gastrochemistry, and specialty and pure chemicals.

Industrial Chemistry. The manufacture of industrial chemicals had the longest tradition at Spolana and was represented by typical heavy chemical products such as sulphuric acid, hydrochloric acid, sodium hydroxide, liquid chlorine, sodium hypochlorite, sodium sulphate, which is a by-product of viscose fiber, ammonium sulphate, a by-product of caprolactam, and caprolactam. Most products in these categories held a dominant position in the domestic market; Caprolactam, for example, accounted for 62 percent and sodium hydroxide for 45 percent of total domestic production.

Man-made Fibers. Spolana's production of fibers also had a long tradition. The production of viscose staple fiber, of which the enterprise was the monopolistic producer in the CSFR, dates back to 1947. The main inputs for this fiber were pulp, mostly from domestic suppliers but some from Germany, carbon disulphide supplied by Siarkopol Co., Poland, and sulphuric acid from in-plant production. Spolana's main competitor in fiber production was Lenzing, Austria.

Plastics. Spolana had produced plastics since 1975, when its petrochemical complex was put into operation. The basic input was ethylene from Chemopetrol Litvinov, one of the major refineries in CSFR, and the principal plastic products were PVC and VCM, the main share of which was used in PVC production, followed by PPO (polyphenylene oxide) and APAD (alkaline polyamide). PVC also gave Spolana a strong domestic position because it amounted to nearly 60 percent of the market share.

Agrochemistry and Gastrochemistry. There were 40 types of products, comprised of many kinds of pesticides and synthetic sweeteners, which made this program the second most diversified after pure chemicals.

Specialty and Pure Chemicals. Spolana's specialties included synthetic hormones and semi-products for medicines, and the pure chemicals included iodine salts and scintillators. The profitability of the last two programs varied from negative values to almost 50 percent.

The applications of Spolana products were very wide, ranging from pulps and papers to textiles, fats, glasses, and uranium, and were used in the electrical engineering and footwear industries, as well as in energy, agriculture, and forestry industries. Plant utilization, after a drop in 1991, was generally very high, ranging from 90 to 100 percent. Only a few production lines were around 60 percent.

MAJOR SHOCKS TO THE FIRM

After 1990, Spolana had to adjust to an unprecedented market squeeze and transform its structure of activities in order to survive and sustain reasonable prosperity. Within a short period of time, the firm was affected by several destabilizing events.

In 1990, the traditional East European markets disintegrated and CMEA markets broke down almost completely. The direct effect on Spolana was minor because, in 1989, its exports into CMEA markets had comprised only 10 percent of its production. However, the indirect effects were much worse. Prices of Russian crude oil increased sharply, first from 1,550 to 5,280 CSK per ton in November 1990. The CMEA carried out transactions in hard currency in January 1991, which, combined with the Persian Gulf war, caused oil prices to peak at 6,200 CSK per ton. Prices then followed world trends and slipped to 4,730 in mid-1992. That caused problems with Spolana's plastics production because prices of ethylene, which is based on oil, bought from Litvinov, tripled. Moreover, because a large part of Czechoslovakia's domestic industry was oriented toward exports to CMEA markets, CMEA's difficulties caused a serious decrease in demand for Spolana products.

In January 1991, 85 percent of all prices and almost all industrial prices were liberalized, causing cost and price patterns to shift significantly. In November 1991, additional prices were decontrolled and the government stopped granting subsidies to most enterprises. Inflation in 1991 was 57.4 percent, although wages in state-owned enterprises were still regulated. Deregulation was planned for January 1993.

The successive devaluations of the national currency, from 14.70 CSK to 17 CSK = $1 in January 1990, to 24 CSK = $1 in October 1990, to 28 CSK = $1 in December 1990, increased the costs of imports. This was problematic for Spolana because it coincided with the construction of a new NAO (normal alpha-olefines) plant, most of the technology for which had been imported from Austria and other Western countries. However, this devaluation was balanced by higher income from exports.

Foreign trade was liberalized and internal convertibility was introduced in January 1991, meaning that all firms could obtain hard currency and were permitted to trade directly with foreign partners. Interest rates increased, peaking in mid-1990 at 24 percent, and a restrictive credit policy followed, particularly in the first half of 1991. This created significant difficulties for Spolana, which needed large bank credits for the increasing construction prices.

These developments caused a slowdown of the entire economy. A gradual decrease in domestic demand for almost all products followed, along with secondary insolvency of individual enterprises. This sales and financial crisis, at different times and with different intensities, also affected the chemical industry, although heavy chemistry was affected only after a considerable delay, which gave the industry time to prepare itself. Thus, most enterprises, especially larger ones, were able to maintain their financial balance. In this environment, Spolana implemented a number of measures.

SHORT-TERM REACTIONS

Corporate Governance

After the breakdown of Communist Party rule, Chemopetrol split apart and Spolana become an independent state enterprise in July 1990. The official founder and supervisor was the Ministry of Chemical Industry of the Czech Republic; however, the firm was relatively independent from state authorities and direct state control was largely a formality. Because the firm had successfully completed the necessary preparations, it was included in the first wave of privatization. The Ministry of Privatization and the Czech government approved its privatization plan, the first step of which was the creation of a state-owned joint stock firm, Spolana, in May 1992.

Organization and Structure of Management

The organization of the firm had not changed much in recent years. It was headed by a managing director with vice-presidents in the six functional areas of production, financial, technical, sales and marketing, personnel, and capital investment. A board of directors and a supervisory board played minor roles. The organizational structure was product-oriented; however, some organizational changes were made in order to respond to changes in the business environment. The structure of the sales department, for example, was modified and some staff added to make up for the loss of Chemapol, the state foreign trade firm, through which all foreign trade had passed.

Production, Output, Costs, Labor, and Short-Term Policy

After a decrease in production caused by the 1991 drop in domestic demand, mainly in specialties, pure chemicals, and agrochemicals, Spolana returned to about 95 percent of its production capacity in mid-1992. Ecological problems, such as excessive emissions of H_2S and CS_2, resulted in a decrease of viscose fiber production. Share core production programs, measured by sales volume, are shown in Table 7. Data about physical production volume are shown in Table 8. The increase in total costs in 1991 was in line with the growth in sales and the prices of raw and other materials. Unit costs declined due to lower specific consumption. The cost structure is shown in Table 3. The financial vice-president commented: "All employees should carry an abacus in their hands. We have found that the majority of operators, and even a number of supervisors and managers, could not give reliable information about the unit cost of the materials they consume, man-hours spent in their departments, or the overhead costs. Although we stress low costs, we know that competitiveness does not rely only on this. It is a combination of customer satisfaction, high quality, low prices, sales services, and good timing."

The new personnel vice-president, the third in three years, said: "We know that we inherited massive overemployment. We do not want to make the cuts too sharp; we prefer to decrease the number of employees by natural departures and find new jobs for our employees in newly constructed plants. We need people with specific skills. We do not complain that engineering and technical skills are inadequate, although in most cases, they are. But there is an urgent demand for people with marketing, foreign trade, accounting and finance, and managerial skills to promote teamwork and the commitment to improve. Another problem is state wage regulations. We have to compete for the best people with private and foreign firms that do not have regulations. Some very valuable employees have already left." (Data on labor at Spolana are presented in Table 10.)

Large enterprises such as Spolana tend to integrate many unrelated activities into a core business, and developments in the firm's department of capital investment demonstrated this. Because the department often had difficulties finding subcontractors, the firm used its own engineers and workers for construction and equipment assembly. These people were required to perform many tasks to coordinate with and sometimes even to replace subcontractors.

A similar situation was found in the social services offered by Spolana. Houses and flats were provided for employees. In 1991, the firm owned 2,169 flats. Spolana also had catering and canteens, health care, and recreation facilities. For example, in 1991, Spolana had five facilities in different locations with 517 beds. The employees also had access to fitness facilities, kindergartens for the employees' children, and an apprentice-training center that became independent in mid-1991. Management had realized that this approach was one reason for overstaffing and it had started to cut down in these areas. The capital investment department was shrinking rapidly and was to be merged with the technical department.

Markets, Prices, and Sales

The market situation was well described by the managing director: "The drop in the Czechoslovak machinery, textile, and building industries, together with the loss of CMEA markets, significantly reduced our previous markets. We managed, however, to recover from most of the losses and, in 1991, we found new foreign markets. In 1990, exports accounted for 22.5 percent of our total sales, and Spolana succeeded in increasing the share of exports to 37.5 percent, which was equivalent to 2.6 billion CSK. In 1992, Spolana lost another market in the former Yugoslavia due to the civil war. Despite this, increases in exports continue and reached almost 50 percent in the first half of 1992. What is even more valuable is that almost all the exports were sent to Western countries."

Exporting to Western countries was not easy because the Western markets were plagued by overcapacity and often dominated by strong firms that erected barriers to entry. The structure of exports by countries is shown in Table 9. While Spolana exported most of its products through Chemapol, the foreign trade firm, it also started to sell some products directly to selected markets.

The firm also tried to get closer to domestic customers, who still accounted for the majority of sales. A significant share of these deliveries was based on long-lasting intra-firm production ties, although these relations may weaken due to changes in industry and in the business environment. In order to increase sales of agro- and gastrochemicals, Spolana also established a firm retail shop that mailed products to customers.

East European demand for Spolana products continued, but the solvency of potential buyers was low. Countertrade became almost compulsory in the former CMEA markets and the shift to hard currency, accompanied by the disruption of the barter mechanism, resulted in a sharp drop in business. However, Spolana planned to return to the Russian market with NAOs to be traded for Russian gas.

Finance, Credit, Subsidies, and Taxes

The firm's overall financial condition improved remarkably with the December 1991 cancellation of the old CSK 657 million debt. This cancellation was part of a state program to decrease the indebtedness that the former regime caused in some companies, a debt that totaled 50 billion CSK. Below is a chart showing the development of bank credits (in million CSK) over the last five years. Their increase since 1990 was caused by construction of the NAO plant, but Spolana had until 1996 to repay this debt.

Year	1987	1988	1989	1990	1991
Credits (at 12/31)	55	676	771	942	2,027

The firm was successful in obtaining credits from Komercni Banka and Investicni Banka, although this was no easy task. Before providing any large credit, banks required that their loans be secured by immovable asset collateral. In Spolana's case, this amounted to 1.3 times the sum of the credit. It was not only a financial guarantee but also a potential instrument of control in the future if the firm were to fail to close its accounts. One of the firm's managers in charge of capital investment planning and control said: "At the beginning, we were promised support from financial institutions to facilitate a flexible reduction of firm debts. As I observe it at present, our new commercial banks are myopic and are not concerned with the recovery of ailing industries."

Taxation of businesses was decreasing. During the communist era, almost all profits were taken by the state and reallocated. Since 1990, the income tax had been 55 percent, but in 1993, the entire tax system was to be changed such that a value-added tax would replace the turnover tax, and income tax would be lowered to 45 percent. Spolana's top management hoped to gain badly needed funds. Management also recognized the need to conform its domestic accounting and financial control systems to Western standards. With the support of Andersen Consulting, these changes began in January 1993.

LONG-TERM RESPONSE

Spolana was privatized in the first wave that ended in December 1992. From a fully state-owned joint-stock firm, it became a stock firm owned by different stockholders, however the state retained 46 percent of the enterprise. Twelve percent of this would be offered to the banks and the rest would remain in the state Fund of National Property for some time. The town of Neratovice received 1 percent for health care and municipal activities, and 3 percent went to the obligatory Restitution Fund.

The public was offered 49 percent of the firm via the voucher scheme. The demand for the shares was quite high. In the first round, Spolana sold 71 percent of the offered amount and, in the second and third rounds, there was overdemand, which meant that no shares were sold and the price in points increased. In the fourth round, the remaining shares were sold. The result of this was that several major investment funds now had a substantial stake in Spolana.

The top management team prepared the firm for the change as was their responsibility. The managing director had this opinion: "In connection with the privatization project, we have prepared new economic rules for the firm, proposed a reorganization of the existing structure that introduces profit centers, and begun the transformation of the accounting system to Western standards."

However, not all the employees were so confident and optimistic. One middle-level manager complained: "The new management uses new terms, but an old management style. I have to say that too many things need to be changed and many of them should have been changed already. The change of the ownership is our last chance. I hope that the investment funds will bring fresh air into the firm management. If not, I am going to leave."

A significant proportion of agrochemical products were made under license, for which Spolana had always collaborated with foreign firms. The most important partners had been ICI and Shell from the United Kingdom, Du Pont, and Ciba-Geigy from Switzerland. The production process for NAO was licensed by Chevron, USA. Spolana was also looking for a foreign partner to create a joint venture. Although some negotiations had taken place, no final decision had been made.

Spolana had a successful R&D department that cooperated on product development with many research institutes and some educational institutions, such as the University for Chemical Technology in Prague. The emphasis was mostly on product innovation and improvement, although the firm developed new products as well. Additionally, there was also collaboration with some foreign enterprises.

Investment

Spolana's major investments over the previous two years had been in the construction of a new plant for NAO production that included a broad range of carboxyl hydrates. NAOs are made from ethylene and are used mainly for the production of plastics, detergents and greases. Only a few enterprises in the world make this product and Spolana's plant was one of three in Europe, the others being Shell in the United Kingdom and Ethyl in Belgium.

Investment in NAO amounted to 921 million CSK in 1990 and 2.025 million in 1991. Total NAO investments were expected to reach about 5 billion CSK, almost the equivalent of all other Spolana assets combined. This plant was put into operation in the autumn of 1992 and, with an annual production capacity of 120,000 tons, it became the principal producer for the enterprise. World production of NAO was 1.8 million tons, but consumption was only 1.2 million tons. Demand, however, was growing by 6–8 percent annually.

The Sales VP stated: "We know that there is overcapacity in the world, but demand for NAO differs significantly and is not met in many market segments. We have a list of 180 potential customers. Moreover, we have succeeded in making contracts to export 12,000 tons, one-half of 1992's planned production, to Russia." To which the Production VP added: "The first samples show that, thanks to our new technology, we are able to meet the quality standards set by our competitors at Chevron, Ethyl, and Shell."

The NAO issue was a hot topic in the firm and many hopes were involved in its production. The managing director saw it this way: "We hope that NAO will boost our sales by 2.5 billion annually and increase profits by 50 percent."

At the same time, Spolana was implementing other minor investment projects such as specialty chemicals, pyrethroids, and glass-filled plastics. In the future, many of the firm's investments were to focus on ecological issues. As an example, the technology used for viscose fiber production, which does not use cesium, should replace old technology. The present technology that produces chlorine and NaOH should also be replaced by one that does not use mercury.

Ecological Issues

The ecological issues inherited from the past created one of the worst problems for Spolana. The head of the ecology department commented: "The firm has to cope these days with the results of ecological mistakes made during the communist era, mainly in the 1960s and 1970s. At that time, ecology was not something to worry about. Moreover, all data on pollution were kept secret by the firm and the state authorities. However, I must say that Spolana has made several very positive steps in this area, such as building a wastewater plant, installing emission filters, and various other things."

During the so-called Velvet Revolution, environmental safety was a hot topic and pressure from Neratovice's citizens was powerful. Even considering the financial constraints, the management was able to develop a very ambitious ecological program. The head of the ecology department added: "To know what to cope with, it was necessary to create an emission monitoring system. Presently, we operate five stationary measuring stations, and in 1991, we purchased a new mobile station with state-of-the-art monitoring equipment for 9 million CSK."

In the future, Spolana intended to switch from fighting pollution to preventing problems. For example, alpha-olefins could be produced without danger to the environment. Many other projects are planned, but their implementation would be a question of money. For 1992, 60 million CSK in investments was used for ecology, and this amount could reach 2 billion CSK by the end of the decade.

MANAGEMENT PERCEPTION OF THE FIRM'S POSITION AND PROSPECTS

In discussions with top management, managers often talked about Spolana's many problems, but they were frequently uncritically optimistic that the firm would overcome them. "We increased our sales at the time of the demand crisis," said one manager. However, if we take into account that the price index increased by about 1.6 for post-1990 prices, the picture changes. Another commented: "We increased our profits a lot." This increase in profits, however, was only possible due to the consumption of inventories of raw materials bought in the past at lower prices. Yet another claimed: "We have boosted our exports to the Western markets." But was this the result of the firm's performance or due to pro-export devaluations of currency? Or, as another commented: "We have decreased the number of employees." Yes, but was this reduction sufficient? Many people argued that the firm could have cut employment by one-third with no problems. "We have chosen thirty-five young prospective postgraduates to be trained for future management posts in specially designed courses provided by the Czechoslovak Management Center," noted another manager. True, managers may have finished their training successfully, but some had already left the firm. Were these young managers and other valuable employees leaving only because of wage regulations, or did they leave because of their working conditions or the firm's prospects?

Top managers believed that the firm had no serious problems, and middle- and lower-level management took a wait-and-see approach that delayed transitional changes. This was true not only for Spolana, but represented a common attitude from the past. A number of problems remained to be tackled after privatization.

MAJOR FINDINGS: IMPLICATIONS FOR CHANGING BEHAVIOR/GOALS

The situation can be summarized by the comments of a middle-level manager: "Change has to start from the top. The firm's management is mostly production-oriented. They have started to recognize the importance of strategy, marketing, foreign trade, accounting, and financial matters, but the transition process is too slow. On the other hand, the passivity of the workers and lower-level managers needs to be changed. People must take the initiative. They have to realize that socialism and state care are over. Workers have to take responsibility for their lives into their own hands, but they need to be motivated to do this."

Spolana's information system needed to be improved radically. It was important that the firm know as much as possible about its customers, its competitors, and industrial and economic development. Its portfolios of activities also needed to be re-evaluated. The oldest facilities had outlived their usefulness and several production lines were on the verge of shutting down; the only question was when this would happen. A number of other processes were in need of modernization, another area in which there was a tremendous need for information.

In spite of these problems, Spolana's future will probably be decided by its human resources. If top management could perform well in this area, the firm's future could be viewed optimistically.

Table 1
Annual Balance Sheet (in million CSK, as of December of the year)

	1990	1991	January–September 1992
Current assets			
Cash	107.3	80.8	183.0
Accounts receivable	536.0	1,491.7	1,268.4
Inventory	834.7	959.2	1,439.1
Prepaid expenses	27.7	0.0	0.0
Total	1,505.7	2,531.7	2,890.5
Noncurrent assets			
Property, plant, equipment	7,922.7	10,572.6	11,412.9
Less depreciation	(3,863.2)	(4,002.1)	(4,035.5)
Intangibles	0.0	2.0	3.0
Total	4,059.5	6,572.5	8,035.8
Total assets	**5,565.2**	**9,104.2**	**10,926.3**
Current liabilities			
Accounts payable	331.9	505.7	608.6
Short-term credits	240.0	843.5	713.6
Other	8.7	137.6	344.5
Total	580.6	1,486.8	1,666.7
Noncurrent liabilities			
Long-term credits	683.9	2,951.7	3,625.1
Other	642.9	61.8	0.0
Total	1,326.8	3,014.5	3,625.1
Total liabilities	**1,907.4**	**4,500.3**	**5,291.8**
Owner's equity	3,556.6	3,687.5	4,108.7
Funds	93.6	722.5	870.4
Retained earnings	7.7	193.9	665.4
Total equity	**3,657.9**	**4,603.9**	**5,634.5**
Total liabilities and equity	**5,565.3**	**9,104.2**	**10,926.3**

Table 2
Annual Income Statement (in million CSK)

	1990	1991	January–September 1992
Sales revenue	4,466.7	7,008.3	5,612.4
Other revenues	412.0	328.4	276.4
Total	4,878.7	7,336.7	5,888.8
Cost of goods sold	4,120.2	6,021.5	4,937.7
Depreciation	197.0	218.5	203.7
Financial costs	299.7	395.4	92.0
Total	4,616.9	6,635.4	5,233.4
Profit before taxation	261.8	701.3	655.4
Income tax	165.9	386.5	343.5
Profit after taxation	95.9	314.8	311.9

HEAVY CHEMICALS: SPOLANA 45

Table 3

Structure of Costs (in percentages)

	1990	1991	January–September 1992
Wages	4.80	4.00	4.80
Materials and energy	84.40	86.80	89.50
Financial costs	6.50	5.90	1.80
Depreciation	4.30	3.30	3.90
Total	100.00	100.00	100.00

Table 4

Main Financial Indices (in million CSK)

	1990	1991	January–September 1992
Sales revenue	4,466.7	7,008.3	5,888.8
Cost of goods sold	4,120.2	6,021.5	4,937.7
Gross margin	346.5	986.8	951.1
Other revenues	412.0	328.4	276.4
Depreciation	197.0	218.5	203.7
Financial costs	299.7	395.4	92.0
Gross profit	261.8	701.3	655.4
Income tax	165.9	386.5	343.5
Net profit	95.9	314.8	311.9

Table 5

Profitability Ratios (in percentages)

	1990	1991	January–September 1992
Gross margin/sales	7.76	14.08	17.58
Gross profits/sales	5.86	10.01	11.68
Gross margin/cost of sales	8.41	16.39	19.90
Gross profit/cost of sales	6.35	11.65	13.20
Net profit/cost of sales	2.33	5.23	6.32

Table 6

Liquidity and Activity Ratios

	1990	1991	January–September 1992
Liquidity ratios			
Working capital/total assets	0.17	0.12	0.12
Current ratio	2.59	1.70	1.73
Quick ratio	1.16	1.06	0.87
Activity ratios			
Accounts receivable turnover	8.33	4.70	6.19
Average collection period (days)	43.80	77.69	58.90
Payments turnover	12.41	11.91	10.82
Average payments period	29.40	30.65	33.74
Inventory turnover	4.94	6.28	4.58
Average inventory turnover (days)	73.94	58.14	79.80

Table 7

Structure of Sales (in percentages)

Production program	1990	1991	January–September 1992
Industrial chemicals	36.1	36.6	37.7
Plastics	27.9	31.5	31.7
Man-made fibers	18.9	18.4	24.2
Agro- and gastrochemicals	8.5	8.1	—
Specialty and pure chemicals	2.3	0.8	6.4
Others	6.3	4.6	—

Table 8

Volume of Production (in thousands of tons)

	1988	1989	1990	1991	January–September 1992
Industrial chemicals					
Caprolactam	43.5	44.4	45.6	44.1	34.7
Sulfuric acid	282.08	279.8	259.0	169.6	161.2
Hydrochloric acid	72.9	69.2	72.2	62.6	48.2
Sodium hydroxide	147.3	147.0	149.7	143.0	104.0
Other	359.4	369.2	377.2	262.6	223.4
Total	905.1	909.6	903.7	681.9	571.5
Man-made fibers	39.5	42.3	40.8	31.7	26.3
Plastics	266.1	266.6	264.5	256.9	196.4

HEAVY CHEMICALS: SPOLANA 47

Table 9

Breakdown of Exports by Destination in 1991 (in percentages)

Germany	35
Benelux	20
Turkey	10
Yugoslavia	8
Italy	7
Switzerland	7
Austria	5
Spain	3
Others	5

Table 10

Changes in Employment since 1987

	1987	1988	1989	1990	1991	January–September 1992
Number of employees	5,508	5,460	5,330	5,183	4,842	4,544

Percentages of white-collar/blue-collar workers in 1991:	
White collars	27
Blue collars	73

Percentages of male/female employees:	
Males	66
Females	34

Note: Share of female employees is 44.3 percent in the CSFR economy.

4

Textiles/Garments: CS-15

Will Inexpensive Labor Help Us to Survive?

Jana Matesová

SECTORAL SETTING

During 1990–92, CS-15 was a state-owned enterprise, based in Prague, that produced high-quality ready-made ladies' and young ladies' clothing. In 1990, the firm had approximately 300 employees. Clothing manufacturing was among the oldest industries in Czechoslovakia and was very labor-intensive. Thus, the skilled labor, the low per-unit labor costs of the Czech garment producers, and the proximity to major markets for textile products generated a competitive advantage for the industry, which had a low price/quality ratio relative to West European and Asian producers.

In 1991, when the demand for clothing on the domestic market declined and the CMEA market collapsed, the Czech and Slovak garment industry lost about 60 percent of its market. CS-15's short- and medium-term strategy was to find new markets. The most important of these became the German garment producers, who started to subcontract the sewing of clothing to CS-15. The firm also introduced credit management, which helped to improve its financial stability. At the end of 1992, CS-15 was privatized and most of the firm was restored to its former owners, a change that might have a significant effect on the long-run behavior of the firm.

The highest concentration of this industry was historically in central Bohemia and central Moravia, where most of the large and medium-sized enterprises were located, but there were other plants of the same size throughout southern and northern Bohemia.[1] Large garment enterprises were also located in western and northern Slovakia. Although, hundreds of new small private garment-producing enterprises had been established after 1989, many had already failed. This industrial sector was very unstable due to particularly low demand for its products on the domestic market and strong competition from clothing imported from Asia, Turkey, and even Western Europe.

After World War II, new investment in the Czech garment industry became rare and most firms operated in old buildings, using mechanical equipment rather than automated machines. In 1990, the Czech garment industry had over 20,000 employees. The majority of material inputs for the industry, such as fabrics, were supplied by the domestic fabric and knitting industry, which had a huge capacity and employed about 160,000 workers. Czech fabric production exceeded garment input requirements almost fivefold.

The major markets for Czech and Slovak clothing were the domestic and CMEA markets, especially the USSR. The quality was mostly standard and designs usually came from firms' own design departments or other domestic designers. A small share of the firms' revenue, however, was earned from subcontracting, i.e., customized tailoring services for Western customers who supplied their own materials and designs and negotiated contracts for delivery of the finished products.

The Czech garment industry had two main competitive advantages. The first was low per-unit labor costs for skilled labor, compared to West European textile producers, and a long history of textile production in the region, which resulted in a low price/quality ratio relative to West European producers. The industry took advantage of its inexpensive but skilled labor force and its proximity to West European markets, while allowing Western partners to supply the raw materials and sell the finished product. The second advantage was the proximity to the West European market, the world's major market for textiles, which resulted in low transportation costs and a short innovation cycle. These last factors were especially advantageous for the industry, relative to the East Asian manufacturers.

In 1991, the Czechoslovak state-owned garment industry was seriously affected by two changes: a sharp decline in the effective demand for clothing on the domestic market, and a collapse of the CMEA market. The former was caused both by a drop in the purchasing power of Czechoslovak currency after the liberalization of prices during a time of severe economic shortages and fixed monopolistic industrial production, and by the liberalization of foreign trade. Prices of raw materials in the textile industry, such as cotton, wool, chemicals, and energy, increased by at least 50 percent and by as much as 150 percent or more.[2] Therefore, if the same production structure were maintained, and no decrease in material inputs occurred, material costs, e.g., of fabrics, threads, yarn, energy, per unit of production in the garment industry would have risen sharply, causing output prices to rise also. Moreover, customers had expected an increase in prices and had hoarded large quantities of consumer goods before the price liberalization.

Liberalization of foreign trade and the expansion of black market dealing in imported goods caused a significant increase in competition on the domestic market.[3] Inexpensive products, particularly from Asia and Turkey, imported through both official and unofficial channels, gained a significant market share, while higher-quality West European goods further weakened demand for domestically produced clothing.

Wholesale trade in Czechoslovakia collapsed during the first and second quarters of 1991. Almost all retail stores were privatized and the number of these retail establishments peaked during the first quarter of 1991, shortly before many of them started to fail. Although boutiques and fashion retail stores were still in the most rapidly growing segment of the expanding retail sector, they mainly used their own distribution channels for imported goods or goods from small family businesses.

The response of the state-owned garment industry was immediate: a reorientation of production. This included all stages of production, from design to the sale of the final product, to wholesale distributors. It also included subcontracting tailor's and seamstress's services to West European, mostly German, firms, which, like U.S. hollow firms, began to focus on design, marketing, and sales, and eliminate manufacturing capacity.

While the total value of sales in the textile and garment industry had dropped by 50–60 percent since the late 1980s, the value added and profits decreased by only a few percent.[4] This small decrease was due to the fact that prices of most subcontracts did not include the cost of fabrics, but covered only labor, depreciation and indirect material costs, and profits.[5] A similar development can be seen in CS-15's data in Tables 1–3. Per-unit material costs decreased significantly, thus per-unit total costs declined as well, but profits from sales and total profits increased during the years 1990–92.

In 1992, with expanding demand, the capacity of the Czech textile and garment industry could no longer meet the demand for customized tailoring services by Western customers. Total employment in the industry had apparently increased rather than decreased since 1990, as a result of a boom in the private sector. It was clear that state-owned firms, particularly in large cities, had difficulty finding qualified labor, although exact figures on employment in the private sector were not yet available.

The paradox is that, while the state-owned garment sector struggled for survival and fought for contracts, hundreds of new businesses were emerging in the same industry. There seem to be two main explanations for this development. First, most of the large state-owned firms were not flexible. They produced large quantities of a limited variety of models, many of which were old-fashioned, while the market demanded very fashionable yet inexpensive clothing. It was fashion and price that mattered, not quality. Also, the output of these enterprises was expensive to produce for the following reasons: a high ratio of managers to laborers and large interest payments on old loans contributed to high overhead costs; the payroll tax paid by state-owned enterprises was high; technology and the organization of labor were efficient only for large volumes; the adjustment to changes in fashion was slow; the quality of design was poor; the labor force was reluctant to change its working habits; the social system was rigid; and last, but not least, the low level of entrepreneurial spirit of most managers prevented them from seeing new opportunities.

Second, due to the above-mentioned poor design and high prices, many households had for years made their own clothing. Also, a market niche existed for small boutiques and workshops selling their products at street stands and, for a while, there was even a tax-free market niche for handy self-trained seamstresses selling their home-made products as second-hand. However, the period of reasonable profit margins for most of these businesses lasted only a few months, before imports of inexpensive Turkish and East Asian products, as well as factory seconds from Western firms, pushed most of these businesses out of the market. In the short- to mid-term, the reorientation exclusively to subcontractors rescued the Czech textile and garment industry, although the cost advantages of cheap labor and proximity to major markets for textiles may not last longer than a decade.

The privatization of the textile and garment state-owned enterprises, which took place in 1992, was mostly by means of restitution, vouchers, and the direct sale of smaller plants, but there were also some management buy-outs. The average number of privatization proposals submitted to the Czech Ministry of Privatization for each firm was five.

HISTORY OF THE FIRM

CS-15, which was established in 1990, consisted of two plants located in Prague and a small workshop outside Prague, at Nova Ves, about 20 miles north of the main plant. The main plant, at Liben, had been founded in the 1930s as a private business that, at that time, manufactured a wide product line, including men's shirts, quilts, and even hats with feathers. The original owners were Jews, and thus the firm was taken over by the Germans at the beginning of World War II. In 1941, the firm was acquired by a Czech family, which also bought the workshop at Nova Ves with its workforce of about 20–30. In the early 1950s, the firm was nationalized and merged with other small firms to form a state-owned enterprise, Pragodev, that manufactured men's and women's clothing. In 1982, Pragodev merged with Triola, a large state-owned shirt and underwear manufacturer with a similar history.

In 1929, a small, private Czech firm built a plant in Michle to produce knitted wear. Since these owners were also Jews, it too was taken over by Germans at the beginning of World War II and remained in Nazi possession until the end of the war, when it was nationalized. In 1952, this enterprise, Mira, became part of Pragodev. The organization brought about a change in product lines and the plant started to manufacture clothing. In 1982, when Pragodev merged with

Triola, Mira was part of that merger. In 1989, Triola split into several independent, state-owned entities, one of which was CSS, later renamed CS-15, and which had the status of state enterprise.[6] In accordance with legal requirements, the employees of this state enterprise elected the managing director.

MAJOR SHOCKS TO THE YOUNG FIRM

CS-15 had faced hard times since the beginning of 1991, with two major problems challenging the firm's management. At the end of 1990, the acting managing director was removed from his position because of self-enrichment at the firm's expense and possible fraud. He, as well as many others with decision-making authority, had misused his position within CS-15 to favor his own private firm, making or mediating in high-margin contracts and allowing for profitable transfers of wealth to his firm. Although such behavior was typical after the Velvet Revolution and was not illegal, it was hardly acceptable from an ethical point of view. One problem with the departure of this director was that he took some people with him; more importantly, he also took the enterprise's network of contacts. As a consequence of this upheaval, the climate and interpersonal relationships inside the enterprise, together with the authority of the management, significantly deteriorated.

Milena Dobrá (a pseudonym), production manager of CS-15 since January 1990, replaced the former director as acting managing director. She had received a MSc in Textile Engineering and Pedagogy, and had worked as a vocational training instructor, a high school teacher, a forewoman at Pragodev and Triola, and finally, as the production manager of Triola and CS-15.

Regarding the departure of the former top management, Mrs. Dobrá said: "The former managing director started to privatize too fast and in his own favor. Unfortunately, our partners left the firm either because of him or with him. My first and crucial task was to gain authority over the workers of CS-15, most of whom are women." In fact, 94 percent of the firm's employees were women, many of whom did not favor Mrs Dobrá's appointment; following the tradition in the region, a large proportion of the employees refused to respect the authority of a female manager.

The second problem was the previously mentioned effects of reduced demand and the collapse of the CMEA. The domestic market had consumed 30–40 percent of the firm's production of ready-made ladies' and young ladies' clothes, blouses, skirts, trousers, and jackets, but the fact that the firm produced mostly higher-quality and luxury clothing made the market loss a disaster. The demand for such products was both price and income elastic and the decline in the purchasing power caused customers to cut their clothing expenditures so that, by early 1991, the lack of the CMEA market had caused CS-15 to lose 40–50 percent of the market for its product.

Another decline in the purchasing power of the population, and thus demand for the firm's products, was expected after the introduction of the new tax system in January 1993. Under the new system, the sales tax was replaced by a value-added tax at two rates, 5 percent and 23 percent, levied on products on which there had formerly been no turnover tax. As a result, the general price level was expected to increase by 5–6 percent. However, nearly all producers and sellers tried to protect themselves against losses in profit margins by increasing prices more than expected immediately after the new tax system was introduced.

The price effect of the value-added tax on garments was rather favorable. In 1991, the sales tax levied on some CS-15 products had been as high as 135 percent, although some products had had negative sales tax rates. In 1992, the average sales tax on CS-15's products was 27 percent and, since 1993, there has been a value-added tax of 23 percent on some products and 5 percent on others.

RESPONSES TO THE SHOCKS

Short- and Medium-Term Responses

As mentioned, as the new managing director, Mrs. Dobrá's first task was to fight for the confidence of employees and her authority over them by means of "less talk and more work," and to ensure that there was sufficient work for all dedicated workers. An improvement in social conditions for women, including the wage policy and the environment inside the enterprise, was another major goal. To this end, one of her first decisions was to increase the low wages as soon as the firm's finances allowed it.[7]

In February–March 1991, the firm's new management had to decide whether to cut jobs radically or to try to keep workers for a limited period of time, but put all efforts into a search for new markets. Employees' wages during the first months of that year were very low. In February, the average monthly wages of laborers fell by 36 percent to CSK 1,704 (approximately $61), less than one-half the average monthly wage in the country. This was aggravated by a 36 percent increase in consumer prices during January and February.[8]

In an effort to find new customers, the managing director took patterns of CS-15's products from one distributor to another, from one potential partner to another, from one customer to another, trying to get contracts to do any kind of work that CS-15 could do. She also started direct sales. With a car full of clothing samples, the firm's people not only visited various plants in an effort to sell the firm's products to the workers, but also opened a store attached to the main plant. The managing director's major concern was to find markets as quickly as possible, believing that this would increase her authority in the firm. Although the first success came early, the enterprise operated far below capacity for a long time. Also, because of low wages and poor prospects, about 10 percent of the workers left at the beginning of 1991, especially since many newly established businesses in Prague had created a demand for trained seamstresses and dressmakers.[9]

In its endeavor to maintain or even increase employment, social policy was the main management tool, and therefore CS-15 financed in-house services such as hairdressing and massages. It also paid the commuting workers' travel expenses, which had substantially increased since 1990. At the beginning of 1993, C-15, the private successor of CS-15, increased wages by 27 percent. This was made possible by the removal of the government wage regulations and the introduction of the new tax system, which decreased the tax burden on the firm.[10]

At the end of 1992, the availability of qualified seamstresses increased, and those employed in small private businesses expected that the financial situation of their firms would deteriorate in 1993. While the new tax system, as a whole, moderated the tax burden levied on corporations, the tax burden of most small businesses, particularly those whose taxable income was close to CSK 0.5 million, was expected to increase. Thus, although small businesses were losing employees, the lower tax burden made it possible for corporations to increase wages, and seamstresses from small private enterprises started to apply for jobs with CS-15 again.

Another shock that CS-15 and most other Czechoslovak firms faced in 1991 and 1992 was a large increase in accounts receivable and a subsequent liquidity crisis. In 1991, accounts receivable reached 23 percent of yearly sales, about one-half of which was overdue. After CS-15 found new, mostly foreign, customers, this problem decreased relative to many other firms. Furthermore, the enterprise began to implement credit management, and even hired detectives to seek out debtors. It also employed the services of credit-rating and credit-management firms that specialized in recovering accounts receivable. Some receivable debts were sold.

New domestic markets absorbed a small amount of CS-15's traditional production of ready-made clothing. Production of each product had to be reduced from several thousand pieces to 200–300-piece units. Distribution channels also changed significantly, from wholesale and retail chains to direct sales to final customers. Furthermore, CS-15 found new markets for its products in Western Europe, particularly in Germany, and inexpensive labor and high quality of products enabled the enterprise to make use of its competitive advantage. The managing director decided to base a survival strategy on subcontracted manufacturing for Western garment producers. These Western firms delivered their designs and materials, and workers in CS-15 sewed the final products, most of which were small quantities of high-quality and luxury ladies' clothing that were then marketed and sold by the Western contractors.

In 1992, demand for the firm's products significantly exceeded its production, and it could easily afford to increase employment. The tabular data at the end of this chapter illustrate the development of sales. The firm was also able to increase the share of products designed by its own employees and to re-establish contacts with Czech fabric producers. Its main business, however, continued to be the processing of fabrics for foreign customers.

In the fall of 1992, the firm's management, with the approval of the restituted owners, decided to restore the workshop at Nova Ves, where a large supply of qualified workers was available, and to create twenty-five new jobs there.

Long-Term Responses

It is important to understand that privatization of state-owned enterprises, a key element of the economic transition in Czechoslovakia, was guided by the owner, the state. The government was the only body that had the authority to decide which enterprises would be privatized, when, and in what form. Although the top managers of all firms were required to submit privatization plans, other bodies were also encouraged to do so, and the government then selected the one privatization plan or a combination of plans. Thus, in some cases, the changes in ownership of Czech and Slovak enterprises in 1992 and 1993 cannot be described as part of the long-term responses of managers to the changing business environment, but only as a significant part of the changes in the business environment itself. This is particularly true of restitutions.

CS-15 was privatized in January 1993. The main plant and the small workshop were restored to their former owners, who registered a new firm, C–15 Ltd., as a limited partnership. They retained the managing director, intending to continue with the same business. CS-15's other plant was acquired by Persa Mode, Inc., a subsidiary of Persa, a recently established local private textile firm. The new owners of C–15 apparently were not interested in changing the firm's production or in formulating a business strategy. Their major concerns were business ethics, including the social environment in the firm and day-to-day responsibilities. Overall, it seemed that the strategy of subcontracting was viable for at least several years. Until the end of 1992, CS-15's supervisory board was kept in place, although its function was rather formal. When this case study was written at the beginning of 1993, the new owner of C–15 was about to establish a new form of corporate governance.

Changes in organization followed the privatization. One of the two major plants, Michle, was spun off and, thus, not only was the firm's workforce decreased from 240 at the end of 1992 to 135 employees, but the size of the management team was reduced at about the same rate. To reduce overhead costs, the shop floor was given more independence in decision-making for production organization and quality and cost control.

The firm was managed by a small team, much like a small business, and the structure of management was simple and informal. It seemed to be a typical one-person firm, with the managing director taking responsibility for marketing and sales, but also being overloaded with many operational decisions that diverted her attention from strategic decision-making.

The managing director was not only involved in quality control, marketing, and sales, but also in decisions about individual production or transportation operations. If a German interpreter were needed, she did the work. Employees were constantly entering her office, asking questions that should have been handled at the lowest operational level. Her efforts at time management were futile and she had little time to think about long-term plans.

The execution of the enterprise's corporate governance of CS-15 and the firm's management did not leave much time for long-term decisions and, as of January 1993, no strategy had yet been formulated.

MAJOR FINDINGS

CS-15's case illustrates a situation in which an old business with a long history gradually lost its markets. Its major competitive advantages were skilled labor, which was inexpensive relative to Western Europe, and proximity to the West European markets, which were important in a business dependent on fashion.

Businesses such as CS-15 found short-term market opportunities in selling labor-intensive products or the labor itself. The combination of short-term responses, such as the managing director canvassing potential customers in search of contracts, medium-term responses, such as subcontracting, credit management, and reconstruction of a workshop, and the long-term response, which was privatization, turned out to be a successful survival strategy and would very likely be a successful growth strategy over the next several years.

Notes

1. Bohemia is the western part of the Czech Republic. The capital is Prague and major cities are Plzen, Liberec, Hradec Kralove, and Usti nad Labem. Moravia is the eastern part of the Czech Republic. Its capital is Brno and major cities are Ostrava and Olomouc.
2. *Vyvoj indexu spotrebitelskych cen za leden az prosinec 1991*, Federal Statistical Office, Prague.
3. There was a strong underground economy in the foreign trade business in the form of nonreported revenues for taxation, nonlicensed and nonreported imports.
4. Estimation of Mr. Smolar, the senior officer responsible for textile industry, Czech Ministry of Industry.
5. If the local garment firm purchased fabrics as inputs, material costs accounted for about 60 percent of total costs. In the case of subcontracting, however, the customer delivered the fabrics for processing and did not charge any transfer price for the delivery.
6. The name *state enterprise* referred to a specific legal status involving ownership, corporate governance, and control of Czechoslovak enterprises between 1988 and 1992. The enterprise was state-owned and corporate governance was executed by a Supervisory Board consisting of members recommended by the enterprise and appointed by the government. A large enterprise could also have managing boards, members of which were both outside and inside directors. The general manager was responsible to the Supervisory Board. Before the economic transition started, state enterprises were controlled by the state plan.
7. Average monthly salary was only CSK 2,523, approximately $90 at the exchange rate in January, 1991, as compared to the average monthly wage in other Czechoslovak industries in excess of CSK 3,800, approximately $135, or in the textile industry at close to CSK 3,100, or $110. Source: Czech Statistical Office, and internal records of CS-15.
8. *Statistical Bulletin, 4/1991*, Federal Statistical Office, Prague.
9. In 1992, the unemployment rate in Prague was below 0.5 percent and the number of vacancies substantially exceeded the number of unemployed.

10. The new tax system introduced a new structure of taxes as well as new tax rates. The corporate income tax rate was decreased from 55 percent to 45 percent; personal income tax rates were changed; and corporate payroll/social security and health insurance taxes were decreased from 50 to 36 percent of wages, of which one-third was to be paid by employees. A compulsory social security and health insurance with a marginal tax rate of 36 percent of taxable income was introduced for all private entrepreneurs with a yearly taxable income of between CSK 20,400–500,000; outside these tax brackets, the tax rate was zero. The sales, or turnover, tax was replaced by the value-added tax of 5–25 percent.

Table 1
Structure of Costs (in thousands of CSK)

	3rd–4th Quarter/90	1991	1st Quarter 1992
Wages	4,471	9,000	2,107
Materials	7,176	9,152	2,365
Energy	66[1]	904	134
Banking charges and interest	105	1,386	236
Depreciation	779	1,943	513
Refinancing assets	160	—	—
Social security payments (payroll tax)[2]	2,382	4,522	1,404
Other overhead	58	599	192
Total costs	15,197	27,506	6,951

[1] Major part of the total cost of energy was paid from a reserve account created from transfers of the "parent" firm Triola at the time of CS–15's spin-off. This amount was not included into costs!
[2] Part of labor cost.

Table 2
Output, Costs, Profit, and Taxes (in thousands of CSK)

	3rd–4th Quarter/90	1991	1st Quarter 1992
Sales plus financial revenues	17,191	30,240	9,538
Total costs	15,197	27,506	6,951
Operating profit	1,994	2,734	2,587
Gross profit	2,228	2,759	2,607
Taxes	1,296	1,698	1,423
After-tax profit/loss	932	1,061	1,184

Table 3
Profitability Ratios (percentages)

	3rd–4th Quarter/90	1991	1st Quarter 1992
Operating profit/sales	11.60	9.04	27.12
Operating profit/total cost	13.12	9.93	37.21
Gross profit/total costs	14.66	10.03	37.50
Net profit/total costs	6.13	3.85	17.03

5

Textiles/Cloth: Veba Broumov
The King of a Declining Industry

Jana Matesová

SECTORAL SETTING

This case study describes the transition of a large textile industry enterprise, Veba, which produced two product lines, damask and terry. Unlike most Czechoslovak enterprises, Veba had a major competitive advantage: among experts, its damask was recognized as the world's top quality. While almost all damask is exported, most of the exports were subcontracted to West European firms that sold Veba's damask under their own trademarks. At the time of this report, many West European textile firms, quality leaders among them, were going out of business, and one of Veba's goals was to increase the proportion of brand-name products exported to the most demanding markets, thereby boosting the firm's market share in these markets.

Although the demand for terry had decreased sharply in 1991, Veba did not have this difficulty with damask. The management knew that hard times were to come and had based the firm's strategy on an attractive quality/price ratio. Unlike most other Czech firms, they also stressed quality.

Veba Broumov was the largest producer of terry in the Czechoslovak industry and, as of 1992, also the largest European producer of top-quality damask. The firm employed about 2,300 people in its six plants located in Broumov, a town of about 7,000 people, and Police, a town of 4,000 people in northeast Bohemia, an area surrounded on three sides by Poland.[1]

Because Veba's output consisted of two product lines with different business cycles, supplies to the two different markets could cross-subsidize one another. The yearly output consisted of approximately 8 million to 10 million meters of damask fabrics, 2 million meters of woven and knitted cotton terry fabrics, and 10 million units of terry toweling, ready-made bedding products, tablecloths, and clothing. About 90 percent of Veba's production of damask was exported to

Western markets, with roughly 65 percent going to Germany and about 20 percent going to other EC countries. Most damask products were, however, re-exported through German and Swiss firms to the West African market.

Approximately 40 percent of Veba's terry was top-quality walk terry that met the standards of West European markets, the remainder being a standard quality that traditionally supplied the domestic market. The West European market purchased about 60 percent of total terry exports, Canada about 10 percent, and the rest went to other non-European markets. Until 1991, almost all of Veba's terry had been sold on the domestic market, but by 1992, about 75 percent was exported.

Veba's dominance among domestic producers and its strength on Western markets were protected by technical barriers, in that high-quality damask and Jacquard woven terry are advanced products that require specific technologies and highly-trained, skilled labor. However, Veba faced competition from producers of less expensive substitutes. For many years, German firms were Veba's major competitors on the international damask market. Recently, however, these firms had to compete with a large volume of Asian substitutes. Many German firms, including leading producers of top-quality damask, went out of business because high wages did not allow many German firms to compete on a cost basis. As a result of these closures, in 1992 Veba became the world's largest damask manufacturer, recognized as a quality leader.

Although the market leader in terry was the Portuguese textile industry, Veba's major competitive advantage over the Asian terry producers was quality. Asian competitors were not yet able to supply such advanced products as damask or Jacquard woven terry, therefore most Asian terry was printed, which made for a significant difference in durability. Low per-unit labor costs also gave Veba a comparative advantage over West European producers, because the hourly wage of workers in comparable German textile mills was often tenfold or higher. Even the greater labor productivity of the German firms could not offset Veba's cost advantage.

Cloth production is an old industry that, even with new technologies, remains labor-intensive. Textiles have a long tradition in Bohemia and Moravia. During the eighteenth and nineteenth centuries, this region was known as the major textile factory of the Austro-Hungarian monarchy. Many of today's cotton-fabric producers continue in the traditions of firms established in the last few centuries, in some cases using the original facilities. Like other industries, cotton manufacturing was fully nationalized in 1945, beginning with large companies and those owned by Germans, and continuing with medium-size firms in 1948 and small manufacturing and trade firms in the early 1950s. Czech textile producers have always had two main competitive advantages: inexpensive skilled labor and proximity to West European markets.

Production of cotton cloth in the Czech part of the country employed about

60,000 people, nearly 2 percent of the labor force. This reflected the industry's goal of fully providing a large volume of relatively inexpensive fabric to the domestic market. Czech cotton manufacturing and processing succeeded in maintaining its position in foreign markets because, for Veba and some other producers, Western markets were much more important than former CMEA markets, where sales had always been negligible.

The world market for cotton products had changed significantly in the last twenty years. A return to cotton from synthetic products, an increase in the prices of cotton, fuel, chemicals for the production of cotton fabrics, and, in particular, tremendously increased competition from inexpensive Asian goods, were the major factors of change. In 1993, there was overcapacity of simple cotton fabrics on the world market, and the only segments of the market that were not yet directly threatened by the price competition of Asian goods were those requiring a great deal of capital or knowledge of advanced labor skills. Because of this knowledge, technologies strongly dependent on labor skills, such as Jacquard, might still have good prospects in Europe.

Until recently, the domestic market for Veba's products, especially terry, had been quite stable, led by demand for inexpensive mid- and low-quality toweling and bedding products. This market reflected the relatively stable purchasing power of the local currency and the slow growth or stagnation of living standards. Unlike like domestic market, however, the international market for damask bedding, clothing products, and terry was typically cyclical, subject to business cycles and fashion. However, cycles varied in regional markets and rarely coincided for damask and terry.

The world's major market for damask is West Africa, where it is usually sold for clothing despite import barriers such as tariffs of up to 100 percent, or even import prohibitions. From the viewpoint of direct exports, West Africa's markets are high-risk, with low liquidity, nonconvertible currency, and an enormous amount of unofficial distribution, including smuggling. Major producers of top-quality damask are West European companies such as Goetzner of Austria, and Irisette-Smail and Erba, both of Germany. As mentioned, most of Veba's damask exports were sold through the distribution networks of these firms and carried their trademarks.

The world's major markets for terry are West Europe, North America, and the most developed Asian countries. European and North American markets are protected by high tariffs and particularly by import quotas, which represents a significant competitive disadvantage for Czechoslovak exporters, compared to these countries and competitors from most developed countries. Leading producers are Portuguese, Brazilian, Pakistani, and Chinese companies, which achieve top quality while still maintaining low labor costs relative to EC countries other than Portugal. A limited quantity of terry production has, however, been maintained by most developed countries, and terry producers in these countries focus on top-quality and luxury-brand products, with a high level of innovation.

Markets for Major Inputs

Veba's technology permitted the manufacture of top-quality products using medium-fiber cotton, which was imported mainly from the CIS, Greece, and Turkey, and represented some 80–90 percent of inputs. Long-fibered cotton was imported from Egypt, the United States, and China. In the past, cotton had been purchased at undetermined prices through a state-owned foreign trade company.[2] Material inputs were carried on the books at government-subsidized prices but, after the Autumn of 1990, Veba had to purchase cotton at world market prices. Although much higher than subsidized input prices, current cotton prices and terms-of-payment were quite favorable, especially from the former USSR.

The supply of skilled labor was limited by low labor mobility, and because Veba's plants were close to the border, they were less accessible to domestic labor. They did, however, provide excellent opportunities for Polish workers. Low wages also limited the market and Veba needed qualified workers.[3] To counteract these situations, the firm operated its own vocational training programs. Also, the management was encouraged to take part in management training programs, both in Czechoslovakia and abroad, in accordance with investment targets determined by the state plan.

Because it was a successful exporter, Veba had fewer barriers to the purchase of Western technology under central planning than many other Czech producers. The firm used advanced spinning and weaving technology from Japanese, German, Swiss, and Italian producers. However, like the entire industry, Veba's fixed assets were highly depreciated; some 72 percent had already been written off. The leased equipment that Veba used significantly modernized its capital stock.

Recent Developments in Czechoslovak Cotton Manufacturing

Economic transition in Czechoslovakia had a severe impact on the cotton industry: cotton prices more than doubled after the removal of state subsidies and devaluation of the currency; domestic market sales declined sharply in the first half of 1991 as a result of a substantial decline in real wages and disintegration of domestic distribution channels; and the combination of the decline in domestic demand and the collapse of the CMEA market caused domestic garment producers to lose on average more than 40 percent of their market.

However, the Czech clothing industry adapted to these changes by changing its markets and the character of its production. Almost the entire industry was given over to subcontracting tailoring services to Western customers; Western firms supplied local manufacturers with their own materials and designs and then purchased the finished product. As a result, traditional relationships between the fabric and garment industries in Czechoslovakia broke down in late 1990 and 1991 and were not re-established until 1992.

The erosion of distribution channels on the domestic market in 1991 presented Veba with another serious obstacle. Like the garment producers, some textile enterprises were exploring new business contacts with West European textile producers. The Czech firms sold the yarn and the West Europeans handled the design and weaving and produced the finished fabric. After a short period, the spinning capacity was almost fully utilized again, and some revival of weaving appeared as well.

HISTORY OF THE FIRM

Most of Veba's plants were built in 1880 by private firms, cotton fabric producers that, for the most part, supplied foreign markets. These firms were among the largest businesses in the region and contributed significantly to its development. The railroad connecting Broumov with the industrial centers of the Austro-Hungarian monarchy was built in the late 1800s to supply local textile mills with cotton and transport their products elsewhere.

During the next 40 years, the government reorganized cotton manufacturing several times in an attempt to find a manageable degree of centralization of state-owned enterprises. In 1988, as a result of the decentralization of Czechoslovak industries, Veba became a state enterprise. Veba's new management followed in these footsteps and decentralized decision-making, separated strategic and operational decision-making levels, changed the organizational structure of the firm, stressed marketing and sales efforts, and began training managers.

ECONOMIC TRANSITION: MAJOR SHOCKS
AND OPPORTUNITIES

The main changes that resulted from economic transition were felt in such areas as macroeconomic stabilization, development of market conditions, and the international business environment.[4] In its reaction to these changes in the business environment in 1990–91, Veba was a typical Czech light industry. Its top managers agreed: "It is not our philosophy to interpret changes in the business environment as shocks. Some changes were hardly predictable, and they seriously hurt the economy of Veba. On the other hand, others brought about opportunities. It is part of the managers' responsibilities to make decisions in a changing environment. When the market for damask is down, it can hurt Veba's economy in a way similar to transitionary changes in the national economy." Like other Czech and Slovak companies in 1991, Veba was most affected by hard budget constraints, i.e., the removal of subsidies for input prices that occurred in the fall of 1990, the devaluation of the currency, and a very tight monetary policy.

Hard Budget Constraints

Cotton prices increased by approximately 100 percent and the removal of subsidies hurt the entire enterprise, particularly in the production of heavy terry. Under the previous system, based on cost-plus pricing, raw materials were both inexpensive and subsidized, and most of Veba's revenue was generated by terry production, which had a large share of material cost and low value added, compared to light damask fabrics.[5] But, after the removal of subsidies, terry product markups became negative. Terry production was also affected by an increase in the sales tax from 2 percent to 29 percent, effective January 1, 1991.

Devaluation of Currency

An undervalued local currency supported exports and hurt imports. Similar to price liberalization, devaluation of the currency affected terry production by increasing material costs. Additional profits from exports, accounting for some 35 percent of total production, were less significant. On the other hand, damask production, which was sold mostly on foreign markets, benefited from devaluation, particularly after its export share increased from 65 percent of total damask production to some 85–90 percent, while production in physical units increased by 2 percent, compared to 1990.

Tight Monetary Policy

The 1991 decline in real wages discouraged customers from buying durable goods and caused domestic demand for Veba's products to fall by more than 50 percent. In addition, interest payments from outstanding long-term loans contributed to further deterioration of cash flow. Veba began to accumulate large inventories of terry products in the first and second quarters of 1991, and needed more financing. But bank loans were expensive and, because of administrative restrictions that still remained, scarce. Limited access to capital to finance these inventories and pay the high interest on outstanding loans contributed to increased commercial inter-firm loans. As a result, it also led to an increase in the mutual indebtedness of enterprises. The management considered this liquidity crisis as the most pressing problem for the firm.

When Veba's situation stabilized after several months, the management, in considering the firm's long-term goals and strategies, decided to invest in a purification station and a finishing facility. However, domestic banks tightly restricted long-term loans with maturity over four years, and therefore Veba had to seek alternative sources of financing.[6]

DEVELOPMENT OF MARKET CONDITIONS

The development of market conditions was supported by two very important steps in government economic policy: liberalization of both foreign trade and prices. The erosion of domestic channels of distribution, caused by privatization, low demand, and low effectiveness of state-owned wholesale and retail channels, also affected the sales of many producers.

Liberalization of Foreign Trade

The liberalization of foreign trade significantly increased competition on the domestic market, where now the more inexpensive Asian terry toweling and damask substitutes competed with Veba's products.

Liberalization of Prices

About 80 percent of prices had been liberalized since January 1, 1991. The liberalization of foreign trade, combined with the need to trade at world market prices, increased most input prices, which in turn caused material costs to rise. The price of cotton more than doubled, the price of the chemicals needed for textile production jumped an average of 160 percent, and the price of energy, which was also now bought at world prices, increased by 75 percent by the middle of 1991, compared to December 1990. These increases were neither one-shot nor typical fluctuations that result from market forces, and prices did not stabilize until about one year later. For most of 1991, Veba's economy was exposed to repeated and unexpected input price variations that increased the uncertainty and risk of business decisions.

Since high inflation after the price liberalization had been fully anticipated, people purchased large inventories of durables before January 1991. As a result, at the end of 1990, Veba's products sold out. Because the firm had many contracts for the first quarter of 1991, it continued production. However, most contracts were repudiated in the first and second quarters of 1991 when distributors realized that demand had substantially declined. Because Veba's business strategy was oriented mostly toward high-quality products and luxury goods, demand for the firm's products was severely affected. The few domestic customers who demanded terry products preferred cheap, lower-quality Asian products, and the prices of these products were generally competitive, even though the domestic market was protected by 13 percent tariffs. In most market sectors, prices, rather than quality, began to play an important role in consumer decision-making.

Breakdown of Distribution Channels

Although there was little in the way of price declines, the decline of the domestic market was followed by a collapse of both wholesale and retail distribution channels. The former was due to the declining market, the latter due partly to privatization of retail establishments. Although thousands of small textile businesses were created in first months of 1991, there was no increase in demand for

Veba's goods. Most small retailers built their image on imported rather than domestic goods.

However, new retailers began to approach Veba, demanding direct delivery of small quantities of goods or direct sales from the warehouse without previous contracts. Although Veba could not respond to everyone immediately, it was able to supply large quantities to a limited number of customers. But there was not enough available in warehouses, and therefore transportation, bookkeeping, and billing became more demanding and expensive. In addition, these hundreds of new firms had no credit history, and credit management was difficult. For these reasons, there was a crucial need for Veba to establish its own wholesale network.

The decline in domestic demand affected both damask and terry. Because almost all damask was exported, Veba's foreign markets were able to absorb a large quantity of excess top-quality production. Inventories of terry, however, started to accumulate. The quantities of standard-quality terry, produced for the domestic market, could not be sold abroad. Moreover, unlike Veba's major foreign markets for damask, those for terry were protected by quotas.

CHANGES IN THE INTERNATIONAL BUSINESS ENVIRONMENT

Except for an indirect effect through garment producers, the collapse of CMEA did not affect Veba. Cotton was imported from the former USSR because it gave a better price-to-quality ratio than cotton from other markets. More important was the lifting of foreign trade restrictions. In 1990, Czechoslovakia was granted Most Favored Nation (MFN) status by the United States, which meant that exports for Czech and Slovak goods to the United States could be greatly expanded. The Association Agreement with the European Community (EC) was completed late in 1991. This would have lowered barriers for textile exports to the EC countries, but the impending division of Czechoslovakia into two independent states meant that the agreement might have to be renegotiated.

Despite the external changes, the economic transition also created important opportunities. Decision-making was decentralized, political constraints were removed, and borders were opened for travel and cooperation with Western partners. On the heels of this, Veba's management then invited foreign consultants and started to study Western management practices.

THE FIRM'S SHORT- AND MEDIUM-TERM RESPONSES

In 1991, when large inventories of terry were accumulating, foreign damask markets were booming. This meant the firm could cross-subsidize the two product lines. Unfortunately, it was at this time that Veba introduced a divisional structure based on product lines, and these divisions were very independent. The damask division had no problems because of the boom in demand, and the devalued currency earned good profits. However, the terry division management thought that a long-term strategy was obvious: textile markets suffer from overcapacity and thus, only producers who offer a favorable price to quality ratio can maintain their share on textile markets. Asian producers offer very low prices, but produce standard or low-quality goods, whereas European producers maintain their market share by producing high-quality products. Veba's high-quality terry was able to compete in West European markets; however, the high-quality terry products accounted for only 40 percent of Veba's production of terry and the firm could not increase this share. Finishing was the limiting factor, in that Veba would have needed a new finishing facility and equipment requiring a large investment. Although the terry division managers sought high profit margins, there was no demand for relatively expensive durable goods. Soon, the terry division recognized the need to sell inventories with high discounts on nontraditional markets such as South Africa, and introduce a new marketing policy.

Because profits earned by the damask division were still high enough to cross-subsidize the losses of the other division, the firm did not accumulate losses. In late 1992, however, the damask boom subsided at the same time as a revival in demand for terry in Czechoslovakia began to bring in profits. This reversal was due to the cyclical nature of damask. It is an old product requiring much care and potential market niches in advanced countries tend to diminish relative to consumers' preferences for easy-care substitutes.

Although profits were not a big problem, Veba's cash flow deteriorated. The management quickly introduced careful control over cash outflow, and tried to have customers pay for deliveries by any means available. Before the end of 1992, this situation had stabilized, and Veba had cash enough for all needs. Also, the large terry inventory that was partly caused by the collapse of domestic wholesale channels in 1991–92 was remedied when distribution was restructured. Veba sought new distribution channels and assisted in their formation, by changing its trade terms to decrease the startup costs and financial burdens on wholesale and retail firms, leasing its warehouses, and so forth.

Veba was able penetrate new market sectors, such as high-quality hotel chains to which it supplied custom-tailored bedding, toweling, and bathrobes. Because these goods were much cheaper than comparable Western goods, hotels became a successful market and some even displayed patterns of Veba's products, which helped attract new customers. The firm also began to export king- and queen-size damask in widths over 100 inches to the United States and Canada. After Czechoslovakia achieved MFN status, Veba became very profitable, yet, it still lacked the finishing capacity to expand production of large-width damask.

LONG-TERM RESPONSES

In 1992, Veba prepared a SWOT analysis (of strengths, weaknesses, opportunities, and threats) based on large surveys both inside and outside the firm. The analysis showed that product quality was the firm's major competitive advantage, and, viewed from the same perspective, that Asian competition was the major threat. Veba's goal, therefore, was to maintain or increase its market share on the most demanding markets, such as Germany. To this end, it opted to establish a brand-name position. Although the firm had sold many products under other trademarks, the management now wanted to reduce this share of re-exports.

After the November 1989 revolution, the political climate in Czechoslovakia demanded changes in managerial positions. Although Veba's prerevolutionary top management had been chosen on the basis of professional ability and skills rather than political loyalty, several members of this management were replaced and all relics of the former Communist Party governance removed. The new management began to rework the business strategy and organizational structure, and a Dutch consulting firm was hired to help with the transfer of managerial knowledge and business analyses.

The first changes in corporate governance had taken place in 1989, before the revolution. Veba became a state enterprise, legally a state-owned entity, and as such, it was guided by the state plan. Two boards—supervisory and managing— were appointed by the Czech Ministry of Industry to represent the owner, that being the state.[7] Most board members were experts in textile production and management, but some were also members of the enterprise's management. The supervisory board exerted a rather formal control over the management. The ministry was willing to listen to proposals by the firm's management regarding appointments and also followed Veba's ideas with respect to the board members.

In May 1992, Veba became a fully state-owned joint stock firm and had to prepare its legal structure for the forthcoming privatization. During the process of privatization, the existing boards continued to execute corporate governance, and this would probably continue until new shareholders were recognized and the general meeting of the firm's shareholders selected new supervisory and managing board members.

According to state requirements, Veba was expected to propose a privatization plan and describe its future business strategy based on the outlook for the industry and markets. All other Czechoslovak bodies were also eligible to submit a competitive plan. The Czech Ministry of Privatization, as a representative of the government, then selected the privatization plan that would be executed.[8]

The approved plan was, in fact, prepared by Veba's management, and stipulated the following: 87 percent of the shares were to be sold through voucher privatization; 2 percent would be sold directly to Veba's employees; 3 percent would go to an account for restitutions to former owners; 3 percent had to be transferred to the State Restitution Fund; and the remaining 5 percent would be sold to banks. Two small units belonging to Veba were privatized through restitutions and their labor forces and equipment moved into the remaining six plants to continue operation as part of Veba.

The first voucher privatization round ended in June 1992. Demand for Veba's shares exceeded the number of shares offered for the voucher privatization at the price set by the government for the first bidding round. Under these conditions, according to rules of the voucher privatization in Czechoslovakia,[9] all shares remained undivided and the price was raised for the second round. In this round, Veba, like most other companies, faced a massive fall-out of investor interest in the firm, so that only 61.8 percent of the shares were sold. The price for the third round, again set by the government, fell to one-half of the original price. At this price, more Veba shares were demanded than were available, therefore no more were sold and the government retained this price for the fourth round. (See Table 1 for details.)

Changes in Organization

Late in 1990, under the previous general manager, Veba's headquarters structure, which involved several plants, was changed into a divisional structure with two separate divisions, one for damask and one for terry. The management structure combined functional and product-line approaches, with the general manager trying to separate the corporate and operational levels. The corporate level was to be responsible for strategic business decisions, and the operational level, headed by the managing director, was responsible for the day-to-day operations of the firm. However, these changes were never fully implemented.

The general manager and two functional managers left the firm in late 1991 and early 1992. The general manager was admitted into an MBA program, one functional manager joined a group that made a management buyout of another firm, and the other became a property owner through the restitution. Josef Novak, the former managing director and head of the damask division, was appointed the new general manager of Veba and promoted three people from within the firm to the top management.

In January 1992, the product-line division was replaced by a vertical system consisting of headquarters and units based on technology and type of activity (e.g., spinning, weaving, supporting services, sales) or responsibility (e.g., accountant or quality manager). These units were managed as cost centers with clearly specified skill levels and responsibilities. The main advantage of this flat organizational structure was its simplicity and the general manager's prior experience with this kind of structure in the damask division.

This general manager, who was responsible for strategic decisions as well as for the quality program, now had five functional managers: a production manager, responsible for textile production and logistics; a financial manager, responsible not only for financial management, but also for the internal economy of the firm, its performance, and managerial information systems; a marketing manager, responsible for marketing strategies, market research, promotion and sales; a technical manager, responsible for fixed-assets maintenance, production services such as transport, heating etc., and investment control; and a personnel manager, responsible for human resources management.

Human Resources

Among the firm's most important long-term goals were a significant change in employees' attitudes, trust in the new personnel, and better internal communication. Trust between the different levels of personnel was lacking and, as was true in post-communist countries, people were often unwilling to take much responsibility because it went unrewarded. Management roles were redefined. Mr. van Sten, president of a Dutch consulting firm assisting Veba and also vice-president of Veba's managing board, put it this way: "We found a team of managers, not a management team. Therefore we had to take several crucial steps. The first task was to develop managers, not doers. It was also important to divide the strategic and the operational level of decision-making. This was difficult. Everyone wanted to work on the operational level. Strategic work was not sufficiently respected, appreciated, and rewarded because strategic decisions, the results of which are never immediately visible, were not considered work."

The members of Veba's staff, however, changed their attitudes. "People should be proud of working for Veba" was a credo of the management and corporate directors. "They have to be appropriately rewarded for their work. Also, when the government takes its hand away, the firm should take over part of the social responsibility. It is a way to increase the confidence of the people," said Mr. van Sten. A new personnel manager was appointed in 1992 and, although at 61 he was older than other top managers, he was trusted by the employees. For many years, he had been their spokesman and had had a very good relationship with the trade unions.

Veba also introduced an incentive system at this time. Although its wages were still subject to government regulation, the firm increased average wages and implemented a new wage policy based on a much higher wage differential. A group of key professionals, whose performance was crucial for the firm, was identified, these people were offered competitive salaries, and a new system of job descriptions was developed. The firm also tried to estimate market prices for every worker. In order to keep labor costs low, the management significantly reduced the size of its staff during 1992, as shown in Table 2, and expected further attrition. Because there were no involuntary lay-offs of local workers, this reduction had not yet caused significant problems. Veba also stopped employing foreign workers to prevent the need to dismiss local people. In addition, some reduction of labor was achieved by retirement and voluntary departures.

Improvement of the internal communication system became part of the quality program. Analyses of strengths and weaknesses showed that there was sufficient transmitted information inside the firm, but very poor communication. Vertical communication was almost missing and people from the shop floor were unwilling to talk to the management. Therefore, the human resources management stressed the notion that people must be aware of the consequences of their actions.

CONCLUSION

Veba's overall goal was to compete with the world's quality and technology leaders, to penetrate new markets such as North America, and to increase its share in other strategic markets as soon as its major West European competitors had left the marketplace. Other goals included long-term stability and profitability, and an increase in the present net value of the firm's shares.

The firm would need to diversify its products and markets to avoid risks and achieve financial stability. In addition to a share of the most demanding markets, the firm also sought to maintain its presence in the domestic market for standard goods and the former CMEA markets. Even as it struggled with these urgent problems, Veba's management continued to work toward its long-term targets.

Strategic alliances with foreign partners were also under consideration in fields that did not threaten the long-term interests of the firm, and under conditions in which Veba retained ownership majority. In 1992, Veba found a foreign financial investor willing to assist in financing the purification station, which was needed to meet environmental requirements, and to start building a facility for high-quality (walk) terry and the production of king- and queen-sized damask. But the firm continued to seek additional finances.

Veba's management was active and approached changes as challenges, rather than as problems. It was able to manage a firm in market conditions, it supported human resources development, and, exceptional among Czechoslovak firms, had a feasible long-term strategy that the management tried to support by short-term decisions. However, the firm would need to contend with competition on the international marketplace, and would require much effort, good decisions at the right time, and luck to win future markets. Its goal of supplying West European markets and the most demanding domestic market sectors seemed feasible, because the enterprise offered high quality at reasonable prices. While it could prove difficult to introduce Veba's trademark in West European markets, it might be easier to sell its products through well-established distribution channels of the top West European firms as they leave the business.

Notes

1. Employment has been cut by approximately 35 percent since 1989 with major cuts since July 1992.
2. All payment conditions were negotiated by a specialized foreign trade company, and Veba had no information about actual contracts between cotton sellers and the foreign trade company. The firm purchased cotton at fixed prices set by the government.
3. For many years, the textile industry, despite its relatively high productivity and high export capacity, has had the lowest average wage level of any industry. In 1991, the average wage in Czechoslovak industries was CSK 4,022, roughly $140 at the current exchange rate, while the average for the textile industry reached only CSK 3,160, approximately $110, during the same period. The average monthly salary of Veba's employees

was CSK 3,844, or $134, in 1991, and was expected to reach approximately CSK 4,400 in 1992. Source: Letter from Mr. Novak, General Manager, Veba, of August 14, 1992, and Mr. Vrchota, Federal Statistical Office.

4. Changes in the business environment are ranked according to their impact on economic activity and decision-making. Ranking of the shocks by importance for Veba's management would, however, give a different sequence, as would a chronological approach. "The most important shock," the general manager says, "was the deteriorating financial discipline of customers" (crisis of liquidity).

5. With standard weight of 120 g/square meter to 180 g/square meter.

6. According to the Country Overview Study, this restriction was due to the commercial banks' caution rather than tight monetary policy.

7. From 1989 to 1992, the Czechoslovak legal system, as in some West European countries, required that corporate governance be executed by two boards, but included only vague provisions on the functions and membership of the boards. Unlike the West European system, it required that both boards have inside and outside directors. No legal requirements regulated the duty of care or loyalty of the outside directors.

8. In some cases, approval of the entire government was required.

9. See J. Matesová, "Czechoslovakia—The Country Overview Study," paper of the joint research project undertaken by the World Bank, the Center for Economic Performance at the London School of Economics, and the Portuguese Catholic University.

Table 1
Bidding for Shares of Veba in the Voucher Privatization

Bidding round	Price (number of shares per 100 voucher points)	Share of ownership sold
1st	3	none
2nd	7/3	61.8%[1]
3rd	6	none
4th	6	n.a.[2]

Source: Center for Voucher Privatization.
[1] Eighty-eight percent of these shares were sold to Mutual Privatization Funds.
[2] As of November 11, 1992.

Table 2
Employment at Veba 1989–1992

Date	Number of employees
December 31, 1989	3,208
December 31, 1990	3,168
December 31, 1991	2,874
March 31, 1992	2,518
June 30, 1992	2,393
October 31, 1992	2,398

Source: Veba internal records.

Table 3
Output, Costs, Margin (in thousands of CSK)

	1991	May–October 1992[1]
Total output	1,133,742	420,327
Sales	1,089,441	406,704
Cost of goods sold	1,040,196	384,731
Markup	49,245	21,973
Operating profit	77,134	16,949
Extraordinary profits minus extraordinary losses	96,905	n.a.
Gross profit/loss	174,039	n.a.

Source: Veba's info-system.

[1] As of May 1, 1992, the balance sheet was restructured when the firm was transformed into a corporate form (a joint stock company).

Table 4
Financial Ratios (as of 1991 and December 31, 1991, respectively, and May–October 1992 and October 31, 1992, respectively)

	1991	May–October 1992[1]
Profitability ratios		
Mark-up/sales	4.52	5.40
Operating profit/COGS*	7.08	4.16
Gross profit/sales	15.98	n.a.
Mark-up/COGS	4.73	5.71
Operating profit/COGS	7.41	4.40
Gross profit/COGS	16.73	n.a.
Liquidity ratios		
Current ratio	1.92	1.98
Quick ratio	0.66	0.63
Activity ratios		
Average collection period (days)	44	57.5
Average payments period (days)	32	41.8
Average inventory turnover/ COGS in days	103	139.2
Leverage		
Debt/equity	0.46	0.56
Equity/total assets	0.68	0.64
Rate of return		
ROE	10.8	3.2[2]

Source: Veba's internal info-system.

[1] As of May 1, 1992, Veba's balance sheet was restructured when the firm was transformed into a corporate form (a joint-stock company).

[2] Adjusted for 365 days.

*Cost of goods sold.

6

Electronics: CS-03

The Transformation of a Television Set Producer

Rudolf Galik

SECTORAL SETTING

Before 1989, the philosophy of the Czechoslovak government was that it was acceptable for firms to produce goods that were suitable for sale only on the domestic market but not for export. Production systems therefore should only use domestic expertise, technology, and components. As a result, sales and profits were not in hard currency and there was no hard currency to purchase high-quality foreign products or the state-of-the-art technology used to produce them. Consequently many domestic enterprises have been liquidated since 1989.

This was also true within the consumer electronics industry. In 1989, the industry consisted of six state firms. Two of these, which produced televisions, were located in Slovakia, and it was clear they would be liquidated. Indeed, one went into bankruptcy, but the second survived the first years of transition. The means by which this was possible and the way in which management coped with various situations present an interesting case.

Until 1989, the enterprise, CS-03, belonged to an industry of mostly low-level domestic technologies and low product quality and was oriented only toward the unsaturated domestic market. Exports were sent to some CMEA countries that had lower technological levels and product qualities compared to the CSFR. The enterprise experienced sales drops in the summers of 1991 and 1992, and increases of sales in 1990 and 1991. These fluctuations were caused by a combination of factors.

CS-03's management had been replaced three times since November 1989. Each new management team had its own strategy for solving the firm's difficulties, but these strategies were often contradictory. The third management team was able to formulate and implement a strategy that helped CS-03 out of its crisis, and this strategy probably provided a base for future growth of the enterprise.

Description of the Industry

The two state firms located in Slovakia that survived the early years of the transition both produced televisions and related products, such as monitors and satellite receivers. One of these, CS-03, had a monopoly because the other, Tesla s.p. Stranice, had been built during 1984–87 and had only a minimal market share in small color televisions. After 1989, the production orientation of both firms changed.

Two other types of enterprises had recently entered the television industry, the first of which was state enterprises. These enterprises had previously produced goods such as radios and gramophones but, because of low quality and credibility, obsolete design, high prices of components and products, and the inability to adapt themselves to new conditions, they had changed their orientation to the more lucrative television industry. The other new entrants were private firms that used contacts with foreign television producers and lower custom tariffs to import components and assemble the televisions in the CSFR.

At the time of this report, the television industry included eight firms, but only CS-03 was an actual producer. The others assembled televisions from imported parts. This group of assemblers was represented by the firms Progreson Dunajská Streda, Tesla Etos Týniště, Tesla Stranice, Tesla Elton Prievidza, Elikon Liberec, and Tesla Cimex. The data on production and imports of televisions in 1989–92 are presented in Table 1.

Table 1 shows that, during 1989–92, CS-03 produced at roughly the same level, despite fluctuations in 1990 and 1991. The assemblers' production level, meanwhile, increased, and imports of televisions decreased. In 1991, 350,000 televisions were sold in the CSFR and presumably the same number would be sold the following year. Taking this figure into account, along with the fact that total delivery was 460,000 units, as shown in Table 1, we could assume that the inventories for 1992 would be about 100,000. Much of this inventory would belong to the importers and assemblers rather than to CS-03, which at the end of the second quarter of 1992 had only 7,500 televisions in stock. Of the importers' stock, most televisions were relatively unknown brands of inferior quality and were as high or higher in price than CS-03's products. The assembler's products, however, were well branded, but were 25–30 percent more expensive than those of CS-03. These were the primary reasons for the larger inventories of assemblers and importers. On the other hand, the future position of assemblers could improve because several Southeast Asian firms had an interest in establishing themselves in CSFR. This would allow them to enter the EC's market with televisions produced in

CSFR, thereby avoiding the tariffs and import limits. As a precondition, however, 40 percent of the components would need to be produced in CSFR.

CS-03 was dominant in the domestic market and its market share was expected to increase. The management estimated that as imports became too expensive, their market share would decrease, and that of assemblers would decrease as well. Because 65 percent of CS-03's televisions were sold in the Czech part of the country, future development would depend both on the economic and social results of Czechoslovakia's split, and on the next round of economic reforms.

External and Internal Constraints

One important external constraint was the government itself. In its 1991 economic program, the government expressed its belief that the industry would be unable to compete. This attitude changed in August 1992, because the firm's management had demonstrated its competence in only six months. Also, whereas many Asian countries protected their markets with high tariffs, the CSFR provided little tariff protection for the domestic television market. The tariffs were higher, at 16.5 percent, for televisions and finished products than for parts, at 2.8 percent. This difference is why the assembly of televisions from imported components remained viable. On the international market, the high tariffs of Central and Eastern European countries constrained CS-03 in that they made exporting difficult. No tariffs or other barriers existed in the EC countries, and therefore CS-03 had free access to their markets.

The government provided further constraints in that it was becoming somewhat lax in its efforts to attract foreign capital. Also, foreign investors were inclined to wait until the CSFR had resolved its difficulties. This situation was made worse by the weak position of the firms' management in negotiations with foreign partners.

The poor financial condition of firms resulted not only from the government's restrictive financial policies, but also from the lack of credit resources. This shortage was caused by the split of the country and the division of property between the Czech and Slovak republics. The banks were only able to provide credits to small businesses and they also lengthened the period of payments. They required accounts to be opened so far in advance that enterprises were unable to generate the greater cash flow needed to meet the banks' requirements. Thus, entrepreneurship became increasingly difficult.

Two other measures were also perceived as constraints; the tax rate on profit, which was 50 percent in 1992 and which would be 45 percent in 1993, and the regulation of wages. State enterprises, even those with good performances and generated resources, had problems motivating employees. Wage regulation kept wages at so-called socialist level, meaning that the average monthly wage in the CSFR had only increased from 3,300 CSK in 1986 to 4,200 CSK in 1992.

CS-03 was also historically constrained. Neither the methods of work nor the relationship between management and workers had changed and this was deemed very important. One of the firm directors said: "The employees fight with the firm for benefits as they did under the last regime. They do not identify themselves with the firm." Another director reacted: "We all are the employees, but only some of us work." The management also viewed the total independence of the firm as a constraint. There was a lack of managerial knowledge and skills for survival in the new market economy, which usually results in poorly made decisions and an unwillingness to take risks.

Description of Technology

CS-03 produced most television parts except for screens, which it purchased. It also purchased some components needed for connection boards, remote controls, and tuners. The technological process consisted of three phases: production, assembly, and control. The production phase involved the manufacture of television boxes and the various metal components, such as connectors and coolers, and the galvanization of their surfaces. This phase also involved production of the connection board, which entailed welding the components on the boards and testing them. In the assembly phase, modules were inserted into the box, which was then rewired, the white color set up, and television tested in a so-called life test that lasted for eight hours. Between 0.5 and 1 percent of the sets proved to be faulty, compared to the rate before 1989, which was between 15 and 16 percent. Finally, after each work shift, consumer control was done. The entire process was very labor-intensive. Automation accounted for only 15 percent of the labor during the setting of the connection board, and the percentage of automation during assembly was even lower. The labor intensity was to decrease from 85 percent to 40 percent in January 1993 with the introduction of new automated centers into the process, thereby resulting in a higher quality television.

TRANSFORMATION OF CS-03

History of the Firm

The firm was created in 1947 as a linen textile plant. It was built in a region of low economic activity, and was to provide jobs for the local labor force, but the lack of raw flax meant that the plant only worked at 25–30 percent capacity. A change occurred in the 1950s when television broadcasting started in the CSFR, at which time few televisions existed. In January 1957, the plant was liquidated and a new enterprise established for the manufacture of televisions. The first sets were produced in 1958, and between 1958 and 1960, the firm produced 57,340 television sets and 172,471 radios.

At the end of the 1960s and the beginning of the 1970s, efforts were made to diversify, and the enterprise began to manufacture monitors and small-class computers in 1968 and color televisions and translators in 1971. It experienced rapid growth during this period, producing and selling 110,000 televisions in 1960, 389,000 in 1980, and 480,000 in 1986. This growth also provided resources for investment in production and social services, and improvements in the computer and translator plants.

Legally, the enterprise was a national enterprise until 1984, meaning that, while it was relatively independent, it was subjected to state-planned targets and was subordinated to the Federal Ministry of Electronics. Between 1985 and 1988, it was a concern enterprise of the so-called production-economic unit, Spotrebna elektronika, Bratislava, which was made up of six concern enterprises. During that period, CS-03 lost most of its independence to the production-economic unit, and its financial resources and investments were determined by the higher concern level in Bratislava.[1]

In 1988, by means of another reorganization, the firm became a state enterprise and regained much of its independence. In 1990, the transformation process began and the enterprise changed its legal form for the last time. In May 1992, CS-03 became a joint-stock firm administered by the Fund of National Property of the Slovak Republic. As of this report, the firm consisted of three plants: a production plant for televisions and satellite receivers, a plant for translators, and a plant for social services.

MAJOR SHOCKS TO THE FIRM

The critical shocks to the firm resulted mostly from the liberalization of prices and the regulation of wages. Free pricing had two influences. First, it permitted suppliers' prices to increase, indeed prices for components increased by an average of 100 percent. This should have resulted in a 60 percent increase in CS-03's prices, from 13,000 CSK per television to 21,000 CSK. However, in January 1991, CS-03 increased prices by 3,500 CSK per unit in response to the pressure from the regulation of wages. The 60 percent inflation rate in the first three months of 1991, combined with the 12 percent limit on the increase in wages, lessened the demand for products of long-term consumption, among them televisions. There were rumors that a new currency would be established, which would result in a growth of prices. The firm sold its entire inventory of televisions at the end of 1990 and beginning of 1991 but increased inventories in 1991, which at that point amounted to 5,135 million CSK. Also, the regulation of wages in state enterprises meant that many specialists and highly skilled workers left state enterprises, attracted by the higher wages in the unregulated private sector. Unfortunately, CS-03 was unable to find a way to convince these workers to remain.

Other changes that affected the firm were the 100 percent devaluation of the

Czechoslovak crown, from 14 CSK/$U.S. to 18 CSK/$U.S. and then to 28 CSK/$U.S., and the need to pay with hard currency for deliveries among the countries of Central and Eastern Europe, especially since CS-03 had imported many components from the former German Democratic Republic. The combination of these factors caused the following reactions: the disintegration of the domestic market; the disintegration of CMEA markets that affected CS-03's imports of components, with export sales rising to only 12 percent of total sales; and the decrease of the firm's profits from 320 million CSK in 1990 to 19.7 million CSK in 1991.

Some government policies were particularly harmful for CS-03—for example, the restrictive fiscal policy, the removal of all subsidies from state budgets, the increase of credit interest to 20–22 percent in 1991, and the restriction of credit resources for banks. At the time, the banks were almost without credit resources, and CS-03's economic director said: "To acquire credit requires the greatest cunning of a firm's management."

The newly regained independence of enterprises was also problematic. The firm had to form units for activities such as marketing, foreign sales, and financing and, during the two years since economic reform began, the management had only partly coped with this task. The general director of the firm commented: "Currently, we think of the immediate future on a functional level. We must learn to manage strategically and for the long term."

Marketing and competition presented new obstacles for CS-03, and the competition from sales organizations and assemblers was keenly felt. In 1991, the sales organizations imported 271,000 televisions and the assemblers delivered 50,000 televisions to the market. Consumers demonstrated two tendencies in that year: a small number expected unbranded foreign televisions to be of better quality and bought imported sets at prices that were the same or a bit higher than those of CS-03. Prices of branded foreign televisions had also increased to 40,000 CSK or more. Most customers bought the domestic televisions and CS-03 was able to sell its entire annual production of 194,187 televisions, compared to 498,552 sold in 1990.

A crash in sales in February 1991 caused CS-03's inventory to increase to 35,000 units, worth more than 420 million CSK. The firm thus decreased its 1991 production target of 405,000 to 200,000 units. This was simultaneously accompanied by another jolt, the privatization of wholesale organizations. Until 1990, CS-03 had had three wholesale customers to whom it sold everything. After privatization began, however, distribution channels were destroyed and the number of customers increased to 840. It took CS-03 four months to find forty newly privatized wholesale organizations. The firm opened twenty-five sales units in various towns throughout the country that sold 10 percent of its production.

Since 1989, the firm has had three different management teams, each one bringing new and often contradictory ideas and strategies. The first management, in 1990, continued the previous strategy, but this was more a desire for status quo than a strategy based on an analysis of the business and the firm. This lack of action caused the workers to lose both motivation and faith in the enterprise. The second management, one year later, attempted to finish the production of domestic televisions and begin importing and assembling the television parts of well-known manufacturers.

This management reorganized the firm according to the advice of a consultant firm by separating it into sixteen relatively independent divisions. Relations between the divisions, however, were not articulated. Consequently, this reorganization resulted in a drop in both output and product quality, and also weakened relations between divisions. In order to rectify this inter-divisional problem, a third management replaced the divisional form with a centralized functional structure. The technical director commented: "Even now, the firm is experiencing the implications of the divisional form."

The 1991 sales problems were solved at the expense of employment. The management laid off 2,474 employees in that year and 162 employees in the first half of 1992. This was not sufficient and therefore the firm stopped all activities for two weeks and, from March to May, shortened the work week by two to three days. However, the most recently installed management team felt that the firm still had about 1,000 employees more than it needed, particularly since it was obvious that other electronics producers had fewer employees and higher productivity.

SHORT-TERM RESPONSES TO THE SHOCKS

In March 1992, the third management was appointed and decided against assembling imported televisions. Instead, it formulated a new strategy to achieve the position of cost leadership mainly through the development of products comparable to the ones sold in Western Europe. This had been considered before, but in early 1992 the conditions were right. Because of the growth in prices of domestic producers' components and stability of the currency, CS-03 was able to acquire foreign suppliers who charged lower prices for higher quality and reliability. The enterprise started to collaborate with firms such as Phillips, Nokia, Siemens, and Thompson, in which the focus was on testing various components for new televisions. These were developed over a ten-month period and gradually introduced to the market. All previous models were replaced by new ones and the final model of the product line was to be introduced in January 1993.

Achieving these objectives influenced production costs. The structure and development of these costs is shown in Table 2, which also shows that total costs of CS-03 increased by 16 percent between 1988 and 1990. In 1991, unit costs decreased by 37 percent due to a 41 percent decrease in output. This meant that CS-03 obtained the same costs per unit as in 1988, before price liberalization, and also obtained the position of cost leader, which allowed it to use price competition to lower prices twice, for a total of 3,500 CSK per television. Thus, since May 1992, CS-03's prices remained at the same level as before 1989.

Because rivals were unable to compete with CS-03's quality/price ratio, its market share increased from 48 percent in 1991 to an estimated 57 percent in 1992. Domestic prices were 15 percent higher than world prices, at least on the European market, and consequently, CS-03 had not been able to generate profits through exports to Western Europe. A comparison of product cost structures shows that material cost were the same for CS-03 as for foreign producers in Western Europe and, although wages were lower at CS-03, overhead costs were 15 percent higher. To strengthen its cost leadership, CS-03 would need to both cut overhead costs by increasing output and obtain economies of scale. The basic strategy for the next two years was to increase output to 450,000 televisions in 1994 and to boost exports to Western markets by 30 percent. CS-03 had taken the first steps toward improving its exports by testing Western markets with new television models and asking for certification for the German market. To enter the Eastern markets, the firm created a joint venture called Tera-Tesla, with a Ukrainian firm, and tested the Ukrainian market by selling 1,000 televisions in 1992.

The technical and production policy was supported by a sales policy designed by the marketing department. This policy offered quantity rebates, promoted new products, and focused on advertisement and good prices, all of which reduced the inventory. In April and July, inventory was 35,000 televisions and production was 4,000 units per month; in August, the inventory dropped to 4,000 and production rose to 32,000. The inventory as of October 1992 was below 3,000 televisions. In 1992, implementation of credit sales also helped. This type of sale, called the Telora system, was based on a credit of 690 million CSK with a 14 percent interest rate. The Slovak government guaranteed the interest. CS-03 planned to sell 36,000 televisions through Telora, but at this point, the firm had already sold 40,000. The advantage of this system was that a large portion of credit was paid off in the first year, and the low costs for repairs of warranty failures helped CS-03 to generate cash flow.

Motivation

Motivation of employees seemed to be a major problem at CS-03. Despite the lay-offs since March 1992, salaries could not be raised because of wage regulation. Although the average wage was 3,282 CSK in 1991 and 3,870 CSK in 1992, 330 CSK lower than the average wage in the CSFR, the economic incentives were strong. The firm was located in a region where there was only one other large firm, and therefore, the loss of a job for a CS-03 worker often meant the loss of the family income. The salaries for engineers and technicians, at 5,000–7,000 CSK, were about one-half that of similar jobs in private business and they lacked responsibility. However, large economic incentives were given to managers, whose salaries were 8,000–11,000 CSK a month. All employees expected to have a raise, perhaps as early as the end of 1992.

Finance

The firm's financial situation seemed to be better than seven months earlier. It generated a stable cash flow and was able to pay its accounts, and gross profits for 1993 were expected to be 190 million CSK, compared to 19.7 million CSK in 1991. These figures are shown in the survey of financial indicators in Table 3. The indicators of the second quarter of the 1992 expressed the same problems the firm had between April and July. Profitability ratios were negative and the losses were 8.7 percent.

Creating cash flow depends on the customers' ability to pay their accounts, and CS-03 tried to outbalance the accounts receivable and accounts payable. It decreased the total value of accounts receivable from 415.24 million CSK in 1990 to 383 million CSK in 1991, and to 317 million CSK in the second quarter of the 1992. The accounts payable to suppliers, except the credits, were 218 million CSK in 1990, 355 million CSK in 1991, and 202 million CSK in the second quarter of 1992.

Other indicators of liquidity and activity are shown in Table 4. With regard to current and quick ratios, the indicators and ratios were calculated from the domestic form of balance sheet. Some categories were modified to better resemble those of Western balance sheets. Furthermore, some categories for the calculation of ratios have been modified. In CS-03's accounts payable and accounts receivable, the credits of 690 million CSK that were provided for credit sales, and the annual credit sales in the average collection period replaced by annual total sales, were included. The other indicators were calculated according to the original form.

The high average inventory turnover was caused by 990.894 million CSK's worth of inventories in the second quarter of 1992. The breakdown of this value was 48 percent material inventories, 11 percent semi-products, 28 percent final products, and 13 percent other inventories. In October 1992, the value of inventories was lower; there were no inventories of final products or miscellaneous inventories. CS-03, however, had high enough material inventories to last for four months.

In order for the firm to maintain its cost leadership position, it would need to cut costs by 15–20 percent, which would mean investing 300 million CSK in technology. The enterprise could generate half of this amount, but the second half would need to be financed by credits, and that could be a problem.

LONG-TERM RESPONSES TO THE SHOCKS

In its privatization plan, the management proposed to privatize state-owned property in the following fashion: 82 percent of property would be sold through coupons, 15 percent sold directly to the Slovak Savings Firm, and 3 percent allocated to a restitution fund. The Slovak government denied the management's and employees' request for permission to buy some of the shares and the response to this decision was critical. Both management and employees had felt that the current strength of the enterprise was a result of their good performance. Also, the firm's improved condition was reflected in the strong interest of the buyers of CS-03's coupons. In the first two rounds of privatization, before June 1992, there had been little interest in CS-03 shares and the prices for the firm's shares decreased very quickly. However, in the third and fourth rounds, demand was so high that the auction had to be canceled and CS-03's management had high hopes that the firm would be sold in fifth round.

In its collaboration with foreign firms, CS-03 developed a 1993–95 strategy with the intent to diversify into related electronics products, thus providing new products and technologies. For example, the management planned to manufacture audio and video sets and expected the first new products to be made in 1993. By 1995, they were expected to account for 30 percent of production.

The investment policy also appeared to be a long-term response. To upgrade the technology, the firm invested both in machines for the automotive assembly of the television sets' boards and in the assembly conveyors. That portion of the automotive assembling was to increase from 15 percent to 60 percent in the beginning of 1993, which will provide the firm with long-term advantage not only in saving costs, but in increased quality as well.

THE MANAGEMENT'S PERCEPTION OF THE FIRM'S POSITION AND ITS PROSPECTS

Generally, the firm had survived the worst of the transition. It had escaped the threat of liquidation and the management believed that its current position was more stable. In addition to generating cash flow, it had implemented programs to sustain this flow, and believed that its ability to pay foreign and domestic suppliers, to pay off its credits, and to obtain payments from customers was reason enough for optimism. In spite of this, the economic director characterized the firm's situation as follows: "I'm not a great optimist. I believe the firm is vulnerable." This vulnerability stemmed from political conditions, especially the proposed split of the country and its property. As of October 1992, the Czech government expected a 10 percent drop in trade between the Slovak and Czech republics. The governments could also impose trade or other restrictions that would make business more difficult for CS-03. Also, the weakening condition of the Slovak economy and the following decline in the standard of living could destroy the demand for televisions. Thus, the economic and political environments would require the firm to adapt.

IMPLICATIONS FOR CHANGING BEHAVIOR AND GOALS

In order to strengthen its position, CS-03 would need to implement the following changes:

- maintain and strengthen its position as cost leader in 1993, decrease costs by 15–20 percent, and offer world prices on the domestic market. These goals could be achieved by investing 300 million CSK in new technology;
- increase output to 350,000 televisions in 1993 and to 450,000 in 1995;
- diversify into related products and increase the sales of these products to 30 percent by 1995. In doing so, it would need to transfer 1,000 employees from work on the original products to the new ones;
- find new foreign markets and increase exports to 30 percent of total output in 1993;
- create strategies for marketing, research and development, finance, and personnel.

To achieve all these goals, a change in the behavior of units, departments, and employees would be required. In discussion with the firm managers, they pointed out the following:

- CS-03 needed to change the culture of the firm by introducing new values, symbols, and norms, and also socialization tactics so that employees would be better able to identify with the firm;
- the firm also needed a new reward system, based on performance appraisal which offered generous monetary incentives;
- specialized education for specific groups should be provided;
- the departments of marketing, research and development, and finance should be modified to play more active roles in the formulation and implementation of strategy;
- the firm would need to maintain an image of high quality and reliability of its products and, lastly, offer them at inexpensive prices.

CONCLUSION

The previous three years had been difficult. The firm needed to adapt to recurrent fluctuations in sales, production, inventories, and financial resources. It was also challenged by large imports and deliveries from the television assemblers. On the other hand, there were some political and economic changes that supported the enterprise, such as rumors about the establishment of a new currency, liberalization of prices, and so forth. Thus, despite the decline in sales that was caused partially by decreasing demand and rising competition, the firm survived the years 1990–91.

After several management team replacements, the last team had been able to formulate and implement a short-term strategy of turnaround by means of low production costs. This strategy was implemented not only by the innovation of the entire production line in ten months, but also by the introduction of a new sales policy. Unlike the economic results in the first half of 1992, which are shown in Table 3, those in the third quarter were positive, and a 200 million CSK profit was supported by other short-term responses that led to decreasing costs, such as laying off employees, decreasing warranty costs, keeping wages and salaries low, making long-term responses in investments, and collaborating with foreign firms.

Thus, the turnaround and survival of the firm in 1992 resulted from the quickness of the management's responses to changes in its environment. The management believed it had taken the first step to pull the firm out of the recession, but most problems still remained. It also announced very progressive objectives, which might be seen as unrealistic, but, confronting them with the management's proven capabilities and the firm's position, they need not go unrealized. The future vulnerability of the firm would be dependent more on the political than the economic situation.

Note

1. The "concern" was a type of "production-economic unit" that was an enterprise composed of "semi-enterprises, or concern enterprises." These concern enterprises received responsibilities and orders from a higher level, the concern. They had limited decision-making power in short-term operations. The "concern" was a subject of state planned targets and was dependent on the state budget, state banks, state insurance companies, and so on. All decisions concerning investments were made at the concern level.

Table 1

Production and Imports of Television Sets in CSFR

Source		1989	1990	1991	1992
CS-03	# of units	486,741	498,552	194,187	260,000
	%	58.59119	64.77925	48.02479	56.51266
Assemblers	# of units	0	0	50,000	80,000
	%	0	0	12.3656	17.38851
Imports	# of units	344,000	271,000	160,100	120,000
	%	41.40881	35.21233	39.59467	26.08277
Total	# of units	830,741	769,616.8	404,347.4	460,073.9
	%	100	100	100	100

Table 2

Structure of Costs of CS-03 (in thousands of CSK)

Indicator	1988	1989	1990	1991	1st Quarter/92	2nd Quarter/92
Materials	2,592,037	2,620,626	2,974,849	1,808,550	511,591	415,926
Energy	13,789	13,657	14,897	27,491	9,063	16,588
Wages	249,862	240,887	24,364	241,624	49,105	51,128
Services	18,413	24,603	0	0	0	0
Overhead	201,300	279,136	316,457	191,620	59,947	73,015
Interest	29,315	28,144	35,021	51,706	27,939	21,861
Depreciation	51,164	55,014	67,074	—	—	—
Penalty	6,846	6,176	4,524	1,747	5,621	14,949
Security payments	50,588	94,797	133,243	123,740	23,775	24,459
Other	63,387	62,675	85,643	14,427	2,612	11,746
Total	3,075,401	3,178,909	3,549,847	2,269,285	629,706	556,657

Table 3

Main Financial Indicators of CS-03 (in thousands of CSK)

Specification	1988	1989	1990	1991	1st Quarter/92	2nd Quarter/92
Net sales	3,559,281	3,063,523	3,717,949	2,157,584	443,144	341,641
Cost of sales	3,075,401	3,178,909	3,549,847	2,269,285	629,706	556,657
Markup	483,880	−115,386	168,102	−111,701	−186,562	−215,016
Remaining revenues	34,993	178,540	142,734	124,431	232,560	178,197
Exchange gains/losses	−27,400	32,647	9,189	0	0	0
Profits/Losses	491,473	95,801	320,025	12,730	45,998	−36,819
Extraordinary profits	0	4,186	755	7,048	1,220	7,057
Extraordinary losses	−128	0	0	0	0	0
Gross profits/losses	491,345	99,987	320,780	19,778	47,218	−29,762
Taxes	33,433	38,308	208,507	11,997	25,970	0
Subsidies	5,473	42,700	−29,284	3,500	0	0
Net profits/losses	463,385	104,379	82,989	11,281	21,248	−29,762
Profitability ratios						
Markup/sales	0.13595	−0.0377	0.04521	−0.0518	−0.421	−0.6294
Gross profits/sales	0.13805	0.03264	0.08628	0.00917	0.10655	−0.0871
Markup/sales costs	0.15734	−0.0363	0.04735	−0.0492	−0.2963	−0.3863
Net profits/sales	0.13019	0.03407	0.02232	0.00523	0.04795	−0.0871
Net profits/sales costs	0.15067	0.03283	0.02338	0.00497	0.03374	−0.0535

Table 4

Liquidity and Activity Ratios of CS-03

Specification	1988	1989	1990	1991	1st Quarter/92	2nd Quarter/92
Liquidity ratios						
Working capital/Total assets	0.747	0.708	0.653	0.709	0.734	0.735
Current ratio	1.157	0.758	1.670	1.532	1.669	1.457
Quick ratio	0.435	0.088	1.061	0.831	0.857	0.710
Activity ratios						
Receivable turnover	11.50	12.15	8.542	3.489	0.633	0.319
Average collection period (days)	31.29	25.50	44.03	62.55	70.76	108.5
Payments turnover	5.25	6.799	7.245	2.490	0.643	0.498
Average payments period (days)	59.28	47.29	49.56	92.18	99.02	113.1
Inventory turnover	0.167	0.168	0.116	0.338	1.439	1.780
Average inventory turnover (days)	2,180	2,174	3,141	1,080	254	205

7

Food Processing/Chocolates and Sweets: CS-07

A Firm's Adaptability in the Transition Period

Rudolf Galik

SECTORAL SETTING

The top management of the state-owned enterprise CS-07 immediately accepted the request of the Czechoslovak Management Center to do a study on the firm for the World Bank. In doing so, it would be able to make known its views on the functioning of the firm. This attitude was rather unusual. During this period of transition to a market economy, enterprises in Czechoslovakia were often reluctant to provide information to outsiders for several reasons: an increase in competition in the new markets; the fact that the process of privatization created conflicts of interest for many groups, the top management among them; and lastly, the desire of managers not to disclose the weaknesses and strengths of their enterprise and its managerial processes.

Even under these conditions, some data could not be included in the List of Quantitative Indicators or in the case study because they were not part of government statistics and to calculate them would have taken too much time. The top management agreed that most of the missing data would be added through calculations from the first data accounts, or alternatively extracted for CS-07 from the former state enterprise statistics. (For details, see History of the Firm below.)

CS-07 was chosen for study for several reasons: the firm was enthusiastic about the project and supported this type of research; its products, chocolates and sweets, were usually supplementary consumer goods, sometimes called border products, bought only when consumers had enough money; and CS-07 had the ability to adapt to the changing conditions of the transition. CS-07 was also interesting because it had continually invested in reconstruction, technology, and product innovations. The political and economic changes had not had much influence on the firm's investment policies and the management had been able to cope with the changes. Despite the fact that the official economic reform began in January 1991, some changes occurred in 1990 when enterprises were to prepare for the reforms. Early responses showed that each enterprise would react differently, particularly in the agriculture and grocery industries. The management of CS-07 tried to anticipate these changes and to estimate their impact. Also, in 1990, incomes were expected to decrease because of rising prices, the increasing inflation rate, and problems of raising wages and employment.

During 1989–92, CS-07 was able to cope with the major changes in the economy, including the liberalization of prices, the twofold devaluation of the Czechoslovak koruna, and the disintegration of distribution channels. But, although the firm had demonstrated strong economic performance, many problems remained. For example, it was just beginning to build its own distribution channels and to market its products. This strategic behavior conformed to Henry Mintzberg's learning model of strategic management: the enterprise's management had decided to base its strategy on learning and understanding the market situation.

CS-07 used the same approach in the privatization process: it adapted its privatization goals and strategies to the current situation in the marketplace, which then resulted in its undertaking negotiations with potential foreign investors. The firm was able to change its strategy and then convince two governments with different political programs, the Ministry of Privatization officers and the officers of the Fund of National Property in the Slovak Republic, to accept the changed proposal. Finally, CS-07 is an interesting case because it seems to have successfully achieved its business and privatization goals. The new situation required totally new approaches and techniques from its management, and new ways of viewing things, especially from a strategic point of view. That was, and still is, a challenge for the firm's management.

Description of the Industry

In the CSFR, the manufacture of chocolate, chocolate sweets, and candies was complementary to the grocery business. The demand for these products occurred only when consumers had satisfied their basic needs. Considering the economic situation in Czechoslovakia, this was as important during transition to a market economy as it had been before 1989, when the state had regulated the industry's prices.

The chocolate and candies industry was the subject of much organizational reform and currently consisted of four enterprises: Čokoládovny a.s. Praha, which owned all the plants that produced chocolates, candies, and durable biscuits in the Czech Republic; CS-07; Figaro a.s. Trnava; and Deva a.s. Trebiov.

The last three were located in the Slovak Republic and produced the four main groups of products: cocoa powder, chocolate, chocolate candies, and sugar candies. CS-07 was the only one of the four firms that produced the semi-product, chocolate mass, which was delivered to Figaro a.s. Trnava and Pecivarne a.s. Sered and used to cover biscuits. The last enterprise was the monopoly producer of durable biscuits in Slovakia. The data on the production capacity of these firms may be found in Table 1, and those on production and exports in Table 4. This table is missing data on Čokoládovny a.s. Praha and imports into Czechoslovakia. Data on Čokoládovny are not available for many reasons, including competition between Czech and Slovak firms, and the problem of dividing the state; thus data on Czechoslovakian imports are unknown. Table 1 shows that Čokoládovny a.s. Praha owned 68.9 percent of the production capacity and three Slovak firms owned 31 percent. CS-07's portion represented 14.2 percent of production capacity in the CSFR.

External Constraints

The top management of the firm viewed several factors as external constraints to business. For example, the process of small privatization, including wholesale organizations, was very slow. This caused the break in the chain between producer, wholesaler, and retailer during November 1991–March/April 1992. In the past, wholesale organizations had purchased about 80 percent of production, but now inventories increased and therefore output had to be decreased by 40 percent.

Until recently, there was no law regarding relations between organizations. When such a law was passed, it provided only weak penalties for those who avoided fulfilling their contracts. Thus, from the first half of 1992 onward, the candy firms still had 90 million CSK in accounts receivable.

Product and packaging quality was strictly regulated in the international markets. Because the firm had not yet acquired the technology for double-rolled chocolate mass and also experienced problems obtaining natural color and aromatic ingredients, its products did not meet the requirements. In addition, the graphic designing and printing of its packaging was inferior because the innovative cycle of packages was a full year.

Another constraint was the rigid behavior of the managers and the administrative staff. Managerial methods had not changed and improvements in the firm were occurring very slowly, especially in sales, marketing, and market analysis. Additionally, there were problems with varying output and the development of new products.

High profit taxes also presented difficulties. A year earlier, the tax in Czechoslovakia had been 55 percent. This year, it was decreased to 45 percent except for grocery enterprises, which would have a 5 percent increase to 50 percent. These taxes consumed resources that could otherwise have been used to update technology. The insolvency of former CMEA countries was another constraint. These countries had been interested in CS-07's products but, aside from Poland and Bulgaria, were unable to pay for deliveries.

Increasing prices were seen as further constraints. For example, the prices of imported ingredients such as cocoa beans and butter, nuts and almonds, and domestic ingredients such as sugar, milk, and nuts had been raised. Changing technology and production had high investment costs. A chocolate-processing machine with a performance parameter of two tons an hour had cost 60 million CSK in 1990, but now cost 200 million CSK. To compound matters, the separation of Czechoslovakia into two independent states would decrease the size of the domestic market for CS-07, and the small Slovak market would not be of interest to foreign investors.

Basic Technological Description

CS-07's operations ranged from processing cocoa beans to packaging the finished product. The technological process consisted of the following:

- preparing the cocoa beans, cleaning, roasting, taking out the scales, and milling the cocoa mass;
- rolling and pressing the cocoa mass and cocoa butter into a chocolate mass;
- forming this chocolate mass into various products, e.g., chocolate bars and desserts;
- using the chocolate mass for covering nuts, almonds, fruits, and so forth to make candies.

THE TRANSFORMATION OF CS-07

History of the Firm

CS-07 was created in 1896 with capital of 300,000 German marks. Its first name was the Austro-Hungarian Royal Court Factory for Producing Chocolate, Stollwerck Brothers, Bratislava. The plant, which produced mainly caramels, was an affiliate of Stollwerck, Köln am Rhein, and employed 700 workers in 1906. By increasing its basic capital to 3 million crowns, it was incorporated in 1907 and renamed Brothers Stollwerck Ltd. Bratislava. In 1918, after the Czechoslovak Republic was formed, the firm lost its Austrian and Hungarian markets and output decreased.

When World War II started, the firm reoriented production toward marmalade and canned fruits, during which time its basic capital increased to 10 million CSK. The change in development occurred after the first defeat of the Germans on the eastern front. Technological reconstruction of the enterprise, which used technology imported from Germany, was stopped. The management was taken over by the national administration in 1945, and remained so until 1948 when the firm was nationalized.

The changes that occurred after 1948 were part of the socialist reforms that attempted to optimize the organization of chocolate and candy production in Czechoslovakia. The latest change occurred in 1988, when all Slovak enterprises that produced chocolate, sweets, and sugar were transformed into one large state enterprise. Six months later, this was split into a number of state enterprises, one of which was CS-07. In 1992, CS-07 was legally transformed from a state enterprise to a state joint stock firm. The sole owner of all shares thus far has been the Fund of National Property of the Slovak Republic, but the shares of the firm were to be sold in the second wave of privatization. Except for CS-07's entry into the chewing gum business in 1988, the products offered by the firm had not changed since the end of World War II.

MAJOR SHOCKS TO THE FIRM

CS-07 was the subject of large privatization, meaning that it was the top management's responsibility to create a plan for the transformation of the firm in the new market economy. This privatization affected the firm in various ways. For example, price liberalization caused the prices of the firm's products to increase by an estimated average of 45–50 percent. This estimate, however, was made by managers who had had little experience in this situation. There was also discordance between price decontrol and the process of privatization. This decontrol had begun before privatization and many monopolies had governed the market during the first half of 1991.

The unprofessional practices in small privatization, especially in privatizing wholesale organizations, made it difficult for producers to put their goods on the market, a situation which lasted from March to July 1991. Because there were no longer wholesale organizations, the firm now accessed the market through small private businesses. Indeed, the number of customers, especially in small and mid-size businesses, increased from 90 to 2,500, which meant more work for the sales personnel. Also, the system of integrative sales by all four Czechoslovak producers, which had been organized to coordinate the production and sales to domestic and foreign markets, broke down in 1990. The system had also helped firms plan their business and was supported by the demand for chocolate and sweets that had, for many years, exceeded the supply. Another breakdown was that of the CMEA markets. The percentage of enterprise exports to these markets, calculated from material indicators, was 77 percent in 1988, 73 percent in 1989, 47 percent in 1990, and 72 percent in 1991.

The change in exchange rates also affected the firm. During 1990–91, the exchange rate of the koruna to hard currencies was changed twice, in the first instance dropping from 14 CSK to 18 CSK per $U.S., and in the second, to 28 CSK per dollar. These changes made CS-07's imported inputs, and thus the final product, more expensive. However, inventories of imported inputs that were bought at lower prices in 1990 allowed the firm to earn large profits in 1991, but because wages and salaries in state enterprises were regulated, consumers' real income decreased, which caused lower demand. The result was that, in 1991, output was reduced by 35–40 percent.

During the two years, the Ministry of Agriculture and Grocery had no power to manage the firm, except to name its general director and annually evaluate its economic results. This lack of outside direction was a major shock for the managers and staff.

The sector's financial situation was adversely affected by a change in the taxes on retail sales. Earlier, the tax on chocolate had been 120 percent and that on caramel 20 percent. These rates were combined into one rate of 29 percent for grocery items, but in November 1991 the rate was cut to 20 percent, meaning that chocolate prices dropped to levels lower than before 1989. Increases in the prices of sugar sweets were necessary to support the increase in the prices of milk and sugar. However, because sugar sweets did not sell well, they were only produced in small volumes. The production of caramel, for example, decreased by 80 percent.

The proposed purchase of 65 percent of Čokoládovny a.s. Praha by the consortium of Nestlé of Switzerland and BSN of France was another surprise to the sector. This purchase, which had already been approved by the Czech government, would make Čokoládovny stronger and therefore a stiffer competitor for CS-07.

A major weakness within the firm was that it was slow to respond to the current social and economic changes. It also lost much time waiting to see what would happen in the economy and the industry, and worrying about government subsidies. The economic independence of the firm, therefore, caught it off guard. Managerial reorganization in response to the changes in society was badly needed. Unfortunately, CS-07 had no previous experience in building management systems.

The inability to adapt quickly to the new conditions caused a decrease in both sales and production and this necessitated a reduction in the work force. On top of this, workers were often required to do more than one job and their jobs changed according to the products required by the market. New customers were hard to find, especially foreign customers, and this was compounded by obsolete products and packaging. Another weakness was caused by the 1991 separation of both Figaro a.s. Trnava and Pecivarne a.s. Sered from the enterprise. The general office of the former state enterprise broke up and 40 people were dismissed.

Some of the effects of these various factors are listed in Table 2. To understand the situation, the decrease in output from 16,636 tons in 1988 to 12,570 tons in 1991 and 1992 must be taken into account. The value of this last figure was even higher than the value of 16,636 tons sold in 1988. Simultaneously, the profitability ratio of gross profit/sales decreased from 6.6 percent in 1988 to 3.7 percent in 1990. Then, because of the liberalization of prices and the enterprise's response to changes, it increased to 14.987 percent in 1991. The same development was characteristic of the ratio of net profit/sales. In 1992, despite seasonal decreases in the first quarter of the year, both ratios kept their values.

SHORT-TERM REACTIONS

Corporate Governance

CS-07 was state-owned from 1948 to 1992 and was governed in two ways. As a socialist enterprise, from 1948 until March 1992, it was managed directly by the Ministry of Agriculture and Grocery. After that, it became a state joint stock firm created and administered by the Fund of National Property of the Slovak Republic. This switch to shareholding was a result of privatization.

The top management created a privatization plan in which ownership of the firm would be sold in the following manner:

- 65 percent of the shares would be sold by means of coupons;
- 22 percent would be directly sold to a chosen Slovak bank;
- 10 percent would be sold to foreign firm(s); and
- 3 percent would be made available for restitutions.

The firm initiated negotiations with four foreign firms but, after ten months, no agreement had been reached, either because the foreign firm was too small or the Slovak government rejected the proposals. At the beginning of 1992, the Swiss firm, Jacobs-Suchard, entered negotiations with CS-07. With their consent, the privatization plan was changed such that 32 percent, or 10 percent + 22 percent, of the shares would be sold to Jacobs-Suchard, and its portion of ownership would increase to 66 percent through future investments. The Fund of National Property of the Slovak Republic, as the administrator of firm shares, named the board of directors and the supervisory board. The former consisted of a general director and four vice-directors and the latter had one representative from the Fund and two from the firm.

Organization

The firm had three managerial levels: the general director, the vice-directors, and four workshops managed individually by foremen and shift leaders, but with a production vice-director overseeing all four. Operation of the firm was divided by market criteria, with each workshop involved in the manufacture of a different good. The top management had made only small changes in the organization so far, but fundamental changes would probably be made after privatization to be consistent with the firm's future strategy. Jacobs-Suchard would be a strong influence during this process.

A number of changes occurred within the firm. In order to streamline the organization, 40 employees were released from the general office of the state enterprise, a marketing department was created that would concentrate on advertising only, and the structure of the sales department was changed and its manager and the manager of the purchasing department were replaced. The sales department now consisted of sales agents, each of whom was responsible for a different region of the country. The EDP department had been updated in 1987 and many jobs and costs were cut, which in turn led to a poor relationship of the firm's employees with this department. And lastly, the department of organizational design collapsed.

Decision-making power was divided such that a great deal of authority was given to the production, marketing, and sales managers, but other powers were given to the general director, who was able to hire and fire managers and determine their salaries, to negotiate with foreign firms, and to make organizational changes. As a means of increasing profitability, the size of the enterprise was decreased and the salaries of the management were raised. CS-07 had 802 employees in 1989, 600 in 1990, and 587 in June 1992. After June 1992, all firm managers received fixed contract salaries that reflected the importance of their positions, the result being that now earnings were double what they had been before that date.

Production, Output, and Short-Term Policy

The fundamental goal of CS-07's management was to successfully privatize the firm and create a decent level of profitability. To accomplish this goal, several things were done after the firm began operating in a market economy. A 1989 agreement was strengthened with Tschunt GmbH Itzgrund/OT Lahm of Germany. This agreement concerned the production of chewing gum and pledged cooperation between the two enterprises. Tschunt agreed to deliver technology and ingredients to CS-07 and then purchase the products, amounting to 400 tons annually, from CS-07 and sell them through its distribution channels.

Production was modified so that caramels and some sweets were almost completely replaced by chocolate and chocolate candies. The structure of 1991's production was 20 percent chocolate mass, 32–35 percent chocolate bars, 32–35 percent chocolate candies, 4–5 percent cocoa powder, and 8–10 percent sugar candies. Also, all packaging materials were replaced over a period of 10 months, and the firm now bought its packages from Austria, Germany, and Italy. They were 25 percent more expensive, but were comparable to those of CS-07's competitors. This improvement, particularly for sweet drops and chewing gums, strengthened the firm's position on the domestic markets.

During the period of privatization of wholesale organizations, the firm formed a sales department to work with small and medium-sized trade firms. Using information gleaned by this department, plans were made to introduce various improvements and innovations in technology, products, and packaging on the domestic market. For example, the plan proposed sterile and double-rolled cocoa mass, hollowed chocolate figures, and hollow-ball chewing gum. Also, the production of milk and cream chocolate bars, chocolate- or sugar-covered fruit, and seasonal items, such as Christmas and Easter chocolate specialties, was suggested.

The enterprise changed its prices because of changes in the retail tax rate and price liberalization. The prices of inputs rose, causing the prices of products to increase, but the increase in product prices created higher sales profits in 1991. That year, profits were 23.44 million CSK more than in 1989, and 108.17 million CSK more than in 1990, despite the 28.3 percent decrease in production compared to 1989, and 11.3 percent decrease compared to 1990. On the other hand, the 40 percent decrease in production from November 1990 through April 1991 was partly offset by exports to Poland and Bulgaria. In eight months, the firm exported 300 tons to Poland and 1,400 tons of products to Bulgaria.

In the fluctuating environment, the firm managed to oriented itself to the domestic markets, despite the fact that exports had increased during the last four years. In 1988, total production was 17,636 tons, of which only 624 tons, or 3.1 percent, were exported. In 1991, production was 12,570 tons and 1,854 tons, or 14.7 percent, were exported. Poland received 121.3 tons, the United States 1,117.16 tons, Germany 85.8 tons, Austria 62.6 tons, Bulgaria 27.6 tons, and Sweden 25.6 tons.

In sum, the short-term goals of the management were:

- to privatize as quickly as possible according to the privatization plan;
- to develop regional sales centers as the bases for new distribution channels;
- to reduce labor costs;
- to develop and strengthen the role of the marketing department;
- to increase the profitability or net profit to total costs, by 10–11 percent and to increase the net profit to 100 million CSK per year within 5 years.

Finance, Credit, Subsidies, and Taxes

The financial situation of the firm seemed satisfactory. The ratio of net profit to total costs had increased by 3.6 percent in 1988, and by 8.95 percent in 1991, and this enabled the firm to make investments from its own resources. The accounts payable were 22.631 million CSK in 1991 and 8.496 million CSK in June 1992. Accounts receivable were 56.545 million CSK in 1991 and 90.293 million CSK in June 1992. Although the accounts payable had decreased regularly, accounts receivable increased, despite efforts made to obtain this money. CS-07's difficulty in obtaining these payments was related to the poor financial situation of small and medium-sized businesses that were unable to generate the cash flow, and therefore unable or unwilling to pay their debts. The firm had one tool to combat the delinquency of these businesses; cut sales to debtors.

Several of the firm's financial indicators are shown in Table 3. Both current and quick ratios had a tendency to increase over the past four years. The current ratio value was much closer to the required value standard for firms in Western market economies, but the quick ratio had not achieved the required value. Short-term liquidity could be a problem if customers are unable to pay for deliveries.

In calculation of the indicators, credit sales in the average collection period have been replaced by total sales. Other indicators were calculated according to original formulas. The firm's total credits were 75.181 million CSK in 1991 and 89.86 million CSK in June 1992. These figures are equivalent to two years of the firm's net profits. Eighty percent of the credits are long-term credits.

In 1989, CS-07 received 46.737 million CSK in subsidies, of which 5.775 million CSK were used to support exports and 40.962 million CSK to buy technology. The state provided the first amount, and the general office of state enterprise the second amount. Most of the plants' profits were collected by this office and redistributed to the individual plants according to the investment plan. In 1990, the firm received subsidies of 1.544 million CSK and the state provided support for the export of products, but all subsidies disappeared in 1991. Thus, the business has received no subsidy for the last two years and, except for credits, has been financed entirely from its own resources.

The tax on profits in agriculture and grocery changed annually since 1988: from 25 percent to 65 percent in 1989, to 55 percent in 1990, and to 50 percent in 1992. Increased profits of more than 100 percent, resulting from the increase in prices, and the 50 percent tax rate combined to produced an increase in taxes of more than 450 percent from 1988 to 1991. The firm responded to this with lower prices and increased output. This strategy was acceptable to CS-07's future partner, Jacobs-Suchard, which had expressed interest in as large a market share of the firm as possible.

CS-07 also paid retail sales taxes of 468.075 million CSK in 1988 and 138.59 million CSK in 1991. This tax represented 20 percent of the sales prices of retail sale organizations. After January 1, 1993, this tax was to be replaced by a value-added tax at a rate of 23 percent. The firm also paid a social security tax, calculated at 50 percent of wages and salaries, which had increased from 14.888 million CSK in 1988 to 19.523 million CSK in 1991.

LONG-TERM RESPONSES

The most important long-term changes were privatization and the future merger with Jacobs-Suchard. As mentioned earlier, Jacobs-Suchard would eventually own 66 percent of the firm, with the remainder belonging to investment funds or individuals. This would create a totally new position for the enterprise on the domestic market. A resultant expansion in European markets through Jacobs-Suchard's distribution channels was also expected. Simultaneously, this merger would change the economic relations between CS-07 and the largest and most powerful manufacturer in the sector, Čokolàdovny a.s. Praha. The previously mentioned five-year contract with Tschunt Gmbh, Itzgrund/OT Lahm, was another long-term proposition. CS-07 also agreed to sell its goods to the Polish firm Wawel Krakow, contracting to export 300 tons of chocolate and sugar sweets annually.

The firm had not yet formed a research and development department, but a number of employees in the production department had been active in development in an ad hoc fashion. The vice-director of productions was responsible for product development, and the results of CS-07's new technology were prepared and offered by their producers. These innovations were based on ideas of the employees formed through both visits to various exhibitions and external contacts.

The purchase of the production line for hollow-ball chewing gum from Cormeck Strassbourgh, France, for 10 million CSK, which produced goods for Tschunt, was an investment that was expected to have a long-term effect. Another such investment was the purchase of two lines for packaging chewing gum, one bought from Eurosigma Milan, Italy, to package individual pieces, and a second one from Asba Homburg, Germany, to package sets of chewing gum. Both investments cost 2.2 million CSK. In addition, four thirty m^3 reservoirs were constructed by Construmex Budapest, Hungary, at a cost of 4.5 million CSK. These were for the short-term storage of both sterile and double-rolled chocolate mass delivered by Jacobs-Suchard, which would be used to manufacture high-quality chocolate bars until CS-07 could amass the technology to produce the chocolate on its own. The reservoirs would then store the chocolate mass to be delivered to Figaro a.s. Trnava and Pecivarne a.s Sered.

The enterprise also signed a contract with Carlo et Montanari, Italy, to reconstruct the cocoa bean mill by the end of 1992 at a cost of 2.2 million CSK, and arranged for the construction of equipment for the compressed air used in hollow-ball chewing gum production at 0.9 million CSK. Further investments included:

- a new packaging line of sweets, purchased in Italy for 0.3 million CSK;
- reconstruction of two technological lifts for 1.9 million CSK;
- reconstruction of the central boiler room, including replacement of the coal boilers by gas ones for 8 million CSK;
- reconstruction of the administrative building for 0.683 million CSK;
- reconstruction of the building for chewing-gum production at 3.5 million CSK;
- construction of the piping network to transport syrup to all workshops at a cost of 5.5 million CSK.

FOOD PROCESSING/CHOCOLATES AND SWEETS   99

All of these investments had long-term effects and, from the firm's perspective, were consistent with its post-privatization plans. Despite the investments and its good financial situation, CS-07's top management presumed that the firm would need an additional 1 billion CSK in investments over the next five years in order to preserve and strengthen its position in domestic European markets, but the firm would not be able to create such resources alone.

MANAGEMENT'S PERCEPTION OF THE FIRM'S POSITION AND PROSPECTS

The management believed that the firm's position was stable and this stability was confirmed by its ability to respond to changes in its environment. These responses have been:

- diversification of production to include hollow chocolate figures, Christmas and Easter chocolate collections, and candies;
- privatization of the firm and the merger with Jacobs-Suchard, which would be a very strong partner;
- build-up of new distribution channels in CSFR and use of the foreign distribution channels of Jacobs-Suchard;
- acquisition of technology for the production and sales of Jacobs-Suchard's high-quality products;
- expansion into former CMEA markets with the intent to become the major producer for these markets.

MAJOR FINDINGS: IMPLICATIONS FOR CHANGING BEHAVIOR AND GOALS

The firm had changed its goals during the transition but, because it did not view the external changes as drastic, it was able to respond to them in a relatively short period of time. A decision was made to increase the proportion of shares sold to foreign firms from 10 percent to 32 percent. To a certain extent, the merger with Jacobs-Suchard ensured the future strength of the firm's market position, but to achieve this position, certain measures would need to be taken, namely:

- in 1992–93 to reconstruct production facilities and introduce new technology for processing cocoa and chocolate masses;
- to seek new niches in the Czechoslovak market for Jacob-Suchard's products, and to extend its own product line, particularly in luxury and high-quality goods;

- to increase export of output to 25 percent, which would require finding new foreign customers, using Jacobs-Suchard's distribution channels where possible;
- to reduce costs and increase output in order to generate net profits of 120 million CSK;
- to improve the managers' knowledge and skills, thus minimizing the gap between the skills of CS-07's managers and those of the Western partner's management.

Despite two years of ongoing economic reform, the behavior of people, especially of workers, had changed very little. In order to fulfill the above-mentioned goals, the firm's management felt a need to change the workers' attitudes in these directions:

- to strengthen economic incentives by introducing a new compensation system for all employees that would hopefully stimulate them to produce more products of better quality;
- to develop the marketing department, particularly the areas of market research and marketing strategy, believing that the enterprise must have not only sellers, but also marketers and marketing strategists.
- to improve the firm by means of learning the culture of Jacobs-Suchard and their way of doing things.

CONCLUSION

CS-07 had performed very well during the planned economy period. It had served domestic markets and had channeled a considerable amount of revenue to the state budgets in the form of taxes. It had also prepared and continuously renewed an investment plan to upgrade its technology. Since 1989, the overall strategy had been to respond to changing political, economic, social, and legal environments, the objective being privatization, so that it would be strong enough to compete with the joint venture created by Čokoládovny a.s. Praha with Nestlé and BSM. This was done; CS-07 found the proper foreign partner, convinced the Slovak government to approve this joint venture, made it functional, and has continued to make long-term planned investments to upgrade its technology.

The enterprise also adapted well to economic reform by cutting the prices of the goods when consumer taxes decreased and by responding to the twofold devaluation of the Czechoslovak koruna that led to an increase in prices of imported ingredients and technologies. Simultaneously, the responses to market situations were adequate and the firm innovated not only technologies but products and their packaging as well. It also made extensive efforts to enter new niches of the domestic market and foreign markets through direct sales and by cooperating with foreign firm.

Cost management seemed to be the second strategic aim of the CS-07 along with privatization. To be competitive from a cost perspective, the firm implemented some very painful measures, for example, laying off employees and emphasizing work discipline.

Thus, the management was the most important element of the firm's transformation. Under its guidance, the firm was successful in adapting to changes and challenges, and in formulating the strategies that were based on learning the markets. In this respect, the management's intentions and plans for the future seemed to be very realistic.

Table 1

Production Capacities of Four Chocolate and Candy Firms

Group of products	CP	CS-07	FT	DT	Total
Cocoa powder/tons	2,000	1,000	0	0	3,000
% of product. cap.	66.67	33.33	0	0	100
% of total cap.	1.791	0.895	0	0	2.685
Chocolate/tons	11,000	2,400	200	1,100	14,700
% of product. cap.	74.83	16.33	1.36	7.48	100
% of total cap.	9.85	2.15	0.179	0.984	13.16
Choc. candies/tons	30,000	8,500	1,500	4,000	44,000
% of product. cap.	68.18	19.32	3.41	9.09	100
% of total cap.	26.86	7.61	1.34	3.58	39.39
Sugar candies/tons	34,000	4,000	6,000	6,000	50,000
% of product. cap.	68	8	12	12	100
% of total cap.	30.44	3.58	5.37	5.37	44.76
Total tons	77,000	15,900	7,700	11,100	111,700
% of total cap.	68.835	14.235	6.894	9.936	100

Key:
CP = Čokoládovny a.s. Praha
FT = Figaro a.s. Trnava
DT = Deva a.s. Trebiov

102 CASE STUDIES OF CZECH AND SLOVAK FIRMS

Table 2

Main Financial Indicators of CS-07 (in thousands of CSK)

Indicator	1988	1989	1990	1991	1st Quarter/ 92	2nd Quarter/ 92
Net sales	616,823	634,749	551,008	659,178	179,846	166,227
Cost of sales	568,039	616,247	520,190	580,544	169,046	149,791
Markup	48,784	18,502	30,818	78,634	10,800	16,436
Extraordinary profit	0	9,934	0	20,159	7,748	6,841
Extraordinary losses	8,024	0	−10,230	0	0	0
Gross profit/loss	40,760	28,436	20,588	98,793	18,548	23,277
Taxes	20,266	14,218	10,300	46,817	9,340	11,639
Net profit/loss	20,494	14,218	10,288	51,976	9,208	11,638
Profitability ratios						
Markup/sale	7.9089	2.9149	5.593	11.929	6.0051	9.8877
Gross profits/sale	6.6081	4.4799	3.7364	14.987	10.313	14.003
Markup/sale costs	8.5881	3.0024	5.9244	13.545	6.3888	10.973
Net profit/sale	3.3225	2.2399	1.8671	7.885	5.1199	7.0013
Net profit/sale cost	3.6079	2.3072	1.9777	8.953	5.4470	7.7695

Table 3

Liquidity and Activity Ratios of CS-07

Specification	1988	1989	1990	1991	1st Quarter/ 92	2nd Quarter/ 92
Liquidity ratios						
WC/TA	0.629	0.605	0.533	0.575	0.517	0.5198
Current ratio	1.276	1.796	1.576	2.658	2.600	2.6092
Quick ratio	0.332	0.634	0.485	1.177	1.187	1.2933
Activity ratios						
Receivable turnover	14.54	18.56	13.42	11.65	1.794	1.841
Avg. collection period (days)	25.09	19.66	27.19	31.31	203.4	198.26
Payments turnover	11.96	7.657	51.40	25.65	10.55	17.631
Avg. payments period (days)	28.09	46.27	6.703	12.53	32.50	18.655
Inventory turnover	0.269	0.274	0.302	0.272	0.922	0.9856
Avg. inventory turnover (days)	1,356	1,329	1,208	1,337	395.6	370.32

Table 4

Production, Sales, and Exports of Two Slovak Companies

Indicator	"CS-07"					Figaro a.s. Trnava				
	1988	1989	1990	1991	1992	1988	1989	1990	1991	1992
Semi-product/tons	3,054	2,665	2,843	2,250	1,242	0	0	0	0	0
Exports/tons	0	0	0	0	0	0	0	0	0	0
Cocoa powder/tons	965	989	854	700	290	0	0	0	0	0
Exports/tons	0	0	0	1	2	0	0	0	0	0
Chocolate/tons	2,504	2,470	2,131	2,738	2,184	302	333	407	391	170
Exports/tons	48	42	0	306	288	0	0	17	52	31
Choc. candy/tons	8,494	8,467	7,704	5,334	2,274	1,453	1,479	1,537	1,295	541
Exports/tons	95	71	131	1,044	274	53	20	30	24	18
Sugar candy/tons	4,619	4,935	3,649	1,548	547	6,266	6,320	6,864	4,710	2,145
Exports/tons	481	498	412	503	162	714	834	654	634	402
Sales/tons	19,639	19,526	17,181	12,570	6,537	8,021	8,132	8,808	6,396	2,856
Exports/tons	624	611	543	1,854	920	767	854	701	710	451
Sales/mil. CSK	616.8	635.7	551	659.2	346	189.5	220.5	220.7	298.4	163
Exports/mil. CSK	8.44	7.68	13.16	82.56	41.9	—	—	—	—	—
Employees	842	802	749	600	587	660	679	665	669	637

8

Footwear: Tipa

Jaroslav Jirasek and Ilja Mracek

SECTORAL SETTING

Life was good for entrepreneurs in Czechoslovakia after the November 1989 Velvet Revolution. Market demand was much greater than supply for almost all goods, and people were willing to pay high prices, thus creating a high margin/profitability ratio. There were no legislative regulations for entrepreneurial activity and the tax system was better for small businesses than large ones. Many new private enterprises chose a particular business because of its profit margins and switched to others when the first one became less profitable. Others simply diversified.

Tipa was one firm that diversified. At the time of this report, it owned agriculture production facilities, a fruit farm, a travel bureau service, a trade service, telecommunications and security systems services, and a construction firm. It was also involved with agricultural machinery, foreign trade, shoe and food production, and investment privatization funding, but the most important parts of the enterprise were the last three.

The production of frozen cream products was technologically demanding and there was much competition because of the high profit margins in this business. This came not only from state-owned firms, many of which were being privatized, but also from large foreign enterprises, such as Juhliever, Algida, and Schuller. External constraints for food production were stiff hygienic requirements and foreign trade barriers, by means of which EC countries protected their own food and agricultural industries. Tipa's output represented only a small fraction of total production and the only reason it offered ice-cream bars was because that technology was available.

Its shoe-production facilities were located in Trebic, a town of 45,000 inhabitants in western Moravia. This region has had a long tradition of shoe production and was home to one large state-owned producer and several smaller ones. Since 1990, there have been four large Czech shoe enterprises and about ten small ones, mostly cooperatives. The larger ones included Svit, with 17,500 employees, Bopo, with 7,800 employees, Sazavan, with 2,600 employees, and Botana with 2,000 employees; the most important cooperatives of the region were Snaha Brno, Snaha Jihlava, and Snaha Mnichovice. A similar market structure also existed in the Slovak Republic.

From June 1990 to June 1991, prices of the industry's products had increased 80–105 percent, with most increases occurring after January 1991. Real industrial output dropped by 66 percent between April 1991 and April 1992, an additional 8 percent between April 1992 and May 1992 and, as of May 1993, it was still falling. Nominal exports fell by 12 percent from April 1991 to April 1992. Relative to April 1991, the labor force employed in this industry had fallen by 15 percent, and productivity was down by 22 percent. In April 1992, the industry average salary was 3,800 CSK per month, which represented a 14 percent increase. According to the Czechoslovak Statistical Office, the average salary was 4,360 CSK in the manufacturing industry as a whole, which represented an increase of 20 percent.

Investment Privatization Funds

In 1990, a large-scale privatization program was introduced in Czechoslovakia and voucher privatization was one method used to transfer ownership from large state-owned enterprises. Any Czechoslovak citizen over the age of 18 who was a permanent resident of the country could purchase and register a voucher book for a total sum of 1,035 CSK. (This sum represented about 30 percent of an average monthly salary.) Each book contained 1,000 points that could be invested, thus giving the holder of the book the right to bid for shares in firms that had submitted privatization proposals and were to be included in the first wave of privatization. Out of the total population of 15.6 million, 8.5 million people, nearly 75 percent of all eligible citizens, registered their voucher books. Most of them, however, had little or no information about the privatized firms and no experience with financial markets.

After the announcement of the voucher privatization plan, many investment funds, which were mutual stock market funds, set up business. Individual investors were encouraged to become shareholders of the funds. The funds' objective was to create a high-return portfolio by bidding for shares of the privatized firms. At that time, the financial markets in Czechoslovakia were just beginning to develop and were far from efficient. The market niche for investment funds was the exchange of information about firms.

There was no real legislative control over the 500 funds in the country. The rules for their establishment were sketchy and their founders were not required to give proof of competence. Few appeared to have any staff qualified to make decisions or, indeed, with any experience in the financial sector. Only a few firms, such as Tipa a.s., established privatization funds and paid for the education of the funds' managers. In most cases, the managers were simply people who thought they knew something about investment. Small investors were encouraged to hand over their voucher books to these funds but they had little or no information with which to analyze the viability or investment preferences of the funds nor were the funds themselves required to publish information concerning financial structure and competence. No one seemed to have information about firms being offered for sale and there was the additional concern about conflicts of interest and insider trading. In fact, most traders had access to information through consultancies, some of which were bankers or members of the government with access to inside information. For example, the Head of the Department of Voucher Privatization at the Federal Ministry of Finance was on the board of at least four investment privatization funds.[1] Senior management in firms slated for privatization were frequently members of these boards.

Few people had any interest in the voucher scheme until one fund, Harvard Capital and Consulting, which had no connection with the university of the same name, promised to pay 10,350 CSK in cash within a year and a day in return for voucher books. As other funds got on this bandwagon, increasingly higher cash payments were offered to those who signed over their books. Roughly 5.8 million citizens, about two-thirds of those involved in the voucher privatization, chose to designate all of their points to investment funds, and a further 0.42 million allocated some portion of their points. Altogether, investment funds received 72 percent of all vouchers in circulation, about 6.13 billion investment points.[2] Because funds did not have to reveal financial data, as is required in most other European countries, many fear that when people begin to demand cash payment the funds will be unable to deliver.

THE CASE OF TIPA

History of the Firm

Tipa a.s. was a private firm established in 1990 by a group of nine former executives from nearby state and cooperative farms. The name of the enterprise was derived from the original businesses of the enterprise, namely, Trade, Travel, Information, Production, Agriculture. All of the founding partners were university graduates who knew each other from past managerial work and had amassed a great deal of experience. As the present CEO said, they had decided to leave their former positions to prove that they were capable of prospering under market conditions. Political pressures following 1989 accelerated this decision. After collecting 500,000 Czechoslovak koruny, ($1 = 14.5 CSK), they registered a joint stock enterprise with a diversified business mission. The firm's first group consisted of services, trade, and a small construction group. The second group, in which almost all the founders were actively involved, began with a fruit farm and a tree nursery. Concurrently, the first travel bureau, which became very successful, was established in a rented house. The foreign trade activities were directed toward selected importers and created several small business niches in trade and agricultural products.

After 1991, Tipa a.s. began to expand into other areas, such as telecommunications and security systems, services for agriculture, an agricultural machines business, and a small bakery and retail shops. The firm bought an older factory and a shoe-making business where it found a market niche in the sale of ladies' Italian sandals, home slippers, and special-purpose shoes such as protective shoes for hospitals and food industries. It was the only producer serving this sector and the footwear division became one of the largest, with a turnover amounting to 100 million CSK. The new frozen-food division was earning an estimated 150 million CSK annually, and recently, the firm began preparations to expand into food production. It also began construction of a plant for wood processing, the technology for which had been purchased on very favorable terms from a bankrupt Swiss cooperative. Lastly, almost all investments had been made using loans or a leasing service.

In the process of privatization, Tipa a.s. registered two investment funds to implement voucher privatization. Altogether, 2,800 private voucher-holders entrusted their coupons to Tipa, and these were expected to have an equity of 110–150 million CSK. The firm continued to expand rapidly. It founded two limited enterprises and opened new divisions, plants, stores, and offices. Its now famous logo and its 350 million CSK turnover and 500 employees, inclusive of two affiliations, made it the largest wholly privately owned firm in the town.

This rapid growth can be demonstrated by the following figures:

	1991	1992 (2nd quarter or annual est.)
Number of shareholders	9	31
Equity (mil. CSK)	0.5	7.7
Share (par 1,000)	3,500	10,000
Number of employees	220	500
Sales (mil. CSK)	35	350 (est.)

Its export trade involved Italy, Germany, and Austria, with exports amounting to 70 million CSK in 1992. As of the second quarter of 1992, the two affiliations of Tipa a.s. had employment amounting to:

Product	Employees
Footwear	80
Simple gardening & agriculture equipment & implements	45
Kitchen steam absorbers	20
Frozen food (icecream bars)	80
Bakery (bread and pastry)	40
Local mobile telecommunication (assembly and maintenance)	15
Building work	35

Services	
Food retail	90
Travel offices	0
Real estate transactions	3

So where were the problems? All the top managers admitted that business was flourishing, but there was a cash flow insufficiency. The balance sheet did not indicate the problem nor did the income statement, but the shortage seemed to stem from a number of factors. The CEO put it this way: "First, it is an inevitable companion of the firm's growth. We have to invest almost everywhere. Second, it is the high interest rates of our banks. They show a self-interest but are not concerned with general business promotion. One day it may happen that the banks will be very rich but the economy will remain poor. Third, we are victimized by the severe secondary indebtedness of our customers."

It was financial restructuring that mattered most. After price deregulation in January 1991, enterprises tried to accumulate as much cash as possible. Industrial firms disposed of large inventories that they had procured at lower prices and not revaluated. Profits skyrocketed as did personal rewards. After the first business cycle, however, raw materials, subcontracts, and services became a problem. Many firms were unable to cover their liabilities and delayed their payments. A few refused to pay completely. Tipa a.s. decided to deliver nothing unless payment had been allocated in advance by means of a single-purpose account or a letter of credit, but receivables from the past remained.

MAJOR SHOCKS AND OPPORTUNITIES FOR THE FIRM

A lack of resources meant that the firm did not have the funds for further expansion. Foreign resources were not easily available and loans were for a maximum of four years and had a high interest rate. A general lack of money in the economy meant that other resources were blocked as accounts receivable after their maturity. Shoe production faced an enormous decline in demand after

January 1991. People had expected a steep increase in prices and had accordingly made necessary purchases at the end of 1990. But the saving grace was that the sector's products were durable and could be stored. In this regard, the leather industry was one of those worst hit by the collapse of the CMEA markets. At least in the food industry, such as ice cream production, there were seasonal demand fluctuations. The greatest advantage for Tipa was that its management understood market conditions. As mentioned earlier, they knew each other from past managerial work, through which they had gained considerable experience and knowledge of the market, and now they worked with a well-known entrepreneur, Mr. F. Cuba, who had Western management techniques even before 1989. Due to the lack of ready cash of Tipa's customers, the managers maintained a tight credit policy.

SHORT-TERM REACTIONS

Organization of Management

The structure of the firm consisted of the CEO, his deputies, the law department, the secretarial department, and seven divisions. The CEO had two deputies: one responsible for production who was simultaneously the purchasing agent, and one responsible for economics and finance. The divisions were business centers, and the firm headquarters retained the right of veto in the human resources, management, and investment areas. Management defined strategies, prepared new programs, assured financed resources, and represented the firm in the community.

Production, Output, Taxes, and Subsidies

Tipa sought market opportunities, preferably ones with a high profit margin. Business decisions were made on the basis of market opportunity and available skills and this approach was expected to continue. The CEO explained: "It was our desire to diversify. However, we were looking for experienced advice. Mr. Cuba, our first adviser, recommended that we diversify in these turbulent times. He said that, unless we diversified and no longer exposed ourselves to a narrow specialty, we could be fatally hit by unexpected changes in the market or legal and financial provisions." Growth was continued in small, sequential steps; only after capital had been accumulated could mid-sized businesses be started.

Tipa a.s. was subject to various taxes. These included VAT and a 12 percent turnover tax a 55 percent tax on profits; payroll and social security payments, which amounted to a 50 percent tax on wages; and local taxes of about 4 percent. To offset this burden, the firm also received total subsidies in 1991 of 5.6 million CSK.

LONG-TERM RESPONSE

Corporate Governance-Ownership Changes

The CEO said that the firm was managed primarily by its owners. The founders served as top managers and divisional directors. The owners and founders were also the top managers of subsidiaries and joint ventures, and served on the board of directors and the supervisory board. These boards appointed the firm's president and the directors of subsidiaries and joint ventures. Other top managers also became shareholders of the firm to increase interest and strengthen the owner relationship to the firm. The CEO served as both general manager and chairman of the board of directors as a means of maintaining a uniform strategy. Nevertheless, founders of the enterprise still maintained control over the decision-making.

At the time of this study, the production facility for frozen creams was under construction and Tipa was faced with the decision of whether or not to centralize the management of this division. This centralization might be needed to work out a division strategy, especially in marketing and pricing, and possibly in the establishment of a joint venture with another producer.

Foreign Collaboration

There was quite a bit of collaboration with foreign partners, but only in the form of common business contacts. However, these contacts, combined with business connections in Italy, Germany, and Austria, helped to expand commerce. Tipa had considered establishing a joint venture in ice-cream production, and a number of other joint ventures were under discussion with Italian and German concerns. A joint venture with Moscow to facilitate barter counter-trade is to be formed soon, and a group of bricklayers and facade-lifters started to work in Germany.

Product Development and Investment

Ice cream production involved seasonal demand problems and therefore an expansion of production to make better use of production capacity would be necessary. These particular problems could also be solved by using a seasonal labor force.

An expansion of food production was also planned. The goal was to double production capacity, which was 350 million CSK, by introducing an entire product range. Also, a milk-processing plant could support the expansion of the frozen-food business. As previously mentioned, construction of a wood-processing plant was already under way.

Estimation of Capacity Utilization (managers' estimation)

Footwear	60 percent
Ice cream	90 percent

MANAGEMENT'S PERCEPTION OF THE FIRM'S POSITION AND PROSPECTS

In 1992 and 1993, Tipa a.s. entered a middle-size group of enterprises. With a turnover of 1 billion CSK, 600 employees, and a growth rate that moved from 500,000 to 1 billion CSK in three years, it had great potential. "All the businesses have proven to be prosperous so far," explained the CEO, "but we see a growing disparity among them." Retail businesses, which were the original base of the firm, were now the least contributing factor. Competition was widespread, but Tipa had a firm foothold and would have little problem continuing as a retail trade firm. "Our main drive is focused on industrial businesses. In 1992, half of our profits came from frozen-food production. And now, our new acquisition will be a packaging plant in Tabor (southern Bohemia) which will enlarge our possibilities."

One ongoing problem was financial constraint. "What we will do immediately, is to consolidate our investment funds. This will be a good foundation for our next step, i.e., to try to develop financial business, such as regional savings firm or a bank, which will facilitate further growth of the firm."

Tipa a.s. felt that the regional boundaries of its businesses were becoming too narrow. "We already need an office in the capital," asserted the CEO. Indeed, this was to become reality. It would be located in the center of Prague together with Tipa's travel bureau. In anticipation of the separation of Czechoslovakia, Tipa a.s. was anxious to begin business in Slovakia. They expected a lower wage level there and could expand their industrial enterprises on Slovak territory. Martin, an industrial town in central Slovakia, was to be Tipa's expansion target. "It is as good as accomplished," concluded the CEO. The management welcomed the challenge. In the early days of the firm, when it was rapidly expanding, personal dedication was sufficient. Now, however, it badly needed a sophisticated management. "We have to acquire not only new businesses but new business knowledge at the same time," stated the CEO.

MAJOR FINDINGS: IMPLICATIONS FOR CHANGING BEHAVIOR/GOALS

Tipa looked for market opportunities with a high profit margin. Therefore, market opportunities and available skills were the rule. This approach was expected to continue into the future. To avoid the risk of unexpected changes in the market or legal and financial provisions, Tipa relied on a high level of diversification in all of its activities.

Tipa exhibits a number of characteristics shared by many new private firms in the Czech Republic and elsewhere in Eastern Europe. First, its founders and owners had been managers under the previous regime. Therefore they were relatively well educated and able to carry out their new responsibilities. No doubt their past work also provided them with a rich network of contacts and connections, which facilitated finding sources of inputs, leads for leasing office and work spaces, and information for identifying likely market niches and takeover opportunities. Another characteristic feature of small and medium enterprises is their focus on services, construction, and retail activities. Indeed, these are the sectors in which the share of the private sector is highest in all economies in transition from socialism to capitalism. Thus Tipa's gradual evolution from heavy involvement in these sectors to one where manufacturing predominates is an interesting development. Similarly, its ifforts to acquire or start a bank or other financial institution in order to reduce its credit constraints reflects the behavior of many conglomerates in market economies. Finally, the central role played by Tipa's manager-owners in its operations is characteristic of new private firms in East and Central Europe and Russia. An interesting question will be whether these entrepreneur-managers will be able to yield control to a new generation of managers or to sell Tipa to a larger firm in the future, or whether today's dynamic entrepreneurs will become the entrenched managers of the future.

Also an interesting question for the future is whether Tipa's management will be able to make the adjustment from a firm that bases its success on identifying and exploiting profitable niches to one that can compete on the basis of strengths in manufaturing, including the ability to organize production in a low-cost and efficient way and to maintain high levels of quality in its production. Clearly, as the transition proceeds, there will be fewer unexploited opportunities and therefore the nature of the competition Tipa faces will change.

Notes

1. Source: *PlanEcon Business Report*, vol. 2, no. 3, (February 5, 1992).
2. Source: *Privatization Newsletter of Czechoslovakia*, No. 6 (May 1992).

Table 1

Annual Balance Sheet

Book value of fixed assets	50 million CSK
Total accounts receivable	25 million CSK
Total accounts payable	15 million CSK
Total bank loans outstanding	
Short-term	15 million CSK
Long-term	51 million CSK

Table 2

Annual Net Profit (Net profit after taxes = 42 million CSK mostly used for reinvestment)

	1991	1992 (est.)
Total sales	35 mil. CSK	350 mil. CSK
Domestic sales		335 mil. CSK
Foreign sales		15 mil. CSK
Footwear sales		100 mil. CSK
Frozen food sales		150 mil. CSK
Total costs		220 mil. CSK
Labor costs		21 mil. CSK
Cost of material inputs		148 mil. CSK
Cost of energy inputs		5 mil. CSK
Overhead costs		46 mil. CSK
Financial costs		11 mil. CSK
Depreciation		2 mil. CSK
Expenditure on research and development		1 mil. CSK
Total workforce	220	500
Number of laborers		437
Number of technicians		50
Number of top managers		15
Number of female workers		350
Number of male workers		150

	1992
Activity ratios	
Accounts receivable turnover	14
Avg. collection period (days)	26.07
Payments turnover	11.6
Avg. payments period (days)	31.47
Gross profit/sales	0.37
Net profit/sales	0.12
Gross profit/cost of goods sold	0.75
Net Profit/cost of goods sold	0.24

9

Plastics: CS-13

Jan Pavek

SECTORAL SETTING

CS-13 was one of the largest and most important manufacturers of plastic goods in Czechoslovakia. Its market share in the CSFR, which is difficult to estimate, was calculated at more than 15 percent when measured by sales. The firm was originally established in 1946 as a state-owned enterprise. In 1963, a new plant was opened in Liberec and, because of the intensified focus on the automotive industry in the 1980s, this plant was renovated and expanded in the latter part of the decade. In April 1993, the automotive sector was CS-13's most important customer and deliveries to this sector accounted for about 48 percent of the firm's sales.

The firm's operations were affected by several factors that could be divided into three areas: effects of the government's macroeconomic policy, effects that were sectoral, and those that were firm-specific. The management's reactions to these social and economic changes were revealed in the personnel and organizational changes within the firm, in the decision to establish a joint venture with a foreign partner, and in the preparation of a long-term strategy with this partner.

The decision to join forces with a foreign concern was based on the close connection between CS-13 and the automotive industry, especially the Skoda enterprise, which had recently joined the German Volkswagen/Audi/Seat Group. A long-term strategy was also needed to immediately overcome the firm's weaknesses. The stagnation of the world economy, especially in the automotive industry, made it necessary for the foreign parent company to re-evaluate its present strategy. New strategies for the firm's subsidiaries were expected in the near future.

CS-13 profited from its privatization and from the clarification of its ownership role. State control was removed and competition was created among both the firm's suppliers and the banks. Currently, the firm had passed the break-even point and its future development depended on the speed of the domestic economy's recovery.

CS-13 concentrated mostly on the production of injection-molding and blow-molding products for technical use, for packaging, and for household use. Deliveries to the automotive industry comprised nearly 50 percent of its production. The industry's plastic goods market was strongly influenced by the recent price liberalization, by the insolvency of a large number of enterprises, and by the loss of export markets in the former CMEA countries, all of which resulted in demand fluctuations and affected the firm's customers.

At the time of this report, the most stable market was the automotive industry, particularly Skoda Mlada Boleslav. Skoda was expected to undergo considerable development and experience an increase in its production, which would increase its purchases from CS-13.

Competition among plastics manufacturers is based on their size, technological equipment, and technical and quality level. In the field of injection molding, where a machine's clamping force determines the size of the product that can be made, there were many manufacturers who were equipped with machines that had a clamping force of 1,600 kN. A limited number of manufacturers in the country had machines with a clamping force of over 7,000 kN. These included Strojplast Tachov, Lisovny novych hmot Vrbno, Technoplast Chropyne in the Czech Republic, and Plastika Nitra and Slovenska armaturka Myjava in the Slovak Republic. These manufacturers were able to produce technically sophisticated plastic parts, but only CS-13 owned injection-molding machines with clamping forces of over 16,000 kN. These machines were used to manufacture larger-sized parts for the automotive industry such as bumpers and dashboards. The stiffest competition existed among those who owned 1,600 kN machines, because, in addition to state enterprises and cooperative businesses that were privatized, new plastics enterprises were being created by private entrepreneurs.

The firm owned about 5 percent of all molding machines in the country. Its output, however, was estimated at 12–15 percent of the domestic market and more than 15 percent when measured by domestic sales. The entire plastics industry in the CSFR was experiencing major difficulties due to the economic reforms. Because plastics manufacturers cooperated with 70 percent of the other manufacturers in the country, including machinery, electrical, and building industries, they were also affected by the problems in those enterprises.

Production was based primarily on domestic plastic materials inputs from three primary suppliers in the Czech Republic and two in the Slovak Republic, and products went mostly to the domestic market. Poor quality of production, low productivity, poor product design, and lengthy product development had resulted in insignificant export demand, but change was on the horizon. It was expected that the share of Czechoslovak exports would grow due to the favorable pricing policy and also that foreign competition would increase. Despite the fact that foreign plastics were more expensive than domestic goods, they were preferred because of their higher quality, better design, and coat finishing. Domestic manufacturers were not yet able to produce technically demanding products.

HISTORY OF THE FIRM AND ITS PRODUCTION STRUCTURE

CS-13 was created in 1946 as a state-owned enterprise through the merger of several private businesses in the Jablonec and Liberec areas. From its onset, it focused on injection- and blow-molded plastics production as well as the manufacture of the molds themselves.

The firm passed through the first stage of its development in 1963, when a new plant was opened in Liberec. The plant was the largest in Central Europe at the time, and the firm's headquarters was moved there. New technologies such as thermosetting resin and heat forming were introduced, and deliveries to the automotive industry increased. In the mid-1980s, the firm controlled eight plants in the Bohemian towns of Liberec, Praha, Modra, Tachov, Liban, Horsovsky Tyn, Plzen, Havlickuv Brod, together employing a total of 4,800 people.

During the 1980s, the intensified focus on the automotive industry, in the case of Skoda Mlada Boleslav, for example, culminated with Skoda's new product line, the S 781 Favorit. This escalation also required that the Liberec plant be renovated and constructed, a project completed in 1990. In January 1991, the state-owned joint stock enterprise CS-13 was established, and one year later, the firm was sold to its designated foreign partner. The firm's economic indicators, used in the previous economic system, are shown in Table 1.

Currently, the Liberec plant had 922 employees, the Havlickuv Brod plant had 374 employees, and 239 were employed at Liban, for a total of 1,535 workers. Output was approximately 918 million CSK, broken down as follows: Liberec produced 73.2 percent; H. Brod, 14.6 percent; Liban, 12.3 percent.

Those parts manufactured for technical cooperation were considered the most important and accounted for 77.6 percent of output. Of those, 48 percent went to the automotive industry, which was the crucial market sector, a situation that would probably continue into the future. The plant's work for Skoda/VW was especially important, with deliveries accounting for 47.2 percent of firm sales at the present time. The other important segment was the electrical industry, which absorbed 13.0 percent of the output. Other segments included 11.3 percent for packaging, 5.8 percent for household goods, and 4.4 percent for molds and tools manufacturing.

The manufacturing technologies of the production were divided as follows: injection molding at 70.2 percent, blow molding at 12.3 percent, thermosetting resin at 4.9 percent, heat forming at 7.4 percent, forms manufacturing at 4.4 percent, and other at 0.8 percent.

CS-13's management believed that the firm's strengths and competitive advantages were the following:

- its long-term tradition in plastics manufacturing and its connection with a well-known trademark;
- its knowledge of injection and blow molding, thermosetting resin, and heat forming;
- its good relations with a wide variety of domestic customers;
- its relatively diverse production, which made its production structure less vulnerable to demand fluctuations;
- its technology for injection and blow molding of large-sized parts for the automotive industry, which was unique in the CSFR;
- its proximity to the main auto-parts customers in Czechoslovakia and potential customers of similar parts in Germany;
- its own tools and forms workshop, and its R&D center, which had the ability to react quickly to possible demand fluctuations.

The firm's weaknesses and disadvantages were as follows:

- its lack of knowledge of the foreign market;
- its lack of experience in the construction of sophisticated technical parts, and insufficient technical equipment for construction of forms (CAD/CAM systems);
- its present inability to communicate with R&D centers of partners or customers who were equipped with these systems;
- its shortage of sufficient financial resources and capital investment to satisfy the demands of the increasing production of Czech cars;
- the low quality of its products, which did not satisfy the standard European automotive industry quality certification requirements.

INFLUENCES OF THE EXTERNAL ENVIRONMENT

The economic environment in the CSFR started to change shortly after the beginning of the political transformations in 1990. Some changes, such as the collapse of the CMEA market, occurred spontaneously while the concept of economic reform was only beginning to develop.

Although Czechoslovakia's economy still operated according to the centrally planned system, the progress toward economic reform began at the end of 1990 with a double devaluation of the koruna. Other macroeconomic changes, such as price liberalization, internal convertibility of the koruna, and tax law restructuring, became effective in January 1991, and the new legislation for 1992 included a Civil Code, a Commercial Code, an Act on Trades, an Act on Accountancy, and a Decree on Depreciation Rates.

A number of the macroeconomic changes that occurred during 1990–92 were considered disadvantages for CS-13. These included:

- the collapse of the CMEA market;
- the demand-side decline that was caused by the state's restrictive monetary policy;
- the increase in prices of material inputs caused by price liberalization;
- the removal of direct subsidies to the plastics industry and of state subsidies for heat and electrical energy production;
- the price increase of imported materials caused by the established CSK exchange rate in October and December 1990;
- the interest rate increase and the decreased access to bank credits due to the restrictive state monetary policy.

Other events that indirectly affected the firm's behavior were the CSFR's total dependence on only one crude oil supplier, that being the former USSR, and the price increase of this crude oil to world levels. The enterprise's operations were also affected by the high share of production concentrated in the automotive industry, especially in one customer, which was the largest Czechoslovak car producer, and the high-quality demand of the automotive industry.

SHORT-TERM REACTIONS

The management's reactions to these social and economic changes can be divided into three areas: personnel and organizational changes in the firm; the decision to participate in a foreign joint venture; and the preparation of a long-term strategy for the firm with the foreign partner.

Organization Structure Changes

A new general director was appointed by the Ministry of Industry of the Czech Republic in May 1990 and his first task was to decentralized the structure of the firm. The collapse of the market had resulted in a 50 percent decrease in the firm's profitability, but the delegation of almost all duties from the headquarters to the plants partially helped to solve this problem. At the Havlickuv Brod plant, for example, about 30 percent of its production program was changed. Other goals of decentralization were autonomy in sales, purchases, assortment, and searches for new product lines for the individual plants; reduction in the size of the headquarters; to make some auxiliary activities, such as the canteen, transportation, and special-machines manufacturing, independent and privatize them later; and lastly, to appoint directors for the newly created plants and departments.

These changes caused a significant reduction in the size of the firm. At the end of December 1989, the firm employed 1,999 individuals; one year later, that number had been reduced to 1,376. The union permitted this because those workers who were laid off were compensated and, because they were the first unemployed in the region, they were able to find other work without much difficulty. The other result of the reduction was that the remaining employees received wage increases.

In the mid-1980s, CS-13 had difficulty financing a new plant to produce parts for the automotive industry, but by 1989, the Ministry of Industry, the Federal Pricing Authority, and CS-13 had managed to secure the necessary resources. Thus, the firm entered the transition period well-equipped with technology and with a program for potential products.

Some macroeconomic changes had a positive influence on the firm's operations. For example, the income tax rate for joint ventures with foreign partners decreased from 75 percent in 1989 to 55 percent in 1990, and to 40 percent in 1992.[1] Also, the government permitted certain viable enterprises to write off some of their debts. CS-13 was allowed to write off 13 million CSK of the total amount of 50 billion CSK. Nevertheless, the firm was severely affected by other changes.

As mentioned before, the management gave the individual divisions of the firm greater independence, especially in budgeting their costs and revenues. This allowed CS-13 to save money by eliminating the least effective profit/cost centers. The increased prices of goods reflected only the increased prices of material inputs, which in turn were due to price liberalization in domestic production, the weak purchasing power of the Czech currency in buying imported materials, and increased energy prices. Since April 1991, increasing productivity and better utilization of production capacity have eliminated any need for increases in the prices of CS-13's goods.

Despite the search for solvent customers and the fact that new payment methods, such as drafts, promissory notes, and mutual clearing had been implemented in the CSFR, CS-13 was unable to cope with the problem of growing accounts receivable. At the end of 1992, the firm was owed more than CSK 200 million. The firm's CEO said: "This is a problem that the government must solve systematically. The state must counterbalance its liabilities, and delay will only make this situation worse. When privatization stalled and the bankruptcy law was postponed, the difficulties of insolvent and nonprofitable businesses were prolonged. As a result, the situation for enterprises already privatized, which already have a clear strategy, is worsened."

After the construction of its new plant was finished and its financial problems were resolved, CS-13 was considered a stable producer and client. It paid all its accounts promptly and thus had relatively easy access to bank loans. The introduction of internal convertibility of the Czech currency also gave CS-13 access to foreign inputs. Previously, it had not exported much of its production, and depended on the state-planned distribution of foreign materials. With greater access to foreign inputs and increased prices of domestic producers it was important for CS-13 to choose its own suppliers.

The firm streamlined its organization and at present was in the process of enlarging production and hiring new employees. But, as the CEO said: "The labor market does not yet exist in this country. There is overemployment, which means that the labor force is not stimulated to become more productive. Conditions are so favorable that unemployed people are not forced to find jobs, and the sluggish privatization process as well as the postponement of the bankruptcy law have preserved this unpleasant situation. Despite the fact that we are an enterprise in a region in which other businesses are going bankrupt, we are not able to hire workers for line/floor positions, nor experienced language experts for the R&D, sales, or marketing departments." He added: "I see the lack of human resource management, in which workers are chosen, trained, and motivated, as one of our biggest weaknesses."

CS-13 was again attempting to reorganize itself to better adapt to the new social and economic conditions. This is shown in Figure 1. There are several reasons for this reorganization: CS-13 was to be connected to a central information system compatible with that of the foreign parent company; to achieve the same or very similar structure as that of other firms within the parent company; and to develop a tighter connection to subordinate plants. A significant overhead saving was expected as a result of better cooperation among sales, marketing, accounting, and budgeting departments, and better economic control of each plant.

The Influence of the Foreign Partner on Short-Term Perspectives

The major changes in CS-13 that resulted from the economic transformation took place before the joint venture was established. Until then, CS-13 had been self-financed and the foreign partner had no control over the firm. The joint venture gave the firm access to technology and know-how for the development and construction of sophisticated technical parts. Cooperation with the foreign enterprise also enabled CS-13 to communicate with partners' and customers' R&D centers during the product-development stage. Moreover, CS-13 paid the same prices with the same terms of payment as did the parent company, both of which were more favorable. This has put CS-13 in a better position because of the competition that has developed between its foreign and domestic suppliers. Such competition also occurred in the banking sector. Through the joint venture, CS-13 had the same access to foreign banks as did its partner, a German enterprise. Therefore, domestic banks began to offer credit conditions comparable to those offered by foreign banks.

LONG-TERM STRATEGY

In choosing a strategic foreign investor, two approaches were used. Offers were evaluated based on the firm's multiple criteria, and the firm hired the foreign consulting firm, DRT, to assist in the choice of a foreign partner, to evaluate the foreign firm on a market-price basis, and to help with the legal aspects of the necessary negotiations. The result of this was that CS-13 and DRT both selected one German multinational corporation as the most suitable candidate for a future joint venture.

The chosen corporation was the largest plastics producer in Europe. It had two subsidiaries, Enterprise A in Boetzingen and Enterprise B in Bonn. CS-13 became a subsidiary of Enterprise A, which had twenty plants throughout Germany, France, Spain, and Czechoslovakia. It employed approximately 8,000 workers and generated annual sales of over 1.5 billion DM. This enterprise delivered goods to many well-known auto manufacturers. Its sales to VW/Audi/Seat group alone amounted to 500 million DM per annum.

CS-13's privatization plan included its sale to the corporation over a three-year period; 51 percent of the shares would be transferred in January 1992, 25 percent in January 1993, and 24 percent in January 1994. The government of the Czech Republic approved the plan in December 1991.

At the time of this report, CS-13 was managed by three members of the managing board, who were elected by the general assembly. This managing board was the top executive body of the firm. The president and CEO was a 35-year old Czech who had studied the economics of industry at the Czech Technical University, and had worked at CS-13 for three years. The other members of the board were the financial director, a 46-year-old German who was a graduate of a business school in that country and had extensive experience, and the production director. The latter had not yet been appointed, but would also be from Germany. The supervisory board consisted of three members appointed by the German partner, one appointed by the National Property Fund, and two employees of CS-13. The managing board met frequently, but the supervisory board met only three times each year. The state had no control over the firm, and only the managing board, with the supervisory board's approval, could make personnel changes.

Corporate Long-Term Strategy

New strategies of the firm's subsidiaries, based on the joint venture, were to be developed. These would probably include greater product diversification and entry into new markets, and all new programs were expected to be in place by the end of 1993.

CS-13 also prepared its own long-term strategy for the domestic and foreign markets. Its primary goal was to strengthen its position on the domestic market, especially in the automobile industry, and to protect its dominance in the region. The firm wanted to add product lines to its auto parts production profile, which would enable it to cope with demand fluctuations. Such product diversification would also reduce the damage caused by sudden insolvency in other industries. Finally, to reach full production capacity, CS-13 intended to look for customers in Western Europe.

The firm's strategy toward its most important domestic customer, the large automobile manufacturer, was obvious. It would significantly increase the technical level of the preproduction stages and it would achieve the quality standard required by the customer and by other automobile manufacturers. This would mean being able to handle the broad scope of plastics-production technology and finish-coating techniques. A somewhat similar strategy was set forth for those customers in other industries, mostly the electrical industry. This was based on the production of high-quality and technically sophisticated plastics, and the introduction of technology enabling the firm to specialize in the production of large-sized parts.

MANAGEMENT'S PERCEPTION OF THE FIRM'S POSITION AND PROSPECTS

CS-13's management felt that the firm had profited from its privatization and the clarification of ownership roles. The firm had advantages over other enterprises. State influence had been removed and competition created. Privatization had been stalled by a weak economic framework in the form of an absence of both bankruptcy laws and a labor market, and this had been aggravated by the uncertainty of the firm's customers about their future. At this point, because roughly one-third of production went to the Slovak Republic, the impact of the split of CSFR on the economic growth of CS-13 could not be estimated,

The management believed that the future development of the firm lay in the increased diversification of product lines, the focus on market sectors, the reorientation toward more technically sophisticated and large-sized parts, and the improvement of customer satisfaction.

MAJOR FINDINGS: IMPLICATIONS FOR CHANGING BEHAVIOR

Even though CS-13 had a significant advantage at the beginning of the economic transition, that being a financially backed strategy for the future, its management still carefully analyzed strengths and weaknesses, the domestic market and the firm's position in it, and external forces such as suppliers, buyers, entry barriers, substitutes, and rivalry. From this analysis, the management decided on a joint venture with a foreign partner. At the time of this study therefore, CS-13 had passed the break-even point and its development should depend on the speed of the domestic economy's recovery.

Note

1. In 1994 there was a single rate of 45 percent for all businesses.

124 CASE STUDIES OF CZECH AND SLOVAK FIRMS

Table 1

The Firm's Economic Indicators

	1989	1990	1991
Number of employees	1,934	1,884	1,376
Workers	1,487	1,459	1,074
Technicians	447	425	302
Average wages (CSK)	2,960	3,146	3,942
Sales and extraordinary revenues (in thds CSK)	624,124	689,534	904,682
Costs (in thds CSK)	621,248	635,566	844,131
Disposable profit (in thds CSK)	6,249	27,248	39,160
Exports (in thds CSK):	37,960	25,005	9,085
to former CMEA countries	34,681	15,566	572
to Western countries	3,279	9,439	8,513
Subsidies (in thds CSK)	16,200	295	0
Deterioration rates (%)	42.84	38.14	35.47

Table 2

Structure of Costs (in percentages)

	1990	1991	1992
Wages	15.78	12.57	13.87
Material	74.04	72.06	70.63
Energy	n.a.	5.24	5.54
Depreciation	6.58	6.10	6.35
Interest expense	2.88	3.83	2.59
Other financial costs	0.72	0.20	1.02
Total	100.00	100.00	100.00

Note: Wages include also the wages volume tax (social security contributions).

Table 3
Main Financial Data (in thousands of CSK)

	1990	1991	January–September 1992
Sales revenues	683,229	899,299	707,270
Cost of goods sold	569,592	757,071	581,129
Gross margin	113,637	142,228	126,141
Extra revenues	6,305	5,383	4,497
Depreciation	41,812	51,464	41,032
Interest expenses	18,301	32,323	16,754
Other financial costs	5,861	3,273	7,585
Gross profit	53,968	60,551	65,267
Income taxes	29,682	33,303	26,107
Net profit	24,286	27,248	39,160

Table 4
Profitability Ratios (in percentages)

	1990	1991	January–September 1992
Gross margin/sales	16.63	15.82	17.84
Gross profit/sales	7.90	6.73	9.23
Gross margin/COGS*	19.95	18.79	21.71
Gross profit/COGS	9.47	8.00	11.23
Net profit/COGS	4.26	3.60	6.74

*Cost of goods sold.

Table 5
Liquidity and Activity Ratios

	1990[1]	1991	January–September 1992[2]
Liquidity ratios			
Working capital/Total assets	0.25	0.19	0.21
Current ratio	4.70	2.93	2.77
Quick ratio	1.71	1.49	1.70
Activity Ratios			
Accounts rec. turnover	7.28	7.85	4.33
Avg. collection period (days)	50	47	63
Payments turnover	79.63	81.67	40.86
Avg. payments period (days)	5	5	7
Inventory turnover	3.11	4.73	4.13
Avg. inventory period (days)	118	77	66

[1] Averages in ratios denominator were replaced by ending numbers for 1990.
[2] The period for 1992 is 273 days.

Figure 1. The Newly Proposed Organizational Structure for CS-13

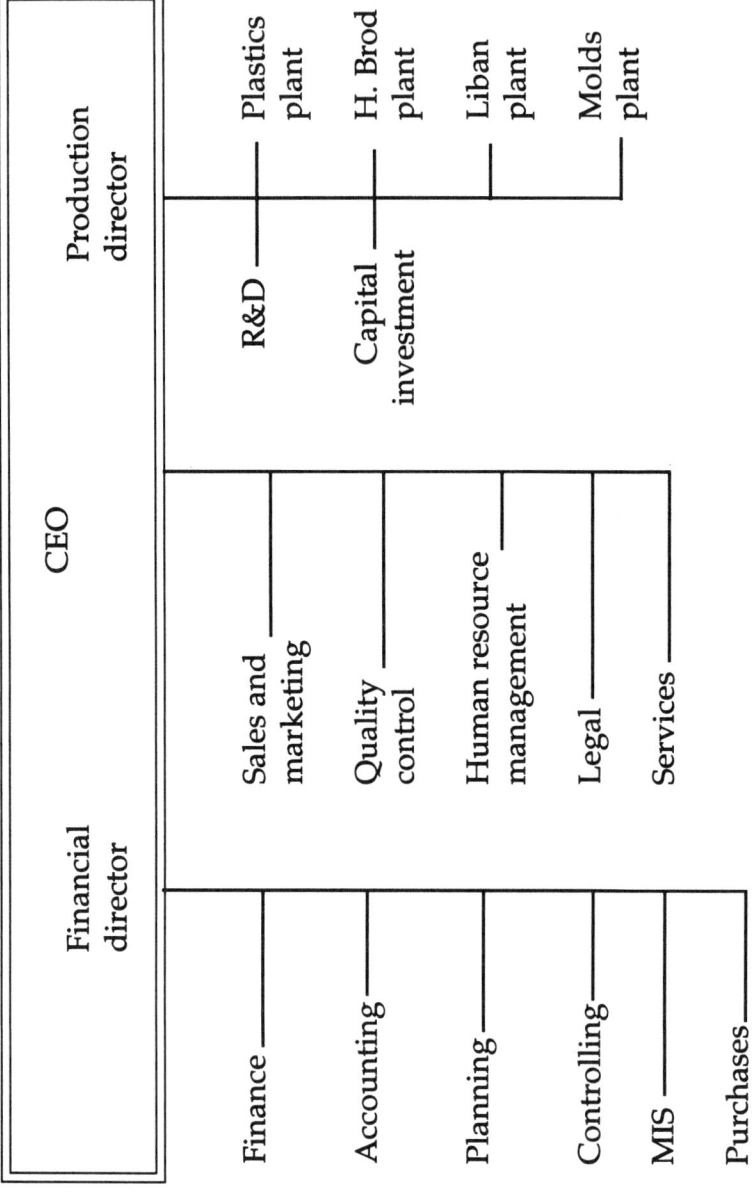

10

Pharmaceuticals: CS-12

Alena Očková

SECTORAL SETTING

CS-12 was one of the major Czechoslovak producers of pharmaceutical products. It was a generic producer with a moderate share of its own R&D, a domestic market leader that had significant export sales and was not much affected by the collapse of CMEA markets. The firm was to have been privatized in the first wave of privatization but the process was postponed due to administrative delay. The future development of the firm and its position on both domestic and foreign markets was based on continuous adaptation to market needs and demands. CS-12's development strategy also included technological improvements, GMP certification, and management development. Not only did the firm's privatization plan reflect these needs, but it would also accelerate the implementation of this strategy.

The pharmaceutical industry worldwide has a moderate but relatively stable growth rate of 6–12 percent per annum. In general, this industry differs significantly from others in various ways. It is R&D-intensive, which is very costly. Due to demanding testing and registration procedures, the time needed to bring a developed product to the market is much longer than in other industries. The industry is highly regulated in most countries and these regulations are mostly concerned with prices, approval procedures, and marketing techniques (promotion, distribution, etc.). The industry is also very competitive. Two main groups of competitors include manufacturers of original products based on their own R&D, and those who manufacture generic products based on the expired patents of major drugs. In spite of high costs and delayed pay-offs, successful firms in both groups are potentially highly profitable. A general trend toward greater patient involvement and self-medication has increased the market for nonprescription drugs relative to the market in ethical drugs, which are available only through a physician's prescription.

In the 1980s Czechoslovakia had a population of about 15.5 million with a moderate market for pharmaceuticals. The level of expenditures for pharmaceutical products was relatively low in value terms because the price level was much lower than the average world price. Imports were regulated only by the obligatory registration of imported products and current tariffs.

The Czechoslovak pharmaceutical market was supplied by six domestic firms and an increasing number of importers. In 1992, CS-12 was the leading domestic producer with about 43 percent of domestic production and a 26.4 percent market share in value terms. The second major domestic producer was Slovakofarma, with about 25 percent of domestic production and a 15.4 percent market share in value terms. Other domestic producers included USOL with 6.3 percent, Galena with 3.9 percent, VUAB with 1.8 percent, and Biotika with 0.8 percent. Foreign producers with important market shares were Polfa (Poland) and Gedeon Richter (Hungary).

The privatization process impacted the distribution of pharmaceutical products in Czechoslovakia. Some large monopolistic distribution firms were abolished or split into smaller ones; others created joint ventures with foreign partners. The privatization of the health services sector, which began in the second wave of large privatizations, was expected to increase the number of customers for pharmaceutical products and create a demand for more sophisticated marketing, with an emphasis on distribution and promotion.

In 1991, CS-12's total sales were 2,357 million CSK, or about $84 million, which represented a 50 percent increase in nominal value since 1988. Domestic sales were 1,830 CSK, or about $65 million in 1992, having increased by 75 percent since 1988, and exports were 527 million, or about $19 million, which was a 34 percent increase since 1988. The depreciated value of the fixed assets of the firm was 696 million CSK, or $25 million, and the gross value, 1,173 million CSK, or $42 million. The number of employees at the end of 1991 was 2,700.

CS-12 IN TRANSITION

History of the Firm

CS-12 was formed by the merger of several plants. The major plant at Dolní Měcholupy, which produced ointments and cough drops, was originally established in 1934 by Bedřich Frágner, a Prague pharmacist. CS-12–National Enterprise was established by combining this firm and three other pharmaceutical plants located in Modřany, Vysočany, and Hořátev. All had been private firms before World War II and were nationalized after 1945. From the 1950s until the end of the 1980s, CS-12 was a member of the pharmaceutical manufacturers group Spofa, but became a separate state enterprise in April 1990, placing it under the jurisdiction of the Czech Ministry of Industry.

CS-12 manufactured about 400 products, down from about 650 in 1990. The dominant product groups were finished human pharmaceuticals, which comprised 78 percent of production, and bulk human pharmaceuticals at 9 percent. Other smaller groups included veterinary pharmaceuticals, sutures, infusions, and cosmetics. The main product lines were antibiotics, at 10 percent, hypertensives, at 9 percent, antirheumatics, at 8 percent, and antidiabetics, 7 percent. CS-12 was also a pure generic producer, with generic versions of products developed by other firms accounting for about 75 percent of total sales. About 16 percent of sales were for licensed products, and the remainder were original products.

In 1990, the domestic market was the primary market for CS-12, with 67 percent of output. The Soviet Union followed with 17 percent, other East European countries received 5 percent, and 11 percent went to Western Europe and developing countries. In 1992, because of the collapse of the Soviet and former East German markets, domestic sales constituted nearly 80 percent of production. But domestic demand for CS-12's products was even higher than the supply. The management believed that the ideal proportion for supply between domestic and foreign markets was 60 percent and 40 percent, respectively.

MAJOR SHOCKS TO CS-12

Despite the fact that the economic environment of the firm was changing daily, with some changes significantly affecting the firm, the top management, especially the managing director, did not consider these changes as shocks, but rather as part of everyday life in the transition period.

The restrictive monetary policy had only an indirect affect on the firm. Health service was financed by the state budget, but increases in its funding did not keep pace with inflation. Therefore, many of CS-12's customers became insolvent and CS-12 was unable to pay its suppliers on time. The management hoped to overcome this problem by the end of 1992.

This problem was demonstrated by the condition of the firm's accounts receivable and payable. In 1991, the accounts receivable increased by 163 percent, reaching 380 million CSK, while the accounts payable increased by 136 percent to 283 million CSK. This trend continued, so that in the first quarter of 1992, the accounts receivable were 527 million CSK and accounts payable 328 million CSK. The firm credited its customers, but had to reserve more current assets to cover the 198 million CSK difference. In the second quarter of 1992, the firm was able to collect more accounts receivable and both accounts receivable and payable decreased by about 30 million CSK. The firm's customers still owe it 200 million CSK. The fact that the major customer was the state insurance agency reflects, in part, the problems in the setting up of this organization and in allocating money from the state budget to it.

Price liberalization started at the beginning of 1991 and its impact was reflected in the firm's financial data. The value of inventories increased by 57 percent, meaning that raw materials were more expensive and more assets were needed to produce the same amount of products. The firm's long-term debts and interest rates were also affected. The interest paid was doubled in 1991, to 70 million CSK, even though the firm increased its debts by only 20 percent.

CS-12's management viewed the internal convertibility of the Czechoslovak crown, introduced at the beginning of 1991 with price liberalization, as a distinct advantage in that it provided unlimited access to imported materials and technology.

One other major macroeconomic change that did not significantly affect the firm was the collapse of the CMEA market. This was because the firm sold its goods mainly on the domestic market. The decrease in exports was not as sharp as in other branches of Czechoslovak industries, and the firm was fortunate that, for its exports, it had negotiated advanced payment in hard currency for most of its sales. The share of exports decreased from 33.6 percent in 1988 to 22.4 percent in 1991, and a similar percentage was expected for 1992. The value of exports had been very important in recent years. In 1988, exports amounted to 530 million CSK; in 1989, 347 million CSK; in 1990, 350 million CSK; and 527 million CSK in 1991. This demonstrated that the firm was able to improve its market position after the CMEA collapsed, but the physical volume of exports remained about 50 percent lower than in the past.

At the time of this report, the Czechoslovak market was the primary target for the firm's products and the management intended both to retain the domestic market share and to increase exports. The firm's competitive advantage lay in the low price of its products relative to Western products. CS-12 could not be certain that the costs of Western producers were higher in all cases, because the profit margins were sometimes very high in the pharmaceutical industry, but it could be sure that Western firms would not sell their products in Czechoslovakia for a lower price than in the rest of Europe. During the privatization process, several Western firms were trying to create joint ventures for production and distribution, and this could impact CS-12's market share significantly.

The state regulated the industry's prices. The maximum margin of 20 percent of the retail price was allowed on domestically produced drugs, but the prices of imported drugs were unregulated. It was very important that firms in the pharmaceutical industry list their products with the Health Insurance Agency. These were the drugs recommended by physicians, and every listed item was fully reimbursed from health insurance money. The price of comparable drugs was a main criterion to the Health Insurance Agency in preparing its list. This meant that the Health Insurance Agency had strong control over prices because financial resources had become very limited and there were only two such agencies, one Czech and one Slovak. However, Czechoslovak producers had the advantage of lower prices relative to imported pharmaceutical products.

The health insurance system in Czechoslovakia was changing. The first step in removing health insurance from state control and the state budget had been taken and, as of the beginning of 1992, there were two Health Insurance Agencies, one in the Czech Republic and one in the Slovak Republic. Previously, the funds of these two agencies had come from the republics' budgets, but the Health Insurance Funds started their own operations in 1993. In 1992, legislation for this insurance system was prepared and the establishment of these Funds also became a part of the program of each republic's government. This removal of the health insurance system from state control was included in the new tax system taking effect in January 1993. Total contribution to the health insurance would be 13.5 percent of wages, paid partly by the firm and partly by the employee. The Health Insurance Fund would provide obligatory health insurance coverage. It was expected that additional health insurance would also be available but not obligatory for special health care. Companies would also be expected to contribute 20.4 percent of wages to Pension Insurance, 3.6 percent to Social Insurance, and 3.0 percent to the Employment Fund. These payments would replace the existing 50 percent wage tax. Moreover, employees would contribute 6.8 percent to Pension Insurance, 1.2 percent to Social Insurance, and 1.0 percent to the Employment Fund.

CS-12'S REACTIONS

CS-12's privatization strategy would determine the future the firm. There were several approaches to privatization depending on the size and profitability of a firm. One was the purchase of a controlling part of the firm by Czechoslovak entrepreneurs—for example, a management buy-out. A second approach was based on the privatization of blocs of shares by a foreign partner. The danger here was that the foreign partner might be more interested in the firm's market position than in the development of its production activities. CS-12's managing director stressed the need to find a strategic owner for the firm. Voucher privatization of a majority of the firm's shares was not considered satisfactory because the intentions of investment funds and private coupon holders were uncertain.

Although the firm was to have been included in the first wave of privatization and its plan had been submitted to the Ministry of Privatization and the Ministry of Industry in October 1991, the plan had not been approved yet by the government as of this writing. The plan was complex in that it involved the restitution claim of the previous owner. The management viewed the approval process as quite bureaucratic: the ministry preferred to deal with those projects with fewer complications. It also intended to prepare firms for the first wave of coupon privatization as soon as possible because there had already been delays. Many complicated privatization projects such as CS-12's were still awaiting completion.

The firm's privatization strategy was based on the following key points:

1. The firm would continue to adapt to new conditions, particularly in the development of market relations in the industry. The management had hired a foreign adviser, PA Consulting, and with its assistance prepared a firm strategy with particular attention to the areas of quality control, and business and investment planning. The firm created a marketing department and increased trade on both the domestic and international markets.

Some important changes had already been implemented. The number of employees was sharply decreased. Between 1988 and mid-1992, 950 workers and 223 technicians and management staff, nearly one-third of the employees, left the firm. This allowed for an increase in wages without an increase in total labor costs, which had remained at less than their 1988 level. The 45 percent increase in technicians' wages was higher than the average 31 percent.

The structure and the costs of different products were changing and new competitors, new health insurance systems, and so forth, made the market unstable. Therefore, the product profile was decreased by one-third, which enabled the firm to be more flexible, to react quickly to market changes, and to retain its position on the domestic market. Important changes were also made in the export structure. Exports of some products, Audiuretin and Rohypnol, for example, increased nearly tenfold during the last two years. The firm also sought new products that would be the basis for improvement in the structure of production, although, because the firm was looking for a foreign partner, changes in the production program and new investments would need to be coordinated with this partner.

The firm's restructuring was to be followed by improvements in technology. The management wanted to obtain GMP certification in order to be able to export its products to Western markets as well as to meet the future requirements of the domestic standards. The management was also considering a new organizational structure because the firm was quite large and had diverse production lines. One possibility was a holding structure with affiliate firms for large production lines and capacities for special products. The affiliates could also have joint ventures with a foreign partner.

2. During the privatization process, the firm wanted to privatize separately some capacities that did not fit its strategy. These included small plants that accounted for only about 15 percent of capacity, and thus could be easily separated.

3. As mentioned earlier, the firm wanted to identify a strategic foreign partner who would improve the firm's management, increase its market opportunities, and provide financial resources for a $45 million investment program. Moreover, the management hoped to find a partner who was also a generic

producer with a strong position on the world market. This partner would need to be interested in the development of the firm and not only in its market share. Because of the extent of the investment program, the partner would be asked not only to buy shares from the National Property Fund but also to increase the firm's equity. PA Consulting was to assist in selecting the partner. The search began in September 1992 and the firm hoped to sign an agreement with the foreign partner by the end of 1993. The firm was aware that the foreign partner might select only a part of CS-12.

4. According to the privatization legislation, it was possible to transfer shares to the Health Insurance Fund. The management wanted to do this because they expected the Health Insurance Agency's interest in collaborating with CS-12 to increase. In such a case, not only would the owner be well known, but it would have an interest in keeping a Czechoslovak generic and cheap producer in business.

5. The relatives of the firm's previous owner, Mr. Frágner, submitted a restitution claim for 10 percent of the firm's equity. The problem with this claim was that the firm was nationalized before 1948, but the owner was not compensated. Compensation should be provided by the state; however, the management included a provision for the restitution claim in its privatization plan and was currently supporting the claim. According to the law, the decision must be made by the court.

6. In order to increase employee support of the firm, employees' shares were also included in privatization plan.

7. The proposed distribution of the shares in the privatization plan was as follows:

- 34 percent strategic partner, including increase of the equity;
- 20 percent Health Insurance Fund preferred shares;
- 30 percent voucher privatization;
- 10 percent to the National Property Fund for restitution claims;
- 3 percent obligatory deposit in the Restitution Fund;
- 3 percent employees' shares.

The time schedule for privatization could not be predicted because of the problems with restitution. However, the following steps could be expected after approval of the plan:

- transfer from the state enterprise form to a joint stock firm;
- distribution of the shares to the specified shareholders;
- creation of a joint venture with a strategic foreign partner;
- preparation of an updated business plan with this partner;
- implementation of the business plan.

IMPACT OF THE NEW TAX SYSTEM

The new tax system, particularly the introduction of value-added tax (VAT), would change economic conditions for the pharmaceutical producers. The VAT would replace the *daň z obratu*, which was currently paid only by consumer goods manufacturers, and only from the part of production that was placed on the domestic consumer market. Because this tax was not paid by distributors of these goods, the costs of distribution were not taxed. Also, services were not taxed under the current system, meaning that the existing tax was not the equivalent of a turnover tax.

There were to be two basic levels of VAT, but some activities would be tax-free. The 23 percent level would be the most common tax rate applied to goods and some services according to a specified list, e.g., restaurants, maintenance, road transport, tourism services, hotel and accommodation services. The 5 percent level would be on food, fuel, coal, drugs, etc., again according to a list, and those services that would be excluded from the 23 percent level, such as building construction, immovable property such as buildings, transfer and usage of rights—for example, leasing. Those goods and services that would not be taxed included financial activities, insurance, the sale of a firm or some part of it, postal services, television and radio broadcasting, transfer and leasing of land and buildings, education, and health services and goods. The introduction of the VAT was expected to increase the general prices of goods and services because much more would be taxed, as would every firm. This contrasted with the current system whereby only the final production stage, which supplied the domestic consumer, was taxed.

Because CS-12 was a pharmaceutical manufacturer, its products would have a 5 percent tax rate, but most of its supplies would be taxed at 23 percent. Therefore, the firm had to generate additional working capital to cover the increase of price in supplies and the time lag in the reimbursement of the VAT. In comparison to the present situation, where the sales tax for CS-12 products was 0 percent, the new tax system would raise the price of pharmaceutical products for final consumers. The components of the new tax system are shown in Table 1.

Due to the introduction of the new tax system, CS-12 would need more current capital to cover its needs. Because all the regulations in the system were not yet available, the financial requirements could only be estimated. One estimate was about 100–150 million CSK, which the firm would need to generate to cover the increased energy and material costs. These costs would represented a significant part of the total cost and the increased value of the total inventory, which was now nearly 1,000 million CSK.

Table 1

Main Taxes Affecting CS-12

Tax	Rates	Comments
VAT	• 23 percent (CS-12's supplies) • 5 percent (CS-12's products) • free (consumers)	increases prices
Corporation income tax	45 percent (the republics had the right to increase it by up to 5 percent)	existing tax 55 percent
Tax on immovables	business buildings: (built up area) 5–10 CSK per year/sq. mile plus 0.75 per additional story	coefficients 0.3–4.5 (Prague 4.5: the tax in Prague will be 45 (CSK per year/sq. mile)
	land: • agricultural: 0.25 or 0.75 percent on the value of land • other: 0.10 or 1.00 CSK per sq. mile	
Road tax	• passenger cars according to the size of the engine • trucks, etc., according to number of axles and weight	new tax (business cars only)
Environment tax	not approved yet	new tax (the legislation had not been completed)

11

Auto Parts: Motorpal

Jaroslav Jirasek, Vratislav Svoboda, and Tomas Varcop

SECTORAL SETTING

The enterprise presented here was among the largest suppliers of the automotive (truck) and engine industries in Czechoslovakia. The main production line, which constituted 70 percent of total production, included eight classes of injection pumps with about 400 variants. Single-purpose equipment and machine tools were also produced. Because of its sophisticated technology and high-quality production, the firm became a monopoly producer of injection devices for Czechoslovakia and former CMEA countries.

During the period of economic transformation, which began in 1990, several factors severely affected the firm. These included the devaluation of CSK, price liberalization, the disintegration of the CMEA market in 1991–92, and the introduction of hard-currency trading with countries of the former Soviet Union. The survival of the firm depended on finding new markets, adjusting production to Western standards, finding ways to finance investment needs, and overcoming difficulties connected with tough monetarist economic reform.

The firm was to be privatized and the management was interested in a joint venture with a strong foreign competitor, in this case, Bosch, a German firm. Changes to create a lean organizational structure had been prepared, and programs for quality improvement and product-upgrading were also taking place. The management was exploring potential markets and ways to finance new technology and quality programs. The firm had the potential to overcome the present problems and once again be one of the best industrial enterprises in the Czech Republic.

Industry and Market Description

The automotive parts industry, especially for fuel injection production, is characterized by high-precision, high-quality production, sophisticated technologies, and economies of scale, all of which create significant entry barriers to newcomers. Brand loyalty is usually high because of high substitution costs and the active participation of fuel injection producers in research and development with engine producers, etc. Flexible customizing was attracting more attention. However, because of the high product quality and a competitive price advantage, penetration into new markets for Motorpal was possible and promising. (See Table 1.)

The domestic industry for fuel injection pumps and the relevant accessories was dominated by Motorpal Jihlava. This monopoly position, combined with advanced technology and competitive price advantage against foreign producers, meant that Motorpal captured practically the entire Czechoslovak market, a situation that continued even after foreign trade barriers were lifted. Motorpal's major domestic customers were the automotive and tractor industries, industrial engines producers, and spare-parts suppliers. (See Table 2.)

All these industries, however, were affected by the collapse of the CMEA. They lost most of their former markets and the remaining customers either did not pay at all, or asked for long-term credits. Many firms were in secondary insolvency, and some truck producers even stopped production for several months. For example, the Tatra firm, formerly the largest truck manufacturer with a production exceeding 15,000 trucks in 1988, had to stop production from May 1992 to November 1992, and was not certain when production would begin again. Tatra faced insolvency and its inventory level was critical. Other large customers of Motorpal, such as Liaz and Zetor, had similar problems. (See Table 4.) The result of this situation was that Motorpal's output and sales dropped sharply.

External Constraints

The period of economic reform in Czechoslovakia was considered a transition toward a market economy. Privatization, liberalization of prices, foreign trade, wages, restrictive monetary and fiscal policies, and a new system of taxation were strongly supported by the government. Despite this support, enterprises faced many problems. A noneffective banking system often delayed foreign transactions and caused serious problems in operations with foreign partners. In addition, there had been no development of investment banking such as that found in Western countries, and long-term credit with reasonable interest was almost impossible to obtain. Restrictive monetary and fiscal policies were seen by many as an obstacle to new investments and acceleration of the economy. Western markets were being captured by well-established large firms with close relations to their customers, but new markets were emerging in the Far East regions.

Basic Technological Characteristics of Production

Production of fuel injection pumps belongs to the high-precision engineering industry. In the late 1950s, Motorpal was the second firm in the world to develop electrotechnology for miniature drilling of injection muzzles. Motorpal attained a sufficient quality standard in its production to be able to export to more than 70 countries, mainly the former Soviet Union and Europe. (See Table 3.) Before the collapse of the CMEA, Motorpal was the leading fuel injection manufacturer within the former socialist countries. The firm cooperated in research and development and created good working relationships with the largest truck producers—Tatra, Liaz, and Avia—and with the tractor producer, Zetor. (See Table 2.)

In addition to the production of fuel injectors, Motorpal also produced special-purpose machines, tools and fixtures, the sales of which reached nearly 18 percent of total net sales in 1991. Foreign competitors, interested in cooperation with the firm, highly valued these machine tools.

MOTORPAL

Enterprise Background

The enterprise was located in Jihlava, a historical, medieval city with a population of 55,000. This city was an important industrial center in western Moravia and is strategically located between Prague and Vienna. The firm was founded at the beginning of the century as a textile plant, but during World War II it was under German occupation as a plant for repairing aircraft engines for the German military. Motorpal was established in 1946, specializing in the production of fuel injection systems for the expanding Czechoslovak truck industry. Later, the firm adopted the technology for miniature drilling of injection muzzles, which provided a promising competitive edge. The Motorpal logo, a combination of an engine and an ignition, was well known in almost 70 countries.

During the 1970s and 1980s, Motorpal was an undisputed industry leader within the former Soviet block. The firm met most of its planned goals and its prosperity seemed secured. In this period, the car industry held a position of prestige in Czechoslovakia and had a priority in obtaining financial resources from the state. The growth of the automotive parts industry was a natural extension of the automobile industry development in the country adopted at the central level. In 1990, at the beginning of the economic transformation, the firm became a joint stock company. Although the state owned the majority share, this was the first step toward overall privatization.

Production Programs

Motorpal also marketed associated products with its fuel injection devices. A rough breakdown for 1991 shows:

Products	Share
Injection pumps	67%
Single-purpose equipment	5%
Machine tools	18%
Services	10%

At the time of this report, Motorpal had seven plants with 3,800 employees, located as follows:

- Jihlava—the headquarters and the main plant, producing in-line fuel injection pumps, longstem nozzles, fuel feed pumps, excess fuel devices, service tools, test benches, and single-purpose machines;
- Jihlava—a second plant that develops and manufactures special machine tools for lapping, honing, and drilling;
- Telc—governors, delivery valves, overpressure correctors;
- Batelov—pistons, barrels, and injection units;
- Jemnice—fuel filters, injection advance devices, tappers;
- Havlickuv Brod—injectors, nozzle testers, fuel feed pumps driven by electric engine;
- Velke Mezirici—shortstem nozzles.

An additional plant at Znojmo, which had been used to produce fuel filters and single-cylinder fuel injection pumps, was sold through small privatization in 1991 for 50 million CSK.

MAJOR SHOCKS TO THE FIRM

During the past three years, the march of the Czechoslovak economy toward a market system had resulted in two major changes that significantly affected trade. These were the 1990 exchange rate changes and the 1991 price liberalization. The Czechoslovak currency was depreciated significantly in 1990 and the exchange ratio was established at about 29 koruny to the U.S. dollar. Because of the positive trade balance of Motorpal, these changes did not negatively influence the economy of the firm. In 1991, about 95 percent of the prices were liberalized. This immediately increased prices of inputs to all producers by a factor of 1.35, but this was much less than in other industries where prices generally doubled. The price index of supplied raw materials went up from 1.5 to 2.5.

The problem of price liberalization was closely connected to that of cost liberalization. Motorpal was able to seize new opportunities, especially in the areas of design, technology, operation, and personnel. However, costs, benefits, capitalization, and similar concerns were not given sufficient consideration. Imminent privatization and foreign cooperation finally pushed these issues to the fore. One CEO commented: "We have to be more transparent." For example, the cost of products was calculated with many miscellaneous items, in particular a sizable overhead.

Calculation Scheme for Products and Parts:

Cost	% of total costs
Labor	7
Raw materials	25
Energy	3
Depreciation	5
Overhead	60

Overhead compared to labor costs is usually around 700–1,400 percent. Motorpal was trying to reduce costs by 2.5–3.5 percent annually.

A second effect of price liberalization was a decrease in the standard of living, which led to some social unrest in an attempt to increase salaries and wages. As a part of macroeconomic stabilization, wages had been frozen for the first two quarters of 1991 and remained regulated until the end of 1992.

Motorpal had relied heavily on orders submitted by truck and tractor makers, as shown in Table 4. The collapse of the Soviet market and the problems in other CMEA countries led to a 60 percent cut in the orders of domestic car, tractor, and engine manufacturers, resulting in a drop in the output of Motorpal during the last few years.

Motorpal Production Volume, 1988–1992

Year	1988	1989	1990	1991	1992
Output (in million CSK)	970	995	992	1,045	650

The transition of a large engineering enterprise also involved complex financial and human resources issues. "Not a single change, not a few changes, but a full conversion of the firm culture," the CEO said when he tried to describe his experience. The financial issues were the most important. There was a growing tendency to chose a more proactive, less restrictive financial policy. The average profit margin oscillated for years in the range of 4–8 percent, but after price deregulation in 1991, the financial situation of Motorpal suddenly improved and profits and management bonuses swelled. However, significant problems occurred soon afterward. Because firms were allowed to set prices freely, many took advantage of their monopolistic position, which led to an increasing delay in payments of anywhere from 14 days to two months on average. Customers' insolvency and impending bankruptcy were serious threats for Motorpal. The government tried to partially solve this problem by canceling the debt for certain enterprises, including Motorpal, but the banks applied this credit to the interest, not the liability of the suppliers. The managers criticized the lack of a banking sector in Czechoslovakia. The underdeveloped commercial banking system and its lack of support of industry were two reasons why Motorpal's management decided to look for a strong partner who could provide capital into the underinvested firm.

SHORT-TERM REACTIONS

Corporate Governance

Motorpal's organization was similar to that of other state enterprises being transformed to private firms in that there were two boards—a board of directors and an advisory board. The board of directors consisted of five members, one of whom was a representative of the Czech Ministry of Industry, one from the Investicni Banka, the CEO and the financial manager from Motorpal, and a professor from the Prague School of Economics.

The advisory board, which acted independently, was in charge of internal audits and reported directly to the owner, that being the state. This Board consisted of three members: a representative of the Czech Ministry of Industry, a representative of the Komerčni Banka, and the head of the Motorpal Control Department. The relationship between the state, represented by the Ministry of Industry, and Motorpal was maintained within these boards in a cooperative way. "Everyone understands that privatization is the most current problem and there is no point in making it more complicated," the CEO stated.

Organizational Changes in Management

A typical question asked at Motorpal was "How do we adjust ourselves to lean times? Assuming that a silver lining will emerge on the horizon, what can be done or ought to be done at present?" The first response was "Slim down."

Underused universal equipment was sold as well as materials, spare parts, and tools, but this did not contribute much. The financial manager said: "What we need more than cash is more attention and responsibility and a higher cost-consciousness." The chief of the newly established marketing department claimed: "Penetration into new markets looks promising. However, as a rule, it takes two to three years to make the deal and start production. The idea that production could be shifted from the East European to the West European marketplace became nonviable. Those markets are dominated by large established firms and protected by high entry barriers."

Therefore, Motorpal began to explore new markets in the Middle East, North Africa, India, Indonesia, and China. In India and Indonesia, in particular, a joint venture seemed promising. Two Asian joint ventures were on the verge of materialization. They would not help tremendously but it would at least keep production going. Motorpal also succeeded in attracting various small production orders, all of which could help to ease critically low demand. "We have good hope," Mr. Karel Jonas (a pseudonym) stated. "But we need immediate alleviation."

Ing. Karel Jonas, CSc, had assumed his position in the firm five years ago. He had a very strong personality and had influenced the pattern and culture of the firm and its business environment. In 1990, when Motorpal was converted into a joint stock firm, Mr. Jonas became both chairman of the board and general manager. While the firm had not changed its structure, this CEO's feeling was that organizational inertia could be a worse rival than competitors.

For the last six years, there had been no change of management. The members of the management team all had university degrees and the average age was about forty. Even though almost all Czechoslovak firms had had major management changes after 1989, Motorpal had not. How was this possible while other firms in the same region replaced all their managers during 1990? Suggested answers to this question were that the CEO possessed great authority and tactics during a very turbulent period and that all top executives were respected among the workers. "The crucial point probably was that people learned about catastrophes from other local firms in which the management was fired, despite its professional credits," mentioned one executive.

Employment, Job Security

The decrease in employment was sharp, although not as severe as that in production, as the following figures show:

Year	1989	1992
Sales (in million CSK)	995	650
Employees	5,500	3,670

Overemployment, however, continued to plague the firm. The chief of the personnel department explained: "The initial layoffs were related to retirement and to foreign workers from Vietnam. Today, we possibly would have been more selective in both categories. At the same time, we dismissed employees with notoriously low work morale. People understand that the switch between employment and unemployment depends on performance, productivity, and quality. From time to time, particularly in 1991, we had to introduce part-time work or temporary layoffs. Through the regional labor office, all those laid off received 20–60 percent of average wages in subsidies paid by the firm. In several cases, however, we lost excellent employees who preferred to join small private businesses or start one themselves. During a recovery in the fall of 1991, we were unable to rehire people with needed skills. Those unemployed persons recommended to us by the labor office were so underskilled as to be almost useless."

The average wage and salary in the firm were low and only partially index-linked. In the second quarter of 1992, the average wage was about 4,000 CSK, lower than the average in the economy, especially considering that Motorpal's production was characterized by high precision and elevated skills.

It took several years to sufficiently train an operator or engineer, and mistakes in recruiting and frequent turnover of manpower were costly. Many small private entrepreneurs could afford to pay higher wages because they evaded taxation and, in some cases, hired registered people who did not pay the 50 percent surplus in labor costs or the mandatory social tax. Another reduction of employment was envisaged for fall 1992, almost exclusively in administrative and functional services, the preliminary goal being an additional 10 percent attrition at the end of 1992.

There was another reason why a reduction in employment and labor costs could not completely offset the drop of production. Some aspects of operation could not be reduced under any circumstances, such as maintenance, energy supply, work safety, and janitorial services. At a certain level of production, employment could become disproportionally higher than output.

Survival Framework

In planning a survival strategy, two factors that appeared to be crucial for the survival of Motorpal were that it manufacture products complying with Western standards and at competitive prices, and that it find new markets with solvent customers.

Motorpal had proven itself capable of adjusting to high-quality products. In 1991–92, two new products were produced within six months and delivered to a leading West European firm. The firm had a significant competitive price advantage: its products could be delivered for less than two-thirds of the typical price level for comparable goods in the West.

Product upgrading proved to be easier than finding solvent customers, however. Customers in Russia and Ukraine, Poland, Romania, and Bulgaria exhibited a need for injection devices, and therefore Motorpal tried to maintain markets in these countries. The customers, however, requested long-term credit. A well-designed countertrade using barter and switch transactions, such as that in these former CMEA countries, could make mutual trade easier, but firms and institutions dealing in this kind of export and import were badly underdeveloped.

Beginning in January 1992, Motorpal refused to deliver unless the customer had completed a letter of credit. This not only improved the balance of payments,

144 CASE STUDIES OF CZECH AND SLOVAK FIRMS

but also captured the demand. It did mean, however, that production capacity was once again underutilized. Generally speaking, despite the alarming aspects of the current situation in that, instead of trimming direct costs, overcapacity and overemployment were augmenting overhead costs, Motorpal's prospects were not bad.

In 1991–92, the domestic market was depressed. The large truck manufacturers, Tatra, which produced off-road heavy trucks, and Liaz, which produced on-road heavy trucks, had large inventories at hand. A rebound was expected in 1993 for this type of vehicle and for the production of industrial diesel engines at CKD Prague, ZTS Martin, and a few smaller producers.

LONG-TERM RESPONSES

Privatization

Privatization in Czechoslovakia was legally imposed and was implemented in two subsequent rounds. The restitution of former private property was negligible and 3 percent of the shares would be reserved for the National Restitution Fund for possible compensation to prior owners.

Motorpal was to be privatized in the second round of voucher privatization and its privatization project had been prepared and submitted to the government. As required by law, four other competitive projects were submitted; however, only one of the plans would be approved by the Ministry of Industry of the Czech Republic.

To improve its market value, Motorpal instituted a number of environmental protective improvements. For example, by 1993, Motorpal intended to have its facilities and surrounding areas environmentally sound. The firm also offered these clean-up services to other firms. Because of the sophisticated technology brought from the West, this business seem to be very profitable and much in demand.

Initially, about 32 percent of the shares was set aside for Bosch A.G., but the German firm was interested in joint ventures and deliveries, not in ownership rights. The management of Motorpal did not expect further complications and almost everyone felt that privatization would be an improvement that would define property rights and bring about a clear power structure. This seemed to be very important and the managers were looking for support in their unpopular decision-making processes. They also believed that the attraction for foreign capital might increase.

MANAGEMENT'S PERCEPTION OF
THE FIRM'S POSITION

From a discussion with Motorpal management came the following thoughts: "It was a bad mistake by our politicians to push the former USSR for trade in hard currency. We have no other option than to buy their crude oil, gas, and ore. Once they have our dollars in their palm, they can buy machinery anywhere. In 1991–92, the Czechoslovak Minister of Foreign Affairs tried to sell a plan to the West for single-purpose funding of Russia and Ukraine to buy Czechoslovak industrial products. But this failed, understandably."

The plant was predicted to grow soon. The general feeling was that this was the nucleus of Motorpal's transformation and that such growth would ensure the future. CEO Jonas said: "What would help us a lot would be a reasonable credit. But our banks are asking for at least 13 percent interest rates. We have no bank that would match the terms of a development bank with consulting services, long-term credits, and low interest rates. For any credit, we have to single out 1.3-fold value of real estate."

"Our accounts payables are fairly acceptable and our receivables amount to almost one-fourth as much, but our clients delay payments. This so-called secondary indebtedness, caused by the insolvency of our clients and not directly by us, slows down our development. We know we will eventually be paid, but we cannot afford to wait. Banks could do so, but they turned away from the growth policy. Instead of being vehicles of recovery, they carry out oppressive financial restriction. In short, what we are experiencing is not so much an economic disbalance as a shortage of cash."

Joint ventures are not an easy international cooperative business arrangement. "First of all, we had to develop mutual knowledge, credibility, and trust," said another manager. Bosch's managers and experts were seen in Motorpal engineering and manufacturing departments, and Motorpal's engineers and workers acquired the local knowledge in Munich. "The professional compatibility is growing, there is no doubt about that," said Mr. Jonas. For a while, the CEO was lured by a Bosch competitor to join forces against Bosch's competitive position. "Not for us," Mr. Jonas continued. "We prefer a strong strategic force, and nobody can match Bosch."

MAJOR FINDINGS: IMPLICATIONS FOR CHANGING BEHAVIOR AND GOALS

The management of the firm was well aware of all the problems. After losing former markets, they were trying to find new customers and means of penetration into new outlets. A great effort was put into seeking partners to cooperate in production, technology and sales, marketing and distribution. Such partners could also help to finance new technology and assist with quality improvement and innovation. Quality and flexibility, which were preconditions for successful competition, were supported by a significant competitive price advantage. The need to streamline the firm's structure was reflected in the new organizational scheme being put into action.

Motorpal could see a silver lining in the future, but was faced with current short-term difficulties. The adjustment to a low level of demand had not yet been finished, and further facilities, production items, work force, and costs could be trimmed without undermining of the firm.

The joint venture was critical. Bosch A.G. maintained a serious approach, provided informational and technological assistance, and sought convincing results. Thus far, this joint venture was promising. If the firm were to prove capable of supplying high quality at low cost, it would obtain a growing portfolio of German orders, in spite of the fact that Bosch's plants suffered from overcapacity. Quality, cost, and flexibility were also crucial points of further expansion into foreign markets. A number of other negotiations were also under way.

Customers in the countries of the former Soviet Union were accustomed to Motorpal's fuel supply systems and would continue to place orders with the firm. Their chronic insolvency was an obstacle; however, several trading companies were trying to reestablish barter transactions to ease the hard currency shortage. The two Asian joint ventures, although not large in size, were expected to be operational in 1993 or 1994, and would contribute to recovery and future growth.

Motorpal needed to enter the world markets and to learn about international marketing and negotiations, but this took time. Meanwhile, individual plants were looking for whatever orders they could find and were adjusting their production programs accordingly. They could at least keep their equipment running.

Restructuring is a process that takes time. We felt that the government economic policy should take this time scale into account by establishing a bank infrastructure including the so-called development banks that could offer midterm and long-term credit at relatively low interest rates. This was perceived by Motorpal and other firms as a missing link.

Table 1

Export to Foreign Countries

	Year 1990 (%)	Year 1992 (%)
USSR	32.0	5.0
England	13.6	2.0
Poland	7.9	1.5
Bulgaria	7.8	—
Italy	6.3	—
Switzerland	5.2	10.0
Germany	4.0	39.5
Austria	—	34.5
China and Hong Kong	—	3.5
India	—	2.0
Turkey	—	0.5
Others	23.2	1.5

Table 2
Main Motorpal Customers

CSFR	Export
Automotive industry Avia Praha Liaz Jablonec Tatra Koprivnice Mototechna Praha (spare parts) **Tractor industry** Zetor Brno ZTS Martin **Industrial Engines** Skoda Praha CKD Horovice Slavia Napajedla CKS Hradec Kralove Diesel Brno	**USSR** VgMZ Volgograd Jazta Jaroslavl **Poland** Andoria Andrychow Cegielski Poznan **Bulgaria** VAMO Varna **German Democratic Republic** MW Schonebeck MW Cunnewalde **India** KCL Puna

Table 3
Business Activities and Contacts

Europe	Africa	The Americas	Asia	Oceania
Albania	Algeria	Argentina	Afghanistan	New Zealand
Austria	Angola	Bolivia	Arabia	Australia
Belgium	Egypt	Brazil	Bangladesh	
Bulgaria	Ethiopia	Canada	Burma	
Canary Islands	Morocco	Colombia	China	
Denmark	Mozambique	Cuba	Cyprus	
Finland	Nigeria	Ecuador	Hong Kong	
France	S. Africa	Chile	India	
Germany	Sudan	Paraguay	Indonesia	
Great Britain	Tunisia	Puerto Rico	Iran	
Greece	Zambia	Uruguay	Iraq	
Holland	Zimbabwe	USA	Japan	
Hungary		Venezuela	Jordan	
Ireland			Korea	
Italy			Kuwait	
Norway			Malaysia	
Poland			Mongolia	
Portugal			Pakistan	
Romania			Philippines	
Spain			Singapore	
Sweden			Syria	
Switzerland			Thailand	
USSR			Taiwan	
Yugoslavia			Turkey	
			Vietnam	

Table 4

Turnover, Profit, Number of Employees, and Debts of Selected Customers

	1989	1990	1991
Turnover (mil. CSK)			
Avia	1,687	1,971	2,523
Tatra	9,013	8,764	11,671
Liaz	5,742	5,454	3,920
Diesel Brno	714	719	794
Profit (mil. CSK)			
Avia	−5.24	97.52	24.91
Tatra	779.81	584.02	1,620.64
Liaz	451.79	401.35	128.09
Diesel Brno	−0.63	−1.80	−56.41
Debt (mil. CSK)			
Avia	749	641	441
Tatra	1,703	1,577	3,571
Liaz	1,316	1,146	984
Diesel Brno	399	552	439
Number of employees			
Avia	4,989	4,668	3,964
Tatra	16,677	16,318	14,635
Liaz	9,471	8,355	6,643
Diesel Brno	781	762	1,127

Table 5

Financial Statements

Balance Sheet

Motorpal Firm Jihlava
(in million CSK)

	Year 1991	Year 1992
Assets		
Cash	38	40
A/R	187	310
Inventories	209	180
Fixed assets	1,405	1,420
Less depreciation	875	980
Total assets	**964**	**970**
Liabilities and Equity		
Debts	276	240
A/P	61	100
Equity	627	630
Total liabilities and Equity	**964**	**970**

Income Statement

Motorpal Firm Jihlava
(in million CSK)

	Year 1991	Year 1992
Sales	1,070	650
COGS[1]	960	584
Other expenses	55	48
Earnings (EBIT)[2]	**55**	**18**

Ratios

	Year 1991	Year 1992
Profit margin	5.14%	2.77%
Asset turnover per year	1.11	0.67
Financial leverage	1.54	1.54
ROE[3]	8.77%	2.86%
ROA[4]	5.71%	1.86%
Debt-to-Assets	28.63%	24.74%

Notes:
[1] Cost of Goods Sold
[2] Earnings before income tax.
[3] Return on equity.
[4] Return on assets.

Figure 1. **Motorpal Organizational Structure**

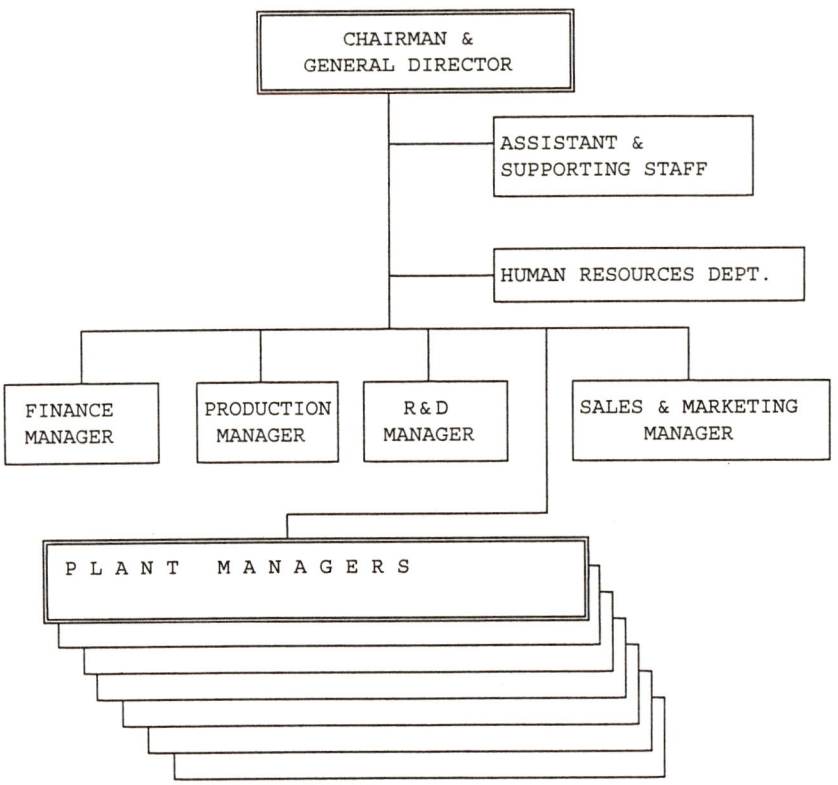

Figure 2. **Motorpal Organization Chart and Functions Responsibility**

General Manager
-international business cooperation -quality promotion -legal services
R&D Manager
-research, development, testing -design, engineering -maintenance -plant for single-purpose machinery and tooling
Finance Manager
-accounting, budgeting -finance
Production Manager
-production and work organization -sourcing and logistics
Sales Manager
-marketing -sales and post-sales services -exports
Chief of Pesonnel Department
-employment -wages, salaries, incentives -training -social policy
Six Plant Managers

Part II

Case Studies of Hungarian Firms

1

Engineering: DKG

Drang nach Osten?

Judit Zsarnay

AN OVERVIEW OF THE INDUSTRY

The Hungarian market for oil and gas equipment has had only one major domestic producer since World War II, that being DKG (Dunántúli Kőolajipari Gépgyár). This firm had 40–50 percent of the domestic market share for its three main products; the remaining domestic demand was satisfied by imports, mostly from Germany and France.

DKG had a few less-important domestic competitors for some of its products, but these Hungarian firms mostly manufactured only the components or building blocks of DKG's products. Therefore, they could have threatened DKG by stopping supplies of these components to DKG and manufacturing the finished product themselves, but otherwise, domestic competition was limited.

These domestic semi-competitors, or rather bargaining partners, of DKG included Ganz-MAVAG and the Alföld Oil and Gas Equipment Factory at Orosháza. Ganz-MAVAG manufactured small quantities of pipeline valves, while Alföld was a larger producer. Because these valves were in different size categories from DKG's, they did not represent a direct threat.

Alföld and the Budapest Oil and Gas Equipment Factory also supplied DKG with special castings and some semi-finished products for pipeline valves. Because the castings could be imported from Slovenia and Czechoslovakia at a lower price, DKG had a very complex relationship with its domestic competitors, but DKG seemed to be in a good negotiating position vis-à-vis them.

HISTORY OF THE FIRM

Although the Nagykanizsa plant was built in 1944, the firm had been an independent enterprise only from January 1950. It then had approximately one-quarter of the total of 1,200 workers who were employed as of June 1992. The establishment of the firm coincided with the onset of production at Hungarian oilfields that had been explored in the late 1930s. The plant's name was chosen in 1954 while the firm was a member of the Hungarian Oil and Gas Trust (OKGT). It became formally independent from OKGT in July 1991, even though the firm's real independence had been granted in 1986.

Although DKG formally became a company limited by shares in July 1992, the transformation process was not completed until the following November, which marked the end of the first phase of the privatization process.

PRODUCT MIX AND SALES PATTERN

DKG manufactured equipment for oil and gas prospecting, production, and processing. It also supplied industries such as mining, chemicals and energy, and the water management sector. The firm was largely self-reliant in R&D and had about 4,000 products of its own creation. These were allowed to carry the certification of the American Petroleum Institute (API) and ASME, the German TÜV (Technische überwachungsverein), and the European ISO 9000. The use of these internationally accepted certificates of quality and the conformity of DKG's products to these standards gave the firm substantial advantage in international markets. In fact, international competitiveness was a major motive behind the firm's continuing effort to modernize its product mix.

Technology and product development benefited from the introduction of modern cost analysis and process management techniques. The firm had an integrated production management system. Moreover, NC and CNC machine tools were used to a great extent and production processes were controlled and backed by CAD/CAM and CIM. DKG's quality management staff constituted about 6 percent of the firm's total manpower, and quality control by the workers themselves was used extensively. A predecessor of Total Quality Management (TQM) was introduced 1982, and the firm now uses TQM exclusively.

The main elements of the product mix were drilling and production equipment for the oil industry, with special emphasis on packers and shock absorbers bearing DKG's own trademark, pipeline valves, and well-head equipment.

The firm's sales pattern had been strongly oriented toward the domestic market, but the firm was now directing efforts toward international markets. The share of exports in sales was 12 percent in 1988 and 11 percent in 1989 and 1990, but it rose to 21 percent in 1991 and reached 27 percent in the first half of 1992.

The structure of exports allowed DKG to retain its traditional access to former CMEA markets. The development of the oil industry was a top priority for the Russian government, with the result that earning convertible currency on the Russian market did not become a serious problem for DKG. Recent structural shifts in DKG's sales were due mainly to the changing role of the Russian market. The Soviet market share in DKG's exports was 20 percent in 1988, 32 percent in 1990, and 37 percent in 1991, reaching 54 percent in the first half of 1992.

The firm's sales strategy seemed to be clear. It would not react to declining domestic markets by competing with heavyweight American, British, and French multinationals in OPEC markets: instead, it sought to outcompete them in selected smaller, formerly Soviet, markets such as Bashkiria or Tatarstan. One important factor in this strategy was DKG's favorable image in Russia. The firm had excellent contacts in ministries and large national oil and gas production trusts and it benefited from a low-profile image as compared to its large Western competitors.

Essentially, DKG had been able to build a reputation as a small but open and honest firm with no interest in special access to, and eventual acquisition of, Russia's natural resources. This image, combined with the firm's well-established reputation for flexibility and reliability, helped it to create and exploit a small but well-defined and uncontestable market niche in Russia.

The other traditional CMEA markets were East Germany, Czechoslovakia, and Poland. Exports to Germany had ceased completely and the two other Central European markets were not important. The firm had an extensive worldwide marketing network, but the effects of the network were not yet evident in DKG's export pattern.

DKG also had an established presence in Austria, Germany, Greece, and, more recently, in Pakistan and Saudi Arabia. Contacts had been established with U.S. and Canadian firms as well. The firm had representative offices in Austria (Petrotech) and Canada (Tridchem) and was the minority owner of the Nagykanizsa-based Hungarian-Canadian joint venture, Merkantoll, also an export-import firm.

Entry into Western markets for oil and gas industry equipment would be very difficult for DKG because of the role played by existing business relationships. In these, quality and reliability were important, but personal contacts also played a very important role. Although DKG's management was very active in this field, the establishment of new markets was difficult, for despite the firm's solid technology base, DKG's marketing staff was much weaker than its R&D and production management, and efforts to upgrade this unit had not yet been successful.[1]

PROPERTY STRUCTURE AND PRIVATIZATION

Organizational and ownership changes occurred at DKG during June and July 1992. The two major changes were the creation of the Hungaro-Russian joint venture, DKG-East Ltd., and the transformation of DKG into a fully state-owned enterprise limited by shares. Both changes were integral parts of management's general strategy and can be evaluated from a strategic perspective.

The DKG-East joint venture was prepared and created after the failure of a planned alliance with an American firm of worldwide repute in the industry. Although few details of these negotiations were available, some reasons for this failure became known. The American firm wanted a joint venture with DKG in order to exploit its contacts with the Russians, but DKG might have become simply the marketing arm of its overseas partner. Moreover, the American firm was reluctant to make a major investment into the new joint venture. In addition, its contribution of technology and know-how would not have been particularly significant.

The failure of these negotiations was strategically important for DKG's management. They realized that DKG could expect to find potential investors among its competitors for the Russian market. Therefore, they needed to identify potential partners in Russia, despite the fact that the shortage of Russian capital available for investment and, even more, for investment abroad, would make it difficult to sell the idea of a Russo-Hungarian joint venture to the Russians. Nevertheless, only an alliance with Russian partners could help DKG in two vital ways: an injection of fresh capital and access to new markets. It was also clear that the Russians needed inexpensive but advanced oil and gas industry technology.

DKG-East had a capital stock of HUF 1.4 billion, or about $17 million. DKG's share of this was 51 percent and the Russian conglomerate, Gasprom, held 47 percent. Two Hungarian trading houses owned the remaining shares. Gasprom was an industrial giant, with an annual output of approximately 650 billion cubic meters of natural gas, and controlled nearly all the gas fields in Russia. Investment by the Russians of approximately $8 million would enable the joint venture to carry out a major technology-development program. This would help DKG as well, because the joint venture was located in part of DKG's central Nagykanizsa plant. DKG-East had close technological ties to DKG, and its Russian co-owner would need to buy products and services from DKG to complement its purchases from the joint venture.

DKG-East had somewhat less than 50 percent of DKG's former capacity. Based on a recent asset valuation, the land, plant, and equipment that DKG invested in the joint venture were accepted by the joint venture partners at a value higher than that on DKG's books. Therefore, the difference between the values of these assets in the books of DKG-East and DKG was subject to capital gains tax, which is simply part of the corporate tax in Hungary.

This posed a serious challenge to DKG because, while it could not expect to make any profit in 1992, it eventually could become profitable as a result of this transaction. The problem, however, was insufficient cash to generate funds to pay the capital gains tax. Therefore, no quick fix was available currently; it would have been a very bad idea to sell part of DKG's assets and thus lose its majority share in the joint venture in order to cover the tax liability.

DKG was transformed into a fully state-owned company limited by shares in

July 1992. As of this report, the privatization of this firm was being prepared. The performance of DKG-East would be a major variable for DKG's management in determining the future role of Russian investors in DKG's privization, especially since they had already expressed strong interest.

DKG'S FINANCIAL SITUATION

Even if the firm's financial situation had deteriorated markedly in the last few years, DKG was financially sound, something that could be considered almost a rarity in Hungarian industry. We have assessed the major financial trends and present them in a table, although some necessary data are missing. The fundamental trends, however, can be highlighted.

DKG was almost debt-free and had no losses yet, although this could change in the future. Nor did it suffer from the so-called queuing problem; that is, it had not acquired a large amount of unpaid short-term obligations. While most indicators had been deteriorating, DKG's relative soundness formed a good basis for strategic thinking by management. DKG was by no means a so-called drifting firm, one that has no strategy for survival, but merely extends its existence by using up its assets.

One indicator of the financial health of a Hungarian state firm was its relative dependence on subsidies during the transition period, a figure that was quite favorable for DKG.

The trends shown in Table 1 can be supplemented by preliminary figures for the first half of 1992. Sales reached HUF 847 million, which represented a slight proportionate increase; gross profit before taxes was HUF 6 million, and taxes paid totaled HUF 120 million. Profit taxes were only HUF 2.4 million, but this could rise almost a hundredfold with the capital gains effect from the joint venture. Subsidies disappeared and after-tax profits were only HUF 3.6 million.

Sales increased by nearly HUF 200 million between 1990 and 1992 and the growth of exports was close to HUF 400 million, but after-tax profits were down by approximately 75 percent. This indicated deteriorating efficiency, a result of a disproportionate increase in costs. The management reacted to this with an ambitious program for cutting labor costs, R&D expenditures, and operating expenses. A new element of this strategy was the exact coordination of designs with the technical details of orders. Thus, customers would only get the functions and technical parameters they actually needed and paid for.

Table 2 shows that DKG was able to offset the relative increase in energy costs and other inevitable items, for example the increased cost of entering and keeping new markets, by pushing down the increase in the costs of materials and wages respectively. Management's ability to carry out a strict financial strategy based on well-controlled production costs would doubtless increase DKG's value for potential investors. Thus, there seemed to be no need for radical financial shock therapy within the firm after privatization.

Although figures for 1991 showed a temporary increase in the share of material costs, preliminary figures for the first half of 1992 pointed to a reversal of this trend. In this period, the share of wages fell even farther, to 17.9 percent, and the costs of materials reached a new low of 44.1 percent. There was, however, an expected increase in other costs, mostly due to the firm's new push for further diversification of sales.

The inventory situation at DKG was also indicative of its solid financial management. The relative share of materials in total inventories oscillated between 70 and 74 percent during the period 1988–91, and the proportion of semi-finished and finished products did not rise above 30 percent in those years. The growing financial uncertainties on Russian markets changed this situation somewhat in the first half of 1992, during which time the relative share of semi-finished and finished products within inventories reached 40 percent. These changes worsened DKG's financial situation to some extent, as was evident from the relative increase in the category, other costs. It seemed quite unlikely that this inventory structure would improve in the coming years, and it could be seen as a negative variable, albeit with a limited impact, in the assessment of DKG's strategic perspectives. DKG's worsening financial situation was not a sign of its crisis. The firm had a solid technology base, well-trained manpower, and a feasible strategy of adjustment to external shocks, but it was suffering from a lack of working capital, which was partly a result of its HUF 50 million or so in unpaid receivables, and it had difficulty securing safe new markets.

Investment was also a growing problem. DKG was still able to spend HUF 198 million on investment in 1988, but only HUF 51 million in 1989 and HUF 12 million in 1990. The HUF 23 million investment budget in 1991 was no major improvement, and only HUF 8 million was spent on investment in the first half of 1992. The origin of funds used for investment sheds more light on the financial strategy of management. Such an investment strategy could be considered very conservative from this point of view. For example, in the period between 1988 and the first half of 1992, necessary funds came partly from the sale of used equipment and partly from profits. This is why a strong link can be seen between the trends of after-tax profits and investment. This was, of course, only partly a result of the efforts of DKG's management. It was evident in the case of many Hungarian firms less fortunate than DKG, such as Hungarian telecommunications or electronics firms, for example, that they had been pressured into major investment projects by the government and were later left alone with their shrinking markets and growing financial commitments.

To a certain extent, DKG was sheltered from the pressures imposed on other Hungarian firms by the country's CMEA-oriented industrial policy in the mid-1980s, as well as from pressures imposed on other engineering firms by the need to adapt production to meet the requirements of the defense sector. This permitted DKG to avoid ambitious high-tech projects that could lead to greater credit exposure toward banks, and the firm was able to coordinate the completion of its technological goals using its own financial resources.

HUMAN RESOURCES, MANAGEMENT, AND LABOR RELATIONS

The relatively high skills of the firm's employees helped the firm to maintain comparatively high standards of quality and efficiency. Approximately 40 percent of the employees were college or university graduates and 75 percent of the blue-collar workers were skilled. Most of the latter had been trained by the firm through on-the-job training. Labor relations were slightly less trouble-free at DKG than at most other firms in our sample. There had been no strikes, but the emergence of two strong trade unions created an unusual trilateral relationship with the management. About two-thirds of DKG's employees were trade-union members, split about equally between the formerly official and the newer more radical trade unions. Both trade unions had a correct working relationship with the DKG management, but the newer trade union often found itself alone at the bargaining table because its older counterpart usually adopted a more conciliatory approach in negotiations with the management.

For instance, the newer trade union normally requested greater wage increases, a more radical approach to ESOP (Employee Stock Ownership Plan), or greater social benefits, whereas the older type more readily accepted the arguments of the management. One recent controversial issue was the request of the newer trade union to accelerate privatization and rapidly increase wages at the same time. The management had some difficulty explaining why these two objectives might conflict with each other if pushed too far.

DKG's management was monolithic in a special sense. All four top managers had climbed the ladder within the firm, which gave them a feeling of team spirit. The prevalence of intra-firm promotion was, however, a handicap with regard to international experience and openness of management. Only the financial director of DKG, who was a graduate of ENI's School of Management in Italy and had a Hungarian economics degree, had significant international experience. The technical director graduated from the Technical University of Budapest and both the director general and the marketing director had two Hungarian degrees, one in technology and one in economics/trade.

DKG's top management team had been in place for only a few months in its current configuration. The director general was appointed in 1990 following the retirement of his predecessor, shortly before DKG gained its independence from OKGT. The financial director was appointed to his position only in May 1992, after his predecessor left to work with a private tax consulting firm. The technical director was appointed CEO of DKG-East: his office would remain on DKG's premises, but he would only indirectly serve the firm.

The management had a clear strategic view of DKG's future. The creation of

DKG-East, the firm's transformation, and the streamlining of its finances and technology base were only elements of a consolidation period. The expansion phase would begin when DKG was able to team up with a major professional investor, had attracted a significant amount of technology and working capital, and had started to capitalize internationally on its strategic presence on the Russian market.

DKG'S FUTURE

The firm's strategy currently included two major but closely inter-related elements: the preparation for privatization and increased export marketing. The privatization tender was announced in December 1992 and at least 51 percent of the firm's stock capital was available for privatization. Priority was to be given to foreign investors in the industry, but domestic financial investors would also be welcome. A smaller number of shares would be available for ESOP only after an increase in the capital stock, but management did not think there would be much interest on the part of the employees. As with other Hungarian firms, setting up ESOP schemes seemed to be difficult due to both financing problems and the fact that such shares could be sold to employees either at a full price, in which case the leverage problem meant an almost insurmountable barrier, or at a 90 percent discount. The latter option would take place with the full guarantee of the government, therefore, it would not really mean the departure of the government from the firm's ownership. The new marketing strategy was based on an increasingly export-oriented sales pattern with a target of 70 percent of sales going abroad and approximately 80 percent of exports sold on Russian and other ex-Soviet markets. It was quite evident that this marketing strategy was part of the firm's preparation for privatization, and its implementation would largely depend on how privatization finally succeeded.

This strategy, and the fact that it was made public, rather correctly stressed that DKG's value for strategic investors consisted mainly of its access to the former Soviet market as well as its high-level technology base.

Note

1. One of the main reasons was that DKG was unable to offer competitive salaries to appropriately qualified salespeople. Such manpower is highly in demand everywhere in the country, and if DKG offered them lucrative remuneration, similar wage demands would immediately spread within the firm. An additional problem is that DKG mostly needs marketing people with good business training and a knowledge of Russian. The supply of such experts is extremely limited in Hungary.

Table 1
DKG's Main Financial Indicators (data in HUF million)

	1988	1989	1990	1991
Annual sales	1,645	1,594	1,499	1,504
Gross profit before tax	175	128	67	11
All taxes paid (incl. social security)	369	414	360	225
Profit taxes	89	72	31	1.4
Subsidies	3.9	3.6	3.9	4.4
Profit after tax	67	45	58	8

Notes:
Figures do not add up due to rounding and minor omissions.
Line 3 (taxes paid) does not include VAT-type taxes.
Dollar–forint exchange rates, 1988: $U.S.1 = HUF50.424; 1989: $U.S.1 = HUF59.066; 1990: $U.S.1 = HUF64.147; 1991: $U.S1 = HUF74.722.

Table 2
DKG's Cost Structure (in percentages)

	1988	1989	1990	1991
Total costs	100	100	100	100
of which:				
Costs of material	54.4	52.2	49.1	53.6
Wage costs	20.6	22.2	23.3	19.6
Energy costs	4.1	3.9	4.9	6.0
Banking costs (incl. interest)	1.5	1.7	1.3	1.0
Depreciation	3.2	3.6	3.5	2.9
Other costs	16.2	16.4	17.9	16.9

2

Defense: Theta Works

A Nuclear Instruments Manufacturer to Be Blown Up?

Gábor Karsai

AN OVERVIEW OF THE INDUSTRY

Theta belonged to the Hungarian military industry, which lost its markets after the collapse of the CMEA and the Warsaw Pact. It must be stressed that this industry included only a small number of weapons firms, because the division of labor among the military industries of the Warsaw Pact states mainly allocated to Hungary the job of supplying military electronics products. Although a string of Hungarian engineering firms manufactured military products, their relatively large number, between twenty and thirty, did not mean that the domestic market was competitive. Sales channels were strictly regulated, technologies and products were different among firms, and even direct links between manufacturers and users were strongly limited in many cases. Theta contributed about 90 percent of the Hungarian production of nuclear instruments and 30 percent of guidance instruments. The second market segment could be considered more or less duopolistic, with Theta controlling 40 percent of the domestic market and several smaller producers accounting for about 30 percent of it.

A BRIEF HISTORY OF THE FIRM

Theta was founded at the beginning of the twentieth century by the Juász brothers for the purpose of manufacturing technologically advanced optical and precision engineering products. Theta became part of the Hungarian military industry after its nationalization in the late 1940s. This gave the firm a special status that it was unable shed even in the late 1980s.

The firm's association with the pre-1990 largely Soviet-oriented Hungarian weapons industry, which was now partly defunct, had limited its options toward transformation and privatization. Theta was paralyzed by the loss of most of its traditional markets in the CMEA area and in Hungary, but its ability to respond to or benefit from the institutional changes in its economic environment was restricted as well.[1]

Theta had a board of directors and a supervisory board, but their functioning was purely formal. Indeed, the board did not meet in 1992. The firm was 100 percent state-owned and was still facing transformation. In spite of its noncorporate legal status, it remained a state enterprise, and had started a sort of spontaneous privatization.

This term might be inaccurate in the case of Theta, because no management-led privatization was taking place. Nevertheless, it is a useful description of developments at Theta because the firm's different plants had separated themselves from Theta and already had acquired a corporate legal status. The problems of the traditionally weapons-industry based, Eastern market-oriented, legally and administratively semi-paralyzed firm had to be solved by what remained of Theta, the former firm's central Budapest plant.

Therefore, at least in Theta's special case, the usual one-dimensional model of privatization preceded by transformation was not applicable. Privatization had to include a spatial dimension, i.e., that of the changing content of what we mean by the entity Theta as well.

The crisis that Theta faced came on with exceptional suddenness. Nineteen eighty-nine was still quite a good year for the firm, and the shocklike collapse of its markets made any kind of strategic response very difficult. The only solution, albeit a temporary one, was to release all the units of the firm with the hope that some of them might survive on their own. Before this peculiar pattern of separation, transformation, and privatization was completed, Theta's sales performance showed abrupt changes, with dramatic drops in sales in 1991 and 1992.

Theta's liquidation began in July 1992. The process was initiated by a government-controlled financial institution, the Pénzintézeti Központ, literally Center of Financial Institutions. The firm's former deputy director for technology and production was appointed official liquidator. The liquidation process was to last at least until the end of the first half of 1993. According to the calculations of the management, a work force of 300 could be maintained at the firm, which would be sufficient to fulfill the remaining contractual obligations in production with some operating profit and to carry out the liquidation.

PRODUCT MIX AND SALES PATTERN

Theta had two major product lines of strategic importance for the firm. One was nuclear instruments, the other was precision guidance instruments. Nuclear instruments had been made partly for regionally restricted military use, but others, such as computer tomographs (CTMs) were fully up to international standards and are widely used within the Hungarian medical equipment industry. These instruments are used basically for measuring radiation, and their importance had been great for the traditional markets for both segments of this product line.

The military and nonmilitary nuclear instruments used in the successor states of the former Soviet Union were mostly made by Theta; management's estimates put the firm's market share there as high as 80 percent. The lack of solvent demand was the only reason why Theta's Eastern sales of these medical instruments dropped so radically in the last years.

The sales of nuclear instruments totaled only HUF 60 million, less than one-tenth of the 1991 figure in the first half of 1992. Of these sales, 70 percent went to former CMEA countries, probably to Czechoslovakia or Poland, but nothing to the successor states of the Soviet Union. The sales of guidance instruments had decreased to HUF 70 million by the first half of 1992, and there were no exports at all.

Domestic sales of nuclear instruments suffered from the increasing financing problems of the national health care system. Theta proposed to pay off its relatively large social security tax liability by delivering the medical equipment to the state health care system. This idea was not accepted because the social security system needed cash in the first place, and its investment plans were strictly liquidity-linked.

Theta's nuclear instruments production was competitive at least in the technological sense. This was why an invitation-based tender was announced in December 1991 to Western industrial investors who might be interested in purchasing the firm's nuclear equipment plant. Because the firm continued to supply products to the Hungarian military, foreign participation in the planned joint venture could not have exceeded 49 percent, but in the end, there was no Western interest in the tender. Other potential investors showed up, but they apparently wanted to acquire Theta's marketing network in the former Soviet Union, and they had little interest in maintaining its production capacity.

The management estimated that there was a $3 million demand for Theta products in the CIS (Commonwealth of Independent States) in 1992, but customers lacked the foreign exchange to pay for imports. The best solution for a Western firm eager to sell in the CIS would be to combine its financial and production background with Theta's brand name and representation on the market, but, at the time of this report, this option was not welcome by Theta.

There were three causes of the dramatic drop in Theta's sales which together made up a fatal external shock to the firm: the collapse of the former Soviet market, the crisis of the Hungarian state health system, and the disappearance of most of the domestic market for military equipment.

While there was no serious chance of a change in the first two causes, the third one could offer some hope for the parts of the firm that survive liquidation. The management believed that international political events, including Yugoslavia's becoming an area of armed conflict and increasing tensions in other countries around Hungary, made the planned speed of Hungarian disarmament unrealistic for the time being. Therefore, part of the domestic weapons industry could eventually be rescued. Employment-linked factors could also have this effect.

The Hungarian government set up an Office of the Military Industry headed by a former state secretary of the Ministry of Industry and Trade in late 1991. Several major domestic manufacturers of military products hoped to be included in the group of firms benefiting from increasing purchases by the Hungarian Army. It was far from clear, however, who would provide the funds necessary for keeping alive part of the Hungarian military industry. Theta wanted to belong to this group of firms, but the State Property Agency (SPA) did not like the idea of selecting out the military part of a firm under liquidation. Theta's arguments in support of joining this group of defense firms were based on the very dramatic nature of the sales crisis of the firm: sales of nuclear instruments finally fell to one-eighth of the 1988 figure, many of the 350 employees were on forced vacation in May and June, and the plant was closed on Fridays. Even a government-sponsored rescue action could not solve this employment problem. If a state-owned nuclear military equipment factory were to be cut out from Theta, its employment could only reach half of the current figure, that is, 170 workers at most. The guidance instruments plant had made the first steps to ensure that it emerged from the crisis. An open tender was announced for its privatization in December 1991, and the tender document offered the whole plant for sale. Two bids were made, one by a Canadian investor, the other by a group of Theta employees, but ultimately these could not be evaluated because of Theta's bankruptcy. A similar effort was made to sell this plant by the liquidator approximately a year later.

THETA'S FINANCIAL SITUATION

Both the firm's demise after 1989 and its best year can be seen from a statistical table (Table 2) containing employment, output, and profit figures. The trends point toward collapse, and this table plus some additional information was the best proof of the inevitability of bankruptcy for the firm.

Figures for the first half of 1992 show the acceleration of negative trends. At the end of this period, the number of employees was down to 510, less than one-third of the 1988 figure, and the firm closed 1992 with 340 employees and gross output to HUF 140 million, almost one-third of the corresponding figure for 1991. The firm continued to be a loss-maker with an operating loss of HUF 66 million in 1990, HUF 92 million in 1991, and HUF 220 million in the first half of 1992 alone.

The firm's cost structure showed increasingly dramatic shifts toward a higher relative share of wage costs. This was initially the result of maintaining employment in a depressed sales situation, and of increasing outlays on lay-off bonuses thereafter. Further developments in Theta's cost structure during the first half of

1992 showed an acceleration of the trends reflecting the phasing out of production while continuing to pay wages and bank costs. The relative share of wages was as high as 48.0 percent and the share of bank costs rose to 13.2 percent. The relative weight of the costs of materials was down to 29.2 percent, a very unusual figure for a manufacturing firm. The figures pertaining to energy costs, depreciation, and other costs reached 3.7 percent, 3.6 percent, and 2.3 percent respectively. The development of the inventory situation at the firm also shows symptoms of agony. These can be seen first of all from the growth of the relative share of inventories of unsold output.

The share of output inventories rose further in the first half of 1992, and it already had reached 48.6 percent by the time liquidation began. Despite the obvious impression of sudden changes, the crisis did not strike unexpectedly at Theta. The first signs of cracks in the Soviet and domestic market based sales pattern were visible around 1984–85. The supply response then consisted of the purchase of a license for the production of high-tech CTM equipment from a U.S. firm.

Theta used the acquisition of this know-how to diversify toward the domestic medical equipment market, challenging the politically backed monopoly of the already defunct high-tech flagship firm MEDICOR in this field. This strategic choice proved correct as far as the deterioration of sales of military equipment and perspectives of exports to the Soviet market were concerned, but no one could foresee the crisis of the Hungarian state health care system. When crisis struck, Theta was not financially and technologically strong enough to respond with new products or to enter new markets.

Theta's management prepared a crisis management plan in 1989, when the firm still seemed to be in full health. The main goals of this plan were realized quickly. Product lines other than the two key ones were eliminated and divisions were organized around the two key product lines, nuclear and guidance instruments. The two divisions enjoyed full autonomy in technology management, production management, and marketing, but they were largely financially dependent on central management.

The problem of components production could not be resolved by management. Similar Western firms do not have component-producing capacities of a comparable size, but Theta had been forced to create such capacities due to import restrictions and the inadequate domestic supply of components. The clear separation of the component-making units from the manufacturing plants and from each other based on the division they served was still unresolved, although this problem was losing its importance because the firm was already selling off its manufacturing units as part of the liquidation.

The crisis-management strategy included the elimination of inefficient small plants outside of Budapest. Just as this part of the crisis-management plan began to be realized, privatization became a legal possibility for Theta. Therefore, the disposition of these little plants became part of the privatization strategy.

TRANSFORMATION AND PRIVATIZATION

Plans for Theta's privatization began in an original manner. The heir of the firm's prenationalization owner showed interest in acquiring the whole firm or part of it in some way. It was still far from clear in 1989 whether restitution would take place at all, and if so, whether it would be part of privatization, or whether there would be reprivatization as such. Therefore the contact with the heir of the former owner seemed to be a starting point for one possible way of privatizing the firm. When it became evident that this Western businessman was only interested in bringing back to the firm an old product line that had been discontinued twenty years earlier, management rejected this approach to privatization.

The government's first privatization program was under preparation in Hungary at that time. Theta had a good reputation as a solid profit-maker within the already-ailing engineering industry, and its contacts with the heir of its former owner also helped it to gain favorable coverage by the press. These may have been the main reasons why the SPA asked Theta to participate in this privatization program. The firm agreed, and, in January 1991, its privatization adviser became the Budapest-based Financial Research Ltd.

The privatization adviser designed a strategy that included many elements of the crisis-management strategy originally worked out by the firm in 1989. The first sequence of steps was the separation of the smaller plants from the central plant and their privatization. This should have been followed first by the transformation of the remaining one-plant Theta firm, and its privatization thereafter. As we already know, the only result of the process was that Theta became a one-plant firm.

Four smaller plants/units were sold in 1991 and early 1992. They were:

- The Sopron plant, with 50 employees, manufacturing geophysical instruments. It was sold to a Hungarian-Swiss joint venture mainly interested in the building. The production of geophysical instruments was discontinued, but 25 percent of the employees were retained by the new owner.
- The metal-cutting plant and foundry at Kisbér, which had served military production within Theta and therefore could not be privatized in one piece. The outcome of the privatization showed the determination of the management and the privatization adviser to carry out privatization: the plant was divided up finally and parceled out among six new owners. Three of the parts were sold on a combined MBO-ESOP basis to Theta employees, one went to a German firm, another was acquired by a Hungarian entrepreneur, and the on-the-job training unit became property of the local municipality.
- A small Budapest plant could easily be sold. The same thing happened to a part of the central plant that produced quartz crystals for the telecommuni-

cation industry. This unit was acquired by a group of Theta employees. They continued production within the central plant, renting the premises.

The four privatized units were operating at a loss; receipts from these sales covered only privatization costs such as severance payments to employees, debt, the adviser's fees, and so forth. Total receipts from privatization amounted to HUF 82.6 million, approximately 8 percent of sales in 1991, and HUF 35.4 million in the first half of 1992, approximately 20 percent of sales.[2]

Theta became a one-plant firm with a focused product profile as a result of these piecemeal privatization steps. By the time this part of the strategy was accomplished, however, Theta was in a deep sales and financial crisis. Its basically import-substituting product mix was uncompetitive imports,[3] and it was too undercapitalized to quickly create a new product mix based on the firm's undeniably high R&D capacity. Thus, Theta was in a bad situation as far its privatization prospects were concerned. Its capacity utilization rate was around 50 percent between 1988 and 1990, but fell to 38 percent in 1991 and to only 20 percent in the first half of 1992. This contrasted with the times when the firm was producing at full speed, with two shifts or more per day, to provide exports for the Soviet market.

Such underutilized capacity probably had a low privatization value as well, mainly because of the weak bargaining position of the current owners and the management, but liquidation could make the sale of the firm's assets necessary even at very low prices. The liquidator had offered the guidance mechanism line of business and half of the plant for sale. Receipts from this sale would help the liquidator move the nuclear instruments line to a smaller plant. The second half of the current plant and the nuclear production line at the new plant would be offered for sale thereafter.

This approach seemed to be feasible, but it depended critically on the price level obtained for these assets. Another problem was the partly military character of the nuclear products line, which would limit its sale to an investor who would accept the legal obligation of maintaining military production. The necessity for such a contractual obligation further depressed the privatization value of the firm's nuclear instruments line.

HUMAN RESOURCES, MANAGEMENT ISSUES, AND LABOR RELATIONS

There had been practically no investments at Theta during the last three or four years, which meant an accelerating depletion of fixed capital assets. The same thing had happened to human capital. While the total number of employees decreased by one-fifth between 1988 and the end of 1992, management and technical staff taken together dwindled by one-third.

The problem was that the firm's human capital base was skimmed off by a wave of desertion, and most of its best managers and technicians were already gone. They could capitalize on the good reputation of the firm for which they had worked, and most of them moved to better-paying jobs.

Theta's management emerged from within the firm in April 1990 when the former director general went into retirement after twenty-five years with the firm. The new, quite highly skilled and efficient management team had basically one task, that being crisis management. As a result of the firm's direct dependence on the Ministry of Industry and Trade, bonuses were determined basically by performance in facilitating bankruptcy and liquidation.

The labor relations situation at the firm was less complex than one would expect, given the disastrous employment situation. The firm had just one trade union, the traditional Trade Union of Ironworkers.

This trade union was a very efficient negotiator with the management in the weeks immediately preceding the beginning of liquidation. The trade union also benefited from the fact that the new legislation on industrial relations came into effect on the same day as liquidation began July 1, 1992. Therefore the trade union could negotiate the new collective bargaining agreement with the firm under liquidation on the basis of the old legal framework, most probably with the tacit agreement of the future liquidator. This agreement included substantial benefits for employees with a long record of service at the firm as well as for those to be dismissed. For example, the employees losing their jobs could be entitled to the equivalent of eighteen months salary, a more generous settlement than the six-month maximum set by the new labor legislation.

THETA'S FUTURE

The causes of Theta's crisis and collapse were summarized by a member of the management team in the following way. The Hungarian precision instruments industry was oversized and based on oversized firms. Both these problems resulted in inappropriate market and technology orientations of former Hungarian industrial policies. Theta was too large a firm for Western industrial investors. Its central building was located on downtown land much better suited for an office complex. The firm would eventually be dismembered, the result of liquidation, and perhaps reorganized in several smaller, assembly-oriented units located on low-cost pieces of land in the outskirts of Budapest. These small plants, or independent little firms, would hopefully be able to continue the high-tech-based Theta tradition.

Notes

1. For example, most Hungarian firms were given at least formal autonomy through the creation of self-management by means of enterprise management councils in the state

sector of the economy in 1985. As a weapons industry firm, Theta was exempted from this, and it remained under the direct control of the Ministry of Industry and Trade even in 1992.

2. One-third of the HUF 18 million price of the small Budapest plant had to be transferred to the SPA.

3. For example, the small electrical motors used for movie cameras cost HUF 800 (approx. $U.S.10) to manufacture, of which HUF 300 (U.S.$3.75) is the cost of imported inputs, and they sell for HUF 1400 on the domestic market. The same products cost only $6 (U.S.$17.50), inclusive of transport, duties, and taxes, if imported from Japan.

Table 1

Theta's Sales of Its Two Strategic Product Lines

	1988	1989	1990	1991
All sales of nuclear instruments (mil. HUF)	767	808	655	617
The share of exports (%)	83.4	83.2	80.8	86.5
Exports to (former) CMEA countries (%)	75.1	74.5	66.0	49.4
Exports to the (former) USSR (%)	49.4	50.1	42.3	36.5
All sales of guidance instruments (mil. HUF)	298	364	355	201
The share of exports (%)	2.4	0.8	0.3	3.5
Exports to (former) CMEA countries (%)	0	0	0	0

Note: Dollar–forint exchange rates, 1988: $U.S.1 = HUF50.424; 1989: $U.S.1 = HUF59.066; 1990: $U.S.1 = HUF64.147; 1991: $U.S.1 = HUF4.722.

Table 2

Theta's Employment Trends, Output, and Profits

	1988	1989	1990	1991
Employment (no. of persons)	1,660	1,540	1,314	964
Gross output (mil. HUF)	1,450	1,583	1,266	949
Gross profits (mil. HUF)	38	50	—	—
Net profits (mil. HUF)	28	39	—	—

Table 3

Theta's Cost Structure (in percentages)

	1988	1989	1990	1991
Total costs	100	100	100	100
of which:				
Costs of material	57.4	60.4	56.1	47.0
Wage costs	28.1	27.4	29.2	34.1
Energy costs	2.9	2.7	3.1	3.2
Banking costs (incl. interest)	6.2	5.3	5.6	8.3
Depreciation	2.9	2.7	2.7	2.8
Other costs	2.5	1.5	3.3	4.6

Table 4

Theta's Inventories (structure in percent)

	1988	1989	1990	1991
Purchased inventories of materials and parts	73.6	74.6	63.6	57.2
Inventories of output	26.4	25.4	36.4	42.8

3

Heavy Chemicals: TVK

An Island of Efficiency in a Depressed Region?

Miklós Szanyi

AN OVERVIEW OF THE INDUSTRY

Petrochemicals producing and processing firms are, strictly speaking, parts of the organic chemistry industry. TVK—Tiszai Vegyi Kombinát (Tisza Chemical Works)—was present in three of the subsectors of this industry: fertilizer manufacturing, the production of plastics and chemical fibers, and plastics processing. All three subsectors were dominated by several large firms in Hungary but none of the market segments was strongly competitive because of the oligopolistic and segmented structure of these markets.

There were twenty domestic fertilizer manufacturers in 1990, four of them with sales above HUF 5 billion, or $70 million; sixteen producers of plastics and chemical fibers, including two companies with sales above HUF 5 billion; and more than 300 plastics processing companies, but only one with more than HUF 5 billion in sales. TVK produced about 9 percent of the output of fertilizers, 38 percent of plastics and chemical fibers, and 25 percent of plastics in Hungary; therefore, it was one of the key firms on the Hungarian markets for these products.

A BRIEF HISTORY OF THE FIRM

The Tisza Chemical Works was the largest one-plant chemical factory in Europe. It was located in northeastern Hungary, the most crisis-ridden region of the country. The firm had exceptional standing within the Hungarian industry for several reasons. Traditionally, it had been a major exporter to the West; it had up-to-date technologies, and about 85 percent of its machinery and equipment was the best available on world markets; and it was one of the few Hungarian firms with a noticeable share of world output.

The value of its gross output of plastic products put this firm, for example, ninth among European ranking firms. It had 1 percent of the world sales of ethylene products, compared, for example, to Dow Chemical's 7 percent, and was seventh in output among ethylene-making firms.

The firm was founded in 1953 by a governmental decree. However, the government program focusing on the production of consumer goods at the expense of investments into heavy industry came into effect soon afterward, and the investment project was significantly delayed due to this program.

TVK's first plant, producing paints, did not become operational until 1961, and the fertilizer plant began production only in 1964. The firm became the basis of the Hungarian-Soviet petrochemicals agreement signed in the mid-1970s. As a result, it started specializing in the production of feed stock for the plastics industry and this remained the firm's main product line in the early 1990s.

The firm was supervised by the Ministry of Industry and Trade.[1] In December 1991, it became a company limited by shares but 100 percent owned by the state. This meant that legal transformation had taken place, but privatization still lay ahead. The firm's shares would be sold after the privatization strategy, to be developed jointly by the SPA and the firm's management, had been completed.

PRODUCT MIX AND SALES PATTERN

TVK's strategy attached great importance to upgrading its product mix by increasing the share of high-value-added products, improving quality, and enlarging the scope of products the firm could offer. This upgrading of the product mix was essential due to the changing market situation of the firm. Among the key changes it faced were the increasing importance of EC markets and the forced withdrawal from some domestic markets that played a key role in TVK's traditional output and sales.

There had been opposite trends in the firm's product mix in the last three years. Output of polyethylene (PE) and polypropylene (PP) materials and semifinished products increased almost to full capacity utilization or remained close to that level, while the production of fertilizers and manufactured plastics decreased to 70 percent and 45 percent below full capacity, respectively. This decline in production was the result of a major decline in demand.

These changes in the firm's markets stemmed from the following sources:

1. The quasi-collapse of a large part of Hungarian agriculture. This, together with the rapidly rising cost of ammoniac, made fertilizer production unprofitable at TVK, and, as a result, this product line was going to be phased out. Plastic bags used for packaging fertilizers would partially disappear from the product mix as well, together with plastic sheets used only in agriculture. The critical

situation of Hungarian agriculture was considered to be a symptom of a long-term sales and structural crisis for the firm by TVK's management. Therefore, more than 10 percent of TVK's employees were dismissed in 1991, and hundreds of others had to be retrained.

The magnitude of this first shock was evident from the fact that fertilizer sales accounted for 9–10 percent of TVK's sales during 1988–1990. Of the total output of fertilizers, 25 percent was exported. Petrochemicals and basic plastic materials had a 60–65 percent share in sales. Of petrochemicals, 40 percent was exported, as was 72 percent of plastics output. Manufactured plastics accounted for 20 percent of the firm's sales, and 15–20 percent of this output was exported. Altogether, 37–40 percent of TVK's sales went to foreign markets, but of this, only 2–3 went to CMEA countries.

2. A relatively small external shock was the disappearance of sales to CMEA markets in 1991, but the overall recession in the Hungarian economy had a much stronger impact on TVK. The share of domestic sales fell from 60 percent to 50 percent in 1991, and only 54 percent was expected for 1992. Restoring the domestic market's share to 60 percent was a strategic target for management, but this increase would need to consist of higher-value-added manufactured plastics.

3. In addition to declining demand, TVK faced competitive pressures from the many low-cost plastics products manufactured by small firms. These firms were small, but due to their low overhead, low labor costs, and easy-to-maintain equipment, their costs were also very low. Large firms like TVK could compete with them only by investing in equipment capable of producing small series. Moreover, TVK believed that its competitive edge lay in cost- and quality-efficient production.

This strategic approach proved basically correct, because a significant number of the firm's traditional Hungarian clients came back to TVK's products after having purchased imports from Eastern Europe.[2] But this strategy also implied an upmarket shift for most parts of the firm's product mix.

4. The dwindling of domestic sales was offset by a stronger export effort toward the West. The share of these markets in sales increased from a 32 to 37 percent range in the previous years to almost 50 percent in 1991. Volume increased in this case more than revenues due to depressed world market prices and increased transport costs.

The worldwide depression on petrochemicals and plastics markets strongly hurt TVK because it exposed one of its former strategic mistakes. The pre-1989 worldwide conjunction boom lured the firm into a major investment program in the second half of the 1980s. The objective of this investment was an upmarket shift in the structure of TVK's product mix, and as a result, polyethylene and the polypropylene-producing capacities were extended. Financing came from bank credits, whose interest rates substantially increased after 1989, and payments of principal and interest peaked in 1992. Moreover, the firm was a net creditor with respect to queuing, meaning that its resources were partly absorbed by its involuntary credits to its customers. These problems taken together made 1992 a critical year for TVK. The firm's survival was probably not at stake, but its prospects for privatization would be very strongly influenced by its performance in 1992.

5. Another element of uncertainty was the input situation. TVK's current product mix was determined largely by the specialization agreements concluded with the Soviet Union in the 1970s. The firm had been very dependent on Soviet deliveries of feed stock ever since. The instability of the supply of inputs from the East was exacerbated by the disappearance of the only domestic source of the fundamental input, because the Hungarian firm DKV (Danube Petroleum Company) stopped the production of industrial gasoline.

The solution to the input problems seemed to lie in both the technological and the trade fields. The technological solution involved the substitution of diesel fuel for gasoline wherever possible, and, to a much larger extent, trade-related measures involving inter-enterprise cooperation with former Soviet suppliers. The cooperation with refineries in the Ukraine seemed to be able to assure a significant part of TVK's long-term needs of inputs. Nevertheless, as a result, it could be necessary for the Hungarian firm to act as a sort of trading house because the Ukrainian side might wish to be paid not in cash from Hungary, but rather in the form of goods because the foreign-exchange-strapped Ukrainian government could always require that the refineries' hard-currency accounts be converted into domestic currency.

The firm's sales promotion strategy also included the creation of new sales channels. TVK had been negotiating with an American company, Columbian Chemicals, on the establishment of a small manufacturing joint venture, and it was continuously seeking to expand its international network of representative offices. The most recent was created in the Netherlands to sell TVK's geotextile products in the EC, and the next one, together with a storage facility, was to be opened in the Far East.

TVK'S FINANCIAL SITUATION

The firm's sales trends worsened in 1991, but this did not cause a sales crisis. The firm was profitable in 1991, despite the fact that its production costs increased faster than sales. The profitability situation had been worsening almost continuously due to rapidly increasing banking fees, even though TVK's credit rating was still good in the Hungarian banking community.

The firm's financial indicators, found in Table 2, showed a dramatic decrease in profits registered so far and expected for 1992. Gross profits were expected to be down by more than HUF 7 billion in 1992 as compared to 1989. One of the reasons was the convergence of trends in sales and costs, already visible in previous years. The development of the cost structure showed the firm's increasing sensitivity to the growth of costs of inputs.

A second factor of reduced profitability, indirectly indicated by the growing relative share of banking costs, was a sudden increase in TVK's short-term debt from 1990 on. The stock of such debt was HUF 0.2 billion in 1989, HUF 2.8 billion in 1990, and HUF 3.7 billion in 1991. This increase in debt resulted in large part from the decision to borrow to cover rising interest costs on short-term debt.

A third reason is that inventories grew by HUF 1 billion in 1990 alone as a result of sudden sales problems. They could not be reduced in 1991, although their increase was much smaller, only HUF 0.4 billion. The structure of inventories was stable.

HUMAN RESOURCES AND LABOR RELATIONS

The firm's first reaction to growing financial imbalance was a tough rationalization program. Employment was cut by 10 percent, from 6,907 to 6,229 in 1990, and further to 5,682 in 1991. The step-wise reduction of employment was a signal to employees as well as to the firm's environment that TVK was not passively accepting external challenges, and it would by no means become a firm that was incapable of adjusting to circumstances, even if external constraints became ever harder.

Labor relations did not suffer much from the management's strong effort toward an increasingly efficient use of human resources, not only because of a relatively good labor–management relationship with the trade unions, but also because of the institution of active job creation and retraining measures by the management in prospective fields of employment. Thus, seventy-seven skilled workers and college-trained employees started their careers at the firm in 1991, and close to 2,000 employees participated in several retraining programs. The firm spent about HUF 40 million, or $500 thousand, on higher education through different foundations and grants in 1991. Its expenditure on welfare and social projects was 4.5 times that much in the same year. Because it was the single large employer in the city of Tiszaújváros, its support of local social and infrastructural programs had a decisive importance for the development of the city, and this indirectly helped to maintain good labor relations climate at the firm.

Reduction of employment, the firm's more complex labor relations policy, the diversification of input sources, and a streamlining of TVK's product mix were, however, only tactical moves.

THE MAJOR STRATEGIC ISSUES:
TRANSFORMATION AND PRIVATIZATION

The management's restructuring concept, backed by the SPA, was based on the strategic role of the petrochemical technology chain for the firm, since this accounted for 75 percent of its output. This focus would need to remain intact, but all the other activities could be separated from it. This would need to be done at least to the extent of creating cost and profit centers, because management needs to have a consistent view of TVK's relative strengths and weaknesses.

This aspect of TVK's strategy was reinforced by privatization experiences of other Hungarian firms. Most foreign investors in Hungary did not wish to purchase huge plants as a whole but, rather, they were interested in buying only precise fields of activities. While it is conceivable that TVK's petrochemical complex could be cut into pieces, it was, by far, the technologically most integrated part of the plant. One investor might eventually be interested in the acquisition of a given part of the petrochemical complex, but then it would be increasingly difficult to sell the remaining elements to other investors. Moreover, serious industrial investors might become reluctant to participate in TVK's privatization if its petrochemical complex were taken apart and eventually distributed among competitors.

The creation of profit centers, including the firm's petrochemical complex as a whole, had already started in 1991. Other profit centers were the paint plant, the geotextiles plant and the plastics plant. These profit centers were supplied with auxiliary capacities such as marketing and maintenance. TVK's central administrative unit was in charge of the petrochemical complex plus all the other activities, such as wage-setting administration and human resources issues, where centralization clearly had a positive impact on cost efficiency.

Privatization was expected to bring new markets, a more rational corporate structure, but also an injection of capital to help TVK carry out its two ambitious investment projects. Both the markets and the injection of capital were needed technologically and would contribute to the much expected upmarket-oriented shift in TVK's product mix. Capacity utilization figures showed that the output of ethylene and propylene was approaching its upper limit. The increase in output of the polymerization plants would require more of these basic materials, which would eventually have to be imported. If the necessary increment were produced by TVK itself, two steps would be required. The first was upgrading existing capacities, but this would only be a short-range solution. The construction of a new petrochemical plant would be necessary in three or four years, but this could be financed only if foreign capital were available.

The second major investment project would help to diversify plastics production and increase TVK's competitiveness vis-à-vis small domestic producers. The target was a substantial increase of value added per physical unit of plastics produced, which would mean a shift in output in favor of manufactured plastics products.

Some parts of TVK had already been privatized as quasi-independent profit centers. The paint-producing plant was already a joint venture with a majority participation of AKZO Coatings of the Netherlands.[3] Another prospective partner was Columbian Chemicals of the United States, and TVK's packaging unit could become a joint venture with the Swedish firm, Ulrikehamns Bleck AB.

The major issue in privatization was, however, the outcome of TVK's efforts to find an appropriate foreign investor for its petrochemical complex. The firm's short-term financial problems were under control. Therefore, factors that would increase

TVK's privatization value in a few years, such as the relative increase in prices of plastics and the consolidation of markets in Hungary and in the region, should predominate. As a result, TVK was in no hurry to find investors for its largest unit. The firm's organizational chart would be not much different from the current one after the privatization of the petrochemical complex, and this structure was basically not open for discussion with the potential investors. The central administrative unit of the firm would not function as an empty-shell-type holding company, but instead, it would retain active management of the petrochemical complex. It would also keep some equity in TVK's other, smaller units that were already semi-independent profit centers and therefore open for privatization even by nonstrategic investors.

Notes

1. This role of the Ministry of Industry and Trade reflects a transitory legal situation in at least two respects. The assets of state firms awaiting privatization are managed by the SPA, but the sectoral ministry representing the owner, the state, exerts strategic control. The control is no longer directed in the case of firms functioning in a corporate structure. The ministry fulfills its strategic role through the company's board members, who are designated by the ministry.

This situation will change specifically with the privatization of each company concerned, and in general when the State Assets Management Corporation (SAMC) is set up. It is not clear yet, however, whether the SAMC will be responsible only for managing the assets of firms where the state wants to keep a long-term strategic equity stake, or also for those that are subject only to preliminary asset management by the state prior to their being turned over to private owners. There are also a few questions regarding the legal status of the SAMC, particularly whether it will be responsible to the Parliament, the SPA, or the government.

2. The share of TVK on the domestic market of polyethylene materials decreased from 100 percent only to 80 percent, and on the domestic market of manufactured plastics from 75 percent to approximately 55 percent after the liberalization of imports.

3. This joint venture was one of the very few firms on Hungarian soil that was accepted as a supplier by General Motors Hungary, an assembly plant producing 15,000 Opel Astra cars per year. TVK-AKZO supplied the auto manufacturing plant with all its inputs of high-tech, environment-friendly water-based body paint.

Table 1

TVK's Volume of Output by Main Product Groups (data in 1,000 tons)

Capacity	1988	1989	1990	1991
Ammonium nitrate (fertilizer)	519	424	151	550
Ethylene	264	234	254	270
Propylene	n.a.	115	127	135
PE (polyethylene) granulates	55	224	248	250
PP (polypropylene) granulates	158	155	150	170
Manufactured plastics	109	79	62	110

Table 2

TVK's Main Financial Indicators (data in HUF billion)

	1988	1989	1990	1991
Annual sales	26.5	32.1	33.3	36.1
Gross profit before tax	4.3	7.0	2.4	1.2
All taxes paid (incl. social security)	n.a.	n.a.	n.a.	n.a.
Profit taxes	1.5	3.6	0.8	0.3
Subsidies	0.0	0.0	0.0	0.0
Profit after tax	2.8	3.4	1.6	0.9

Notes:
Figures do not add up due to rounding and minor omissions.
Line 3 (taxes paid) does not include VAT-type taxes.
Dollar–forint exchange rates, 1988: U.S.$1 = HUF50.424; 1989: U.S.$1 = HUF59.066; 1990: U.S.$1 = HUF64.147; 1991: U.S.$1 = HUF.74.722

Table 3

TVK's Cost Structure (in percentages)

	1988	1989	1990	1991
Total costs	100	100	100	100
of which:				
Costs of material	58.4	60.6	54.3	69.0
Wage costs	7.7	8.7	7.6	8.0
Energy costs	11.1	10.4	11.1	*
Banking costs (incl. interest)	3.8	3.2	4.8	5.2
Depreciation	4.6	3.8	3.1	3.1
Other costs	14.4	13.1	18.9	14.7

*Included in the cost of materials.

Table 4

TVK's Inventories (structure in percentages)

	1988	1989	1990	1991
Purchased inventories of materials and parts	83.9	82.8	82.1	82.3
Inventories of output	16.1	17.2	17.9	17.7

4

Textiles/Garments: Elegant Charm

An Elegant Strategy for Expansion?

László Toth

AN OVERVIEW OF THE INDUSTRY

The Hungarian textile clothing industry had an annual output of about $300 million. Its share of the output of light industry was about 12 percent, and about 60 percent of its output was exported. There was a large number of firms on the domestic market, but they competed more with imports than with each other. There are two reasons for the low intensity of competition among Hungarian textile clothing producers: the first was their narrow specialization; the second was that few producers had direct access to the retail market, and, therefore, the retail firms mostly worked with their own network of suppliers.

A BRIEF HISTORY OF THE FIRM

The first predecessor of Elegant Charm was founded in 1930. It was a firm indirectly affiliated with the military. Its shareholders were army officers, and its 150 employees manufactured officers' uniforms. After its nationalization in 1948, the firm was renamed Uniforms Industry Enterprise. Besides the army, it also supplied the railways, the postal and customs services, and public transport firms with uniforms. The number of its employees grew to 2,000 by 1953. It was renamed First of May Clothing Factory in 1952, and, at the same time, it started growing through the absorption of smaller firms. It also completely changed its product mix in 1954–55, abandoning the production of uniforms in favor of civilian clothes. As a result of this change in output profile, the Ministry of Light Industry became its supervisory ministry.

The First of May factory became the largest producer on the Hungarian clothing market in the early 1980s when its share of the domestic output reached 25–30 percent. It sold only about 30 percent of its output in Hungary; a similar percentage of its production was exported to the Soviet Union; and the rest was sold on Western markets. This strong dependence on the Soviet market had already become a source of increasing problems by the mid-1980s.

A Swiss firm was asked to make a thorough audit, business analysis, and strategy assessment of the firm in 1986. The evaluation pointed to inadequate marketing, a deep gap between production and marketing capabilities, and a lack of cooperation and coordination between the two activities. Privatization was not an option for solving these problems at that time. Although these problems were of a strategic character, at the same time, the firm still seemed successful in its sales efforts and was financially sound; therefore, the analysis wrought no fundamental changes in the firm's operations and organization. First of May was still a profit-maker in 1985 and 1986, mainly due to its advantageous cooperation agreement with Levi Strauss. This agreement made it possible for First of May to make Levi's blue jeans in the firm's Marcali factory. Of this output, 60 percent was exported, and First of May could realize a large profit from domestic sales, because it was authorized to set domestic prices on the same level as competitive imports.[1]

Another part of First of May's product mix at that time was leather clothing. The high capital intensity of this product line was not yet a problem, because First of May's needs in terms of working capital could be financed by cheap credits. The sharp increase in interest rates from 1988 onward changed this situation significantly, because the refinancing of routine short-term credits used up an increasing part of the firm's profits. First of May went into the red in 1989.

A further strategic problem was the existence of wide gaps in technology among the different plants of the First of May conglomerate. In 1986, First of May still had ten plants around Hungary, but only some of them were able to produce for Western exports. Management had a predominantly technological orientation at that time, and did not understand the importance of modernizing the backward plants as part of a sound marketing strategy. As time passed, some of these plants became technologically obsolescent and financially a drain on the firm's resource.

The idea of getting rid of some parts of the First of May empire first surfaced in 1988. The idea was put forward by the then director general, who started thinking in terms of the viability of individual units of First of May versus the viability of the entire group. Privatization was not a legal possibility at that time, and, therefore, the splitting up the group began within a short period of time. One of the spin-off firms, Elegant Charm, was created as a company limited by shares in January 1990.

Elegant Charm's starting equity capital was very low, only HUF 15.7 million. This consisted of HUF 7.7 million in cash, with the rest consisting of equipment and inventories. There were initially five shareholders. The largest shareholder, the First of May factory, had only 48.9 percent of the shares. Moreover, the fact that First of May's contribution consisted of machinery and equipment, whose value was determined somewhat arbitrarily, led to subsequent problems. The other owners were the OTP Bank with 25.5 percent of the shares and several smaller firms with 25.6 percent combined. The structure of the firm's ownership had changed very little thus far. The only difference was that the equity stake of the three smaller firms now belonged to only one small private firm.

PRODUCT MIX AND SALES PATTERN 1 (CHALLENGES AND CONSTRAINTS)

Elegant Charm was a new firm. It had no exact predecessor because it inherited only part of the product mix and the markets of the First of May factory. Its output structure and access to markets depended on quite special factors that were linked to the circumstances in which Elegant Charm was created, to the firm's factor endowment, and to the typical problems of marketing encountered by any medium-size Hungarian light industry firm. The firm had a high probability of long-term viability in a very depressed sectoral environment, but it also had a multitude of external and internal challenges to which it had to react. These were closely linked to production and marketing, and they are assessed in this chapter as exogenous and endogenous factors.

Exogenous Factors

1. Since its creation, the firm had had to struggle with a lasting under-capitalization problem. It did not have access to First of May's traditional sources of credit because it was a much smaller firm that, therefore, could offer much less collateral than did its predecessor. Moreover, it had to operate in a much worse financial environment where conditions of creditworthiness were becoming stricter.[2]

The firm was suffering from a lack of normal credits from banks, from the absence of a domestic venture capital market, and from the difficulty of obtaining export credits. Its relationship with banks was loaded with tensions. In addition to its poor access to credits, it faced a situation in which, despite high banking fees, monetary transfers through banks were very slow. This was a risk factor, given the firm's shaky liquidity situation.

2. The firm faced a drastic manpower situation. Although it sounds odd, Elegant Charm would have been glad to employ 200 additional workers, but it was unable to do so. There were several reasons for this. The traditional training system for skilled workers had totally collapsed, because governmental funds for training were no longer available and apprentices were unable to finance their own training. Even if they could afford it, it would be a poor human-capital investment because of the low wages in the textile industry.

In fact, many skilled workers refused employment in this industry because unemployment benefits were only slightly less than after-tax wages in this sector. Very low wage levels were a consequence of the depressed profits in the industry. The poor profitability of even a relatively well-performing firm like Elegant Charm was linked to several factors by management, with high taxes at the top of their list.

3. The firm faced increasingly intense competition on its main export market segment, subcontracting. Subcontracting agreements with West European firms were now highly in demand in Bulgaria, Czechoslovakia, and even in Ukraine, whereas, in the past, most subcontracting agreements had been concluded with Hungarian, Polish, and some Yugoslav firms. Low-cost competitors were becoming a very serious challenge for the firm on its subcontracting-based export market as well as on the domestic market for finished products. The domestic clothing market had shrunk due to the fall in household consumption, causing a quasi-boom in sales of second-hand clothing, and this smaller market was attacked by imports owing to quick liberalization of the foreign trade regime.

Endogenous Factors

1. The exogenous undercapitalization problem was worsened by the adverse age structure and the poor condition of physical capital at the firm. Machinery and equipment received from the First of May factory were grossly overvalued; indeed, some of this equipment was thirty to forty years old, and it needed urgent replacement. Elegant Charm was insufficiently capitalized to do this.

2. The poor relationship between Elegant Charm and First of May was further complicated by their leasing agreement. The premises used by Elegant Charm were rented from its co-owner and the rent was very high—HUF 10 million, or approximately $120,000 per year—as compared to the building's HUF 200 million market value and the firm's HUF 15.7 million starting equity capital. The best option would be the purchase of the building, but the undercapitalization problem of the firm prevented this.

3. The structure of production capacities among themselves, and as compared to infrastructure, was very unbalanced. This was a result of the spin-off nature of the firm. For example, at the beginning, it lacked marketing and design units and the existing production capacities did not match one another. The elimination of these inherited bottlenecks would probably require significant investment, because the firm could not expect much help from First of May.

4. A very serious constraint on the firm's sales pattern was included in its founding document. Elegant Charm was not allowed to enter into any sort of business relationship with First of May's partners for the five years following its creation. It is true that First of May, in return, guaranteed a 120 percent utilization of Elegant Charm's capacities for the same period. The forfeit stipulated in the agreement was, however, very low, and it proved worthwhile for First of

May to use only a small part of Elegant Charm's capacities. Elegant Charm had to find new markets outside First of May's orbit in order to survive.

5. The firm's ownership structure had been only seemingly stable since its creation. In fact, all three small owners—a small trading house called Modex, an agricultural cooperative, and a small private firm—underwent major crises. Some were liquidated, others had to sell their shares in Elegant Charm, but their participation in strategic management was virtually nonexistent. By the time these shares were in the hands of a single owner, the First of May factory was in a critical situation. It was now in liquidation and Elegant Charm's strategic prospects were complicated by the uncertainty concerning the future ownership of the shares held by First of May.

PRODUCT MIX AND SALES PATTERN 2

The firm started its operations in a very difficult situation, but it was able to ease some of the constraints by appointing a very effective management team. This team correctly identified the major tasks to be fulfilled to assure the firm's long-term survival. Steps could be taken to eliminate or to ease endogenous constraints, while adjustment to exogenous ones required a high degree of strategic flexibility.

The first problem to be solved was the absorption of capacities left unused by the failure of First of May to utilize Elegant Charm's capacity. This was an especially hard task for the management of a firm lacking a marketing department. The solution was massive subcontracting and the resulting orders assured a 108 percent degree of nominal capacity utilization by 1990, and the number of the firm's clients rose to seven in that year, increasing to over twenty-five by mid-1992. This aggressive marketing strategy resulted in a curious situation: while the capacities of most clothing firms in Hungary are standing at least half idle, Elegant Charm struggles with bottlenecks in almost every part of its technology chain.[3]

The second strategic weakness, also due to the firm's weak foundations, was the lack of an independent design department. The gradual buildup of such a unit had made it possible for approximately 15 percent of the firm's sales to be made up of models of its own design. Of these, 90 percent went to the domestic market, but more of these upmarket products could be sold if more production capacity were available.

The success of aggressive marketing was shown by the upward trend in sales. The firm's sales totaled HUF 119 million in 1990, HUF 143 million in 1991, and already HUF 81 million in the first half of 1992. Domestic sales were HUF 20 million, 40 million, and approximately 25 million respectively.

The third major strategic response was a thorough restructuring of the firm's product mix. Several loss-making product lines, such as ready-to-wear leather clothing and fur products, were swiftly phased out and these capacities were converted to textile-sewing.

The change in product mix was based on a radical upmarket shift with a growing percentage of exclusive products. This shift had been taking place without any significant investment, thus helping the firm to improve quality. The first major investment would be completed only in the second half of 1992 when new ironing equipment was to be installed.

A further shift upmarket could be blocked by the lack of adequately skilled manpower. The firm's training program received no government support, and it had to be stopped. The lack of supply in this peculiar segment of the labor market was illustrated by the following: the firm registered with the Labor Exchange Office for hiring 200 people; it received only 18 names; and it could finally employ only 1.

The lack of new employees was aggravated by the fact that labor fluctuations were serious: 61 persons left the firm voluntarily in 1990, 108 in 1991, and 28 in the first half of 1992 as compared to total employment numbers for those years of 306, 297, and 292, respectively.

The serious employment tensions within the firm could be explained by the extremely low level of average wages for blue collars: HUF 12,000 per month before tax, only about 20 percent above the minimum wage, which meant roughly the minimum wage after taxes.

The firm's still rather low level of profitability and its permanent liquidity problems precluded any major strategic response to this challenge. Although average wages had been increased by 60 percent in nominal terms since the firm's creation, this failed to increase real wages. The danger of loss of manpower could be countered more through administrative reorganization: cutting inventories, creating a modern information network, and rationalizing logistics could eliminate a few jobs.

The management had some trouble in the field of labor relations, but not with the trade unions. About 60 percent of the employees were unionized, but the trade union played only a symbolic role. It could have exerted some influence on the collective bargaining agreement, but the firm had not signed such an agreement. The director general refused to sign the agreement because it stipulated that the trade union leader at the firm could have fifteen days of paid leave per year for retraining purposes. No agreement was subsequently reached on this point.

The trade union cooperated with the national headquarters of the MOSZ, or the Hungarian National Trade Union, with respect to wage increase claims, but this cooperation had not led to any conflict with management. The reason for the relatively good labor relations climate was that there had been wage increases on a regular basis. For instance, wages were raised twice in 1992, at a combined average rate of 29 percent. It was true, on the other hand, that management spent practically nothing on social benefits, such as kindergartens, support for vacations, or medical service at the plant. The only social benefit to workers was their free access to work clothes and soap.

THE FIRM'S FINANCIAL SITUATION

By 1991, the successful sales efforts had helped to consolidate the firm's finances. The amount of short-term payables declined from HUF 35.7 million in 1990 to HUF 21.8 million in 1991. Working capital loans decreased from HUF 14.6 million to HUF 6 million in the same time, but these signs of improving financial health did not compensate for the fact that costs had increased faster than sales, compressing profits from HUF 8.5 million in 1990 to HUF 3.2 million in 1991.

The main source of cost increases could not be identified due to the lack of clear trends in the table, but the rising share of materials and depreciation as a new item certainly played a role. The structure of inventories cannot be much analyzed either, because the firm had inventories of output, 35 percent of its total inventories, only in the first half of 1992.

The main factor behind problems in cost containment was undercapitalization: the firm was handicapped by its inability to take advantage of economies of scale. The increase in most elements of production costs was not accompanied by a corresponding elimination of bottlenecks, and the opportunity cost of investment needed to make them disappear was growing rapidly.

HUMAN CAPITAL AND MANAGEMENT

The quality of management was unusually high at the firm. This fact made the contrast between well-educated and performing white collars on the one hand and underskilled and underpaid blue collars on the other even more striking. The top management team consisted of four persons. The director general was seconded by a technical director, an economic director, and a financial director. The team was the same as the one with which Elegant Charm started in January 1990. Three of them had college degrees in their respective fields, and everyone on the team had at least ten years, and in two cases, more than twenty-five years, of professional experience. Two persons had worked within First of May while the other two came from competitors to help launch the new firm in 1990.

The professional record of the director general was impressive. She had been the head of the trade and cooperation department at First of May before she was given the task of transforming the firm's plant at Komló into a joint stock company. Although she had not agreed with the strategy of splitting up the First of May's Budapest plant into several smaller units, including Elegant Charm, she became a CEO who was very loyal to her new firm, even in its conflicts with First of May.

The bonus system of the top management system was a mixed one, but it proved successful in its two-and-a-half years of functioning. The director general, the technical director, and the financial director received a predetermined share of the firm's annual profit as their bonus, while the economic director had a task-linked bonus system whereby each task had its bonus counterpart expressed in a percentage of the annual salary.

STRATEGIC CHOICES FOR ELEGANT CHARM

The set of strategic objectives of the firm had undergone a significant transformation since 1990. The major tasks in the first eighteen months were avoiding financial collapse and fixing the damage caused by the legal shortcomings of the founding document. The basic strategic goal in the current period was maintaining continuous growth and reaching a match between order books and the firm's productive capacities. This meant an investment-oriented financial strategy with less emphasis on increasing labor outlays. A possible solution to the firm's labor shortage could be the hiring of large numbers of low-cost Ukrainian workers if the approval of the authorities could be obtained. The emphasis on investment could result in a more extensive domestic subcontracting system combined with leasing of new equipment.

A special part of the strategy mix was privatization. Privatization in this particular case meant the buyout of the firm's shares from their state-owned owners. The management did not envisage finding a majority owner from abroad because it feared a loss of existing channels to markets. It wanted to have some influence on who would purchase the shares that belonged to First of May.

A favorable outcome would be if the shares owned by First of May could be acquired by Elegant Charm. This HUF 7.7 million (about $90 thousand) worth of shares was now for sale. Elegant Charm's management thought the shares would be available at 75 percent of their face value. Half of these shares could be acquired by Elegant Charm's management, and the other half by the firm's employees. This solution would depend on the willingness of the employees to participate, since most of the sales price would have to be paid in cash because entrepreneurial loans would be too time-consuming and a leasing-based acquisition deal too expensive. Moreover, the management also started negotiations for the acquisition of the firm's shares now owned by OTP Bank.

Several privatization or takeover deals could eventually be subject to discussion, but only after First of May's future was made clear. A positive outcome of the crisis of the ailing First of May could also be helpful to Elegant Charm because it could eventually become the owner of the premises it was using. Elegant Charm already had an interest in purchasing the Dorog plant from First of May. Although no final decision had been reached yet on these possibilities, the management had begun modernizing the plant now operated by Elegant Charm by leasing new equipment.

The management thought it was urgent to build up the marketing and trade department of the firm because they currently sold through trading houses, which added 4–5 percent to their final sales prices.

The main strategic problem to be solved was to develop and produce models of the firm's own design on Western markets. This would require an injection of capital, but institutionalized access to Western markets with the firm's own brand products would be the real key to Elegant Charm's long-term survival and expansion.

Notes

1. A fundamental assumption of the so-called import-following or import-emulating pricing system in existence during most of the 1980s was that domestic products identical to imported or importable ones could be priced as if they were sold on the world market. This assumption was not based on a deep knowledge of standard economic theory. First, the existence of a monolithic and fully competitive, one product–one price type world market is no more than a working assumption. Second, if products a and b are identical, but they are offered by the different producers A and B, the sales prices of products a and b depend on (1) the degree to which the segment of the world market is competitive where they are sold, and (2) the relative strength of the price-setting position of producers A and B on the world market. A good example for factor 2 was the difference between Levi's and First of May as price-setters on the world market.

2. This was due to three reasons: the accumulation of bad receivables (assets) of banks and the wave of bankruptcies in 1992; high real interest rates; and the crisis of three smaller Hungarian commercial banks in June 1992 and the danger of the collapse of at least three others. The first and last reasons directly, and the second, indirectly, combined with a huge budget deficit, made the treasury bonds and other state-issued securities market by far the most lucrative field of investment for banks.

3. An instructive fact shedding some light on differences between old and new style marketing attitudes can be mentioned here. Although Elegant Charm's access to markets was restricted by the agreement with First of May that prohibited business with the partners of the bigger firm, one client of First of May became interested in cooperating with Elegant Charm. When it learned of the legal constraint, it simply broke its relationship with First of May and took that business to the smaller company.

Table 1
Elegant Charm's Cost Structure (in percentages)

	1990	1991	1992
Total costs	100	100	100
of which:			
Costs of material	13	21	19
Wage costs	39	31	35
Energy costs	7	6	7
Banking costs (incl. interest)	3	3	2
Depreciation	—	—	5
Other costs	38	39	33

5

Textiles/Cloth: Hungartextile Holding

The Fate of a Textile Giant: Nothing More Than a Small Office?

Márta Kiefer

A SECTORAL OVERVIEW

The most recent complete figures available for the Hungarian textile industry at the time this case was written were those from 1990. The industry's share of gross industrial output was 3.7 percent; it had 6.1 percent of total industrial employment and 3.0 percent of the gross capital stock of Hungarian industry. These figures have declined somewhat since 1990, but they nevertheless reveal the highly labor-intensive nature of the industry. Figures from 1991 are not entirely comparable with previous years as a result of the major structural and organizational changes within the industry, changes that are clearly illustrated by this case study.

The Hungarian textile sector was a $1 billion industry that exported 25 percent of its output. It had about 70,000 employees and was a very segmented sector, comprised of many small and medium-sized firms with plants scattered across the country with rather limited product mixes. Therefore, the multi-participant nature of the market did not imply that the market was highly competitive.

A BRIEF HISTORY OF THE FIRM

Hungartextile Pamutnyomóipari Vállalat (Hungartextile PNYV, or Hungartextile Cotton Print Enterprise), was founded in 1963.[1] It was the result of a merger with Goldberger Textile Works, a firm that had been on the Hungarian market for more than 200 years, and several other textile factories. This combination made the resulting enterprise the largest cotton textiles firm in Hungary, and it remained the market leader for decades. In 1988, it had a 30 percent share of the output of the Hungarian cotton textile industry.

The firm was a traditional manufacturer of cotton goods such as yard, thread, raw, and finished cotton or cotton-type print, but, more recently, the firm had begun to manufacture clothing and knitted fabrics as well. Hungartextile PNYV's plants became independent subsidiaries in June 1989, on the basis of the 1988 Act on Economic Associations. The former central-administrative unit of the enterprise became a holding company called Hungartextile PNYV Holding. It functioned as an asset management center, managing assets that were operated by the subsidiaries. The objective of this spontaneous transformation, according to the management, was to make the former plants independent and to establish direct links between producers and the market.[2] The main elements of the group's manufacturing structure were the large traditional producers such as Goldberger Textile Works Ltd. and Secotex Textile Dyeing Ltd.

The legal founder of Hungartextile as a state enterprise, whose legal successor was the holding company, was the Ministry of Light Industry, one of the predecessors of the current Ministry of Industry and Trade. The Ministry of Industry and Trade exercised the founder's rights as a representative of the Hungarian state. The legal status of the holding was changed in March 1992 from a self-administered enterprise to one supervised by the government. The main motive behind this change was to accelerate the privatization of the holding and its subsidiaries. Government supervision was being exerted by the State Property Agency, which also exercised the increasingly more nominal rights of the founder. More than 90 percent of the assets of Hungartextile Holding were operated by its subsidiaries.

THE STRUCTURE OF THE HUNGARTEXTILE GROUP

The group was organized as a holding company with two branches, one for manufacturing and one for services. The manufacturing branch had five subsidiaries and the service branch had four. The subsidiaries were as follows, with the property share of the holding shown in parentheses:

Manufacturing subsidiaries
  Hungartextile Goldberger Ltd. (99.8 percent),
  Hungartextile Secotex Ltd. (80.2 percent; the other owners were banks, trading houses and individuals),
  Hungartextile Cotton Industry Ltd., Sopron (98.6 percent),
  Dunamarket Ltd. (a subsidiary of the more than 90 percent Hungartextile-owned Hungartextile Utex Ltd., currently in liquidation),
  Dunavecse Clothing Ltd. (46 percent, the majority owner being Margareta Ltd.; see below).

Trading subsidiaries
Margareta Trading Ltd. (90 percent; other owners were Hungarian enterprises and a foreign firm),
Dunaker Ltd. (98 percent),
Goldker Ltd. (87.3 percent; the other owners were individuals),
Goldtex Ltd. (90.3 percent; the other owners were individuals).

The government believed that the holding should assist with the privatization of the subsidiaries, transfer the state assets managed by it to the new firms operated in corporate forms, and cease to exist if the privatization of the whole group were accomplished.

The holding itself was a small firm with a staff of twenty-nine and a transitional structure. This meant that the holding's structure did not include the departments such as logistics, production management, marketing, and so on that are found in a normal manufacturing firm. Rather it had the relatively large organizational units needed for the privatization of the group, for example, the legal and accounting departments.

THE STRATEGIC PRIORITY OF THE HOLDING: PRIVATIZATION

Privatization of the group could follow one of three strategies: the group as a whole could be purchased by one investor; some portion of the subsidiaries could be purchased by one investor and thus probably remain as an individual firm; the individual subsidiaries could be sold to various investors.

The holding company had already taken some steps toward privatization, but all of these steps included the possibility of any of these three strategies and thus choices were still open. The preparatory steps taken so far included the auditing of the holding and its subsidiaries; asset valuation of the holding and the subsidiaries, which would be subject to revision every quarter or so; the implementation of the privatization strategy; and the initial identification of possible investors.[3]

The auditing and asset valuation were performed by Portfolio Bank Ltd. and the auditing was completed by Europe 92 Ltd. of Germany, which is part of the Coopers Lybrand network. The latter was given the task of seeking investors on a success-fee basis, a role undertaken by Portfolio Bank Ltd. and AGIC Treuhand Ltd. Potential investors included foreign companies, the management of the holding and the subsidiaries, as well as the group's employees. Hungarian firms might eventually also participate in the process, but this was unlikely at the moment.

Because privatization was proceeding only at Margareta Ltd., the future capital structure of the firm could not yet be visualized. As a matter of fact, the group's privatization strategy had no precise timetable and major steps were expected only in 1993. This delay was due not only to the uncertainty of potential investors, but also to the vagueness of some parts of the legal framework for privatization.

The firm's privatization strategy had to be implemented with respect to a number of constraints. The combined book value of the group's assets was HUF 7.2 billion, or approximately $90 million, excluding real estate. Most land used by the group was the property of the Hungarian state and was leased by the holding or by the subsidiaries. Although the textile industry was generally known as a labor-intensive sector, most production at the Hungartextile plants— e.g., spinning, weaving, and finishing—was actually rather capital-intensive. Privatization, which would provide a substantial injection of capital, was therefore a priority for most subsidiaries. Furthermore, because the textile industry was viewed as a depressed sector in most European countries, Hungartextile affiliates were unlikely to become highly rated investment targets.

A management buyout or ESOP-type privatization would probably not be a major consideration in the Hungartextile privatization. This was due partly to the lack of a transparent legal framework for privatization and partly to the lack of savings and appropriate credit facilities for such investment by Hungartextile employees. After all, the textile industry had the lowest wage level in Hungarian manufacturing. There was also a lack of confidence in the future on the part of most Hungartextile companies. While a successful privatization could mean entry to new markets, many investors were attracted only by existing market shares. One goal of new owners would have to be to raise capacity utilization, possibly by increasing the current level of combined output of the group to about 40–45 percent of the output in the peak year, 1988.[4] This level of output would be necessary to maintain a normal rate of capacity utilization; however, more output could not be sold in Hungary competitively. The currently available capacity, therefore, would have to be reduced, mostly by subleasing the plants or by selling land.

THE FINANCIAL SITUATION OF THE HOLDING

Since the transformation of the Hungartextile firm into a holding-based group, the financial situation of the holding company had been deteriorating. A comparison between 1989 and 1990 is difficult because figures for 1989 still show the monolithic state enterprise, Hungartextile, while data after that are only for the holding, as shown in Table 1.

Table 1 shows a relatively smaller decrease in assets, investments, and overhead plus other expenditures. This means the holding company was partly an asset management firm, but most of the group's assets were on its books.

The efficiency and the performance of the holding company could be estimated only by starting with the expected yield of its assets, but this would depend on the development of the manufacturing parts of the group. The book value of the holding's portfolio increased in 1991, but its sales fell.

While the 1990 sales roughly equaled the holding's costs, so that, theoretically, the yield on the assets managed by it could have been close to zero, its 1991 costs were nearly 90 percent higher than its sales. These sharply increasing costs were due mainly to an 85 percent increase in direct costs and to a more than 30 percent increase in costs of administration, management, and sales. Wage costs, on the other hand, increased much less than the CPI in 1991, and even banking costs decreased in nominal terms.

This strange development in the firm's cost structure was mainly the result of the one-sided nature the firm acquired after the creation of the holding. While it had to perform many administrative functions and assume some others from the subsidiaries, the costs of these functions could only be covered by income generated through asset management. This scheme did not work because most subsidiaries quickly became loss-makers themselves.

The sudden increase in costs meant that the profitability of the holding company had to be much higher in 1991 than it was in 1990 in order to break even and thus avoid decreases in assets. Even this would have meant only an approximately 8 percent return on assets, much below normal interest rates. In fact, the holding's operating loss in 1991 was HUF 12.6 million, which reflected the poor performance of the group as a whole.

While sales of the group reached HUF 8.803 billion in 1990, only 70.7 percent of this, or HUF 6.226 billion, was realized in 1991, with an employment level of 3,977 or more. The decline in sales was due first of all to falling demand on the domestic market. Exports fell less than total sales despite the fact that practically no export revenue was earned on former CMEA markets in 1991. Exports decreased from HUF 1.711 billion to HUF 1.611 billion between 1990 and 1991, a 5.8 percent drop, while the share of the former CMEA markets dropped from 42.5 percent of exports to zero.

The development of inventories was proof enough that the transformation of the former state firm into a holding company brought about significant changes in its functions as a firm. Although we usually refer to the holding-based group as the successor of the state enterprise, Hungartextile, the legal successor is *stricto sensu* the holding company only. It lost most, and then all, of its production but kept part of its predecessor's purchasing and sales functions. For this reason, inventories from its own production decreased much more radically than purchased inventories.

The value of inventories of its own production was still HUF 144.1 million, or approximately $2 million, when the holding was created in June 1989, but most of this was transferred to the subsidiaries. Therefore, the value of inventories from its own production reached only HUF 15 million at the end of both 1989 and 1990, and decreased to zero by the end of 1991. Purchased inventories had a value of HUF 360.1 million, or approximately $5 million, in June 1989. This decreased to HUF 3.7 million by the end of the same year, but it grew to HUF 140.6 million by the end of 1990 and still reached HUF 90.7 million in December 1991.

One positive conclusion can be drawn from the recent sales trends. The group was successful in shifting exports from East to West European markets, which meant that it had the potential to increase competitiveness. This was at least partly due to technological factors.

THE TECHNOLOGY BASE

The result of the discouraging financial performance of recent years was an almost total lack of investment in technology. The last significant investment project was carried out during 1989–90, and it helped the group to move upmarket. The group spent HUF 1,350 million on fixed investment in each of those years and another HUF 117 million on leased equipment in 1989. Its only investment expenditure in 1991 was HUF 26 million for leasing. The new production capabilities made it possible to include higher-value-added products such as batiste, satin, and balloon-cloth in the product mix of the group.

This investment, however, increased the differences in efficiency and the average age of equipment among the elements of the technology chain and created more technological bottlenecks. The complete technology chain of the group consisted of three main stages: spinning, weaving, and finishing. The first two stages had four phases each, the third had two, with a combined total of ten elements in the chain. The share of equipment less than ten years old was 95 percent in phase 7, or between 60 and 80 percent in phases 1 and 10; in the 50–70 percent range in phases 4, 5, 6, 8, and 9; and 30–50 percent in phases 2 and 3. Therefore, it can be seen that major technological bottlenecks would occur almost immediately after the beginning of the production process, while the technology level of the middle elements of the chain was remarkably balanced. The weaving stage had the greatest need for major investment. The assessment of the management was that about 60–70 percent of the technology chain was more or less up-to-date, even by West European standards. But the criteria applied to the product mix produced an estimate of only 50 percent. This was unacceptable because the group now had to sell most of its output on highly competitive markets. Although the product mix could clearly be improved if fresh capital were injected, the group itself was unable to generate such funds.

HUMAN RESOURCES, LABOR RELATIONS, AND MANAGEMENT

As the level of employment within the group decreased, the problem of human resources became less significant. Although lay offs per se may or may not have been a good method of crisis management, part of this group, as well as the Hungarian textile sector as a whole, was faced with both a declining industry and problems of undercapitalization, low skill levels, and disappearing markets.

This unambiguous trend might be one reason why trade unions did not strongly resist the on-going attrition in the group. The other reason was linked to the crisis within the trade unions themselves. In Hungarian manufacturing firms with a more or less stable future, there were two types of trade unions: the usually well-organized and financially stable successor of the former, so-called official, communist-dominated trade unions, and the newly emerging trade unions, which were usually smaller and rather uncooperative among themselves, not to mention with the other trade union type. The management had to negotiate with both types. In the case of shrinking firms such as Hungartextile, trade unions were relatively inactive. For example, the Hungartextile group had only a few scattered remnants of the old trade unions, and no new ones. The firm's management clearly had no interest in cooperating with these weak trade unionists during the holding's transformation and privatization, and it was not forced to do so.

The professional competence of managers employed at different subsidiaries of the holding was assessed in two ways, both of which gave a surprisingly favorable picture of the management's quality. The average level of training of managers in the group should have been at 75–80 percent of European standards, whereas their ability and motivation would lie 40–45 percent below European levels. More or less the same was true for the quality of employees in general, but the textile sector was normally one of the least skilled labor-intensive industries worldwide. The approximately 30 percent decrease in employment during 1990–91 and an additional 20 percent or more decrease in the second half of 1992 seemed to have improved the picture to a certain extent.

Although we do not have sufficient information to doubt the competence of the management, our knowledge of Hungarian industry in general makes us a bit skeptical as to the value of these estimates. The experience of the second half of 1992 seemed to confirm this skepticism. The State Property Agency's increasing role in the firm's crisis management resulted in an almost total replacement of the upper and middle levels of management.

The management was structured in two ways within the group. The management of the holding was very much like a traditional Hungarian state enterprise, the only difference being that the director general was formally delegated by and represented the government. Before mid-1992, he reported directly to the Ministry of Industry and Trade, but this role was assumed by the SPA thereafter.

The subsidiaries of the holding functioned in a corporate structure. The interests of the holding as a partial owner and/or an asset manager were represented by board members delegated by the holding. These representatives had a voting majority in all the firms where the holding was the majority owner, which, in practice, meant that the strategy of all such subsidiaries was determined by the holding. The strategic role of the holding within the group was to be gradually transferred to the new owners of the subsidiaries as privatization progressed.

Notes

1. The firm that is the subject of this study was only a holding company. Therefore, it did not have plants as such in the traditional sense of the word. Its only location was the former central-administrative building of the now nonexistent Hungartextile state enterprise. The subsidiaries of the holding were located at different plants across the country and these will be presented when the structure of the group is described.
2. We can add another argument. Our experience with other transformations of state firms into holding-based groups taught us that one of the basic objectives of such transformations was usually the elimination of direct state control over the subsidiaries. The state-owned assets of these affiliates are thereafter managed by the holding company, which remains the only traditional-type state-owned firm in the group.
3. The expression currently used for auditing in Hungary is "X-raying." This means more than normal auditing because it includes the conversion of the company's books to Western bookkeeping standards. Moreover, it has a negative connotation in some cases. It could also mean pointing out details of extreme interest for any would-be investor, such as dubious assets or invisible liabilities, i.e., costs of eliminating environmental damage caused by the firm, financial responsibilities toward employees, etc.
4. The total Hungarian output of cotton and cotton-type yard decreased by 57.5 percent between 1988 and 1991, and its 1991 level was approximately equal to Hungartextile's output of this product in 1988. The group suffered an even more significant setback in production, but an accurate comparison is impossible due to the firm's subsequent transformation. The firm's output decreased by approximately 60 percent in this period, one-third of which was due to the collapse of sales to East European markets, another one-third to the decline in domestic demand, and the remaining part to the very fast liberalization of Hungarian textile imports.

Table 1
Basic Financial Data for Hungartextile Holding

	1989	1990	1991
Sales (VAT not included)	3,752.7	226.4	146.8
Direct costs	2,530.5	21.9	38.7
Wage costs	563.6	14.6	15.9
Depreciation	112.3	23.5	21.9
Overhead	789.2	61.5	89.7
Other expenditures	180.3	93.7	94.8
Long-term debt service	344.5	7.5	7.5
Own assets	3,282.7	2,769.6	2,795.7
Investment	2,653.5	2,218.6	2,541.5

Notes:
The columns for 1990 and 1991 are related to the holding only. This explains the sudden drop in figures compared to the year before (the holding was created in June 1989).

Dollar–forint exchange rates, 1988: U.S.$1 = HUF50.424; 1989: U.S.$1 = HUF59.066; 1990: U.S.$1 = HUF64.147; 1991: U.S.$1 = HUF74.722.

6

Electronics: Radion Radio and Electrical Works

A Whiz-Kid Grown Old?

Gábor Hoványi

A SECTORAL ASSESSMENT

Radion, whose two main product groups were televisions and microwave equipment, was a major participant in the Hungarian telecommunications equipment and consumer electronics industry. This industrial sector was in dire straits because of the collapse of the CMEA markets and the profound impact of the liberalization of imports. In 1992, the industry had sales of $200 million, reflecting a drop in sales volume of more than 40 percent since 1988.

The domestic television market had been duopolistic until 1986 when ITT Nokia set up a small assembly plant in the country. Even so, Radion retained a solid 30–35 percent market share and its rival, Videoton, had approximately 60 percent. The rest belonged to ITT Nokia and a few downmarket brands imported from the USSR, East Germany, and China. This market structure was drastically affected by import liberalization, with the result that Radion's market share fell below 10 percent.

The microwave equipment market was much less competitive due to the strongly consumer-oriented nature of these products. Although several other Hungarian telecom firms offered such products, most did not compete directly with Radion, but rather served other clients requiring different technical specifications.

THE HISTORY OF THE FIRM

The original firm was founded in Budapest in 1913 by a Viennese entrepreneur, and it soon became a leading high-tech firm of its time. Production of radio receivers began in 1926, with daily output reaching 50 units in 1930, and a wide range of export markets, including Germany, Sweden, Switzerland, Norway, Finland, and Poland, was developed. The firm had an internationally registered trademark and employed 600 people.

Annual output reached 50–60 thousand units in the 1940s, with 25–30 percent of output exported. Because rapid technological development and market expansion enabled the firm to withstand the 1948 nationalization, output rose to 116,000 units in 1951 and 257,000 in 1954. The AR 306 receiver was awarded a gold medal at the 1958 Brussels Expo.

In 1963, however, the firm ceased production of radio receivers. This was due to a specialization agreement among CMEA countries, which stipulated that radios would become a wholly Bulgarian industry. Radion then concentrated on the assembly of televisions, the manufacture of which resulted from R&D begun at the firm in 1955.

Output showed dynamic growth in the 1960s and 1970s, with 25 to 40 percent exported. Because this rapid expansion required new capacity, the firm acquired new plants within the country that provided diverse components, electrical accessories, and wooden frames.

Radion's products achieved a good international reputation in those years because of their high quality and technical standards. To move farther upmarket, the firm had to acquire color television manufacturing technology, which was accomplished in 1975 through a licensing agreement with SEL of Germany. The first license-based series was followed by proprietary designs equipped with 32, 56, and 67 cm tubes. Exports of these products totaled almost 200,000 units during the next fifteen years. Finally, in 1988, Radion's R&D staff started to develop digital color televisions.

The firm's other important product line, microwave telecom equipment, mostly consisted of wholesale electronics products that were sold on CMEA markets. In 1988, the value of this output was equal to 25 percent of the firm's television production.

Radion expanded almost continuously until the late 1980s. This trend required a restructuring of management and reorganization of the firm, which brought about the transformation of the firm into a division-based group of quasi-independent subsidiaries, each with its own accounting system. This divisional structure, based on self-accounting, was designed to help Radion cut costs, accelerate decision-making, and smooth the adjustment of each divisional unit to different markets.

MARKET STRUCTURE AND PERFORMANCE

Market trends took a drastic turn for the worse in the late 1980s and, as a result, Radion was forced to declare bankruptcy in 1991. Liquidation began in 1992. Sales developments showed how rapidly Radion's markets collapsed.

Table 1 takes 1988 as the first year. Three sales trends created the impression of distributed lags, but in fact, the points of inflexion of these trends followed one another from 1989.

During 1990, domestic sales collapsed by 50 percent; exports fell by more than 90 percent in just two years; and sales trends were closely followed by output. These figures are presented by main product lines in Table 2. In any event, the production of black-and-white televisions would have been sharply reduced. Production had already been halted in the mid-1980s by Radion's main domestic competitor, Videoton. Black-and-white televisions could be marketed only as second sets to below-average income households or in some East European markets, and this demand fell steadily in the second half of the 1980s. In a normal market environment, this decline in demand would have been offset by increasing buyer interest in color televisions, but this was not the case for either Radion's products or Videoton's, especially after 1989. The main reasons for this were a decline in Hungarian living standards and widespread liberalization of imports.

The three product lines did not suffer equally from the crisis: the ratio of their output values in 1988 was 20 (B&W TVs) : 66 (C TVs) : 14 (MW eqpt), and the ratio in 1991 was 9:82:9. This meant the firm's survival depended increasingly on the sales prospects of color televisions.

The decline in output was followed by a fall in capacity utilization. The management gave the following estimates, where full capacity utilization = 100 percent: 78 percent in 1988; 80 percent in 1989; 67 in percent 1990; 42 percent in 1991. This trend shows a temporary peak in utilization in 1989, but this did not prove decisive. Moreover, this peak could be correctly assessed only if profitability figures were known in appropriate detail and if capacity utilization rates could be linked to shifts in the firm's sales pattern. Although such analyses are not available, management's analysis of the firm's woes could be taken as indirect proof of a link between changes in market patterns and overall firm performance. The management cited three external shocks as having a profound influence: the liberalization of imports, the collapse of sales to the Soviet Union, and no redirection of exports to OECD markets.

The liberalization of imports had a sweeping impact on the domestic market for consumer electronics goods. Upmarket products from Western Europe and the Far East, as well as attractive and inexpensive products at the lower end of the market, flowed into Hungary. The real appreciation of the Hungarian currency enhanced the impact of import liberalization. Thus, Radion suddenly found itself in a highly competitive market with household demand shrinking due to an overall slump in economic activity that was estimated at 25–30 percent. Although the firm sold products in the same quality range as foreign competitors, the competitors' prices were lower and, therefore, Radion lost much of its market share.

Radion's biggest export market, the Soviet Union, collapsed within weeks.

This loss had a catastrophic impact on exports of televisions, but sales of microwave telecom equipment suffered even more. CMEA countries took 58, 83, and 87 percent of the firm's exports in 1988, 1989, and 1990 respectively, but there were almost no exports to these countries in 1991. Moreover, the firm proved unable to redirect exports to OECD markets. According to the management, the main reasons for this were a saturation of the television markets in Western Europe and the ongoing economic recession in the West.

These arguments are basically valid, but we think at least one detail can be added to the picture. The firm's share of exports to the CMEA countries increased from 58 percent to 87 percent in the brief period of 1988–90, that is, prior to the collapse of the CMEA. This meant that Radion's products were already losing ground in Western markets.

RADION'S FINANCIAL SITUATION

The changes to Radion's cost structure are shown in Table 3. The costs of materials followed roughly the same lines as output and sales until 1990, when materials costs dropped sharply, declining by almost 10 percentage points more than sales and output between 1988 and 1991.

For the most part, wage and fixed costs remained unchanged during this period, and even the intermediate fluctuations were not significant. There were no major cuts in employment, nor was the manufacturing staff streamlined. The proportion of wage costs to materials costs was about 16 percent in 1988 and 15 percent in 1989 and 1990, but rose to 31 percent in 1991, showing the inflexibility of the firm's overall behavior.

The firm's inventory position during the last few years had been relatively sound, but the increase of the share of outputs in the value of inventories reflected sales problems. Between 1988 and 1991, sales decreased by 56.5 percent and output by 59 percent, but total costs were down by only 34 percent, which was evidence of a significant worsening in the firm's total factor productivity. As the firm faced the growing threat of bankruptcy and liquidation, it was unable to find an appropriate supply-side response to the economic changes that were occurring. This did not imply that Radion's crisis resulted only from inappropriate reactions to external shocks. Outside trends such as changes in fiscal burdens were extremely unfavorable for the firm, as shown in Tables 5 and 6. The growth of tax liabilities was mainly due to the fact that relative taxes, in proportion to the firm's tax base, continued to increase during the period examined.

Trends in the firm's fiscal burdens, together with its output and sales performance, dictated that Radion's profitability would dramatically worsen during the four-year period analyzed. Table 7 presents the trends in Radion's financial performance that explain the firm's final collapse.

The worsening of the profitability of the firm was accompanied by decapitalization, which can also be called "asset-subtraction." The value of fixed assets decreased because investment funds were becoming less available, and inventories grew relative to output, due to a faster collapse of sales than of purchases of inputs. In order to understand Table 8, it should be noted that the book value of fixed assets, particularly as a result of the specific features of the pre-1992 accounting standard in Hungary, does not necessarily reflect their market value.

The growth of material and all inventories quite closely followed trends in sales and output by 1990, but they virtually exploded in 1991. This fact also contributed to the firm's ultimate collapse, either by aggravating its crisis or by weakening the financial basis of crisis management.

Unfavorable developments in sales or inventories can be considered tactical elements of the crisis of a firm, because they are mostly, although not exclusively, due to short-term changes in the firm's environment. There are strategic elements as well, of which technology-linked ones have a great importance for an electronics firm with a high-tech past.

It is instructive to see that Radion spent a decreasing part of its sales receipts on R&D. R&D expenditures as a percentage of sales were 4.8 percent in 1988, 4.1 percent in 1989, 3.3 percent in 1990, and 2.0 percent in 1991. The absolute amount of R&D expenditure in 1990 was 64 percent of the 1988 level; by 1991 it had fallen to 16 percent.

The above trend shows that Radion practically gave up its ambitions of remaining close to, or even within seeing distance of, its high-tech competitors. It is natural that this passive strategic attitude was the result of its increasingly dire financial situation, but it can be rightly assumed that Radion's crisis started about the time when management decided to cut R&D expenditure in order to save money for other short-term commitments.

The decrease in R&D expenditure also shows that the firm could not get sufficient external financing to fulfill its major strategic goals, and its internal cost structure began to bear increasingly less resemblance to normal patterns in the electronics industry. The worsening of its financial situation could be initially mitigated through credits, but the growing indebtedness of the firm made a soft landing in the financial sense an increasingly remote possibility. Table 9 shows Radion's receivables and payables. These figures give the ultimate explanation for bankruptcy and liquidation.

The financial trends show a dramatic increase in corporate debt. There is a growing gap between payables and receivables; the latter shrink by nearly one-half between 1988 and 1991, while payables increase by one-third. Payables decrease somewhat in 1991, but the firm's financial situation was tragic. Therefore, this seemingly favorable development can only help emphasize the difference between the partial character of debt management and the general character of crisis management in the case of a firm threatened by collapse, at least in the case of Radion.

HUMAN RESOURCES, CORPORATE MANAGEMENT, AND LABOR RELATIONS

Radion's level of employment was 3,274 in 1988, 3,009 in 1989, 2,537 in 1990 and 1,776 in 1991. The firm's employment structure is shown by Table 10.

The decrease in employment was 13 percentage points slower than the fall in output between 1988 and 1991. This trend might seem to speak of increasing overemployment, but it was mostly high-quality manpower that left the firm. The number of employees leaving the company was 1,170 in 1988, 1,067 in 1989, 1,098 in 1990, and 1,267 in 1991. The percentage within this figure of those deliberately leaving oscillated around 20 percent between 1988 and 1990, but increased to 24 percent in 1991. This was not a result of a worsening working climate; there were no strikes at Radion at all. Average wages by employment categories were as shown in Table 11, where 74 HUF was the equivalent of $U.S.1 in June 1991.

These wages did not reflect the inflation taking place in Hungary. The CPI increased approximately 25–27 percent in 1990 and 35–37 percent in 1991. It is astonishing that wage growth was very unfavorable for technicians in 1991. This fact is proof from another aspect that Radion's deepening crisis forced management to gradually give up all illusions of the firm's high-tech-based future.

The qualitative aspect of Radion's human resources policy suffered another blow from the decrease in the firm's expenditure on education and training from 1989 on. All training-related expenditure declined from HUF 24 million in 1989 to HUF 3 million in 1991, and the average annual training expenditure per employee decreased from HUF 8 thousand to HUF 1.7 thousand. Although it was still nominally a high-tech firm, the ratio of skilled to semi-skilled workers at Radion was only 60:40 in May 1992.

The quality of Radion's upper management showed a much more encouraging picture. The director general had degrees in engineering and economics and twenty-five years of professional background in the industry. The technical director had an engineering degree, the same amount of professional experience, and a similar employment record. The financial director had an economics degree and twenty years' professional experience, most of it in the industry and at the firm. The marketing director could be considered an exception, with a degree in marketing but only five years' professional experience, mostly at a trading house.

The director general at the time of this report was appointed in early 1991 when his predecessor retired. His task was crisis management, but he was unable to rescue the firm. In 1991, the top management received no annual bonuses because the firm had become a loss-maker. Liquidation was then begun, directed by a professional liquidator representing the creditors.

The future of the firm would not necessarily be a total disappearance, but it would be unable to survive in its present form. Parts of it would be privatized and probably belong to a new joint stock company. The future of the members of the management team with the successors of the firm is unclear, but they do not have any property share in the firm because Radion is being liquidated as a state enterprise.

Radion had been free of labor conflicts. Such conflicts would not have been legal prior to 1988, but even after that, there were no such problems. Two main reasons for this, characteristic for most industrial firms in Hungary, should be mentioned here. First, the trade unions were very segmented and split. The older unions, i.e., those that were authorized by the communists and cooperated with them, wanted to preserve at least part of their former bastions and privileges, whereas the new trade unions lacked the organizational background and financial means to gain influence over the firm as a whole. The primary conflict between the old and new trade unions concerned the partition of the assets created by organized labor.

The government, of course, had an interest in preserving the weakness of the unions, which helped it to carry out unpopular economic policy measures. Its strategy toward the trade unions was linked to the second main reason behind the passivity of labor relations within this firm and others. This was that most employees were increasingly concerned with their job security and the safety of their income. Since they were well aware of the critical situation of the firm, they tried to avoid any industrial action that might accelerate the sinking of Radion's drifting ship.

THE ASSESSMENT OF RADION'S PERSPECTIVES BY THE MANAGEMENT

The main reason behind bankruptcy and liquidation was a lack of liquidity, a problem that consisted of a number of components:

1. Former defense industry–linked investment, with its accompanying interest and principal payments, was typical of investment projects that were more or less directly forced on the firm by the government. However, high inflation, a loss of market shares, and a total disappearance of market outlets for military products made the financing of such debt an impossible task.

2. The liberalization of imports was too rapid. A more gradual approach might have enabled Radion to keep a significant part of its domestic market shares.

3. A slump in domestic demand for the firm's products, also due to the deep economic recession.

4. The collapse of the firm's largest export market, the Soviet Union. Much the same happened to other former CMEA markets.

5. Radion complained that its Western components suppliers, aware of Radion's liquidity problems, usually charged the firm 15 percent more than they charged the other European buyers.

6. Because of its liquidity problem, Radion had to build up its own component-manufacturing capacities in fields where this was very uneconomical.
7. The firm's military production lost all its markets, both at home and abroad.
8. The firm's reorganization toward a division-based structure had begun, but the administrative overheads were still much too high.

Management's assessment was that Radion still had the human capital necessary to catch up with Western competitors. The lack of up-to-date technology was offset by a more intensive use of cheap Hungarian labor. Even these incremental wage costs added a mere 15 percent to the total costs of output.

According to management, the crisis could be remedied by privatization, but Radion's current financial burdens were too high for any potential buyer. The only serious candidate for buying the firm as a whole was only interested in its post-Soviet (CIS) markets, but it wanted to use Radion's sales channels mostly for the purpose of selling its own products.

Management's strategy for privatization was as follows:

- Liquidation would help to make the firm debt-free;
- The likely opening up of CIS markets would help to make use of the firm's former sales channels. It could sell 120,000 televisions in 1988, 30,000 still in 1991, and, by May 1992, there were already 40,000 orders.
- A technological renewal could be financed from this export income and this renewal could bring Radion back to Western markets.

ASSESSMENT OF THE FUTURE OF RADION AND THE STRATEGIC CHOICES OF MANAGEMENT

The strategy based on export expansion to CIS markets and a technological reconstruction financed from this export drive looked attractive. It had, however, several variables exogeneous to Radion. The re-emergence of solvent demand for imported televisions might not be a short-term development in the CIS countries. Because the CIS was becoming an increasingly loose group of countries with few chances of economic integration among them, its trends of import demand might diverge strongly.

Also, if there were a sudden growth in the Russian or Ukrainian or other demand for imported televisions, the question of why Radion's products, prior to technological reconstruction, would be more competitive than products from Western Europe or the Far East would be asked. If this export expansion were nevertheless to take place, it would remain to be seen whether it would generate enough funds for technological reconstruction. Lastly, the reconstruction would be possible only after serious debt relief for Radion. Who would finance this without selling off chunks of the firm's assets? To date, neither the state nor any private investor had shown any readiness to purchase Radion as a whole or to guarantee its total debt.

A management buyout had not been seriously considered thus far. The lack of interest of even these possible investors in Radion could be linked to several factors:

- the lack of funds and the unavailability of credits;
- undercapitalization was accompanied by a rapidly increasing technology gap, so that any injection of capital would make sense only if it were linked to a major program of technological and product renewal at the firm;
- the serious market and sales problem;
- the strict bankruptcy and liquidation legislation in Hungary.

Hungary had no Chapter 11–type bankruptcy proceedings, and the existing system provided almost no protection to the debtor at all. The grace period was only three months, but there was no legal requirement for cooperation between the creditors and the debtor, even during this period—a one-sided regulation that was to change as of January 1, 1993.

Our assessment of the management's reconstruction plan was thus quite negative, although we did recognize that the new manager took over the firm at a moment when there were few other choices. The firm's perspectives strongly depended on exogenous factors, among which policy-linked factors played an important role. When we evaluated the policy options of the government vis-à-vis the firm, we gave our assessment from the point of view of the firm. These might differ significantly from the policies the government would consider reasonable or acceptable for both domestic and international reasons.

First, there was a need for a definite industrial-policy stance by the Hungarian government. It needed to make clear which firms would be kept in state ownership during the next few years and what sort of commitments could be taken for them by the government. These commitments were debt-relief programs and/or injections of funds needed for technology renewal. If the government were unable or not ready to take such commitments, it would need to make it clear for firms such as Radion, which suffered from a gap between a relatively good technological potential and the current financial straits of the firm. Moreover, an active industrial policy would have serious trade policy implications.

The management of this firm, along with that of other Hungarian electronics firms, was calling for at least temporary protection of the domestic industry from the dramatic increase in foreign competition. The abolition of the import-licensing system was not accompanied by the imposition of any significant tariffs on imports, and the sudden liberalization of imports did not leave time for the domestic manufacturers to adjust. If Radion was not selected for government assistance programs for ailing mid-size firms, in which a dozen crisis-stricken but salvageable state firms were to receive budget-financed therapy, management would need to prepare for privatization with a number of urgent, determined measures. For these, they would need to secure the agreement of the official liquidator.

The firm would need to be split immediately into divisions involved in (a) manufacturing televisions; (b) manufacturing microwave equipment; (c) making printed circuits; and (d) providing services. The central administrative staff would have to be cut significantly.

A comprehensive debt management plan that would include selling some real estate and manufacturing units would need to be implemented. As no real cooperation could be expected from the Hungarian banks, the firm was unable to rely on the domestic capital market to raise funds for a debt relief plan. Domestic banks had no interest in heavily indebted manufacturing firms because they were unable to judge the crisis management perspectives of such firms. Moreover, banks were already risk-averse as a result of the poor quality of their existing portfolio of loans to the domestic manufacturing sector. A technologically promising but financially unstable manufacturing firm was a less-than-attractive partner for a Hungarian commercial bank in late 1992.

Radion's remaining divisions would have to be privatized with the participation of West European or Far East investors. The main factor in choosing partners should be guarantees regarding employment, production, and infusions of capital and technology, not price. The future owner should focus on the development of technology and boost exports.

Privatization should become profitable for the crisis manager, or liquidator. Rather than passively waiting for foreign investors to appear, he should try to identify interested firms in Hungary, North America, Western Europe, or the Far East.

The Radion case has some interesting similarities to Polish and Czech electronics and other engineering firms in that the specialization patterns of firms in the three countries were comparable. The CMEA-market-oriented sales pattern, with its similar product content, was dominant in all three countries. This sales pattern collapsed at the same time, while survival problems linked to undercapitalization and the technology gap relative to Western competitors surfaced in 1989 and 1990. The structural similarities in the three countries meant that their electronic industry capacities were being simultaneously offered for privatization, which tended to push acquisition prices down for Western investors.

Radion was in a desperate situation, and privatizing it was no easy task. While it would certainly help if Hungary began to experience some economic growth, management could have done more to put an end to the disarray within the firm. As just one example, it would be difficult to sell Radion as a firm while its central building continued to sport the giant letters "DION," a minor but telling problem that has existed for months.

Table 1
Radion's Sales (1988 = 100)

	1988	1989	1990	1991
Domestic sales	100	106	100	51.0
Exports	100	97	58	8.5
Total sales	100	105	93	43.5

Table 2
Radion's Main Product Lines (1988 = 100)

	1988	1989	1990	1991
Volume of output				
Black and white TVs	100	66	63	28
Color TVs	100	129	132	55
Microwave telecom. equip.	100	94	61	21
Total	100	108	90	41

Table 3
Changes in Radion's Cost Structure (1988 = 100)

	1988	1989	1990	1991
Total costs	100	110	107	67
of which:				
Costs of material	100	130	110	52
Wage costs	100	107	102	100
Fixed costs	100	105	107	97

Table 4
Radion's Inventories (structure in percentages)

	1988	1989	1990	1991
Purchased inventory of materials and parts	76.7	78.2	74.6	67.1
Inventories of output	23.2	21.8	25.4	22.9

Table 5

Radion's Tax Liabilities (1988 = 100)

	1988	1989	1990	1991
Total taxes paid	100	268	484	271
of which:				
Product taxes (VAT)	100	64	263	*
Profit/corporate taxes	100	76	—	—
Wage taxes	100	115	110	106

* The firm was unable to pay these taxes; they were added to its tax debt.

Table 6

Relative Taxes

	1988	1989	1990	1991
Product taxes as % of sales	2.5	1.5	7.1	*
Product taxes as % of material costs	4.7	2.6	11.3	*
Wage taxes as % of wages paid	40.2	43.2	43.2	42.7

* The firm was unable to pay these taxes; they were added to its tax debt.

Table 7

Radion's Financial Performance

	1988	1989	1990	1991
Pre-tax (gross) profit				
In value (HUF million)	116	78	−497	−662
1988 = 100	100	67	−429	−575
After-tax (net) profit				
In value (HUF million)	76	40	—	—
1988 = 100	100	52.5	—	—

Note: Dollar–forint exchange rates, 1988: U.S.$1 = HUF50.424; 1989: U.S.$1 = HUF59.066; 1990: U.S.$1 = HUF64.147; 1991: U.S.$1 = HUF74.722.

ELECTRONICS: RADION RADIO AND ELECTRICAL WORKS

Table 8
Value of Radion's Assets (1988 = 100)

	1988	1989	1990	1991
Book value of fixed assets	100	94	92	84
Value of stock of material inputs	100	115	78	62
Value of all inventories	100	113	81	71
Value of inventories, % of output	42	44	37	72

Table 9
Radion's Receivables and Payables

	1988	1989	1990	1991
Receivables as % of annual sales	18	20	28	24
Dues as % of annual sales	43	49	71	129
Receivables, 1988 = 100	100	117	145	57
Dues, 1988 = 100	100	119	154	132

Table 10
Radion's Employment Structure

	1988	1989	1990	1991
Operatives, 1988 = 100	100	91	76	54
Technicians, 1988 = 100	100	115	98	68
Managers, 1988 = 100	100	106	110	54
Operatives/employees (%)	94	94	93	94
Technicians/employees (%)	2.8	3.5	3.5	3.5
Managers/employees (%)	2.7	3.2	3.9	2.8

Table 11
Average Monthly Wages by Employment Categories (in HUF)

	1988	1989	1990	1991
Operatives	81	93	100	124
Technicians	136	152	171	180
Managers	181	216	296	379

7

Glass: Salgglas

Peering Through Broken Glass?

Miklós Somai

AN OVERVIEW OF THE INDUSTRY

The Hungarian glass industry had a only one firm until 1988, a conglomerate called Glass Industry Works. After the dissolution of this enterprise, both low-value-added basic glass and flat glass were produced by two firms in Hungary. Basic glass was supplied by Salgglas, as well as by the Orosháza Glass Factory, which, since 1989, had been part of the United States–based Guardian Group and renamed Hunguard Co. This latter firm had also supplied modern float glass since February 1991. Flat glass was produced at Salgglas, as well as at the seven or eight plants of Pannonglas, the last member of the former Glass Industry Works empire.

A BRIEF HISTORY OF THE FIRM

The predecessor of Salgglas was founded by the Budapest-based trading house, A. Schwarz and Sons. Its production had to be halted several times, once in 1896 due to sales problems, and as a result of World Wars I and II, and it also underwent numerous changes of ownership. The major technological development of the firm occurred because of an ownership change. In 1929, based on a 1914 invention by the Belgian engineer E. Fourcault, manual production of glass was replaced by continuous mechanical-pulling technology. The Fourcault oven-based technology was still in use by Salgglas as of 1992.

The firm's products were purchased mainly by the construction industry and by the Hungarian State Railways in the prewar period. The demand for its output increased very rapidly after World War II due to the country's reconstruction. The firm, with a two-thirds foreign majority ownership, was nationalized in 1949.

Demand for Salgglas's products sharply increased again in the 1960s when the number of automobiles in Hungary began to increase. Electrical ovens for tempered flat glass production were installed. In the post-1968 period, the increased autonomy of the firm made it possible to invest in new technology. The technology cycle in the glass industry is normally fifteen years long and, for this reason, the firm had to embark upon a major modernization of its technology, starting in the early 1970s and ending in 1983.

About HUF 1.2 billion, or approximately HUF 2 billion at 1992 prices, was budgeted for this modernization. Know-how was purchased from Asahi of Japan, and this helped the firm to improve the optical parameters of its glass, and it also upgraded the last element of the technology chain, that being packaging. After 1983, the technology development program continued at a somewhat slower pace. At the time of this report, the firm was able to produce heat-resistant glass, construction glass, smash-safe security glass for burglar-alarm equipment, and glass products for gardening.

The firm gained its independence from the national glass industry conglomerate, Glass Industry Works, in 1988. After that, it became a part of the basically duopolistic structure of the Hungarian glass industry.

Salgglas was transformed into a joint stock company in July 1991. The State Property Agency held 94 percent of its shares and 6 percent belonged to the municipalities of Salgótarján, Balatonalmádi, and Jászárokszállás. When this report was written, the firm was under liquidation because the management and the main creditors, mostly banks, had been unable to agree upon any feasible program for the settlement of Salgglas's debts. Reorg Ltd., the state-owned firm for liquidating bankrupt state enterprises, had already offered several of Salgglas's production lines, storage facilities, and parcels of real estate for sale.

PRODUCT MIX AND SALES PATTERN

The Hungarian flat glass market had been very depressed from the late 1980s, and the industry's capacity utilization ratio was around one-third. The flat glass market was closely linked to the construction market, which was known to be a sensitive barometer of the overall economic and investment climate.

The collapse of the domestic construction industry was accompanied by a crisis in the bus industry, a major customer for Salgglas.[1] In addition to these problems, import liberalization reduced the firm's sales, and could be considered the first major external shock for Salgglas. At the time of this report, approximately 15 percent of the annual domestic consumption of 10 million square meters of flat glass was imported. Effective protection in the industry was very low; flat glass could be imported at a tariff rate of 7.7 percent while one of the firm's important inputs, plastic sheets needed for making glued glass, was in the 16 percent tariff bracket.

The worldwide excess supply in the industry resulted in a growing level of protection internationally. This tended to reduce Salgglas's exports, but the firm was unable to lobby for more protection in Hungary. It was also recently hurt by the introduction of a 15 percent customs tariff on its products in Czechoslovakia, one of its major export markets. The introduction of this tariff was negotiated by the Belgian firm Glaverbel as a condition for investing in the Czechoslovak glass industry.

Two points should be stressed. First, the firm was affected by protectionism on one of its major foreign markets while faced with increased import competition on its domestic market. Second, its privatization seemed to have been hampered by the reluctance of the Hungarian government to provide protection from import competition to foreign investors in the glass industry.

The European flat glass market is oligopolistic and each of the five major players was interested in large investments in East Europe. Pilkington Glass of the United Kingdom invested in Poland, the French group Saint-Gobain in Yugoslavia and the eastern part of Germany, Guardian in Hungary, and Asahi of Japan and Glaverbel in Czechoslovakia. Salgglas had been unable to team up with any of these giants and now its maneuvering ability depended largely on their decisions.[2]

Salgglas's share of the domestic market had dwindled, but it also faced tough challenges abroad. It mainly lost market shares to competitors from countries where open or hidden export subsidies, such as lower energy prices, were still a standard practice. For example, Salgglas could sell 2 million square meters of gardening glass per year in the Netherlands, but Polish glass with weaker transparency parameters was offered for DM1 less per square meter. The successor countries of the Soviet Union, along with Romania and Czechoslovakia, were also serious competitors in Western Europe, as were the People's Republic of China and South Africa.

All these discouraging signs still did not mean that Salgglas was in a desperate situation, at least as far as its sales pattern and prospects were concerned. The firm had a good chance of reorganization after its present form was liquidated. Even if its share of the domestic flat glass market were only 20 percent, it still had 40–45 percent of the market of insulating glass and 80–85 percent of the market of security glass products used in the motor vehicle industry.

The firm also had good prospects of becoming a major supplier in the so-called Suzuki project, a factory for producing Suzuki Swift cars in Hungary. Salgglas had invested in the construction of a Glasstech oven for high-tech thermal glass tempering, which was needed to produce high-quality windscreen glass for passenger cars.

The first sets were tested by Suzuki in September 1991 and Salgglas management believed that there was a 95 percent probability that Salgglas would be able to supply Suzuki Hungary with all the windscreen glass sets the factory needed. This would mean an approximately 15–25 percent increase in annual sales starting in 1993. The Total Quality Management system installed at the request of Suzuki would also help Salgglas sell its products elsewhere. The geographical pattern of the firm's new marketing strategy seemed, at the same time, to be rather radical.

Salgglas was aware of the fact that its competitive edge was unlikely to improve in Western Europe in the near future, although its recent export efforts had yielded surprisingly good results, increasing from $5.4 million to $6.8 million between 1990 and 1991. Half of these sales went to Germany, 25 percent to the Netherlands, 10 percent to France, and 5 percent to Italy. The firm also had good access to special market niches such as glaze glass, gardening glass, and special glass products for electrical household equipment and furniture. The share of former CMEA countries in this export structure was very low relative to the size and the proximity of East European markets, even if the ability to pay was currently a problem there.

The firm launched a wide-scale export offensive in the East European markets with a special emphasis on Ukraine, Slovenia, and Croatia. The bottom line of this strategy was the idea that Salgglas could offer its marketing experience and contacts in these countries to Western firms that wished to enter these markets, but were hesitant to do so before the situation in these countries had stabilized. Therefore, the firm needed to strengthen its positions on these markets, even by accepting barter agreements or other forms of cooperation. It could then serve as a stepping stone for Western companies interested in those markets.

TRANSFORMATION AND PRIVATIZATION

The oligopolistic nature of European glass markets and the high capital intensity of the industry would have made privatization inevitable for the firm. The firm's record of failed privatization initiatives was mentioned briefly earlier. As a matter of fact, privatization had been of prime importance ever since it became clear that Salgglas would be unable to finance those investment projects necessary to maintain the firm's presence on key markets, and that the minimal legal and institutional framework necessary for privatization existed in Hungary.

Salgglas negotiated the terms of a joint venture with several major international players in the industry, including Guardian of the United States, Warimpex of Austria, Pilkington Glass of the UK, Saint-Gobain of France, SIV of Italy, and Asahi-Glaverbel, a Japanese-Belgian group. The best offer was made by Asahi-Glaverbel, which promised to contribute to the development of both basic glass and float glass production and access to the group's markets worldwide.

The Hungarian firm requested inclusion in the first privatization program in August 1990, shortly before the joint venture agreement with Asahi-Glaverbel was to be signed. Within a few weeks, the State Property Agency (SPA) rejected the firm's request to participate in the first privatization program on the unusual ground that privatization deals concluded in this program had to be exemplary cases that would serve as models for privatization of Hungarian firms.

The SPA suggested an open tender for Salgglas's privatization, but the Belgian-Japanese group insisted on exclusivity even in further negotiations. When this condition was rejected, Asahi-Glaverbel withdrew from negotiations. It was decided not to announce the tender; as a result, Salgglas did not team up with a foreign investor, and a new Hungarian float glass factory was built by Hunguard.[3] Eighteen months later, Asahi-Glaverbel invested $48 million in the Czech glass industry, thereby gaining part of Salgglas's traditional markets in the region. The damage caused Salgglas by the SPA's behavior was far from complete. The most important consequence was the drastic financial shock to the firm, the second in a series of major external shocks.

Salgglas started ambitious investment projects, which were absolutely necessary for both technological and marketing reasons, but risky in the financial sense. Salgglas therefore undertook these investments only because the likelihood of receiving a major injection of foreign capital through the expected joint venture was very high. The technological and marketing justification of this investment effort could not be questioned, but it became the major cause of insurmountable financial trouble for the firm once the foreign partner failed to materialize. The management made a strategic mistake in this respect only in that its assessment of the probability of privatization was too optimistic.

When the joint venture negotiations collapsed, Salgglas was left with the financial burdens caused by the as yet unfinished investment projects.[4] The firm had to finance these investment projects through short-term loans bearing interest rates of 40 percent. Mainly due to these financial problems, the firm was in a crisis when this report was written and had to declare bankruptcy in April 1992.

The financial problems had to be tackled immediately by management, even though privatization was again in the offing. The privatization adviser of the firm, Daiwa-MKB, had identified three possible investors. One of them, a foreign company comparable to Salgglas in size but in much better financial condition, did not want to drive the Hungarian firm from the market. On the contrary, it wanted to establish its first production base in Europe at Salgótarján and thus was interested in the acquisition of a majority equity stake in Salgglas. We already know that the SPA did not approve this privatization deal, very probably because it found the financial parameters of the transaction unacceptable.

SALGGLAS'S FINANCIAL SITUATION

The firm's shortage of working capital worsened in December 1991, when it had to stop its turnover and personal income tax payments. It also started to make its main suppliers, like those of electricity, natural gas, and soda, queue for payments in late 1991. The financial record of Salgglas developed as follows, with the figures as of December 31 of each year:

- profits were at a HUF 173 million level in 1988 and HUF 155 million in 1989; the firm was HUF 120 million in the red in 1990 and HUF 241 million in the red in 1991;[5]
- the stock of short-term debt was HUF 67 million in 1989, HUF 282 million in 1990, and HUF 370 million in 1991;

- the stock of long-term debt reached HUF 67 million in 1989, HUF 540 million in 1990, and HUF 452 million in 1991;
- the stock of the firm's unpaid receivables, mostly from motor vehicles and construction firms, had also grown drastically during recent years. This stock, which amounted to only HUF 50 million in 1988, reached HUF 135 million in 1989. The latest figure, from June 1992, was HUF 300 million for all receivables, of which approximately 80 percent was the share of overdue claims. The percentage of overdue claims had been 45 percent two years earlier.

Preliminary figures for the first half of 1992 were of HUF 427 million in sales, 32 percent from exports, HUF –88 million in pre-tax profits, which meant losses, HUF 95 million with all taxes paid, no profit taxes, no subsidies, and no after-tax profits. Although the sharp downward trend in sales pointed to a crisis, even this did not necessarily mean that Salgglas would inevitably collapse and disappear.

The dramatic slump in sales was due partly to structural and business cycles, such as the crisis of the Hungarian building sector and the uncertain future of the bus industry. Another set of factors, however, was of a transitory nature—for example, the time lag between the completion of the Glasstech investment and the start of its sales to Suzuki. An analogous problem was the time and money spent on the marketing efforts in Ukraine, Romania, Croatia, and Slovenia, which had not yet yielded the expected return. Salgglas's cost structure showed dramatic changes that reflected the impending crisis as well as the desperate efforts of management to prevent it.

The rationalization of the work force, together with slow wage growth, resulted in a sharp decline in the relative share of wages and related costs. The decrease of the relative weight of material costs was also necessary to offset the increase in bank costs, which, without intervention by the management, could easily have reached an intolerable level. The shock therapy started by the new management in 1991 resulted in a reversal of these trends. Figures for the first half of 1992 showed an increased share of wage costs of 19.8 percent, a lower relative level of material costs of 37.7 percent, and a stabilization of bank costs at 11.9 percent.

The structure of inventories at Salgglas showed the other side of the coin, that being the lack of success of the marketing efforts of the new management; there had been a permanent increase in the share of finished products in the firm's inventories.

The trend toward increasing unsold output accelerated in the first half of 1992 when its relative share reached 25.0 percent. This fact raised doubts about the marketing component of the crisis-management program and seemed to justify a skeptical approach to management's optimism with respect to the firm's strategic prospects.

Management believed that the firm's technology base and sales prospects were adequate for long-term survival. If an agreement with the crediting banks on rescheduling Salgglas's debts with a grace period until 1994–95 could have been reached, or if privatization could have taken place so as to include the necessary injection of capital into the firm, the firm's future could have been taken for granted. This was not the case, although the option finally taken by creditors did not seem to rule out the survival scenario.

HUMAN CAPITAL AND MANAGEMENT

The deteriorating profitability of the firm could be attributed to mistakes in corporate strategy and financial management, especially to financial overstretch, but a failed reform of the operational setup and structure of the firm also contributed to the crisis.

The organizational changes made in March 1990 included the creation of a profit-center-like division-based manufacturing structure within the firm. It was soon discovered that this system disrupted fundamental logistic linkages within the firm, because divisions supplying other units within the firm always had the choice of selling outside the firm. When they did so, production at the upper part of the production chain was halted and the firm as a whole incurred losses.

Crisis management began with the appointment of Sandor Toth as director general in March 1991. His first steps included the elimination of the division-based corporate structure; the creation of a simple intra-firm organizational pattern consisting of only three main units—production, finances, and marketing; and radical cuts in employment.

The necessary cuts in employment required the modification of the collective bargaining agreement of the firm. This occurred in the summer of 1991. These modifications included substantial financial benefits linked to early retirement and voluntary departure. The number of Salgglas's employees decreased by nearly 700 persons in 1991 alone, a 37 percent reduction in employment achieved in just one year. The number of operatives was still 1,631 in 1988 and 1,468 in 1990, but it decreased to 1,185 by the end of 1991 and to 907 by mid-year 1992. Sales per employee increased by 45 percent in 1991 alone. The number of technical staff decreased from 60 in 1989 to 53 in June 1992, and the number of top and medium-level managers declined from 63 to 48 over the same period.

The new management's employment policy was similar to that of other Hungarian companies, such as DKG, for example. The decline of female and part-time employment was much faster than for full-time workers: the number of female employees was 701 in 1988, 586 in 1989, 501 in 1991, and only 385 in mid-June 1992. The number of part-time employees decreased from 23 in 1988 to 3 in 1992. Both trends had started well before the new employment policy was implemented, so it can be assumed that the new management merely accelerated already observable trends in employment.

We have no indication of any serious deterioration of labor relations at the firm as a consequence of the rather fast decline of employment. This was probably the result of the generous early retirement plans and other benefits linked to the voluntary departure of employees. There seemed to have been a peculiar trade-off between tensions in labor relations and further financial problems for the firm. Management opted to avoid layoff-linked conflicts with the employees, even at the price of higher corporate debt, because it correctly thought crisis management would be impossible without the cooperation of the employees. Debt, on the other hand, would only slow the process down.

A key factor in determining Salgglas's prospects for survival could be the unusually high quality and dynamism of management. The director general, Sandor Toth, was only thirty-three years old when appointed in 1991, but he had an impressive training background and professional experience. He held an M.A. in Transport Engineering from the Technical University of Budapest and a Diploma of Management Studies from the Buckinghamshire Wolsey Oxford School of Management in Britain. Except for his studies abroad, he had spent his entire professional career with Salgglas.

The technical director also had some international experience due to his work on an investment project in Nigeria. A special case was the marketing director, whose predecessor had a high level of culture and a command of several languages, but apparently much less talent for business. The new marketing director was seriously handicapped by the lack of the knowledge of any foreign language, but he had a considerable amount of managerial and marketing ability. While working on developing new markets, he was also building a young marketing team in order to be able to handpick his successor.

STRATEGIC CHOICES FOR SALGGLAS

The firm was literally drifting because negotiations with creditors were not completed and the new privatization plan was not ready. Salgglas was, in spite of its limited scope for action, not a lost cause like other companies facing eventual liquidation.

This glass firm was stripped of cash, but it had a good technological background and a promising marketing strategy. Therefore its management had to convince investors that the key to success was more responsible financial management; but new funds to be managed would also be required. After liquidation, Salgglas could still reappear on the market with part of its current capacities and without its present financial liabilities.

The liquidation of Salgglas finally resulted in a modified version of privatization based on a debt-equity swap. The three creditor banks—Inter-Európa Bank, the Postabank, and the Hungarian Credit Bank—agreed with the firm's management on the terms of reorganization during the bankruptcy proceedings. After liquidation became inevitable, the tender for buying the firm's assets gave priority to investors ready to acquire the firm as a productive entity.

The tender was won by Glasunion Ltd., a recently founded limited liability company owned by the three banks mentioned, the Hungarian Foreign Trade Bank, and the foreign trade company Ferunion. This deal gave hope for the survival of glass production at the former Salgglas plant. Estimates were that the subcontracting work for Suzuki itself could profitably ensure a 60–70 percent capacity utilization rate for the firm's present physical assets.

Notes

1. Salgglas's orders from the Hungarian motor vehicle industry decreased by about 40 percent in 1989, the company's first bad year. This was the equivalent of approximately 15 percent of the total order book of the firm. Moreover, conditions of payment by the motor vehicle industry had steadily worsened since then and transfers took at least two months instead of eight days prior to 1989. The cost efficiency of glued vehicle glass used to be almost twice as high as that of flat glass. These negative trends in the company's sales to the motor vehicle industry had a dramatic impact on Salgglas' profitability. The firm's profits were down from a HUF 173 million level in 1988 to HUF 155 million in 1989, and it became a loss-maker with losses of HUF 120 million in 1990 and HUF 241 million in 1991.

2. Salgglas had not been passive in this respect. It planned to create a joint venture with Asahi-Glaverbel of Japan and Belgium in 1989, but Hungary needed only one modern float glass factory. Guardian planned to invest $15 million in Hungary, Asahi's offer was $20 million, but the Hungarian government preferred Guardian for some reason. The Hunguard factory was built within eighteen months' time and the strong new competitor proved a strong challenger for Salgglas on the market. Hunguard lured away the technical director of Salgglas, which could not have happened in West Europe, and could thereby learn much about his competitor's practices. The result was that Salgglas was permanently losing domestic market shares and its former approximately 50 percent share of the float glass market would decline to 20 percent in 1992.

3. At the time of this report, this firm, as Salgglas's major domestic competitor, had the best equipment in Hungary for the production of high-quality basic glass. Therefore, Salgglas could not avoid buying the semi-finished product from it needed for the Suzuki product line and therefore became Hunguard's major customer in Hungary.

4. The decision to start the Glasstech tempered glass investment project was taken in late 1988. The original budget of the project was HUF 627 million, but HUF 176 million were guaranteed through several channels, such as export-related tax credit and a special subsidy for the introduction of TQM, by the government, and a HUF 236 million long-term credit was offered by the Hungarian Foreign Trade Bank. The Hungarian Credit Bank (MHB) was in charge of the financial management of the investment, but it quit the next year. Inter-Európa Bank took over the credits, but with Ferunion Trading House, one of Salgglas's competitors on the domestic market, as a guarantor. This bank also offered HUF 200 million more as a short-term credit in order to help the company to complete the investment, but this credit also became a serious liability for Salgglas. Moreover, a supplementary investment project of HUF 130 million to upgrade the input side of Glasstech was started in 1989. HUF 96 million was supplied for this by a credit from Postabank.

5. A significant part of losses incurred in 1991 was not due to mismanagement, but inherited problems or to attempts to find a way out from the crisis. Banking costs alone equaled the HUF 241 million in losses, costs linked to employment cuts were at HUF 50 million, and depreciation costs were up by HUF 15 million because of the increase of depreciation rates for new equipment. All this means that operating profits were already realized in 1991.

Table 1

Salgglas's Main Financial Indicators (data in HUF million)

	1988	1989	1990	1991
Annual sales	1,763	1,864	1,809	1,989
Exports/sales (in %)	18.0	15.0	25.0	33.0
Gross profit before tax	173	155	−120	−275
All taxes paid (incl. social security)	167	382	267	236
Profit taxes	20	360	—	—
Subsidies	1	2	2	1
Profit after tax	72	90	−120	−278

Notes:
The 1988 figure in Line 4 is only for the last four months of the year.
Except for Line 2, figures do not add up due to rounding and minor omissions.
Line 4 (taxes paid) does not include VAT-type taxes.
Dollar–forint exchange rates, 1988: $U.S.1 = HUF50.424; 1989: $U.S.1 = HUF59.066; 1990: $U.S.1 = HUF64.147; 1991: $U.S.1 = HUF74.722.

Table 2

Salgglas's Cost Structure (in percentages)

	1988	1989	1990	1991
Total costs	100	100	100	100
of which:				
Costs of material	57.2	52.7	44.6	42.9
Wage costs	23.2	24.0	24.6	17.9
Energy costs	13.5	13.2	16.7	18.0
Banking costs (incl. interest)	1.1	2.6	6.5	12.3
Other costs	2.1	4.7	5.4	4.2

Table 3

Salgglas's Inventories (structure in percentages)

	1988	1989	1990	1991
Purchased inventories of materials and parts	95.6	92.6	90.2	80.7
Inventories of output	4.4	7.4	9.8	19.3

8

Food Processing/Chocolate and Sweets: Intercsokoládé Kft

A Sweet Strategic Alliance?

Lilli Berkó

AN OVERVIEW OF THE INDUSTRY

The Hungarian confectionery industry had sales of approximately $230 million in 1992. The most recent figures on its subsectors were from 1990. In that year, 13.3 percent of output consisted of flour products, 10.6 percent of candies, 7.4 percent of cocoa and cocoa products, 30.3 percent of chocolate, chocolate products, and nougats, 28.2 percent of coffee and coffee-related products, and the rest, 10.1 percent, consisted mainly of semi-finished products. Intercsokoládé Kft, later Globalfood Hungary Ltd., a pseudonym, represented about 60 percent of the sales of chocolate and related products in Hungary in 1990. This market share gave it a decisive role on the market for that product group, but the company was not the strongest Hungarian firm in the industry.

The Hungarian confectionery industry was quite competitive in 1987 when its participants included four state enterprises, thirty-seven bakery firms owned by municipalities, and about thirty different cooperatives. The market structure then changed profoundly and the industry came to be dominated by three firms in 1991. The important players were now Quintie Sweets Industry Ltd., Compack Douwe Egberts Ltd., and Globalfood Hungary Ltd. Ranked by their net sales, these companies were, respectively, numbers 19, 32, and 98 on the top 200 list of Hungarian industrial firms in 1991. The next largest firm from this industry on the list, Biscuits Plc. of Győr, was ranked 153. Globalfood Hungary Ltd. also ranked seventh on the list of joint ventures in Hungary, based on the size of foreign-owned equity capital, while Biscuits Plc. of Győr was ranked twentieth.

A BRIEF HISTORY OF THE FIRM

The predecessor of Globalfood Hungary Ltd. was the Szerencs Sweets Factory, originally established in 1923 as a Swiss-Hungarian joint venture called Szerencs Chocolate Factory. By the late 1920s, it had became the second-largest chocolate factory in Hungary. Its manager was Swiss and most of the skilled workers were foreigners as well. Hungarians trained by them gradually took all the jobs at the company. Szerencs is located some distance from Hungary's traditional industrial regions, so it was quite natural that generations of skilled workers followed each other in the service of the company.

The company was nationalized in 1947. Its next major institutional change took place in 1963, when all the chocolate and sweets factories in Hungary were put under a single organization or trust. This situation existed until 1981 when a wave of decentralization in the Hungarian industry swept away most such trusts. The company was glad to regain its autonomy, but, for various reasons, it suffered significant losses from the dissolution of the trust. For one thing, it inherited the most obsolete equipment. Second, it was amalgamated against its will with the Szerencs Sugar Factory, a firm with an approximately HUF 300 million uncompleted investment. Moreover, the sugar industry was suffering from a worldwide crisis, and depressed prices led to a depletion of the company's financial reserves so that no funds were available for R&D and investment.

The chocolate factory parted with the sugar firm in 1985, but the money and time wasted in maintaining the artificial alliance were lost forever. Management immediately understood that it was facing a crisis and responded as best it could. Agreement was reached with the trade union that wages would be increased only minimally over the next five-year period in order to use all available profits for reconstruction. However, even this strategy was not sufficient to make up for the decline in domestic demand for the company's products that began around 1988 due to the economic recession in Hungary.

The management, therefore, felt that the firm needed a reliable strategic partner. An extensive search for potential partners across Europe convinced the management that Globalfood of Switzerland was the best candidate, and not only because of the Hungarian company's Swiss roots. By 1988, when it concluded a cooperation agreement with the Szerencs firm, Globalfood had been present on the Hungarian market for twenty years.[1]

The cooperation agreement included a detailed plan for the transfer of licenses and know-how. The Hungarian factory managed to produce the volume of Globalfood products planned for the tenth year of the cooperation in its first year, in the quality required by the Swiss company. This extremely favorable experience turned out to be one of Globalfood's motives for the acquisition of a majority equity stake in the Szerencs company. Globalfood became an almost exclusive owner of the firm in 1992, and its presence proved decisive in shaping the company's current sales pattern and product mix.

PRODUCT MIX AND SALES PATTERN

The transformation of the product mix of the Szerencs factory had begun even before the takeover by Globalfood, but it gained speed thereafter. Management decided to gradually phase out lozenges because of the obsolete technology used to produce this product. The two other major product lines, especially chocolate products, gained importance after 1988. Sales of chocolate products went up from HUF 1.77 billion to HUF 2.77 billion between 1988 and 1991; candies grew from HUF 0.25 billion to HUF 0.30 billion; but sales of lozenges stagnated at the HUF 0.05 billion level. The physical volume of output showed these structural changes even more clearly: output of chocolate was 10.2 thousand tons both in 1988 and in 1991, with an upmarket shift of the product mix; the output of candies decreased from 5.4 to 4.7 thousand tons; and the production of lozenges declined from 1.2 to 0.5 thousand tons.

The share of chocolate products also increased because this was the product line with by far the highest licensed technology content. The company's newest products showed an attempt to diversify away from a too strongly chocolate-based product mix. The new products were Chokitto, Pralinette, and Globalcafé, all bottled in Hungary. These appeared on the market in early 1992. Also helping to boost sales was the fact that Globalfood purchased the right to decorate all its products sold in Europe with Walt Disney figures, because these figures had considerable appeal for Hungarian consumers.

The joint venture with Globalfood also helped the chronically undercapitalized Hungarian firm through a substantial injection of capital. The ten-year business plan worked out as a basis for the strategic partnership set a goal of a 60 percent increase in the Hungarian affiliate's capacity. The short-term part of the business plan outlined an investment program between HUF 1.5 and 2 billion by the end of 1992. HUF 1.4 billion was invested within this framework in 1991. Half of these funds was spent on new equipment, and a new storage building and several social facilities were constructed using the other half. These investment projects would doubtless help Globalfood Hungary Ltd. to catch up technologically with other members of the Globalfood empire, and they would also dispel suspicions that Intercsokoládé was to be relegated to a backward technological status within the Globalfood group.

The Hungarian company's sales pattern had been shifting toward greater internationalization before subsidies for exports were abolished. It still exported 15 percent of its sales in 1991; the comparable share was below 10 percent in the years before Globalfood's appearance as a strategic partner. Since sales totaled HUF 3.5 billion in 1991, this meant more than HUF 500 million, or $6.5 million, in exports, and exports had tripled since 1988. One-fifth of exports was chocolate and chocolate products, while cocoa butter was second on the export list. The abolition of export subsidies caused an unexpected and very serious decline in exports, but the exact size of this decline was not yet clear. The management wanted to rebuild exports in parallel with the introduction of new technology through its investment. The export push was to be aimed toward both the other Globalfood affiliates and other foreign buyers.

The company's export and import strategy were strongly influenced by its role in the worldwide Globalfood group. The Hungarian firm was also the group's general importer in Hungary, and all other members of the group could sell only through it in Hungary. While this was an advantage for the company as an importer, its export channels were, in a certain sense, limited by the application of this rule in markets outside Hungary because the company had to use the Globalfood subsidiaries as its trading partners in each country where the group was represented. This could, in some cases, be a handicap, especially if the Hungarian regulatory environment were to change toward a system based increasingly on direct promotion of exports.

TRANSFORMATION AND PRIVATIZATION

Globalfood first appeared as a potential investor at Szerencs in 1988, when the Hungarian government had not yet formulated a privatization strategy, and consequently, the institutional and legal basis for the process was insufficiently developed. The government took privatization decisions almost at random, and it was normally reluctant to give foreign investors majority ownership in Hungarian firms that had a large share of the domestic market.

As a result, Globalfood was at first offered only 33 percent of the equity of the Szerencs company. This share was increased to 51 percent only in early 1990 when State Property Agency (SPA) was already in place. Not much later, Globalfood was allowed to become an almost 100 percent owner of the firm, with only 2.3 percent of the shares, representing the value of the land occupied by the firm's facilities remaining in Hungarian hands. These latter shares were held by the municipalities of Szerencs, Miskolc, and five other towns in which the firm had its facilities. This, then, was the equity structure of Globalfood Hungary Ltd., established in January 1991, with a capital stock of HUF 2.8 billion.

The price at which the Hungarian company's capital was sold to Globalfood was higher than expected on the basis of the original asset valuations, and reflected new asset valuations made by an Austrian and a Hungarian auditing firm. The reason the Swiss partner was ready to acquire an East European chocolate factory at such favorable terms was that the Hungarian company had a strategic importance for Globalfood, which wanted to establish its first joint venture in postcommunist Eastern Europe with a Hungarian firm with whom it was already familiar. Globalfood also placed considerable emphasis on acquiring a quasi 100 percent equity stake in the Hungarian firm in order to be able to incorporate the Hungarian subsidiary into the worldwide Globalfood data processing and administrative system.

As a result, Globalfood Hungary Ltd. was integrated into Globalfood's European divisional system together with the group's Austrian and, subsequently, Czech, subsidiaries. The three subsidiaries had joint export and import strategies, and the top management of the three was controlled by Austrians. Top management was closely linked with the group's EC-level Regional Board, which was chaired by the president of Central European Subregion of Globalfood.

Intercsokoládé's privatization put the Hungarian chocolate firm on an equal footing with all the other members of the international Globalfood group, and it gave the company access to the capital, technology, and managerial skills available within the group. While this approach to privatization could be considered exemplary, unfortunately, it was not open to many other Hungarian firms of comparable size, because only a few of them could attract a major foreign investor the way the Szerencs company did.

The industry setting had also been special in the Intercsokoládé/Globalfood case. International competition was less intense in the chocolate industry than in most other sectors due to the oligopolistic structure of the world, and even more the European, market, because it is dominated by a small number of well-established Swiss, French, and Belgian firms, all of whom have strong brand names and reputations for quality. As a result, newcomers to the international market have only one realistic option, that of joining one of the big multinationals. This option was taken by the Szerencs firm without hesitation, and as a result, it was able to enter the world market through Globalfood. Such an approach also quickly integrated the Hungarian market of chocolate products into the world market.

INTERCSOKOLÁDÉ'S FINANCIAL SITUATION

The firm's cost structure underwent major changes between 1988 and 1991. Total costs increased by 77 percent in this period, but wages increased by 138 percent and fixed costs by 142 percent. Costs of material and energy showed much slower increases, 43 percent and 62 percent respectively. The divergences in cost trends reflected, in part, different rates of inflation, but they also reflected the impact of the privatization-related changes in factor intensities. A major explanation for the increasing share of wage costs was the rapid increases in wages without significant lay offs, whereas a more efficient use of physical inputs resulted in below-average increases in expenditure on materials. This latter trend was extremely remarkable due to the fact that the share of costs of material was such a large part of the company's total costs.

Taxes had been a rapidly increasing burden on the company basically as a result of its rapid wage increases. Taxes increased by 53 percent between 1988 and 1991, and by 9.0 percent in 1991 alone, whereas the increase of wage taxes in these periods was 740 percent and 121 percent respectively. Taxes on profits were not paid in 1991 due to the approximately HUF 60 million loss in that year, but we can observe an interesting crowding-out effect here among taxes. If the special wage tax had not existed and the promise of its elimination had been one of the carrots accompanying the stick of the introduction of the new income tax system in 1988, the company would have probably paid a comparable amount in profit taxes.

Subsidies were of special interest in the case of the chocolate firm. Although the firm received subsidies each year prior to 1990 whenever requested, these subsidies were not used to compensate for losses, but were used exclusively as export subsidies, which the company did not receive after 1990. The elimination of these subsidies led to a significant decline in the company's export performance; moreover, this was not the only external financial shock facing the company.

The financial stability of the company seriously suffered from the increase of its stock of accumulated debt. The amount of its total bank debt rose from HUF 57 million in 1988 to HUF 578 million in 1991, mainly due to higher interest rates, inflation, and the queuing problem. Queuing had been an increasingly serious source of trouble for the firm, because it forced Globalfood/ Intercsokoládé to rely very heavily on short-term credits. The amount of its short-term debt was HUF 573.7 million in 1991 as compared to its long-term debt of only HUF 4.9 million. The very low level of long-term debt reflected a conservative investment policy based upon self-reliance, although decreasing sales figures did not dissuade management from launching long-term investment projects. The strong short-term debt exposure was a result of the irredeemability of most receivables, which were HUF 486 million in 1990, but soared to HUF 817 million in 1991. The company's accounting system was thoroughly changed in early 1992. This change made it possible to do a very accurate screening of the cost structure of each product, which would allow a far-reaching restructuring of the company's price structure.

Although in 1991 the firm achieved a modest loss of HUF 60 million, the financial plan for 1992 foresaw a net operating profit. Its size was not known exactly, because the role of exogenous factors was strong in this industry. For instance, price fluctuations on the sugar market are quite large. The ability of a chocolate firm to buy sugar at the end of a bearish or at the beginning of a bullish price trend has considerable effect on profits. At any rate, the structure of the company's inventories showed the increasing strategic importance of logistics only after privatization was completed. This was a signal of a change of strategic thinking by the management.

HUMAN CAPITAL AND MANAGEMENT

The company's situation was exceptional among recently privatized Hungarian firms with respect to its employment situation. Globalfood declared that it would maintain the level of employment at the company. Since the creation of Intercsokoládé Kft, i.e., during one-and-a-half years, employment decreased at the firm through retirements and the elimination of part-time employees on term contracts. About 80 percent of the employees were women. This relatively high figure was linked to the fact that chocolate production required a great amount of semi-skilled labor.

The use of working time had become more flexible during 1991. The use of part-time, seasonal workers linked to peaks in the supply of sugar and in the demand of chocolate products before Christmas was replaced with overtime work. This was one of the reasons why personal incomes increased by 51 percent in 1991.[2] Wages of blue collars increased by 50 percent, technical staff had a 100 percent increase, and management a 300 percent wage increase in 1991. Annual bonuses were abolished. The only stimulus for top management was the possibility of an extra month's salary, which was dependent on the company's performance.

The employees' loyalty to the company was certainly strengthened by the new owner's determination to maintain employment and to keep real wages stable. This was the main reason why there had been no industrial action or other tensions in labor relations at the firm. There was only one trade union at the company. It was not very active and even the workers' council had yet to be elected. However, this exemplary situation in labor relations would not be sustainable if management could not fulfill its promise of a wage policy that fully covered increases in the price level. The monthly pre-tax wage level for operators was HUF 13,600, or approximately $160, in October 1992, around the average for the industry.

Exemplary work discipline was enhanced by the management's efforts to improve social facilities around the plants. This was a quite exceptional approach in today's Hungarian industry because social facilities quite often became the first victims of efforts to cut operating costs.

Finally, it was difficult to get workers accustomed to Globalfood's very high hygienic standards. Workers mostly lived in villages around Szerencs and Miskolc and worked on their household plots in addition to their work at the factory, and they were used to coming to work directly from working on their plots, without washing or changing their clothes. Therefore, they had to undergo a sort of social transformation while working in the same factory, but for different owners.

Globalfood retained the top management and technical staff, thus following its traditional policy of leaving local management in place for two years in order to test it. The grace period expired in October 1992. Top management already had several new members in January 1993. The new marketing director was brought in from abroad, and the former director general became deputy director general.

The latter individual, currently president and CEO, had had an impressive employment record with the company. He started working for the company's Diósgyôr (Miskolc) plant in 1961, and became the director of the Szerencs plant in 1977. One of his important achievements was his successful lobbying for the quick and efficient privatization of the company. He was replaced as director general by a Hungarian manager well known for his experience in the international trade of food products. This manager, in his mid-forties, was fluent in several languages and had a wide network of professional contacts both abroad and in the country.

The firm's top management was lean while being internationally oriented, reflecting Globalfood's philosophy. The Hungarian president and CEO was assisted by the members of the Board of the Subregional Directorate of Globalfood headquartered in Vienna and by the members of the local management team in Hungary.

STRATEGIC CHOICES FOR THE COMPANY

As has been stressed, Globalfood Hungary was in an exceptional situation as compared to other Hungarian industrial enterprises recently privatized. The firm became a full-fledged member of the Globalfood empire, which was a guarantee of its long-term survival. R&D acquired a new role for the firm. Like marketing, it lost its traditional autonomy and both functions had to become integrated in the worldwide R&D and marketing strategy of Globalfood.

In assessing the firm's fate, this seeming loss of autonomy should not be overemphasized. To a large extent, as part of the Globalfood group, the firm also gained certain advantages in terms of its export possibilities, capacity for expansion, and technical development that would have been impossible for a Hungarian-owned firm. More important, its employment was almost entirely maintained, its development was assured, and it was integrating into a multinational company with a high standing around the world. To sum up, a problem for Hungarian regional and industrial policy became an asset for the region and for a multinational company as well.

Notes

1. It had a cooperation agreement with the Debrecen Canning Factory for the production of the Global product line of soups and sauces, it cooperated with a Budapest-based confectionery company for packaging and selling Globalquick chocolate powder, and also had an agreement with the trading house, Compack, for jointly providing granulated Globalcafé on the Hungarian market.

2. Another reason might have been the Hungarian wage regulation system, which punitively taxes wage increases exceeding a centrally fixed limit. Newly established firms are, however, free to set starting wages. Intercsokoládé was considered a new company, because it was created in 1991.

Table 1

Intercsokoládé Kft's Cost Structure (in percentages)

	1988	1989	1990	1991
Total costs	100	100	100	100
of which:				
Costs of material	69.2	67.6	60.1	56.1
Wage costs	7.0	7.8	8.6	9.5
Energy costs	3.1	2.7	2.6	2.9
Banking costs (incl. interest)	0.9	1.7	3.0	4.3
Depreciation	1.0	1.0	1.0	1.5
Other costs	18.5	19.2	24.7	25.6

Table 2

Intercsokoládé's Inventories (structure in percentages)

	1988	1989	1990	1991
Purchased inventories of materials and parts	70.4	70.9	70.4	73.4
Inventories of output	29.6	29.1	29.6	26.6

9

Food Processing/Brewing: Kanizsa Brewery Ltd.

Privatization Brewing?

Judit Zsarnay

THE SECTORAL OVERVIEW

Despite Hungary's overall industrial decline during 1987–92, the brewery industry remained exceptionally stable. Of the twenty-seven industrial subsectors, brewing was the only one in which output increased, even in 1991, the worst year for industry as a whole. This stability was the result of several factors: widespread modernization of the industry, combined with the introduction through license agreements of domestically brewed foreign brands in the product mix of most domestic firms; a boom in consumption mostly due to increased tourism; and the disappearance of inexpensive East German, Czechoslovak, and Polish beers from the domestic market. Although most of these brands were still available in Hungary, their prices had soared as a result of the abolition of intra-CMEA trade at arbitrarily determined clearing prices.

The brewery sector was undergoing major structural changes resulting from privatization, which took place in July 1992. By the end of 1991, four of the seven breweries in the country had already been privatized, all with the majority participation of foreign strategic investors. The Sopron and the Martfü breweries were acquired by Brau AG of Austria, which then owned 13 percent of the Hungarian market. Interbrew of Belgium became the majority owner of Borsod Brewery Ltd. with 27 percent of the domestic market. The smallest brewery, that of Komárom, which only had 1 percent of the market, was acquired by Heineken of the Netherlands. The result of these acquisitions was that, altogether, more than 40 percent of the Hungarian beer output was under foreign ownership.

The largest brewery, Kôbánya Brewery Ltd., had yet to be privatized. This firm, comprising about 35 percent of the domestic market, had been available for sale, but its carefully prepared memorandum excluded the participation in the tender of any of the foreign investors mentioned above.

Kanizsa Brewery Ltd. (Kanizsa Sörgyár Rt.), the third largest brewery in Hungary, was the largest of those still under Hungarian ownership. This brewery comprised about 12 percent of the domestic market, which amounted to 11 billion liters in 1991. Kanizsa's privatization is a special story, which will be presented in detail. As of 1993, the last brewery, Pannonia Brewery Ltd. in the city of Pecs, was still available for privatization.

THE HISTORY OF THE FIRM

The Kanizsa Brewery was founded in 1892 by Vilmos Gelsei Guttmann as a company limited by shares. It was nationalized in 1948, after which its ownership or legal form changed five times. It was a state enterprise until 1985, then became a state enterprise controlled by a management council, i.e., self-management, and was directly supervised by the government during January–September 1990. The brewery functioned as a limited liability company until January 1992, then once again became a company limited by shares. All shares but one were retained by the State Property Agency until July 1992. That single share belonged to the director general of the firm, allegedly to limit the SPA's control over and responsibility for the firm.

PRODUCT MIX AND SALES PATTERN

The Kanizsa Brewery's output was sold only on the domestic market, although it had made efforts to explore markets in Russia and Romania. The two major elements of its product mix were a light, nonpasteurized beer called Balaton Light, and Holsten Beer, which was brewed under a 1984 license from the German brewery.

Balaton Light was made mostly for local consumption, and included sales in the Balaton area, one of the major Central European sites of international tourism. Its sales, therefore, were strongly seasonal, but these fluctuations had not yet been a major threat to the stability of the firm. Holsten beer was an upmarket product in Hungary, competing mostly with imported beers. Its relatively low price, which was due to both the lack of customs duties and to lower production costs, did not necessarily increase its competitiveness in all domestic market niches, e.g., luxury hotels. Domestically produced Holsten had been generally successful as a substitute for expensive high-quality imported beers. Table 1 presents the brewery's major figures of output in value and volume.

Figures for the first half of 1992 were HUF 1,458 million for total gross output—HUF 461 million of output in value and 23 million liters in volume for Product 1 (Balaton Light), and HUF 397 million of output in value and 12 million liters of volume for Product 2 (Holsten).

There was a slow but continuous shift in the firm's product mix toward its upmarket product, a trend that reflected a change in domestic demand due to the purchasing power decline of Balaton Light's traditional working-class consumers. The brewery's homogeneous product mix and the slow pace of technology change in this industry gave it a low level of exposure to external shocks of a technological origin. Furthermore, because it had acquired world-class knowhow and equipment from Holsten, the firm could feel quite secure as far as its technology base was concerned. Its market situation was not discouraging either. Kanizsa had preserved its 12 percent share of the domestic market between 1988 and 1991. The share of imports increased from 2 to 7 percent in the same period, while the brewery's major domestic competitor, Kôbánya Brewery, lost 8 percent of its market share. The Kôbánya Brewery had continued to brew only its own current brands plus its former pre-war brand, Dreher, while Kanizsa Brewery had increased the share of licensed and internationally known brands in its product mix.

The fact that Kanizsa Brewery was able to maintain its share of the domestic market was a proof of the success of its license-based upmarket-oriented strategy. As a matter of fact, there had been greater expansion of foreign brands than of imported beers on the domestic market and Kanizsa had adjusted to this process.

Kanizsa was vulnerable to financial challenges that originated from the growing instability of the domestic financial environment. To respond to these challenges successfully, the brewery needed to create an ownership structure that would make the firm much more secure in a financial sense.

TRANSFORMATION AND PRIVATIZATION

Because of delays in privatization, the firm had changed legal form several times in its brief history. The first privatization attempt failed because the foreign investor, Les Mechtler and Vanbrew Ltd. of Australia, did not meet its financial obligations within the six-month period of its purchase option. Therefore, the State Property Agency discarded this privatization plan in November 1990. The next privatization round started in December 1990, but a few months later the firm's new management decided to create a new privatization strategy, which further delayed the process.

The services of foreign consulting firms, such as Morgan Grenfell, Coopers and Lybrand, and McKenna, were used to elaborate this strategy. The consultants assisted the firm in presenting a reliable assessment of its financial situation and in determining estimates of the capital expected from the new foreign investor. Although Hungarian investors were also able to participate in the privatization tender, the firm's management preferred foreign firms. The reasons for this biased attitude are still not completely clear more than one year later.

Sixteen potential foreign investors expressed an interest in the tender documents, but only a few entered the competition. Among them, Holsten of Germany, Steierbrau AG of Austria, and Courage of the United Kingdom were perhaps the best-known names. Holsten simply wanted to expand its relationship with Kanizsa Brewery, while Steierbrau's acquisition of the firm would have increased the market share of Brau AG in Hungary.

Brau AG had a majority stake in Steierbrau, but it also controlled 60.3 percent of Martfû Brewery and had 37.5 percent of the shares of Sopron Brewery with an option for the rest. Therefore, Steierbrau's interest in Kanizsa Brewery was part of Brau AG's strategy of acquiring a decisive role in the Hungarian brewery industry. Some sectors of Hungarian industry, such as sugar, cement, paper, and vegetable oil, were now entirely under foreign control and this could also happen to the brewing industry.

The interest of foreign investors in acquiring entire industries in Hungary was not country-specific, but it might be interesting to note that Austrian firms had been successful in gaining strategic control over a significant part of the sugar and the paper industries, and the brewery sector could be next.

The Kanizsa Brewery's privatization appeared to have included a special combination of MBOs (Management Buy Outs) and ESOPs. This original solution, called M+E (Managers and Employees—M+D in Hungarian), was only formally a blend of MBOs and ESOPs, because managers and employees acquired the ownership not of the brewery itself, but of a special holding called M+D Kft (M+E Ltd.). In this form of privatization, neither managers nor employees had priority, nor could compensation bonds be used for this type of buy out.

There was no formal distinction between managers and employees in this program. Both groups could use only their personal savings or personal entrepreneurship. Employment with the brewery did not entitle them to a discount, as was usually the case with MBOs or ESOPs in Hungary, because they did not acquire direct ownership of the firm in which they were employed. Instead, they invested in the formation of a new holding company.

The decision by the SPA to allow M+D Kft (M+E Ltd.) to buy 80 percent of the brewery's HUF 1 billion equity capital was made in July 1992. The M+D Kft was able to assist 419 people, or more than 40 percent of the firm's employees, in becoming owners of the firm. The conditions were favorable. Only 25 percent of the investment was to be paid in cash, and credits were made available for the rest. This privatization plan was popular among employees because they had confidence in the future of the firm, but they were also concerned about their employment security. This was because it had been stated that ownership in the Ltd. was no guarantee *per se* of permanent employment at the brewery.

Hungarian press coverage of this privatization deal had some political overtones: M+E Ltd. became a winner, beating out such world-famous firms as Holsten, Steierbrau, and Forest/Courage, and this fact was interpreted by some as an expression of the government's intention to not allow the entire brewing industry to fall under foreign control. Although the terms of the deal were not made public, M+E insisted that their offer had been the best, and that, for example, Holsten was unsuccessful in its bid because of the low price it offered, a price that was the result of the German firm's knowledge of the brewery's financial problems.

THE FIRM'S FINANCIAL PERFORMANCE

Management was somewhat concerned about the firm's financial situation, although the figures available do not entirely substantiate this concern. Interestingly enough, management complained about the excessive degree of deregulation of the domestic market. This attitude differed from most popular political or macroeconomic assessments of the Hungarian situation, but it was more or less well founded in the special case of the brewery.

The reason for this was the above-mentioned special, strongly regionally oriented sales pattern of the firm. Its sales were distributed less through national wholesale channels than directly to smaller local or regional retailers, including individual hotels and restaurants. Therefore, the firm was more exposed to liquidity or payment-related risk. These problems constituted the most important external shock to the firm in recent years.

Kanizsa had given supplier credits to a host of small limited liability companies, mostly local catering or retail firms, that subsequently did not pay their bills and eventually went bankrupt, only to resume their operations under a different name but with the same entrepreneurial and financial background. The firm incurred losses approaching HUF 100 million, and it was unable to proceed legally to recover the money lost in sales to these small firms. Management's complaints about the government's growing inability to control the economy and to promote honest entrepreneurship had a grain of truth, but more with respect to deficiencies in legislation than to administrative power.[1]

Figures for the first half of 1992 showed a slightly declining, but not discouraging, performance for the firm. Sales totaled HUF 1,655 million in this period with a total absence of exports, as in almost all previous years. There was a relatively insignificant operating loss of HUF 20 million, and taxes totaled HUF 1,174 million. No profit taxes were paid, but after-tax profits of HUF 8 million could be earned due to the nonrecurring surplus of extraordinary receipts over extraordinary expenditure, a balance that had been negative during the entire 1988–91 period and in each of its years.

The firm's cost structure reflected the low capital intensity of its production and also the modest level of value added peculiar to the brewing industry. This meant a high exposure to other cost elements, primarily to increasing prices of material and energy.

Figures for the first half of 1992 reveal changes in the firm's cost structure. These changes could be interpreted as the first evidence of the strategic changes accomplished by management. The share of material costs and energy decreased to 35.9 percent and 9.0 percent respectively and the share of wages decreased to 35.9 percent, while the proportion of other costs increased to 29.1 percent. This meant a growing importance for sales and marketing expenditures, financed through a more efficient use of material inputs.

The relatively modest growth of labor costs shows two important and interrelated characteristics. The smoothness of labor relations at the firm and the fact that an important segment of employees became *de facto* owners helped management to get slow wage increases accepted by the firm's work force.

Management had relatively little freedom in its inventory policy due to the high material intensity of production. It was true, however, that successful marketing and a good programming of production, adjusted to the strongly seasonal character of demand, helped to keep output inventories at a low level.

The low technological level and capital intensity of the brewery industry in general is evident in the extremely low level of R&D and investment expenditure by the firm. It spent the minuscule amounts of HUF 2.9 million in 1988, HUF 0.8 million in 1989, HUF 6.6 million in 1990, HUF 0.3 million in 1991, and nothing in the first half of 1992 on R&D, and its expenditure on gross fixed investment remained at fairly constant levels in nominal terms, e.g., between HUF 140 million in 1988 and HUF 166 million in 1989. One remarkable increase occurred in the first half of 1992 when HUF 169 million was spent on investment, more than in the entire previous year. However, this did not imply that a radical change in the firm's rather low-profile investment strategy had occurred.

The conservatism of the firm's financial strategy was demonstrated by the fact that it had avoided financing investment from external funds. Nineteen eighty-eight had been the last year that the firm used banking credit for investment, when it accounted for 56 percent of its investment expenditure in that year. This approach could at least partly explain why the firm's debt exposure toward the banking sector did not increase substantially between 1988 and 1991. Its stock of bank debt was HUF 606 million in 1988, HUF 523 million in 1989, HUF 647 million in 1990, and HUF 729 million in 1991. There was, however, a marked increase in the first half of 1992, when the debt grew to HUF 1.633 million.

This negative turn helps explain the management's growing pessimism about the deterioration of the business climate in Hungary. During 1990–91, the amount of unpaid receivables literally exploded from HUF 466 million to HUF 1.025 million. The firm felt obliged to rely on services of firms specialized in recovering bad debt, but this was normally a procedure that cost 20–25 percent of the value of the recoverable assets. A significant part of other bad assets had to be written off and refinanced. For this reason, the decrease of unpaid receivables from HUF 1.025 million in 1991 to HUF 695 million in the first half of 1992 was accompanied by an increase in bank debt.

HUMAN RESOURCES AND MANAGEMENT

The brewery's manpower structure showed a marked shift toward a higher share of skilled labor during 1988–92. The number of operatives decreased from 1,024 to 855 between 1988 and the first half of 1992, whereas the number of engineers and technicians grew from 16 to 20 in the same period. There was also a relatively significant increase, from 29 to 35, in the number of managers. Another important trend in employment was the total disappearance of part-time employees, whose number had been at 24 in 1988. This latter trend could be at least partly explained by the decrease in female employment from 413 to 377 in the period analyzed.

Many women had entered part-time employment in industry in the Nagykanizsa region, where households normally had multiple sources of income from industry and household plots. Growing tensions in the labor market, increasing tax burdens and the decreasing dependence of social security on regular employment, as well as most employers' policies against part-time employment, led to the decline of the part-time employment of housewives in industry. This was the case not only in Nagykanizsa, but in Hungary as a whole.

Labor relations were not a problem at the firm and there was no information on any labor conflict. Moreover, even the trade unions were very much in the background, and their function was mostly formal. The reason for this was mainly the high level of employee participation in ownership, combined with the fact that the strategic role of the employees in shaping the firm's future was stressed repeatedly by consecutive managements. The brewery industry belonged, by the way, to the less unionized sectors of Hungarian industry.

The brewery's management consisted of the director general and his four deputies: a financial deputy, a technical deputy, and a marketing director, plus a deputy director general in charge of strategic issues and privatization. The director general had earned a biochemistry degree in Prague and all his deputies had Hungarian master's degrees in their respective fields. Although management had no training background or experience from the West, this was not a major handicap, given the firm's low, or even nonexistent, dependence on exports. Moreover, all members of the firm's top management had risen within the firm. The average age of the approximately thirty high- and medium-level managers, below forty years, was low.

THE FIRM'S STRATEGY

The brewery's business strategy focused on three major inter-related issues. The first priority was privatization, which was aided by a strong effort to improve quality, and the second, the exploration of new markets. The last major step in quality improvement had been the increase of the share of products with a warranty of 180 days to above 50 percent.

After privatization was accomplished, management had to create a new strategy. This had as its focal points both a continued marketing offensive and restructuring. The marketing offensive was to be based on the creation of a new corporate image reflecting much higher quality requirements and an ever-increasing level of quality of products and services offered to consumers.

Restructuring was closely linked to the marketing push. The firm had a strongly decentralized system of sales channels and points, including distribution, storage, and bottling plants. The strategy was to privatize these as well, so that these small local plants would initially become the firm's majority-owned subsidiaries. When they were strong enough to survive without direct links with the brewery, they would be offered for sale to their managers and employees.

The Kanizsa Brewery's management was clearly focused on improving performance at the firm's central plant, with special emphasis on production. Ongoing technological modernization was a key strategic priority. The sources of its financing were not yet clear, with financing from banks or the participation of outside investors being possible options, but the management insisted on keeping the firm in the majority ownership of M+E Ltd. This did not mean forcing an ESOP within the holding, M+E Ltd., because they thought the current ownership form would be able to attract more capital from employees and managers, even without formally creating an ESOP scheme.

The firm's good product mix, its relatively high level of corporate culture with stable labor relations, and a more or less sound financial situation made Kanizsa a good candidate for expansion. The long-term survival of the firm could not be questioned at all.

Notes

1. Hungarian business law is a blend of Anglo-Saxon and continental, primarily German, legal systems in the sense that, like German law, it allows limited liability-based corporate forms, but, like Anglo-Saxon legal systems, it makes it possible to clearly separate corporate assets from private ones. Moreover, it sets a very low legal capital stock limit for founding private firms. Therefore, the risk of individual investors with respect to the failure or liquidation of the limited-liability corporate forms owned by them can be very low.

Their corporate creditors are further handicapped by the fact that state claims, such as social security, the Tax Office, and the Customs Office, have a legally fixed priority over corporate claims. All this means that small firms with an inadequate capitalization ratio might find it relatively risk-free to contract debt with corporate suppliers. Companies like Kanizsa Brewery, whose clientele mostly consisted of smaller and largely undercapitalized private firms, could therefore find themselves exposed to an above-average level of business risk.

Table 1

Kariza Brewery Net Structure (data in HUF million, and in million liters for volume of output)

	1988	1989	1990	1991
Gross output, total	1,306	1,552	2,401	2,879
Product 1 (Balaton Light)				
Value of output	486	424	594	832
Volume of output	69	49	49	52
Product 2 (Holsten)				
Value of output	255	331	578	731
Volume of output	16	20	24	23

Notes: Dollar–forint exchange rates, 1988: $U.S.1 = HUF50.424; 1989: $U.S.1 = HUF59.066; 1990: $U.S.1 = HUF64.147; 1991: $U.S.1 = HUF74.722.

Table 2

Kanizsa Brewery's Main Financial Indicators (data in HUF million)

	1988	1989	1990	1991
Annual sales	1,507	1,937	2,752	3,503
Gross profit before tax	88	144	313	228
All taxes paid (incl. social security)	1,470	1,731	2,320	2,328
Profit taxes	41	46	145	39
Subsidies	—	—	—	—
Profit after tax	79	60	172	156

Notes:
Figures do not add up due to rounding and minor omissions.
Line 3 (taxes paid) does not include VAT-type taxes.
Dollar–forint exchange rates, 1988: $U.S.1 = HUF50.424; 1989: $U.S.1 = HUF59.066; 1990: $U.S.1 = HUF64.147; 1991: $U.S.1 = HUF74.722.

Table 3

Kanizsa Brewery's Cost Structure (in percentages)

	1988	1989	1990	1991
Total costs	100	100	100	100
of which:				
Costs of material	50.1	46.2	47.1	43.8
Wage costs	9.1	9.7	9.7	9.9
Energy costs	10.9	9.9	9.6	10.7
Banking costs (incl. interest)	6.1	6.1	8.8	10.6
Depreciation	4.3	4.5	4.2	4.4
Other costs	19.5	23.6	20.6	20.6

Table 4

Kanizsa Brewery's Inventories (structure in percentages)

	1988	1989	1990	1991
Purchased inventory of materials and parts	92	95	92	91
Inventories of output	8	5	8	9

Note: The proportion for the first half of 1992 was the same as for 1991, i.e., 91:9.

10

Pharmaceuticals: EGIS Pharmaceutical Works Ltd.

No Prescriptions for Healthy Firms?

Judit Karsai

THE PHARMACEUTICAL INDUSTRY IN HUNGARY

The Hungarian pharmaceutical industry consisted of six firms with a combined output of HUF 60 billion, or about $800 million, in 1991. The share of this among the different firms was as follows: Gedeon Richter 29 percent, Chinoin 23 percent, EGIS 22 percent, Biogal 14 percent, Alkaloida 11 percent, Reanal 1 percent.

On average, 50 percent of each firm's output was exported. The industry had an employment level of 20,000, with wages totaling 8 percent of the combined output. Initial figures for 1992 suggested a 10 percent increase in output, a trend contrary to the overall development of Hungarian industry.

A BRIEF HISTORY OF THE FIRM

EGIS was founded in 1913 as the Hungarian subsidiary of the Swiss firm, Dr. Albert Wander AG. This Berne-based enterprise wanted to find a stable outlet in the Austro-Hungarian Monarchy, Italy, and the Balkans. Its product mix included the still-famous Ovomaltine nutriment and numerous other over-the-counter items like throat lozenges, candies, malt products, and bonbons. Its Hungarian subsidiary enjoyed a sales boom from the mid-1920s on. This boom entailed diversification, and the firm's product mix came to include cosmetics, household articles, and packaging products. The firm also progressed in pharmaceutical R&D and components production. World War II had grievous effects; the firm lost most of its markets, and its buildings were seriously damaged.

After the war, the firm was nationalized with other pharmaceutical firms. The resulting group of firms was renamed Egyesült Gyógyszer-és Tápszergyár

(Amalgamated Pharmaceutical and Nutriments Works). The 1950s and 1960s were a period of fast growth for the firm both in the field of dosage-form pharmaceuticals and pharmaceutical agents. It established major capacities for the production of pharmaceutical agents and new laboratories were put in place for R&D and quality control.

The most important development of the 1970s was the establishment of the firm's new plant at the town of Körmend, close to the border with Austria. Modern packaging facilities were added to this small plant later on.

The firm received its current name, EGIS, in the early 1980s. It became a self-administered firm in 1985, and its five-year plan for 1986–90 was discussed and adopted by its new management council. It established a new plant in Budapest in 1989. This meant EGIS was able to expand within a generally staggering economy. The firm had operated under a joint stock company form, with majority ownership by the state, since December 1991.

PRODUCT MIX AND SALES PATTERN

EGIS was the second or third largest firm within the Hungarian pharmaceutical industry. Probably this is the top sector of Hungarian industry as far as international competitiveness and R&D capacity are concerned. If the closing of the technology gap between Hungarian firms and major multinationals could ever be achieved, it would most likely occur in this industry.

EGIS had a product mix consisting of 98 percent pharmaceuticals and related products. One-quarter of its sales was accounted for by active ingredients in bulk form, three-quarters by dosage-form drugs ready for consumption. Medicines made by EGIS can help to combat nearly twenty different diseases, but the firm earned a good reputation primarily in the field of traditional neurology and the treatment of circulatory illnesses. It was one of the leading pharmaceutical firms in central Europe and its sales pattern had been traditionally very balanced. This meant the relative shares of the three main markets, domestic, East and West, had been roughly equal.

This balanced sales structure helped EGIS maintain its financial stability during the past few decades, because negative effects from one market could be more or less successfully offset with increased sales efforts on another. This approach was used when EGIS had to abandon most of its former CMEA markets, as the loss was made up by price increases on domestic and Western markets and by a favorable change in the regulations pertaining to CMEA exports. The lifting of the so-called output tax[1] helped the firm to realize much higher after-tax profits even from considerably lower sales on the former CMEA markets in 1991. Table 1 shows the sales structure of EGIS.

Domestic sales had a special importance for the firm. EGIS did not stand out among its domestic competitors in this respect, because domestic sales had usually been a major factor for all of them. Overhead costs of such sales were disproportionately low as compared with sales to other markets. Therefore, a higher percentage of EGIS's profits came from domestic sales than the relative share of these sales. This is why the above average increase in domestic sales in 1991 had a very beneficial impact on EGIS's profits in that year.

It is worth mentioning at this point that management had to put less effort into the sales success on the domestic market than into maintaining the firm's even modest presence on traditional markets of East and Central Europe. There was no need for any major change in the product mix. Boosting domestic sales required the creation of a completely new sales channel, direct sales to hospitals, and more efficient marketing. More efficient marketing in the former CMEA countries required, however, much more of a policy of small steps. This included the creation of storage facilities for consignment sales and very significant sales promotion efforts paying much attention to less important clients and low-value sales.

The role of the domestic market as a major source of profits for EGIS could have been even stronger if the pharmaceutical market had not been one of the few remaining markets in Hungary where state regulation still existed before 1991. This special form of state regulation was known as the supply responsibility of domestic producers. This regulatory device was used to force domestic producers to supply the domestic markets with shortage goods even if these sales generated losses for them.

The specific characteristics of the health sector, including the large role of the state as a buyer of pharmaceuticals, the limited substitutability between domestic and imported products, and the major legal risks linked to shortages seemed to justify a certain degree of regulation of the pharmaceutical market. Before 1991, Hungarian pharmaceutical firms were legally obliged to sign domestic sales contracts and to honor them for those drugs that were registered in Hungary. The Health Act stipulated that the registration of a drug made in Hungary automatically obliged the manufacturer to supply the domestic market with that medicine in quantities sufficient to meet commercial demand.

Although this regulation was contrary to the Competition Act while not legally superseding it, EGIS's management did not openly reject this limitation on competition. They thought that the domestic supply of medicines was a major political issue and that any imbalance on the market would probably have had a very damaging impact on the image of drug manufacturers. It is certainly true that most of the EGIS products sold on the domestic market had roughly similar profitability levels, so non-price preferences among them would not damage the firm. Even in case EGIS were forced to produce and sell a loss-making product, the firm's major concern with capacity utilization would easily help it overcome this problem.

The security of EGIS's sales on a hitherto regulated but also protected domestic market has been slowly undermined by institutional changes in sales channels, such as the liberalization of wholesale trade and the gradual liberalization of pharmaceutical imports. The impact of these changes was felt by EGIS only from the more sporadic character of orders from domestic wholesale firms in

1991, and domestic sales are expected to fall in 1992. The low degree of monopolization of the wholesale trade in drugs does not really mean that EGIS could make its clients compete with each other to sell more of its products. More important side-effects of these developments were the increasing uncertainty of market forecasts and the lower dependability of orders.

Wholesale firms struggled with inventory and payments problems and EGIS had to be careful not to get caught up in these problems. It had become necessary for the firm to increase the flexibility of its supply, which also required increased inventories, especially in the most recent period.

The share of output in inventories had reached 58.1 percent in the first half of 1992. The increasing instability of the domestic market forced EGIS to look for another more effective supply-side reaction to this instability. The solution was a much stronger effort in direct marketing. For example, the firm had put together a staff of twenty so-called visitors. The members of this group regularly visited medical doctors in order to familiarize them with new EGIS products and R&D strategy, to discuss side-effects or special suggestions for use, and to get acquainted with the special needs of the medical profession.

Increasing import competition was very likely to worsen EGIS's competitive position on the domestic market, especially in the long run. Most import licenses had been available only for drugs of vital importance, but now the domestic producers of other medicines had to face increased foreign competition as well. It could also be expected that competition between drugs that are substitutes for each other would be strong, because the number of medicines legally available in Hungary was much less than the number of drugs available in West European countries.

This new situation would make life more difficult for domestic firms manufacturing modern foreign drugs on the basis of licenses, because the Western providers of know-how would be increasingly interested in selling their own products to Hungary. EGIS would be strongly affected by such changes in the policies of major foreign pharmaceutical firms because it had been successful in purchasing and implementing licenses under favorable terms. At the same time, it also felt the favorable impact of import liberalization on the input side. This provided better access to imports of pharmaceutical agents and chemicals and, due to this competition, improved conditions under which it bought from domestic suppliers who accounted for about 40 percent of EGIS's inputs.

The former CMEA markets played a very important role in the sales of EGIS for decades. The normal 30 percent share of output taken by this market decreased by half in 1991. As a rule, EGIS was more successful in maintaining its presence on the market in countries where the transition to the market economy has been less disorganized. The firm had to invest massively in each of these markets[2] to be able to stay there. In this way, it was able to regain its temporarily lost market shares in Poland, Czechoslovakia, and the former German Democratic Republic. Moreover, EGIS showed itself capable of quick adjustment to the different markets by flexibly serving all the newly appearing local distributors of medical products. It was helped, of course, by its good image on those markets and by its network of local contacts.

The major problem with respect to maintaining former positions on ex-CMEA markets appeared in the former Soviet Union. This was an outlet for about one-fourth of EGIS's sales in the past, but the market deteriorated into anarchy. There were neither distributors nor storage firms, and pharmacy networks seemed to have disappeared, therefore there was no negotiating partner for the firm. EGIS tried to open missions or representative offices in most successor countries, but such efforts seemed to be premature in some cases. EGIS was not even paid for part of its exports made on the basis of a payments guarantee of the Soviet government in 1991.[3] The current unsatisfactory situation on this market seemed to effectively disprove the old argument of EGIS's management that "there will always be sick people on such a big market."

It is true that the management was very innovative in trying to identify any possibility to boost sales in the former USSR. One such attempt was linked to economic diplomacy. EGIS wanted to be included in the Western aid programs to Russia and the other successor states. Another effort was being made in Hungary where EGIS was trying to get a share of the export credit package offered by the government to help pharmaceutical exports to the former USSR. This credit line, worth $10 million, was, however, far from sufficient. EGIS had no other choice than to try to cope with losses linked to missing receipts from exports to the East. The firm could find comfort in the fact that the profitability of its remaining sales to the former Soviet Union had vastly increased, but this favorable development alone did not offer any solution to the capacity utilization problem.

The decrease in the volume of sales reduced capacity utilization, which was down by 10 percentage points from the 90 percent average of the last few years. There had been a decline in production efficiency, as measured per working hour, but production halts had not been required as yet.

Profitability trends show that EGIS's current structure of sales could be profitable only with a relatively low level of sales to the West, because losses from these sales had to be covered by profits earned elsewhere. A massive export offensive directed toward Western markets to increase sales there above their traditional share of around 30 percent of output would have required a significant improvement in the profitability of those sales.

EGIS's exports to the West consisted of a product mix quite different from sales on the two other markets. Whereas dosage-form drugs were the most important part of sales in Hungary and former CMEA countries, 90 percent of the exports to the West consisted of bulk sales of pharmaceutical ingredients. Most of the dosage-form drugs sales took place on the basis of tenders. Competition was very strong on the markets for these mass products because their patents had either already expired or their patent protection could be bypassed. Some more extensive dosage-form drugs were sold to private hospitals or doctors, but these were almost exclusively brand products.

EGIS had dropped some unprofitable items from its Western exports during the past several years. This led to cuts in the firm's exports to the Third World. Reexports were eliminated and more emphasis was put on serving only solvent foreign clients. These changes improved export profitability but further deteriorated capacity utilization. Another improvement in the profitability of Western exports occurred due to unexpectedly high price increases of sales by foreign agents. These price increases could be linked to a particularly favorable sales climate and to a more efficient negotiating policy of the firm.

EGIS's marketing strategy on Western markets was to be focused on special products that had no competitors. Unfortunately, EGIS had a technological monopoly for only about 5 percent of its current sales. Therefore, the firm had to extend its R&D base and make its R&D as well as its marketing truly international. In order to achieve these goals, it would need a substantial injectio of capital. In addition to this, it would need to decide how to organize its marketing operations in the future.

EGIS had no full-fledged marketing division at the moment. Rather, it used the services of a trading house and the EGIS management thought there was no need to create a corporate marketing division. Instead, the management appeared to be concentrating on bringing the largest possible number of original medicines to the market, because the increasingly competitive market environment meant for EGIS that its future could not be built on non-original products to such an extent as was the case before 1992.

THE FINANCIAL SITUATION OF EGIS

EGIS was in an exceptionally stable financial situation for a Hungarian firm. Its sales amounted to nearly HUF 12 billion in 1991. This was a 9 percent growth over 1990, and 36 percent over 1988. Half of the revenues came from the domestic market in 1991, which was a stabilizing factor as described in the previous section. In fact, EGIS's domestic sales increased by 44 percent in 1991, which was proof of active adjustment to the changing market environment.

The firm's good performance in 1991 was backed by a well-managed change in the product mix. This was reflected in a decrease of the share of materials in inputs, which was beneficial in terms of direct costs. The considerable fall in direct costs had a favorable impact on profit rates, despite the increase in the share of fixed costs. The expected improvement in the cost structure could not be fully realized due to the sudden increase in banking costs.

The firm had a record year in 1991, with its profits at an unprecedented high—three times higher than in 1990. This profit of HUF 1.802 billion was more than 15 percent of sales, as compared to 5 percent in the previous year, and the increase of the profit/assets ratio from 9 percent to 26 percent was also spectacular. All key financial indicators improved substantially between 1990 and 1991. Thus, gross output grew by 29.0 percent, net sales by 9.0 percent, value added by 41.7 percent, net output by 45.7 percent, and after-tax profit by 46.0 percent.

The indicators of EGIS's debt also turned out favorably in 1991, with a considerable improvement over 1990. The liquidity ratio showed that the firm had 2.2 times more liquid resources than its debt with a less-than-one-year maturity. The debt service ratio was 2.9, i.e., the sum of after-tax profit and depreciation was 2.9 times higher than debt service in 1992. The firm's financial strategy focused on diminishing its long-term debt exposure, and long-term debt amounted to only 9 percent of the book value of assets.

HUMAN CAPITAL, MANAGEMENT AND LABOR RELATIONS

The firm's financial stability was clearly evident in the field of human resources. Continued growth was helpful for avoiding drastic lay-offs and management preferred the slow erosion of redundant manpower to serious labor cuts. EGIS had 3,743 employees at the end of 1991, 5 percent fewer than a year before. Employees leaving voluntarily or retiring were replaced from within the firm. The firm's human resources policy was flexible, partly due to its average wage level, which was high even by pharmaceutical industry standards.

Gross wages averaged HUF 307,000 in 1991, 25,000 per month, and employees also received free asset coupons convertible into company shares. Earnings showed an above average growth for technology-linked managers, and this was the only employment category in which employment increased.

The firm's prosperity had to be linked to the ability and efforts of its upper management, whose members normally were promoted from within. A partial generational change took place in 1989 when the research and the marketing directors retired simultaneously.

The firm's CEO was trained as a chemical engineer on a scholarship provided by the firm. He had worked at EGIS since 1964 and he took twenty-one years to become its CEO. He was a well-known figure in the economic and political life of Hungary through his role as the president of the Economic Chamber of Hungary.

The financial director, who had a degree in economics, had worked for almost ten years with the then Ministry of Heavy Industry before he came to the firm in 1981. The technical director, who was educated as a chemical engineer, had been with EGIS since 1962. The marketing director had a degree in pharmacology. He had spent ten years with the firm, beginning in 1969, and, after working abroad, he was appointed to his current position twenty years later.

There were currently two trade unions active within EGIS. About 65–70 percent of the employees belonged to the successor of the old trade union, which was considered part of the communist political heritage by the other trade union, and which had only 5 percent—approximately eighty people—of the firm's employees among its ranks. The second union was much more aggressive and active, but part of its energy was used against its formerly communist competitor. For example, it took a firm stand against the ESOP proposal because it considered the ESOP proposal to be an attempt to preserve the economic power of the former management.

The firm's privatization process was closely followed by the trade unions and mostly supported by them. The trade unions requested, however, that they be accepted as full-fledged partners of the State Property Agency (SPA) during the privatization negotiations. They also expected the SPA to be obliged to conclude a legally binding agreement with them on job and wage security and on the maintenance of the social network and infrastructure within the firm. The SPA refused to accept the trade unions as independent negotiating partners, but it agreed to represent their requests to the new owners, with the exception of the one request for maintaining the existing social infrastructure.

THE ONLY STRATEGIC OPTION: TRANSFORMATION AND PRIVATIZATION

The book value of the firm's total assets was HUF 6.771 billion in 1991, with an 85 percent ownership held by the state. This less-than-total state ownership was the result of privatization efforts that had been practically uninterrupted since 1989. The first ideas for privatization did not exclude the possibility of an ESOP, but the employees' lack of interest in this solution brought to the fore the possibilities of finding a strategic investor or the sale of the firm's shares on the stock exchange as the two most viable options. EGIS had sought, above all, two things from privatization: injections of capital into R&D and marketing, and better access to new product and marketing information. As a firm with steady profits, it also had a serious interest in teaming up with a foreign investor for financial reasons. By teaming up with a foreign firm, EGIS could take advantage of the considerable tax breaks enjoyed by joint ventures in high-tech sectors.

The strategic commitment to privatization was not pursued by means of hasty steps. Rather, the management took a cautious approach. This caution had a mostly psychological basis resulting from the fact that the firm had very seasoned and experienced managers who preferred a low-profile approach to business decisions. EGIS's management had a reputation for being reluctant to take excessive risks and to try to be first in any new field, but they were also known for being ready to prepare important strategic measures that could be implemented when circumstances were appropriate. This was true also in the case of the firm's privatization. The strategy and key measures for implementing it were prepared but not made public.

In line with this philosophy, management made auditing and asset valuation a first priority. The firm approached the SPA only after these had been completed. The privatization process was placed on hold until summer 1991. At that time, one of the central privatization initiatives, which ultimately did not get the status of a privatization program, focused on firms facing collapse due to the loss of their former CMEA markets.

EGIS was, for some reason, considered as one of such firms, although even a glance at the firm's balance sheet would have made it clear that this firm could have remained in good financial health despite the undeniable losses that the quasi-collapse of its Eastern sales inflicted upon it. Nevertheless, with EGIS categorized as a firm vulnerable to external shocks of an East European origin, its transformation process could finally begin. This process was relatively smooth, and EGIS became a company limited by shares in late 1991, with 85 percent of its shares owned by the state, 10 percent owned by employees, and 5 percent by municipalities in which its facilities were located.

Further privatization proposals were prepared by Credit Suisse First Boston (CSFB). Some options, such as sales to a large domestic investor or an MBO, were immediately ruled out. Domestic investors were considered uninterested because of the large amount of capital required for such an investment. The managers themselves rejected the MBO option, recognizing that "this is too good a firm, and the SPA will not stay out of a promising privatization deal because it needs some successes in its portfolio of holdings."

The SPA and the management jointly took the decision that 51 percent of EGIS's state-owned shares would be sold to a single strategic investor through a closed tender.[4] The Public Offering Memorandum was sent by CSFB to more than seventy potential investors in January 1992, and it was very likely that EGIS would start 1993 as an international firm.

The management stressed that EGIS was an attractive investment target. Through it, the foreign investor could get access to a domestic market that had a national health system that was quite comprehensive by regional standards. The firm's tradition, its R&D potential, low operating costs, considerable export know-how, financial stability, and good geographical location were all major assets. EGIS also had an excellent image on East European markets.

Privatization seemed promising, but it has to be emphasized that the firm had no other strategic choice. Because it had not yet been privatized, the State Assets Management Corporation (SAMC) became the holder of its shares. SAMC could be expected to act as an enlightened monarch, and could be willing to help EGIS, but it was unable to inject capital into EGIS and to get it access to foreign markets. Nor could SAMC be expected to help EGIS create a more efficient internal structure. All these tasks would require the assistance of a foreign strategic partner.

The need for a major foreign investor was, to begin with, based on EGIS's considerable need for fresh capital. The size of the necessary amount, in all probability, excluded domestic investors. Moreover, EGIS placed great emphasis on an investment by a foreign pharmaceutical firm, because its R&D capacity could be brought to the international scene only if its access to the world market were assured by a foreign partner who had an extensive global distribution network. Therefore, other Hungarian pharmaceutical firms, also in need of injections of capital themselves, would hardly be able to become a major partner in EGIS since they shared the same strategic liabilities in marketing with EGIS.

Given these considerations, it is evident that a partnership with a major multinational pharmaceutical firm would be the ideal way of addressing EGIS's strategic objectives.

Notes

1. This tax had been introduced in order to centralize profits earned from exports to the CMEA by enterprises active in sectors selling overpriced so-called hard goods to CMEA markets, mostly the Soviet Union. It was initially used completely to compensate exporters selling there at depressed prices, e.g., Bakony in our sample, but later on such receipts were probably partly used to help diminish the budget deficit. The last marginal rate of this tax was as high as 40 percent in 1990 before it was completely lifted in 1991.
2. This investment meant the creation of regional centers of distribution, storage facilities and visitor teams.
3. A proof for the collapse of sales to CIS states was the 150 percent increase of the long-term moving average of inventory of finished goods between 1990 and 1991.
4. As a matter of fact, CSFB persuaded the Hungarians that their proposal of selling only 30 percent, the minimum required for tax break eligibility, to a foreign investor would make the transaction much less attractive than a 51 percent offer.

The role of the SPA in the process also needs clarification. EGIS did not really feel that the SPA was the firm's owner. SPA did not intervene in the firm's strategy because it lacked the professional competence to do so. After the firm's transformation, the role of was taken over by the Board of Directors. The State Assets Management Corporation was to have the firm's shares in its portfolio, which did not imply any interference with the firm's strategy, but could delay its privatization.

Table 1

The Sales Structure of EGIS (shares to main markets in percentages)

	1988	1989	1990	1991
Domestic sales	39	33	39	51
Exports (CMEA or former CMEA)	30	32	28	14
Exports (OECD and Third World)	27	30	27	32
Other exports (e.g., China)	4	5	6	3
Total sales	100	100	100	100

Note: The changes in the relative shares of the different markets are reflected in the divergence of growth trends of these different sales.

Table 2

The Development of the Sales of EGIS (1988 = 100)

	1988	1989	1990	1991
Domestic sales	100	86	123	177
Exports (CMEA or former CMEA)	100	110	116	64
Exports (OECD and Third World)	100	112	123	161
Other exports (e.g., China)	100	155	211	105
Total sales	100	103	125	136

Table 3

The Structure of EGIS's Inventories (in percentages)

	1988	1989	1990	1991
Inventories of inputs	68.8	64.7	61.1	43.0
Inventories of outputs	31.2	35.3	38.9	57.0

Table 4

The Profitability of the Sales of EGIS by Main Markets (in percentages)

	1988	1989	1990	1991
Domestic sales	27.2	21.5	23.5	21.5
Exports (CMEA or former CMEA)	4.8	−18.5	−10.6	32.0
Exports (OECD and Third World)	−1.1	−5.6	−6.6	−1.6
Total sales	13.3	2.1	5.5	15.3

Table 5

The Cost Structure of EGIS's Output (in percentages)

	1988	1989	1990	1991
Wages	10.6	9.8	10.0	11.2
Other wage-linked costs	4.2	4.3	4.3	4.8
Materials	51.8	51.0	47.2	44.8
Energy	4.8	3.3	4.1	4.1
Banking costs (incl. interest)	5.9	6.2	10.0	10.7
Depreciation	4.2	4.6	4.1	3.4
Other costs	19.3	20.7	20.2	20.9

11

Auto Parts: Bakony Metal and Electrical Appliance Works

Hot Spark Plugs?

Miklós Somai

AN OVERVIEW OF THE INDUSTRY

The auto parts industry in Hungary was vertically structured. This meant most individual components manufacturers were technologically linked to their clients. Therefore, the markets for most auto parts made in Hungary were virtually monopsonistic.

A large number of these firms had specialized in supplying the strongest manufacturers on the traditionally highly protected Hungarian market for passenger cars and utility vehicles. These included, for passenger cars made in East Europe, Lada, Polski Fiat, Dacia, and Zastava; for utility vehicles in Hungary, Ikarus and Csepel; and for those produced in the Soviet Union/Russia, KAMAZ. Therefore, very few Hungarian manufacturers of auto parts competed with each other. Where this did occur, it was for products whose demand was less dependent on the technology of the auto manufacturer. Such products included glass, tires, and batteries, but not the products made by Bakony.

Bakony became a auto parts manufacturer in the early 1970s in conjunction with the Soviet Union's effort to create its own modern passenger car industry, in cooperation with Fiat. Therefore, Bakony still had a more or less Fiat-based technology and production culture, while the newest domestic manufacturers of auto parts in Hungary were already linked to those Western passenger car manufacturers, Opel and Suzuki, who had established manufacturing operations in Hungary. For example, another firm analyzed by our case studies, Salgglas, was likely to become a supplier to Suzuki.

A BRIEF HISTORY OF THE FIRM

The predecessor of Bakony, the Hungarian Ammunition Works Ltd., was founded in 1938 as part of the Hungarian armament program when the country was preparing for war. Originally, the Royal Treasury of Hungary owned 59.4 percent of the firm, and the rest was divided among a savings bank, a copper mill, and members of the board. The postwar period reparations and efforts were directed toward the creation a civilian product mix. With the nationalization in 1949, there was a temporary reconversion to military production.

The production of electric products in the form of small switches for household use began in 1959. Electrical appliances and auto components had been in production since 1963. The firm adopted its current name, Bakony Metal and Electrical Appliances Works, in 1968, at which time its founding document was also changed. Bakony became one of the first firms to build up extensive international cooperation on the basis of enterprise autonomy resulting from the 1968 economic reform, and to adopt specialization agreements in the framework of socialist economic integration.

The cooperation with VAZ (Lada) Automobile Works began in 1970, by means of which Bakony became one of the major components suppliers to the Soviet passenger car factory with an annual output of 700,000. This agreement was of the so-called balanced barter type, i.e., the Soviet Union delivered cars to Hungary in exchange for kits of auto parts. One car was the equivalent of approximately fifty kits consisting of horns, ignition systems, windshield wipers, and spark plugs.

Similar agreements were concluded in 1973 with FSM of Poland, the producer of the small Polski Fiat 126p, and Zastava of Yugoslavia in 1981. The three cooperation agreements were similar in their balanced barter payments system and their technological background: all three models were assembled in East Europe on the basis of licenses purchased in the late 1960s from Fiat. Therefore Bakony became loosely integrated into Fiat's international network of licensed producers, including Spanish, Turkish, Argentinean, Brazilian, and Indian as well as Soviet, Polish and Yugoslav firms.

Interestingly, most of these producers, including Bakony, did not follow Fiat's modernization of its products and technologies, but continued to manufacture components for the Fiat 120 product line, including the Fiat 124, 125, 126, 127 and 128, even in the late 1980s. The Italian firm had ceased to manufacture this product line in the late 1970s, replacing it with the Ritmo-based product line introduced in 1978, and the Tipo family in 1989.

In addition to its technological integration with the Fiat group and its East European licensees, Bakony was active on other East European markets. It became a supplier to the Romanian passenger car factory, Dacia, which was based on Renault technology, the Ukrainian producer of small ZAZ passenger cars, and the giant Russian truck manufacturer, KAMAZ. Bakony was equally successful in teaming up with major multinational firms other than Fiat.[1]

Bakony acquired licensed Bosch technology in 1974 for the production of auto repair and maintenance equipment; it started producing industrial ceramics in 1976; and capacity utilization became more efficient with the purchase of a license of KLG spark plugs from Smiths Industries of the United Kingdom in 1980. The last major step in the creation of the firm's current structure of output was taken in 1990 when ammunition production was completely stopped.

The firm's expansion, aided by several international cooperation agreements, made it necessary to invest in new plants. The Hungarian government's regional industrial policy in the 1970s gave priority, and sometimes also financial support, to job creation in underdeveloped areas. The seven plants of Bakony outside the city of Veszprém, where the firm had its headquarters, were all established or acquired in the decade 1969–78. The firm ceased to expand domestically in 1978, but domestic expansion resumed in a different legal form in 1988 when Bakony began to create subsidiaries, although only in Veszprém to date.

Its first subsidiary, Flexmont Ltd., assumed Bakony's production of repair and service equipment. The second subsidiary, Bakony Spark Plugs and Ceramics Ltd., was created in late 1991. The parent firm, Bakony, completed transformation in 1992 and took the form of a company limited by shares in July 1992. The new firm's Board of Directors considered privatization its first strategic priority.

PRODUCT MIX AND SALES PATTERN

The last chapter in Bakony's history was written by the sweeping political changes in East Europe beginning in 1989. The firm had a high degree of exposure to East European customers and had to face several demand-side shocks from East Europe. The first external shock came from the firm's main traditional client: in December 1989, its Soviet partner stated that part of Bakony's supply would no longer be needed. This was due to a fundamental change in VAZ's business philosophy[2] and in the intra-CMEA payments system. Not only did import prices begin to convey clear market signals to VAZ, but the Soviet firm lost interest in obtaining components whose combined price might well exceed the selling price of the car they were to manufacture. However, Bakony's Russian partner changed its attitude soon afterward and sales to Lada continued to account for 60 percent of Bakony's total sales in 1992.

Given that 70 percent of Bakony's sales went to CMEA markets, this was a dire warning for the firm. The collapse of some of Bakony's East European markets was not the only consequence of the change of the traditional Hungarian export pattern in intra-car-industry cooperation within the CMEA; also, the rapid liberalization of passenger car imports to Hungary nearly drove out Soviet-made Lada cars, which had been the market leader from 1973. In fact, their share in new car registrations declined from about 35 percent to well below 10 percent between 1988 and 1990. Therefore, somewhat paradoxically, a shift in the Hungarian demand for imports contributed to the dramatic external shock facing an exporter.

The same thing happened, although on a much smaller scale, to Bakony's other East European markets for components. Its sales to Romania stopped in 1989, exports to Yugoslavia and to the rest of the firm's Soviet market—ZAZ cars made in Ukraine by a firm different from VAZ and KAMAZ trucks—ceased in 1991, and Bakony finally lost its Polish market in 1992. The reasons were largely the same as those with the Lada connection.

The decline of Bakony's presence on its traditional East European markets for auto parts was primarily due to changes in the intra-CMEA payments system, followed soon after by the dissolution of the CMEA itself. Another factor was the opening up of East European markets to Western suppliers, especially to firms whose entry into these markets was facilitated by subsidies or by the acquisition of an East European market niche as a result of privatization.

Bakony's exports of horns to the VAZ factory were replaced by deliveries by a former East German firm, which had a very successful formula for invading the Russian market. The East German firm combined its contacts from within the former GDR and its knowledge of its Russian partners with a newly acquired solid technology base and German government support for creation of jobs and exports for the New Federal Länder.

Bakony's sales to Poland became a victim of the new Polish partnership with Fiat. The Italian multinational company upgraded its relationship with the Polish automobile industry to joint venture status. Both FSM's old 126 and the new Cinquecento assembly lines were supplied by Fiat's mostly Italian and German subcontractors.

Bakony's business strategy still largely depended on the cooperation with VAZ. The Russian firm originally wanted to substitute almost all components purchased from Bakony with Russian-made products, but this would have required substantial investment that neither VAZ nor its domestic partners could afford. The strategy of Bakony's new director general, Mr. Jüttner, who was appointed in December 1990, was also based on continuing cooperation with the Russian firm, at least until Western markets could be found for Bakony.

Bakony currently provided 50–60 percent of VAZ's input of windshield wipers and ignition systems, but it had little access to the international market for spare parts for Lada cars. Acquiring a larger share of the market in windshield wipers would be profitable because the average passenger car used three to five sets during its life cycle.

Two things must be explained in order to understand the strategic role of the VAZ connection. One factor was the status of the VAZ factory in the Russian economy. It was built in the 1960s as a prestige investment project and was meant to become the major supplier of passenger cars to the Soviet Union and the CMEA. VAZ had always enjoyed a special status in the Soviet, and later Russian, economy as a firm able to produce a car closer to world standards than other former Soviet cars, such as the Moskvich and Volga made in Russia and ZAZ made in Ukraine.

VAZ had special access to capital, imports, and skilled manpower and was the only Soviet/Russian firm able to export sophisticated engineering products for civilian use to the West. In fact, it exported about half of its 700,000 output in 1992 and 60,000 Lada cars were sold in Germany. For these reasons, VAZ could probably remain a relatively reliable partner for Bakony with more or less the necessary level of liquidity, as compared to Bakony's other traditional Soviet or post-Soviet clients to whom only a marginal sales level could be maintained after 1990.

The other factor was the system of payments between VAZ and Bakony. Before 1990, the method of payments for Bakony's products consisted of two parts: one between the Soviet Union and Hungary whereby kits of components were traded directly for cars, the other between the Hungarian government and Bakony. The nominal export price of components and the nominal import price of cars were both artificially low. A Lada Samara 2108 car, for example, could be purchased for $2,800 in 1988 in the Hungarian hard-currency shops, and the government compensated Bakony for its loss. For instance, the firm received HUF 275 million in 1988 and HUF 283 million in 1989 in compensation for its deficit from the Lada cooperation, while its pre-tax profits were HUF 201 and 157 million respectively. Thus, Bakony received more than its profit from the state budget.

This payment scheme changed in 1990 when the firm ceased to receive compensation for the deficit that Lada received directly from the state budget. It received a fixed amount of HUF 20,000 in turnover tax for each Lada car sold by Merkur, the state-owned monopolistic car retailer. The final amount of the compensation was HUF 644 million in that year, together with the relatively small amount paid for Polski Fiat 126p cars. As a result, Bakony's profits soared to HUF 334 million in 1990.

The barter scheme was discontinued in 1991 because of the introduction of trade paid in U.S. dollars between Hungary and the other CMEA countries. However, during 1991, VAZ did not have enough dollar liquidity to pay for its imports from Hungary in cash. There were times when Bakony had claims amounting to $4 million on VAZ, which resulted in an increase in Bakony's bank fees because of the high interest rates in Hungary and the relative appreciation of HUF with respect to the dollar. The increase of Bakony's short-term banking debt from HUF 351 million to HUF 650 million between late 1990 and late 1991 originated mainly from Bakony's need to have its receivables from VAZ refinanced in Hungary.

The problem of financing Bakony's sales to VAZ seemed to be solved by the creation of a Russo-Hungarian joint venture called Hungaro-Lada Ltd. Of this joint venture, 40 percent was owned by the trading house of VAZ and 10 percent by each of the six Hungarian trading partners of VAZ, Bakony among them. But after VAZ repaid its debt to Bakony in December 1991, it acquired Hungaro-Lada Ltd. At the time of this report, this 100 percent Russian-owned trading firm was selling Lada cars on its own account in Hungary and paid the factory's Hungarian suppliers with revenues from the car sales. Because the Hungarian passenger car market fell victim to the economic slump in the country and Lada cars did not have a very good reputation in a fully liberalized market, Bakony was normally an involuntary creditor to Hungaro-Lada.[3]

According to some of Bakony's managers, it might have been wiser to create a directly dollar-based payments system between Bakony and VAZ on the one hand and between VAZ and its Hungarian importer on the other. Such a system could have been made possible by the fact that VAZ had a substantial amount of receipts in U.S. dollars. It also had a high degree of financial autonomy within Russia because of its privileged status as a significant hard-currency earner outside the primary sector.

The current system of sales to and payments from VAZ was the same for Bakony as for its domestic clients. Because Lada cars imported in return for Bakony products were, in effect, produced by the same automobile industry in Hungary, Bakony believed that Lada cars should have been treated as Hungarian products by the government, much more so than the Opel or Suzuki cars that were assembled in Hungary and sold duty-free, but contained only some Hungarian value added. Lada cars were subject to an 18 percent customs duty. which was a serious handicap for them given that the products were of a downmarket nature and demand was very price-elastic.

The request for duty-free imports of Lada cars was quite unrealistic. Therefore, Bakony needed to find a strategic response to alleviate its dependence on Lada sales in Hungary. To this end, it chose to become part of Lada's dealer network in Hungary, which generated trade-related income for the firm. The value of imports of Lada cars to Hungary was expected to meet the $20 million target in 1992.

The other key element of Bakony's new sales strategy was a more active appearance on Western markets. There had already been remarkable success in this field; the firm's exports to the West rose by 61.4 percent in 1991 alone, and their share of Bakony's total sales reached 13.5 percent for that year. The product mix that the firm could offer for export to Western markets was, however, even less technologically intensive and its value-added component was lower than with exports to Russia.

The key product in Bakony's exports to Western markets was spark plugs. As a result of a 85.8 percent increase of this product's exports in that year alone, sales of these products in the West accounted for 56 percent of Bakony's total exports to the West in 1991. This spectacular achievement occurred as a result of a partnership with the U.S. firm, AC Rochester, a member of the General Motors group.[4]

Other partnerships were established in 1991 with German subsidiaries of the ITT group. One firm, SWF, leased equipment to Bakony for the production of the mechanical parts of windshield wipers. The output of this product was worth only HUF 20 million in 1991, but it quickly helped Bakony to become a supplier to VW, SEAT, Opel, Fiat, and Volvo. The management estimated that these sales would increase eight to ten times in 1992 to a value of about DM 4 million worth of exports because capacity was available and access to West European markets had been secured by the good quality of the first deliveries.

Another German ITT subsidiary, Teves, helped Bakony to become a supplier of emergency brake locks to BMW and of front seat elements to Audi. The Teves cooperation was expected to bring Bakony DM 2.1 million in exports during 1992. The Hungarian firm was also preparing to join the new Ford Sierra program with a special mechanical component of front door hinges.

These changes in Bakony's market pattern and product mix showed that the firm understood the need to abandon its traditional electrical appliances profile and switch to mechanical components. This shift in the firm's product mix constituted a strategic response to the collapse of Bakony's traditional sales pattern.

Such a shift was understandable if, in general, the image of a Hungarian auto parts manufacturer in Russia or in the West were considered. Its image was more upmarket, high-value-added and technologically intensive in Russia than in West Europe, quite independent of its real factors of competitiveness. Bakony also tried to develop its more upmarket type image in the West by introducing a comprehensive new quality management system in conformity with the international ISO 9000 quality standard.

This management system was essential for another key element of Bakony's new marketing strategy: that of becoming part of the network that supplied the two Hungarian passenger car assembly plants, co-owned by GM-Opel and Suzuki.

Negotiations with Opel, however, had not progressed very far because Bakony rejected Opel's cautious approach. Before ordering complete windshield wiper sets from Bakony, Opel wanted to make the Hungarian firm subject to a longer quality and in-time-delivery test while ordering only mechanical parts of these sets. GM-Opel believed that the evidence of quality derived from Bakony's Russian business was insufficient to make the Hungarian firm more than an indirect or second-tier supplier to a GM plant.

Bakony's Suzuki connection was in much better shape because of a license purchase for horns and windshield wipers from Matsuba Industries Ltd. of Japan. This HUF 150 million investment project, which was supported by the government through preferential credits, made Bakony one of the Hungarian suppliers officially accepted by Suzuki.

TRANSFORMATION AND PRIVATIZATION

Bakony was an exceptional Hungarian industrial enterprise in that transformation and privatization had apparently been quite low on its list of strategic priorities for a long time. Top priorities had been given to the transformation of the firm's product mix and the necessary adjustments in its sales pattern. The management declared that its most important strategic task was privatization but believed that the firm had to be made more lucrative for foreign investors. First, two major tasks had to be resolved before managers could begin the search for investors: the structure of Bakony's shares on different markets had to be optimized because access to markets that were highly evaluated by investors could increase the firm's privatization value; and Bakony had to be transformed into a company limited by shares.

Part of the first task was accomplished by the changes in the firm's product mix. The second task was finally completed in July 1992, despite the fact that the SPA seemed to want to delay the process. The SPA apparently believed that the transformation would only make sense if serious investors appeared, but Bakony's view was that the firm would be more financially and technologically understandable and transparent to possible Western investors if it were in a corporate form.

Bakony probably would not be privatized in its entirety because its product mix was too diversified, its geographical structure too scattered, and its strategic relationship with a Russian firm too strong. The privatization optimism still prevalent in 1990 was now gone and the firm had to be cleaned up before privatization could occur. The new management made important steps in this direction and started to eliminate the small rural plants that supplied former CMEA partners with low-value-added products. Bakony's plant at Kerta was closed and the plant at Mezôlak, which had formerly sold components to an East German firm that manufactured harvesters for the Soviet market, was closed in 1992.

BAKONY'S FINANCIAL SITUATION

We have seen from the examples that Bakony's *de facto* profit was markedly different from its operating profit because the firm was generously compensated for losses incurred as a result of excessively low sales prices on the Soviet market. On the other hand, many of its losses were due to high bank fees as a result of the Russian purchaser's liquidity problems.

Preliminary figures for the first half of 1992 showed the most spectacular change in the export/sales ratio, which decreased to only 18.6 percent. The explanation was the new legal status of Bakony's sales to VAZ: these were no longer considered exports because the buyer was Hungaro-Lada Ltd., a firm operating in Hungary. Total sales declined to HUF 1,395 million; all taxes paid declined to HUF 198 million, subsidies disappeared completely, and there was a relatively minor pre-tax loss of HUF 30 million.

Although Bakony's financial situation had deteriorated significantly, the firm could still be considered relatively sound financially, with no survival problems. Receivables totaled HUF 690 million in June 1992, compared to liabilities worth HUF 925 million. Of the latter, HUF 612 million was bank debt, which was normally significantly easier to manage than unpaid suppliers' credits. Furthermore, even though the bankruptcy law was quite severe, the firm was not threatened by bankruptcy.

The firm's cost structure reflected the impact of two major trends: an increase in bank fees resulting from the deteriorating liquidity situation of the firm's major client, and a corresponding decline in the degree of the material intensity of production. Labor intensity of production, on the other hand, increased slowly but surely. The other major cost elements have shown a remarkable stability in recent years.

The above-mentioned trends in the cost structure of Bakony changed, at least temporarily, in the first half of 1992. The decrease in the relative share of material costs was reversed by an increase to 42.5 percent while human resource costs declined to 28.7 percent. This was of strategic importance because it was one of the first signs of conservative manpower management at Bakony as part of the new, more privately oriented strategic approach.

The further increase of the share of bank costs to 9.8 percent was a warning signal stressing the urgency of paying much more attention to financial problems at the firm. Management agreed with us that the most obvious response to this challenge was privatization.

Unfavorable financial developments and an increasingly grim sales picture were also reflected by the changes in the structure of inventories, as shown in Table 3. The share of output in inventories reached 12.0 percent in the first half of 1992. This percentage was still quite low compared to levels experienced by firms such as Salgglas, which faced major financial trouble, but it did call for a major strategic intervention by management in order to transform the firm's sales pattern.

HUMAN RESOURCES AND LABOR RELATIONS

Employment at Bakony had declined significantly since 1988. The number of operatives went down from 3,437 to 2,351 between December 31, 1988 and June 30, 1992; the number of technicians from 141 to 92; and the number of managers from 249 to 182. These changes accelerated after early 1991 when the new management took control. Four hundred jobs were cut in 1991, resulting in a 20 percent improvement in per capita sales. Approximately the same number of jobs was cut in 1992.

The management's policy of accepting a hardening employment constraint was not only the result of decreasing sales. It can be traced back to technological changes. For example, with the old technology 50 workers were needed to produce approximately 4,000 windshield wipers per day, whereas at the SWF operation, 5–6 workers produced 5,000 wipers daily. Labor relations did not seem to constitute a major barrier to the strong-handed manpower policy of Bakony's management. One of the reasons for this is historical: Veszprém had a traditional reputation of freedom from political conflict as a university city with a strong presence of intellectuals and clergy, but a relatively low level of unionization. A more practical explanation was linked to Bakony's plant structure. The firm had a string of smaller rural plants scattered around the region employing many housewives from double-income households who were reluctant to organize or to participate in industrial action.

STRATEGIC CHOICES FOR BAKONY

Management had embarked on an ambitious program of reversing the firm's technological decline and loss of market share. The first results were encouraging and provide a good example of semi-successful reconversion from a strongly CMEA-oriented market pattern to a more Western sales orientation. The term semi-successful only means that Bakony was unable to abandon its dependence on the VAZ connection, although the financial rules of the game have markedly changed. A complete rupture with VAZ would not be feasible in the coming four to five years. Bakony had to be prepared to bear the costs, bank costs, for example, of the market pattern inherited from the days of the safe Soviet market. Indeed, Bakony was lucky to be linked to one of the very few Russian firms in a relatively good financial situation. VAZ's liquidity problems were dwarfed by the dramatic payments problems of many other Russian firms, of which many had a host of Hungarian firms among their traditional suppliers.

Bakony's strategy would include a more aggressive approach to transformation and privatization in the first half of 1993. Nevertheless, it remains to be seen whether the foreign investors the firm was looking for would come from among those firms currently supplying it with technology and helping it find new markets. Bakony's value to foreign investors might strongly depend on how they evaluate its strong supplier position in the Lada components market. This assessment depends on a variety of uncertain factors such as the future of the Russian economy and industry.

Notes

1. This happened at a time when joint ventures with Western firms were a rarity, even though they were legally possible in Hungary from 1972. Bakony followed a conscious strategic alliance policy with Western firms supplying technology and with eastern countries offering access to their markets. It is interesting to see that the concept of strategic

alliances was not unfamiliar to Hungarian industrial enterprises already in the early 1970s. It is true, of course, that this strategy was carried out in an embryonic form due to the isolation of Hungarian firms from world markets, but the behavioral pattern was remarkable.

2. The rule had been that the Soviet car factory obtained approximately two-thirds of the supply of each imported component from CMEA partners, the rest was produced in the Soviet Union, although at a lower quality. The imported components went into exported cars and those sold on exclusive segments of the domestic (Soviet) market. The reason for this unjustified high dependence on domestic inputs was the effort to avoid excessive dependence on imports. On the other hand, barter agreements with East European governments or firms were a secure source of relatively high-quality inputs for VAZ at prices that conveyed no market signals to VAZ, because their prices were only expressed in cars. The terms of trade fixed in the early 1970s in the barter agreements proved increasingly more beneficial for VAZ, because international price trends of components and of cars became divergent in favor of components.

3. Its claims on Hungaro-Lada reached HUF 400 million by June 1992, and the planned amount of Bakony's banking costs was HUF 250 million for 1992.

4. This partnership started in 1988, but it became a close one only in early 1991 when the two companies decided to create a joint venture with Rochester's 51 percent equity stake. The product of the joint venture would have been AC spark plugs with an annual output of 20 million, twice Bakony's annual output of the old KLG models. The joint venture was established in late 1991 with minimal equity capital, but a few months later, Rochester decided to quit because GM's losses had created problems in financing the joint venture. However, the joint venture was not liquidated because Bakony bought out Rochester's equity stake and the U.S. firm agreed to leave its technology and equipment in Hungary in the hope of a strategic alliance with Bakony.

Table 1

Bakony's Main Financial Indicators (data in HUF million)

	1988	1989	1990	1991
Annual sales	2,032	2,323	2,217	3,085
Exports/sales (in %)	52.4	57.8	61.6	77.0
Gross profit before tax	201	157	334	196
All taxes paid (incl. social security)	322	447	446	566
Profit taxes	90	94	120	116
Subsidies	273	293	656	13
Profits after tax	110	55	214	121

Notes:

1. Except for Line 2, figures do not add up due to rounding and minor omissions.

2. Line 4 (taxes paid) does not include VAT-type taxes.

3. Dollar–forint exchange rates, 1988: $U.S.1 = HUF50.424; 1989: $U.S.1 = HUF59.066; 1990: $U.S.1 = HUF64.147; 1991: $U.S1 = HUF74.722.

Table 2

Bakony's Cost Structure (in percentages)

	1988	1989	1990	1991
Total costs	100	100	100	100
of which:				
Costs of material	50.1	51.9	44.8	41.0
Wage costs	27.3	26.2	29.7	32.4
Energy costs	5.6	4.7	5.8	6.3
Banking costs (incl. interest)	4.1	5.6	6.7	8.2
Other costs	9.5	8.8	10.3	9.6

Table 3

Bakony's Inventories (structure in percentages)

	1988	1989	1990	1991
Purchased inventories of materials and parts	97.0	95.8	90.5	89.1
Inventories of output	3.0	6.2	9.5	10.9

Part III

Case Studies of Polish Firms

1

Engineering/Railway Rolling Stock: Pafawag Enterprise

Stefan Krajewski

SECTORAL SETTING

The railway rolling stock industry in Poland consisted of ten enterprises that produced railway rolling stock for the Polish railways, city transport, internal transport for industry, and for export. One characteristic of this sector was the fact that many firms oriented their production toward export to the CMEA countries, especially the USSR. In fact, some firms exported about 70 percent of their output. The decrease in the volume of exports posed a serious threat to many. The export of their products to other foreign markets became difficult because their technical and organizational backwardness made it virtually impossible for these firms to launch a competitively priced modern product that could be sold abroad without major input of foreign capital. In consequence, the industry possessed large unutilized—and largely obsolete—production capacities.

The railway rolling stock producing enterprises were also affected by cuts in budgetary subsidies in the system of financing railway and city transport. The needs of the Polish railways and city transport firms were great but there was a shortage of resources to subsidize purchases of rolling stock. According to some forecasts, the Polish railways would only be able to purchase 10 to 15 electric locomotives annually during the next few years. In 1989, 51 locomotives and 20–30 multipartite electric sets were produced in 1989, and 52 such sets were produced in 1990.

For these reasons, the output of rolling stock fell considerably. In some product lines, the output in 1991 was 70–80 percent lower than in 1988, and this trend continued in 1992. Profitability also declined. In September 1992, the ratio of gross profit to costs of sales in the entire industry was 3.0 percent and the ratio of net profit to costs of sales was a –3.7 percent, indicating that some enterprises had little chance of survival.

HISTORY AND GENERAL DESCRIPTION OF PAFAWAG

Pafawag was a state-owned firm established on July 17, 1945, only two months after the Polish authorities took over Wroclaw, which had belonged to Germany before World War II. The enterprise was located on the site of the former railway car factory Linke Hoffman Werke, which had existed since 1856. About 30 percent of the buildings lay in ruins and only 20 percent of the machines and equipment had been left behind by the Germans. At the end of 1945, the firm produced the first freight cars for coal transport. Production of passenger cars was launched one year later. In 1949, the firm began export of its railway cars with the sale of freight cars for salt transport to Holland. In 1956, 2,600 special cars were exported to India. Passenger-car production was expanded to about 600 cars in 1958, and a crucial moment in Pafawag's history occurred in 1957 when the firm began to produce electric locomotives. They were based on Polish design but used an engine produced under Soviet license. The following year, production of Polish multipartite electric sets was begun, also with the engine made under license. Earlier sets produced after 1953 had been equipped with imported engines. The production of a modern postal car and a new type of electric locomotive was launched in 1964.

Pafawag was the largest enterprise in the railway rolling stock industry, the largest producer of electric locomotives, and the sole Polish manufacturer of multipartite electric sets. Sales amounted to $32 million in 1991, but dropped to about $15 million in 1992. Employment had also fallen from 3,140 in 1988 to 2,184 in 1988.

The main buyer of Pafawag's railway rolling stock was Polskie Koleje Panstwowe (PKP), the Polish State Railways. Throughout its history, Pafawag had exported its products to the USSR, China, India, Iraq, Bulgaria, Hungary, Yugoslavia, Czechoslovakia, Morocco, and Syria. However, interest in Pafawag's products abroad was declining because they did not usually fulfill the technical requirements of customers. In 1988, only 5.9 percent of total output was exported. In subsequent years, this dropped to 1–2 percent and in early 1992 virtually ceased, with the exception of a contract with Czechoslovakia, signed in the second half of 1992, that raised the export share for the year to about 5 percent of total sales.

The firm's production capacities were largely underutilized. The utilization of production capacity on the first shift had fallen steadily from about 86 percent in 1988 to 72 percent in 1991 and to 54 percent in the first six months of 1992. The shift coefficient had been little higher than 1 for many years: it was 1.1 in 1988 and 1.05 in 1992. Pafawag possessed a large but considerably depleted capital stock. Fixed assets in 1988 were depreciated at 57.5 percent and in 1991 at about 63 percent. Most of the buildings had been erected before World War II and most machines had been in service for more than twenty years. Their usage was costly but the firm did not have the resources for new equipment. During the last five years, its investments had been financed exclusively from its own resources, but these were insufficient to prevent a steady deterioration of fixed assets.

Pafawag had its own research and development facilities and conducted studies on new construction and technologies. However, because Pafawag could not match the technological standards of leading foreign firms, the gap widened and no resources were available to buy lucrative licenses. Apart from its productive assets, Pafawag had a large portfolio of social assets. These included a large housing district, medical clinic, vocational and technical secondary schools, culture center, sports clubs, holiday resorts, and canteens. At present, however, the firm did not have the resources to make proper use of these facilities.

Management

At the time the new economic system was being introduced, no major changes had occurred in Pafawag's management. Before 1989, all directors had had a university background, and no political activists had been imposed from outside without professional qualifications. Most directors had started their professional careers at this firm and had gradually been promoted. Economists and lawyers were seldom found among the top management: technical knowledge and production management skills had been considered more important. This type of management selection prevailed, although it underwent some modifications. Economic knowledge and marketing skills became increasingly more appreciated. Nevertheless, most managers, particularly those at intermediate and lower levels, still believed that technical and production knowledge had priority. The general belief was that the present difficulties of the firm were largely due to a lack of the financial resources that were needed to replace obsolete machines and equipment and thereby modernize production. The view that conducting an effective marketing campaign was quite simple and required no particular skills was also expressed.

The current top management of Pafawag consisted of the managing director and three deputies: one deputy for production; one for technology, development and marketing; and one for economics. The managing director, who was fifty-five years old, was a technical university graduate who started working for the firm in 1962, immediately after graduating. He worked his way through the positions of constructor, manager of the construction section, deputy chief constructor, manager of the Railway Rolling Stock Research and Development Center, and in 1982, deputy technical director; since a 1984 open contest, he had been managing director. In May 1992 a new contest for the post of managing director was organized and he was reappointed.

The deputy director for production, a forty-year-old with a technical university background, started his work at Pafawag in 1972 as a quality-control inspector. He was next appointed manager of the production department, then chief of production, and finally deputy director in July 1991. The deputy director for technology, development, and marketing, forty-three years old, also with a technical university background, had worked for the firm since he graduated from the technical university. His subsequent positions were as technologist, chief welder, deputy chief technologist, assistant to the commercial director, and finally, in 1992, deputy director for technology, development, and marketing.

The economic director, who was also the chief accountant, was a thirty-four-year-old economist who had worked at Pafawag since 1982. He had held the positions of planner, manager of the planning bureau in the production department, manager of the economic department in the iron casting division, and since 1990, economic director. This information about the firm's top management indicates that only those persons who had been linked with Pafawag since the very beginning of their careers were appointed to such posts. In each case, the technical university background was salient, and their previous posts, connected with developing new technologies and with production processes, had paved the way for the present appointments. None of them, however, had much experience in marketing.

Their pay had somewhat improved in the last years, but was still relatively low. Those with similar qualifications who worked in private firms generally had much higher salaries. In 1988, the engineers and technicians at Pafawag earned wages and a profit bonus that was equal to about 94 percent of the blue-collar workers' average wage. The director's salary was 213 percent higher. These proportions did not change until 1991. In the first half of 1992, the director's salary was 332 percent that of workers, while that of the engineers and technicians was about 109 percent. This differentiation increased, but probably not enough to create adequate incentives for the directors and the technical personnel.

Changes in the remuneration system were introduced in April 1992. Until then, the pay of the management had consisted of three elements: a basic wage, a premium, and a commission that depended on the profit made. The premium was 50 percent of basic wage and was paid every month on the instruction of the managing director after ascertaining that a given organizational division had fulfilled its tasks. Since April 1992 the premium has been included in the basic wage. The old premium had been replaced by a new one for all white-collar employees, but was dependent on the attainment of a planned level of gross profit and sales. The aim of the new motivation system was to create stronger incentives to find ways to improve the firm's finances. The managing director was excluded from this premium because the principles of his remuneration were determined by the workers' council, but his deputies received premiums equivalent to 25 percent of their basic pay.

EVOLUTION OF THE SITUATION OF THE FIRM IN THE 1990S

Shocks of the Transition

Before the changes in the Polish economy occurred, Pafawag had held a stable although increasingly less advantageous market position. On the domestic market, it was a monopolist in the main assortment groups. Its most important customer, the Polish State Railways, only bought rolling stock from the Polish producer, thereby obtaining large subsidies from the central budget. In this way, the government had long given preference to, and financially assisted, domestic producers. However, the technical standards of these products had steadily declined relative to similar products of leading foreign firms. These stable and convenient circumstances for Pafawag lasted until 1990, and, even then, Polish State Railways used substantial subsidies to purchase rolling stock, which allowed Pafawag to maintain a high level of production and sales. In particular, this applied to tripartite electric sets, of which 38 sets were produced in 1988, 52 sets in 1990, and 45 sets in 1991, and to freight car trucks, of which 1,733 units were produced in 1988 and 1,822 units in 1990. The production of electric locomotives was the first to decrease, with 61 units produced in 1988, 44 units in 1989, 4 units in 1990, 6 units in 1991, and 12 units in 1992.

Rapidly shrinking budgetary subsidies for the Polish State Railways forced Pafawag to make substantial production cuts. Thus, for example, only 71 freight car trucks were produced in 1991 and, in 1992, their production was abandoned completely. The production of tripartite electric sets remained stable for the longest time, but dropped from 45 sets in 1991 to 10 sets in 1992. Summing up, the drop in domestic demand occurred relatively late, but it was much sharper than in most other industries and was spread unevenly among the various product groups.

Inflation in the late 1980s disturbed the stability of the firm, but combined with the liberalization of prices, it enabled Pafawag to substantially raise the prices of rolling stock, reaping high profits. As the data in Table 3 indicate, the profitability ratios were exorbitant in 1989 and 1990, then began to drop rapidly in 1991. In 1992 the enterprise experienced substantial losses, both net and gross. The primary cause of the profitability decline was rapidly shrinking demand, which made additional price increases impossible despite growing production costs.

The high interest rate on credits that was introduced at the beginning of 1990 presented another problem. Pafawag was not using long-term credit but had obtained large credits to finance its working capital. In 1989, bank charges combined with interest made up almost 10 percent of total costs. In order to avoid a growing burden of financial costs, short-term credits were restricted and a search begun for suppliers who would provide materials on convenient terms of payment.

For a firm like Pafawag that depended strongly on the state as principal customer (like the vast majority of State-Owned Enterprises, PKP cannot be considered an autonomous, market-oriented entity), the switch from a system based on commands and central allocation of production supplies to a market economy necessitated amendments to most legal regulations. Frequent changes of economic conceptions and programs, partly due to an unstable political situation and repeated changes of government, further destabilized the firm's operating conditions and made it practically impossible to develop and implement a consistent long-term strategy.

Apart from these negative elements, however, the new economic policy created greater freedom for the firm. Prices could be freely set, meaning that Pafawag, as the nearly sole Polish producer of many products, recorded high profitability rates until the end of 1990. Due to the abandonment of central allocation of industrial supplies and easier access to many factors of production, the firm was able to find suppliers who offered either cheaper products or more favorable terms of payment.

Markets, Production, Sales

As Pafawag sold most of its products on the domestic market, mainly to the Polish State Railways, PKP's deteriorating financial condition led to a sharp drop in output. Worst affected were locomotives and freight cars. Only the production level of tripartite electric sets was maintained, and even increased, from 38 sets in 1988 to 52 in 1990 and 45 in 1991, but in 1992 this dropped to 10. However, before the transformation crisis, these units had only accounted for about 15 percent of sales. To make up for the losses, Pafawag increased production of items unconnected with the rolling stock market. For several years, the firm produced car trailers, welded steel construction including devices for environmental protection, forging wares, and iron castings. The sales potential of these products was limited. Many firms faced a situation similar to Pafawag's. They, too, had underutilized production capacity in their casting, forging, and tool departments, which was why they were able offer their products and services at lower prices. Thus, increasing competition limited the demand for this part of Pafawag's product line. The firm had not yet developed products that would find an adequate market in Poland or abroad. The enterprise's export capacity was diminishing because its capital stock was obsolete; there had been modest investment in the last few years, and little allocated for research and development.

The reduced demand did not lead to accumulation of large inventories of finished goods since the firm's main product, railway rolling stock, was not produced until orders were received. Until 1991 the firm had no inventories of finished goods and they did not begin to accumulate until 1992. However, even though sales and output in the other product lines revived significantly in the second half of 1992, the inventories-output ratio remained at a relatively high level. Inventory dynamics are shown in Table 2.

Financial Indicators and Structure of Costs

In 1991, a sharp drop in sales led to a deterioration of financial conditions at Pafawag. The information contained in Table 2 is almost self-explanatory, but let us briefly note that the significant losses were due not only to the growth of costs in relation to sales but also to a high level of losses in that period. For example, in 1991 the balance of gains to losses reached an amount of –41 billion zloty, while the net loss was only 9 billion zloty. This balance was roughly the same the following year, at –40 billion zloty; however, the operating profit and dividend tax increased the net loss to 44 billion zloty, a large part of which was the penalty interest for delayed payments to banks and suppliers.

The rapid decline in output led to significant changes in the cost structure, as shown in Table 4. The percentage of material costs fell, which is to be expected in a firm whose output, and therefore material consumption, declined. The share of all other cost elements, especially labor, increased, despite a decline in employment of 956 persons, or 30.4 percent of the 1988 work force. This was due to the fact that output fell more rapidly than employment. Until this time, dismissals were on an individual basis only, although group lay-offs were organized for those able to benefit from early retirement schemes. For economic reasons, several hundred more workers should have been dismissed by the end of 1992, but the firm's financial situation was such that severance payments for those dismissed in a group lay-off could not be guaranteed.

Pafawag attempted to lower costs of materials, energy, and transport, but because of cuts in production, the decline in profitability ratios was only briefly halted. Difficulty in separating the various elements of its technology lines and a lack of potential buyers meant that the firm was unable to sell its unnecessary property. Furthermore, it had trouble selling its large social assets and only a significant part of the property had been leased.

Organizational Changes

Pafawag was a one-plant firm. Until recently it had had two subsidiaries, located in Trzebnica and Zmigrod, small towns near Wroclaw, but in November 1992 these became independent enterprises. The firm also had its own research and development center. The following changes had taken place in the enterprise:

- the position of deputy director in charge of technical affairs was merged with that of marketing director to streamline the organization in the face of reduced production volume by reducing the number of employees;
- in the last two or three years, the number of employees in marketing and accounting had been increased and wage levels raised;
- the number of employees in many organizational units was decreased due to substantial production cuts and the ensuing smaller work load;
- many low-level managerial posts were eliminated;
- the financial and marketing autonomy of particular departments was increased;
- because casting was no longer needed, the department was liquidated in 1992.

HOW TO SURVIVE?

While these modest measures could not eliminate the threat to the firm's existence, the directors envisioned a long-term program that would not only allow it to survive but also ensure its growth. The main elements were the following:

- transforming Pafawag into a one-person partnership of the State Treasury as the first step in privatization;
- establishing a joint venture with the aid of foreign capital;
- obtaining enough financial resources from a foreign partner or shareholder to restructure production;
- launching products that could compete with those of the leading European enterprises.

In May 1992 an application to transform the firm into a one-person partnership was submitted and later accepted by the Ministry of Ownership Transformation, and Pafawag was to be commercialized by the end of January 1993. The management had begun negotiations with several leading European manufacturers of railway rolling stock, including ABB and Alstom. These firms had indicated a willingness to cooperate with Pafawag by investing the capital needed (several tens of millions of U.S. dollars) to ensure production of modern stock within a short time. For example, Alstom, the French firm, was ready to help launch production in 1995 of a modern electric locomotive based on its own technology. According to Pafawag's managing director, this was the only way to preserve the firm's position in the rolling stock market. The electric locomotive that Pafawag currently produced, from its own design, had been introduced one year earlier, but, because the design process had taken ten years, the product was immediately technically obsolete. It was unlikely that Pafawag would manage to solve its problems on its own without access to modern technologies, financial resources, and outlets abroad. The establishment of a joint venture with Pafawag would also allow the foreign partners to enter the potentially lucrative Polish market, thus easing access to the former USSR markets. No one knew what the long-term strategy of potential foreign owners would be, and the directors were aware of dangers of such a solution, especially since foreign partners would want to control most shares. Still, this seemed to be the only realistic solution to Pafawag's problems.

The firm also had a contingency plan for the production of trams and cooperation in the construction of an underground railway. In the directors' opinion, however, this did not guarantee the firm's survival. As the latest government decisions indicated, the carriages for the Warsaw underground would in fact be built at Mielec, another embattled enterprise in a depressed region in southern Poland, and not at Pafawag.

SOME CONCLUDING REMARKS

The Polish railway stock industry as a whole was in a state of crisis. The CMEA markets were gone, and this, combined with permanent changes in domestic demand, meant that the firm's structural character was reinforced by the extent of the fiscal crisis of the state budget. However, even though the railways would probably not play as dominant a role in transport as they had in the past, Pafawag potentially had greater chances to survive the shock of transition than other enterprises in the industry for the following reasons:

- production was not oriented toward exports to the CMEA and the USSR;
- the decline in output had been spread over a longer time period;
- the firm had begun to diversify production beyond the typical industry profile several years earlier;
- the firm did not carry the burden of long-term credits.

Since 1991, a combination of decreased demand and large losses have caused the financial condition of the firm to deteriorate, and the efforts on the part of the management have not been sufficient to prevent imminent bankruptcy. One could argue that Pafawag would be better off with a more active marketing effort, something virtually unknown in the past; but, on the other hand, selling railway carriages and locomotives is not like selling clothing or refrigerators. You must have a good product for a well-defined customer. Without major capital investment, it would be impossible to have a good product in this industry. Thus, the management's errors of omission probably did not make much difference overall.

A foreign partner or buyer, willing to risk investing a substantial amount of money in the development of new products, could do much to improve the survival chances of this enterprise. However, the negotiation skills of the Ministry of Ownership Transformation, and possibly the management, would need to be efficiently combined. As the experiences of the last few years have shown, foreign investors are more readily attracted to a firm in good, or at least improving, condition, even if the market value and price are consequently higher, than a firm on the verge of bankruptcy. Thus, the management should continue to find means of cost-cutting to make the firm look healthy; passive waiting would necessarily be counterproductive.

The prospects of finding an interesting and serious partner seemed to have improved when the second half of 1992 showed signs of a reversal of the negative trend. PKP ordered a delivery of multipartite electric sets for short-distance transportation, and a contract was signed for a delivery of small carriages to the Czech Republic. According to an optimistic scenario presented to us by the management, output in 1993 was expected to grow by 60–70 percent relative to 1992, with net profitability reattained by the end of the year.

Table 1
Basic Data about the Railway Rolling Stock Industry

Specification	1988	1989	1990	1991	1st–3rd Quarter/92
Sales in current prices (in billion zloty)	191.3	548.8	4,928.4	2,313.6	1,271.5
Sales in constant prices (preceding year = 100)	—	—	—	29.8	60.3
Production of selected items locomotives (units)	133	108	51	6	12
passenger and postal cars (units)	294	230	160	83	23
freight cars (units)	6,500	4,600	4,200	1,135	526
multipartite electric sets	38	33	52	45	10
Number of employees (in thousand persons)	23.2	21.8	20.8	9.4	9.8
Average monthly pay (in thousand zloty)	55.9	219.0	1,114.2	1,785.2	2,141.4
Profitability ratios gross profit/costs of sales	—	66.9	62.3	17.4	3.0
net profit/costs of sales	—	—	—	4.9	–3.7

Source: Statistical Yearbooks of Industry, (Central Statistical Office, Warsaw 1989, 1990, 1991). *Naklady i wyniki przemyslu I–III kwartal* 1992, Central Statistical Office, Warsaw, December 1992.

Table 2

Inventories at Pafawag (in percentage of sales)

	1988	1989	1990	1991	January–May 1992	January–December 1992
Total inventories	36.0	43.5	31.0	40.5	215.9	77.8
of which						
Materials	25.3	22.0	25.6	29.1	120.3	—
Works in progress	8.8	19.2	5.3	9.3	86.2	—
Finished goods	—	—	—	2.0	9.5	—

Table 3
Main Financial Indices of Pafawag

Specification	1988	1989	1990	1991	1992
Profitability ratios					
Gross profit/costs of sales	26.7	50.2	62.4	0.8	—
Net profit/costs of sales	8.5	28.5	31.1	−3.1	—
Ratio of costs to sales	79.0	78.1	56.6	81.2	88.7
Liquidity ratios					
Current ratio	2.04	1.55	1.65	1.32	1.44
Quick ratio	0.55	0.80	0.64	0.69	0.50

	1988	1989	1990	1991	January–May 1992
Activity ratios					
Inventory turnover	—	3.33	5.66	2.63	1.38
Receivables turnover	—	3.74	8.67	2.98	1.84

Table 4
Structure of Costs at Pafawag (in percentages)

Specification	1988	1989	1990	1991	1992
Labor costs	16.5	23.0	18.0	22.3	37.8
Material costs	68.8	54.4	58.4	54.9	35.7
Energy	1.9	2.1	4.5	6.7	8.7
Banking charges and interest	1.5	9.9	6.3	8.1	8.2
Depreciation	1.2	0.7	2.3	5.4	6.2
Property tax	1.0	0.4	0.1	1.6	3.3
Others	9.1	9.5	10.4	1.0	0.1
Total	100.0	100.0	100.0	100.0	100.0

2

Engineering/Machine Tools: PO/5

Stefan Krajewski

SECTORAL SETTING

Approximately sixty companies in Poland were involved in the production of machine tools. They possessed large production capacities that were poorly utilized, and, for the most part, their capital stock was worn out and obsolete. The gross value of capital stock per employee amounted to 67.3 million zloty in 1990, little higher than in the entire engineering sector, which was 65.3 million zloty, but lower than the average 90.8 million zloty for Polish industry. The depreciation rate of fixed assets, especially machines and equipment, in the machine tools industry was very high, reaching almost 80 percent.

Polish machine tools generally represented a lower technical standard and quality than those offered by the leading foreign firms. For many years, they had been sold primarily on the domestc market and in the CMEA countries, but, because of a recession, a marked drop in domestic demand, and major cuts in investments, recent sales to the former CMEA had rapidly declined. Meanwhile, imports of competitive products had been growing rapidly, being of much better quality, while price differences were tending to diminish.

Output declined by about 20 percent in 1990 relative to 1989, and by a further 33.3 percent in 1991. It fell also in the first three quarters of 1992 by an exceptional 25 percent, as shown in Table 1. The employment in this industry decreased as well, but much more slowly: by 7.5 percent in 1990, 14.5 percent in 1991, and 15 percent in the first three quarters of 1992. The net average monthly pay in the traditionally high-paying machine tools industry reached 1,910,800 zloty in September 1992, about 15 percent lower than in the entire machine tools industry and 24 percent lower than in the industry as a whole.

In 1991, total inventories represented almost 50 percent of the value of working capital, and inventories of manufactured products, 11.1 percent. Payments arrears had become a major problem, with the ratio of payables to receivables about 73.3 percent, and receivables and claims representing 46.9 percent of the working capital value. A 91.9 percent profitability ratio, attained in 1989, was the result of the inflationary growth of prices of machine tools and a much slower increase of prices of production factors, but this slid to negative values by 1992. This drop was primarily due to a small but constant decline in demand for machine tools, increasingly greater import competition, and a rapid growth of production costs (the industry received no significant subsidies, either before or after the economic reform). The dramatic financial situation of the industry in 1992 could be improved by either the growth of demand or a substantial reduction of its production potential.

HISTORY AND CHARACTERISTICS OF PO/5

The enterprise dated back to 1881, when a private metal-working factory that produced, among other things, fire pumps and artillery shells for the Russian army, was established on its present site in Pruszkow, near Warsaw. During World War I the factory was badly damaged. After Poland regained independence in 1919, it was taken over by a new owner, the Association of Polish Engineers in America S.A., which had its headquarters in Warsaw, and began to produce machine tools. The name was changed to Factory of Machine Tools and Implements in Pruszkow, and in 1921 its work force was strengthened by a large group of employees from the oldest Polish machine tools factory, Gerlach and Pulst. A dynamic designing office was established and in 1929 the factory expanded its production line to a wide range of metal-working machines and tools. It became a leading producer of machine tools in Poland, representing a high technical standard in line with the world standard. In 1936 the factory launched the production of armaments under the Bofors license, including anti-tank weapons. During World War II it shared the destiny of all of Polish industry and was taken over by Germany in November 1939.

Rebuilding commenced immediately after the liberation of Poland. In 1947, the first thirty machine tools were produced. In 1948, PO/5 Machine Tools Company was nationalized; in 1950, the former Designing Office became the Central Designing Office of Machine Tools, its task being to supply blueprints to the reviving Polish machine tools industry. This office employed and cooperated with the leading designers from the Warsaw Polytechnic.

Major organizational changes took place in 1970. On the strength of the government decisions, most companies producing machine tools in Poland were merged into one large industrial combine.[1] PO/5 was designated as a leading plant in the Polar-Koso Combine, set up in January 1970, and its directors became simultaneously the directors of the entire combine. PO/5 returned to its former organizational structure in the 1980s, when the combine system was abandoned.

The 1970s witnessed the greatest prosperity of the company; it was enlarged and considerably modernized, becoming the largest and most modern machine tools producer in Poland, with some of its products matching world standards.

These successes were due to its own research and development center, as well as the application of new foreign technologies. For example, in the FYJ-40RN milling machine, which is still produced, third-generation systems supplied by the General Electric Company were used for continuous control; the control system of the Swedish firm ASEA was used for production of the first metal working centers, FYJ-40RNM; and blueprints supplied by the Japanese firm Mitsui-Seiki enabled the production of modern vertical metal working centers, FYM-63NM, and horizontal metal working centers, HP-5, which is also still produced.

In the 1980s, all major investment projects were abandoned and, consequently, the capital stock of PO/5 steadily deteriorated, its depreciation rate reaching 61.6 percent in 1988 and 69.6 percent in 1991. The company could no longer afford to purchase foreign technologies. Basic information about production and employment is as follows:

	1991	1992
Total income	$4.8 million	$3.0 million
Value of sales	$4.5 million	$2.7 million
Value of exports	$1.0 million	$0.7 million
Number of employees	774	550
(1,161 in 1988)		

SHOCKS CAUSED BY THE REFORM

The reform radically altered the conditions in which the company operated. To start with the positive aspects, the firm was equipped with much greater autonomy, allowing it to make decisions compatible with its own interest. The most important change was the removal of administrative price regulation, which enabled the enterprise to raise the prices of machine tools on the domestic market and reap an inflationary profit. Similar effects were produced by a several hundred percent increase in the dollar exchange rate in late 1989. This resulted in a much higher profitability of exports, in spite of the fact that the company applied elastic prices to induce potential customers to buy its products. The positive effect of the increased exchange rate of the dollar, however, was partly neutralized by a large share of imports in production costs during 1988–89. For example, about 40 percent of the value of production supplies was represented by the imports from the dollar zone.

The possibility of increasing prices on the domestic market had already been exhausted by 1990. The barrier here became a rapidly shrinking demand, accompanied by even more rapidly rising prices of production factors such as materials, energy, transport, and wages. Ultimately, relations between the prices of machine tools and their production costs steadily worsened, and this situation was further aggravated by the stable dollar exchange rate in 1990–91.

The greatest shock proved to be a drastic drop in both domestic demand and demand on the CMEA markets. During 1987–88, the company had not faced any difficulties in selling its machine tools, since these markets were very absorptive and many customers had to wait as long as two to three years for their orders to be executed. The firm was able to sell even technically obsolete and defective products. Moreover, the production of machine tools was treated preferentially by the government, partly because many of these tools were earmarked for military use, and export sales to the CMEA were regulated by long-term intergovernmental agreements. About 400 metal-working centers created by PO/5 still operate in the former USSR, mostly in armaments factories, all of which created a very convenient and stable situation for the company.

Since 1989, the demand in Poland and on the CMEA markets has declined, but at first the financial effects on the company were very slight owing to a substantial growth of machine tools prices. The number of orders collected on the domestic market continued to decrease as a result of cuts in investments and a deficit of financial resources felt by an ever larger number of enterprises. Those firms manufacturing armaments, previously very reliable customers, were increasingly unable to fulfill their financial obligations to PO/5, since they were unable to collect their receivables from the army; army indebtedness to the national economy grew steadily due to cuts in budgetary expenditures.

Moreover, PO/5 had greater difficulty collecting receivables from domestic customers and the former CMEA, and especially the former USSR. Consequently, it could not fulfill its own obligations to its suppliers. High interest rates made short-term loans to cover overdue payables or to purchase materials, pay wages, and so on the least favorable solution, and the firm's worsening financial standing caused banks to refuse credit. Thus, financial resources for investments, debts, and taxes were lacking.

Before 1989, PO/5 had held a monopolistic position on the domestic market; no other company in Poland manufactured similar products, nor were they imported from abroad, but this situation changed for two reasons: many firms attempted to sell superfluous used, and sometimes almost new, machine tools at low prices; and the number of imported machine tools increased. This, in turn, was due to two factors. First, the growth of domestic prices reduced the price differential between domestic and imported machines, so that, given the higher quality and flexibility (multiple uses) of imported products, they became more and more competitive. Second, in the case of investment projects financed or credited by foreign companies and banks, foreign partners often insisted that machines and equipment be purchased abroad.

Although it is difficult to identify any sectoral determinants that affected the nature and intensity of the shock, it is quite easy to perceive the specific character of the company itself. Some of its characteristics exerted a favorable influence on its recent circumstances, and others a negative influence.

Positive influences:
- the firm had no rivals in Poland;
- it received few subsidies before the reform and hence did not experience destabilization once these were suspended by the government;
- it had a large number of highly qualified employees, mainly technicians, who could be expected to quickly come up with effective ways of adapting to the new conditions even in the absence of economists and marketing practitioners.

Negative influences:
- a large portion of its exports went to the CMEA countries, particularly the USSR;
- rapid technological change, characteristic for the machine tools industry in general, imposed an urgent need to invest in order to maintain a position on the market—a need that PO/5, due to shortage of resources, was unable to fulfill;
- the proximity of Warsaw allowed highly qualified employees to find attractive work relatively easily when the financial straits of PO/5 were too difficult to ensure high wages for its best employees.

EVOLUTION OF THE SITUATION IN THE 1990s: SHORT-TERM RESPONSES

Organization and Management Structure

The organization and management structure of the company, which was not changed to any great extent, consisted of three divisions controlled by the deputy directors for production, technical affairs, and accounting. Eleven organizational units were directly subordinated to the managing director, including guards, legal adviser, and the departments of organization and management, employment and wages, trade and marketing, and quality control. There was no separate trade and economic division, although the difficulties encountered in finding new outlets and in promoting and selling the firm's products were the most troublesome. The department of trade and marketing had eleven employees, but its effectiveness was quite insignificant; the department of organization and management employed fifteen people, but ten of them were manual workers. This organizational structure made pursuit of an effective market-oriented policy, linked with the firm's financial and technical possibilities, quite difficult.

Drastic cuts in output forced the directors to reduce the number of employees. In 1988, 1,161 persons were employed, as compared to 550 in 1992, although group reductions were avoided, since it was the firm's policy to avoid large lay-offs in those organizational units that the directors considered vital to the firm's survival. These included the department of chief technologist, which employed 27 persons, and the department of chief designer, with 16 persons; although they were underutilized at present, the expectation was that they should be preserved until such time as the demand for machine tools increased. Most specialists and managers were dissatisfied with the low pay, stagnation, and uncertainty about the future, and those who could, found work elsewhere, although not always in their previous occupations.

In recent years, the wages within the company, including profit bonuses, had been lower than the average for the industry, representing 91.2 percent of the industry average in 1988, 97.7 percent in 1989, 120.6 percent in 1990 (due to high inflationary profits), 83.3 percent in 1991, and only 65.0 percent in 1992.

As might be expected, wages in the enterprise were set according to egalitarian principles: the pay of the top management, consisting of thirty persons, was 60 percent higher than the firm average in 1991–92, which was more than in the past, but only slightly exceeded the national average, 3.6 million gross.

The principles of remunerating the directors were determined by the workers' council. For the managing director, the council determined how many times higher than the average pay within the firm his pay would be, while the pay of the deputy directors was fixed to some multiple of the average in six main sectors of the economy.

Characteristics of the Directors

All three directors were in their early-to-mid fifties and were mechanical engineers who had graduated from the Warsaw Polytechnic. The managing director had worked at PO/5 for twenty five years and had been in his present position since March 1992, before which he was a chief technologist. The technical director, who had worked at PO/5 since 1968, had been at his present post since 1990, before which he had been manager of the design laboratory. He had also served as chairman of the workers' council during 1988–90. The production director, in his present post for fourteen years, had worked at PO/5 since 1961, and had spent seven years as manager of the mechanical department. The chief accountant was seventy years old and retired, but still working. He was a chartered accountant who had been in his present post for seventeen years. At PO/5, as at the vast majority of state-owned companies, engineers predominated among the management. They had typically been linked with one enterprise since the beginning of their professional careers, dealing with technical issues, but lacking expertise in marketing or financial management.

The former managing director did not appear for the March 1992 competition. He had been a party member and had belonged to the nomenklatura, which meant that he had no chance of winning the post again. He now operated his own firm, set up a few years ago, which, until 1992, had also been partly owned by his wife. The former technical director also joined a private partnership, becoming its chairman.

Markets, Sales, Production

The drop in demand for machine tools resulted in a substantial decrease in output and, therefore, sales, as confirmed by the figures below, which refer to changes in units of output in two main product lines:

	Numerically controlled machine tools (metal-working centers)	Milling machines
1988	72	86
1989	57	71
1990	52	56
1991	41	35
January–May 1992	2	6

The cuts in production in 1992 were prompted by the need to first sell those machine tools stored in warehouses or in the production process. Given the present demand, these machine tools could suffice even for several years.

The company had managed recently to expand export sales outside the former CMEA. In 1991–92, contracts for small deliveries to Turkey, Iran, and Great Britain were signed, a trial lot was sent to the United States, and a modest joint venture with a German firm was initiated. But these were very difficult markets, demanding high-quality products and efficient marketing, and PO/5 was not always able to meet the requirements. In fact, despite the collapse of exports to the former CMEA from about 50 percent of the total value of sales in 1988–89 to 2.1 percent in 1991 and 0 percent in 1992, the share of exports in total sales continued to be high in 1992, reaching 41.9 percent, as compared to 62 percent during 1988–90. However, the exports in physical terms decreased very distinctly, which can be seen below:

	Metal-working centers	Milling machines
1988	44	54
1989	33	38
1990	14	15
1991	5	6
January–May 1992	2	4

Failure to retain its outlets was an inducement to change the product mix and, to this end, the firm began to modernize previously produced machine tools. According to the managing director, about 60 percent of items produced in 1992 differed considerably from those produced in 1990. Following a radical reduction of output in 1991, attempts were made to use the existing production capacities in a different way, including the provision of repair services for companies possessing unique machine tools, made not only by PO/5, but also by foreign companies, and also the production of tooling and software for machine tools.

It is also worth noting that the company tried to change the markets where it bought raw materials. The increase in the dollar exchange rate at the end of 1989 increased the costs of raw materials from outside the CMEA and, as a result, the share of imported materials in the value of all used materials went from 43 percent in 1989 to 62.9 percent in 1990, while the share of materials in total costs rose from 28.5 percent to 32.9 percent in that period. In 1988–89, raw materials imported from outside the CMEA accounted for about 40 percent of the value of all materials used by PO/5, but that share declined to 27.2 percent in 1991 and 20.5 percent in the first months of 1992.

Costs Structure and Financial Standing of PO/5

The drop in output also led to major changes in the structure of costs. A comparison between 1988 and the first half of 1992, as shown in Table 2, allows one to draw the following conclusions:

- The share of material costs in total costs declined rapidly, from 43.8 percent in 1988 to 13.0 percent in May 1992, an obvious reflection of a significant growth of fixed costs due to reduced output.
- The costs of energy rose very significantly, from 5.8 percent to 20.0 percent of total costs, as a result of both a growing share of fixed costs and higher energy prices. The firm was equipped with computers that required constant temperatures and, although they were not in great use, large outlays were needed to maintain them. The heating of large halls to maintain the same temperature was also a heavy burden. In late 1992, there was a decision to stop heating much of the firm's space, meaning that these areas were then excluded from the production process for a longer time.
- As a result of repeated revaluations of fixed assets, the costs of depreciation increased from 5.7 percent to 12.4 percent.
- The share of wages rose from 27.8 percent to 41.4 percent, as a result of a faster drop in production than employment, and of growing social security fees.
- Bank charges and interest paid by the firm also increased, from 1.5 percent to 4.6 percent. This increase of costs was fully a result of high interest rates, since the firm used bank credit only to a small extent. This minimal use of credit was in part a result of a deliberate decision of the directors and in part due to the firm's weak financial standing, which made access to credit difficult.

- The share of costs of external services declined from 14.2 percent in 1988 to 5.9 percent in May 1992. To an ever greater degree, such services, which prior to 1990 were performed by external units, were now performed by the company's employees.

In spite of the fact that output and sales of machine tools had already begun to decrease in 1989, it did not immediately affect the firm's financial standing. On the contrary, 1989 was exceptionally favorable for the company. As can be seen in Table 3, the ratio of gross profit to sales rose from 31.3 percent in 1988 to 66.9 percent in 1989. This growth surge was due to the following factors:

- Owing to the liberalization of prices, the company began to raise the prices of its products and, because of the current healthy financial situation of most state-owned companies, prices could be increased without fear of demand barriers or financial difficulties of the customers.
- Apart from wages, production costs, including materials and costs of external services, were rising relatively slowly, while the prices of fuels, energy, and transport services were still controlled by the state.
- Banking charges and interest remained at a low level.
- The firm obtained extraordinary profits mainly as a result of foreign currency revaluations.

In 1990, PO/5's profitability dropped significantly. The recession and declining demand for machine tools restricted the possibility of raising prices and resulted in a major drop in output. Consequently, fixed costs per product unit and financial costs rose, while the firm's ability to improve its financial condition by selling foreign currency balances was gradually exhausted, and extraordinary losses in the form of penalties for unpaid invoices and overdue taxes steadily increased. Despite the intensification of negative circumstances, the 1990 net profit reached 7 billion zloty, and the ratio of net profit to sales amounted to 11.6 percent.

Although difficulties began to accumulate in 1991, the company continued to earn a positive markup from its production activity. But high costs and rapidly growing losses caused ever greater deterioration of the firm's financial standing and the company finished 1991 with a negative balance, a situation that was even worse in 1992. This sudden deterioration in financial standing, and an accumulation of payments arrears that hampered normal operation, are shown by the liquidity and activity ratios in Table 4. During the analyzed period, the company had had a high liquidity ratio, ranging from 2.50 in 1989 to 1.53 in 1992. However, because a relatively large part of its working capital consisted of inventories, the quick ratio, with the exception of 1989, remained at a level lower than 1; 1991's quick ratio of 0.37 and 1992's of 0.26 indicate that a considerably restricted liquidity of the company threatened its survival. This was also confirmed by a rapid decrease in the share of working capital in total assets, which dropped to 0.16 in 1992. Most disturbing, however, were rapidly deteriorating ratios of payment and inventory turnover in 1991.

LONG-TERM RESPONSES

A long-term adaptation process, which could pave the way for stabilization, had not yet been begun, nor did there seem to be a clear program of such adaptations. In the directors' opinion, the appraisal made by the German consulting firm F.G.U., which was financed by the World Bank, and the Polish Agency of Industrial Development, proved useless in practice.

The directors did not envisage any change in ownership, and claimed that privatization of the company would not produce any greater benefits for the company under the current conditions. The managing director advanced the following argument: "At present, the company does not pay the excess wage tax (PPWW), because wages are low and there are no resources allowing an increase. We do not pay the dividend either, since we do not have financial resources for fulfilling our obligations toward the budget. The workers' council is not too active, nor does it interfere in the directors' decisions in a troublesome manner." This rather narrow and short-sighted perception of the effects of privatization also reflected the directors' approach to the problems facing the company.

In a truly desperate situation, a search for foreign partners ready to invest or acquire a stake in the firm began. There had already been preliminary talks with two potential partners from Canada and Great Britain. According to the managers, they were appreciative of the company's potential, particularly the qualifications of its personnel and the technical level of some of the installations, and a large order from Canada of 100 working centers was contemplated, but no concrete measures had been taken so far. Perhaps the company was too little involved in this search for investors, but probably of greater importance was the fact that the company was no longer attractive. It badly needed major modernization, and its financial situation made mobilization of its own resources, even on a modest scale, impossible. It also could not obtain bank credit, nor was there any indication that assistance would be provided by the government.

In practice, PO/5 tried to survive the recession by engaging its capacities in secondary forms of activity, such as repairs of atypical machine tools used in other companies, and preparing tooling and software for machine tools. This, at least, made some use of the high qualifications of its employees and did not involve large outlays for purchases of materials. The directors seemed to have accepted two assumptions:

- The government would not liquidate the company, although it was unable to fulfill its obligations to the budget or to suppliers. This assumption was prompted by a conviction that the enterprise was important to the national economy, particularly for the production of armaments.

- The recession would eventually end, and the demand for machine tools in Poland and the former CMEA would grow rapidly, allowing the company to regain its previous markets.

Explicit evaluation of these assumptions is difficult, but it seems that they were too risky and exerted a harmful influence, since they justified a passive wait for the reappearance of favorable external conditions. It probably would have been better to adopt a program of deeper restructuring on the assumption that, when the recession had ended, the firm would fundamentally change its profile. But the question was how to do this without any financial resources. As mentioned, some changes had already been made, but they were treated only as transitional measures, to be accepted in the present conditions and abandoned as soon as possible.

There had been no success in reducing production capacity, which, at only a little more than 10 percent in 1992, was utilized very poorly. In recent years, fixed assets in the amount of about 450 million zloty had been sold, and some space in buildings had been leased, but the directors claimed that they had had difficulty selling buildings for the following reasons: the property ownership status had not been regulated; it was hard to separate the needed premises from those no longer needed; there were no buyers willing to purchase the main part of the buildings; the firm did not have the financial resources to move machines and equipment onto a smaller and more compact area, since the machines required specific conditions of temperature, humidity, and lighting.

As a result, the company's fixed costs were quite high. For instance, energy costs, mainly heating, represented over 20 percent of total costs between January and May 1992 and rose even higher after the mid-1992 increase in energy prices.

The negative consequences of recession were perhaps more visible in PO/5 than in most other Polish SOEs. The company seemed to drift, with no clear perspective or program of deep adjustment, and the short-term responses could only be effective if external conditions were to change dramatically. The other problem was that, even if the general situation changed, the market would not be waiting for PO/5; rather the firm would need to find the market again, and it was unlikely that it would be able to sell the same products in the same ways as before.

To conclude the story with a faint glimmer of optimism: some cost reduction was achieved in the second half of 1992, and sales stabilized. The managers hoped that a positive gross profit could be attained by the same period in 1993. This hope was based on a conviction that demand for machine tools by domestic private firms would increase. In late 1992, for the first time since World War II, a working center was sold to a private Polish entrepreneur.

Note

1. The establishment of combines by grouping companies with a similar product line encompassed many branches of industry at that time. It was one of the elements in improvements of the economic system introduced by the government, following the

model of the organizational structure of industry in the GDR, where combines were very common. However, in the GDR, combines often grouped so-called vertically linked companies, i.e., different phases of a production cycle, from raw material to final product, while in Poland, the major combines grouped companies with the same production line, resulting in horizontal integration.

Table 1
Basic Data About the Machine Tools Industry

Specification	1988	1989	1990	1991	1st–3rd Quarter/92
Sales in current prices (billion zloty)	144.3	471.2	2,266.5	2,125	1,282.7
Sales in constant prices (preceding year = 100)	107.9	100.5	80.4	66.7	75.1
Production of selected goods (tons)					
metal working machines	32,445	29,828	27,033	15,291	6,038
Of which:					
numerically controlled machine tools	2,876	3,429	2,203	1,263	497
metal plastic working machine tools	7,388	6,949	4,898	2,579	1,334
Number of employees (thousands)	31.8	30.5	28.2	24.1	20.5
Average net monthly pay (thousand zloty)	57.4	216.4	1,057.2	1,532.0	1,910.8
Profitability ratios					
gross profit/costs of sales	—	91.9	49.3	13.7	–4.4
net profit/costs of sales	—	—	—	0.9	–11.6

Source: Statistical Yearbooks of Industry (Central Statistical Office, Warsaw, 1989, 1990, 1991). *Naklady i wyniki przemyslu I–III kwartal 1992* (Central Statistical Office, Warsaw, December 1992).

Table 2
Structure of Costs in PO/5 (in percentages)

Specification	1988	1989	1990	1991	January–May 1992
Wages	27.8	41.1	31.5	33.1	41.4
Materials	43.8	28.5	39.2	25.9	13.0
Energy	5.8	6.8	9.2	11.5	20.8
Banking charges and interest	1.5	6.5	5.0	5.8	4.6
Depreciation	5.7	2.1	5.7	12.7	12.4
Property tax	1.2	2.6	0.9	1.5	1.9
External services	14.2	12.4	8.5	9.5	5.9
Total	100	100	100	100	100

Table 3

Main Financial Data on PO/5 (in million zloty)

Specification	1988	1989	1990	1991	1992
Net sales	6,049	18,975	60,009	50,741	35,576
Costs of sales	4,101	9,112	45,439	43,675	42,011
Markup	1,948	9,863	14,570	7,066	−6,435
Remaining revenues	5	80	886	2,725	3,434
Costs of obtaining revenues	—	260	—	—	920
Financial revenues	—	50	—	696	600
Financial costs	62	689	2,845	4,629	2,480
Operating profit	1,891	9,044	12,611	5,858	−5,801
Extraordinary gains	122	4,042	5,270	191	—
Extraordinary loss	118	393	2,585	6,839	6,808
Gross profit/loss	1,895	12,693	15,296	−790	−12,609
Taxes	1,210	4,403	8,318	3,337	1,291
Gross profit/loss	685	8,290	6,978	−4,127	13,900
Profitability ratios (in percentage)					
Markup/sales	32.2	52.0	24.3	13.9	−18.1
Gross profit/sales	31.3	66.9	25.5	−1.6	−35.4
Net profit/sales	11.3	43.7	11.6	−8.1	−39.1

Table 4

Liquidity and Activity Ratios

Specification	1988	1989	1990	1991	January–May 1992
Liquidity ratios					
Working capital/total assets	0.32	0.52	0.15	0.21	0.16
Current ratio	1.98	2.50	1.92	1.96	1.53
Quick ratio	0.76	1.83	0.57	0.37	0.26
Activity ratios					
Receivables turnover	3.83	3.28	6.48	5.23	3.00
Average collection period (days)	94	110	56	69	50
Payments turnover	2.95	3.50	4.93	2.19	1.26
Average payments period (days)	122	103	73	164	188
Inventory turnover	1.82	3.88	3.39	1.31	0.51
Average inventory turnover (days)	198	93	106	275	292

3

Textiles/Garments: Wolczanka S.A.

Marek Belka

SECTORAL SETTING

Wolczanka, a large and well-regarded producer of men's shirts and women's blouses in Lodz, was probably the largest enterprise in the Polish garment industry. It employed over 4,000 people, with yearly sales in 1991 approaching $22 million. Wolczanka was one of the first SOEs privatized through a public offer of shares, and it was listed on the Warsaw stock exchange.

The garment industry has long been an important sector of manufacturing in Poland, employing over 180,000 people in approximately 30,000 small firms, most of which were family workshops. About 400 large and mid-sized units were recorded by the Central Statistical Office and the majority of the statistical information in this study is based on data collected by this office.

In 1990, real sales dropped by 24 percent and virtually maintained this level throughout 1991. They dropped an additional 8.3 percent in the first quarter of 1992 compared to the same period of 1991. Sales then revived and for the next three quarters the garment industry recorded growth in real terms of 7 percent. In late 1991, both the industry as a whole and the group of the largest 400 firms improved somewhat in volume of sales and in profit rate. Although nearly half of the larger and mid-sized firms regularly recorded losses, the industry as a whole maintained a positive net profit. The gross profit rate fell from 55.3 percent in 1989 to 20.9 percent in 1990 and to 4.2 percent in 1991, only to recover in the first three quarters of 1992 to 6.3 percent. The net profitability in 1991–92 was correspondingly lower, only slightly above zero. Compared to most subsectors of textiles and light industry, the garment producers had fared quite well. Sales revived due to a halt in the real appreciation of the Polish zloty, higher import tariffs, and better enforcement of customs duties. Relaxation of export restrictions by the European Economic Community probably also helped.

An interesting development in the industry's cost structure was that, although wages in 1991 increased only modestly (23 percent compared to 70 percent inflation), the share of labor costs in total costs continued to grow at the expense of material costs. The latter stabilized due to a virtual freeze of textile prices and improved inventory management, but the managers were understandably unhappy at not being able to pass their rising costs on to their customers. Wolczanka was a leader of the industry both in terms of size and in the reputation of its products and management. Although its economic condition was better than average, it still had the same problems as the smaller, less well-established enterprises.

HISTORY AND DESCRIPTION OF THE ENTERPRISE

Historical Sketch

Wolczanka was founded in 1946 on the basis of a garment factory that was previously owned by a German industrialist but nationalized after the war. Over time, five other larger units were added, forming a multi-plant enterprise called Zjednoczone Zaklady Przemyslu Odziezowego Wolczanka (United Garment Factories Wolczanka). One of these plants was built on the foundation of the German-owned firm, but the other four resulted from investments in the 1970s. With the exception of the smallest plant at Lodz, where the headquarters were located, the rest of the enterprise was spread over the towns of Lask, Opatow, Wieruszow, and Ostrowiec, all of which were 30–100 km from Lodz.

In December 1990 Wolczanka became a one-person partnership of the State Treasury under its current name, Wolczanka S.A. Its shares were sold publicly, and in July 1991 it formally became a private corporation and was privatized in the second group of five big SOEs. The details and consequences of this will be discussed later.

Products, Market Position

Wolczanka's principal products were men's shirts and women's blouses, the first accounting for 78 percent of total output as measured in physical units, the second for 15 percent. The men's shirts were considered to be the best in quality and design in the country. The firm also produced a variety of shirts for all uses. At $8–$15 each, they were relatively expensive for Polish consumers, but the enterprise's strategy was to move up-market, at least in terms of domestic demand.

Wolczanka's share in the market was estimated at 20 percent but growing. In the past its share had been much greater, but one of the firm's largest shirt-producing plants was separated to fulfill the anti-monopoly requirements of privatization. According to Polish law, in order to privatize an SOE, or even to transform it into a joint stock company, permission had to be obtained from the Anti-Monopoly Office. The policy was to block transformation of SOEs with a market share of over 30 percent, and so the Wolczanka plant at Lask was leased by its employees, thereby becoming a separate enterprise.

Wolczanka had always been a significant exporter. For example, in 1991, of a total of 4.977 million shirts and blouses, about 3.4 million pieces, or 68 percent, were exported. Export sales accounted for 53.5 percent of sales value but only 47 percent of profits. Of exports, 96 percent was made up of so-called processing exports, meaning the sale of labor services. Foreign customers delivered designs, fabrics, and all finishing elements, and the resulting product was sold under foreign labels. About 75 percent of total export sales went to Germany and the remainder went to Denmark, Holland, and Austria.

Fixed Assets

Wolczanka's management stressed that the firm was modern and well-equipped and the figures seemed to verify this. Average annual investment in the early 1990s was regularly over $1 million and the pace had not slowed in 1992. Most machinery had been purchased abroad, which became possible in the 1980s through the introduction of foreign currency retention accounts. Although these accounts were fiercely criticized by nonexporters, they decentralized the investment process in exporting enterprises. In the 1990s Wolczanka financed its own investment from profits. The firm could afford not only new machines but also new construction. Consequently, fixed assets were depreciated by only 44 percent.

Labor Force, Management

The firm's total employment exceeded 5,000 people before 1990 but dropped to around 4,400 after the Lask plant was separated and then stabilized at 4,200. No future reductions have been planned. On the contrary, some increase was probable as output resumed its upward trend. The managers explained that the structure of employment had changed in the last few years, and that the share of production employees was now increasing at the expense of administration and auxiliary workers.

Wages at Wolczanka were roughly equal to the national average, which was not very high considering the firm was a stable, profitable one. There were three factors that explained this: 93 percent of the workers were women; the garment industry had traditionally paid low wages; and most of the employment was in small towns in predominantly rural areas where job alternatives were limited and unattractive. Nevertheless, the best workers earned 3–5 million zloty, a good wage for light industry. Also, the wage system was simple in that there were no bonuses, and workers were paid in strict proportion to their quantitative and qualitative performance.

The management of Wolczanka, called the board of directors, consisted of four persons: a general manager, a deputy in charge of financial affairs, a deputy in charge of production and marketing, and a chief accountant. The general manager, who was forty-nine years old, had an M.A. in economics. He was well known in both Lodz and the industry, and had a reputation as an efficient manager. He had been promoted to the present post in 1981, and therefore must have been accepted by Solidarity in the early days and made politically useful contacts with the then-young economists who were now in important political and economic positions. The deputy in charge of financial affairs, sixty-three years old, had the same education as the manager, but had been at his post since 1971. He had also served as chief accountant until 1990. The deputy in charge of production and marketing, forty years old, was an engineer and had been member of the management since 1982. The chief accountant, a forty-four-year-old woman, had been promoted to this post in 1990, after serving five years as deputy chief accountant at Wolczanka.

Overall, the management consisted of insiders, most of whom were economists. During 1989–90 the structure of the management changed. The deputies in charge of technology and sales left and their positions were eliminated and merged with that of the deputy in charge of production. The new management team consisted of sixteen people including the chief specialists and, most important, the managers of the five plants. In conversation, this was the group referred to as management, and its role was reflected in the distribution of shares.

Before privatization, the remuneration of the management was typical for Polish SOEs in that the workers' council set managerial wages at approximately five times the national average. After commercialization, or after becoming a regular public limited company, the system changed entirely. The supervisory board set the wages of the board of directors and these wages were kept confidential. The general manager then set the wage levels for the rest of the management team, and these, too, were not divulged. The wage level of the top management was thought to be much higher than average for SOEs. In addition, the management received a fixed percentage of net profit that could even double their income level.

Internal Organization of the Enterprise

With five plants dispersed over a significant area of central Poland, management was a problem, especially since the plants were partly autonomous. The annual budget was prepared for the entire enterprise and export sales were centralized in a separate export division. Cost calculations were prepared by the various plant management teams as administration and management became decentralized.

Individual plants did their own purchasing of material inputs, which was mostly for fabrics, but this only applied to domestic sales. Most export transactions involved fabrics and other materials that were imported. Wolczanka had a well-developed central supply that in most cases was able to pay less for domestic inputs, so the plants only rarely purchased on their own. The plants' choices of designs were limited to domestic sales. They mostly used the services of the central design workshop in Lodz. Given the centralized nature of export activity, the autonomy of the separate plants was actually quite limited.

WOLCZANKA'S ECONOMIC SITUATION IN THE 1990s

According to Wolczanka's management, the new economic policy stimulated the expansion of the firm. With its export orientation, modern equipment, and minimal credit burden, this enterprise was not much affected by the restrictions introduced by the Balcerowicz Plan. That did not mean, however, that no adjustment was necessary. Domestic demand declined, causing a decrease in the sales level and an accumulation of receivables from domestic customers. Also, Wolczanka had been a traditional supplier to the Soviet Union and; in fact, in the late 1980s, about 15 percent of all exports had been directed to this market. In 1990, however, these sales virtually disappeared. The consequent slump in output apparently lasted for two months, but it was alleviated by new export contracts with Western clients.

In 1989, the volume of output fell somewhat, from 6.6 million pieces to 6.3 million in 1990. In 1991, output reached a level of 4.9 million pieces, but, despite the separation of the Lask plant, it actually grew by a few percentage points. The upward trend intensified in the first five months of 1992 and a 16 percent growth over the previous year, or over 2.5 million pieces sold, was recorded. Because of the size and stable nature of the processing export, output volume was not a problem for Wolczanka.

Profit evolution, however, was. As was true for the entire garment industry, the rates of profit had never been very high. At Wolczanka, they reached 22 percent gross and 11.3 percent net in 1988. After a one-time surge in 1989 in which they attained 56 percent and 25.5 percent, they dropped again to 34 percent and 14 percent in 1990, and to 14 percent and 8 percent in 1991. The volume of net profit, fluctuating at $1.5–$2.0 million, was enough to meet the current needs of the enterprise and to finance the ongoing investment program. However, a constant squeeze on profits due to rising costs, particularly labor costs and depreciation of the dollar, was undermining the long-run position of the firm.

NEW SALES STRATEGY

Both export and domestic prices were virtually stable. Price inflation for Wolczanka's products from April 1991 to April 1992 was about 15 percent. Now the problem of costs became crucial for profitability. In mid-1993, in the annual report prepared for the general assembly of shareholders, management expressed the view that the most efficient way to minimize costs was to increase the scale of output. Bearing in mind the sales–profit relationships for exports and domestic sales mentioned earlier, the new strategy would naturally be to expand sales on the domestic market. Export sales, at least in their present form, would remain as a stabilizing, but not primary, source of profit.

The increase in domestic sales in 1992 inflated the share of domestic sales in the firm's total sales from 47 percent in 1991 to 58 percent in mid-1993—not bad, considering that export sales in real terms also grew. The profit response was immediate. Gross profit for 1991 was 27.8 billion zloty, reached 21.1 billion after five months in 1992 and, after eleven months, amounted to 38.3 billion. Net profit after five months reached 11.9 billion, and after eleven months, 21.2 billion relative to 15.5 billion for all of 1991. In real terms, the volume of net profit in 1992 could have reached the level of the previous year.

This latest success was due to the introduction of higher-quality shirts on the domestic market. One problem in recent years had been increasing competition in the form of attractive but poorly finished products from such places as Thailand, Hong Kong, and Korea. To combat this, Wolczanka increased purchases of fashionable fabrics from abroad, including the Far East. It tried to match the design and originality of the competitors' goods and it was able to surpass the quality by adding Western-type finishing details.

The sales intensification on the Polish market was accompanied by market organization. After 1990, the collapse of state-owned wholesale trade led to the spontaneous development of many small, financially unviable firms that tried to do business with the larger producers. These firms frequently were unable to fulfill their credit obligations. After Wolczanka organized a debt collection squad to extract part of the overdue receivables, it made a decision to limit its domestic sales to a small number of serious customers. The policy in recent years had been to avoid trade contacts with limited liability partnerships because they often were financially fragile and neglected their obligations. To reinforce the need for payment, the remuneration system of the sales section was radically changed. If sales and payments proceeded smoothly, the employees in this section could earn as much as three times more than before. However, if delays began to accumulate, the reverse would be true.

In late 1991, agreements were signed with twenty-five large wholesale firms all over the country that gave wholesalers the right to distribute shirts and blouses to retail shops in Wolczanka's name. These distributors generally received a 10 percent rebate, which was their primary source of profit because the producer determined the price. Terms of payment were thirty days, which was rather generous, but delivery was effected against collateral in the form of a confirmed bill of exchange. If a customer delayed payments, he was charged with penalty interest or the contract was revoked.

Because Wolczanka produced quality goods and could set standards with trade companies, the volume of receivables grew throughout the years, causing liquidity problems. To avoid delayed tax payments or payments to its suppliers, the firm resorted to working capital credit because it was cheaper than penalty interest rates. Also, the terms at which the enterprise received zloty-denominated short-term credit from Polish banks were relatively favorable. As a prime customer, it paid 44–46 percent, whereas refinancing credit at the National Bank of Poland was 38 percent, and twelve-month time deposits brought about 42–45 percent. By late 1992, Wolczanka managed to decrease its volume of inter-firm receivables by some 20 percent, or about forty days' sales, which made it possible to trim the outstanding volume of working capital credit by one-third.

Although Wolczanka was paying more attention to the domestic market, it had no intention of reducing exports. The plan was to be more selective in accepting orders from abroad and to try marketing its own brand, using its own designs and material. It was too soon to evaluate the progress of this venture, but the share of processing exports in all export had dropped by a few percentage points over the last eighteen months. At over 90 percent, that might have been sheer coincidence. The management claimed that it had recently negotiated better prices for processing exports and ascribed the success to the new sales strategy of the enterprise, which increased its bargaining power with foreign customers.

Management also claimed that its knowledge of profitability pointed to the need to stress domestic sales at the expense of processing exports. However, the present form of exports gave stability, which was of value in Poland's current economy, and management did not want to risk losing it.

PRIVATIZATION

Wolczanka's privatization resulted from the implementation of national policy, and thus it should not been seen as part of its reaction to the new economic situation. The ownership transformation nevertheless helped the enterprise, and it will most probably be beneficial for the firm in the long run.

In the summer of 1989, when the first Polish noncommunist government came into power, the government plenipotentiary in charge of privatization, whose office was later transformed into the Ministry of Ownership Transformation (MOT), made the privatization of SOEs one of his top priorities. The implementation of this privatization, similar to that which occurred in Britain in the 1980s, actually began in mid-1990 with the privatization of five firms through the public sale of shares and, despite technical problems, it was completed later in that year. As a means of quick ownership transformation, public-offer privatization was a complete failure, its merit lay in the knowledge gained from the experience, which is still beneficial.

Wolczanka, in the second group of five to be privatized, was chosen because of its sound economic condition and solid reputation on the market. Its privatization process was formally begun in November 1990, when the new enterprise,

Wolczanka S.A., was founded with an equity capital of 30 billion zloty, at which time the Treasury formally acquired 1,500,000 shares, each worth 20,000 zloty. Six months later, the Treasury sold part of these shares through public offer. Altogether, 64 percent of the shares, at 50,000 zloty each, was sold within the period of the initial offer. Bank guarantees were unnecessary and the sales campaign was successful. The remaining shares were distributed in the following way:

- 1 percent was acquired by the bank and its employees as payment for services;
- 20 percent was offered at half price to the workers of Wolczanka. Solidarity, to which the majority of the 30 percent union membership at Wolczanka belonged, played an active role in convincing the workers to accept the idea of privatization and stock ownership;
- 3 percent was bought by the sixteen-person management team at Wolczanka in the initial offer period;
- 12 percent was held by the Treasury, but could be bought by the management within five years as long as the above-mentioned 3 percent had been bought initially and the management team then paid 1 percent of the option in advance. They did so and will become owners of the next 12 percent of shares, which they now own in terms of voting rights. The cost of this buyout was negotiated separately with the Ministry of Ownership Transformations and was not disclosed to us.

Of the 64 percent of the shares offered for sale, 18.3 percent was purchased by Bank Handlowo-Kredytowy, a private bank in Katowice. The bank thus became a powerful stockholder and was very active during the first assembly of shareholders convened after privatization in August 1991. A new nine-member supervisory board was elected and consisted of the following: two employees of Wolczanka, who were both economists, one from the central administration, the other from one of the plants; two representatives of banks that were long-time partners of Wolczanka; a high-ranking official of the Ministry of Ownership Transformation who was currently in private business; three representatives of the Katowice bank; and lastly, the chairman of the board, who was an academic from the University of Lodz and a well-known economic consultant. Of these members, six represented the interests of the insiders and three those of Bank Handlowo-Kredytowy. The practical role of the Supervisory Board, at least of its insider faction, was involvement in strategic decision-making and problem-solving of major issues. For the most part, the initiative seemed to be controlled by the management and the board played a supportive but strong role.

In spring 1992, during preparations for the second general assembly of shareholders, two fundamental differences between the three representatives of Bank Handlowo-Kredytowy and the rest of the supervisory board became evident. One concerned the issue of the yearly dividend. The insiders wanted to retain all profit for reinvestment and other purposes, but the outsiders wanted to pay a dividend to shareholders. The other difference concerned the personal composition of the future supervisory board. The controversy increased to the point where, at least in the managers' opinion, a hostile takeover attempt had been made, probably the first in post-communist Poland. However, the 15 percent of shares controlled by the management, supplemented by part of the employees' ownership, was enough to outvote the outsider bank. The new supervisory board then had only six members because the three representatives of the bank from Katowice had been removed from their posts. As the management had wanted, the dividend was retained in the enterprise, but Wolczanka's performance on the Warsaw stock exchange was not very impressive.

Something should be said here about the Warsaw stock exchange and Bank Handlowo-Kredytowy. At the end of 1992, sixteen enterprises were listed on the Warsaw Stock Exchange. This small number was due to the slow pace of public-offer privatization and the rigid stance of the Polish Securities and Exchange Commission, which applied international standards to the listing of new securities for public trading. The sessions of the Polish exchange, which took place twice a week for most of 1992, increased to three times per week later in the year, with aggregate turnover reaching $20 million in one month.

Many problems hampered the development of the stock market in Poland, but one obvious fundamental factor was a lack of demand. The returns on shares were disastrous, only a few outpaced inflation, and none had a return comparable to the bank interest rate on time deposits. In addition, the need to mobilize resources to finance the state budget deficit was leading to a sale of government bonds that absorbed much of the existing savings. This did not mean that the smart short-term investor was unable to earn a profit, but the stock exchange held little attraction for the long-term investor. In late July 1992, the Warsaw Stock Exchange Index (or WIG) stood at 72.0 with 100.0 as the starting point about one year earlier, climbing to 92–95 at the end of 1992. Shares of Wolczanka, nominally worth 50,000 zloty, recorded a market price in the range of 38,000–43,000, occasionally falling below this level. Little else could be expected with a net profit rate below 10 percent, no dividend payment, and an interest rate on three-months treasury securities of around 45 percent.

Bank Handlowo-Kredytowy made news when it figured in the biggest financial scandal in recent years in Poland. This bank was the primary creditor and financial partner of Art B., a private conglomerate with an annual turnover believed to be near $1 billion. This conglomerate was founded in 1990 by three musicians and earned considerable income by taking advantage of the existing loopholes in the banking law and the backwardness of banking procedures and techniques, for example through multiple deposits of checks, which was legal but morally dubious. The crime, apparently committed when the enterprise was first founded, occurred when the musicians used a bad check to earn their first million dollars. The group was politically well connected. It had financed political parties and Walesa's presidential campaign, and most recently the papal visit. Indeed, the musicians were to have a private audience with the pope in Czestochowa, but then the scandal broke and the three musicians fled to Israel.

Bank Handlowo-Kredytowy then took over Art B., apparently for debts, but unfortunately the enterprise's debts were larger than its assets. For reasons not made clear to us, the chairman of the National Bank eventually liquidated Bank Handlowo-Kredytowy, and its assets and obligations were assumed by other banks and the Treasury. Because the scandal occurred after the last assembly of shareholders, the 18.3 percent of Wolczanka's stock that the bank had owned was apparently still controlled by the bank liquidator, and it was not clear what the new owners would try to do with it. In effect, Wolczanka continued to be controlled by insiders who proved capable not only of managing the enterprise but also of defending their own interests in the newly emerging market environment.

To briefly summarize the immediate consequences of Wolczanka's privatization: the firm's tax liabilities were slashed, but in 1990 Wolczanka paid about 7 billion zloty in tax penalties on high wage increases and a 775 million zloty dividend. This could grow to 9–10 billion altogether in 1991, making a serious dent in the investment capabilities of the firm. It would be fair to say, then, that privatization had an initially positive effect on Wolczanka's economic condition. The tax concessions were partly neutralized by a significant wage increase. In 1991, the average wage was 81 percent higher than in 1990. On the surface, this was a sizable increase, but, with inflation at 70 percent, the increase was not much and exceeded the national average growth rate by only a few points. Most important, these wages did not undermine the cost structure of the enterprise. The budget lost the current tax revenues of about 9–10 billion zloty, but the proceeds from the sale of shares, which exceeded 50 billion, more than compensated for this loss. Besides, allowing for supply-side effects, the budget could be better off in the long run.

The clear winner from the transformation was the management team, whose income grew significantly. The incentive structure at Wolczanka improved, promising a more efficient profit- and asset-oriented management. In fact, privatization resulted in the establishment of close working relationships with foreign and local consulting firms, auditors, and so on, which opened up new horizons for the people involved and fostered interest in acquiring more education. An extensive training program for managers at all levels was established and the supervisory board and its chairman were taking part in it. So far, the only losers seemed to be the shareholders, who financed the transformation of Wolczanka with the expectation of a decent return on their investment.

CONCLUDING REMARKS

Wolczanka's case is included because of its successful privatization process and because the enterprise survived the transformation in good shape. It preserved stability in the unstable environment of the Polish economy of 1990–92, building a solid foundation for future expansion. Also, because it was included in the public-offer privatization, its chances for long-run success were vastly improved.

Table 1

Structure of Costs (in percentages)

Specification	1988	1989	1990	1991	January–May 1992
Wages	35.37	38.76	52.31	49.03	55.91
Materials	62.65	54.91	38.76	41.41	36.59
Energy	0.43	0.38	1.51	1.15	1.18
Banking charges (incl. interest)	0.56	1.82	5.11	5.31	3.54
Depreciation	0.76	0.45	2.01	2.79	2.34
Property tax	0.28	0.09	0.3	0.31	0.36
External services	—	3.59	—	—	—
Total	100	100	100	100	100

Table 2

Main Financial Indices (in million zloty)

Specification	1988	1989	1990	1991	January–May 1992
Net sales	16,155.6	55,027.6	175,057.2	225,779.7	159,538.0
Costs of sales	13,368.3	40,607.3	128,262.3	199,528.0	135,812.0
Markup	2,787.3	14,420.3	46,794.9	26,251.7	23,726.0
Remaining revenues	232.0	494.4	2,564.9	1,458.8	21.0
Costs of obtaining revenues	—	—	—	—	—
Financial revenues	111.0	1,248.5	1,459.1	937.0	1,487.0
Financial costs	109.0	565.0	2,325.0	6,497.0	4,742.0
Operating profit $[3 + (4-5) + (6-7)]$	3,021.3	16,163.2	48,493.9	22,150.5	20,492.0
Extraordinary profits	452.7	16,055.1	15,277.7	8,533.0	2,178.0
Extraordinary losses	123.3	3,455.4	10,868.2	3,549.0	1,478.0
Gross profit/loss $(8 + 9 - 10)$	3,350.7	28,762.9	52,903.4	2,713.5	21,192.0
Taxes	1,431.0	112,513.6	35,348.5	12,286.0	9,242.0
Gross profit/loss $(11 - 12)$	1,919.7	16,249.3	17,554.9	14,848.5	1,195.0

Table 3

Profitability Ratios

Specification	1988	1989	1990	1991	January–May 1992
Markup (operating profit)/sales	17.25	26.21	26.73	11.63	14.87
Gross profits/sales	20.74	52.27	30.22	12.02	13.28
Mark-up (operating profit)/cost of sales	20.85	35.51	36.48	13.16	17.47
Gross profits/costs of sales	25.06	70.83	41.25	13.60	15.60
Net profit/cost of sales	14.36	40.02	13.69	7.44	8.80

Table 4

Liquidity and Activity Ratios

Specification	1988	1989	1990	1991	January–May 1992
Liquidity ratios					
Working capital/total assets	0.29	0.20	0.11	0.18	0.25
Current ratio	1.77	1.51	1.35	1.57	1.78
Quick ratio	0.88	0.80	0.67	0.88	1.05
Activity ratios					
Account receivable turnover	7.82	5.34	8.44	7.54	2.88
Average collection period (days)	46	67	43	48	52
Payments turnover	5.60	3.65	5.21	5.17	2.78
Average payments period	64	99	69	70	54
Inventory turnover	6.36	5.01	7.47	7.54	3.82
Average inventory turnover (days)	57	72	48	48	39

4

Textiles/Cloth: Textilpol

Marek Belka

SECTORAL SETTING

The textile industry was among the worst hit during Poland's recent political and economic transtion. Loss of the Soviet market, dollarization of trade in the CMEA (with imports of cotton from the former USSR suffering most), poor domestic demand due to falling real wages, and, most important, effective import competition combined with unfavorable internal organization of the sector resulted in falling output and profitability, leaving the textile industry in a deep recession. Within the sector there were great differences, with fabrics-producing and yarn-producing enterprises being in poor condition and knitting and garment subsectors managing to escape most of the misfortunes.

Textilpol is a producer of fabrics made of wool and woolen-like chemical fibers as well as of woolen yarn. In this study, we concentrate on the situation of the woolen cloth- and yarn-producing subsector.

At the end of 1992, the wool industry in Poland employed around 30,000 people, only half of the number of 1988. In 1991 total output reached $300 million; in 1990 it was $370 million. The data for the first three quarters of 1992 showed that output in real terms was more than 25 percent less than in the same period of 1991, and with no apparent tendency to rebound from the bottom of recession. The slump of the sector could be illustrated by the output dynamics of principal products. Data on profitability also illustrate the depth of the crisis.

	1988	1989	1990	1991	January–March 1992
Yarn (in thousands of tons)	83.7	77.2	25.5	16.6	8.6
Fabrics (in millions of meters)	101.0	95.8	64.7	44.2	9.3

The textile industry was an important source of budget revenues in the past, mainly in the form of turnover tax. In 1989, the woolen products industry recorded a gross rate of profit of 42.3 percent, which dropped in 1990 to 6.4 percent, continued to −27.4 percent in 1991, and reached −22.6 in 1992. The rates of net profit were correspondingly lower by some 4 percentage points. It should be noted that all of the observed enterprises in the subsector were loss-making, in most cases for at least one year. Consequently, the liquidity situation was dramatic, and insolvency, bank account sequestration, liquidations, and bankruptcies commonplace. Overall, the situation of the woolen industry in 1992 could be described as a total collapse and, against this background, the fate of Textilpol did not appear so dismal.

HISTORY AND DESCRIPTION OF THE FIRM

History, Product, and Current Market Position

Textilpol was founded in Lodz in 1951 through the merger of four smaller private firms nationalized under the 1946 Law on Nationalization of Industry. These firms had been established between 1911 and 1927 by German and Jewish industrialists, as was typical for Lodz. When the owners did not reappear after the war, the factories were taken over by the state.

In mid-1992 Textilpol, consisting of four neighboring plants, was a typical mid-size state-owned enterprise with a typical organizational and management structure. It produced fabrics made of wool and wool-type chemical fibers of different quality and weight. For many years the principal product was cloth for military uniforms and heavy overcoat material. Textilpol also produced coarse, low-quality woolen yarn, mainly for its own purposes, which was frequently made of recycled fabrics or low-quality domestic wool. Better yarn, such as worsted or cheviot yarn, which was used for more delicate cloth, was purchased in specialized spinning mills in Poland. Textilpol also sold the services of its finishing mill.

The firm's share of the industry's output and sales was estimated at about 2–3 percent, which placed it among the top ten producers of woolen fabrics in Poland. Its total sales in 1990 amounted to 67 billion zloty, or $7 million, and in 1991, almost 81 billion zloty, or $7.7 million. However, given the real depreciation of foreign currencies in recent years, this did not mean a growth in real zloty sales.

Textilpol had always been considered one of the best, if not the best, firms in the subsector. Its general manager was a chairman of the National Chamber of Wool Industry and an unquestioned leader of the unofficial industrial lobby. For the last thirty-five years the firm had supplied cloth for uniforms to the army, and thus was a monopolist in this respect. It also had a 70 percent share in the country's production of elana-argon, a cloth made of a wool-type chemical fiber, which was popular in Poland for men's suits. Besides the army, its main customers were Polish garment-producing firms.

Traditionally, export sales accounted for about 15–20 percent of total sales, the principal markets being Great Britain, Ireland, and China. In 1990, Textilpol tried to expand its exports to the USSR with disastrous results, but recently, due to falling domestic demand, the share of exports has grown.

Fixed Assets

Textilpol, as a fabric producer with a full cycle of production, had a spinning mill, two weaving mills, a finishing department, and a dyeing mill. The firm was also known for its design workshop, which rendered services for other enterprises within the industry. Fixed assets were depreciated at about 75 percent, which is average for the textile industry in Poland, with buildings depreciated at 85 percent and machines at approximately 65 percent. Investment had been limited in recent years, and the overall level of technology was not high, but some aspects of the equipment were considered to be very modern.

Among recently purchased assets were sixty nearly new weaving machines obtained in 1991 from a liquidated enterprise in southwest Poland, and a finishing line purchased from Germany in 1989 for LIBOR-linked credit from the Bank of Export Promotion, a state-owned bank begun in the late 1980s and recently privatized.

Labor Force

Textilpol currently employs 450–460 people, compared with 1,022 people in 1988 and 956 in 1989. The labor force reduction roughly reflects the decline in real output over the same period. Although radical compared with most other cases we are analyzing, the evolution of employment in Textilpol is somewhat characteristic of the textile industry. However, factors specific to Lodz also meant that Textilpol was able to reduce employment to this extent. Lodz is a large industrial center of over 1 million inhabitants, where skilled labor has few problems finding better-paying jobs in the shadow economy, both in the service sector and in the small, private textile firms that have been mushrooming around Lodz for the last few years.

As expected, unions at Textilpol were not very strong: at the end of 1990, Solidarity had only 75 members and the formerly official OPZZ union 214 members. After the group lay-offs in 1991 and 1992, Solidarity's membership fell to some 20 people and OPZZ's to about 100, including retirees. Although the unions tried to stage a protest in early 1992, there was no support from the workers. The position of the firm's general manager seemed to be such that the unions had little function, especially since the manager also seemed to have full control of the workers' council.

By Polish standards, wages at Textilpol were not low. In 1991 they reached nearly $180 per month, which was 30 percent more than the national average for the subsector. It was possible that the wage policy had gained the support of the workers, so that management had fewer personnel problems; for example, wages of white-collar workers were about 27 percent higher than the firm's average, suggesting a rather egalitarian policy. Although it had paid an analogous tax before 1990, Textilpol had avoided paying *popiwek*, or PPWW—a penalty tax on excess wage hikes—because wages in September 1989, to which the base wage after January 1990 was keyed, had already been increased.

Management

Textilpol's management consisted of three persons: a general manager, his deputy in charge of production and sales, and a deputy in charge of financial affairs. The latter also served as chief accountant. The general manager, who had an M.A. in economics and was about fifty years old, had been in this position since 1978, before which he had been a deputy for economic and financial affairs in another wool enterprise in Lodz. As mentioned previously, he had an exceptionally strong position within both the industry and the enterprise. In 1991, intending to break with the communist nomenklatura, he resigned his post to enter a competition organized by the workers' council, which he eventually won. It was somewhat surprising that a man so well placed in the former regime, although not a Communist Party dignitary, would not only survive but even strengthen his position (this had not been the case for other prominent managers who had been former members of the Polish United Workers' Party). He hinted during our discussions that he had received attractive offers from both Polish and foreign private firms, and that he would need to decide in the near future whether to leave Textilpol, since he is getting on in years.

The professional level of management in Poland in the 1980s was generally much higher than in earlier decades, but in 1989–91, the majority of many management teams were dismissed for a variety of reasons. Those who survived, particularly in larger cities, must have been the cream of Polish management, however mediocre that may have been. In many cases these people were among the most valuable assets of their enterprises. That the unions, for whatever reason, saw this situation as compromising could have been detrimental to the survival of these enterprises.

At Textilpol, the deputy in charge of production and sales was an engineer in his early thirties, formerly in the production steering section of Textilpol, who had recently moved into this position from that of associate to the general manager. The latter had been dismissed, together with the sales section manager, over a disagreement on the sales strategy in the domestic market. The third member of the core management was the financial and accounting manager, who also had an M.A. in economics and long practice in accounting. Previously, there had been two other top managerial posts, deputy for economic affairs, which had merged with the functions of the general manager, and deputy in charge of technology, which was downgraded to the level of chief specialist. The management now consisted of three managers and five chief specialists. One of the latter, a young economist who had formerly led the export section, was now responsible for marketing, having been promoted to the post of chief specialist early in 1993.

The system of managerial remuneration was typical for an SOE, with the exception that the workers' council determined the basic wage of the general manager at four times the firm average, as opposed to the national average, plus a bonus equal to one month's average wage, and the deputies received 70 percent of the general manager's income. With no net profit in Textilpol, there were no additional bonuses for the managers.

WHAT HAPPENED IN TEXTILPOL AFTER JANUARY 1990? THE NATURE OF EXTERNAL SHOCKS

The new economic situation resulted in severe setbacks for Textilpol. We shall describe both those that affected the demand side—such as a poor and disintegrated domestic market; insolvency of the principal customer, the army; the collapse of both barter trade with China and a large Soviet contract—and those on the supply side; such as rising costs. We shall also evaluate the 1990–91 survival strategy and the program of restructuring initiated in the second half of 1991.

Deliveries for the Army

As mentioned before, Textilpol had been a traditional supplier of uniform fabric to the Polish army. About, 35 percent of total output in physical terms went to the military, but although it was a stable business, it was not very profitable. In 1990, after a bulk order had been placed to Textilpol, as it was every year, the army's budget was suddenly reduced. The enterprise borrowed working capital at 90 percent to complete the order. The army then decided that it did not want the product after all and put it into military storage without paying Textilpol. Finally, in June 1992, after agreeing to a price reduction of 25 percent, Textilpol succeeded in extracting payment, and the financial section immediately demanded penalty interest on the delayed payment, but with little hope of receiving it. According to the firm's estimate, the loss suffered by Textilpol on this contract amounted to 10 billion zloty, or 400 percent of the net loss recorded in 1991. Normally, it would be possible to minimize such a loss by delivering the cloth to other customers in the garment industry. The market demand for khaki-colored fabric was very small, however, and garment-producing firms were even withdrawing their usual orders and switching to other business.

Disruption of Demand and Existing Structures on the Domestic Market

Civilian domestic demand fell to a similar extent. Traditional garment industry customers, crowded out of the market by cheap imports from the Far East, switched to exporting their services, and most of them survived by accepting Western processing orders for production according to foreign design and with imported material. Consequently, they had no need for deliveries of domestic fabrics producers and Textilpol estimated that civilian domestic demand for its products fell from about 1.5 million meters in 1988–89 to 0.5–0.6 million in the last two years. Moreover, the customers had changed entirely. In the 1980s, Textilpol had ten major customers; now it was dealing with over 500 small clients, with small-quantity demand, frequently as little as 100–200 meters. Such production was costly, not only because the production machines had to be changed very often, but also because small quantities of cheviot yarn had to be bought, obviously at higher prices.

Export Fortunes and Misfortunes

Faced with mounting difficulties in the domestic market, the management of Textilpol tried to use an apparently golden opportunity on the Soviet market to make up for the losses. The enterprise had had positive past experiences in trade with the Soviets, who would buy large quantities of low-quality coarse woolen fabric, paying decent prices in transfer rubles, but this trade had disappeared in the late 1980s. In 1990, a consortium of light industry enterprises, led by a large local foreign trade company, tried to revive export sales to the USSR. This was to be a big barter transaction, with the Soviets paying in crude oil and helicopters.

After obtaining a license from the Polish government, but before signing the contract, Textilpol began production with 350,000 meters of ordered cloth. Credit was obtained to buy raw materials, again at 90 percent, other costs were carried in full, and the product was put into storage. In the meantime, the USSR ceased to exist. Negotiations over the contract were delayed; it was finally signed in mid-1991. But the prospective customers were not able to pay: that is, to deliver the promised goods. In an attempt to recover at least part of the cost, the ordered cloth was used for men's suits and overcoats, but the products turned out to be unsalable in Poland and Textilpol was still trying to get rid of this stock, sometimes at 20 percent of the total cost. The transaction finally ended with losses estimated at 10 billion zloty, similar to the deal with the army.

There were no plans to reenter the Eastern market in the near future, although numerous barter transactions were being prepared in Lodz. In our discussions, the general manager pointed to the weak financial standing of potential partners in the East and to the falling profitability of such exports due to growing price competition from Finnish and East German firms trying to return to that market with substantial assistance from their governments.

China had been a customer of Textilpol for many years. This was also barter trade, but the goods offered by the Chinese—cotton T-shirts, for example—were in demand in the 1980s. Textilpol had sold these goods in its own shops and the business was profitable and fairly easy. After 1990, the situation changed completely. The Chinese continued to offer products of the same type and quality, such as vacuum flasks and sweatshirts, but the Poles would no longer buy these products and, as a result, trade with China was ended.

There were some brighter spots in the export activity. British and Irish customers regularly bought as much as 0.5 million meters of high-quality cheviot woolen fabric, and the prospects for expansion of these deliveries were good. Additionally, smaller quantities were sold to Finland, Cyprus, Lebanon, the United States, Panama, Iran, and Singapore. In fact, probably up to 65 percent of the reduced output of Textilpol was, at this point, export-oriented.

Cost Evolution

The events of 1990–91 could justifiably be called a cost revolution. All costs grew substantially, although at uneven rates, changing the cost structure of Textilpol. Material and labor costs traditionally dominated the total cost of output, their share fluctuating around 85–87 percent, or 20 and 65 percent respectively. The three main cost-oriented problems at Textilpol were the following:

- There was a dramatic growth in total cost, which could not be fully compensated by price increases. Total cost per unit between 1989 and 1991 grew approximately ten-fold. Price increase possibilities were practically exhausted in early 1991, leading to a serious profit squeeze. To preserve the modest net profitability from the previous year, the price level would have to have been 60 percent higher.
- Output in physical terms in 1989–91 declined by more than 50 percent, from 3.1 million units in 1989 to just 1.45 million units in 1991. In such a case, the dynamics of fixed cost per unit was very important, as shown by a study in the framework of a restructuring program that was prepared by a local consulting firm, and which estimated that the fixed cost per unit grew twenty-five-fold.
- Several special problems ensued with labor costs, energy costs, and interest charges. A short comment on this will also shed some light on what could be considered fixed cost in our firm.

Labor Cost. Its share in total cost fell from 22.7 percent in 1989 to 21 percent in 1990, but grew to an astonishing 30.8 percent in 1991 and was still high at 28.3 percent in early 1992. Bearing in mind the sizable reduction of employment that occurred at Textilpol, one would expect a different tendency. However, if a firm undertook a group lay-off instead of reducing employment by natural attrition, it had to bear the three-to-six-month-wage severance payment, which inflated the recorded labor cost. Only later could the cost diminish. Group lay-offs took place every year, leading to extra costs of this nature. A high-wage policy was another partial explanation for the observed evolution.

Energy. The rise in energy prices was particularly painful: the enterprise's energy bill skyrocketed in 1990 and continued to grow rapidly. Between 1989 and early 1992, its share in total cost of output increased from 3.1 percent to 16.9 percent, partly due to penalty interest charges on unpaid energy bills being added to the current bill. Also, energy costs in Poland were like fixed costs. At the beginning of each year, a firm determines its needs and places an order to the energy supplier. If, however, due to reduced output, the firm does not use the entire ordered quantity, it still has to pay the full amount. Only after some six months of the contract have expired can it modify the order.

Interest Charges. Insignificant in the distant past, its share grew to a serious 5.5 percent of total cost in 1989, continued to grow in 1990–91, and reached 11.7 percent in 1992. The volume of credit obtained was not very big, but the unfortunate business transactions of 1990 inflated Textilpol's short-term bank debt to about two months' sales by the end of 1990, after which the scale of bank indebtedness was reduced. At the same time, Textilpol had a long-term investment denominated in German marks that was to be repaid by the end of October 1992. The interest on this was moderate, but the multiple devaluations of zloty caused the credit to weigh increasingly more in the balance of the enterprise. It is fair to say that the policy of high interest rates pursued after January 1990 seriously affected Textilpol, even though it had not entered the transformation period with a backlog of old debts.

SHORT-TERM SURVIVAL STRATEGY

The first reaction to falling domestic demand, both civilian and military, was an attempt to fill the gap by increasing export sales. Unfortunately, this was a complete failure and Textilpol found itself in a dramatic situation. The scale of output was adjusted quickly, employment reduced, but costs continued to grow and inventories accumulated to a level of six months' sales by the beginning of 1992. However, the recent high level of work-in-progress inventories was deceptive in that these goods were actually finished-goods inventories in disguise, to look better for the banks and the regional representative of the Ministry of Finance.

The worst situation occurred in the third quarter of 1991, when sales virtually stopped, the cash flow ceased completely, and the management needed to make a decision about the optimal structure of debts. Faced with obligations including repayment and servicing of bank credit, tax payments, and suppliers' bills, with energy bills at the forefront, management decided that preserving good relations with banks was absolutely crucial. All available cash was used for bank interest and principal payments, and significant arrears were allowed to accumulate in relations with the suppliers and the budget. The justification was straightforward: the penalty interest rate at the bank was higher than either inter-firm credit or the overdue budget obligations, and besides, the state was

the owner and it should bear the consequences of its policy. (The latter statement was only partly true, since the Soviet deal was, unlike the army deal, a mistake of the management.)
The result of these optimization decisions at the end of 1991 was:

- 20 billion zloty tax arrears;
- 24 billion zloty inter-firm payables (most overdue);
- 40 billion zloty in finished goods inventories;
- access to working capital credit and decent relations with the banks.

It should be noted that, throughout most of the period, the enterprise maintained both a positive gross profit and a decent margin of operating profit on current activity that, nevertheless, translated into a net loss after the inclusion of obligatory deductions—income tax and a very small dividend. High income tax obligations compared with a very modest amount of gross profit were due to the fact that the latter was reduced by extraordinary losses, including penalty interest charges on tax arrears, which could not legitimately be included in total costs to reduce income tax obligations. Another interesting feature at Textilpol was a significant amount of revenue from such miscellaneous activity as the services of the finishing mill. The statistical data concerning volume of output include this kind of production and thus show higher quantities of fabrics than actually produced.

It would seem that the management made the right decision to preserve current liquidity from complete disruption at the risk of being liquidated or declaring bankruptcy due to the mounting overdue tax obligations. Their implicit bet that the state would think twice before eliminating Textilpol, one of the best firms in the industry, was correct. The enterprise became a candidate for debt rescheduling and a partial cancellation program, particularly because it was in the course of meaningful restructuring.

RESTRUCTURING PROGRAM AND ITS FIRST RESULTS

In mid-1991, the management invited a local consulting firm to assist in the preparation of a comprehensive restructuring program encompassing all basic aspects of the enterprise. An immediate reason for preparing such a program may have been a competition organized by the Ministry of Ownership Transformation; to have not participated would have tarnished the image of the manager. Nevertheless, this program was quickly put in operation. We will not evaluate the program here, but only mention its essential elements.

Cost reduction was naturally considered the most urgent aim for Textilpol. Reducing employment to the level of 450–500 people was recommended because, although after redundancy costs this would result in immediate cost savings of only 700 million zloty, there were prospects of more significant long-term gains. As we know, this has already been accomplished.

Fixed assets utilization at the current level of output did not exceed 40–45 percent and an obvious recommendation was to eliminate redundant space and unused machinery. By mid-1992, Textilpol had rented the majority of the space in the administration building and in one of the four plants, which brought in about 300 million zloty in cash and saved 150 million zloty in maintenance fees. Although these amounts were annual and not decisive for the enterprise, they were used for some immediate needs. At the time of this analysis, an even deeper program of asset restructuring was under way. Since coarse yarn could be bought cheaply at specialized producers, the yarn-producing mill had been closed, and the two existing weaving mills were to be merged. This would entail a further reshuffling of machinery and equipment, which we will not describe, but, in sum, Textilpol would eventually concentrate production in two plants, instead of four. According to a rather conservative estimate prepared by the consulting firm, this could reduce the total cost by some 5 percent.

To improve sales, two things were needed: an enhanced sales effort on the domestic market and modification of the product mix to offer a more attractive export package. As previously mentioned, a reshuffling of the sales and marketing sections within the firm had begun. To the existing two retail shops and one warehouse, a second warehouse was added, located in one of the liquidated plants. Although the concentration would be on textiles, this combination of facilities would offer the full spectrum of Textilpol's production. The establishment of a country-wide sales force was also under way. In the past, arrangements of this type had brought mixed results in the form of unreliable customers who took delivery but never paid, but, with the many smaller, new wholesale and retail firms growing in strength, the prospects were better. People from outside the firm, but also employees from the sales section, enticed by a 4 percent commission on sold products, were encouraged to become salespeople.

The high quality of the design workshop facilitated an upgrade in the product mix. However, to attain a quality in additional product lines that would be accepted in Western markets, some new investment in machinery was indispensable. According to the management's estimate, to effectively modernize the enterprise, $1.2 million was needed immediately, followed by an additional $2.5 million within three years. Given the present situation, the implementation of such a program did not appear likely. Textilpol also intended to maintain the sales volume of its finishing mill's services to outside producers of textiles, since these have proven quite profitable.

A successful restructuring program would have to take into account the firm's existing backlog of debts and huge inventories. Textilpol was negotiating with its suppliers a rescheduling of its obligations, or at least a freeze on the accumulating penalty interest charges. The chemical fibers supplier, a monopolist on the Polish market, was the most difficult partner. As the volume of payables in late 1992 grew to four months' sales, the pressure on the part of the suppliers mounted. Similar negotiations were under way with the regional office of the

Ministry of Finance concerning tax obligations. Although Textilpol would not, in the foreseeable future, be able to pay its obligations in full, it had resumed meeting most current tax obligations by the latter part of 1992. The purpose of these negotiations was not so much to set a timetable for debt repayment as to present the firm as a viable, serious partner, and possibly obtain a freeze on penalty charges or their partial cancellation.

One option that was considered at Textilpol was privatization. In 1991, after time-consuming preparation of necessary documents, the firm was placed on the Lista 400, meant for mass privatization. However, due to a deterioration of its financial situation, it was withdrawn from the program and the effort was never resumed, since regulations about the tax on capital paid by one-person partnerships of the state made it unattractive for Textilpol to seek this kind of transformation. Prospective foreign buyers had appeared in the past but were not presenting any serious financial offer. At present, then, the issue of privatization seems to have been put to rest at Textilpol. This could change rapidly if the Ministry of Industry were to decide to liquidate the enterprise, but that seems unlikely.

FINAL REMARKS

Textilpol, and the entire woolen products industry, was in a very difficult situation, but it may have survived the worst period, 1991, by adopting the smart but slightly cynical attitude of optimizing the portfolio of overdue obligations. In 1992, slack domestic sales and growing liquidity problems resulted in a decrease in real output to some 1.1–1.2 million meters of fabric. The management decided to try more aggressively to eliminate the remaining inventory of finished goods from the unfortunate Soviet and army deals. Forced to sell these products much below historical cost, Textilpol recorded substantial losses in the second half of 1992, but managed to find resources to survive, and even to decrease the volume of bank credit.

One should stress once again that there had been much adjustment in terms of employment level, fixed assets restructuring, and increased selling efforts, not to mention preserving positive profitability on current operations and successfully expanding export sales, other than the 1990 Soviet deal. But notwithstanding the management's efforts, the situation of the enterprise was extremely difficult and, without some sort of emergency package, would probably have augured nothing more than prolonged agony.

However, there was a glimmer of hope on the horizon. The Ministry of Industry decided to begin a restructuring program in the woolen industry in the Lodz region and Textilpol's general manager was appointed the ministry's official plenipotentiary in charge of this program. It might thus seem that the future of the enterprise would be secure. The idea, shared by a consortium of local consulting firms charged with preparation of a general plan, was to liquidate most of the sixteen existing firms and concentrate production in the remaining few that were most productive, thus ensuring their survival. Chances were good that Textilpol would be among the latter group. At the time of this report, it was too early to write an epilogue to the story. Still the example of Textilpol may demonstrate whether it is possible to stage a successful restructuring effort in a branch of industry in total collapse.

Table 1
Structure of Costs (in percentages)

Specification	1988	1989	1990	1991	January–May 1992
Wages	19.73	22.72	21.03	28.69	28.30
Materials	67.86	65.16	55.01	42.86	43.59
Energy	3.97	3.06	8.06	12.59	16.91
Banking charges (incl. interest)	1.0	5.55	7.42	10.88	0.20
Depreciation	1.98	0.73	2.30	3.96	4.33
Property tax	0.4	0.11	0.50	0.84	1.59
External services	5.06	22.67	5.68	0.17	5.08
Total	100	100	100	100	100

Table 2
Main Financial Indices (in million zloty)

Specification	1988	1989	1990	1991	January–May 1992
Net sales	5,646.9	20,087.1	61,058.6	67,045.0	21,159.0
Costs of sales	4,640.4	12,465.1	49,531.0	53,784.0	19,531.0
Markup	1,006.5	7,622.0	11,527.6	13,261.0	1,628.0
Remaining revenues	—	—	—	5,194.0	2,133.0
Costs of obtaining revenues	13.7	0.36	60.0	5,048.0	2,091.0
Financial revenues	0.13	66.5	–336.0	901.0	236.0
Financial costs	46.2	835.94	4,709.0	8,140.0	966.0
Operating profit $[3 + (4 – 5) + (6 – 7)]$	946.73	6,852.2	6,422.6	6,168.0	940.0
Extraordinary profits	61.2	1,380.4	4,737.0	4,097.0	931.0
Extraordinary losses	78.3	302.8	766.0	10,203.0	1,815.0
Gross profit/loss $(8 + 9 – 10)$	929.63	7,929.8	10,393.6	62.0	56.0
Taxes	381.05	2,455.92	4,504.0	3,121.0	358.0
Gross profit/loss $(11 – 12)$	548.58	5,473.88	5,889.6	–3,061.0	–302.0

Table 3

Profitability Ratios

Specification	1988	1989	1990	1991	January–May 1992
Markup (operating profit)/sales	17.82	37.94	18.88	19.78	7.69
Gross profits/sales	16.41	39.48	17.02	0.09	0.26
Markup (operating profit)/cost of sales	21.69	61.15	23.27	24.66	8.34
Gross profits/costs of sales	20.03	63.62	20.98	0.12	0.29
Net profit/cost of sales	11.82	43.91	11.89	−5.69	−1.55

Table 4

Liquidity and Activity Ratios

Specification	1988	1989	1990	1991	January–May 1992
Liquidity ratios:					
Working capital/total assets	0.44	0.38	0.34	0.14	—
Current ratio	2.12	1.78	2.10	1.23	—
Quick ratio	0.80	0.69	0.97	0.58	0.31
Activity ratios:					
Accounts receivable turnover	4.65	4.46	4.30	2.73	1.49
Average collection period (days)	75	78	80	128	101
Payments turnover	3.52	2.54	3.38	1.83	0.43
Average payments period (days)	99	138	104	191	349
Inventory turnover	3.70	4.31	5.07	2.72	0.49
Average inventory turnover (days)	95	81	69	129	306

5

Electronics: Miflex Radio Components Firm S.A.

Stefan Krajewski

SECTORAL SETTING

In the 1970s, the purchase of new licenses and import of modern machinery from the West greatly modernized and expanded the Polish electronics industry. As a result, some parts of the industry, which had absorptive outlets in both Poland and the CMEA, attained a leading position in the CMEA countries. For a while, this industry was also the pride of both the Polish authorities and Polish society and many talented and energetic young people sought jobs there. Therefore, it came as surprise that this industry, formerly so strong, seemed unable to adapt to conditions of a market economy and foreign competition.

The greatest threat for the firm studied here was an increase in the supply of high-quality, low-priced imported goods. Firms selling these products, most of which were from Western Europe and the Far East, promptly organized a distribution network, thereby gaining many customers. Meanwhile, state-owned wholesalers selling Polish electronic products did not respond to the new challenges as elastically.

Other problems that besieged the industry included the collapse of exports to the USSR and the CMEA countries, a deepening fiscal crisis that caused a reduction or even elimination of government orders for the army, and a decline in living standards, which reduced demand for electronic equipment.

The output of this industry declined each year, not only for the entire industry, but also for most individual items. For some product ranges, the cut in production was quite severe. For example, the 1991 output of radios and semi-conductor devices represented about 22 percent of 1988 production, and this situation worsened in 1992. (See Table 1.)

During 1991–92, the electronics industry as a whole began to experience losses. Many state-owned electronics firms were liquidated and some were forced to negotiate with banks, suppliers, and the Treasury to reschedule their debt payments. Arrears continued to grow. Even the most successful firms had difficulty selling the new products that had been developed in the course of ambitious restructuring programs.

GENERAL INFORMATION ABOUT MIFLEX

Miflex Radio Components State-Owned Company was established in Kutno in 1957. Later, a plant was opened at Krosniewice, near Kutno. The firm produced radio components and electronic parts, with the latter predominating in the firm's present assortment structure. Miflex's products were utilized by enterprises manufacturing televisions, telecommunications equipment, household appliances, lighting devices, and so on. In 1990 its production structure was as follows:

- condensers (about 65 percent of sales);
- high-voltage multipliers (15 percent of sales);
- amplifiers (14 percent);
- transformers (4 percent);
- electronic transmitters; (2 percent).

The group of products closest to world standards were foil and split transformers and fluidized condensers. For many years, Miflex had sold its products on the domestic market and in the CMEA countries. Until recently, it held a near monopoly on the Polish market, the only competition being the insignificant imports from some of the East European countries.

The firm possessed a large production capacity. The majority of the machines and equipment were purchased in Western Europe, but had been in use for many years and were depreciated by 62 percent as of 1991.

Miflex had its own research and development center. It employed many highly qualified and experienced constructors and technologists, who were the designers of most products manufactured. Proximity to Warsaw and Lodz also allowed the firm to attract good specialists.

In March 1992, Miflex was transformed into a one-person partnership of the State Treasury. The main statistical information is as follows:

	1991	1992
Value of sales	$14 million	about $10 million
Share of exports	32.2 percent	15 percent
Employment	2,474 people	1,450 people

IMPACT OF THE TRANSITION

Among the changes occurring after 1989, several seemed to have a profound influence on the firm. For example, the rapid increase in prices both in costs and for products manufactured by Miflex shook the hitherto stable conditions of the firm's operation and set off a feeling of uncertainty.

The share of banking charges and interest in the overall costs rose from 1.0 percent in 1988 to 8.9 percent in 1989 and 11.2 percent in 1990. At the same time, the current situation forced Miflex to obtain greater amounts of short-term credits, because some customers began to accumulate sizable debts to Miflex due to their own financial troubles. Also, demand for some of Miflex's products decreased, causing inventories of manufactured goods to grow, leading to a further freeze of financial resources. Lastly, the firm was buying larger quantities of materials because it expected further increases.

The liberalization of foreign trade and mitigation of tariffs prompted rapid growth in imports of electronic goods. A rich assortment of these goods imported from West European countries Japan, the United States, Hong Kong, Taiwan, Singapore, and Thailand appeared on the Polish market. Their importers were dynamic private firms that organized an effective distribution network and reached many potential customers of Miflex by using an elastic pricing policy of differentiated margins and successful advertising. New plants for the assembly of televisions and radios using imported parts began to emerge and expand. The result of this was that demand for Polish electronic equipment by former customers of Miflex also began to decline rapidly in 1990.

For many years, the second major source of domestic demand for products other than televisions and radios was the army. However, the recession necessitated substantial cuts in military expenditures, particularly with regard to the purchase of equipment. The army suspended payments for previously ordered goods and stopped ordering new supplies.

Another major shock was the collapse of the CMEA markets. Exports had constituted nearly 17 percent of total sales in 1988, with about 90 percent going to the CMEA—a convenient and stable market. But from 1990 on it was impossible to make reliable predictions about the size of transactions or terms of their fulfillment.

The destabilized conditions in which firms were operating after 1989 coincided with a withdrawal of the government from interference in affairs of individual firms. The government's declarations that it would not support ineffective firms that were unable to adapt themselves to the new conditions were accepted with a great deal of anxiety by the directors of Miflex. In their view Miflex's situation was like that of a man thrown into deep and turbulent water who could not swim well and did not know which way to go to save his life. For the management of Miflex, it was this sense of isolation and sole responsibility for the firm's destiny that was perhaps the greatest shock. The remaining employees felt it later, when the drop in demand forced lay-offs.

Several factors hamper Miflex's adaptation to the new conditions. These included its reliance on a narrow circle of domestic customers who were manufacturers of final electronic products and, consequently, on these customers' ability to survive on the market. Also hampering the firm was its obsolete and depreciated machinery and equipment; the needed investment outlays would be particularly large in a technology-intensive industry such as electronics.

In turn, some characteristics of the firm might be considered as facilitating the adjustment process. The firm had a monopoly in the main production lines in Poland; it had low domestic dividend and wage (PPWW) tax burdens (although these are endogenous to the performance of the firm); there was no need to repay long-term credits, which improved the current profitability position and made it easier for the firm to obtain credit in the future; and, since the firm had not received any direct government subsidies in the late 1980s, it did not face problems connected with their sudden elimination.

THE SITUATION AFTER THE "BIG BANG": FIRST RESPONSES

Markets, Sales, Production

The collapse of former outlets made it necessary to find new sales opportunities. To this end, Miflex sought new customers such as small workshops and service centers. The previous system of sales through large state-owned wholesaler distributors had disappeared. Therefore, Miflex organized its own network of wholesalers, with about 100 trading firms covering the entire country. A wholesale center attached to Miflex had been already opened and preparations were under way to establish wholesale centers or conclude agreements on wholesale deliveries in Ukraine, Belorussia, Lithuania, and Czechoslovakia. Efforts were also being made to expand sales to the West European markets, so far without much success, although a cooperation deal with a German firm was in prospect.

Miflex intended to increase the number of its canvassers and to participate in fairs and exhibitions in Western and Eastern Europe. Also, the employees in the research and development center were working on new applications for Miflex's existing products.

The difficulties in finding new outlets resulted in decreasing sales, which dropped significantly in 1991, although this tendency seemed to have been reversed in the first part of 1992, as shown in the data in Table 2. This situation affected the volume and structure of inventories. Before 1990, Miflex had accumulated large quantities of cheap raw materials such that the ratio of inventories to sales value reached about 25 percent in 1988. In the following years, these inventories were consumed, which led to a reduction of material costs. However, a part of those inventories proved to be unnecessary for production and remained in storage for several years. The inventories/sales ratio rose in 1991 to 34 percent and by May 1992 had reached 117.5 percent. Now, moreover, the internal structure of inventories had changed. The intensifying difficulty of selling products was reflected by an increased share of finished goods in total inventories (see Table 3).

To avoid producing goods for which there were no customers, the sales plan for the second half of 1992 and the first half of 1993 was drafted on the basis of submitted orders and visits of canvassers, technicians, and employees to the production divisions of fifty-five competitors. These trips provided a valuable, although sometimes bitter, lesson that what counts is not so much producing what one considers to be a good quality item but selling it.

As a result of insufficient demand, the sales plan for 1992–93 envisaged the need to liquidate or reduce a large part of the existing production capacities, a decision that largely concerned condensers. The plan was that 37 percent of the value of production in the second half of 1992 and the first half of 1993 would be represented by new products that were better adapted to the market requirements, i.e., split and impulse transformers, MKSP and MKSE condensers. Attempts were made to extend production beyond the traditional assortment range. A newly introduced welding machine turned out to be a market success because of its high quality and moderate price.

Profitability, Liquidity, Taxes

Throughout the analyzed period, the firm had realized an operating profit on its main activities. In 1991, both the volume of profit and profitability ratios dropped by about 50 percent (Table 4) and continued to decrease during 1992, the result being losses for the whole year. This was mainly due to the growth of prices of materials, energy, and various charges and fees; an excessive level of employment; and underutilization of production capacities, i.e., high fixed costs.

A high nominal interest rate inflated financial costs such that they amounted to 23.6 billion zloty in 1991 and almost 10 billion zloty in the period January–May 1992. While the volume of operating profit decreased, an increasingly larger influence on the firm's financial results was exerted by the balance of extraordinary profits and losses. Until the end of 1990, extraordinary losses were offset by differences in currency exchange rates, i.e., the revaluation of dollar balances, which operated in the firm's favor. However, in 1991 extraordinary losses increased sharply to more than six times the level of profits, largely due to penalty interest charges on delayed tax payments and overdue invoices.

The poor financial situation of the firm was reflected in worsening liquidity and activity ratios. The share of working capital in total assets sharply decreased, liquidity dried up, and collection periods of receivables continued to lengthen at least until the end of 1991, all of which virtually paralyzed the normal operation of the firm.

Because Miflex's customers were having their own financial difficulties, it seemed sensible for Miflex to accept payments in finished goods such as televisions that were then sold in the firm shops. But even practices like this did not prevent Miflex from falling into an indebtedness trap with suppliers, banks, and the state.

During 1988–90, when its profitability was high, the firm paid all its debts to the state with no difficulty. The dividend did not represent a big burden for the firm (see Table 5). Since the management conducted a cautious wage policy, there was no PPWW tax burden; on the other hand, the low wage level maintained over a period of years had became a cause of a growing dissatisfaction among employees. The firm found it difficult to pay the taxes due in 1991, when its gross profit of 557 million zloty turned out to be 8.7 times lower than its debts to the state budget, 2,232 million zloty in income tax and 2,626 million zloty in dividend. The situation in 1992 was even worse, as the minimal gross loss recorded after eleven months of 1992 grew to a serious amount after allowing for the due taxes.

Management Changes

The Solidarity trade union and the workers' council (before its dissolution at the time of commercialization) jointly recognized that major changes in the management, especially top management of the firm, were indispensable. The firm's unsatisfactory financial situation and intensifying concerns of its employees, such as lay-offs, low wages, and cuts in the welfare fund, were given as the primary reasons for the frequent changes in managerial posts since 1989.

The information obtained from the enterprise indicates that promotion to the top managerial positions at Miflex was guided by the same factors as in most other Polish firms: most directors had a technical university background, had previously been responsible for production or technical affairs, had worked for the firm for a long time, and had little experience in marketing or contact with foreign partners.

The chairman was a forty-year-old electronic engineer. He had assumed his post in December 1992, after having been division manager in a large transport equipment-manufacturing firm in southern Poland. His predecessor, forty-five years old, also an engineer and a machinery construction specialist, had worked at Miflex since 1971, and took over as chairman of the board in late 1991. As a result of a conflict with the Solidarity, he left the firm in mid-1992 to manage his own small electronics firm.

The deputy in charge of trade was a forty-one-year-old technical university graduate, in the current position since 1984. From 1982 until 1984, he had been chief engineer, and still earlier, manager of the production preparation department. He had worked for Miflex throughout his entire professional career. The deputy in charge of finance was fifty-two, had an M.A. in economics, and had held the present position since October 1990. From 1985 until 1990 he had served as deputy chief accountant and before that, as manager of the costs department. The production director was a man of forty-seven years, a technical university graduate, in the present position since January 1992, before which he had been chief technologist. Miflex was his first and only employer.

The former managing director and several deputy directors had left the firm because they had not attained results that were satisfactory to the workers' council or trade unions. The chairman and vice-chairman of the supervisory board had been replaced recently for the same reason. The result of this management turnover could be regarded as an excessive destabilization of the top management that negatively affected the firm's performance and diminished any interest in being appointed to managerial posts. Many potentially good candidates were unwilling to apply, discouraged by low pay, much responsibility, and a tense relationship between the management and trade unions. In fact, the post of the chairman of the board was vacant for nearly six months due to the lack of an appropriate candidate.

In 1991, the salaries of the directors, including profit bonus, sometimes called a commission, were 2.6 times higher than average pay in the firm, and this pay differentiation increased when Miflex was commercialized. As a result, the pay of the directors rose in mid-1992 to 3.75 times the average pay, despite disapproval of some employees. The low level and poor differentiation led to an outflow of highly qualified employees, who could find well-paid jobs elsewhere with relative ease. This prompted the board to prepare a policy to encourage the retention of the firm's more highly qualified personnel. At present, those employees who were especially useful to the firm were identified and their pay was to be doubled. The remaining employees received 20 percent wage increases in January 1993. The most acute shortage of highly qualified employees existed in the trade and finance divisions and in the development departments, i.e., construction and technology.

ORGANIZATION AND MANAGEMENT STRUCTURE

The were four divisions at Miflex: trade, headed by a deputy; finance, headed by another deputy; production, headed by the production director; and development, under the chief specialist for development. Great effort was made to strengthen the divisions of trade and finance; they were managed by deputies, which emphasized their priority. The number of employees was increased, their pay was raised, and the divisions were better equipped. The employees were trained outside the firm in such areas as marketing, data processing, finance, and accounting, while some directors got practical training abroad at the American Management Association, Dupont, and MEET.

The emphasis laid on the divisions of trade and finance encountered a great deal of resistance among some managerial staff on various levels who had difficulty accepting the idea that the problems of production were to be of secondary importance relative to marketing and finance.

LONG-TERM RESPONSES

The main long-term strategic goals of Miflex were the following: to gain a position as the best manufacturer of condensers in Poland and Eastern Europe; to implement a program of mechanization and automation of production processes; and to improve the quality of production processes in terms of environmental protection. It was recognized that the drop in demand on the domestic market was not going to change in the near future; therefore, emphasis was to be placed on expanding exports.

Management of the Firm and Ownership Changes

The board intended to enhance the effectiveness of individual units in Miflex by establishing a holding of partnerships in the future by means of the following:

- changing the department of machines construction into an association of capital with Miflex;
- changing the department of semi-manufactures, tool shop, and electroplating section into an association of capital with Miflex;
- changing the remaining departments of condensers and transformers into partnerships.

Each partnership would assume responsibility for repair and financial services, procurement of supplies, and marketing to the degree it considered desirable. For the departments of energy supply and auxiliary production services, the board submitted two suggestions for using their oversized production capacities:

- Internal privatization, i.e., setting up partnerships on the basis of these departments and providing services for Miflex and other economic entities. Apart from Miflex, however, there were no other firms willing to use these services.
- Merging these two departments, accompanied by a considerable reduction of employment. Some qualified employees could be moved to the production departments.

These moves were to be preceded by an across-the-board reduction in employment that would decrease costs significantly, without which such reorganization would be ineffective. Of course, the growth of individual partnerships would not be possible until they became independent and were able to collect a number of orders.

An American consulting firm, Company Assistance Ltd., which had prepared a business plan for Miflex, thought that it was possible to sell the enterprise to a foreign partner. However, selling the entire firm to one investor would be difficult because various departments dealt with different types of production. This also meant that each department could exist independently, thereby being profitable to more than one potential investor. The management was also interested in acquiring the firm by means of a management buyout (MBO) in the future, but only if favorable terms were available and the firm had a decent financial standing.

Investments and Changes in Production Structure

Export provided the best means of increasing sales, but this would involve significant investments of as much as $2.5 to $3 million in the coming years. Miflex did not have enough of its own financial resources for such investments and it was seeking external financing in the form of bank credits and a loan from the Industrial Development Agency. As already mentioned, permanent changes on the market made it necessary to abandon the production of certain types of condensers and electronic units. Company Assistance had advised Miflex to produce condensers, products in which Miflex could best compete in technology and quality terms, with large inputs of labor. Since present productive capacity was too large for expected demand, a plan to liquidate part of fixed assets was prepared. Unnecessary machines and equipment were to be sold. Production halls at Krosniewice, totaling 3,000 m^2, and one of the firm's buildings in Kutno, at 1,700m^2, would either be sold or given to creditors. Another building in Kutno became a trade center and was partly leased. The sale of buildings was expected to reap about 7–10 billion zloty. The board also intended to sell the firm's seaside holiday resort, which was currently being leased. The remaining holiday resorts have been leased to a partnership called Relax that was set up by Miflex and its trade unions.

Company Assistance Ltd. also recommended the following:

- creation of a motivation system based on piece rates, with premiums for low absenteeism;
- improved packaging and external appearance of products;
- finding new applications for existing products and preparing new products for production;
- preserving present markets in Poland and the former USSR, and only then seeking entry into new markets.

One last recommendation was to reduce employment. Overemployment was one of the main causes for low profitability throughout the firm. The percentage of labor costs in total costs rose from 31.5 percent in 1988 to 40.5 percent in 1992, and the management estimated that, relative to planned production, there was an excess of about 430 employees. Therefore, about 180 persons in basic production, roughly 150 persons from auxiliary production, and about 100 administrative employees needed to be dismissed.

EVALUATION OF ADAPTATION MEASURES AND PROSPECTS OF MIFLEX

The management recognized the dire situation of Miflex and the threat of bankruptcy, and prepared a program of long-term adjustment. But only a small part of it could be executed immediately. The short-term measures taken so far had not dramatically changed the picture. For Miflex to survive, it would need to reduce its production capacities, modernize, and find new markets for its products.

An unclear power structure within the enterprise caused some sluggishness in undertaking strategic measures. Although the workers' council was eliminated when the firm was commercialized, the local trade unions, especially Solidarity, continued to exert a powerful influence on the selection of managers and directors, and on the program of activity.

Internal privatization was to take place in early 1992, with the bulk of the changes occurring later in that year and in 1993. But this timetable proved to be rather unrealistic because neither the individual departments nor the enterprise as a whole were prepared for it. Moreover, given the firm's financial situation, the credit needed for restructuring would be impossible to obtain. Plans to sell some of the firm's buildings in an attempt to reduce capacity also seemed too optimistic. And finally, the firm would probably have some difficulty finding a market large enough for its products. However, at least a part of Miflex could probably be salvaged by selling its individual departments to foreign investors.

Table 1

Basic Data about the Electronics Industry

Specification	1988	1989	1990	1991	1st–3rd 1992
Sales in current prices (billion zloty)	655	2,225	8,491	6,947	5,203
Sales in constant prices (preceding year = 100)	111.8	103.8	79.8	72.0	105.2*
Production of selected goods					
Radios (thousand units)	2,684	2,523	1,433	594	234
Televisions (thousand units)	749	772	748	443	298
Semi-conductor devices (million units)	368	373	208	81	26.6
Number of employees (thousand persons)	113.6	110.5	101.8	77.9	54.6
Mean monthly pay (thousand zlotys)	55.2	210.3	911.1	1,455.7	2,076.6
Profitability ratios:					
Gross profit/costs of sales	—	49.0	17.1	–31.2	–25.4
Net profit/costs of sales	—	—	—	–34.8	–28.0

Source: Statistical Yearbooks of Industry, (Central Statistical Office, Warsaw 1989, 1990, 1991). *Nakłady i wyniki przemysłu I–III kwartał 1992,* Central Statistical Office, Warsaw, December 1992.

* I–IIIQ 1991 = 100.

Table 2

Volume of Output in Particular Assortments

Specification	1988	1989	1990	1991	January–May 1992
Metallized polyester condensers					
thousand units	129,327	125,751	84,254	42,647	20,989
% (1988 = 100%)	100.0	97.2	65.1	33.0	16.2
Alternating current condensers					
thousand units	2,054	1,084	1,274	558	430
%	100.0	52.8	62.0	27.2	20.3
High-voltage multipliers for color televisions					
thousand units	915	596	379	443	196
%	100.0	65.1	41.4	48.4	21.4

Table 3

Structure of Inventories (in percentages)

Share in total inventories	1988	1989	1990	1991	January–May 1992
Of materials	67.8	69.2	53.2	36.3	25.6
Of works-in-progress	24.8	20.0	28.9	26.3	31.6
Of finished goods	5.7	8.3	13.9	30.4	39.5
Of products (in firm stores)	0.7	2.5	4.0	7.0	3.3

Table 4

Financial Results of Miflex for 1988–1992 (in million zloty)

Specification	1988	1989	1990	1991	January–November 1992
Net sales	10,919	39,279	159,998	158,564	110,726
Costs of sales	8,628	25,160	104,736	128,836	102,514
Operating profit	2,291	14,113	55,262	29,728	8,212
Gross profit	2,199	12,851	40,704	557	–122
Tax burden	1,093	5,041	17,946	4,858	3,098
Net profit	1,106	7,810	22,758	–4,301	3,220
Profitability ratios (%)					
Operating profit/sales	21.0	35.9	34.5	18.7	7.4
Gross profit/costs of sales	25.5	51.1	38.9	4.3	–0.1
Net profit/costs of sales	12.8	31.0	21.7	–3.3	–2.9

Table 5

Burden of Taxes Paid from Gross Profit (gross profit = 100)

Types of taxes	1988	1989	1990	1991	1992
Income tax	37.8	27.8	39.8	400.7	44.7
Dividend	—	2.8	4.3	471.5	83.5
Tax on wage increases	5.7	8.6	—	—	—
Total tax burden	43.5	39.2	44.1	872.2	128.2

6

Glass: Huta Szkla Hortensja

Marek Belka

SECTORAL SETTING

The Polish glass industry employed 25,000–30,000 people in 1988–91, accounting for approximately 0.8 percent of total manufacturing industry employment. Total industry sales in 1991 reached $74 million. Glass has always been a low-paying industry, especially when compared to other sectors characterized by similarly harsh working conditions, such as metallurgy and mining. This can be ascribed to the industry's low bargaining power, a crucial factor in determining wage levels under socialism.

The glass industry underwent a major transformation between 1990 and 1992. Its output declined in real terms by 27.3 percent in 1990, by an additional 13.3 percent in 1991, and by 13.1 percent in the first quarter of 1992. It is worth noting that the output of industrial glass dropped in 1990 much more abruptly than that of table (household) glass. The latter continued its downward trend in subsequent years (a decline reflected in the developments at Hortensja). Overall employment in the industry dropped from about 32,000 in 1988 to 23,300 in the first quarter of 1992, i.e., by about 27 percent, a change similar to that recorded in all manufacturing. The gross profitability of the glass sector, measured by the relation of gross profit to the cost of sales, was higher than average both in 1989 and in 1990, although it fell from 52.2 percent to 25 percent. Profitability deteriorated dramatically in 1991, when the sector began incurring gross losses, a tendency that deepened in the first months of 1992.

The decline of profitability in the sector was reflected in disastrous changes in the asset structure. Whereas the inventories of raw materials and work-in-progress increased at the rate of sectoral inflation, about 25 percent annually for the first half of 1992, which was much lower than the aggregate rate of industrial inflation, inventories of finished goods grew much more quickly, reaching a nominal level three times that of January 1991. Simultaneously, the volume of payables skyrocketed in 1991, increasing by 250 percent, thereby bringing the average payables rotation to 114 days; in December 1991 it reached 251 days.

As a result, both current and quick ratios for the sector indicate a situation of total disruption of the glass industry's liquidity position. Such symptoms were not surprising, given that the industry had been registering gross losses since May 1991. Of the 56 enterprises in the sector, 23 were in the red at the end of 1991.

HISTORY AND DESCRIPTION OF THE FIRM

History

In 1889 a Belgian industrialist named Hoebler established two glass factories in Piotrkow Trybunalski and named them after his two daughters, Kara and Hortensja. Both firms still exist; Kara specializes in flat glass and Hortensja in table glass. In 1945, Hortensja became a state-owned enterprise under the Industry Nationalization Act. The current production profile dates back to the 1970s when the factory was modernized and expanded.

Products and Markets

Hortensja produces high-quality glass products, often of considerable artistic value. Glasses, vases, ornaments, and miscellaneous items of white and colored glass, richly decorated and sometimes resembling sculptures, are typical of the firm. Elaborate techniques are used to obtain new and original combinations of colors, types of glass, and relief-type shapes. A so-called covered glass consisting of different layers is an object of particular pride to the firm.

Management boasts employing the best glass technologists in Poland. The nearest competitors in Poland, the glassworks at Tarnow and Krosno, are oriented toward standardized table-glass products, although both are known to produce items of good quality. Hortensja concentrates on hand-made products, having abandoned the production of both standard table glass and crystal glass, since not only domestic but also foreign competition in this market is intense. Thus, it is fair to say that Hortensja is a producer of unique goods, some internationally renowned.

As a consequence, Hortensja has always been a substantial exporter, exclusively to hard-currency Western markets. Export sales accounted for 21 percent of total sales in 1988, nearly 29 percent in 1989, and reached 40–42 percent at the point when domestic sales declined. In 1992 export sales exceeded 50 percent of total sales. These numbers do not tell the whole story of Hortensja's dependence on foreign markets. The vast majority of product patterns are export-oriented, which means that only 7 of the 51 brigades, or 15 percent of the work force, is normally engaged in the preparation of goods for domestic customers. Recently, that number has been reduced even further.

Production is structured around a system of brigades, a brigade being a team of 15–20 people with different skills, working in a full-cycle system around a glass tube, which is a particular type of oven. This resembles a nest system in a modern car factory. Some workers keep the glass tube in operation, others blow the necessary shapes, still others engage in the most difficult and demanding job, the formation of the raw shape and the combination of different parts into a finished product. The rest of the team provides auxiliary services.

The strong export orientation of the enterprise has both positive and negative aspects, as was shown between 1990 and 1992. It secures a stable market and profitable sales with clear prospects for expansion. At the same time, manual production, particularly in the field of artistic glass, frequently results in goods that are of varying, although not necessarily inferior, quality levels. As a rule, these goods do not qualify for export sales and must be sold instead on the domestic market, usually at a lower price. There is little problem as long as domestic demand is strong enough to absorb the second-quality export items, thereby securing additional revenue flow. However, export prices are not always high enough to compensate for the possible loss of domestic sales.

Management has never treated the domestic market as a viable alternative to foreign markets, indicating either that products of the firm are too expensive for Poles or that people in Poland do not keep up with the latest fashion trends. Judging by the immense number of patterns at the disposal of the design section, the expertise in preparing new patterns, and the tastes of the individual team members, the managers of Hortensja have never really attempted to conquer the domestic market, offering instead goods that do not necessarily appeal aesthetically to potential Polish customers.

Size, Fixed Assets, Sales, Cost Structure

Hortensja consists of one plant located in a mid-sized industrial city in central Poland and supplies about 7 percent of the nation's glass. The only enterprise in the Polish glass industry that is substantially larger is the Krosno glass factory, a multi-plant firm that was one of the first five state-owned enterprises privatized in 1990 through the public sale of shares. In the 1970s, Hortensja's optimal employment was estimated to be 2,600 people and an expansion of floor space was undertaken in order to increase productive capacity. However, insufficient money was put into the project and the firm was left with less than adequate equipment, in terms of the number of glass tubes, and inadequate use of space. As a result, at the end of 1992, Hortensja employed slightly fewer than 900 people, or about 40 percent fewer than in 1988.

Most of Hortensja's buildings are old and in poor condition. The basic equipment is the glass tube mentioned above, which can be used for five years before replacement is necessary. Because this technology requires regular investment, fixed assets have depreciated only slightly more than 50 percent and, in management's opinion, the overall technological level of production at Hortensja is satisfactory and a technology gap is not a problem. The immediate investment needs of Hortensja are minimal, according to management's estimates, and concern focuses on the peripheries of the basic production process.

Labor costs make up almost 50 percent of total costs. This is a direct consequence of the production profile of the enterprise. It is notable that the share of labor costs dropped from 52–54 percent in 1988–89 to 47 percent after 1990. This can be explained both by real wage decreases, a tendency observed in all sectors of the Polish economy in 1990, and by the growing importance of other cost items, such as materials, energy, and interest.

Material costs accounted for over 30 percent of total cost and were the most volatile item, rising from 23 percent in 1989 to 36 percent in 1991. This seems to be the consequence both of price changes in the past and of the specific meaning of material costs in a glass mill, comprising not only typical raw materials but also the costs of semi-fixed assets, such as tubes and their parts. In fact, the share of typical raw materials is as low as 4 percent of total cost, with the cost of imported material being negligible. Hortensja uses gas as an energy source, and the expenditure for energy accounted for about 5 percent of total costs in 1991, twice that of 1988–89. Energy prices grew dramatically in 1990 and 1991, whereas the increase in 1992 was moderate enough to be fully offset by conservation measures.

Interest costs also increased over the past four years, but they have never exceeded 6 percent of total cost. It is interesting to note that they had risen already in 1989 to 3.3 percent from a previous mere 0.5 percent and remained constant in 1990, reaching 5.9 percent only in 1991. This seems to typify the whole manufacturing sector, probably reflecting the reluctance of enterprises to incur high-priced credit in 1990. Only in 1991, when the situation worsened dramatically, did firms need to resort to bank credit to finance their working capital. In many cases, this was more a doubling-the-bet strategy than normal, prudent behavior. Throughout most of 1992, with industrial prices growing at an annual rate of 25 percent per year and banks lending at 55 percent, firms could maintain a sound cost structure only with a very low volume of credit. This made the problem of inter-firm credit, more precisely the problem of overdue payables and receivables, the so-called settlement jams, so important. The example of Hortensja illustrated the changing liquidity situation in Polish enterprises over this period.

Labor Force, Wages, Social Situation

Hortensja's 1992–93 labor force of fewer than 900 people was the smallest it had been in twenty-five years, mostly due to the decreasing scale of production and certain steps that were taken to rationalize the employment structure. However, the shortage of qualified labor was a recurring theme in discussions with the management. Voluntary departure of 50–60 employees over a year was not too bad, but it was interesting that, during a period of rising unemployment, more people left the firm voluntarily than in 1988–89. Most serious was the outflow of qualified workers, which was not compensated by an equivalent inflow.

In a local vocational school, a class for glass handicraft was sponsored by

Hortensja, but of twenty graduates per year, only five usually took up employment with the enterprise, some finding jobs in other glass works in Piotrkow or in small private firms. In the near future, Hortensja would be forced to compete with a huge private enterprise being constructed in the vicinity that would be specialized in flat glass and serial, automated production that requires lower qualifications and provides better working conditions.

The main reason for the labor shortage was, of course, the low wage level. The average wage at Hortensja at the end of 1992 was over 30 percent lower than the national average. Monthly gross earnings of about $125 were not attractive for young, qualified people. Further, the extent of wage dispersion in the enterprise was minimal. Most experienced workers, on whom the firm's production and good reputation depended, earned just $U.S.140–145 a month. It was surprising that these people would still work in Hortensja as they would have no problem in finding more remunerative jobs in the private sector. The reason for this seems to be that, aside from emotional factors in the case of the core workers, such as that it was a family tradition to work at Hortensja, there was greater job security at Hortensja than would be found in a small private firm. The best craftsmen could earn additional income from moonlighting in small private firms, but either they were not willing to take up a permanent job in such firms or the owners had no interest in employing additional people. In any case, the labor shortage became so acute that the management contemplated employing workers from abroad, for example, from Lithuania.

Labor unions in the enterprise were quite large compared with those in other enterprises. The Solidarity union was very active and the dominant union with about 300 members. The post-communist OPZZ branch union had more members but most of them were retired. The labor movement in Hortensja had a long tradition and the firm was perceived in Piotrkow as a leader in this respect. In 1980 the first strikes in the region, resulting in the founding of the Solidarity union, started in Hortensja. In recent years the unions had concentrated their efforts on the wage issue and in late 1989 wage demands led to a strike. Shortly after the new year began, the general director, who refused to acquiesce to the workers' demands, was forced to resign. For about four months his post was left unfilled. After that there were no more strikes at Hortensja, although the social situation in the enterprise remained tense. This was not surprising as wages had barely risen since July 1991. With nominal wages frozen the unions were uncompromising on the issue of labor shedding and in January 1992, when the management wanted to dismiss ten people, the unions rejected the idea.

Management

Until mid-1992, the management of Hortensja consisted of four people: the general director, the deputy director in charge of technology and development, the deputy director in charge of production and sales, and the chief accountant.

With the exception of the last, all were engineers, specialists in glass technology or mechanical equipment. The general director had worked in Hortensja for thirty years, and had become director two and a half years earlier, having won an open competition organized after the resignation of his predecessor. Previously he had spent six years as deputy director in charge of production. The deputy director in charge of technology and development had worked at Hortensja for the last six years and was the only member of management with significant professional experience earned outside the Hortensja glass factory. The chief accountant, typical of Polish SOEs, was female, had no university education, and was promoted to the present job after many years of employment within the administration of the firm.

Thus, Hortensja had basically been managed by engineers. Production and design mattered more than marketing and sales. For many years, however, marketing had been easy, even on foreign markets where Hortensja used the services of Minex, a foreign trade enterprise and sole exporter of Polish glass products. In addition, the members of the management team were typical insiders who knew most of the employees and aspects of the production process, but relatively little about the outside world, particularly concerning business techniques, modern accounting, etc. In July 1992, due to the serious financial condition of the firm, the *voivod* (local political subdivision) nominated a commissary manager, or *komisar,* to replace the general manager. This manager has managed Hortensja ever since. All the rules applying to such a situation, as well as the results of his efforts, are described below.

One disturbing fact at Hortensja concerned the system of management remuneration. As was mentioned before, wages in the enterprise were differentiated very little, resulting in a direct impact on the system and the level of managerial wages. By law, wages and bonuses of the general manager or director were determined by a contract signed following a competitive selection process. There were certain nonobligatory guidelines which stated that the basic wage of a director could not exceed a level five times higher than the national average. The workers' council, whose opinion could determine the outcome, often decided on a different level; for example, one linked to the average wage within the enterprise. At Hortensja the workers' council had been very conservative with the manager's wage level. The general director had been awarded a wage three times the national average, his deputies 2.7 times. This level was set in September 1990 at the time of the signing of the managerial contract and had been kept frozen in nominal terms since then. As a result, the director general was earning about $300 by mid-1992, almost as little as a university professor. Since Hortensja operated at a loss, there had been no bonuses since July 1991 when the annual balance was verified. Bonuses were paid out when the enterprise made a profit, or more precisely, after verification of the annual balance and in the middle of the following year. In both cases they were paid out according to certain general rules linking profit to the amount of these bonuses.

WHAT HAPPENED AT HORTENSJA AFTER JANUARY 1990: MAJOR SHOCKS OF THE TRANSFORMATION PROCESS

The year 1991 was good for Hortensja. Strong domestic and foreign sales produced unusually high profits. A series of severe devaluations of the Polish zloty, which occurred throughout the year, bringing the official exchange rate close to the free market rate, were of importance for all exporting firms. Production costs lagged behind the pace of devaluation, even in the inflationary times of 1989, making exports increasingly more profitable.

Both gross and net profitability of Hortensja were high enough to prevent liquidity problems. This enabled the firm to avoid substantial bank indebtedness. Indeed the volume of credit outstanding at the end of 1989 was 500 million zloty, 5 percent of annual sales.

The introduction of the Balcerowicz Plan in January 1990 changed Hortensja's economic environment in many respects, including an increase in costs, particularly of energy and interest, and also a higher tax burden. Crucial, however, were the changed demand conditions on the domestic market; suddenly it became quite difficult to market second-quality goods originally intended for export.

The energy bill in 1990 rose 9.5-fold in nominal terms, reaching 5 percent of total costs. Other items rose much less dramatically, but the increase in material costs and depreciation was greater than revenue from sales, the latter being the result of an across-the-board revaluation of fixed assets carried out at the beginning of the year. Disproportionate growth of material costs was a periodically unstable factor at Hortensja because the glass tube had to be replaced every five to six years, which resulted in a loss of two months' production time. This cost never appeared in the account ledgers as an investment, since only a small portion of the process could be described as machinery, the rest being mostly construction materials.

Property taxes and pollution penalties had also begun to cloud Hortensja's overall economic situation. The enterprise occupied a large tract of land in the middle of the city and had to pay a land and property tax levied by local governments, or communes. Heavy fines for pollution became a serious problem in 1990, but, as production declined, management was able to shut down some of the more pollution-creating areas of the enterprise.

Overall, the 1990 gross margin of Hortensja, measured as the relation of gross profit to its own costs of sales, declined from the previous year's 47.2 percent but remained at a level decidedly higher than in 1988, reaching almost 30 percent. However, net profitability decreased almost threefold from the previous year, attaining just 9.2 percent, which, although still higher than in 1988, reflected the growing burden of taxes paid out of profit. With the loss of all income-tax concessions linked to export and investment activity and the need to pay an obligatory dividend tax six times higher than in 1989 as a result of revaluation of fixed assets, the enterprise faced a share of taxes on its gross profit rising to 68.8 percent. In this way the new economic policy influenced Hortensja from the supply side.

Weakening domestic demand created stockpiles of finished goods. In physical terms they grew from 150,000 units in the beginning of 1990, to 450,000 units by the end of 1990, to 750,000 units by the end of 1991, and reached a record level of 1 million units of glass products at the end of May 1992. Domestic sales dropped by 23 percent from about 3.9 million units in 1989 to about 3 million units in 1990 and by 20 percent to 2.4 million units in 1991. This was not an unusual amount for the Polish manufacturing industry during this period. One could even say that, compared to many other SOEs, Hortensja was not badly affected. Moreover, for an exporting firm like Hortensja, the policy of the undervalued real exchange rate of the Polish zloty helped cushion the blow. In fact, export sales in physical terms grew in 1990 by 20 percent, and in dollars by 25 percent, so that exports accounted for almost 41 percent of total sales revenue, an increase of 12 percentage points compared to the previous year.

Another favorable circumstance was that large quantities of certain types of glass products, such as silicone-calcium glass, were in stock in 1989 and sold later at much higher prices, improving the liquidity position of the enterprise. This was also briefly true for the dollar deposits that Hortensja had inherited from the old system of so-called retention accounts from export activity. However, the enterprise did not sell these dollars until 1991, when their real value was much lower. One may observe that the art of financial management was unknown at Hortensja. Nevertheless, the enterprise survived 1990 in relatively good condition.

Problems began the following year, and these brought into question both the popularly held and the official view. The latter, held by both the Polish government and international financial organizations, was that the economic decline was not due to the dissolution of the CMEA and the dollarization of trade with the Soviet Union. Domestic sales dropped by another 20 percent, which could not be compensated by export sales. Moreover, a significant real appreciation of the zloty, which occurred as a consequence of the fixed exchange rate policy for most of 1991, squeezed the profitability of export sales. The managers estimated that production costs grew by 30 percent over the year, but prices in the domestic market were virtually stable for items sold by Hortensja.

The firm began to experience losses during May 1991, accumulating tax arrears and overdue obligations to suppliers, mostly in the form of energy bills, amounting to 20 billion zloty at the end of 1991 and to nearly 33 billion zloty at the end of November 1992, about 40 percent of 1991 sales. The banks revoked credit for Hortensja for part of the year. Eventually the firm became totally insolvent and even lacked money for wages and materials. Fortunately, the production of a glass factory is not material-intensive and several long-standing foreign customers offered favorable terms of payment, frequently pre-paying part of the invoice. Despite keeping within the budget and paying no taxes in 1991, Hortensja found itself at the brink of bankruptcy.

Paradoxically, the situation improved somewhat the following year. The crawling peg of the zloty, introduced in November 1991, coupled with a 10 percent plus devaluation in February 1992, once again made export sales more attractive. Although rather stagnant in the first half of 1992, these sales accelerated somewhat during the rest of the year. Large inventories of finished goods, which had haunted Hortensja in recent years, stabilized throughout the year at a level of three to four months' sales and, in late 1992, the firm recorded some modest reduction of inventories. As a result, Hortensja managed to stay afloat, avoiding any significant gross losses and finishing November 1992 with losses amounting to 191 million zloty. But with taxes due, the net loss of Hortensja exceeded 2 billion zloty in 1992 and, of course, the firm could not deal with the backlog of overdue payments to both the budget and the suppliers.

A note should be made here of managers' reaction to our question about new opportunities created by the transition to a market economy. Admitting that the availability of inputs, but not of labor, had improved, they hurried to add that, for the first time in many years, problems with gas deliveries occurred in the winter of 1992 as a consequence of the disruption of the post-Soviet economy. Before speculating what could happen to Hortensja, let us return to the 1990–91 period and analyze what had been done in the firm to avoid imminent disaster and what had not.

REACTIONS TO THE SHOCKS

In the case of Hortensja, we examine the following aspects of enterprise behavior: scale of output and product mix, costs, internal organization, and sales effort. Attempts to privatize will also be discussed.

Scale of Output and Product Mix

The output in physical units of glass products declined in 1990, and more significantly in 1991, but this could only partly be attributed to conscious efforts to avoid overproduction in times of weak demand. A plan to change the product mix from simple, undecorated items to more elaborate, labor-intensive and more expensive goods had been implemented as early as 1986. Consequently output in unit terms declined as follows:

1986	6.7 million
1987	6.1 million
1988	5.3 million
1989	4.7 million
1990	4.5 million
1991	3.5 million
1992	3 million (estimate)

These figures show that the scale of output in 1990 was maintained at near the 1989 level, decreasing in a more pronounced way in 1991. It must be asked why management allowed continued production of goods at a rate leading to a massive accumulation of inventories. The explanation is fourfold.

The only means by which this situation could be remedied was through an improvement in the average quality of products, which would enable Hortensja to decrease the quantity of inferior, domestic market-oriented second-quality goods. However, as this was a function of labor qualifications and motivation, such improvement could not be accomplished in the short run, particularly at the low wages prevalent throughout the firm.

Because of Hortensja's cost structure, the curtailment of output was not a viable method of ameliorating a difficult situation. The glass factory was planned in the 1970s for some 2,600 employees, a much larger scale of production than currently existed. As a result, some elements of fixed assets, such as space and construction, were unnecessarily very large, thereby leading to high fixed costs such as dividend tax, depreciation, land tax, maintenance cost, etc. Material costs in glass production were insignificant except for the glass tube installation, which was necessary for production. Even labor costs, clearly the most important item in total costs, seemed to behave like fixed costs, due to the fierce resistance of the labor unions. If management decided to maintain the current level of output, the employment level would be automatically determined, since only reductions with respect to administration and auxiliary workers could be considered and, in fact, did occur with the union's agreement.

Another reason for the apparent passivity was linked to the social situation in Hortensja at the end of 1989. After the competitive selection process, the new director took over only four months after the dismissal of the previous director, and, since this effectively meant being appointed by the unions, he was therefore in no position to initiate a harsh adjustment program. Finally, the situation in 1990 did not appear bleak enough to require any drastic measures.

Costs and Internal Organization

The effect of cost-saving measures is not easily detected, although many were attempted. Employment declined only by means of natural attrition, because the idea of active labor-shedding was rejected by the unions. Employment between 1989 and late 1992 declined by about 40 percent, which is less than the unit output decline, but, considering the increased labor intensity required by new patterns, it is hard to say whether the employment adjustment was correct. One should note that the share of labor costs in total costs was lower than before 1990, and grew by only a few percentage points in 1992. However, this should be attributed to lack of investment in material costs during this period.

Excess employment in the administration of Polish SOEs was common, although most workers, including union members, desired the dismissal of the more unproductive white-collar workers. This situation existed at Hortensja, but the ratio of workers to nonworkers had already been improved and, between 1988 and 1992, remained surprisingly stable. The real problem concerning white-collar employees in Polish SOEs was not so much overemployment as prevailing low professional qualifications and an employment structure that did not correspond to the needs of the market economy—poorly staffed marketing and sales sections, for example.

Hortensja managed to achieve considerable savings in material and energy costs by concentrating production. The reduction in the number of shifts and of glass tubes in operation at any one time was reflected in an 80 percent capacity utilization during the first shift of 1992, as opposed to 60 percent in 1988–89. Although these were only estimates of the management, they should probably be taken seriously. One other bit of evidence was the growth of the energy bill, which had been stemmed despite rising energy prices.

Sales Effort

One of the factors aggravating domestic sales was the sudden disintegration of the wholesale trade system in Poland. Traditionally dominated by large state-owned organizations, it was literally smashed in 1990 by the policy of high interest rates. This proved particularly painful for large state-owned manufacturers who could not find an alternative form of access to the domestic market. The reconstruction of wholesale trade was gradual, beginning with small, private, often financially unsound firms, which often proved unfortunate for the established SOEs. This partly explains the success of import competition in many consumer markets, even where Polish products were both price- and quality-competitive. This institutional factor hit the manufacturing industry in 1990–91. Hortensja was not an exception. Only in early 1992 did the firm start successfully rebuilding its network of trade partners on the domestic market. By granting serious customers preferential terms of payment and bigger rebates, Hortensja tried to support them and create conditions for long-term relations.

Polish law required standard payment within two weeks, after which the seller incurred an obligation to pay a turnover tax. Hortensja's policy for sales to new, unknown, usually very small customers for cash utilized the two-week term for regular customers and a four-to-six-week payment term for preferred wholesalers. As a result, the wholesaler's share in total domestic sales grew to about 30 percent and was still growing in mid-1993. Hortensja did not attempt to control the market prices of its products, although the main wholesalers received rebates on basic prices, but were free to set retail price levels.

Strangely, Hortensja never had serious problems selling to the United States, Great Britain, Canada, Australia, and several countries in Western Europe. It used the services of an intermediary, a foreign trade enterprise in Warsaw called Minex, paying a 3–5 percent commission, which was modest in the manager's opinion. Occasionally goods were sold abroad directly, but Hortensja was apparently satisfied with the services of Minex.

With the exception of early 1992, when export sales inexplicably collapsed, Hortensja had almost always operated at export capacity, although the seasonal nature of export demand could destabilize or even disrupt the production process. Weak and unstable domestic sales remained the principal problem but apparently there had been no effort to study the Polish market in order to bring Hortensja's production profile closer to the needs of the domestic consumer.

To sum up, most conscious adjustment to the new economic situation took place in technology and production because this is what appealed most to engineers and was their area of expertise. Very little or no attempt had been made to intensify the marketing and selling effort, to change the organization of the financial and accounting sections, to find an outside investor, or to improve cost and price calculation techniques, despite the fact that existing methods had obviously produced unreliable results.

A PRIVATIZATION EPISODE

In early 1990, Hortensja's management expressed an intent to privatize, without specifying the method. The workers' council rejected the idea because of a conflict over wages, but accepted it after the nomination of the new general manager.

The Ministry of Ownership Transformation sought to privatize firms in decent financial condition, i.e., net profitability, no budget arrears, and a proper asset structure. Although the enterprise was placed on a list of 400 SOEs to be privatized as a group, in mid-1991 Hortensja withdrew its application because its economic situation had deteriorated. Another means of privatization for a firm such as Hortensja was privatization by restructuring. In this case, an outside managerial group was given access to the enterprise to prepare it for sale within two or three years, a program in which Kara, the other Piotrkow glass mill, was participating. As of May 1991, no privatization had occurred at Hortensja.

EPILOGUE: THE MENDING PROCEDURE

Debt accumulation and poor profitability, combined with a tense atmosphere in the firm, produced a critical situation. The *voivod*, representative of government for the region, which had taken over from the Ministry of Industry, had to decide whether Hortensja should be liquidated. On the advice of a consulting firm from Lodz, it was decided that a so-called mending procedure would be initiated, changing the formal situation of the enterprise entirely. The decision, a complete surprise for Hortensja's managers, was apparently made in three days. Let us give some basic information on this procedure.

The 1981 Law on SOEs stipulates that, when an enterprise incurs losses, or its profit is not high enough to pay the obligatory dividend, the founding organ can initiate a mending procedure by installing a temporary manager, or *komisar*. This appointment by the founding organ may not be appealed by the enterprise and the immediate consequence is the suspension of the workers' council and recall of the previous general manager. The *komisar* is a one-person body, but may employ a team of managers consisting of one or more members of the previous management team. The *komisar* is appointed for a set period of time, six months in the case of Hortensja, but his appointment may be renewed. His wage is set by the founding organ and is paid by the enterprise but, as a rule, the *komisar's* wages are considerably higher than those of the former managers and, in Hortensja's case, were three times higher.

By law, the first and foremost duty of the *komisar* is the presentation of a restructuring and improvement program, the objective of which is to determine the possibility of saving the firm from liquidation or bankruptcy. Commissary management could result in major restructuring of the firm, usually connected with liquidation and sale of its parts, but also in one of the following decisions:

- liquidation of the SOE;
- some method of privatization;
- a request to the court to declare bankruptcy.

There are many questions about certain formal competencies and rules of the *komisar's* behavior, and one issue is always how to avoid having the workers and members of the former management treat the outsider as an intruder. Questions arise as to the proper system of incentives and there is the possibility that the *komisar* would attempt to keep his well-paid job for longer than necessary.

Hortensja was fortunate in that many of these problems were avoided. Its commissary team decided to leave all production issues in the hands of the previous management team, thereby gaining their cooperation, and to concentrate most efforts on sales and marketing and on initiating preparations for ownership changes.

The decision was that the domestic market, although important in the long run, could not at present secure a sufficient level of demand, and therefore Hortensja must, for the time being, depend on export sales. Better access to foreign markets was to become one of the top priorities, but first, steps would also be taken to begin a more active sales strategy on the domestic market. A marketing section was established, factory-sponsored retail stores were set up, and sales agents throughout the country were hired. These measures, which were aided by generally better market conditions, led to a 60 percent growth of sales in the second half of 1992 over the first half, with exports accounting for an unprecedented 70 percent of total sales in this period.

The new management also initiated a conciliation procedure with the enterprise's creditors and, in fact, Hortensja's payables diminished slightly, although they were still at a level of three months' sales. This strategy resulted in frozen or partly canceled penalty interest charges. Similarly, partial payment of current taxes improved relations with the Treasury Chamber, and bank credit, by no means high at mid-year, was fully repaid by the end of 1992. All in all, the backlog of past obligations remained large, exceeding six months' sales, but the combination of the above efforts, the favorable terms of payments offered by Minex, and more active and disciplined financial management secured a flow of cash sufficient to avoid any major disaster.

The new management estimated that ownership changes were crucial to Hortensja's long-run prospects and, to facilitate this, the firm initiated a painful and time-consuming procedure to transform the enterprise into a one-person partnership of the State Treasury. This was accomplished at the beginning of 1993. In the course of these preparations, many legal questions connected with the ownership of land and assets, including social assets, were tackled and partially cleared up.

Considering that the usual attitude of the Ministry of Ownership Transformation is reluctance to give consent for commercialization to firms in poor economic condition, the transformation of Hortensja had to be considered a management success. Also, a change of legal form meant the revocation of all previously existing organs of the enterprise, including commissary management and, contrary to prevailing practice, the *komisar* finished his work quickly, though he himself stressed that the actual job of saving Hortensja had only started. Surely he deserved credit for speed, despite the high wages involved. In fact, his appointment was to last until mid-1993.

Commercialization was beneficial in the short term in that it helped rid a firm owned directly by the State Treasury of redundant social assets and floor space, since the firm, as a traditional SOE, did not need to buy assets previously used to dispose of them. If the new Pact on Enterprises were to be passed, commercialization would become a prerequisite for a full-fledged conciliatory procedure, and is ultimately seen as facilitating negotiations leading to more fundamental ownership changes.

In the case of Hortensja two possibilities emerge. A Price Waterhouse-prepared sectoral study proposed a consortium of five glass factories. Alternatively, Hortensja could form a joint venture with Minex, but it was too early to evaluate either solution and their potential consequences. At this point, Hortensja needed more aggressive marketing, both at home and abroad, help in financial restructuring, and continued efforts to strengthen internal accountability and financial discipline in order to offer attractive products and a physical material base for expansion.

GENERAL CONCLUSIONS

Hortensja provided a good example of the misfortunes of Polish SOEs in the transition period. It was a firm with a good reputation, long-standing traditions, and well-established foreign markets, but, at the same time, it was typical in that it had been entirely production and design oriented with a total neglect of marketing and sales activity. Accounting had been crude and active financial management unknown.

Hortensja, though hit by the shocks of transition, did not simply drift. There were attempts to avoid imminent collapse including cost-cutting and a consistent management policy on wages, though the latter led to permanent conflict with the unions. Only after a long delay and little immediate success did the management try to improve domestic sales, but the internal market, with its presumably less-stringent quality requirements, did become important as a backup for Hortensja's export sales.

The introduction of modern, more precise cost accounting could help in selecting foreign customers. Once the backlog of second-quality, unsalable items was taken into account, the profitability of some export contracts could prove illusory.

Installation of the commissary management seemed to have been a success, because it began the process of marketization of the firm and radically improved its prospects in a relatively short period of time by changing the legal form. Thus, the future of Hortensja should be more stable.

Table 1
Structure of Costs (in percentages)

Specification	1988	1989	1990	1991	January–April 1992
Wages	51.79	54.09	47.42	46.66	50.72
Materials	29.74	23.26	31.42	36.19	32.68
Energy	2.72	2.57	5.08	5.57	5.66
Banking charges (incl. interest)	0.56	3.36	3.35	5.93	0.43
Depreciation	1.27	0.61	2.13	3.57	3.76
Property tax	0.84	0.28	0.73	0.4	1.27
External services	13.08	15.86	9.93	1.14	5.48
Total	100	100	100	100	100

Table 2
Profitability Ratios

Specification	1988	1989	1990	1991	January–April 1992
Markup (operating profit)/sales	17.64	24.60	25.65	6.84	15.53
Gross profits/sales	17.44	35.58	21.96	−3.43	6.30
Markup (operating profit)/cost of sales	21.42	32.62	34.49	7.34	18.38
Gross profits/costs of sales	21.18	47.18	29.54	−3.68	7.46
Net profit/cost of sales	7.48	26.23	9.21	−9.27	−5.80

Table 3
Main Financial Indices (in million zloty)

Specification	1988	1989	1990	1991	January–April 1992
Net sales	2,930.34	8,041.0	42,193	47,352	15,133
Costs of sales	2,413.43	6,741.8	311,372	44,115	12,783
Markup	516.91	2,199.2	10,821	3,237	2,350
Remaining revenues	11.84	—	—	—	171
Costs of obtaining revenues	19.37	1.3	—	—	66
Financial revenues	11.71	55	220	241	4
Financial costs	14.02	251.2	1,199	3,216	1,137
Operating profit [3 + (4 − 5) + (6 − 7)]	507.07	2,166.7	9,842	262	1,322
Extraordinary profits	14.91	1,296.27	1,592	590	73
Extraordinary losses	10.86	118.41	2,168	2,478	441
Gross profit/loss (8 + 9 − 10)	511.13	3,180.9	9,266	−1,625	954
Taxes	330.71	1,412.68	6,376	2,464	1,696
Gross profit/loss (11 − 12)	180.42	1,768.19	2,890	−4,090	−742

Table 4
Liquidity and Activity Ratios

Specification	1988	1989	1990	1991	January–April 1992
Liquidity ratios					
Working capital/total assets	0.35	0.47	0.17	0.07	—
Current ratio	3.25	2.28	2.07	1.21	—
Quick ratio	0.86	1.23	0.68	0.63	0.23
Activity ratios					
Account receivable turnover	9.24	6.69	11.20	7.14	—
Average collection period (days)	39	54	32	50	—
Payments turnover	7.92	5.42	6.65	3.16	—
Average payments period (days)	45	66	54	114	—
Inventory turnover	6.50	9.92	10.51	4.96	—
Average inventory turnover (days)	55	36	34	73	—

7

Food Processing/ Chocolate and Sweets: Drops

Marek Belka

SECTORAL SETTING

During the period of transition, the food-processing industry was among the healthiest sectors of the Polish manufacturing industry, with the confectionery and sweets-producing subsector one of the more successful. This was due mainly to the relative stability of domestic demand for its products in 1990–91, a good export performance, and successful adjustment behavior by enterprises. A microeconomic study carried out by Pinto, Belka, and Krajewski, covering the first five quarters of the new economic policy in Poland, even established that, measured by a standardized synthetic coefficient of adjustment, food-processing was the least changed among the sectors examined.

The confectionery and sweets-producing industry in Poland was a fairly significant sector of manufacturing. Sales in 1991 reached about $700 million, and employment fluctuated between 25,000 and 29,000 people. Real sales dropped in 1990 by a typical 24 percent, compared to 1989 when they fell by 6 percent, but recovered in 1991 to attain a surprising 122 percent of the previous year's level. Sales grew by 7 percent in the first nine months of 1992 and thus it was fair to say that the industry had effectively returned to a normal, pre-recession level. In fact, the production of chocolate in early 1992 was twice that of 1988, with other sweets lagging considerably behind. Under the new system of internal convertibility of the zloty, better access to imports of cocoa beans allowed the industry to satisfy the normal level of domestic demand for chocolate. Overall, employment in the industry was very stable in the third quarter of 1992, holding at the 1988 level of 28,600 people. Only in 1990 did it temporarily drop to 25,300.

Traditionally, the industry has never been very profitable. The rate of gross profit in 1989, at 35 percent, was lower than in most other sectors but declined very little in 1990 to 32 percent, and to just 27.8 percent in 1991. Compared to the rest of the Polish economy, the confectionery and sweets-producing industry stands out as an exceptional example of stability and good health.

The share of material costs as a proportion of total costs dropped from a 1990 high of 74.5 percent to 72.6 percent, and dropped again in 1991, stabilizing at the level of 67.7 percent the next year. This suggested that both the devaluation of the zloty in 1990 and the collapse in 1990–91 of the clearing trade with China, a traditional supplier of inputs such as sesame seeds, did not greatly affect the industry. This favorable outlook was marred slightly by declining profitability in early 1993. It was still much higher than average in the manufacturing industry at a 13.6 percent gross profit and 5.8 percent net profit rate in the first three quarters of 1992, but every fourth firm in the sector had experienced losses, a result of growing costs of output rather than of weak sales. With a stable share of material costs, labor costs became more critical.

The structure of assets in the industry has remained normal and inventories, inter-firm payables, and receivables have tended to grow at a rate lower than the 1991 sectoral inflation rate of 33 percent. The only dark spot in an otherwise bright picture was the increase in bank credit. This helped to maintain financial ratios but, at Polish interest rates, could create problems in the near future. In Poland, most sectors with declining profitability attempted save their liquidity by means of working capital credits, only to find themselves in an insolvency trap. In May 1993, however, the volume of credit in the industry was still less than 50 percent of monthly sales, as opposed to credit from domestic sources, which has had diverse effects in Poland. The confectionery and sweets industry was therefore in good shape, with Drops reflecting most of the characteristics observed in the sector.

HISTORY AND DESCRIPTION OF THE FIRM

Drops was established in 1945 when three private factories, which had existed before the war, merged. The enterprise then consisted of four plants of roughly similar size, employing 300, 200, 150, and 150 people respectively. All plants are located in Bralin, the principal town of Pomerania, a relatively well-developed and affluent region in the northwestern part of Poland.

In 1993, employment and sales at this enterprise, which was one of the larger manufacturers of confectionery products in Poland, accounted for about 3 percent of those of the value of the entire sector. Wedel S.A. of Warsaw, which was five times the size of Drops, was bought out by Pepsico in 1991. Of the remaining five or six second-tier producers, including Drops, none dominated the market, although they were all well known throughout the country.

The enterprise's range of production was wide and covered biscuits, traditionally the leading item with a good market reputation, dragées, fudges, chocolate covered products, and jellies. While Drops did not specialize in chocolate bars, its share of chocolate-covered products had always been substantial and was growing fast. In Polish market conditions success required an upgrading of the product mix.

Drops's 1991 sales reached 223 billion zloty, or approximately $21 million, compared to $15.3 million a year earlier. The growth in dollar terms of about 37 percent should not be taken too seriously, since the output in constant zloty prices, using the sectoral price index for 1991, increased by a more modest 15.5 percent. The process of rapid real appreciation of the Polish currency in 1990 and most of 1991 makes international comparisons over time difficult. The dynamics of Drops's output was another question for which we needed to rely on management estimates.

Drops had never been a big exporter, its main market being northwestern Poland. In the 1980s it sold large quantities of biscuits to Canada and the Arab countries but this did not prove profitable. In 1990, due to the abnormally high exchange rate of the dollar, Drops increased its export sales to about 7 percent of total sales, but in 1991, exports fell to an insignificant 0.5 percent of total sales. In 1988–90, Drops increased its sale of sweets to the Soviet Union and, while this market never weighed much in the firm's total business, management had again attempted to revive former contacts in the East for the purpose of possible export expansion.

A well-founded reprivatization claim to one of the plants had been presented recently, and management was prepared to relinquish this plant as soon as the reprivatization law had been passed by the parliament. The machinery from this plant would be moved to the other three so that the production capacity of the entire enterprise would not be impaired. A joint venture of some sort with a new owner had not been ruled out.

Fixed Assets

The firm was located in old buildings, some eighty years old. The only exception was a 1970s building in the leading plant. Most machinery and equipment were also old and in many respects obsolete. This was very advantageous in 1990, when the new increased level of obligatory dividends was determined. The smaller the net book value of fixed assets, the smaller the amount of dividend levied on the value of a proportion of these assets. So the dividend at Drops was less than 1 percent of sales.

Although the highly depreciated fixed assets were advantageous in some respects, they also caused serious problems in recent years. The firm lacked modern packaging machinery, particularly important for keeping the domestic market share, given the increase in foreign competition and the visible improvement in quality of domestic production. Sweets and confectionery were one of the best examples of dramatic progress in quality in response to import competition. The enterprise now operated in a fully competitive environment.

The dividend tax referred to above was fiercely criticized as unfair and skewed against more modern enterprises. Sectors of manufacturing industry that were underfunded in terms of central investment under socialism, such as the food-processing industry, generally had a low dividend burden. This was apparently one explanation for their success during the transition period. Conversely, sectors that enjoyed high bargaining power in the past, or where investment was a matter of survival, as in the chemical industry, now paid a high price in the form of high dividend payments.

The Pinto-Belka-Krajewski study found that, of the seventy-five big SOEs from five sectors of manufacturing industry, the dividend burden was inversely correlated with the average age of machinery in the enterprise, with older firms paying less. Moreover, it was established that these older firms had bigger cash flows, determined by gross profit plus depreciation, and therefore the argument about the perverse impact of the dividend seemed to be confirmed.

The need to relax or eliminate *popiwek*—PPWW, or tax on excessive wage growth—was stressed in discussions of the tax system for SOEs in Poland. Parliament passed an amendment to the law on *popiwek*, relaxing its rules somewhat. However it seemed more appropriate to change the dividend rules, particularly since the tax only generated 3.3 percent of budget revenues.

As the buildings were quite old, they could not house modern, heavy production lines. Faced with this problem in 1990, Drops initiated a considerable investment program, financed entirely from 1991 by its own resources. We had the impression, however, that the level of technical equipment was still far from modern.

Labor Force

At the end of 1992, Drops employed 760 people, about 15 percent fewer than in 1988 but roughly the same as in 1990. Seventy-three percent of the crew were women, reflecting previous patterns of wage relations in Polish industry, where food-processing was characterized by low wages. This situation changed in the early 1990s, with wages becoming a function of the firm's financial standing rather than of the bargaining power of the branch and location of the firm. Confectionery moved from the bottom of the wage ladder to a position above the national average. Drops had always paid higher wages than the sector as a whole, but the gap narrowed. The average net monthly wage in the enterprise was about $200 in 1993. Interestingly, *popiwek* payments in Drops were quite moderate. In 1989 management apparently received information that the September 1989 wage levels would determine the base level for the new wage policy. Relative wages were gradually changing in favor of white-collar workers, up from 121 percent of the firm's average in 1989 to 147 percent in mid-1992. Thus the moderate *popiwek* payments might have been due to inside information or luck rather than the consequence of wage restraint.

Within Drops, labor unions were quite strong. Membership was about 50 percent of total employment with two unions, Solidarity and the old OPZZ, roughly equal in terms of numbers. There were no strikes in the enterprise in the last few years, but the workers' council, mostly dominated by Solidarity, had a long record of conflict with management. In early 1990, and again in February 1992, the council dismissed the general manager, in the latter case because of awkward attempts to initiate a privatization procedure in Drops. This issue is discussed below.

Management

Management consisted of three persons: a general manager, a deputy for finance and economic affairs, and a deputy for technology. When we first visited Drops the general manager had been in the enterprise for only two months, after having emerged as winner in a competitive selection process and having been accepted by the workers' council. He was an engineer by profession but with managerial experience. He had spent the previous two years as general manager and, after transformation of the firm into a joint stock company, as chairman of the board of directors of a large bicycle-producing enterprise in Bralin. He had only recently resigned from the last post over a conflict about the method of selling the firm to private investors in a situation of rapidly deteriorating liquidity. His deputy responsible for financial and economic affairs, who was also chief accountant, had an M.A. in economics and was also a licensed accountant. Because of a conflict with the workers' council he left Drops after only one year of employment and, in January 1993, a new person filled the post. The third member of the management team, the deputy in charge of technological affairs, was a food-processing engineer who had been working at Drops for the previous five years. Deputies were nominated and their wages determined by the general manager after a positive opinion from the workers' council, a system that was to be renegotiated after two years.

The remuneration of the management team was not typical of Polish SOEs. The basic wage of the general manager was set at a fairly high, although fixed, level of $800–$1,000, which was about five times the national average but did not grow with inflation. There was no bonus system except for a so-called commission on net profit, which was regulated centrally. In the case of a profitable firm like Drops, this could create a payment of about $2,000 a year.

WHAT HAPPENED TO DROPS AS A RESULT OF THE NEW ECONOMIC POLICY?

Shocks to the Firm

The introduction of the Balcerowicz Plan in January 1990 created no disasters for the enterprise. There was no cost revolution, although the prices of imported inputs increased nearly fourteen-fold. The share of total cost, even material cost, was small and did not undermine the cost/revenue ratio. In fact, material costs rose less than the total cost of output. Increases in the energy bill, in depreciation, and in interest charges, which were so important in most enterprises, were hardly noticed at Drops. It was probably surprising to an observer of the Polish situation that the share of labor cost in total cost actually rose in 1990 by 1 percentage point, as a result of an almost sixfold increase in the average nominal wage. However, workers at Drops suffered no real wage drop during this period.

With an estimated 1990 drop of output and sales of about 15 percent, the ability to pass on costs in the form of price increases was essential for maintaining the favorable condition of the firm. Profitability did fall compared to 1989, when paper profits had been inflated by a revaluation of inventories and foreign currency accounts, but they were quite favorable compared to 1988: a 19.5 percent gross rate of profit, and an 8.7 percent net rate of profit. In 1991 these rates both climbed by about 4 percentage points, and dropped back approximately to their 1990 levels in 1992.

Liquidity was no problem during this period, as reflected in a sharp drop in inter-firm credit to sales ratio in 1990–91. However, in early 1992 both receivables and payables grew, causing managers to complain about liquidity shortages. Many firms in the sector resorted to expensive bank credit in this situation, but Drops avoided this. Inventories were at a low level throughout the period, which, for finished goods, was partly due to the perishable nature of confectionery products. Given this situation, it was not surprising that personnel at Drops had many positive things to say about the transition to a market economy. They noted that the new system had eliminated several negative aspects of the old system, such as rationing of inputs, export subsidies, and foreign currency retention accounts for exporters.

Rationing of inputs, particularly of imported raw materials, meant that the production structure diverged significantly from the structure of demand, with chocolate, chocolate-covered sweets, and jellies treated almost as a luxury. The elimination of this obstacle, made possible by introducing zloty convertibility, created an advantage for the entire sector by changing the product mix, the average price level and profitability.

Two other aspects of the former system were disadvantageous for nonexporters. The foreign currency retention accounts, although stimulating export sales, tended to distort supplier–customer relations, with most suppliers demanding certain quotas of dollars from their domestic customers. This in turn led to a controlled free market for foreign currency in the form of auctions organized by the National Bank in 1989, which probably brought the economy closer to exchange rate unification. Access to inputs generally improved after January 1990, with the notable exception of bank credit. The existence of external controls, which were eliminated under the new system, also created problems. The worst for Drops came after 1990 with the collapse of wholesale trade and the overall system of state-owned trade infrastructure. Previously, most production had been sold to big trade organizations during quarterly meetings of the industry, during which good contacts among the managers of competing enterprises were nourished.

At the time of this report, state-owned customers bought only 10 percent of production, with small, private, newly founded firms buying the rest, which, at first, created a problem by causing work stoppages. However, in the analysis of past data, one can note that the number of hours lost through paid work stoppages was greater in 1988–89 than later. Previously, the causes were of a supply-side character, such as shortage of inputs, while in the 1990s the causes were on the demand side.

REACTION OF THE FIRM TO CHANGING MARKET CONDITIONS

The immediate response to the introduction of the new economic policy was entirely typical: output fell in line with declining demand, and an attempt was made to defend profitability by means of price increases, which proved very effective in the short run. Coupled with the changing product mix, which was delivered without any investment, Drops improved its position in 1991. These maneuvers, however, were clearly not enough to create long-run survival, and both the previous and the new management seemed to understand this. The long-run strategy consisted basically of three elements:

- building up a stable sales network in the country, supported by an expanded advertising campaign;
- continuation of the investment program started in 1990;
- reorganization of the firm's administration.

Sales Network

In the early 1990s, several private trade companies grew sufficiently to become viable partners for big and medium-size manufacturing enterprises. Taking this into account, Drops had built up a network of sponsored wholesale stores consisting of 55–65 units in Poland. Some would be eliminated after having proved to be unreliable, but the network at this time sold approximately 70 percent of the total output of the firm. The system was set up in a surprisingly short time in the spring of 1992 and, as early as mid-1992, was already absorbing up to 50 percent of domestic sales.

Drops attempted to control the prices of its products by means of wholesalers negotiating and receiving rebates on the recommended price. Drops did not require exclusivity from its trading partners, unlike some of its domestic competitors, nor did it grant local monopoly status; in fact, in some large cities there was more than one sponsored wholesale store. In addition, Drops operated six retail shops, which sold about 10 percent of the total production and which also carried goods produced by other firms. Until very recently, Drops had just two such establishments and the decision to expand the network was among the first measures taken by the new manager.

The popularity of propriety retail shops among many Polish producers increased during the liquidity crunch because revenues from this source were sure money for firms. If an enterprise were failing, with its bank accounts sequestrated to satisfy the debtors, sales proceeds from its own retail shops would be beyond external control and they could thus help secure money for more urgent purposes.

Drops began an advertising campaign to bolster sales. As there was no experience in this field, management considered it a risky but indispensable business strategy because, to succeed in terms of profitability, one zloty spent on advertising would need to bring in four zloty of increased sales. About 1 percent of sales proceeds were spent on the campaign in the second half of 1992. Judging by the spectacular sales growth in this period, which is 40 percent higher in nominal terms than the first half, the campaign was apparently successful.

Investment Program

In the previous year approximately 50 percent of net profit was used for investment, as foreseen in 1992. Management considered it out of the question to take bank credit for this purpose. Even the possibility of applying for LIBOR-linked credit from foreign sources did not seem attractive to Drops's general manager because of the danger of devaluation of the zloty. The investment program covered three areas: computerization of the firm's administration and accounting; an upgrading of packaging; and expansion of production capacity, particularly the creation of new product lines. The accounting section claimed to have had full knowledge of the profitability of separate products and thus a clear vision of necessary product mix restructuring; however, the existing buildings were not suitable for some types of equipment and the firm could not risk engaging itself in time-consuming and expensive investments in construction.

Organizational Change

The most important organizational changes undertaken very recently have been:

- reinforcement of the sales department with subordination directly to the general manager;
- strengthening of the marketing section with subordination directly to the general manager;
- merger of the functions of the deputy in charge of production and the deputy in charge of technology (which had already been accomplished);

- assignment of the duties of general engineer or chief of production to the manager of the leading plant;
- creation of a department of internal control, subordinated to the general manager.

According to the general manager, the principal aim of these changes was to create a market-oriented enterprise instead of a production-oriented one.

OWNERSHIP CHANGES AT DROPS

The previous manager was dismissed due to an unsuccessful attempt at privatization. The method of privatization had not been determined clearly, possibly to avoid discouragement of the workers' council, which, as a prerequisite of the whole procedure, must accept the plan with an application for commercialization addressed to the Ministry of Ownership Transformation.

As feared, the council rejected privatization for two reasons. The first was that, in a private firm, the workers would lose the currently provided social benefits such as subsidized holidays, interest-free housing loans, and so on. The second reason was a reluctance to change anything in an enterprise that had heretofore fared so well.

Ownership change was approached cautiously in this climate, however. The new manager considered two possible solutions to the dilemma. The first of these was a managerial contract, in which the manager would take over the firm with a goal of preparing the enterprise for sale within two years. However, since the workers' council was unlikely to approve this idea, the only realistic solution, given the social situation at Drops, was that of employee leasing.

To describe employee leasing, let us define the basic rules for enterprise transformation. According to the Polish Privatization Law of 1990, the liquidation of an SOE for the purpose of privatization can lead to the following: the sale of the SOE or its component parts, the creation of a partnership or joint venture from the SOE or its component parts, or the rental or lease of the SOE or part of it for a predetermined period. We shall expound here on the third case, which, in Polish practice, has been by far the most popular method of transforming a state-owned enterprise.

The SOE is liquidated and a new unit, a civil partnership acting according to rules set out by the civil code, is created. Partners in the new enterprise may be individuals, including employees and managers of the former SOE, other Polish investors, and foreign investors. Polish investors are encouraged, as the policy of the Ministry of Ownership Transformation is to have a strategic shareholder or group of shareholders possessing a sizable percentage of the shares. The share of foreign investors, in principle, should not exceed 20 percent. In most cases, partners should be individuals, not legal entities, but exceptions to this rule could be made by the minister.

Before an SOE can be liquidated and a new unit created in its place, a sum equal to 20 percent of the sum of its founding and enterprise funds must be collected, an amount frequently too high for the employees themselves. This fund is then left in the newly founded firm, thereby increasing its capital and serving as assurance to the state that the assets will be properly managed.

The next step is to assess the market value of these assets, which is crucial in the determination of the leasing fee to be paid to the state budget for the use of the assets. This fee is comprised of two parts: a quarterly installment and a payment analogous to interest, where the interest rate applied is equal to 75 percent of the actual refinancing rate of the Polish National Bank, but does not exceed 30 percent.

Let us assume that the market value of the firm's assets is determined at 50 billion zloty and a ten-year repayment period is agreed upon. The quarterly installment would be 1,250 million zloty throughout the whole period as the initial market value is not revalued afterward. The additional fee, at the rate of 28.5 percent, three-quarters of the current refinancing rate of 38 percent, would be 3,562 million, 3,473 million, 3,384 million, and 3,295 million zloty in the first four quarters. In sum, the yearly leasing fee would be 18,714 million: 5,000 million the capital installment and 13,714 million the interest charges. The latter part supports the new enterprise, a crucial benefit. At the existing rate of income tax, 40 percent, the yearly payment for leasing the firm would slightly exceed 13 billion zloty.

To be fair, there is a possibility in the existing system for the new firm to pay only one-third of the additional interest charge in the first year and one-half in the second year of the contract. However, the difference should be repaid in the third year of the contract. It is obvious that a danger of frequent bankruptcies of leased firms may take place in 1994–95. In the currently negotiated pact between the government and the trade unions on SOEs, a possibility of spreading the repayment of this difference over the whole remaining period is mentioned.

Assume that, at 1992 levels, in order to sign a contract, the employees of Drops would need to collect about 6 billion, or 8 million zloty per person, which was over two months' wages. The interest charge would inflate costs, thereby reducing gross profit. Given an income tax of 40 percent, no dividend tax or *popiwek*, the net profit could still attain a level capable of financing the current rate of investment. Using the two-year partial grace period, as foreseen by the law, Drops could postpone any major problems for two more years. Therefore, if the above-mentioned extension of payments were available, if interest rates declined, or if the firm's sales expand, as the manager hoped, Drops could avoid financial difficulties.

Encouraged by simulations similar to the above, and by the good results scored by the firm in late 1992, bringing the total sales for the whole year to some 290 billion zloty (that is, real sales equal to last year's level), and net profit to about 21 billion, management decided on the leasing solution. To obtain the necessary funds for a lease, the employees used undistributed profit from the previous year as a source of credit. They could purchase up to 70 percent of their shares, which, in the initial payment, were proportional to shares in the future stock of the firm. This credit was cheaper than bank credit, and could be repaid from the current wages over a period of five years. Thus, with money to finance the initial payment, the workers overcame their initial resistance. Only current employees were permitted to participate, and all did so, with purchases ranging from 1 to 400 shares. One group of managers bought about 35 percent of the stock, and we were told this was a guarantee of effective and sound control.

The general manager himself was quoted as having invested "all family savings and five years of future wages" into the venture, which was taken as an expression of unqualified optimism and self-confidence.

During the second visit to Drops the privatization process was in full swing. Final consent from the Ministry of Ownership Transformation was pending, and a temporary liquidator of the SOE had been nominated by the voivodship in order to clear up legal aspects of the existing assets. The new partnership was to take over Drops at the beginning of April 1993.

SUMMARY

Drops was fortunate. It had a stable domestic market, reserves in production capacity to enable it to increase output by as much as 20 percent and to significantly change the product mix, and a good general manager. We felt that anyone who replaced a person dismissed after a conflict with the workers over privatization and who then succeeded in privatizing the firm in less than one year deserved full respect. If the investment program were to continue at the same pace, the enterprise could remain stable.

Management was aware that a more meaningful and quantitative expansion of sales on the domestic market was highly improbable and, for this reason, Drops began to look toward the expansion of its market to the East. It planned to participate in a series of trade fairs in the states of the former Soviet Union, and first contacts had already been established in Belarus. Sales, even when bringing initial losses, are considered important for future expansion.

A potential danger for the future of Drops may lie in the repayment schedule of the leasing fees, with the third year being crucial. If major problems were to arise, there would always be a possibility of renewed conflict between the ambitious manager and the workers, who may not behave like co-owners and may demand higher wages at the cost of undermining the long-run prospects of the firm.

Table 1

Structure of Costs (in percentages)

Specification	1988	1989	1990	1991	January–May 1992
Wages	11.78	14.92	15.88	18.84	21.21
Materials	84.90	80.20	77.60	75.62	64.69
Energy	2.14	0.78	1.50	2.36	2.24
Banking charges (incl. interest)	0.49	1.07	1.11	1.89	0.51
Depreciation	0.47	0.14	0.52	1.05	0.95
Property tax	0.15	0.04	0.14	0.18	0.51
External services	0.07	2.85	3.25	0.06	0.89
Total	100	100	100	100	100

Table 2

Main Financial Indices (in million zloty)

Specification	1988	1989	1990	1991	January–May 1992
Net sales	8,331.90	32,891.12	129,128.0	190,039	88,751
Costs of sales	6,665.00	25,942.21	108,080.0	161,485	75,897
Markup	1,666.90	6,948.91	21,048.0	37,554	12,854
Remaining revenues	—	—	—	623	1,666
Costs of obtaining revenues	—	—	—	–882	1,217
Financial revenues	1.00	28.10	5.0	257	90
Financial costs	34.30	289.00	1,220.0	3,122	450
Operating profit [3 + (4 – 5) + (6 – 7)]	1,633.60	6,688.00	19,833.0	36,198	12,943
Extraordinary profits	10.11	4,324.10	2,6180	1,195	288
Extraordinary losses	15.61	31.95	1,096.0	1,464	216
Gross profit/loss (8 + 9 – 10)	1,628.10	10,980.00	21,335.0	35,925	13,015
Taxes	1,086.22	4,459.22	8,875.8	17,767	5,500
Gross profit/loss (11 – 12)	541.88	6,520.78	12,479.2	18,162	7,515

Table 3

Profitability Ratios

Specification	1988	1989	1990	1991	January–May 1992
Markup (operating profit)/sales	20.01	21.13	16.30	19.76	14.48
Gross profits/sales	19.54	33.38	16.52	18.91	14.66
Markup (operating profit)/cost of sales	25.01	26.79	19.47	23.26	16.94
Gross profits/costs of sales	24.43	42.32	19.74	22.25	17.15
Net profit/cost of sales	8.13	25.14	9.66	11.25	9.90

Table 4

Liquidity and Activity Ratios

Specification	1988	1989	1990	1991	January–May 1992
Liquidity ratios					
Working capital/total assets	0.59	0.57	0.56	0.44	0.29
Current ratio	3.38	2.43	4.28	4.45	3.49
Quick ratio	0.81	1.23	1.19	2.21	1.91
Activity ratios					
Account receivable turnover	12.01	7.97	15.49	16.81	—
Average collection period (days)	30	45	23	21	—
Payments turnover	9.47	7.41	13.71	21.46	—
Average payments period (days)	37	47	26	16	—
Inventory turnover	9.62	12.14	16.02	14.47	—
Average inventory turnover (days)	36	29	22	24	—

8

Wood Products: Lodzkie Fabryki Mebli

Marek Belka

SECTORAL SETTING

Furniture production was an important sector of Polish industry. In 1991, total sales amounted to about $900 million, 20 percent of which was exported, mainly to the EC. The share of smaller, rapidly expanding private firms had grown in the last two years such that, by the end of 1992, four large state-owned enterprises had been privatized. Three were sold to individual investors, and one, the largest furniture producer in Poland, was sold through a public offer of shares and was listed on the Warsaw Stock Exchange. According to the plans of the Ministry of Ownership Transformation, three more state-owned firms were to be privatized in the near future.

The industry had suffered a major setback in 1990 when real output fell by more than 25 percent. In 1991, real sales dropped by an additional 18 percent, but recovered in late 1991 and early 1992. This decline occurred entirely in furniture sold in sets, with sales of single pieces of bent-wood furniture staying at the pre-1990 level. Both the recession in the construction industry and the pauperization of much of the population explained this tendency. Employment trends paralleled those in output and sales only to a limited extent, however. The labor force was reduced in 1990 to 76,000, a 17 percent drop, but grew in 1991 to reach 84,600, probably due to the emergence of new firms on the market; then, in the first three quarters of 1992, employment dropped to 75,000.

Profitability behaved in a similar fashion. After an unprecedentedly good 1989, when the gross profit rate reached 51 percent, the next period brought a deep slide. While in 1990, gross profitability was low but still positive at 13.5 percent for the entire industry; in 1991, the gross loss was –3.8 percent, with a net loss of –7.3 percent. Most larger and mid-sized enterprises observed by the Central Statistical Office were in the red, and rising output and sales in late 1991 were not enough to make up for rapid cost expansion, even when unit prices grew by nearly 50 percent. In late 1991, the economic downturn in furniture production seemed to be reversed and, although sales in 1992 were quite erratic, they grew in real terms by almost 5 percent in the first three quarters of 1992. Finally, with costs growing only very slightly, so that in January 1992, they were only 5 percent greater than one year earlier, profitability improved in the first three quarters of 1992, but the gross profit rate remained near zero. The percentage of loss-making firms fell from 57 percent to 41 percent, but the industry as a whole still recorded net losses. In early 1992, the deterioration of liquidity in the industry was reflected in a rapid accumulation of overdue payables, which led to some increase in working capital credit and attendant consequences for cost structures. Overall the sector was in difficulty but better off than one year previously. There was higher dispersion within the sector and export-oriented enterprises were generally doing much better than the rest.

HISTORY AND DESCRIPTION OF THE FIRM

History

Lodzkie Fabryki Mebli, or Lodz Furniture Factories (LFF), is one of the older furniture manufacturers in Poland, dating back to 1928 when it existed as a mid-sized privately owned factory supplying the local market. It was nationalized in the late 1940s, merged with other firms, and finally, in 1951, established with its present name and legal form. Over time, LFF grew by absorbing a number of smaller furniture manufacturers in Lodz and the region. This process of centralization, so characteristic of the Polish economy under central planning, resulted in an awkward, artificial structure such that, at the end of the 1980s, LFF consisted of 14 plants scattered throughout Lodz and adjacent districts (voivodships), some being as far as 100 km from the headquarters.

Product and Market Position

In terms of sales, LFF was one of the five or six largest furniture producers in Poland, producing a variety of typical furniture for living rooms, bedrooms, and kitchens. In the past, upholstered furniture had been part of the product mix, but was discontinued because it did not sell well. Most of LFF's products were made not of wood but of sawdust sheets, supplemented with hardboard and timber. They were simple items meant for the small flats typical of Poland and were produced and delivered in segments for self-assembly. This type of furniture had been extremely popular in the past and most Polish families, particularly the poorer ones, still used it.

The production profile was imposed on the enterprise by the branch association, an intermediate organizational structure existing in centrally planned economies. In the 1960s, LFF strengthened its position as a producer of this type of furniture by founding a national center of design and technology. The firm's share of exports in total sales never exceeded 10 percent. The rest of the output went to the domestic market, but this had negative long-run consequences because the firm always lacked investment and modem technology. This was a result of centralized resource allocation providing resources to export-oriented enterprises. It was not by chance that transformation to privatized joint stock status improved the financial situation.

LFF's annual sales in 1990 reached $13.3 million, but dropped in 1991 in nominal terms in both zloty and dollars. In this period, its percentage of total sales in the industry dropped from 2.2 percent to 1.2 percent. Due to its heterogenous character, it was virtually impossible to present synthetic data on output and sales in physical units, but the scale of activity can be shown by the following sales figures from the first half of 1991:

- furniture for children: 2,784 sets,
- kitchen furniture: 1,699 sets,
- bedroom furniture: 277 sets,
- living-room furniture: 366 sets,
- upholstered furniture (armchairs, chairs, sofas): 7,036 pieces,
- miscellaneous: about 23,500 pieces accounting for 60 percent of total sales.

Fixed Assets

The overall state of fixed assets in mid-1992 could be described as poor, since statistics on their gross and net value were quite misleading. Their 56 percent depreciation suggested a decent state of technology, and investment expenditures up to 1990 had been ten times or more yearly depreciation. But a closer look gave a completely different view. The enterprise was a rather accidental conglomerate of plants with different historical backgrounds. Some plants were actually small private workshops from prewar times, others were cooperatives liquidated in the 1960s and 1970s, and some had been built from scratch, mostly in the 1970s.

The size of the various plants was quite different. Only four employed more than 100 people, totaling nearly 50 percent of LFF's overall employment, with 6 other plants employing fewer than 50 people. In terms of net assets, the two largest plants accounted for 74 percent of the total. The average age of machinery and equipment was eight years, which concealed the fact that in five plants machines were depreciated by nearly 100 percent, and only in two by less than 50 percent. Frequent breakdowns, increasing maintenance costs, and low quality of products from some suggested a need to liquidate within the framework of a deeper restructuring. In the past, liquidation of plants had been very difficult. For example, one plant, which should have been closed years before, produced steam for a local hospital and its liquidation was fiercely resisted by local authorities. The distance of some plants from the headquarters was a problem in that it increased transportation costs and complicated the management process. In addition, the LFF shared headquarters with a spare-parts warehouse and central repairing services section, and was thus separated from the production facilities.

The most important factor concerned the history of the construction of the largest and most modern plant of the LFF. As early as 1978, a centrally financed investment was begun in one of the Lodz plants to expand the production capacity of the standard segment-type furniture. The current management's opinion was that the plant had been designed improperly, allowing only massive production of a limited choice of products; to attain flexibility in the production profile, additional significant investment might be needed. This investment had to be stopped several times in the 1980s as the government tried to restrain investment in the economy. This was a classic example of Kornai-type investment in an economy of shortage.

Due to decentralization of the investment process, in 1988 the enterprise took over its own investment management. In November 1989, in an attempt to complete this project, LFF obtained a foreign currency–denominated long-term credit for $2 million, to be repaid in 1992–93. Although only one-half of this credit was used, LFF was unable to repay this debt and therefore had to negotiate a settlement with the crediting bank to reschedule payment. After many technical problems, the new plant began operation in late 1990 but has been a complete failure. Lack of money meant the technical equipment was incomplete and production much smaller than planned. Hence the plant incurred losses.

To summarize, LFF had a chaotic background and internally inconsistent technology in need of radical restructuring. The need for restructuring was such that a few modern elements could not change the overall burden to the enterprise in this respect.

LABOR, WAGES, MANAGEMENT

LFF's employment had fallen steadily, from 1,701 employees in 1988, to 1,634 in 1989, 1,570 in 1990, 1,407 in 1991, and reached 800 by the end of 1992. Until mid-1992, this reduction was more limited than that in real output and only recently did a more radical reduction of employment occur. This was the result of the liquidation of some plants and a concentration of output in a smaller number of production facilities.

Wages at LFF had always been lower than the national average for the industry, because most LFF plants were located in rural areas outside Lodz. In 1991, the firm average was about $115/month, more than 17 percent less than the industry average. Surprisingly, given the financial circumstances, in mid-1992, they rose to the national average for the sector of $133/month because of labor shortage. The uncompetitive wage policy of SOEs was one of the main reasons for their degeneration into second-class labor pools. Inevitably, there were outflows of qualified labor to the private sector or the shadow economy, despite the growth of registered unemployment.

LFF's management was aware of this and tried to defend the discrepancy that had grown over the years between the wages of the engineering and supervisory staff and those of blue-collar workers. LFF had always had problems retaining good craftsmen and technologists because the industry vocational schools were located in Warsaw and Poznan, which was the center of Polish furniture production. An earlier housing shortage followed by currently high rents made it virtually impossible to employ graduates of these schools who were not permanent residents of Lodz or the region. A furniture and carpentry class sponsored by the enterprise in a nearby vocational school did not solve the problem since graduates were reluctant to take low-paying jobs in an enterprise that had hazy prospects.

LFF had a typical Polish SOE wage regulation system. According to a 1984 Wage Agreement for the Enterprise, the determination of wages and other payments at LFF was comprised of the following elements:

- remuneration rules for workers employed in piece-work and day-work systems;
- remuneration rules for nonworker employees;
- a qualification scale for all types of employees, based on the 1980s job valuation system that mimicked the labor market;
- rules of bonus payments for all types of jobs;
- rules for allowances for arduous and health-aggravating labor conditions;
- rules for premiums for long working experience;
- rules for anniversary premiums;
- rules for one-time retirement payments;
- rules of payment for the monetary equivalent for coal and wood shavings, which was an in-kind payment in the past; and
- rules of payment for work stoppages.

Labor union membership in LFF was not very strong. The old OPZZ union had about 190 members and Solidarity about 130. Atypically, the OPZZ-affiliated union was more active because its chairwoman happened to be the national leader of the furniture-producers union and was well-informed and tough in negotiations. The managers clearly did not like the unions and described their behavior as destructive, recalling a conflict in 1990 with some former regime members of the enterprise's management. The conflict was not with top management but concerned members of supervisory staff who were good craftsmen and valuable to the firm and were forced to leave the firm. The people in question chose to retire before schedule, which was encouraged at that time. This satisfied the demands of Solidarity to get rid of the old nomenklatura. The workers' council's activity in the enterprise was complicated by the fact that, in order to convene its meetings, delegates from fourteen widespread plants had to assemble. This created immense logistical problems when an opinion of the council was needed.

The top management of LFF consisted of three persons: a general manager, a deputy in charge of economic affairs, and a deputy in charge of technology and production. The general manager, an economist in his early fifties with an M.A. from the University of Lodz, had been in this position since 1985, before which he had worked in a textile firm. His job combined the duties of CEO with those of deputy for sales and marketing. In early 1992, when his term expired, he entered, and subsequently won, an open competitive selection for the position of general manager. He seemed to be a well-educated, intelligent man, depressed by his mostly unsuccessful efforts to improve the situation of the firm. The deputy for economic affairs was also the chief accountant. She had an M.A. in economics and was a licensed auditor, and had worked at LFF for twenty-one years, seven of them in her present position. The second deputy was an engineer and a specialist in timber processing who had thirty years' experience in the industry and had been at his post since 1978.

Remuneration of the management was typical for Polish SOEs. The workers' council determined the general manager's wage relative to other enterprises and set the deputies' wages according to the firm's qualification scale. Before 1992, deputies' wages had been a proportion of those of the general manager, but the present system is less favorable, meaning the council had effectively voted to lower deputies' wages.

Internal Organization

Managing an enterprise that consisted of so many widespread units, particularly in a material- and transport-intensive industry, was complicated, especially in light of the relationship between the headquarters and the production plants. Before 1989, the enterprise had functioned as a typical centralistic organization, with the administration, accounting, design, engineering, supply, and sales services located at the center. In 1989, internal financial accountability was introduced in an effort to transform the separate plants into autonomous cost and profit centers. This proved impossible and inefficient, apparently for two reasons. First, due to a lack of qualified people, the small plants were not prepared to assume what had been the responsibility of the central administration in the field of purchases, sales, and especially, cost accounting. Second, in the past, there had been overspecialization of labor between plants, meaning semi-products and parts were sent from plant to plant for further processing or finishing. This practice, typical of socialist economies, was justified in the production process because it inflated costs and prices in a system of regulated price-setting. Thus, deepening these ties inflated each plant's apparent contribution to the gross value added of the firm. However, the sudden increase in costs after 1990 could not be carried over into higher prices as easily.

The idea of internal financial accountability was abandoned and important changes in production introduced. Plants became independent centers, each with a full production cycle. This required some reallocation of assets such as machines, tools, and labor, but eliminated most transportation needs and simplified management. Plant employment consisted of a plant manager, supervisors such as foremen and brigade leaders, and workers; everything else was centralized. The managers admitted that, although the production process had been somewhat rationalized, some cost savings achieved, and the management process simplified, many old deficiencies remained. Even computerized central accounting, introduced in 1990, did not alleviate the imprecision of cost accounting since it is often not possible to ascribe many cost items to separate products or even to separate plants.

SHOCKS OF TRANSITION AND IMMEDIATE CONSEQUENCES

With its domestic market orientation, obsolete technology, and complicated internal organization, LFF was sensitive to massive external shocks as early as 1990. It was not possible to increase export sales to compensate for falling domestic demand, a dramatic increase in production costs, and taxes. These factors caused profitability to decline in 1989 from a 24.2 percent net rate of profit to a net loss of about $0.25 million. The net rate of profit was measured as the ratio of net profit to the firm's own costs of sales, which was the highest in the history of LFF. This was followed by a real disaster in 1991 when the net loss reached a depressing $3.77 million.

Demand and Sales

In 1990, compared to the previous year, output dropped by 40–45 percent in real terms, due entirely to the slump on the domestic market, since export sales remained relatively unchanged. The share of exports in the 1980s had always been around 10 percent, with a slight but indecisive tendency to grow. This explained the inability of LFF to at least partly make up for the losses suffered on the domestic market by increasing sales abroad. Without suitable products and good business channels, the enterprise was fully dependent on domestic market conditions.

Considering the management's estimate of the scale of the slump in real sales, which was extremely difficult to verify given product heterogeneity, selling prices would have to have risen almost nine-fold. This roughly reflected the tendencies of the market, although the actual rise was probably less dramatic. Most important, the condition of the domestic market in 1990 allowed LFF, and the industry, to cushion the blow of rising costs and taxes by shifting them to the consumer. As a result, the enterprise maintained a modest gross positive profit rate of some 4.4 percent even though real sales dropped by one-half.

A steep price increase in 1990 drove prices to their market ceiling, although it is hard to speak in terms of world price levels since this type of furniture is not usually an object of international trade. The managers admitted that they were not afraid of import competition, a fact that was also true for the entire industry. However, private carpentry firms, which previously had had no interest in furniture, or at least in furniture sets, now found this market attractive. These small firms were price-competitive, even though, according to LFF, they offered rather low-quality goods. Nonetheless, they began to make significant inroads in a market previously dominated by large state-owned furniture producers.

The price bonanza did not last long and in 1991 the firm was only able to increase prices by 25 percent. Rising costs and other difficulties caused LFF's financial and economic situation to collapse entirely. Disintegration of traditional trade channels—large state-owned wholesale stores, for example—aggravated the situation, creating difficulties in both sales and the receipt of payment for deliveries.

Costs and Taxes

In January 1990 all costs grew, but energy prices and the drastic change in interest rates were most painful. The 1990 energy bill grew eleven-fold, its share in total cost increasing from 2.3 percent to 3.3 percent. In 1991 it doubled again and reached 5.2 percent of total cost. Managers of insolvent enterprises feared arrears in payments for energy more than most other unsettled debts since the penalty charged by energy suppliers was higher than that of other suppliers and, more importantly, electricity could be shut off, paralyzing the firm.

Interest costs were a different matter. Their percentage of total cost actually dropped in 1990, only to climb in 1991. The high cost of credit prevented the enterprise from obtaining the necessary amount of working capital credit, at least from the technological point of view. The problem was that timber for furniture had to be stored and seasoned for some time in order to prevent warping. If the firm could not afford it, or if the banks were not willing to lend, the quality of furniture tended to deteriorate.

The dubious privilege of acquiring central investment for new capacity was translated into an obligation to pay increased dividends, which grew sixfold in 1990. In addition, in nominal terms the *popiwek,* or PPWW, increased fourfold and as a consequence gross profit in 1990 fell by one-third, from 6.68 billion to 4.484 billion zloty, but taxes on it grew by more than 100 percent, from 3.482 billion to 6.964 billion. A modest gross profit thus turned into a serious net loss.

Collapse

Compared to 1990, 1991 output and sales remained stable. The sale of furniture, being seasonal, typically dropped in the second quarter and revived in the fourth quarter. But the firm was unable to survive this mid-year slump due to accumulating receivables and payables, and LFF stopped paying taxes. Worse, it began to have problems with bank credit. In the summer of 1991, the main crediting bank revoked overnight working capital credit, the last nail in the coffin. The bank may have had good reasons, but its methods suggested that LFF's management had experienced poor relations with the bank, probably the result of trying to put bank credit on a par with other debts. Both energy suppliers and banks had the means to vindicate debts quickly. This was a fatal mistake that the management of Textilpol, for example, had skillfully avoided.

By the end of 1991 LFF was on the verge of bankruptcy, with huge net losses symptomatic of mounting debts. Suppliers were owed 47 billion zloty, tax arrears totaled 25 billion, bank credit was 18 billion—10 billion in long-term credit (more if zloty devaluation was taken into account) and 8 billion in short-term credit, half of which was overdue.

Lacking working capital, the enterprise had problems continuing production, a situation that did not change in 1992. Debts grew, almost reaching the value of yearly sales. Although for the first time LFF had found export customers, mostly in Germany, contracts for both domestic and foreign markets were realized with increasing difficulty. Consequently, in nominal terms, 1992 sales were even smaller than in the previous miserable year. The enterprise faced bankruptcy or liquidation; the *voivod* had done nothing to prevent this.

REACTION TO THE SHOCKS AND RESTRUCTURING EFFORTS

The immediate response to the economic changes was to curtail output and raise prices, a policy that worked only briefly. A long-run restructuring program was prepared in 1991, before the actual collapse of the enterprise, and included a change in the product mix and search for export possibilities, a reorganization of the domestic sales network, and better organization by means of the elimination of redundant assets and liquidation of some plants.

This program was the joint product of a local consulting firm and the management but contained no recommendations for the financial restructuring that was crucial to survival of the firm. Nevertheless, some progress had been made in this area. First the bank, Handlowy S.A., was willing to reschedule repayment of the investment credit obtained in 1989. Similar efforts with the working capital credit and the inter-firm payables were less successful, leading to some rather hopeless efforts to find new creditors. LFF's overdue working capital credit consisted of 80 percent penalty interest but only 20 percent unpaid principal. The firm paid a few monthly installments in 1992, to try to come to terms with the bank, but these funds were treated as interest due and not, as the management had hoped, as partial repayment of the principal. LFF then decided to stop paying this credit and remained at war with its bank. Relations with suppliers of materials, however, improved and many agreed to disregard the old debts and accrued interest, and supply the firm with necessary inputs on a cash payment basis. This was regarded as a fair deal by LFF management.

LFF also attempted to ease mounting tax arrears. A deal was made with the Treasury Chamber whereby the repayment of all past debts would be postponed for approximately six months and penalty interest frozen, but current taxes would be due in full. Unfortunately, LFF could not afford to pay any taxes, so arrears, contrary to inter-firm payables, continued to grow. The restructuring program had emphasized that some recommendations should be taken very seriously by the firm. This was partly done, and brought some results, but given LFF's present dire straits, the measures were not sufficient.

Change of Product Mix, New Markets

One of the benefits of the firm's complicated structure was the diversity of its production possibilities. In recent years LFF had acquired greater capacity in one of the larger plants where modern, exportable furniture could be produced. During the past five to seven years efforts had been made to upgrade the production profile from the standard segmented pieces to more elaborate and expensive products. A 1991 profitability analysis, done within the framework of the restructuring plan, showed that only two product groups, bedroom sets and children's furniture, were profitable. Some of the loss-making products were immediately eliminated, but others were retained in the hope that increased production volume would result in cost reduction and eliminate losses.

Efforts to expand export sales were intensified, with new products exhibited at the international furniture fair in Poznan. Also, negotiations with prospective customers in Russia, Ukraine, and Latvia were started. The enterprise was also contemplating a barter deal, furniture against machinery, which could partly upgrade the firm's technology base. Preliminary results of these efforts were already visible. About 25 percent of 1992 sales were export sales and, according to the management, contracts worth about 65–60 billion zloty had already been signed. However, the firm did not have enough working capital. Some foreign customers made prepayments, financing necessary working capital, in return for lower prices. We were not able to get data on the profitability of these exports since this information was confidential, but it could be decisive for the prospects of the enterprise.

Domestic Market

The characteristics of the customer base were changing. After the 1990 collapse of state-owned traders, the number of customers grew from 10–20 to almost 300. Payment problems followed, worsening the cash-flow situation. However, after this, things changed for the better. LFF consciously limited the number of its customers, and reduced the number of solid wholesalers to 8–10. Even so, receipt of payment for deliveries within 30 days proved impossible; the average length of time was closer to 60 days. The two existing factory retail shops were a valuable asset to the firm because their sales proceeds helped to cover the most urgent financial needs. There were even plans to found a large wholesale store in one of the liquidated plants in Lodz.

Liquidation and Sales of Assets

Liquidation seemed to be the most natural way to reduce costs and simplify management. Indeed, this process, which was well under way in early 1992, was accelerated later in the year. Seven plants, most of them smaller units, were closed and most of the production transferred to the remaining plants. The headquarters were moved from an old building to the newest and biggest factory. At present, three plants are in full operation, one consisting of a cluster of four smaller shops located very close to each other.

Technically, it would have been possible to concentrate the existing production process in two larger plants, but, because of the immobility of labor, this was difficult. The workers at two liquidated plants were offered jobs at different plants within the enterprise, which would have entailed some commuting, but not more than 20 km. Of a total of 130 workers, only 15 accepted the offer. Others left, still eligible for a three-month severance payment. Therefore, in order to make the best possible use of relocated machines, the firm had to train new employees. Of a group of 30 people, however, only one stayed at LFF after the training period.

Some assets, buildings, and depreciated machines were being sold or rented, but the sales procedure was very complicated. An assessment had to be made to determine the value, below which the price could not be set. In order to acquire the right to sell an asset, the enterprise first had to buy it from the *voivod*. The *voivod* determined the terms of payment, usually 30 days, but since the enterprise did not have this much money, it then had to find a buyer who would pay cash or pay within 30 days. The fact that the market was crowded with redundant assets from liquidated SOEs also hampered the selling process. In addition, ownership of most of LFF's materials was not clear. The enterprise had title only to the newest plant. In all other cases, it was owner by usucaption, meaning that claims of former owners could appear as the reprivatization process in Poland got started. In fact, several had already been submitted. A seaside vacation house owned by LFF was also on the market. Since LFF wholly owned this property, it would receive the entire sale amount rather than the surplus of sale proceeds over book value; but because real estate demand was weak, the prospects of a sale were uncertain. Selling assets can save costs of current operations but would not improve cash flow.

Much space in the LFF had already been rented, bringing in approximately 450 million zloty per year. This was only about 0.5 percent of the annual sales value, but it helped with maintenance costs and was a source of ready cash. According to the restructuring program, assets sales and rent should have amounted to about 2.5 billion zloty in 1992. While this alone could not have remedied the financial troubles of the firm, it should have brought some relief.

Overall, the changes introduced were insufficient to visibly improve the situation. A serious shortage of liquidity constrained the scale of output, making it impossible for the firm to take advantage of existing demand and eliminate losses. Drastic cost-cutting measures in 1992 resulted in a net loss that was one-half of 1991's loss, but the fact that the assets were rearranged was, in our opinion, far more helpful in implementing any kind of privatization program.

Privatization

A plan to transform the enterprise into a joint stock company was presented in 1991. All necessary documents for the Ministry of Ownership Transformation were prepared but, because of the rapid financial deterioration, this plan was shelved. However, privatization of the enterprise, or what was left of it, seemed vital. Both foreign and domestic investors had shown some interest and, in the latter case, an offer had been made to rent the largest plant, which would supply the firm with sufficient working capital. One large German customer simply wanted to buy part of the enterprise. It was too early to judge whether both offers were serious and, if so, which the *voivod* would choose, but one could assume that some sort of ownership change would take place.

CONCLUDING REMARKS

It seemed that the implementation of the restructuring program would not be enough for the enterprise to survive. The backlog of debts was so large that the firm could not cope with it alone. From the very beginning of the transition period, LFF had been the underdog, a victim of the vagaries of the central planners in such areas as investment process and artificial concentration. The result of this was helplessness when confronted with a new economic situation. It was only a medium-sized enterprise and therefore would receive no aid from the state, as would some giants of the Polish mining or electromechanical industries. Privatization seemed to be the only solution other than to close down entirely. However, there was always the chance of attracting an outside investor because relatively low costs of timber and labor meant the Polish furniture industry was competitive on the European market, particularly in Germany. Crucial adjustment in this respect had already been made and, instead of low-quality items intended for the domestic market, LFF had been able to become a producer of exportable furniture.

Table 1

Structure of Costs (in percentages)

Specification	1988	1989	1990	1991	January–May 1992
Wages	29.48	37.99	21.61	28.36	38.59
Materials	50.22	53.36	48.15	38.66	34.28
Energy	2.22	2.35	3.69	5.72	7.28
Banking charges (incl. interest)	2.11	6.04	5.09	7.56	4.70
Depreciation	1.40	0.60	1.70	4.27	4.82
Property tax	0.40	0.29	0.71	1.33	2.29
External services	13.73	—	19.05	14.10	8.04
Total	100	100	100	100	100

Table 2

Main Financial Indices (in million zloty)

Specification	1988	1989	1990	1991	January–May 1992
Net sales	5,883	2,067.3	113,258.6	104,652	35,693.5
Costs of sales	5,041	13,222.9	101,976	112,453	41,998
Markup (1 – 2)	842	7,450.1	11,282.6	–7,801	–6,304.5
Remaining revenues	75	203	225.4	69.1	298
Costs of obtaining revenues	—	—	—	—	—
Financial revenues	6	16	101.8	497.4	149
Financial costs	111	916	5,472	9,197	2,080
Operating profit [3 + (4 – 5) + (6 – 7)]	812	6,753.1	6,137.8	–16,431.5	–7,937.5
Extraordinary profits	15	419	1,531	437	99
Extraordinary losses	43	462	3,152	20,774	1,608
Gross profit/loss (8 + 9 – 10)	784	6,710.1	4,516.8	–36,768.5	9,602.0
Taxes	444	3,482	6,964	2,911	1,213
Gross profit/loss (11 – 12)	340	3,228.1	–2,447.2	–39,679.5	–10,815

Table 3

Profitability Ratios

Specification	1988	1989	1990	1991	January–May 1992
Markup (operating profit)/sales	14.31	36.04	9.96	−7.45	−17.66
Gross profits/sales	13.33	32.46	3.99	−35.13	−26.70
Markup (operating profit)/cost of sales	16.70	56.34	11.06	−6.94	−15.01
Gross profits/costs of sales	15.55	50.75	4.43	−32.70	−22.86
Net profit/cost of sales	6.74	24.41	−2.40	−35.29	−25.75

Table 4

Liquidity and Activity Ratios

Specification	1988	1989	1990	1991	January–May 1992
Liquidity ratios					
Working capital/total assets	0.25	0.37	—	—	—
Current ratio	1.75	1.78	0.93	0.45	—
Quick ratio	0.43	0.59	0.43	0.24	0.25
Activity ratios					
Account receivable turnover	12.18	7.49	9.83	5.90	1.77
Average collection period (days)	30	48	37	61	85
Payments turnover	3.67	3.49	4.10	1.67	0.42
Average payments period (days)	98	103	88	216	353
Inventory turnover	4.59	6.34	11.48	6.69	1.83
Average inventory turnover (days)	78	57	31	54	82

9

Iron/Steel: Czestochowa Steelworks

Stefan Krajewski

SECTORAL SETTING

In 1992, there were twenty-seven iron- and steelworks in Poland. In the past, the material-intensive nature of the economy and the central allocation of output safeguarded their existence. The transition to a market economy revealed a number of weaknesses of the Polish iron and steel industry, among them:

- excess production capacity for products of low quality, produced in the wrong assortment;
- obsolete and inefficient technologies, which also caused grave environmental damage;
- inefficient management;
- absence of competent marketing specialists who understood Western markets.

A drop in demand for iron and steel products caused substantial cuts in output. The production decline started in 1989 when output fell by 8.5, and intensified in the following years with a 17.1 percent drop in 1990 and 24 percent in 1991. In some product lines, the output in 1991 represented about 50–60 percent of the 1988 output (see Table 1). The decline in production continued in 1992. In the first nine months of 1992, real output of the sector fell by 10 percent compared to the corresponding period of 1991.

The financial situation of iron- and steelworks worsened quite rapidly. In 1990, the ratio of gross profit to costs of sales amounted to 31.1 percent. In 1991, it declined steadily, reaching a value of −3.9 percent for the entire iron and steel industry at the year's end. It declined further to −4.1 percent in the first three quarters of 1992.

In 1992, most iron- and steelworks recorded losses and only a few showed any profit whatsoever. Aggregate losses in 1991 reached 2 trillion zloty or about $180 million, and in 1992 were estimated at 3.5 trillion or about $250 million. There was almost no investment in 1991, and the steel mills' indebtedness to suppliers grew rapidly.

The restructuring programs of the iron and steel industry, such as one prepared by a Canadian consortium, recommended the following modifications to be made within the next few years:

- liquidation of unprofitable iron- and steelworks and a 50 percent reduction in steel production;
- reduction of the work force by as much as two-thirds by the year 2000;
- acceleration of changes in organization and management;
- intensification of technological innovation not requiring large investment outlay;
- investment of about $4.5 billion over the next ten years for technical restructuring.

HISTORY AND GENERAL INFORMATION ON CZESTOCHOWA STEELWORKS

The steelworks was established in 1896, based on relatively poor-quality ore deposits that can be found in the vicinity of Czestochowa. A favorable circumstance was the proximity of Silesia with its considerable production of coal and coke. In 1934, Czestochowa Steelworks was incorporated into the Modrzejow-Hantke concern. After World War II, it was nationalized and expanded in the 1950s as a result of rapid industrialization and growing military demand.

Czestochowa Steelworks was one of the largest steelworks in Poland; only Katowice Steelworks in Katowice and Sedzimir Steelworks in Cracow were larger. In 1992, with 8,300 employees, its sales amounted to more than $210 million, and in the last few years, its exports have accounted for about 20–25 percent of total sales.

New open-hearth furnaces were put into operation in 1951, and one year later a pipe mill of the Calmes-Innocenti type was added. In 1953, two new blast furnaces and an agglomerating plant began operation. The department of steel constructions was established in 1954 and the department of mechanical working was built two years later. During the next decade, investment was focused on the coking plant, and by 1960–62, four coke oven batteries were brought on stream, followed by two more in 1972 and 1973. The last major investment project was the construction of the plate mill in 1972, and partial modernization of the steel plant was performed in 1990.

Czestochowa Steelworks consisted of a raw material processing part and a manufacturing part. The raw material part consisted of the following:

- an agglomerating plant equipped with two sinter belts, with a production capacity of 800,000 tons per year;

- blast furnaces with a production capacity of 650,000 tons, of which two were currently operational; this capacity represented a few percent of the total domestic output, producing 600,000 tons of steelmaking pig iron and 50,000 tons of foundry pig iron;
- a coking plant with an annual production capacity of one million tons, or about 8 percent of total domestic output; three batteries were currently functional, but the remaining three were shut down for several reasons, including excessive pollution.

The manufacturing part of the steelworks encompassed the following:

- A steel plant that could produce 800,000 tons of steel ingots a year, which was a few percent of the total domestic production. It was equipped with four furnaces, each with a capacity of 170 tons. Preparations are under way to install furnaces and equipment for continuous casting of steel.
- A plate mill with a capacity of one million tons per year, or 76 percent of total 1990 domestic output. It produced construction, ship, and boiler steel plates 5–40 mm thick from slab ingots cast in the steel plant.
- A pipe mill with an annual output of about 120,000 tons of seamless pipes, which was about 85 percent of total domestic output. These pipes were also made from ingots produced in the steel plant.
- Steel constructions produced for the steelworks' own needs in working, assembling, and processing services, and for sale.
- The regeneration of parts for machines and equipment through metallic coating.

Because most of the machines and equipment had been in use for many years, the depreciation rate of fixed assets reached 64.5 percent in 1991. The equipment in the sheet and plate mill was the least depreciated because most of it had been used for only twenty years. In sum, Czestochowa Steelworks required modernization to alleviate its harmful impact on the environment, to reduce costs, and to change its product profile.

The enterprise had its own research and development center and laboratory for mechanical and chemical testing. It also possessed a large portfolio of social assets including a housing district, workers' hostels, culture center, holiday resorts, medical clinic, schools, sports facilities, kindergartens, creches, and canteens. Despite the present financial troubles, they were all in operation.

EFFECTS OF THE REFORM

The directors claim that the reform was not a total surprise for the steelworks. In the second half of the 1980s, it was already preparing to operate under conditions of a market economy. Attempts had been made to improve efficiency and quality, a cautious wage policy was pursued, and the firm made some effort toward financial independence.

However, the changes that had occurred since 1989 had had a major impact on the enterprise. One of the more important aspects of economic reform was the liberalization of prices. Before July 1989, the prices of steel products had been controlled by the state, but the liberalization of prices allowed the steelworks to raise them significantly in the second half of 1989 and in 1990. Immediately after the liberalization, prices of steel products were linked to the exchange rate of the zloty, whose rate of depreciation exceeded the rate of domestic inflation.

The next stage was the transition to prices shaped freely by the market forces. In 1990, the prices of products manufactured by Czestochowa Steelworks rose by 778 percent, in contrast to a 15 percent growth in 1991 and 10 percent in 1992. The growth of steel prices slowed at the end of 1990 as two barriers appeared. First, the level of domestic prices began to approach that of world prices and a further increase would have encouraged imports. Second, domestic demand declined rapidly and price competition among domestic producers became increasingly more pronounced. The policy of the Czestochowa Steelworks was to set prices at a level about 2 percent lower than that of its closest competitors.

At the same time, the prices of raw materials, energy, water, and transport services used by the steelworks were rising, albeit more slowly in 1990. However, their rate of increase was greater than that of steel products. This difference between the rates of growth of input and output prices was the main cause of the very high profitability recorded by the steelworks in 1989 and 1990 and the subsequent decline during 1991–92.

These price changes, while very advantageous for the steelworks during the initial phase of the reform, became increasingly more troublesome later. As mentioned previously, in 1990 the decline in domestic demand for metallurgical products intensified. This was a result of a combination of recession, a decreasing demand for investment goods, and structural changes within the Polish economy.

The next shock was the collapse of the CMEA market. In 1988, exports to that market constituted 62 percent of total exports of the steelworks industry. The USSR alone absorbed 45 percent of exports. In 1991, exports to the former CMEA accounted for only 1.1 percent of total exports. The managers of Czestochowa Steelworks claimed that they had expected such a decline and had been making efforts to preserve the firm's position on this market and also to find new markets.

Managers expressed considerable dissatisfaction with the steadily decreasing effectiveness of exports caused by the fixed exchange rate policy in effect after December 1989. The sharp increase in interest rates did not directly affect this enterprise because it had not obtained a large amount of credits. In early 1990, however, it exerted a destabilizing impact on customers and suppliers, who began to have their own financial problems.

The nature and intensity of the changes connected with the reform were affected, to some extent, by specific characteristics of the iron and steel industry. The absence of competitive imports had a cushioning effect but a number of factors hampered adaptation to the new conditions. First of all, production capacity was too large for the market requirements. Also, the enterprise previously had relied heavily on the CMEA countries, both as a source of raw materials and as a market for finished goods. Lastly, and perhaps most important, obsolete technologies not only polluted the environment but also accounted for high operations costs.

These negative factors were partly offset by positive effects of economic reform. The enterprise had received insignificant subsidies from the budget in the past, amounting to 1.5 billion zloty in 1988, 2.2 billion zloty in 1989, and 4 billion zloty in 1990; carried a minimal burden of credits; and had a stable management that allowed for continuous adaptations to changes.

EVOLUTION OF THE SITUATION IN THE 1990s: SHORT-TERM RESPONSES

Organization and Management Structure

The managing director of Czestochowa Steelworks was fifty-three years old, had both a technical and economic university background, and had started his professional career in this enterprise. He then became managing director of Zawiercie Steelworks, but returned to Czestochowa after winning an open competition for the position of managing director in 1986. He again won a similar competition in May 1992. For many years, he had been a member of the Polish United Workers' Party and a party activist in the province of Czestochowa.

The steelworks was divided into seven divisions, each headed by a deputy director. The economic division was headed by the sixty-three-year-old first deputy. He had a master's degree in economics and had held this position since 1974, the steelworks being his first and only job. In the past, he too had been a member and activist of the Polish United Workers' Party.

The director of the trade division was thirty-five years old, a graduate of a polytechnic, in this position since 1990. Prior to that, he had been chairman of the workers' council for two years and a Solidarity activist. He had been employed at the steelworks throughout his professional career. The chief accountant was a fifty-eight-year-old university graduate with an M.A. in economics. He had been in this post since 1971, after having been the manager of the costs department. He had spent his entire career at the steelworks and had also been a member and an activist of the Polish United Workers' Party.

The technical division was headed by a forty-year-old who had a technical university background and had been in this position since 1990. Previously, he had been the manager of the production department. Again, his professional career had been connected with the steelworks. The production division head was forty-three years old. A graduate of a technical university, he had held the present position since 1991, after having worked as the manager of the steel plant. He had always worked for the steelworks.

The development division director was forty-two years old, an engineer, and in the present position since 1986. Before that, he had been chairman of the workers' council, and his career, too, had been linked with Czestochowa Steelworks. The personnel division was headed by a thirty-five-year-old graduate of a secondary technical school, at the present post since 1991. In the past, he had been both chairman of Solidarity in the steelworks and chairman of the workers' council and his only job had been with this enterprise.

As is evident, the directors had different political orientations and their harmonious cooperation was not common in Poland in recent years. The older directors were linked with the former Polish United Workers' Party, while those appointed to their posts within the last two years were connected with Solidarity. There were no conflicts between these two groups and there seemed to be a gradual passing of powers in the enterprise that avoided social tensions. This allowed the younger directors to benefit from the experience of the older top management and to continue the operation of the steelworks in the spirit of cooperation.

Four deputy directors had left the steelworks during the last four years; two had retired and the other two were removed from their posts because they were unable to manage their division effectively under the new conditions. One of those removed, who was soon to retire, had been a party activist and was transferred to the post of chief of production.

A great deal of attention was given to the training of managers and directors. Numerous courses and traineeship programs were organized, frequently abroad. Trade union and workers' council leaders were among the participants, allowing them to better understand the intentions of the top management and the need of taking unpopular decisions, and enabling them to participate actively in the adjustment of the enterprise to the economic changes.

No radical changes in organization and management had taken place in recent years. Rather, emphasis was placed on systematic and consistent improvements including the following: expanding marketing activities; the direct sale by the steelworks of its products; increasing the effectiveness of costs and output recording by using computers; increasing financial and trade autonomy of certain departments; privatizing auxiliary services such as transport, tool shop, cleaning, designing office, and canteens by means of employee partnerships; and leasing and sales to foreign investors.

The top management's pay was quite low. For example, in 1989, the directors' pay was only 2.4 times higher than the average pay within the steelworks, including profit bonus. In 1989 and 1990, it was 2.9 and 3.5 times higher respectively, rising next to 4.5 times in 1992. However, any attempt at greater differentiation, which could raise the efficiency and active involvement of managers, encountered resistance from the employees. The remuneration of the directors was also small relative to the incomes of moderately successful owners of small private firms in trade and services. At the time of this study, the general director's remuneration consisted of two parts: a fixed wage equal to five times the national average pay and a bonus related to the volume of profit. His first deputy received 70 percent of this wage plus a profit bonus, and the other deputies received 65 percent of the director's wage.

The improved work organization in the steelworks was reflected in a decrease in the number of overtime hours, from 1,104,000 in 1988 to 186,000 in 1991. Moreover, an equally marked decrease in the number of unjustified absences was further proof of a growing respect for work. These absences declined from 81,300 hours in 1989 to 6,600 hours in 1991, and the number of persons leaving jobs voluntarily fell from 380 in 1989 to about 10 in the following years.

Markets, Sales, Production

In the 1980s, the steelworks was easily able to sell its entire output. The domestic market was absorptive and customers were ready to buy everything the steelworks produced, including obsolete and defective products. At the beginning of the 1990s, however, the domestic market shrank at the same time as the markets in the former CMEA collapsed.

Where possible, steps were taken to preserve existing markets, and a search was begun to find new ones. Even before the reform, the steelworks had given a great deal of attention to market analysis. Most transactions on the domestic market were concluded directly with customers and only coke, which constituted about 6 percent of the value of output in 1989, was sold through trade middlemen. Similarly, nearly all production supplies were purchased directly from domestic producers.

Before the reform, all imports and exports had been handled by specialized foreign trade organizations (FTOs). The general opinion at Czestochowa Steelworks was that these organizations were not very effective and could not ensure trade transactions on favorable terms. For this reason, the steelworks opened its own FTO in 1990 to handle all export and import activities and, by 1992, 80 percent of foreign sales were carried out by this unit. The suppliers of imported iron ore and mazut were also changed. They had been mainly imported from the USSR in the past but today they are sourced increasingly from Sweden and Mexico. Although these new suppliers charge higher prices, they also guaranteed both better quality and on-time delivery.

Various attempts made to strengthen the enterprise's position on the markets of Western Europe and enter the U.S. market have met with some success. The share of exports in total sales has been maintained and even increased. More information on the firm's export sales can be found in Table 2. This success was possible because of elastic prices, which were often lower than the prices on the domestic market. This resulted in an accusation by representatives of the U.S. steel industry against Czestochowa Steelworks of dumping on the American market. The charges concerned the sale of 13,000 tons of steel sheets at low prices.

One major obstacle to an increase in sales on foreign markets was the fact that the steelworks did not have international quality certification for some of its products, especially pipes, which were in great demand in many countries. When measured in aggregated volumes, the profitability rates of sales in Poland and abroad were similar. However, there were differences between certain assortments. Thus, for example, pipes and coke could be sold at higher prices abroad and steel sheets at higher prices in Poland.

Some attempts were made to enter new markets in Poland, particularly to sell various types of steel constructions. Thus far, these attempts have not been very successful because of little demand for investment goods and keen competition from other domestic producers. An expanding but secondary market was the sale of surplus electric energy to the city of Czestochowa, a surplus that resulted from cuts in production.

Substantial inventories of manufactured products appeared in 1991 and 1992 was a result of the declining sales, a problem that had not existed during 1988–90. The ratio of total inventories to sales decreased from 7.2 percent in 1988 to 6.9 percent in 1989 and 5.9 percent in 1990 and rose to 7.6 percent in 1991 and 12.7 percent in the period of January–August 1992. The decrease from 1988 to 1990 was because, before the transition started, raw materials and components had been purchased in large quantities to protect the steelworks against irregular supplies, especially from the USSR. Because the steelworks had terminated transactions with unreliable suppliers, there was no longer a need to maintain such large quantities of materials.

As mentioned, shrinking sales on the domestic and foreign markets resulted in production cuts. These were also made necessary by diminishing profitability of exports due to a continuing real appreciation of zloty and by pressure from the local authorities to restrict coke production to prevent excessive pollution of the environment. Since 1989, real output of all leading products has declined by about 35–45 percent, as shown in Table 3.

Although employment at Czestochowa Steelworks had decreased by 27 percent since 1988—from 11,355 at the end of 1988 to about 8,300 in 1992—this reduction was slower than the drop in output. That was partly due to the specific technology employed in iron metallurgy, because the operation of production lines requires the same number of workers regardless of output, and partly due to a deliberate policy pursued by the management. The management had not yet resorted to group lay-offs, and the decreasing employment was chiefly a result of attrition through disability, retirement, and voluntary departures.

Credits, Finance, Taxes

For many years, the steelworks had needed no long-term credits. The financial outlays in 1988–92 were fully financed from its own resources. Working capital credits were obtained only when necssary and consequently, the enterprise had insignificant banking charges and interest payment, representing 0.4 percent of total production costs in 1990 and 0.6 percent in 1991 and the first half of 1992. Throughout the time period of this study, Czestochowa Steelworks had good liquidity ratios. The current liquidity ratio and the quick ratio indicated that the steelworks could completely manage its financial obligations, as shown in Table 4. The declining share of working capital in total assets observed since 1990 was largely due to several revaluations of fixed assets, which resulted in a changed relation between fixed assets and working capital.

After recording an inflationary 66.8 percent ratio of gross profit to costs of sales in 1989, this ratio declined to 36.2 percent in 1990, 11.6 percent in 1991, and 5.0 percent after the first eight months of 1992. There were several reasons for this. The prices of imported raw materials had increased, as had prices of energy and transport services. Moreover, the stable exchange rate of the dollar caused the profitability of exports to decline, and production cuts resulted in a growth of fixed costs. Thus, although costs were growing, the possibility of selling the steelwork's output at prices that would offset these costs was exhausted in mid-1991.

Until the end of 1990, the profit earned by Czestochowa Steelworks was large enough so that the obligatory dividend and the PPWW did not impose too great a financial burden. In 1991–92, this situation altered, as shown in Table 5, such that there was even a slight net loss in 1992. Relaxation of the dividend, which was introduced in mid-1992, combined with an imminent dilution of the PPWW tax, would, the management hoped, help the steelworks to restore a positive rate of profit in 1993.

LONG-TERM RESPONSES

There was no possibility of immediately privatizing Czestochowa Steelworks; at best, it could be commercialized. The huge capital stock of the steelworks would make its acquisition by domestic investors practically impossible, and no foreign investors have shown any interest so far. The plan was to transform the enterprise into a holding company within the next few years, where the parent company would be the production part of the steelworks and would remain a state property. Those auxiliary parts concerned with production services, such as transport, tool shop, and designing office, would be privatized, perhaps as employee partnerships or joint ventures with foreign capital participation, but they would continue to be linked to the steelworks through capital. An employee partnership that organized catering services for canteens and the cafeteria had already been established.

The most important long-term goal was a restructuring to modernize the facilities and change the production mix of the steelworks. The plan was to gradually abandon the production of raw materials and switch, to a great extent, to the production of manufactured items. Within this framework, the enterprise had already reduced coke production and it now had three batteries operating as compared to six in 1989. In a few years, its production is to be completely abandoned as public concern over its environmental effects increases.

There was also a possibility of abandoning the production of pig iron and purchasing it at Katowice Steelworks instead. Both blast furnaces installed at Czestochowa Steelworks were already obsolete, having been in operation since 1953; and in addition to this, the costs of their exploitation were high and they threatened the environment.

As a result of the previous modernization program, which ended in 1990, only four of the nine open-hearth furnaces remained, and these were equipped with dust collectors, heat-recovery devices, and other environment-protecting devices. A contract for the installation of continuous steel-casting technology has been signed with the Austrian firm Voest-Alpina, and its costs were to be repaid through deliveries of coke to Austria.

Modernization of the pipe mill would also be necessary within the next few years, but this would enable the steelworks to manufacture a product that would meet the requirements for international certification. The problem here is that such a project would involve significant investment outlays that could probably only be covered by foreign investors. But thus far, no foreign firms had shown a serious interested in this investment.

There were no plans to modernize the steel sheet and plate mill yet because there were no financial resources for this purpose. Delaying its modernization long also could endanger the Czestochowa Steelworks because the sales of steel sheets were now the most important source of income, and constituted a major part of hard currency revenues.

EVALUATION OF FIRM'S FUTURE PROSPECTS BY THE DIRECTORS

According to the directors, Czestochowa Steelworks had already begun its adaptation to the market economy in the 1980s. For several years, it has had a long-term program executed by its management with no assistance from the Polish government or outside consulting firms. The one expert study prepared by a Canadian consortium was of little use.

The steelworks has implemented its program consistently and successfully. Compared with the entire iron and steel industry, Czestochowa Steelworks was in sound financial condition and had good prospects. The management believed that success lay in an efficient management system reinforced by highly qualified and experienced managers, who could react quickly to changes in the economy; a good working relationship among employees; and effective cooperation between the top management, the workers' council, and the trade unions.

Management was pursuing a cautious financial policy that avoided credits and large wage increases and advocated prompt payment of financial obligations to suppliers and the state budget. The weakness of the steelworks was its slow, fragmentary restructuring, which was a result of relying solely on its own financial resources. The directors did not see any current major threats to the survival of the steelworks, nor, unfortunately, any possibility of considerable improvement in its financial situation.

CONCLUSION

It is our opinion that the directors were quite realistic about the present situation and prospects of the steelworks. We did not discover any serious errors in the way in which the steelworks was managed. However, it seemed that the process of privatizing the auxiliary segments of the production part was being delayed too much, and similarly, decisions concerning the liquidation of its raw materials part have been postponed too long also. Attempts to involve foreign capital in financing the modernization of the manufacturing part of the steelworks were very cautious, a result of the enterprise's relatively stable financial condition. The bottom line is that the goal of becoming a first-class internationally competitive modern enterprise would probably go unrealized.

Table 1

Basic Data About the Iron and Steel Industry

Specification	1988	1989	1990	1991	January–September 1992
Sales in current prices (billion zloty)	1,850	6,110	43,188	38,921	31,782
Sales in constant prices (preceding year/period = 100)	99.4	92.5	82.9	76.0	88.9
Production of selected goods (thousand tons)					
Pig iron	16,873	15,094	13,625	10,438	7,480
Rolled products	12,424	11,272	9,836	8,059	5,662
Steel pipes	1,053	971	567	517	384
Cold-rolled steel sheets	1,530	1,467	1,047	739	117.2
Number of employees (thousands)	147.8	141.1	131.3	121.6	117.2
Mean monthly pay (thousand zloty)	67.0	266.3	1,384.5	2,160.5	2,671.4
Profitability ratios					
Gross profit/costs of sales	—	48.6	31.1	–3.9	–4.1
Net profit/costs of sales	—	—	—	–11.1	–9.5

Source: Statistical Yearbooks of Industry (Central Statistical Office, Warsaw 1989, 1990, 1991). *Naklady i wyniki przemyslu, I–III kwartal 1992,* Central Statistical Office, Warsaw, December 1992.

Table 2

Share in Total Sales and Structure of Exports (in percentages)

	1988	1989	1990	1991	January–August 1992
Share of exports in total value of sales	20.4	17.7	23.7	22.8	25.6
of which:					
USSR	45.0	36.0	32.0	1.1	12.5
Remaining CMEA	17.0	7.0	7.0	0	0

Table 3

Volume of Production in Main Product Groups

Types of product	1988	1989	1990	1991	January–May 1992
Steel sheets (thousand tons)	985	876	703	548	285
1988 = 100	100.0	88.9	71.4	55.6	—
Steel pipes (thousand tons)	137	128	94	88	36
1988 = 100	100.0	93.4	68.6	64.2	—
Coke (thousand tons)	1,552	1,390	1,105	868	364
1988 = 100	100.0	89.6	71.2	55.9	—

Table 4

Liquidity and Activity Ratios

Specification	1988	1989	1990	1991	January–August 1992
Liquidity ratios					
Working capital/total assets	0.20	0.39	0.20	0.10	—
Current ratio	1.73	1.90	2.17	1.50	1.37
Quick ratio	0.76	1.22	1.20	0.85	1.03
Activity ratios					
Receivables turnover	5.96	3.40	5.90	4.27	—
Average collection period (days)	60	106	61	84	—
Payables turnover	5.90	4.07	6.84	4.26	—
Average payment period (days)	61	88	53	85	—
Inventory turnover	13.77	21.75	28.57	14.13	—
Average inventory turnover (days)	26	17	13	25	—

Table 5

Tax Burden on Gross Profit (in percentages)

Specification	1988	1989	1990	1991	January–August 1992
Total tax burden	47.4	47.6	47.9	84.3	100.3
Income tax	47.4	30.8	32.9	41.9	44.9
Dividend	—	7.9	6.2	32.9	52.2
PPWW tax	—	8.9	8.8	8.6	3.2

10

White Goods—Refrigerators, Washers and Dryers: Polar Enterprise

Stefan Krajewski

SECTORAL SETTING

The metal consumer goods industry consists of about eighty enterprises manufacturing a wide range of products for the domestic market. Among them are several producers of electrical household appliances including the Polar firm, which was the largest domestic washing machine and refrigerator manufacturer.

Previously, the firms in this branch faced no domestic competition; this allowed them to hold a comfortable monopolistic position and to cushion the problems connected with adaptation to the requirements of the market economy. A specific characteristic of these firms was their spatial dispersal and a large number of customers. In the new situation in which the industry finds itself, producers must acquire the skill to reach a large number of small customers because the transition process has eliminated large, state-owned trade companies that, in the previous system, acted as middlemen between producers and end users.

HISTORY AND CHARACTERISTICS OF POLAR

Polar Electrical Household Appliances State-Owned Enterprise was established in 1952. It was located on the premises of a former paper works that had been operating even before World War II. Initially nobody knew what to produce at Polar, so its products were varied, including gas ovens, post carts, parts for excavators, and motorbikes. The first refrigerator, with capacity of forty liters, was produced in 1957; three years later, Polar began to export refrigerators. A branch plant that manufactured box freezers and wood-paneled refrigerators was opened at Zagan in 1968. During 1972–77, Polar was considerably expanded. Later investments were of a supplementary nature. One of the latest major investments was a polystyrene boards production line completed in 1981. In 1970, Polar opened its Experimental Plant, transformed in 1976 into the Research and Development Center employing highly qualified personnel.

The firm was equipped with production lines of the leading Western firms that specialized in the manufacture of washing machines. These included a Scarioni condenser production line, a Miramondi casing production line, and a Flowling aggregates assembly carousel. However, all these machines were quite obsolete; about 90 percent of the machines and equipment were about 10–20 years old. Polar specialized in the manufacture of cooling equipment such as two-door refrigerators and cabinet and box freezers, and automatic washing machines. Its remaining assortment of soft drink and milk coolers played a marginal role.

General information about the firm is as follows:

- gross value of capital stock: 827 billion zloty ($72 million), net value of capital stock: 378 billion zloty ($33 million), both at the end of 1991;
- sales value: $103 mil in 1991, $96 million in January–November 1992;
- share of exports in total sales: 15 percent (for 1991–92);
- employment: 5,393 persons in 1991, 4,969 in 1992, 7,153 in 1988.

The production capacity of the firm then greatly exceeded its sales potential. The shift rate amounted to 1.37, relative to 1.6 in 1989, and estimates of the utilization rates of machines and equipment during the main shift were set at 50–60 percent.

Polar had at its disposal a large portfolio of social assets including hundreds of flats, a hotel for workers, a creche, a kindergarten, a medical clinic, three holiday resorts, a culture center, a canteen, several cafeterias, and a sports stadium.

IMPACT OF THE REFORM

The newly introduced high interest rates had the fastest and most acute effect on the company. Fear of an excessive burden of financial costs connected with repayment and servicing of working capital credits forced the firm to reduce volume of production, although the demand for its products had not changed yet.

Payments arrears proved to be a major impediment for the firm. Domestic customers were unable to fulfill their financial obligations to Polar on time, which, in turn, made it very difficult for Polar to make settlements with its suppliers, and this ultimately necessitated the reduction of output.

The next factor exerting a negative influence on profitability of the firm's exports was the policy of stable exchange rate of the dollar accompanied by growing prices of materials, wages, and energy, and no possibility to reduce costs per production unit. A major factor restricting output was a sharp drop in domestic demand in 1991. However, the demand for the firm's products increased again in 1992 to such an extent that, in July, the entire current production of Polar was sold out while inventories of manufactured products were less than two days' production.

This branch of industry recorded the sharpest drop in its output in 1990, a drop of about 25 percent. In the following years, output declined by an additional 5–7 percent per year. The 1991 drop in demand for refrigerators, freezers, and washing machines was caused by the following factors:

- lower incomes of the population;
- the rapidly decreasing number of new flats and the resulting smaller outlays on their equipment;
- rapid growth of competitive imports from the Soviet Union and the West, especially in 1991, when customs regulations were deregulated; launching the production of refrigerators from imported parts by the Elmex Company;
- illegal import and trade in small washing machines from the USSR. The import of these small, poor-quality washing machines peaked in 1991 and declined rapidly during 1992 due to both a decrease in the Polish buyers' confidence in them and decreasing profitability in importing them into Poland given the rapid growth of prices in the USSR.

Certain specific characteristics made survival possible for Polar during the period of fundamental changes in the Polish economy. First of all, the firm had not received any government subsidies at the end of the 1980s and, therefore, was not affected by their discontinuation. Second, the firm had only an insignificant burden of credits from the previous period. Lastly, the size of the obligatory dividend and the burden of tax on excessive wage growth were small.

At the same time the obsolete and worn-out capital stock, which made for high production costs, was a major weakness for the firm. Environmental protection regulations dictated that some of its machines would have to be eliminated within the next two or three years; however, there were not enough resources to make such an investment.

Apart from these problems, the transition to a market economy created new opportunities for the firm. Polar now had greater freedom in determining its prices such that it was able to maintain high profitability in 1990.

The firm also had freedom of access to raw materials and components and in choosing its sub-suppliers. It now had independence in making all decisions about organizational changes, subsidiaries, etc. A substantial increase in the dollar exchange rate in 1989 proved to be beneficial for Polar. It had accumulated reserves of foreign currency in retention accounts that could be used later to ease the liquidity shortage common to most firms after the introduction of the new economic policy.

In sum, the immediate consequences of the Balcerowicz Plan on Polar seemed to have been a reduced volume of output, a substantial increase of production costs due to the higher cost of credit, a revaluation of the firm's property, price liberalization or hikes of administered prices of inputs, and increased fixed cost per unit as a result of the drop in output. Also, after the initial increase, export sales profitability gradually declined.

Taking into account the two basic assortment groups, output (1988=100) was as follows:

	Washing machines	Refrigerators/ freezers
1989	102.2	105.0
1990	47.6	119.0
1991	37.3	88.0

In turn, the volume of exports was as follows (1988 = 100):

	Washing machines	Refrigerators/ freezers
1989	101.6	102.3
1990	81.4	110.8
1991	0	110.5

SHORT-TERM RESPONSES

Management

Since the beginning of the transformation process in 1989, Polar's most important problem has been to find and retain good directors and managers for the firm. All directors had been replaced by 1990 because the workers' council and trade unions did not feel that the previous directors could guarantee effective management of the firm, and they had not enjoyed the confidence of the workers. However, the process of finding appropriate directors proved to be quite difficult. Consequently, deputy directors were changed fourteen times during the appointment period.

The present managing director, a forty-year-old technical university graduate, had worked at Polar since 1975, before which he worked for an aircraft company. In 1985–86, he was the chairman of the workers' council and in March 1991 he became managing director, after having been in the position of deputy technical director. He was responsible for all issues connected with Polar's technical innovation.

Polar was a one-plant firm with five organizational divisions controlled by deputy directors. The director of the division of technology and development was a 35-year-old technical university graduate who had managed this division since April 1991. His previous job was deputy manager of the technical department and he had worked for the firm since 1980.

The division of production and material supplies was headed by another forty-year-old technical university graduate who had held this position since 1990, after being a manager of the import department. He had worked at Polar since 1978. The deputy director of the division of maintenance operations, forty years old and a technical university graduate, had been responsible for the division since July 1991. Earlier he had managed the electrical section, and had worked for Polar from the beginning of his professional career.

The economic-financial division manager was a forty-year-old woman who had an M.A. in economics and who had held this position since 1990. Her previous post was that of a manager of the economics department and she had been with Polar since 1975. The marketing and service division had as its deputy director a man, thirty-five years old, with an M.A. in economics, who had been at this post since 1991. His earlier post was that of manager of the foreign trade office and he had worked for Polar since 1983.

The chief accountant, also a member of the management board, was fifty-seven years old, had an M.A. in economics, and had been responsible for the firm's finances since December 1991. Before that, he had been a deputy director for economic affairs and a chief accountant in a road and bridge construction enterprise.

This information shows that the directors of Polar were mostly people who had been associated with the firm for a long time. Most were engineers and none had any professional experience abroad. The fact that the position of chief accountant was held by someone hired from another enterprise was indicative of the difficulty in finding well-qualified people in this field within Polar.

Frequent changes were also made among intermediate and lower-level management, e.g., managers of departments or sections and foremen. At the time, it was difficult to assess the effects of these changes. It seemed that political criteria as well as qualifications and organizational skills were taken into consideration. Changes in attitude and priorities occurred steadily among the firm's management. Although increasingly greater attention was given to marketing, the conviction that the production process was the most important aspect of the firm's operations still prevailed among managers at different levels.

Organizational Structure

In March 1991 the plant at Zagan (150 km from Wroclaw), which had been employing 800 people and specialized in the production of box freezers and wood-paneled refrigerators, was separated and became an autonomous enterprise. There was no close cooperation between the subsidiary at Zagan and Polar Enterprise in Wroclaw. The management and self-governed representatives of the subsidiary believed that their market position and financial effects, as well as development prospects, were better than those of the parent company. Therefore, they had advanced a proposal that the subsidiary be transformed into an independent firm. The idea had won the acceptance of Polar's management and workers' council and the permission of the Ministry of Industry and Trade. The directors of Polar did not feel that the separation of the subsidiary exerted a negative influence on the firm's present situation or on its development prospects. There were no permanent contacts between the firms at present.

There were several plans to enable the firm to adapt to the new economic conditions. After the collapse of big state-owned wholesale enterprises, the main customers of the firm throughout the postwar period, a new distribution system was organized. Polar also established its own network of wholesale warehouses and agents throughout Poland to supply retailers. Moreover, the firm introduced a system of price preferences for different customers.

The organizational units dealing with marketing and finance were better equipped: they increased their number of employees and had pay preferences created. Organizational units responsible for sales and purchases both in Poland and abroad were given greater autonomy in making decisions. The autonomy and financial responsibility of production departments was enhanced. In order to identify those areas of activity that should be curtailed or expanded, the system of costs recording was improved.

The improved organization of work yielded the following positive effects: the number of overtime hours was decreased from 500,000 in 1988 to about 200,000 in 1991; the number of remunerated dead-time hours was reduced from 161,400 to 78,400; and the number of unjustified absences decreased from 9,100 to 2,100.

Markets, Prices, Sales, Production

Economic recession and the growth of competitive imports from Western Europe and the former USSR created disturbances on the domestic market that caused a drop in demand for the firm. These difficulties seemed to mobilize marketing efforts at Polar. First of all, an efficient system of distribution in Poland that allowed the firm to reach the greatest possible number of potential buyers was created. Also, the freedom to determine prices obtained during the initial period of the economic reform allowed the firm to have a flexible pricing policy. Despite significant price increases in 1990, the firm maintained a strong competitive position on the market and only in 1991 were the possibilities of further price increases considerably limited.

As early as 1990, the firm had begun to lower its prices for certain types of washing machines in an attempt to win new customers. This enabled it to compete successfully with technically better but much more expensive washing machines from the West. However, even a marked price reduction could not eliminate the competition of the low-priced Russian Viatka washing machine.

Still, due to poor quality, the increasing prices as a result of inflation in Russia, and the difficulty in bringing these machines into Poland, their sales on the Polish market declined quite rapidly.

Owing to more active market research, elastic prices, and stronger intra-firm stimuli, Polar succeeded in increasing its exports of refrigerators and freezers from 157,000 units in 1988 to 173,000 in 1991. On the negative side, the export of washing machines had almost completely stopped. Washing machines produced by Polar were technically obsolete compared to those from the West, and even a substantial price reduction did not make them salable.

The share of exports in total sales rose from 9.3 percent in 1988 to 15.6 percent in 1991 and, according to management's estimates, should have attained this level in 1992. The firm's exports to the former CMEA countries, which were 9.2 percent of overall exports in 1988, 5.8 percent in 1989, 4.8 percent in 1990, and 7.2 percent in 1991, remained unchanged. Polar's main importers were the FRG, Great Britain, France, Czechoslovakia, Canada, and Austria. Due to a stable exchange rate of the Polish currency, export production was less profitable than production for the domestic market. Polar's intentions to expand its export volume were prompted by the following considerations: the domestic market was too small compared to the firm's production capacities; a larger scale of production would make it possible to lower product unit costs; and competition with foreign products and the requirements of customers abroad could stimulate a higher technical level, which would strengthen the firm's position on the Polish market as well.

Until three years ago, the firm had no Polish competitors on the domestic market. Then an Elmex Company became a major competitor. This Elmex enterprise first imported refrigerators but then changed to importing parts and assembling them in Poland.

Various efforts have been made by Polar to lower its production costs. Thus, for example, many suppliers of materials have been replaced in the last three years because their products were too expensive, or the quality was too low, or the terms of payment were not attractive. This freedom of choice was one of the most positive effects of the reform. However, these cost-saving measures were offset by other factors that led to a growth of production costs, including increases of prices of raw materials and components, energy, banking services and interest, and depreciation as a result of repeated revaluation of fixed assets. Consequently, the relation between costs of production and sales value worsened such that, from 59.7 percent in 1989, the share of costs in sales value rose to 68.0 percent in 1990 and 82.4 percent in 1991. However, this ratio increased to 71.5 percent in 1992 (see Table 2). No major differences in the internal structure of costs could be observed during that period. The share of material costs maintained constant and the financial costs of banking services and interest increased by several percentage points. However, the firm recorded a marked drop in the costs of transport and other external services. This meant that Polar continued to reduce its reliance on external services, seeking to use its own potential more effectively.

The growth of wage costs in 1992 was caused by a combination of collecting the social security contribution from the gross wages, the base of which increased by 20 percent, raising its rate from 43 percent to 45 percent, and a faster decline in output than in employment size.

Credits, Finance, Taxes

During the initial period of economic transformation, the firm was not burdened with servicing on long-term credits. However, the high interest on working capital credits was a problem that affected the operation of the firm. In 1989, Polar was using short-term credits, which were abandoned to a large extent in the following years to avoid an excessive burden of interest charges. At the same time, however, Polar had to reduce its output. Later, particularly in 1991, the firm used fewer credits than required by production needs, due not only to the high interest but also to the difficulty state-owened firms experienced in obtaining credits. We were told that banks made it difficult for Polar to obtain both working capital and long-term credits, although the financial condition of the firm was good. This unwillingness on the part of banks to extend credits for state-owned enterprises was common, not exceptional for Polar. In 1991, Polar obtained a foreign-currency-denominated credit to finance an investment project—the modernization of an automatic washing machine. The bank credit amounted to $374,000 and the firm contributed $522,000 from its own resources.

The data in Table 3 give insight into the firm's financial results and its liquidity. The inflationary results of 1989 could not be repeated in subsequent years: the ratio of gross profit to sales dropped from 23.1 percent in 1989 to 19.2 percent in 1990, and next to 3.1 percent in 1991. However, those results achieved in 1992, namely 9.4 percent in May and 9.9 percent in November, (cumulative from the beginning of the year), point to some improvement in the firm's financial standing. A major factor that improved the firm's profitability in 1992 was the reimbursement of 60 billion zloty in customs duties paid on imported materials used for export production. Other profitability indices changed in a similar way.

The firm recorded a high current liquidity ratio, but because a substantial part of assets was tied up in inventories and financial settlements, its quick ratio was low. The receivables and inventory turnover ratios increased in 1990, but in 1991, a trend of delayed collection cycles again appeared along with a freezing of excessive working capital in inventories. The taxation of gross profit is shown in Table 4.

During 1989–90, the dividend Polar paid was not imposing a heavy burden on profit (4 percent). However, in 1991, when gross profit decreased sharply, the dividend rose to 26.8 percent of profit. This situation changed in 1992 as profits increased and the rate of dividend was slashed at mid-year from 22 percent to 10 percent of the founding fund.

Throughout the entire period, the firm paid wages that exceeded the limit set by the inflation-adjusted wage index. The PPWW tax increased to 10.2 percent of gross profit in 1991 but fell to a mere 1.2 percent in 1992. On average, taxes consumed about 50–60 percent of profit, which rose to almost 85 percent in 1991. In 1990–91, the firm had no net profit for development. Also in 1991, the entire surplus of profit above obligatory taxes and other burdens was used for profit bonus for the employees and the socio-welfare fund. Again, the situation in 1992 improved dramatically. Profit reached $5.3 million and, according to the plan, a significant part of it was to be reinvested.

LONG-TERM RESPONSES

The adjustment measures adopted by Polar had enabled it to survive, but they could not completely eliminate the main threats facing it. Although the enterprise had been successful so far compared to most other SOEs, most of its behavior was short-run–oriented and it still needed to implement its long-term strategy. Thus, the extent to which this strategy would be successful could not yet be estimated.

The most important elements of the firm's long-term program included:

- privatization;
- establishing stable links with foreign capital;
- securing financial resources for investment in machinery and equipment;
- strengthening the firm's position on both domestic and foreign markets involving, among other things, the use of the distribution network of a foreign partner.

In 1991, the management of Polar prepared a plan to commercialize the firm, i.e., transform it into a one-person partnership of the State Treasury, and consultations with the Ministry of Ownership Transformation followed. The project suggested that auxiliary services units be separated from the firm and transformed into a stock company, with employees holding 51 percent of shares. The next stage in privatization of Polar would be its transformation into a joint venture with the participation of foreign capital.

This project, however, was not accepted by the workers' council and trade unions. They also objected to including Polar in a program of mass privatization because they did not feel that privatization of the company would guarantee clear benefits. Indeed, it contained many elements of risk because the goals of a foreign owner or co-owner were unknown. The workers were afraid that a new owner might drastically reduce employment, cease production of final goods such as washing machines and refrigerators, or switch the focus of manufacture to simple components supplied to producers of final products abroad. Representatives of self-government organizations had quoted incidents of such moves in privatized Polish companies sold to foreign firms and the results had never been very satisfactory.

Consequently, privatization was suspended for the time being, but this hampered, and even made finding a serious foreign partner who was willing to invest in the modernization of Polar, virtually impossible. Many foreign firms were interested in this firm, its production potential, and its development prospects; however, such contacts usually ended after preliminary talks. Foreign partners would withdraw from further negotiations, suggesting that they resume when the social situation within the firm stabilized and the firm had been privatized, decreasing the risk for foreign investments.

Polar had no intention of changing the present structure of production, but it still faced an urgent need to make major investments within the next three or four years; those modernization investments carried out since 1988 were financed mainly from the firm's own resources. It was only in 1991 that a credit of several hundred thousand DM was obtained from a German bank. It was allocated to replacement of the equipment used to produce tumblers for automatic washing machines. A new investment credit of about $1.5 million had been in the negotiation stage since mid-1992. This was to be paid in two installments and was to be used for modernizing the painting shop. The present shop had been in use for twenty-five years, was obsolete, expensive to use, and very harmful to the environment. It would also be necessary to modernize the enameling shop. The furnaces could only be used effectively for 8–12 hours per day. This department worked on one to one-and-a-half·shifts, and these furnaces had to be left on constantly because they needed a long time to reheat. The new furnaces that the firm wanted to purchase could be switched off and on as the need arose, allowing for a considerable conservation of electrical energy. The banks to which Polar submitted its offer refused to grant a credit for this investment, claiming that the financial situation of the firm was poor.

The most important investment project would be changing the production technology of cooling equipment based on freon. Poland had signed an international agreement to stop using freon, given its detrimental effects on the ozone layer, but this would require an investment amounting to about $8 million. The firm had not yet made an attempt to obtain credits for this purpose, but perhaps it would apply for credit from the World Bank.

MANAGEMENT'S PERCEPTION OF THE FIRM'S PRESENT POSITION AND PROSPECTS

According to the firm's management, the current difficulties faced by the firm were caused by the following factors:

- the government's restrictive fiscal policy toward state-owned enterprises in the form of a dividend and PPWW tax;
- defective credit policy of a high interest rate and a reluctance on the part of banks to provide credits to state-owned enterprises;
- an absence of a consistent government policy toward state-owned enterprises regarding privatization, financial assistance, and payment arrears problems.

The management realized that they could not depend on any substantial external assistance in their struggle for survival: almost everything would depend on the adopted strategy and its consistent execution. They believed that the firm's major advantages were its well-qualified personnel, spacious although ineffectively utilized premises, developed distribution network in Poland, and good location. The main weaknesses of the firm were a shortage of resources for modernization, the difficulties encountered in expanding its outlets, especially in Western Europe, and resistance of the workers' council and trade unions to new ideas advanced by the management, even though most present directors were former leaders of these bodies.

The management was also aware that the process of adapting employees, including managers, to new conditions and requirements was proceeding too slowly. This negatively affected the possibility of ownership transformation being carried out, made it difficult to create an effective system of incentives and select appropriate management staff, and hampered the process of drafting and executing the program of restructuring.

CONCLUDING REMARKS

Any more significant, long-term-oriented measures that would be decisive for the future of the firm were still to be taken. The management pursued a reasonable policy of short-term adaptations of the market, production, and investment type. However, the firm's financial situation continued to be problematic, in spite of the fact that it had avoided large wage increases or an excessive burden of long-term credits.

A rapid decision concerning ownership changes would seem to be indispensable and should have been made much earlier. However, the directors had little leverage to enable them to carry out their program of long-term adaptations. In turn, the employees themselves were slow to accept the challenges facing the firm as a result of transition to a market economy. Moreover, the directors could not fight the employees' resistance to privatization, a greater differentiation of pay, and distrust of foreign capital.

Table 1

Basic Data about the Metal Consumer Goods Industry

Specification	1988	1989	1990	1991	January–September 1992
Sales in current prices (billion zloty)	377	1,297	5,893	8,169	6,884
Sales in constant prices (preceding year = 100)	104.8	105.6	74.4	96.9	94.6*
Production of selected goods (thousand units)					
Electrical washing machines	761	811	482	335	252
Home refrigerators and freezers	484	516	604	563	360
Vacuum cleaners	1,081	1,086	913	856	694
Number of employees (thousands)	63.4	61.2	58.3	59.0	53.5
Average monthly pay (thousand zloty)	51.5	207.7	913.8	1,517.2	1,926.9
Profitability ratios					
Gross profit/costs of sales	—	59.5	31.7	4.2	5.6
Net profit/costs of sales	—	—	—	–2.0	–0.4

Source: Statistical Yearbooks of Industry (Central Statistical Office, Warsaw 1989, 1990, 1991). *Naklady i wyniki przemyslu, I–III kwartal 1992,* Central Statistical Office, Warsaw, December, 1992.
* (1st–3rd Quarter 1991 = 100)

Table 2

Structure of Production Costs at Polar in 1988–1992 (in percentages)

Specification	1988	1989	1990	1991	January–September 1992
Labor costs	14.8	19.8	14.3	15.5	19.9
Material costs	67.8	62.5	64.9	64.8	64.3
Energy	1.0	1.1	1.6	1.9	2.1
Banking charges (incl. interest)	1.4	4.8	7.7	7.8	4.3
Depreciation	1.2	0.5	1.3	2.5	2.9
Property tax	0.5	0.2	0.4	0.4	0.7
Transport services	5.1	4.3	2.1	2.5	2.2
External services	8.2	6.8	6.7	4.6	3.6
Costs of production	100.0	100.0	100.0	100.0	100.0
Share of costs in value of sales	65.4	59.7	68.0	82.4	71.5

Table 3

Main Financial Indices of Polar in 1988–1992

Specification	1988	1989	1990	1991	January–November 1992
Profitability ratios					
Gross profit/sales	16.1	23.1	19.2	3.1	9.9
Net profit/sales	6.3	9.8	9.8	0.5	3.6
Liquidity ratios					
Current ratio	2.99	1.59	2.23	1.53	—
Quick ratio	0.88	0.77	0.47	0.54	—
Net working capital/total assets	0.49	0.34	0.30	0.16	—
Activity ratios					
Receivables turnover	—	5.93	13.29	10.26	—
Average collection period (days)	—	61	27	35	—
Payables turnover	—	3.17	6.09	4.50	—
Average payment period (days)	—	114	59	80	—
Inventory turnover	—	6.33	6.63	4.19	—
Average inventory turnover (days)	—	57	54	86	—

Table 4

Burden of Taxes Paid from Profit (in percentages; gross profit = 100)

Type of tax	1988	1989	1990	1991	January–November 1992
Total tax burden	60.6	57.8	49.2	84.8	46.1
Income tax	55.7	45.1	42.0	47.8	40.3
Dividend	—	4.1	3.6	26.8	4.6
Tax on wage increases	4.3	8.6	3.6	10.2	1.2

11

Footwear: Mokasyn

Marek Belka

SECTORAL SETTING

The footwear industry was an important traditional sector that once employed almost 100,000 people. The state-owned part of the industry, which consisted of about thirty-five large and medium-size enterprises, had 50,000 employees. One Western marketing firm, preparing a review for the program of sectoral privatization, estimated the production capacity of the sector at 200 million pairs of shoes per year.

This industry was among the manufacturing sectors most severely affected by the recent fall in real income, tough import competition, and the collapse of the Soviet market, all of which contributed to a large drop in sales and production. During 1990–91, real sales decreased at more than 30 percent per year, a tendency that intensified in the first quarter of 1992. This is illustrated by the following data: in 1988, over 155 million pairs of shoes were produced; in 1989, 151 million; in 1990, 78 million; in 1991, 71 million; and in the first quarter of 1992, 13 million pairs.

Employment fell by one-third during this period, from 97,000 to 65,000 people, leading to a significant decrease in labor productivity. This eliminated the most important source of comparative advantage the industry had in exports to the Western markets. Sectoral wages, at about 80 percent of the national average, were among the lowest in the economy. While the footwear industry had never been known for its high salaries, the financial difficulties of the last two years forced many enterprises to limit the growth of wages or even to cut nominal wages. The sectoral profitability crisis began in 1990, earlier than in most industries, with the aggregate gross profit rate reaching 10.7 percent and net profits virtually disappearing. During 1990–92, the industry regularly experienced both net and gross losses, and a vast majority of SOEs faced bankruptcy or liquidation. In fact, we had difficulty finding a firm that roughly satisfied our criteria yet was not in a state of liquidation. The situation at Mokasyn reflected the problems of the Polish footwear industry and was therefore an interesting study. Nevertheless, we were aware that the firm could cease to exist next year, in which case we would have to find another firm.

HISTORY AND DESCRIPTION OF THE FIRM

History

Mokasyn dated back to 1949. It was founded when former employees of closed local footwear factories formed two small workers' cooperatives. In 1960, one of the founders invested a considerable amount of his own resources in the buildings and infrastructure, and the current enterprise came into being. In 1979, these two cooperatives, Orkan and Mokasyn, merged with a neighboring state-owned enterprise called Odra. This merger was contrary to the will of the shareholders of the cooperatives, but the policy of centralization pursued by the central authorities in the 1970s prevailed over the vaguely defined autonomy of socialist cooperatives.

Three years later, a reverse trend became fashionable and the state-owned Mokasyn was separated from Odra, appropriating most of the assets of the two cooperatives. Mokasyn consisted of three plants, one located in Rybowo and two others in small towns in the vicinity. Old workers, former members of the cooperative, whom we met during our visits to Mokasyn, expressed regret about the juggling to which Mokasyn was exposed, adding that part of the assets were stolen from them in the process. Namely there was still another plant, a fourth one, located outside Rybowo (presumably quite well equipped), that was not reunited with Mokasyn after 1982. Also, some of Odra's machines disappeared in the rearrangement.

In the 1980s, then, Mokasyn consisted of three plants. The one located in Rybowo was by far the largest, possessing most of the fixed assets and employing 75 percent of the labor force. The second plant, at Ptaszkowo, a rural town in the nearby lake district, played an auxiliary role, but was prepared for full-cycle production of shoes. The third and smallest part of Mokasyn was a sewing mill where products were semi-produced, to be assembled in Rybowo. This plant employed only twenty-two people on a full-time basis and a varying number of seamstresses working in their homes. It was closed in 1990. All regular employees were offered a job at the main plant in Rybowo but, due to rising transportation costs, none accepted the offer.

The economic situation of the enterprise deteriorated rapidly after 1989 and on May 1, 1992, liquidation was initiated. The main purpose of liquidation was to sell the firm in order to preserve most of its assets and, if possible, jobs. The details of the process will be discussed later.

Product and Markets

Mokasyn produced men's casual, hand-sewn shoes of the moccasin type. Shoes from Mokasyn, unlike those from the neighboring giant, Odra, were not well known but were mainly sold on the local, rural market. Also, Mokasyn had been a significant exporter to the Soviet Union; in some years, over 80 percent of its output was sold there. While visiting the enterprise, we tried to buy shoes in the factory-sponsored shop but found the products very cheap and unattractive. Typical of many shoe producers in Poland, the available goods were long-lasting but poorly designed.

In the early 1980s, Mokasyn produced over 800,000 pairs of shoes, but this figure dropped to 600,000 later in the decade. In quantity terms, Mokasyn could be described as a mid-size shoe manufacturer. The largest firms in Poland produced ten times that many each year.

Fixed Assets

Most buildings in the leading plant in Rybowo dated back to the 1960s and were in decent condition, although not roomy enough to house modern assembly lines. We did not visit the plant at Ptaszkowo, but our host said that its buildings were in much worse condition. Machinery and equipment there had been bought in the mid-1970s, with only minor additions in the 1980s, and virtually no investment had been made in the last five years. Given this situation, it was surprising that fixed assets at Mokasyn had been depreciated by 55 percent, the machines alone by 70 percent.

Labor Force and Management

Mokasyn had employed over 500 people, but that number was reduced to 305 by the end of 1991, and fell to a mere 235 as a result of the recent separation of the Ptaszkowo plant. There were no lay-offs in the enterprise, and the figures reflect natural attrition. Labor shortages, always a problem at Mokasyn, led to output reduction during the 1980s. Second shifts had to be eliminated, even when the demand was high, because people were not attracted by the low wages, hard working conditions, and modest level of social benefits. In this respect, Mokasyn could not equal the larger Odra, which had facilities and holiday houses at the seaside.

This situation, especially with regard to qualified labor, improved somewhat in early 1991 when the liquidation of Odra began. Good craftsmen from that enterprise could survive on their severance pay and unemployment benefit and, therefore, were unwilling to take jobs at Mokasyn at the going wages. Paradoxically, wages at Odra had not been higher than at Mokasyn, but laid-off employees, after some period of idleness, were normally able to find some source of income in the shadow economy and did not want to resume employment in the state-owned sector at the standard wage. Managers at Mokasyn told us that they had been willing to employ some of the workers who had been released by Odra on a temporary contract basis, which would enable Mokasyn to pay them higher wages. This proved to be impossible because of the protests of the regular employees.

Wages at Mokasyn, which usually lagged behind the low national average for the sector, reached $95 per month in 1990 and, despite a 70 percent inflation rate, grew the next year in nominal zloty terms by only 46 percent to a level of $124. Let us add that wage dispersion at Mokasyn had always been low. White-collar employees earned about 120 percent of the firm's average wage, and between 1988 and 1991 this dispersion gradually increased.

Unions had never been strong at Mokasyn in terms of numbers, but it would be a mistake to infer weakness in terms of representation from this fact. The OPZZ union was small and passive, but Solidarity had an active leadership. The chairman was a high-ranking official of the regional authorities, employed by the union rather than the enterprise. He was very outspoken, frequently attacking not only the management, but also the voivod, for not doing enough to save the firm. We were shown newspapers with his fiery statements, and the situation was widely discussed in the city. The unions at Mokasyn had a long record of conflict with the management, and the management said that the unions had undermined all efforts to restructure the enterprise. Interestingly, the workers' council was not dominated by the union and remained on good terms with the management. This may have been because the workers' council was mainly composed of administrative and supervisory staff, whereas the unions exclusively represented the blue-collar workers. The conflict in Mokasyn was perceived as a class conflict.

Mokasyn has had little luck with management in the last few years. Problems began in 1990 when the Solidarity committee accused the manager of being a die-hard communist and forced him to resign. In fact, he had been in his post for twelve years and therefore must have had good relations with the local party chiefs. Probably no harm would have been done to the firm had a new manager been chosen and assumed his duties immediately. However, no appointment of new management was made for the next six months. In order to find a manager, the *voivod* sponsored a public competition. The chosen candidate was a young engineer from Mokasyn. The workers' council accepted him, but, on the day he was to assume his new job, the union attacked the results of the competition. In early 1990, it was not difficult for Solidarity to cancel the nomination, even though it was against the law. Not surprisingly, no candidates appeared for the second competition. The worried *voivod* (the enterprise's "founding organ") took the initiative and organized a third round, suggested a candidate from outside the enterprise, and obtained all necessary approval for him. This new general manager was an engineer with some managerial practice in another SOE in Rybowo. However, the damage was done, and for half the year, no meaningful decision was made and current business was run by the deputy manager in charge of technology. This deputy manager was respected and friendly, but could not have been a candidate for manager because he had no university education and was a practitioner who had worked for Mokasyn from its inception. Recently he had suffered a heart attack and was now resting. Asked about the roots of the conflict between the workers and management, he pointed to the cooperative traditions surviving at Mokasyn. What he had in mind was that in a cooperative, all workers were formal co-owners and had the right to participate in the decision-making process, or at least to speak out at one of the regular meetings of shareholders.

The third member of the management, the deputy in charge of economic affairs and sales, had reached pensionable age two years before and subsequently that post had been left open. Only in July 1991 did the chief accountant absorb some of these duties and become chief economist. Overall, the management at Mokasyn was in a poor state for most of the difficult period of 1990–92. With vaguely defined job descriptions, frequent vacancies, and no solid economic education, the people running the enterprise, all of whom were in their late fifties and thinking in traditional terms, were ill-equipped to put it in order.

On top of this, the wages of management were disastrously low. Suffice it to say that the latest wage of the general manager was 3.2 million zloty plus 800,000 zloty as a functional bonus, i.e., under $300 a month. This was an obvious consequence of the conflict with the unions, which the manager did not want to intensify with managerial pay raises at a time of general wage restraint in the enterprise. In a sense, the problems with management ended with the introduction of the liquidator and his team in May 1992.

SHOCKS OF TRANSFORMATION AND THE INSUFFICIENT REACTION TO THEM

In the prevalent shortage economy of the 1980s, even poor-quality products could be sold on the domestic market. The always-hungry Polish consumer would accept nearly anything, although this situation started to change during the second half of the decade. The Soviet market was open and could readily absorb everything that was left. Production runs were long, design uncomplicated, and quality requirements not very stringent. The cozy position of the producer was only slightly limited by the need to adhere to the delivery terms. Soviet customers characteristically demanded on-time deliveries and immediately charged penalties for any delay. Workers in Soviet-oriented enterprises therefore worked overtime when necessary but produced very low-quality goods.

Mokasyn was an exporter to the Soviet Union, but even there, with sales fluctuating widely over the last decade, its position did not seem stable. For example, one year the entire output might be exported, but the next, only 40 percent. It was safe to say that Mokasyn's market position and its future had always been uncertain. In such a situation, even in the old system, it was difficult to make long-term plans, invest, and consciously build the profile of the firm.

In 1990, Mokasyn was granted a large export contract to the Soviet Union that was a part of protocol trade. The agreement was made centrally and run exclusively by Skorimpex, a foreign trade enterprise from Lodz and a sole exporter of leather products from SOEs. Mokasyn had no part in negotiating the contract and was merely to deliver the shoes on time. The contract must have been a decent one, with prices exceeding the level usually obtained in Poland. All in all, the USSR bought almost 230,000 pairs, roughly one half of yearly output, and the enterprise even received payment from the foreign trade enterprise with no delay.

But costs grew faster than prices, and even the income from the Soviet contract could not prevent a serious drop in profitability. In 1990 profits remained at roughly the nominal level of the previous year, which translated into a rate of profit decrease of 37 percent gross and 16.7 net in 1989, falling to just 7 percent and 4 percent in 1990, bearing in mind that output in physical units dropped by one-sixth.

In 1991 the real troubles began and, with the collapse of Polish-Soviet trade even for more "serious products" than shoes, the enterprise had nothing to bail it out. In another study of light industry that we carried out, we got the impression that the disappearance of the Soviet market probably hit the footwear industry harder than any other subsector of light industry in Poland. We know that two much bigger and better shoe manufacturers experienced similar problems and also ended in liquidation or bankruptcy. One may only add that those firms were even less fortunate than Mokasyn because their contracts with the Soviet Union broke down as early as 1990, and they did not have time to adjust as Mokasyn apparently had.

With the deliveries to the East absent in 1991, output in pairs fell by half, exactly the volume sold to the USSR; domestic sales continued to decrease. Inventories of finished goods at the end of 1991 reached a level of 5.1 billion zloty compared to 1.5 billion a year earlier. In terms of average monthly sales, inventories grew from fifteen days' to two months' sales, not much at normal liquidity flows. These data were based on inventories accounting and, judging from the data on output, inventories must have reached a level of about three months' sales.

Although our discussion partners either did not know or deliberately gave us a low figure, according to our rough calculations, the selling price in 1991 doubled in comparison to the previous year, and yet the sales of Mokasyn in nominal terms went down from 34.3 billion zloty to 30.6 billion in 1991. This shows the depth of the crisis. In the middle of the year, Mokasyn began to register increasingly larger losses. For the whole of 1991, the net loss reached 4.6 billion zloty; in the first five months of 1992 it grew to 3.9 billion.

Let us note that the gross margin on the current sales, even with the turnover tax, was positive in 1991, but the interest costs and extraordinary losses, such as penalty interest on overdue payments, drowned the enterprise. In fact, it is surprising, even immoral, that a firm maintained a positive gross margin using 40 percent of its production capacity.

This focuses our attention on the immediate consequences of the slumping sales, i.e., the mounting liquidity problems that led to the accumulation of debts. Inter-firm credit payables nearly doubled in 1991, increasing from 5 billion to 9 billion zloty. Tax arrears on a larger scale appeared in 1991, with short-term bank credit stabilizing at over 3 billion. It is interesting that, because of maneuvering and trickery, Mokasyn officially lost creditworthiness only very belatedly, just before the liquidation procedure started. Previously, the overdue credit was reclassified, despite the fact that the enterprise was not able to service it from the beginning of 1992. This is reflected in the fact that overdue credit appeared in the books as late as May 1992.

Growing interest costs and the impact of increasing penalty charges proved to be too great a burden for Mokasyn. According to the management's estimates, in order to maintain net profitability in light of these additional costs, the firm would have to sell about 1,600 pairs of shoes per day. During 1991, however, the level of output slipped to 500 pairs per day. Moreover, with weak domestic sales, stagnant wages, and poor prospects of the firm in general, the whole production process seemed to disintegrate. Qualified workers began to leave gradually, forcing production to be limited to one shift. This was at the time when the firm wanted to employ laid-off people from Odra, but union resistance made this impossible and the labor force, paradoxically, became a bottleneck. In 1992, when the firm signed an export contract with an American firm, problems became acute, leading to overtime work.

A 1991 shortage of liquidity caused frequent work stoppages. Mokasyn could not afford to buy raw materials, and delays in wages further aggravated the lingering conflict with the unions. Faced with this rapidly deteriorating situation, the management's first reaction was to allow debts to accumulate. Output was curtailed, but not sufficiently, as shown by the growing inventories. Further, no one had the marketing experience to launch a sales campaign to increase sales, and there were no means with which to hire specialists, nor any investment to significantly change the product mix. Management tried two options. Because of increased fixed costs, a decision was made to liquidate one of the plants located outside Rybowo. Machines were sold, the building rented out, and the workers laid off. They were offered jobs in the leading plant, but rejected this idea.

The most valuable employees, especially qualified craftsmen, tended to leave the firm, but the weaker, less productive workers stayed. Also, a large number of administration employees, remnants of the days when the enterprise consisted of more units, produced more shoes, and employed more people, were a burden. Therefore, an attempt was made to rationalize employment. The necessary attrition met with strong resistance from the workers' council and both unions, the latter reacting with a hint that the first to go should be the general manager.

A casual analysis of the 1991 cost structure suggests that labor costs were the only item of significant growth, despite output decreasing by half. Cost cutting was not a practical option to save Mokasyn. While an expansion of production and sales was feasible, such expansion required working capital, good designs, and markets, none of which was available. The management realized that external assistance was indispensable.

In early 1991, the general manager got the workers' council's consent to prepare the firm for privatization. Mokasyn was addressed by American Financial Services, an investment promotion enterprise from Warsaw examining the possibilities of American investments in Poland. They sent a consulting firm to analyze the economic situation and a potential buyer. This was presented to us as a capital group from Missouri. Mokasyn seemed to be ready for sale by means of privatization through liquidation. A price of 13 billion zloty, about $1.25 million, was quoted unofficially, but, because of the rapidly deteriorating financial situation at Mokasyn, the Americans withdrew, although they remained in touch and have not entirely lost interest.

A by-product of the contacts with American Financial Services was an export contract for an undetermined quantity of shoes. An American trade enterprise called Pagoda supplied the design and cardboard boxes for packaging, made a prepayment for leather and other materials, and virtually started financing Mokasyn. As a result, about half of the diminished output was then directed to the United States. This is not fully reflected in the statistics because the contract had only just been signed, even though negotiations started in 1991. The contract with Pagoda was not a panacea, but instead prolonged the agony. The negotiated price was very low because it had been determined many months before and costs had grown. It was agreed, however, that the price would increase after the first successful delivery, thus assuring a minimal rate of profit for Mokasyn. A positive consequence of the contract was the necessity to reorient the production process and to change the attitude of the workers. The operation seemed to be successful and could be beneficial in the long run, if not for Mokasyn itself, then for its next owner.

Overall, the very modest adjustment efforts proved unsuccessful but were not totally useless. Admittedly, not much could be done by an incomplete management in deep conflict with the unions. Any contact with the Western market would be beneficial both for Mokasyn's management and for the workers confronted with new quality requirements.

LIQUIDATION

With Mokasyn submerged in debts and internal conflict, the very existence of the enterprise was challenged. At any moment creditors could lodge claims and bring about bankruptcy. They did not do this, however, fearing that their chances of extracting dues were poor, as the state budget and banks would have priority in debt repayment. It was even suggested that Mokasyn declare bankruptcy but continue operations. This is usually very damaging for the creditors because the proceeds from sales are not used to repay debts but rather for current needs such as wages and raw materials. At the same time, as in most bankruptcy cases, all overdue obligations are frozen and penalty interest charges stop accumulating. In fact, the financing bank had already done this for Mokasyn in 1992, granting yet another favor for the embattled enterprise.

The *voivod* started the liquidation procedure at the request of the workers' council. The aim was to save as much as possible of the enterprise and try to secure the jobs if possible. Mokasyn's liquidation was based on Article 19 or the 1981 Law on State-Owned Enterprises, concerning enterprises in bad economic conditions. This law is very similar to that for liquidation for privatization (Article 37 of the 1990 Law on Privatization), except that the latter is initiated in a situation where the prospects of privatizing a firm are clear. A fundamental difference between these two cases is that a firm liquidated according to the SOE law cannot be rented or leased, for example, to the employees and management. It should be sold entirely or in part, or its assets may be put into a new joint-venture company. Also the role of the Ministry of Ownership Transformation differs, being an active one in the liquidation-for-privatization procedure.

The liquidator is nominated by the *voivod* or the Minister of Industry and assumes the responsibilities of general manager. The *voivod* determines his wages, usually much higher than that of the former manager, but the firm must cover this and all other costs of his activity. The liquidator can, and in most cases does, nominate a team of plenipotentiaries, who need not come from within the enterprise. He is not expected to prepare a restructuring plan or to try to preserve the enterprise in its existing form. Rather, his role is to sell the assets of the liquidated firm in the best interest of the owner, which in this case was the state. The notion of "best interest" is a little vague because it may mean the highest price; or selling to a person able and willing to use the resources in a proper way; or selling the firm as a unit or in parts, to keep the assets intact. This latter tendency can be spotted when an insider, such as the former manager, is in charge of liquidation and tries to find an apparently painless solution, either by seeking a buyer who will keep the firm and its employment intact, or by implementing some sort of restructuring program, engaging in debt rescheduling negotiations, signing new contracts, incurring additional credits, etc. In most cases this is a waste of time and decreases the value of the disposable assets. A preferred solution is thus to have a liquidator from outside the enterprise.

A firm in a state of liquidation is not free of obligations. As long as it continues to produce, it must pay the dividend due the state. This covers the costs of sick pay, and the number of people on sick leave during liquidation grows by leaps and bounds. Maternity pay is assumed by ZUS, the state social security system, but the enterprise must cover all current and liquidation costs from revenues. As a rule, these are insufficient to cover costs, and the longer the liquidation process, the worse the financial circumstances of the enterprise.

At Mokasyn, the liquidator was an outsider, the chairman of a local consulting firm. He gave the impression that he was not going to waste time. After all, he had his own consulting firm to run. Under his auspices, the former management was dismissed, but still received wages because, formally, they were on leave. The liquidator nominated two plenipotentiaries, an engineer from outside the firm to run the production process, and the former chief accountant to be in charge of financial and economic affairs. Because the assets of a liquidated firm may be sold to the public, announcements were placed in newspapers informing the prospective buyers of the terms and procedures of the sale.

It was decided to sell the two plants of Mokasyn separately. The price of the main plant was set at 13 billion zloty, or under $1 million, and the Ptaszkowo plant at 1.4 billion zloty. The sale of Mokasyn was difficult. There was no interest shown in the initial price offer. When we visited in mid-July 1992, the sale of the Ptaszkowo plant had progressed as far as the notary's office, with a few problems yet to be cleared up. It was purchased by a private investor from Poland for 600 million zloty. This covered the buildings, machinery and equipment, and land in the form of an "eternal" rent for ninety-nine years, and all obligations and receivables were assumed by the state. The new owner intended to produce footwear using machines from Odra and the former GDR. Because space in the Ptaszkowo buildings was scarce and modern assembly lines would not fit there, a nest system of production was to be used. This is less modern, but in light of the poorly qualified labor force, would be cheaper and more efficient. In July, talks with the former employees of Mokasyn were under way to determine who would and could continue to work there.

Selling the Rybowo plant was even more difficult. There was no response to the first offer. Finally, after additional offers, negotiations were started with a group of local private entrepreneurs who owned a chain of large wholesale stores and had some interest in Mokasyn. However, by July, negotiations were still far from finalized. The most recent offer was a managerial contract whereby the firm would remain an SOE, a new management would be installed by the managerial group, and the workers' council would be disbanded. This managerial group would have the right to buy the firm before other customers, after a certain time period to be negotiated in the contract. There was no guarantee, however, that this purchase would be made, in which case a declaration of bankruptcy would be seriously considered.

CONCLUDING REMARKS

Mokasyn was never a leading enterprise in the industry. Thus, when the sector found itself in a crisis, it was no surprise that this firm was hit very hard. In our opinion, the difficulties faced by Mokasyn were not inevitable. Being a small firm, it probably had a relatively good chance of adjusting and surviving in the harsh conditions of the transition.

We had the impression that the problem was not so much the mediocrity of the firm's products, as it was able to adjust quickly to the requirements of the American client. Rather, it was the lack of managerial skills in dealing with the union leadership that prevented the firm's restructuring. After a period of hopeless drifting, ended by the *voivod*'s decision to liquidate the firm, the future of the firm would depend on the liquidator's efforts and negotiation skills.

Table 1

Structure of Costs (in percentages)

Specification	1988	1989	1990	1991	January–May 1992
Wages	21.04	26.43	20.62	31.82	46.16
Materials	69.15	62.82	65.54	58.67	36.70
Energy	0.81	1.04	1.25	—	2.45
Banking charges (incl. interest)	0.40	1.87	7.72	4.56	14.09
Depreciation	0.43	0.17	0.49	1.52	2.43
Property tax	0.13	0.03	0.14	0.30	—
External services	8.07	7.64	4.24	3.13	—
Total	100	100	100	100	100

Table 2

Main Financial Indices (in million zloty)

Specification	1988	1989	1990	1991	January–May 1992
Net sales	2,041.5	8,059.5	32,064.0	26,110.0	6,241.0
Costs of sales	1,695.3	5,804.9	28,646.0	25,278.0	7,279.01
Markup (1 − 2)	346.2	2,254.6	3,418.0	832.0	−1,038
Costs of obtaining revenues	—	—	—	—	1,157
Financial revenues	0.6	11.3	56	41	1,162
Financial costs	—	—	—	2,596	600
Operating profit [3 + (4 − 5) + (6 − 7)]	346.8	2,265.9	3,474	−1,723	−1,543
Extraordinary profits	1.95	2.8	190	88	29
Extraordinary losses	13.4	107.8	1,656	3.061	1,044
Gross profit/loss (8 + 9 − 10)	335.3	2,160.5	2,008.0	−4,696.0	2,558
Taxes	223.1	1,252.2	890.0	74.0	15.0
Gross profit/loss (11 − 12)	112.2	908.7	1,118	−4,746	−2,573

Table 3

Profitability Ratios

Specification	1988	1989	1990	1991	January–May 1992
Markup (operating profit)/sales	16.96	27.97	10.66	3.19	−16.63
Gross profits/sales	16.42	26.81	6.26	−17.99	−40.99
Markup (operating profit)/cost of sales	20.42	38.84	10.66	3.29	−14.26
Gross profits/costs of sales	19.78	37.22	6.98	−18.58	−35.14
Net profit/cost of sales	6.62	15.65	3.90	−18.78	−35.35

Table 4

Liquidity and Activity Ratios

Specification	1988	1989	1990	1991	January–May 1992
Liquidity ratios					
Working capital/total assets	0.81	0.46	0.20	—	—
Current ratio	6.87	1.91	1.35	0.86	0.74
Quick ratio	0.93	0.65	0.65	0.42	0.40
Activity ratios					
Account receivable turnover	7.18	10.24	9.04	4.38	0.99
Average collection period (days)	50	35	40	82	364
Payments turnover	6.48	5.60	5.34	2.15	0.41
Average payments period (days)	56	64	67	167	878
Inventory turnover	9.37	7.58	8.59	4.35	1.26
Average inventory turnover (days)	38	47	42	83	286

12

Plastics: Boryszew-Erg

Anna Krajewska

SECTORAL SETTING

The production line of Boryszew-Erg, S.A. (in Sochaczew, near Warsaw) was quite differentiated, and included radiator fluids, floor coverings, thermal stabilizers for plastics, and plastic barrels. It is rather difficult to classify the firm in any single industrial branch, but, since most of its output can be classified among the plastics industry products, the industry will be treated here as a reference point.

The plastics industry consisted of five state-owned companies, which, in the early 1980s, belonged to an amalgamation. Later, amalgamations were replaced by voluntary associations of enterprises, most frequently grouping firms from different industries, but there were no institutions uniting or coordinating the firms in the industry; instead, they competed with each other.

The financial circumstances of plastics-producing enterprises were difficult, but none was currently on the verge of bankruptcy. Until 1991, the best economic results were found at Gamrat-Erg of Jaslo, which was also the largest firm in the sector. At the time of this report, however, this firm was confronted with a strong competitor, a West European firm that was entering the Polish market with plans to launch large-scale production of plastic pipes. Of the remaining firms, the one producing mainly for the army had the greatest chances for survival and the government intended to preserve it.

Plastics production, based mainly on domestic raw materials, was primarily intended for the domestic market; due to the low quality of products and ineffectiveness of production, exports did not play a large role. Competitive imports had been rather insignificant, but recent changes in price relations were beginning to cause domestic customers to purchase foreign plastic products because of higher quality and diminishing price differentials between the foreign and domestic goods.

The capital stock, particularly of machinery and equipment, of the plastics industry was rather obsolete, not having been replaced, for the most part, since the 1970s. In 1990, the total depreciation rate of fixed assets amounted to 54 percent, of which buildings constituted 37.8 percent, machines and equipment 71.9 percent, and means of transportation 62.8 percent. Due to major cuts in investment expenditures, which meant fewer available resources, and high interest on credits and difficult access to them in recent years, fixed assets depreciation rates had grown. Total employment in the industry decreased from 8,500 in 1989 to 8,300 in 1991 and 7,800 in September 1992.

The sales of plastics in constant prices had declined during 1989–91 by over 10 percent each year, mainly as a result of shrinking domestic demand and intensified financial difficulties (see Table 1 for basic data). Data for the first nine months of 1992 indicated, however, that sales had rebounded and a healthy growth rate for 1992 would be recorded.

The financial condition of the firms had also deteriorated rapidly, as may be seen in Table 1. Subsidies were quite insignificant, at 0.3 percent of the value of sales during 1988–90, and about 0.1 percent in 1991. Also, in 1991, receivables and claims constituted over 50 percent of working capital, inventories of manufactured products about 12 percent, and cash over 7 percent. Short-term bonds were very rare, and the ratio of payables to receivables amounted to about 70 percent.

HISTORY OF BORYSZEW-ERG, S.A.

The firm was established in 1911, the first owner being the Belgian Association of Rayon Factories. During World War I, rayon production was abandoned and the manufacturing of smokeless powder was begun. In 1922, the firm was acquired by the French-Polish concern Pocisk i Nitrat, which expanded the production of powder and initiated the manufacture of pharmaceutical products, including dental cement, which was well known in Europe. Smokeless powder production was expanded on a large scale before World War II. During the war the factory was seriously damaged and most of the production equipment was removed to Germany. A forced labor camp, which later became a POW camp for Soviet soldiers, was opened in the area of the factory, and the Germans started both an alcohol distillery and an installation for the rectification of ethyl alcohol.

After the war, the factory was rebuilt using equipment from the disassembly of other plants and equipment revindicated from Germany. The production of radiator fluids, *borygo*, was launched in 1948, and in 1950, the first plasticizer in Poland was installed. Plastics were first made from dibutyl ph-thalate and, then from dioctyl ph-thalate, which is still used today.

During the Korean War, production for the army rapidly expanded. In the late 1950s, the current production profile gradually emerged, and the firm began to specialize in the production of auxiliary items for the manufacturing of plastics at a time when plastics production was steadily growing. Polyvinyl chloride was introduced for the production of floor coverings. In the 1970s, the department for this product was enlarged and the technology of its production was mechanized and automatized. This time period also witnessed a large-scale development of miscellaneous plastics such as large containers, pipes, boxes, barrels, baskets, and bowls.

PRESENT POTENTIAL OF BORYSZEW-ERG., S.A

In 1992 sales reached $18 million; average employment in the same period amounted to 714, as compared to 985 in 1988. Main products manufactured in 1991 included radiator fluids, which amounted to 21.8 percent of sales, floor coverings, at 15.8 percent of sales, and thermal stabilizers for plastics, at 11.7 percent of sales. Production was based only on Polish technology, since no foreign license had been bought. The enterprise had its own research and development laboratory and a construction department, and cooperated with the Warsaw Polytechnic, the Institute of Organic Industry, and the Institute of Industrial Chemistry. The management personnel were graduates of the Warsaw Polytechnic and vocational schools, and most employees were from families of which the second or the third generation was linked with the firm.

Since the capital stock was outmoded, production costs were quite high and new items seldom introduced. In addition, the available production capacities were underutilized, the capacity utilization rate having dropped from about 63 percent in 1988 to about 35 percent during 1990–92. The shift coefficient was 1.27, and had not undergone any major changes in recent years. For technological reasons, some machines and equipment were operated twenty-four hours a day, which necessitated four six-hour shifts.

Before 1992, the enterprise had owned a large portfolio of social assets, including several hundred flats, a sixty-bed hotel for workers, a canteen, a few cafeterias, a seventy-bed holiday resort, and a cultural center. However, due to the shortage of financial resources, this social-welfare activity had become restricted. In 1992, all social assets were transferred to the local, or communal, authorities. Moreover, the firm donated about 3 billion zloty to the commune to cover part of the exploitation costs of these objects. The operation was one of the conditions set by the Ministry of Ownership Transformation when the enterprise applied for commercialization.

SHOCK CAUSED BY THE TRANSFORMATION

The system transformation initiated at the beginning of 1990 seemed to be a big shock for the firm. Both the withdrawal of the government from its role as owner-supervisor and protector and the new fiscal and monetary policy surprised the management. Until 1989, the firm had been certain of its extreme usefulness, as confirmed by the great demand, difficult to satisfy, for its products. In 1990, however, the firm first realized that its future existence was not unquestionable and obvious.

The most important changes resulting from the transformation included:

- the elimination of administrative control over prices;
- the collapse of domestic demand, especially for products used in agriculture;
- the adoption of a stringent tax system whereby high taxation of profits was accompanied by a consistent departure from government subsidies, tax reliefs, exemptions, and postponements; and
- the introduction of a very restrictive credit policy.

These changes resulted in a 40 percent decrease in output over two years, and created increasing difficulties for the firm in fulfilling its obligations. This was reflected in decreasing profitability, as shown in Table 2; a growing tax burden, accumulating payments arrears, especially in 1992, when the relation between receivables and payables changed very unfavorably; and rapidly diminishing possibilities of modernizing the capital stock.

In 1990, the firm had not yet perceived any major threats. Because of favorable circumstances delaying the deterioration of its financial standing, its profitability was still high, and at the same time the new economic policy created numerous opportunities, the most important being increased autonomy, especially regarding price setting, which permitted high profitability until the demand barrier appeared on the domestic market, and easier access to production factors (until 1989, the shortage of materials, machines, and labor was the main factor restricting the firm's activity).

Certain specific sectoral characteristics, which facilitated the transition of plastics-producing enterprises through a period of shock, included insignificant subsidies at the end of the 1980s; small burden of outstanding credits; weak foreign competition; modest links with foreign markets, including export, import, capital, and technological; stable assortment structure of production; a friendly attitude and some degree of protection from the state, partly as a result of production for the army. These factors appeared in the analyzed firm. We could also mention some specific features of Boryszew-Erg, such as the insignificant burden of the dividend and the tax on excessive wage increases, the stable and relatively well trained personnel, diversified production allowing a flexible adjustment to fluctuations in demand on different markets, and the small expansiveness of domestic competitors in their struggle to preserve the market position, the only exception being the newly launched production of brake fluid for cars by Plock Refinery, sold under the brand name Petrygo, which closely resembled the Borygo brake fluid produced by Boryszew-Erg. As a result, Boryszew-Erg brought a suit against Plock, accusing it of stealing its brand name. The charge was decided by the court in the second half of 1992 in favor of Boryszew.

The early easy possibilities of obtaining a gratifying profit could hardly exert a pressure on the management to adapt to the new system. In the second half of 1990, the possibilities of raising prices radically diminished, while the costs tended to grow. In 1992, the prices of goods sold by Boryszew grew by a mere 15 percent, because of low domestic demand and intensifying import competition, and it became necessary to search for new ways of operation, which led to changes in organization and management of the firm.

CHANGES IN ORGANIZATION AND MANAGEMENT

All the directors were replaced in 1990. Since it was recognized that the previous directors had not managed to work out a program that would guarantee survival of the firm, the workers' council announced a competition for the post of managing director. In May 1990, the current manager of the production department, a 46-year-old chemist, became the managing director. He was activist of the regional committee of Solidarity, and had worked for Boryszew-Erg since 1970, the beginning of his professional career. The previous chief engineer, thirty-six years old, was appointed deputy in charge of technical matters, and the previous chief of production, fifty-two years old, took the post of deputy in charge of production and marketing. All the above were graduates of Warsaw Polytechnic. The previous deputy chief accountant assumed the position of the chief accountant. She was fifty years old, with a secondary school background, but had completed various training courses. All the directors and the chief accountant had started their careers at Boryszew-Erg.

Since 1989, there had been several changes in the organizational structure of the firm, including the establishment of a marketing department and the strengthening of the trade, economic, and financial departments by increasing the number of employees and their wages, and reducing the role of the hitherto dominant divisions of production and production services. It should be noted that these changes marked only the beginning of what was desired. Unfortunately, there was a shortage of highly qualified employees in these fields, and older employees had difficulty adapting themselves to the new economic system, while younger ones lacked the proper experience. These problems were also confirmed by the top management composition: an engineer was responsible for the economic and trade division; the chief accountant had only a secondary school education; the economic and trade departments were too weak as yet to be able to put forth a realistic long-term program of sales opportunities, based on market research, and propose directions of changes in the firm; and the management responsible for the divisions of production and production services was greatly dissatisfied with its steadily lowered position in recent years, and tried to push through technical criteria to solve the firm's problems.

SHORT-TERM RESPONSES

In 1990, the goods manufactured by Boryszew-Erg were still in deficit on the domestic market. The firm could sell all its products, even obsolete ones, without difficulty, but this changed radically, probably in late 1990. Demand declined rapidly as higher quality and price considerations became crucial for the consumer. Output dropped by about 40 percent in 1991 as compared to 1989. Particularly acute was the decrease in demand for plastic products used in agriculture, forcing the firm to reduce output of these goods by about 70 percent. Progressive growth of production costs squeezed the profitability of export sales to the extent that its share of total sales declined from 10.8 percent in 1988 to 8.3 percent in 1989, 5.3 percent in 1990, 4.5 percent in 1991 and, in 1992, export production was completely abandoned.

Besides giving up this unprofitable sales sector, the firm undertook a series of positive measures as a response to changing market conditions, the most important of which seemed to be the following:

- *changes in the product mix:* after 1990, new products accounting for about 20 percent of total output had been introduced at Boryszew, however, a more fundamental restructuring in this respect was hampered by lack of sufficient financial resources;
- *efforts to reduce costs,* mainly through a search for suppliers of cheaper materials, savings of water and energy, and rationalization of transport costs; here, also, major investments were needed to bring about more significant savings;
- *reconstruction of distribution practices:* before 1990, the main customers had been large state-owned manufacturing and trade companies. During 1990–91, the majority of state-owned trade companies were liquidated or they restricted their activities drastically. The demand for state manufacturing companies also decreased substantially. On the other hand, there was increasing demand from small private firms, the result being that the firm needed to maintain contacts with several hundred firms and not with ten or so, as was the case a few years earlier. The role of the sales department also increased, as more in-depth market analyses and a more aggressive sales policy became necessary;
- *attempts to sell or lease the redundant productive and nonproductive assets:* the enterprise had sold a small part of its unnecessary productive property, but further sales were difficult because of the technical nature of the property and a lack of buyers; also, the workers' council and trade unions objected to the sale of the social assets;
- *changes in the wage system:* the system was simplified and made more transparent for the workers, and many nonfixed elements and bonuses were eliminated. Wages of the rank-and-file employees now consisted of two parts: a fixed salary and a flexible increment dependent on the sales volume. Wages of the top management depended partly on the volume of net profit, and more dispersion of wages was allowed in order to stimulate efficiency and strengthen the incentives for the supervisory staff.

It is not that easy to say whether any of these measures contributed to the improvement of the firm's situation, but the fact is that, particularly in the second half of 1992, sales accelerated visibly. It was estimated that 1993 sales would attain a level of 330 billion zloty, or $19–$20 million, with net profit climbing to around 18 billion zloty.

LONG-TERM RESPONSES

The main element of the enterprise's long-term adjustment program was privatization. The plan, prepared by the managing director, was privatization through liquidation of the state-owned property, followed by a takeover of assets in the form of leasing by the present employees. This meant that they would control the majority of shares in the future. Within this framework, a stock firm was formed in December 1991, with the managing director as chairman, and the deputies as members of the board. The firm was to be liquidated in December 1991. However, serious delays occurred, mainly due to the sluggishness of the central administration, especially the Ministry of Ownership Transformation. A liquidator, though not the one proposed by the managing director, sent from Warsaw by the ministry, did not appear until late June 1992. He did not interfere with the current management of the firm, but performed only his formal duties.

Some employees and the trade unions—Solidarity, with its approximately 500 members was the strongest in the firm, while the OPZZ-affiliated branch trade union numbered only 15 persons—were critical of the privatization program, fearing that it would allow the top management to reap excessive benefits. Despite these problems, in July 1992 the stock partnership Boryszew-Erg, S.A., began operations. Only legal persons, mostly employees of the former SOE, Boryszew-Erg, were shareholders. Equity capital was about 32.2 billion zloty, or $2.3 million, and the top management acquired 10 percent of stock, the rest of the shareholders about 80 percent. Because there was no demand within the firm for the last 10 percent, people from outside Boryszew were allowed to buy it. At the end, about 72 percent of the current employees and many retired workers owned shares of the firm. The acquisition of these shares was greatly facilitated by the firm itself. Employees could take credit, at a symbolic interest rate of 1 percent annually, from a special fund created from the undistributed profits of 1990–91, and there was no limit as to how much one person could buy. At the beginning, hesitation and lack of confidence prevailed, but later, the mood changed so that almost no one was willing to sell shares, although there were persons willing to buy. The management hoped to repay all obligations incurred in the leasing contract as early as 1993–94 and, according to the managers, in three to four years, a sizable dividend could be expected to be paid out regularly.

The next important element of the long-term adjustment was to be an investment program that would improve quality and reduce costs. Several million dollars would be needed to implement this program, although the enterprise did not have the necessary financial resources, and was not seeking credit in Polish banks because the interest rate was too high. One French bank had agreed to grant such credit, but Boryszew-Erg did not obtain a guarantee from Polish banks, since its financial condition was considered unsatisfactory, and therefore the project had to be put off for the moment.

No serious attempts had been made to link the firm with foreign capital on a more permanent basis. In fact, many talks had been held, but potential investors had not entered into concrete negotiations, most probably discouraged by the protracted nature of the firm's privatization, its highly differentiated production profile, and the unstable political and economic situation in Poland. The managers, moreover, had no clear vision of the extent to which cooperation with foreign partners should be taken.

MANAGEMENT'S PERCEPTION OF THE FIRM'S POSITION AND PROSPECTS

According to the board of directors, the present situation in Boryszew was evaluated as difficult, but better than in most other enterprises in the industry or in the town where the firm had its headquarters. The directors did not perceive at present any major threats to the firm's existence, and the situation was expected to improve if the following occurred: the government elaborated and began consistently implementing an industrial policy that would support firms in their restructuring efforts; the firm obtained cheaper investment credit; and the recession ended and domestic demand grew.

CONCLUDING REMARKS

One could agree with the general evaluation of the firm's situation as presented by the members of the management team; however, according to them, possibilities of improving the situation were dependent on favorable external circumstances. This may very well be true, but changes in internal organization and management effected thus far seemed fairly shallow. The process of changing mentality and implanting a market-oriented approach had just begun and would need to be continued, but a more active policy of strengthening the firm's position on the market and seeking new selling opportunities was also necessary.

A well-conceived investment program that would secure a comparative advantage on the market could be necessary to survive in the long run, since the market for chemical products was becoming more competitive, although at a slower pace than some other markets. The firm did not see any immediate possibilities of using a zloty-denominated investment credit, because it carried too high an interest rate, but instead was investigating the possibilities of obtaining foreign credit. There was, however, a trap here. With rapidly declining exports, a drop in the exchange rate of the zloty could considerably increase the real costs of such credit and undermine the viability of the whole project. For this reason, among others, the enterprise would need to more actively seek opportunities to export its products, especially to the Eastern markets, which were less demanding of quality.

Table 1

Basic Data about the Plastics Industry

Specification	1988	1989	1990	1991	1st–3rd Quarter/92
Sales in current prices (billion zloty)	107	2,981	2,343	2,447	2,188
Sales in constant prices (preceding year = 100)	106.4	101.8	75.4	84.8	101.4*
Production of plastics (thousands of tons)	723	721	627	593	466
Number of employees (thousands)	8.6	8.5	8.4	8.3	7.8
Average monthly pay (thousand zloty)	61.6	220.6	1,051.9	1,776.8	2,311.5
Profitability ratios:					
Gross profit/cost of sales	—	56.4	34.8	14.9	8.9
Net profit/costs of sales	—	—	—	2.5	2.3

Source: Statistical Yearbooks of Industry (Central Statistical Office, Warsaw 1989, 1990, 1991). *Naklady i wyniki przemyslu I–III kwartal 1992*, Central Statistical Office, Warsaw, December 1992.

*1st–3rd Quarter 1991 = 100.

Table 2

Main Financial Indicators of Boryszew-Erg (in percentages)

Specification	1988	1989	1990	1991	January–November 1992
Profitability ratios					
Gross profit/costs of sales	21.5	57.7	50.3	16.1	11.2
Net profit/costs of sales	12.9	28.7	26.4	7.3	5.1
Tax on gross profit	40.1	46.7	47.5	54.4	54.3
Share in gross profit of:					
Income tax	40.0	37.3	39.3	36.3	39.0
Dividend	—	5.3	3.8	12.1	9.3
PPWW tax	0.1	4.1	4.4	6.0	6.0

Specification	1988	1989	1990	1991	January–May 1992
Relation between receivables and sales	15.5	22.1	11.0	16.1	59.4
Relation between payables and sales	12.6	25.1	14.8	14.3	49.5
Relation between investment outlays and net value of fixed assets	17.9	49.7	9.1	15.1	2.1

13

Pharmaceuticals: Polfa Enterprise

Anna Krajewska

SECTORAL SETTING

The Polish pharmaceutical industry consisted of thirteen enterprises. Most were large entities comprised of several plants with a rich production profile that included the production of bulk pharmaceuticals through chemical synthesis and fermentation as well as the manufacture of dosage-form products such as tablets, suppositories, etc. There were also several smaller firms making mainly dosage-form products. All firms had formerly belonged to a compulsory amalgamation called Polfa, and later to an association of similar enterprises. Major research and development projects of this industry were handled by the Pharmaceutical Institute, established especially for this purpose, but, in addition, all enterprises had their own research and development units. A new partnership, called the Scientific Information Center, Polfa, that grouped all pharmaceutical establishments, had been established recently.

Pharmaceuticals produced by Polfa supplied about 65 percent of the domestic market's needs. Herbal medicine and vaccination- and antidote-producing enterprises, along with some twenty smaller, recently established private firms, supplied another 20 percent, and the remaining 15 percent was imported.

In the past, the pharmaceutical firms had been very profitable, largely as the result of exports, especially to the USSR. Even quite recently, Polfa had been the main supplier to Eastern markets, satisfying about 15 percent of their needs. The firm's current situation was not as bright as it had been in the past, but was still much better than that of the sector as a whole, as the data in Table 1 show. The following factors were contributors to the decline of financial stability:

- the collapse of exports to the former CMEA;
- continuation of administrative price regulation covering about 50 percent of the drugs produced in Poland, meaning that prices were 25 percent lower

419

than production costs, and firms then had to make up the losses by increasing nonregulated prices;
- growth of imports, stimulated by real depreciation of foreign currencies and deregulation of their prices; private pharmacies preferred to deal in imported drugs, due to their higher prices and higher margins. Imported pharmaceuticals were, on average, four times more expensive than their domestic counterparts;
- drop in domestic demand for drugs, a result of the pauperization of society, price increases, and the previous introduction of a full payment policy for certain drugs;
- declining profitability of exports to the West, caused by both the relative stability of the dollar exchange rate and strong domestic inflation.

Financial stability deteriorated most in the large pharmaceutical firms dealing with chemical synthesis and bio-synthesis, while those involved exclusively with the manufacture of dosage-form products fared much better. The entire Polish pharmaceutical industry, however, was facing the need for substantial investment outlays to introduce the technology for sterile production and to obtain the necessary certification for their products in the West. Currently, most firms were unable to accomplish these tasks by relying solely on their own resources, but the industrial policy designed by the government a year earlier designated the pharmaceutical industry as a sector needing greater assistance from the state.

In 1991, when the Ministry of Ownership Transformation was preparing both a mass privatization project and one on sectoral privatization, Polfa was an object of interest. Up to then, only two pharmaceutical firms had been commercialized, the others having developed no vision of their ownership transformations as yet. It was often pointed out that the best solution would be to form a holding company of all interested pharmaceutical enterprises, the argument being that this would be the best way to fend off foreign competition. This idea had many supporters within the industry who wanted more concentrated efforts in the fields of research and development, investments, and marketing. Some managers, however, were very cautious about the idea, fearing a loss of independence and a possible revival of centralizing tendencies.

HISTORY AND GENERAL CHARACTERISTICS OF POLFA IN PABIANICE

Polfa, in Pabianice, dated back to 1889, when Ludwik Schweikert established the Factory of Destructive Wood Distillation. The factory also supplied synthetic dyes to manufacturers of cotton wool and silk fabrics both locally and in nearby Lodz. In 1899, the German owners, Schweikert and E. Froechlich, who had become a joint owner in 1894, entered into an agreement with the well-known Swiss pharmaceutical firm, Ciba. After World War II, the factory was nationalized.

The sodium sulfide department accounted for the largest share of production, followed by sulfur and azo dyes, and then formic acid. In 1951, the Amalgamation of Pharmaceutical Industry Companies took over the factory's production line, and Polfa gradually expanded into a chemical and pharmaceutical complex consisting of six separate plants. During the early postwar years, the enterprise manufactured a variety of products based on relatively simple technology. In the course of time, especially after an investment project completed in 1963, the firm's production profile became that of a highly specialized pharmaceutical firm with complex technology at its disposal. The production of dyes, however, was never neglected.

At the time of this report, Polfa's production included the following: pharmaceutical synthesis, dye synthesis, pharmaceutical bio-synthesis, bio-synthesis for agriculture needs, dosage-form drugs and their necessary punches and molds for all pharmaceutical firms in Poland, and final forms of dyes (standardization). To sum up, the firm produced about 110 different drugs for human and veterinary use, accounting for 85 percent of total sales; the remainder consisted of dyestuffs for the textile and leather industries. Total sales in 1990 amounted to $30 million, in 1991, $36 million, and in 1992, $21 million.

In 1991, exports accounted for 25 percent of total sales, 89 percent of which was pharmaceuticals sold exclusively to the former CMEA, and 11 percent consisted of dyestuffs, sold mainly to Western countries, such as the United States, Italy, Portugal, and Turkey. The capital stock of Polfa was quite varied. A small percentage of the machines and equipment reached world standards, but most were about twenty years old, with some being much older. The rather poor research and development facilities allowed only imitation of external achievements, with no possibility of self-improvement through the development of new products. The firm's range of social facilities, however, had become fairly extensive, with its own 180-bed seaside holiday resort, full catering equipment, cultural and recreational amenities, and a nearby forest holiday center for children that had 120 beds, many recreational facilities, a sports field, video equipment, and computer games.

SHOCKS CAUSED BY THE TRANSFORMATION

Major macroeconomic shocks included a restrictive fiscal and monetary policy, stringent financial discipline imposed on the firm, and an overly liberal customs policy. Foreign drugs were imported free of duty. Customs tariffs of 3–50 percent were introduced on imported raw materials, but customs duties on raw materials from the EC were suspended in 1992. This was of little help, because Polfa imported most of its supplies from India and South Korea. Another shock was a drop in living standards, leading to shrinking domestic demand for drugs. Additional factors restricting the demand for Polish-made drugs included the import of competing drugs by private pharmacies, supplies of medicines donated to hospitals by the West, and the removal of state subsidies for some drugs. These factors caused a 40–50 percent decline in domestic demand for Polfa's drugs.

The collapse of exports to the former CMEA markets also created problems. The entire pharmaceutical industry, including Polfa, had been strongly linked to these markets. In 1988, 56.5 percent, and, in 1989, 55.2 percent of Polfa's output had been exported, with the majority going to the CMEA countries. The CMEA received 93.3 percent of total exports in 1988, 89.8 percent in 1989, and 85.7 percent in 1990 but, in 1991–93 this dropped to about 40–50 percent. The collection of payments for exports to the USSR also became difficult, further aggravating Polfa's financial condition. In 1991, the governments of Poland and the USSR agreed on a barter deal whereby drugs imported from Poland were to be paid for with Russian natural gas. The Soviet government fulfilled its obligations, leaving an appropriate quantity of gas at the disposal of Ciech Foreign Trade Organization, which was supervising the execution of this agreement. Ciech, in turn, sent the gas to Polish power-generating enterprises. These firms, however, did not fulfill their financial obligations toward Ciech, which consequently could not pay Polfa. This also happened to other pharmaceutical firms and, by the end of 1992, Polish exporters of drugs to the USSR had accumulated receivables worth of $128 million, i.e., 60 percent of the amount due from the 1991 barter deal. At Pabianice, these overdue receivables totaled 54 billion zloty, or some $4 million. Because identification of the economic entity that did not fulfill its obligations toward Polfa was difficult, it was decided that the amount would be treated as an extraordinary loss.

Also problematic were changes in the distribution network. In the centrally planned economy, the entire output for the domestic market had been distributed to pharmacies and hospitals by Cefarm, the state-owned wholesaler. Now, however, Cefarm handled only about 50 percent of domestic sales, the remainder being purchased directly from Polfa by about 380 small private wholesalers.

The combination of these factors produced a number of negative consequences. Among the most important were the following:

- substantial cuts in output: no major drop in production was recorded in 1990, but in 1991, production fell by about 40–50 percent of the preceding years' output: in 1992, there was a further decline of about 20 percent;
- an increase in average fixed costs that decreased profitability;
- an increase in the prices of many inputs, while 50 percent of output was subject to price regulation; this was reflected in a decline of the mark-up from 95.1 percent in 1989 to 28.8 percent in 1992. The mark-up is the difference between value of sales and costs of sales, reduced by the turnover tax;
- the extraordinary 54 billion zloty loss mentioned earlier, recorded in mid-1992: because current production was profitable, the net loss for the year only amounted to 30 billion zloty, as shown in Table 2;

- growing inventories of both finished goods and raw materials: the former increased from 4.6 percent of total inventories in 1989 to 34.8 percent in mid-1992, while the latter grew from 9.4 percent in 1989 to 18.7 percent in 1992. Cuts in output and sales caused an ever greater part of working capital to be tied up in inventories so that by May 1992, total inventories equaled 105.4 percent of sales during the first five months of 1992.

SHORT-TERM RESPONSES

Changes in Organization and Management

Polfa was a one-plant enterprise headed by a managing director and four deputy directors: a deputy in charge of production and technology, a deputy for development, a deputy for administration and marketing, and a chief accountant responsible for finance. Since the early 1980s, the top management of the enterprise had remained almost unchanged. The managing director and the production director had held their positions since 1982, and the administrative and marketing director had held theirs since 1980. A new director for development had been appointed in 1990, and a new chief accountant in 1989, because their predecessors had retired. The managing director and the deputies were 47 to 59 years old and, with the exception of the chief accountant, were graduates of the Lodz Polytechnic. All had worked at Polfa for many years and, with one exception, they had started their professional careers there and had been gradually promoted to higher posts. One director was hired after completing secondary school, but graduated from the Lodz Polytechnic in the course of his employment. Only the chief accountant had a secondary school economic education. She had been working at Polfa since 1989, before which she worked in the financial department of the paper industry amalgamation. All directors maintain contacts with several Western pharmaceutical firms through trade contacts, seminars, and exhibitions.

The present directors were accepted by the workers' council and by both Solidarity and the OPZZ-affiliated trade unions. An open competition for the position of managing director was organized in 1990 and, although there were several candidates, from both within the firm and outside it, the winner was the current managing director, who kept all other directors in their posts. The principles of remunerating the management were changed after the competition. Previously, the founding organ, the Ministry of Industry and Trade, had determined the salary of the managing director, while the remuneration of the deputies was regulated by the so-called autonomous, or intra-firm, wage system. Currently, however, this remuneration system remained at the discretion of the workers' council. The managing director's pay consisted of a basic salary, which was 6.5 times the mean national wage of the preceding three months, a seniority bonus, and a commission from profit. The deputies' pay was comprised of a basic salary, a functional allowance, a seniority bonus, a premium of about 30 percent of basic salary, and a commission from profit. The latter was figured at 200 percent of the managing director's commission, divided among four deputy directors. After the competition, the pay of the managing director rose considerably, while that of the other directors increased by about 10 percent.

Because there were no plans to change the existing structure of the management, the most significant organizational changes would include the creation of a marketing department (in July 1992) and of a firm-owned wholesale center and store, and changes in the information flow system. These changes were among recommendations of a French firm, Bossard Consulting, which was hired by the Ministry of Ownership Transformation in 1991 to prepare a program of sectoral privatization for the industry.

Short-Term Adaptations in Production and Employment

As previously mentioned, reduced demand led to a 40–50 percent drop in output in 1991, and 20 percent in 1992. The enterprise was surprised by the new situation, and it was unable to develop a quick survival strategy. It therefore responded in a passive way. Among other things, it cut production and exports, increased inventories of finished goods, and did not pay its debts. The only symptom of more active adjustment was an attempt to broaden the product range to give potential customers a wider choice, and to ensure prompt deliveries. But this did not work, and inventories of finished goods continued to grow, especially in 1992.

In the short run, it was difficult to cut costs. Also, some costs were increasing. Depreciation costs rose because of the revaluation of fixed assets. Property taxes increased. Social security contributions increased to 43–45 percent of the wage bill. Standard income tax increased by 20 percent in 1992, and interest costs rose. Employment had been stable over the years, reaching nearly 1,300 people at the end of 1992, as compared to 1,447 in 1988. This made employment reductions difficult, due to both social and economic reasons. The Lodz region had been acutely affected by unemployment. Moreover, training newly hired personnel, or paying severance payments in group lay-offs, meant that maintaining the present level of employment was generally sensible from an economic point of view. This was reinforced by the belief that demand would soon pick up. In a situation like this, even if the share of labor cost in total costs were to grow, temporary work stoppages and mandatory holidays would be preferable. See Table 3 for details on production costs.

Markets, Prices, Sales

The collapse of the CMEA markets, which had absorbed nearly 50 percent of the firm's entire production, resulted in rapid cuts in production. The barter deal between Poland and the USSR, and its unfortunate execution in 1991, created losses reaching 54 billion zloty. A complete collapse of exports to the former Soviet Union occurred in 1992. In the first half of 1992, exports to the former Soviet Union represented 1.3 percent of the total exports, as compared to 60.8 percent in 1991. This did not mean, however, that Polfa intended to abandon the former Soviet market. During 1992, the firm continued to maintain contacts with potential customers in Ukraine, Belarus, and Russia. Moreover, in 1993, a government agreement, worth U.S. $94 million, on drug exports between Poland and the Commonwealth of Independent States was being prepared, and Polfa hoped to play a large part in this transaction. There was also possible participation in drug deliveries to the Ukraine using U.S. $12 million allocated by the EEC.

The management believed there was a chance to regain a considerable part of the former USSR market, despite increasing competition from numerous Western companies. Also, more postcommunist countries were entering these markets. For instance, according to the managers, in 1992, Czechoslovakia purchased from Polfa a drug called Biseptol in quantities far exceeding the needs of its internal market, and started selling it in Ukraine.

A two-price system was used by Polfa. It consisted of free prices for dye-stuffs and about 50 percent of its drugs, and official prices for about 50 percent of pharmaceuticals on the official list of drugs, which covered about 60 percent of all drugs produced by Polfa. Official prices were changed once or twice a year, which, given the constant growth of the production costs, reduced the profitability of production.

The firm viewed export expansion as a chance to maintain a good financial standing for two reasons. The fixed costs per unit produced would be reduced, and profitability would be higher than in domestic trading. In 1991, export profitability was more than three times higher than the overall profitability of the firm's sales.

Another short-term adaptation concerned the distribution system. Formerly, the state-owned Cefarm Wholesale Company had been the only wholesaler, but as a result of the transformation, Cefarm now handled only about 50 percent of sales. Another 380 or so private wholesalers sold the rest, and a reorganization of the sales department and expansion of the marketing department were necessary. The firm also became more actively involved in the direct sales of its products. It opened a wholesale center and a pharmacy, and intended to use some buildings at its holiday center for the next wholesale warehouse or to lease them to another firm for this purpose.

Taxes, Credits, Finance

Polfa had not obtained any government subsidies in the period under review. Until 1990, it had paid its taxes to the state. In 1991 and 1992, however, the payment of these taxes was delayed because it was having trouble collecting payments from its customers. At the end of 1992, its tax liabilities reached 10 billion zloty. Taxes on the gross profit grew from 63.8 percent in 1991 to 85.4

percent in 1992, mostly due to a declining volume of profit. The dividend tax was not a major burden for the firm, but the growth rate of excess wage taxes was, as shown in Table 4. Even in mid-1992, when Polfa was recording losses, it continued paying wages higher than the inflation-indexed limit would allow, and thus it incurred sizable tax debts. The management believed, however, that the markup obtained on the current production, at a profitability rate of about 30 percent, and the prospects of collecting the amount due for the exports to the USSR in 1991, justified the wage increase and was not a problem for the firm. And, indeed, in June and July the firm obtained a part of the money due it. We should note, however, that the wage level at the Pabianice firm was about 15 percent lower than in the pharmaceutical industry as a whole.

Thus far, Polfa had used little short-term credit, and had obtained no long-term credit. In 1990, it obtained a loan of 9 billion zloty from the Committee of Scientific-Technical Progress to be used for an investment project on environmental protection. This committee was a governmental agency in charge of stimulating national research and technological progress. However, in 1993, Polfa also planned to seek long-term credit to finance a production line that would meet the requirements of the Good Manufacturing Practice (GMP).

Polfa had attained a satisfactory profitability level from its current operations, and cash-flow problems only occurred because the firm could not stop the accumulation of overdue receivables. We mentioned the consequences of the Soviet deal, but Cefarm also caused problems. The former wholesaler was still Polfa's most important customer, but regularly delayed payments for up to six months. The firm had to tolerate this because Cefarm was Polfa's main access to the domestic market. Without this wholesaler, the market would be flooded with imported drugs. As a result, both receivables and payables grew, and Polfa was forced to finance its customers. (For details, see Table 5.)

LONG-TERM RESPONSES

Ownership Changes

In 1991, because Polfa was interested in privatization, it was included in a list of 400 enterprises selected for mass privatization. In July 1991, it was to be commercialized, and Polfa employees were chosen for the supervisory and management boards. Later, however, the Ministry of Ownership Transformation (MOT) changed its concept of mass privatization and decided to privatize only 200 firms at one time. Polfa was also of interest to the MOT when sectoral privatization was being organized. A French firm, Bossard Consulting, worked at Polfa for two months, preparing a program to include Polfa in this type of privatization. This firm was financed by the Western assistance funds for Poland. Polfa paid the consultants' living costs, and employed two interpreters for the two months, each of whom earned 32 million zloty a month. These high wages were required by the consulting firm, but were an outrage for the local people. The consultants prepared an organizational format and a timetable for restructuring. According to the top management, this program was not well suited to the present needs of Polfa. The consulting firm found it very difficult to compile a cost account and conduct economic analyses in such conditions of high inflation.

At the time of this report, there were no immediate privatization plans at Polfa. This decision was probably influenced by the experiences of two other pharmaceutical firms that were commercialized. Commercialization is not the same as privatization, but rather a first step toward it. These firms did not reap any greater tax benefits as a result of commercialization and, in fact, they had less independence in decision-making, due to the interference of the supervisory board. Polfa's management was convinced that the firm should continue to be state-owned for some time. It also felt that the firm's best organizational form would be that of a holding company that would control the existing pharmaceutical firms.

Changes in Structure of Production, Investments, and Cooperation with Foreign Partners

Polfa believed that its survival and growth lay in regaining lost markets and maintaining or expanding the present level of exports to the West. It also felt that only large-scale production would be profitable. For these plans to be realized, however, the production of internationally certified drugs under sterile conditions (GMP) was necessary, and this would require investment. The firm had received two offers of investment in this project, an Italian one and a Czech-Austrian one. The project would cost about U.S. $10–$11 million, and Polfa had financial resources for about 20 percent of the cost. This amount would be sufficient to cover the costs of the construction. The firm also planned to secure the necessary funds for equipment and technology by means of a World Bank credit, and had already made the first moves toward obtaining these funds. The project was expected to expand the production profile by about 30 percent, which would maintain exports to the East at the previous level and expand exports to the West.

The firm's next goal was to establish stable cooperation with well-known French, Swiss, and Austrian pharmaceutical firms and conduct joint marketing ventures with them. A few years ago, these firms had expressed interest in cooperating directly with Polfa, but Poland's political instability had been given as the reason for a lack of concrete plans on the part of these parties.

Evaluation of Adaptation Processes and Polfa's Prospects

The directors of Polfa were very optimistic about its chances for survival. Much of this optimism rested on the possibility of long-term, foreign-currency-denominated credit granted on better terms than those offered by the domestic banks. If the capital investment were properly used, production could be diversified, and the necessary certification for exports to the West secured.

Management's conviction that the state would not leave the firm on its own, because it was a major producer of drugs, was a bit disturbing to us. It was also possible that the government would be neither willing nor able to offer much assistance to enterprises in trouble. Besides, Polfa's situation was comfortable compared to most other Polish firms, and it had enough potential and reserves to continue on its own. Indeed, the directors seemed to underestimate both the present problems and the opportunities that could be alleviated by disciplined and competent internal management and more aggressive marketing. Maintaining the traditional production range and not trying to enter the booming market for paramedical products that bordered on cosmetic may have been a mistake. A private firm specializing in paramedicals had been established in the area, and it was flourishing.

At the same time, external factors were blamed for the deterioration of Polfa's financial circumstances. These included the collapse of the Eastern markets, the faulty economic policy of the state, a poor tariff policy, a lack of guarantees supporting exports to the East, price regulations, and excessive taxes. Even if these factors did contribute to the firm's financial straits, stressing them seemed counterproductive to the current needs of the enterprise.

Because most of the managing personnel had a technical university background, they perceived the firm from the viewpoint of its production potentialities. Cost and financial management, market research, and the like, were things they had only started to learn. Because Polfa had been in good economic shape in 1990, and in some respects in 1991, this learning process began later than in those firms that were hit badly from the onset of transformation.

Table 1

Basic Pharmaceutical Industry Data

Specification	1988	1989	1990	1991	1st–3rd Quarter 1992
Sales in current prices (billion zloty)	267.2	671.9	3,995.9	7,409.5	4,822.0
Sales in constant prices (preceding year/period = 100)	106.8	102.6	75.4	114.5	66.6
Employment/(thousands)	21.8	21.3	20.2	21.0	21.0
Mean monthly pay (thousand zloty)	61.9	220.0	1,071.4	1,878.2	2,493.3
Profitability ratios					
Gross profit/costs of sales	—	92.3	72.3	75.3	25.6
Net profit/costs of sales	—	—	—	35.2	11.5

Source: Statistical Yearbooks of Industry (Central Statistical Office, 1989, 1990, 1991). *Naklady i wyniki przemyslu I–III kwartal 1992*, Central Statistical Office, Warsaw, December 1992.

Table 2

Financial Results of Polfa/Pabianice in 1988–1992 (in million zloty)

Specification	1988	1989	1990	1991	January–April 1992	1992
Net sales	18,695	47,732	290,425	416,204	124,959	331,965
Costs of sales	11,397	24,462	157,749	262,200	97,011	257,792
Markup	7,298	23,270	132,676	154,004	27,948	74,173
Remaining incomes	239	650	108	23,751	8,735	21,813
Costs of obtaining revenues	8	—	—	20,264	7,630	17,786
Financial revenues	—	—	—	2,969	1,084	11,416
Financial costs	—	—	—	10,453	9,426	16,321
Operating profit	7,529	23,920	132,784	150,007	20,711	73,295
Extraordinary gains	69	3,965	10,266	17,314	7,361	36,366
Extraordinary losses	184	453	11,260	10,942	58,351	65,537
Gross profit/loss	7,414	27,432	131,790	156,379	–30,279	44,124
Tax burden	4,390	5,632	60,861	99,742	8,045	37,683
Net profit/loss	3,024	21,800	70,929	56,637	–38,324	6,441
Profitability ratios (in %)						
Operating profit/costs of sales	64.0	95.1	84.1	58.7	28.8	28.8
Gross profit/costs of sales	65.1	112.1	83.5	59.6	–31.2	17.1
Net profit/costs of sales	26.5	89.1	45.0	21.6	–39.5	2.5

Table 3

Structure of Production Costs (in percentages)

Specification	1988	1989	1990	1991	1992
Labor cost	11.3	20.5	14.6	15.4	22.6
Material inputs and energy	75.0	62.0	70.2	68.5	60.4
Banking charges (incl. interest)	1.0	0.4	3.3	3.5	5.6
Depreciation	1.7	1.3	2.7	4.3	4.9
Land and property taxes	0.5	0.2	0.5	0.5	0.8
External services and other	10.5	15.6	8.7	7.8	5.7
Total costs	100.0	100.0	100.0	100.0	100.0

Table 4

Taxes Paid from Gross Profit (gross profit = 100)

Types of taxes	1988	1989	1990	1991	1992
Income tax	59.0	15.3	37.5	43.0	44.1
Dividend tax	—	2.5	1.1	1.0	2.5
Tax on wage increases	0.2	2.7	7.6	19.8	38.8
Total tax burden	59.2	20.5	46.2	63.8	85.4

Table 5

Payables and Receivables of Polfa

Specification	1988	1989	1990	1991	January–November 1992
Receivables (mil. zl)	1.652	11.882	27.398	75.534	67.896
Payables (mil. zl)	1.447	12.772	14.080	15.155	3.226
Receivables/payables	1.14	0.97	1.98	4.98	22.54

14

Auto Parts: Polmo Enterprise

Anna Krajewska

SECTORAL SETTING

Polmo was one of twenty-six state-owned enterprises that made up the Polish automobile industry. This group included seven assembly plants, including two enterprises manufacturing passenger cars, and nineteen firms manufacturing automobile parts. The output and assortment of particular enterprises depended on the needs of automobile manufacturers. Production specialization was narrow and, in principle, each firm in the automobile industry held a monopolistic position on the domestic market. Polmo in Lodz produced carburetors, fuel pumps, brake suspensions for automobiles, and compressors for tractors.

In the 1970s and 1980s, the auto industry held a prestigious position in Poland and was able to obtain financial resources readily for central investments, research and development, and purchases of licenses and patents. The growth of individual enterprises was determined by growth of the auto industry as a whole, which was centrally determined.

During the period of economic transformations and recession, the industry experienced a collapse that, in 1991, resulted in a 40 percent decline in real output compared to the preceding year, and a gross profit rate for the entire industry of −15.3 percent. Truck and military equipment manufacturers had little chance of survival, but those that manufactured passenger cars began to establish cooperative ties with Western firms such as Fiat, Peugeot, Volvo, General Motors, and Volkswagen. In turn, the survival of auto parts manufacturers depended on the car and truck manufacturers. An overall policy and an active role on the part of the state were perceived as crucial to the survival of the industry.

Only one enterprise in the industry had been privatized. Fiat purchased 90 percent of stock in FSM, which now produces the small Fiat 126p and, more recently, Fiat's new sub-compact, the Cinquecento. FSO, an automobile manufacturer from Warsaw (Polonez), was negotiating a deal with General Motors, but other firms with deteriorating financial condition had less chance of attracting foreign capital, and this was made worse by the growing interest of Western automobile manufacturers in investments in the former Soviet Union.

HISTORY AND GENERAL INFORMATION ABOUT POLMO

The state-owned firm Polmo was formed in 1948 through the merger of eight castings and auto-parts manufacturers that had been established at the beginning of the twentieth century. The oldest, Ferrum Iron Foundry in Lodz, established in 1908, had had a production profile similar to that of the present firm. One of the prewar plants, incorporated into Polmo in the 1930s, had produced not only auto parts but also aircraft and motorcycle parts, engines, garage equipment, and trailers. In 1936, it had about 300 employees.

Polmo consisted of three plants: Plants A and B in Lodz, and another in Dabie, a township 70 km from Lodz. The value of the firm's 1991 sales was $16 million, and its 1992 sales, $12 million. Export sales accounted for only 4.3 percent in 1991 and 6.1 percent one year later. The 1991 employment of 1,547 persons had shrunk to 1,360 in 1992. The enterprise had always manufactured auto parts, beginning with engines for agriculture and radiators for Ursus tractors and Star 20 trucks, followed by carburetors for motorcycles. In 1968, the firm opened a subsidiary at Dabie and started to manufacture carburetors and fuel pumps for the Fiat 125p under licenses from the Weber and Corona enterprises. The next important step came in 1971, when the production of compressors was moved from FSM Bielsko-Biala to Lodz. Polmo was expanding quickly and had, at that time, 2,700 employees. Other items were produced under a Westinghouse license, and output was augmented by products designed by the firm itself.

The production of tractors in Poland under the Ferguson-Perkins license was seen as a further means of expanding the firm. Investment credit was obtained in the second half of the 1980s to construct Plant B at Lodz to manufacture the compressors and pumps for this tractor. The investment project came on line in 1987, giving Plant B a production capacity of 120,000 compressors for tractors per year. It was built according to plan and 80 percent of its equipment was installed. However, because the agreement with Ferguson-Perkins was suspended and the prospects of tractor production in Poland were unclear, much of Plant B has been idle. Only 20,000 compressors were produced in 1988 and production was completely suspended in 1992. This was because Ursus limited its orders to such an extent that inventories could cover the demand for the next two years. Machines, equipment, and buildings remained idle. Meanwhile, Polmo systematically repaid both the principal and the accrued interest of the investment credit. However, a deal was agreed upon whereby the yearly installments were fixed in nominal terms up to 1996. The effective use of this investment project would depend on decisions by the Ursus firm concerning the production of tractors. For 1993, a preliminary order of 8,000–10,000 compressors had been already placed.

IMPACT OF ECONOMIC REFORM

Polmo was a typical sub-supplier that relied heavily on orders from automobile manufacturers. In 1988, 56 percent of the firm's production went to auto manufacturers and 7 percent to producers of agricultural machines. The collapse of the automobile industry, a result of reduced domestic demand, lower exports and government orders, and increased competitive imports, led to sharp cuts in orders for auto parts. Of the remaining 1988 production, 14 percent was exported and the rest consisted of spare parts sold to auto owners. Because 93 percent of exports were intended for the markets of Czechoslovakia and Hungary, and 5 percent went to the USSR, the economic difficulties of these countries also resulted in shrinking demand for Polmo's products.

Another factor undermining the firm's position was increasing imports of competitive products. The liberal customs policy of 1990–91 caused an influx of imported carburetors and other auto parts manufactured by Western firms, mainly in Italy and Germany.

Naturally, the reduced demand for the firm's products necessitated major cuts in output. With 1988 as 100, management estimated that output during 1989–92 was as follows:

1989	90–95 percent
1990	80 percent
1991	60–65 percent
1992	42–45 percent (estimated)

Output of the main assortments produced by the firm, where 1988 = 100 was as follows:

	1989	1990	1991
Carburetors	88.5	95.3	68.1
Fuel pumps	91.7	81.9	54.0
Air compressors	90.4	40.8	21.7

The declining demand of its traditional customers made it necessary for the firm to broaden its position as a typical sub-supplier to that of a producer for the market, and to change its market orientation from exports to the former CMEA to exports to Western Europe.

The new economic policy also caused an increase in unit production costs, namely in average fixed costs due to lower output, in material costs due to price liberalization, in labor costs because of a slower decline in the size of employment than in output, and in the cost of credit. On the other hand, the economic transformation created opportunities for the firm by giving it the freedom to change prices and product mix and to choose suppliers and customers.

SHORT-TERM RESPONSES

Changes in Management and Organizational Structure

The firm was headed by the managing director and was divided into the technical division, the production division, the economic division, and the accounting division, all of which reported to the managing director. The most important recently introduced organizational changes were the establishment of a marketing department and the enlargement of the firm's two stores.

An open competition for the position of managing director took place in 1990. Several people from both inside and outside the firm applied for it but it was won by the incumbent managing director. This man had been with Polmo since 1958. He had started as a blue-collar worker but then completed a secondary vocational school course and finished at the Lodz Polytechnic with a degree in mechanical engineering. A few years later, he took a two-year economic course for engineers. During his thirty-five years of work at Polmo, he passed through all levels of employment, holding the posts of chief engineer from 1975 to 1978, deputy director for technical affairs from 1978 to 1982, and managing director from 1982 onward. After winning the open competition, he then made two changes in the top management team. He dismissed the technical director for reasons of incompetence, and he shifted the production director to the position of a plenipotentiary responsible for a new quality system. This decision was prompted by both political and professional reasons: the former director, who had been a member of the Polish United Workers' Party Central Committee, had been appointed to that post by the Communist Party. He was an inefficient manager and the employees were glad to have him dismissed.

There was no change in the positions of economic and trade affairs director or chief accountant. The former had held this post for nine years, was forty-eight years old, and had an M.A. in economics. The previous chief accountant retired in 1991 after many years of service at this post. The job then passed to a forty-eight-year-old woman with a secondary school economic education and about fifteen years' experience in Polmo's financial department, much of it spent as deputy manager. The newly appointed technical and production directors were graduates of technical universities and had worked for the firm for about twenty-five years.

The careers of the directors indicate that they could be classified as the former nomenklatura; however, the managing director and his deputies were all accepted by the workers' council and the trade unions. The relationships between them were quite satisfactory and there had been no major conflicts. In the turbulent month of December 1992, when the regional committee of Solidarity polled its membership on staging industrial action, only 12 percent of Polmo employees voted to strike.

The management style of the directors could be described as paternalistic. Despite major cuts in production, group lay-offs were avoided. The several-percent-per-year employment reduction was due to retirements and voluntary departures. For economic reasons, the plant at Dabie, which employed 120 people, needed to be liquidated, but the management delayed this decision mainly for social reasons. Dabie is a small town and people who were dismissed would be unable to find another job. In hindsight, the managers admitted that they should have closed down the plant three years ago when labor shortages were still common. At present, they claimed employees would "resort to scythes, if they saw their machines being moved to Lodz."

The wage and welfare policies were also affected by social concerns. The directors were doing what they could to maintain wages at a level higher than the inflation-adjusted wage index, but this also made it necessary to earmark part of profit for the excess wage tax.

Polmo had no intention of disposing of its social assets: a holiday center, which consisted of lakeside summer cottages equipped with a canteen and sanitary facilities. The costs of maintaining this center were covered partly from the firm's social-welfare fund and partly by employees who used it, and the management said that they would continue to do so as long as possible because of their long attachment to the firm and the need to protect employees' interests. This was possible because of the relatively good financial condition of the firm. They did realize, however, that in the near future, especially once the firm obtains a foreign partner or investors, this center may need to be abandoned.

Production and Sales

During the 1980s, Polmo had a monopoly on manufacturing carburetors, fuel pumps, and specific types of compressors. Under the "economics of shortage," the demand for its products was much greater than its production capacities, and priority was given to exports and to supplies for those automobile manufacturers who dealt with the firm. This was part of the existing system of input rationing and the system of incentives for management and employees. In 1992, output was 50 percent of that in 1988 and would have been much less except that the firm decided to supply auto parts directly to end users of cars and trucks. To this end, the firm expanded the marketing department, created a network of its own dealers, and enlarged the two stores attached to its production plants in Lodz and Dabie.

At the time of this report, Polmo contracted with about fifty dealers in Poland. These dealers could buy parts on preferential terms, such as a lower margin and a thirty-day collection period. Agreements were signed with dealers specifying the volume of sales and terms of payment, and these contracts were re-evaluated annually. At first, the firm experienced difficulty in collecting receivables from some dealers, but this situation had been remedied and cooperation with dealers was proceeding smoothly. As may be expected, the structure of the firm's customers has undergone major changes, as shown in Table 2.

Profitability of Polmo

The data depicting the firm's financial situation are found in Table 3. Throughout the period of this study, the firm achieved very good financial results as measured by different profitability ratios. These results were considerably different from those recorded in the automobile industry, a difference that was most pronounced in 1991; the ratio of gross profit to sales reached 23.3 percent at Polmo while the automobile industry as a whole recorded losses (Table 1). In 1992, the firm still had a decent financial situation, with a gross profit rate of 14.0 percent.

The extremely high gross profit rate of 1989 was inflationary in nature, whereas the high profits in the following years were caused by totally different factors. For example, in 1990, Polmo's change from sub-supplier to direct-market supplier of spare parts produced a profitability that was about 50 percent higher than that for the industry, a result of the weak financial standing of the automobile manufacturers.

Also in 1990, the firm had hard currency reserves, which, when exchanged for zloty at a favorable exchange rate, provided a financial cushion. Moreover, during the last few years, including 1992, Polmo relied on inventories of materials, raw materials, and semi-manufactures purchased earlier at relatively low prices.

An increasingly large amount of total income was coming from sources other than direct market sales, i.e., sales of products in the firm's stores, leasing some of both its productive and nonproductive assets, shares in other firms, interest on its savings in banks, etc. Part of its production premises was leased as a wholesale warehouse, and the previous canteen and all its facilities had become a disco. Whereas in 1988, 99.7 percent of the firm's income had come from sales of its products, in May 1992 this represented only 81.9 percent.

During the period of this study, the firm had adopted measures aimed at improving its performance. In order to reduce costs, employees began to perform part of material and nonmaterial services, thus replacing the services of external units. Moreover, the firm quickly switched to the manufacture of many components previously purchased from outside and also provided many services for other firms. In addition to reducing production costs, these measures also created additional work for Polmo's employees. In fact, the share of external services in the firm's total costs dropped from 13.8 percent in 1988 to 4.6 percent in 1992. These data are shown in Table 4.

The work force was also reduced from 1,885 in 1988 to about 1,370 in 1992, a decrease of 11.4 percent. To further cut costs, the use of bank credits was reduced. Despite a considerable increase in interest rates, the share of banking charges and interest in total costs remained at a fairly constant level of 5.1 percent in 1988 and 4.8 percent in 1992. Lastly, one cost-cutting measure was the rational use of inventories.

Inventory Management at Polmo

Polmo was a prime example of the changes in inventory management in the new economic environment in Poland. In 1988–89, the firm maintained huge inventories of materials such that, at the end of 1989, its level exceeded annual consumption by 16.2 percent. This excessive accumulation had been deemed necessary for several reasons. First, large material inventories helped to maintain an uninterrupted flow of production and also reduced the fairly common risk of delays in supplies. Furthermore, because credit was cheap and easily accessible, rational financial management was unnecessary. Also, excessive inventories of certain materials were sometimes imposed by monopoly suppliers who would refuse to deliver small quantities of goods. Lastly, there was a deliberate accumulation of inventories of cheap materials in an attempt to reap a profit from the inflationary growth of prices.

All these reasons for accumulating inventories have lost their meaning under the present circumstances, although monopolies still sometimes try to force larger deliveries than needed, even though the quality of their products remains poor. Because of the high interest rates, speculative storing of inventories declined, although at a slower rate than would be expected, given the economic constraints. Additionally, some inventories were materials that were either not very useful in production or had become unnecessary because of major changes in the assortment structure of production.

Another problem in the unwanted accumulation of inventories was the growing quantity of finished goods and work-in-progress, the latter often hiding inventories of the former. This was a result of deficient demand, the consequence of which is that the positive effect of diminishing inventories of materials was being neutralized by growing inventories of finished goods, which in turn reduced the liquidity of working capital of the firm. For data on this, see Table 5.

Liquidity and Working Capital Turnover

The data in Table 6 indicate that, despite positive profitability during the analyzed period, Polmo had difficulty maintaining a satisfactory level of liquidity. The share of working capital in total assets increased somewhat and the current ratio improved also, but the quick ratio fell to 0.87 in 1992. Moreover, turnover ratios of inventories and inter-firm credit were also deteriorating.

Taxes and the Distribution of Profit

During 1988–92, Polmo had not obtained any subsidies from the budget and had managed to pay its debts to the state budget promptly. The share of taxes in all expenses of the firm is shown in Table 7.

Because of the small founding fund, the obligatory dividend was not a major burden for the firm in 1989 and 1990, but this burden became more significant in 1992 as profits shrank. During the period of this study, the firm also paid a PPWW tax on excessive wage growth, which, before 1992, was a small burden on gross profit. However, in 1992, the PPWW tax accounted for nearly one-sixth of gross profit. It should be mentioned, however, that the PPWW payments in absolute terms were not as high as in 1991, and wages at Polmo were about 25 percent lower than the national average.

Lower profits also affected the firm's distribution pattern. With the profit bonus and both social-welfare and housing funds stable relative to the wage bill in 1989–91, the share of nondistributed profit, which enlarged the enterprise fund and was a potential source of investment, dropped from 88.2 percent in 1990 to 31.2 percent in 1991 (Table 8). The 1992 profit would probably be distributed in a similar way.

LONG-TERM RESPONSES

Until now, the firm was fully owned by the state, and this will probably not change in the near future. In 1991, the firm was included in an analysis performed within the framework of sectoral privatization, but Polmo did not obtain any information about the progress made or about the firm's place in this program. Unofficial information reached Polmo that the Ministry of Ownership Transformation was withdrawing from this form of privatization.

As a result, the firm was still awaiting crucial decisions concerning the prospects of the automobile industry, because these decisions would ultimately determine, to a great extent, the future structure of production and the possibility of domestic and/or foreign joint ventures. At the moment, the firm could only seek potential partners and wait for a response.

The management of Polmo believed the firm's long-run prospects lay in becoming a sub-supplier of parts to modern, possibly foreign, producers of automobiles in Poland. Because the future of the industry was vague, steps were taken in mid-1992 to broaden the product mix of the enterprise. Some employees designed and manufactured such items as wood- and glass-processing machines for handicrafts, fuel-injection electric pumps, safety valves, fuel pumps for various automobiles such as the Lada, Wartburg, and Skoda, and solar water-heating cells, which was an ecological product subsidized by local authorities.

These items were produced using existing assets and minimal investment input. This broadening of the production mix could help Polmo survive until the prospects of the automobile industry become clear.

GENERAL EVALUATION OF THE FIRM AND ITS PROSPECTS

Polmo was in good financial condition thus far, much better than the other firms in the auto industry in Poland. However, Polmo's current situation could only minimally be attributed to its management; rather it was due to the following factors:

- high technical standards and the multiple-use nature of its capital stock, as well as a history of broad product assortments, resulting in greater flexibility in the choice of production profile;
- a change from auto-parts manufacturing to the production of spare parts sold to car owners, combined with the liberalization of prices, which ensured profitable production;
- when the economic transformation began, the firm was in a good financial position and there were reserves of profitability growth that could easily be tapped, i.e., hard currency reserves and inventories of cheap materials. However, these reserves were being depleting rapidly, while the firm's prospects remained unclear.

The future of the firm could be either positive, as in establishing joint ventures with Polish and foreign automobile manufacturers, or negative, as in the firm being left on its own without stable links to automobile manufacturers.

Even under positive circumstances, the firm's chances for survival in its present organizational form are slim. Streamlining would be necessary to reduce diversification and condense activities. With regard to joint ventures, it is probable that foreign or domestic manufacturers would only be interested in acquiring work establishing cooperation with a part of the firm as it stands now. As a result of its evolution, Polmo was heavily overinvested with fixed assets and excess spaces that would most likely never be used.

However, despite doubt about the future and the adjustment measures taken so far, we felt that the management had made good use of the existing opportunities and prevented the firm from sliding deeper than it might have.

440 CASE STUDIES OF POLISH FIRMS

Table 1

Basic Data about the Polish Auto Industry

Specification	1988	1989	1990	1991	1st–3rd Quarter/92
Sales in current prices (billion zloty)	1,041.4	3,209.2	15,829.9	14,394.8	14,664.2
Sales in constant prices (preceding year = 100)	106.5	94.6	74.8	68.2	117.6
Production (thousand units)					
Passenger cars					
of which:	293	285	266	167	143
FSO 1300 and 1500	38.7	23.1	25.7	—	—
Fiat 126p	206	208	190	—	—
Polonez	48.3	54.5	51.1	—	—
Buses	10.4	9.2	3.9	1.9	1.0
Trucks	46.8	43.9	39.0	10.1	9.0
Number of employees (thousands)	114.8	114.1	105.9	94.9	84.4
Mean net monthly pay (thousand zloty)	56.9	223.8	1,029.9	1,584.7	2,197.4
Profitability ratios					
Gross profit/costs of sales	—	38.7	22.4	−15.3	−12.3
Net profit/costs of sales	—	—	—	−19.5	−16.3

Source: Statistical Yearbooks of Industry (Central Statistical Office, Warsaw 1989, 1990, 1991). *Naklady i wyniki przemyslu: I–III kwartal 1992,* Central Statistical Office, Warsaw, December 1992.

Table 2

Customers of Polmo (in percentage of sales)

					Forecast	
Types of customers	1988	1989	1990	1991	1992	1993
Automobile industry	56	60	56	38	43	41
Domestic market	23	26	35	54	47	47
Export	14	7	6	5	7	9
Other customers	7	7	3	3	3	3
Total	100	100	100	100	100	100

AUTO PARTS: POLMO ENTERPRISE 441

Table 3

Basic Financial Data of Polmo in 1988–1992 (in million zloty)

Specification	1988	1989	1990	1991	1992
Net sales (sales minus turnover tax)	19,113	25,995	171,725	166,617	173,400
Costs of sales	7,153	14,220	100,456	130,798	141,600
Underlying profit	2,960	11,775	71,269	35,819	31,800
Financial revenues	36	2,549	1,234	25,037	36,600
Financial costs	—	1,481	17	13,661	43,200
Operating profit	2,996	12,843	72,486	47,195	25,200
Extraordinary gains	101	3,528	7,026	4,010	4,970
Extraordinary losses	80	678	7,859	12,424	5,940
Gross profit	3,017	15,693	71,653	38,781	24,230
Tax burden	2,238	8,534	37,415	30,141	16,624
Net profit	779	7,159	34,238	8,640	7,606
Profitability ratios (in %):					
Underlying profit/net sales	29.3	45.3	41.5	21.5	18.3
Gross profit/net sales	29.8	60.4	41.7	23.3	14.0
Net profit/net sales	7.7	27.5	19.9	5.2	4.4

Table 4

Structure of Costs (in percentages)

Specification	1988	1989	1990	1991	1992
Labor costs	24.9	38.6	25.6	31.2	34.5
Materials	46.4	35.4	45.0	33.5	38.9
Energy	2.6	4.1	5.6	7.8	7.6
Banking charges (incl. interest)	5.1	4.7	7.1	6.0	4.8
Depreciation	6.3	4.3	5.5	11.0	7.9
Property tax	0.9	0.6	0.8	1.5	1.7
External services	13.8	12.3	10.4	9.0	4.6
Total	100.0	100.0	100.0	100.0	100.0

Table 5

Structure of Inventories in Polmo (in percentages)

Items	1988	1989	1990	1991	1992
Materials	71.8	67.5	48.9	41.4	34.1
Work-in-progress	19.5	29.6	40.0	37.1	48.8
Finished goods	8.7	2.3	10.5	18.5	13.4
Goods*	0.0	0.6	0.6	3.0	3.7
Total	100.0	100.0	100.0	100.0	100.0

* "Goods" are finished products stocked in the factory retail shops rather than in the general storage.

Table 6

Liquidity and Activity Ratios

Specification	1988	1989	1990	1991	1992
Liquidity ratios					
Working capital/total assets	0.15	0.23	0.21	0.27	0.23
Current ratio	1.64	1.48	3.84	2.98	2.23
Quick ratio	0.60	0.77	1.85	1.35	0.87
Activity ratios					
Inventory turnover	—	3.97	7.09	3.17	2.16
Average inventory turnover (days)	—	92	52	115	169
Receivables turnover	—	5.74	7.60	3.84	3.35
Average collection period (days)	—	64	48	95	109
Payables turnover	—	3.03	9.93	5.44	3.25
Average payment period (days)	—	121	37	67	112

Table 7

Tax Burden (in percentages)

Specification	1988	1989	1990	1991	1992
Total tax burden (from profit and counted into costs) in relation to sales	30.3	52.5	33.9	36.6	28.9
Share of taxes paid from profit in gross profit	70.9	66.2	52.3	77.8	68.6
Share in gross profit					
of income tax	62.2	50.6	41.8	54.9	38.5
of dividend	—	3.4	5.3	13.5	15.7
of PPWW tax	8.7	12.2	5.2	9.4	14.4

Table 8

Distribution of Net Profit (in percentages)

Specification	1988	1989	1990	1991
Enterprise fund	86.0	56.6	88.2	31.2
Profit bonus	8.4	39.0	7.0	38.8
Enlarging social-welfare fund	3.0	3.6	2.9	11.6
Enlarging housing fund	2.6	0.7	1.8	17.4
Other purposes	—	0.1	0.1	1.0
Total	100.0	100.0	100.0	100.0

Index

AGIC Treuhand Ltd., 193
Agrochemistry (Spolana), 35, 41
AKZO Coatings, 179
Alföld Oil and Gas Equipment Factory, 155
Alkaloida, 241
American Financial Services, 404
American Petroleum Institute (API), 156
Asahi, 214–16, 220n. 2
ASME, 156
Assets, fixed. See Fixed assets
Automation/robotics (Desta), 7
Auto parts
    Bakony Metal and Electrical Appliance Works, 252–63
    Motorpal, 136–51
    Polmo Enterprise, 431–43

Bakony Metal and Electrical Appliance Works, 252–63
    cost structure, 260, 263
    employment, 260–61
    exports, 255–58
    financial indicators, 259–60, 262
    history, 253–54
    Hungaro-Lada Ltd. joint venture, 256–57
    industry overview, 252
    inventories, 260, 263
    labor relations, 261
    privatization, 259
    profits, 259
    sales pattern, 254–58
    strategic objectives, 261
    VAZ, cooperation with, 255–57, 261
Bakony Spark Plugs and Ceramics Ltd., 254
Balcerowicz Plan, 348–49, 387
Bank Handlowo-Kredytowy, 297–99
Biogal, 241
Biscuits Plc., 222

Boryszew-Erg, 409–18
    cost reductions, 414
    external shocks, 411–13
    financial indicators, 418
    history, 410–11
    management, 413
    organizational changes, 413
    present potential, 411
    product mix, 414
    sectoral setting, 409–10
    strategic objectives, 415–16
    wages, 414
Bosch A.G., 144
Bossard Consulting, 426
Brewing (Kanizsa Brewery Ltd.), 231–40
Budapest Oil and Gas Equipment Factory, 155

Capital investments
    CS-07 (chocolate/sweets), 98–99
    Drops (chocolate/sweets), 351
    Hungartextile Holding, 196
    Huta Szkla Hortensja (glass), 329–30
    Lodzkie Fabryki Mebli (wood products), 360
    Spolana (heavy chemicals), 41–42
    Tipa (footwear), 110
    Wolczanka S.A. (garments), 292
Carlo et Montanari, 98
Case-study method, xii
Cefarm, 422, 425, 426
Chemapol, 39
Chemical manufacturing. See Heavy chemicals
Chinoin, 241
Chocolate/sweets
    CS-07, 88–103
    Drops, 344–56
    Intercsokoládé Ltd., 222–30
CKD, 20–21

445

Cloth
  Hungartextile Holding, 191–98
  Textilpol, 302–14
  Veba Broumov, 58–72
Compack Douwe Egberts Ltd., 222
Company Assistance Ltd., 322, 323
Competitiveness
  CS-03 (televisions), 78
  CS-15 (textiles/garments), 49
  Desta (forklift trucks), 6–8
  EGIS Pharmaceutical Works Ltd., 244
  PSP (heavy industry), 19
Construmex, 98
Cormeck Strassbourgh, 98
Corona, 432
Corruption
  CS-15 (textiles/garments), 52
  Wolczanka S.A. (garments), 297–99
Cost reductions
  Boryszew-Erg (plastics), 414
  Polfa Enterprise (pharmaceuticals), 424
Cost structure
  Bakony Metal and Electrical Appliance Works, 260, 263
  CS-03 (electronics), 79–80, 85
  CS-13 (plastics), 124
  CS-15 (textiles/garments), 57
  DKG (oil and gas equipment), 163
  Drops (chocolate/sweets), 355
  EGIS Pharmaceutical Works Ltd., 251
  Elegant Charm (garments), 190
  Hungartextile Holding, 195
  Huta Szkla Hortensja (glass), 330, 336, 341
  Intercsokoládé Ltd., 226, 230
  Kanizsa Brewery Ltd., 235–36, 239
  Lodzkie Fabryki Mebli (wood products), 369
  Mokasyn (footwear), 407
  Pafawag Enterprise (railway rolling stock), 273, 276
  PO/5 (engineering/machine tools), 284–85, 288
  Polar Enterprise (white goods), 390–91, 395
  Polmo Enterprise (auto parts), 441
  PSP (heavy industry), 29
  Radion Radio and Electrical Works, 209
  Salgglas, 221

Cost structure *(continued)*
  Spolana (heavy chemicals), 45
  Textilpol, 308–9, 313
  Theta Works (defense), 173
  TVK (heavy chemicals), 181
  Veba Broumov (textiles/cloth), 72
  Wolczanka S.A. (garments), 300
Cotton manufacturing techniques (Veba Broumov), 61–62
Courage, 234
Credits
  Polar Enterprise (white goods), 391
  Spolana (heavy chemicals), 39–40
Credit Suisse First Boston (CSFB), 249
CS-07 (chocolate/sweets), 88–103
  corporate governance, 94
  decision-making, 95
  exports, 103
  external constraints, 90–91
  external shocks, 92–94
  financial indicators, 92–93, 96–97, 102
  history, 91–92
  investments by, 98–99
  Jacobs-Suchard, merger with, 94, 97–98
  liquidity/activity ratios, 102
  operations of, 91
  organization, 94–95
  output, 96
  privatization, 89
  production output, 95, 101, 103
  prospects, 99
  sales policy, 95–96
  sectoral setting, 89–91
CSFB (Credit Suisse First Boston), 249
CS-12 (pharmaceuticals), 127–35
  external shocks, 129–31
  health insurance, 131
  history, 128–29
  monetary policy, 129
  price liberalization, effect of, 130
  privatization strategy, 131–33
  sectoral setting, 127–28
  taxation, 134–35
CS-13 (plastics), 115–25
  cost structure, 124
  economic indicators, 124
  external environment, 118–19
  financial data, 125

INDEX   447

CS-13 (plastics) *(continued)*
  foreign investor, choice of, 121–22
  history, 117
  liquidity/activity ratios, 125
  organization changes, 119–21, 126
  production structure, 117–18
  profitability ratios, 125
  prospects, 123
  sectoral setting, 116–17
  strategic planning, 122–23
CS-03 (televisions), 73–87
  cost structure, 79–80, 85
  employee motivation, 80–81
  external/internal constraints, 75–76
  external shocks, 77–78
  financial indicators, 81, 86
  history, 76–77
  liquidity/activity ratios, 81, 87
  privatization of, 81–82
  prospects, 82
  sales policy, 80
  sectoral settings, 74–76
  technological considerations, 76
CS-15 (textiles/garments), 48–57
  competitiveness, 49
  corruption at, 52
  cost structure, 57
  external shocks, 52–53
  history, 51–52
  labor shortage, 50
  liquidity crisis at, 54
  organization, 55
  output, 57
  privatization of, 55
  profitability ratios, 57
  sectoral setting, 48–51
  social policy of, 53–54
  wages, 49
Currency devaluation
  CS-03 (electronics), 78
  Veba Broumov (textiles/cloth), 63
Czech and Slovak firms
  CS-03 (electronics), 73–87
  CS-07 (food processing), 88–103
  CS-12 (pharmaceuticals), 127–35
  CS-13 (plastics), 115–25
  CS-15 (textiles/garments), 48–57
  Desta (forklift tractors), 3–15

Czech and Slovak firms *(continued)*
  Motorpal (auto parts), 136–51
  PSP (heavy industry), 16–32
  Spolana (heavy chemicals), 33–47
  Tipa (footwear), 104–14
  Veba Broumov (textiles/cloth), 58–72
Czestochowa Steel Works, 371–83
  exports, 377–78, 382
  external shocks, 373–75
  history, 372–73
  liquidity/activity ratios, 382
  management, 375–77
  prices, 374
  production volume (table), 382
  profits, 379
  restructuring, 379–80
  sectoral setting, 371–72
  strategic objectives, 380–81
  tax burden (table), 383

Debrecen Canning Factory, 229*n. 1*
Decision-making
  CS-07 (chocolate/sweets), 95
  PSP (heavy industry), 26
Defense (Theta Works), 164–73
Desta, 3–15
  capital/time constraints, 9–10
  competitiveness, 6–8
  employment, 10–11
  management, 4–5
  marketing, 8–9
  1960s vs. 1990s at, 12–13
  organization, 15
  product innovation, 7–8
  profitability, 11–12
  research and development, 7–8
  sectoral setting, 5–6
  transformation strategy, 13–14
DKG-East Ltd., 157–59
DKG (engineering), 155–63
  cost structure (table), 163
  DKG-East joint venture, 157–59
  exports, 156–57
  financial indicators, 159–61, 163
  history, 155–56
  inventory, 160
  labor/employment, 161
  management, 161–62

DKG (engineering) *(continued)*
  product mix, 156
  salaries, 162n. 1
  sales pattern, 156–57
  strategic planning, 162
Dr. Albert Wander AG, 241
Drops (chocolate/sweets), 344–56
  cost structure (table), 355
  employment, 347
  external shocks, 348–50
  financial indicators, 355
  fixed assets, 346–47
  history, 345–46
  investment program, 351
  labor relations, 347–48
  liquidity/activity ratios, 356
  management, 348
  organizational changes, 351–52
  privatization, 352–54
  profitability ratios, 356
  sales network, 350–51
  sectoral setting, 344–45
  taxation, 346–47

Ecological issues (Spolana), 42
EGIS Pharmaceutical Works Ltd., 241–51
  competitiveness, 244
  cost strucutre (table), 251
EGIS Pharmaceutical Works Ltd.
  employees, 247
  exports, 245–46
  financial indicators, 246–47
  history, 241–42
  industry overview, 241
  inventories, 251
  labor relations, 247–48
  management, 247
  privatization, 248–49
  product mix, 242
  sales, 242–46, 250, 251
  strategic objectives, 249–50
  wages, 247
Electronics
  CS-03 (televisions), 73–87
  Miflex Radio Components Firm S.A., 315–26
  Radion Radio and Electrical Works, 199–211

Elegant Charm (textiles), 182–90
  cost structure (table), 190
  financial indicators, 188
  and First of May, 185–86
  history, 182–84
  labor relations, 187
  labor shortage, 184–85
  management, 186, 188–89
  marketing, 186
  ownership structure, 186
  privatization, 189
  product mix, 185, 186–87
  strategic objectives, 186–87, 189–90
  subcontracting agreements, 185
  undercapitalization, 184, 185
Employment. *See also* Labor relations
  Bakony Metal and Electrical Appliance Works, 260–61
  CS-03 (electronics), 80–81
  Desta (forklift trucks), 10–11
  DKG (oil and gas equipment), 161
  Drops (chocolate/sweets), 347
  EGIS Pharmaceutical Works Ltd., 247
  Hungartextile Holding, 196–97
  Huta Szkla Hortensja (glass), 330
  Intercsokoládé Ltd., 227–28
  Kanizsa Brewery Ltd., 237
  Lodzkie Fabryki Mebli (wood products), 360–61
  Mokasyn (footwear), 399–400
  Motorpal (auto parts), 142–43, 148
  PO/5 (engineering/machine tools), 281–82
  PSP (heavy industry), 28
  Radion Radio and Electrical Works, 204, 211
  Salgglas, 218
  Spolana (heavy chemicals), 47
  Textilpol, 304
  Theta Works (defense), 170–71
  Veba Broumov (textiles/cloth), 69
Energy costs
  Huta Szkla Hortensja (glass), 333
  Textilpol, 309
Engineering
  Desta (forklift trucks), 3–15
  DKG (oil and gas equipment), 155–63

INDEX 449

Engineering *(continued)*
  Pafawag Enterprise (railway rolling stock), 267–76
  PO/5 (machine tools), 277–89
  PSP (heavy industry), 16–32
Exports
  Bakony Metal and Electrical Appliance Works, 255–58
  CS-07 (chocolate/sweets), 103
  Czestochowa Steel Works, 377–78, 382
  DKG (oil and gas equipment), 156–57
  EGIS Pharmaceutical Works Ltd., 245–46
  Huta Szkla Hortensja (glass), 328, 329, 337–38
  Intercsokoládé Ltd., 224–25
  Lodzkie Fabryki Mebli (wood products), 363, 366
  Miflex Radio Components Firm S.A., 323
  Motorpal (auto parts), 146
  PO/5 (engineering/machine tools), 283–84
  Polar Enterprise (white goods), 390
  Polfa Enterprise (pharmaceuticals), 421
  PSP (heavy industry), 29
  Salgglas, 215
  Spolana (heavy chemicals), 39, 47
  Textilpol, 303–4, 307–8
  Wolczanka S.A. (garments), 292

Factor markets, development of, xiv
Ferrum Iron Foundry, 432
F.G.U., 286
Fibers, man-made (Spolana), 35
Financial independence, xiii
Financial indicators. *See also* Cost structure; Profits and profitability
  Bakony Metal and Electrical Appliance Works, 259–60, 262
  Boryszew-Erg (plastics), 418
  CS-07 (chocolate/sweets), 92–93, 96–97, 102
  CS-03 (electronics), 81, 86
  CS-13 (plastics), 124, 125
  Desta (forklift trucks), 9–10
  DKG (oil and gas equipment), 159–61, 163
  Drops (chocolate/sweets), 355

Financial indicators *(continued)*
  EGIS Pharmaceutical Works Ltd., 246–47
  Elegant Charm (garments), 188
  Hungartextile Holding, 194–96, 198
  Huta Szkla Hortensja (glass), 342
  Intercsokoládé Ltd., 226–27
  Kanizsa Brewery Ltd., 235–36, 239
  Lodzkie Fabryki Mebli (wood products), 369
  Miflex Radio Components Firm S.A., 325
  Mokasyn (footwear), 407
  Motorpal (auto parts), 140–41, 149
  Pafawag Enterprise (railway rolling stock), 272–73, 276
  PO/5 (engineering/machine tools), 284–86, 289
  Polar Enterprise (white goods), 391, 396
  Polfa Enterprise (pharmaceuticals), 429
  Polmo Enterprise (auto parts), 441
  PSP (heavy industry), 30, 31
  Radion Radio and Electrical Works, 202–3
  Salgglas, 216–18, 221
  Spolana (heavy chemicals), 44, 45
  Textilpol, 313
  Theta Works (defense), 167–68
  Tipa (footwear), 112
  TVK (heavy chemicals), 177–78, 181
  Veba Broumov (textiles/cloth), 72
  Wolczanka S.A. (garments), 300
First of May Clothing Factory, 182–86
Fixed assets
  Drops (chocolate/sweets), 346–47
  Lodzkie Fabryki Mebli (wood products), 359–60
  Mokasyn (footwear), 399
  Radion Radio and Electrical Works, 211
  Textilpol, 304
Flexmont Ltd., 254
Food processing
  CS-07 (chocolate/sweets), 88–103
  Drops (chocolate/sweets), 344–56
  Intercsokoládé Ltd., 222–30
  Kanizsa Brewery Ltd., 231–40

Footwear
   Mokasyn, 397–408
   Tipa, 104–14
Foreign activities/contacts
   CS-13 (plastics), 121–22
   Motorpal (auto parts), 147
   PSP (heavy industry), 22–23
   Tipa (footwear), 110
Forklift trucks (Desta), 3–15
Fourcault, E., 212
Froechlich, E., 420
FSM, 253, 255

Gamrat-Erg, 409
Ganz-MAVAG, 155
Garments
   CS-15, 48–57
   Elegant Charm, 182–90
   Wolczanka S.A., 290–301
Gastrochemistry (Spolana), 35
GDR, 288n. 1
Gedeon Richter, 241
General Electric, 279
Glass
   Huta Szkla Hortensja, 327–43
   Salgglas, 212–21
Glasunion Ltd., 219
Glaverbel, 214–16, 220n. 2
Globalfood, 222–26, 228
Goldberger Textile Works, 191–92
Guardian, 214, 215
Guttmann, Vilmos Gelsei, 232

Health insurance (CS-12), 131
Heavy chemicals
   Spolana, 33–47
   TVK, 174–81
Heavy industry
   Czestochowa Steel Works, 371–83
   PSP, 16–32
Holsten, 232, 234
Human resources. See Employment
Hungarian Ammunition Works Ltd., 253
Hungarian firms
   Bakony (auto parts), 252–63
   DKG (engineering), 155–63
   EGIS (pharmaceuticals), 241–51

Hungarian firms *(continued)*
   Elegant Charm (textiles/garments), 182–90
   Hungartextile Holding (textiles/cloth), 191–98
   Intercsokoládé (food processing), 222–30
   Kanizsa Brewery, 231–40
   Radion (electronics), 199–211
   Salgglas (glass), 212–21
   Theta Works (defense), 164–73
   TVK (heavy chemicals), 174–81
Hungarian Oil and Gas Trust (OKGT), 156
Hungaro-Lada Ltd., 256–57
Hungartextile Holding, 191–98
   capital investments, 196
   cost structure, 195
   employment, 196–97
   financial indicators, 194–96, 198
   history, 191–92
   inventories, 195
   labor relations, 197
   management, 197
   privatization, 193–94
   sales, 195–96
   sectoral overview, 191
   strategic objectives, 193–94
   subsidiaries, 192–93, 197
   technology base, 196
Hunguard Co., 212
Huta Szkla Hortensja (glass), 327–43
   cost structure, 330, 336, 341
   employment, 330
   energy costs, 333
   exports, 328, 329, 337–38
   external shocks, 333–35
   financial indicators, 342
   history, 328
   investment needs, 329–30
   labor relations, 331
   labor shortage, 330–31
   liquidity/activity ratios, 343
   management, 331–32
   organizational structure, 336–37
   output, 335–36
   privatization initiative, 338
   production brigades at, 328–29
   product mix, 328
   profitability ratios, 342

Huta Szkla Hortensja (glass) *(continued)*
  sales strategy, 337–38
  sectoral setting, 327–28
  taxation, 333
  training, 330–31

Inflation, effect of
  Miflex Radio Components Firm S.A., 319
  Pafawag Enterprise (railway rolling stock), 271
Interbrew, 231
Intercsokoládé Ltd., 222–30
  cost structure, 226, 230
  employment, 227–28
  exports, 224–25
  financial indicators, 226–27
  Globalfood joint venture, 224
  history, 223
  industry overview, 222
  inventories (table), 230
  labor relations, 228
  management, 228–29
  privatization, 225–26
  product mix, 224
  profits, 227
  sales pattern, 224–25
  strategic objectives, 229
  taxation, 226–27
Interest costs
  Huta Szkla Hortensja (glass), 330
  Lodzkie Fabryki Mebli (wood products), 364
  Textilpol, 309
Inventories
  Bakony Metal and Electrical Appliance Works, 260, 263
  DKG (oil and gas equipment), 160
  EGIS Pharmaceutical Works Ltd., 251
  Hungartextile Holding, 195
  Intercsokoládé Ltd., 230
  Kanizsa Brewery Ltd., 236, 240
  Miflex Radio Components Firm S.A., 325
  Pafawag Enterprise (railway rolling stock), 272, 276
  Polmo Enterprise (auto parts), 437, 442
  Radion Radio and Electrical Works, 209
  Salgglas, 217, 221

Inventories *(continued)*
  Theta Works (defense), 173
  TVK (heavy chemicals), 181
Investments. *See* Capital investments
Iron/steel (Czestochowa Steel Works), 371–83
ISO 9000, 156
ITT Nokia, 199

Jacobs-Suchard, 94, 97–98
Jüttner, Mr., 255
Kanizsa Brewery Ltd., 231–40
  cost structure, 235–36, 239
  employment, 237
  financial indicators, 235–36, 239
  history, 232
  inventories, 236, 240
  labor relations, 237
  management, 237
  output (table), 239
  privatization, 233–35
  product mix, 232–33
  research and development, 236
  sales pattern, 232–33
  sectoral overview, 231–32
  strategic objectives, 237–38

Katowice Steelworks, 372
Kôbánya Brewery Ltd., 231–33
Krivoi Rog, 16, 20–22, 26, 27

Labor force. *See* Employment
Labor relations
  Bakony Metal and Electrical Appliance Works, 261
  Drops (chocolate/sweets), 347–48
  EGIS Pharmaceutical Works Ltd., 247–48
  Elegant Charm (garments), 187
  Hungartextile Holding, 197
  Huta Szkla Hortensja (glass), 331
  Intercsokoládé Ltd., 228
  Kanizsa Brewery Ltd., 237
  Lodzkie Fabryki Mebli (wood products), 361
  Mokasyn (footwear), 400
  Radion Radio and Electrical Works, 205
  Salgglas, 218–19
  Textilpol, 304

Labor relations *(continued)*
  Theta Works (defense), 171
Labor shortage
  CS-15 (textiles/garments), 50
  Elegant Charm (garments), 184–85
  Huta Szkla Hortensja (glass), 330–31
Levi Strauss, 183
Liquidity/activity ratios
  CS-07 (chocolate/sweets), 102
  CS-03 (electronics), 81, 87
  CS-13 (plastics), 125
  Czestochowa Steel Works, 382
  Drops (chocolate/sweets), 356
  Huta Szkla Hortensja (glass), 343
  Lodzkie Fabryki Mebli (wood products), 370
  Miflex Radio Components Firm S.A., 319
  Mokasyn (footwear), 408
  PO/5 (engineering/machine tools), 289
  Polmo Enterprise (auto parts), 442
  Spolana (heavy chemicals), 46
  Textilpol, 314
  Wolczanka S.A. (garments), 301
Lodzkie Fabryki Mebli, 357–70
  capital investments, 360
  cost structure (table), 369
  employment, 360–61
  exports, 363, 366
  external shocks, 363–65
  financial indicators, 369
  fixed assets, 359–60
  history, 358
  interest costs, 364
  labor relations, 361
  liquidity/activity ratios, 370
  management, 362
  market position, 358–59
  organizational structure, 362–63
  privatization, 368
  product mix, 358, 366
  profitability, 357, 370
  sales, 359, 367–68
  sectoral setting, 357–58
  taxation, 364
  wages, 360–61

Machine tools (PO/5), 277–89
Management. *See also* Organization and organizational changes
  Boryszew-Erg (plastics), 413
  CS-03 (electronics), 78–79
  Czestochowa Steel Works, 375–77
  DKG (oil and gas equipment), 161–62
  Drops (chocolate/sweets), 348
  EGIS Pharmaceutical Works Ltd., 247
  Elegant Charm (garments), 186, 188–89
  Hungartextile Holding, 197
  Huta Szkla Hortensja (glass), 331–32
  Intercsokoládé Ltd., 228–29
  Kanizsa Brewery Ltd., 237
  Lodzkie Fabryki Mebli (wood products), 362
  Miflex Radio Components Firm S.A., 320–21
  Mokasyn (footwear), 400–401
  Pafawag Enterprise (railway rolling stock), 269–70
  PO/5 (engineering/machine tools), 282
  Polar Enterprise (white goods), 387–88
  Polfa Enterprise (pharmaceuticals), 423–24
  Polmo Enterprise (auto parts), 434–35
  PSP (heavy industry), 32
  Radion Radio and Electrical Works, 204
  Spolana (heavy chemicals), 37, 40–41
  Textilpol, 305–6
  Theta Works (defense), 171
  Tipa (footwear), 109
  Wolczanka S.A. (garments), 293
Managerial autonomy, xiii
Managerial motivation, xxi
Margareta Ltd., 193
Markets and marketing. *See also* Sales
  CS-03 (electronics), 78
  Desta (forklift trucks), 8–9
  Elegant Charm (garments), 186
  Lodzkie Fabryki Mebli (wood products), 358–59
  PSP (heavy industry), 18, 19, 22–23, 28
  Spolana (heavy chemicals), 39
  Veba Broumov (textiles/cloth), 61
  Wolczanka S.A. (garments), 291–92
Matsuba Industries Ltd., 258
Mechtler, Les, 233

INDEX 453

MEDICOR, 168
Merkantoll, 157
Miflex Radio Components Firm S.A., 315–26
  exports, 323
  external shocks, 316–18
  financial results, 325
  history, 316
  inflation, effect of, 319
  inventories (table), 325
  liquidity/activity ratios, 319
  management, 320–21
  organizational structure, 321
  output volume (table), 325
  profitability, 319
  sales strategy, 318–19
  sectoral setting, 315–16
  strategic goals, 322–23
  survival strategy, 323–24
  taxation, 320, 326
Minex, 340
Mira, 51–52
Mitsui-Seiki, 279
Mokasyn, 397–408
  cost structure (table), 407
  employment, 399–400
  external shocks, 401–4
  financial indicators, 407
  fixed assets, 399
  history, 398
  labor relations, 400
  liquidation, 404–6
  liquidity/activity ratios, 408
  management, 400–401
  product mix, 398–99
  profitability ratios, 408
  sectoral setting, 397–98
Monetary policy
  CS-12 (pharmaceuticals), 129
  Veba Broumov (textiles/cloth), 63
Motorpal, 136–51
  corporate governance, 141
  debt, 148
  employment, 142–43, 148
  exports, 146
  external constraints, 137
  external shocks, 139–41
  financial policy, 140–41

Motorpal *(continued)*
  financial statements, 149
  foreign activities/contacts, 147
  history, 138
  job security, 143
  main customers of, 147
  organizational structure, 141–42, 150–51
  overemployment, 142
  and price liberalization, 139–40
  privatization of, 144
  production programs, 138–39
  production volume, 140
  profit, 148
  sectoral setting, 136–38
  survival strategy of, 143–44
  technological considerations, 137–38
  turnover, 148

Nuclear instruments (Theta Works), 164–73

Odra, 398, 399
Oil and gas equipment (DKG), 155–63
OKGT (Hungarian Oil and Gas Trust), 156
One-man leadership (Desta), 4–5
Opel, 252, 258
Organization and organizational changes. *See also* Management
  Boryszew-Erg (plastics), 413
  CS-07 (chocolate/sweets), 94–95
  CS-13 (plastics), 119–21, 126
  CS-15 (textiles/garments), 55
  Czestochowa Steel Works, 375
  Desta (forklift trucks), 15
  Drops (chocolate/sweets), 351–52
  Huta Szkla Hortensja (glass), 336–37
  Lodzkie Fabryki Mebli (wood products), 362–63
  Miflex Radio Components Firm S.A., 321
  Motorpal (auto parts), 141–42, 150–51
  Pafawag Enterprise (railway rolling stock), 273
  PO/5 (engineering/machine tools), 281
  Polar Enterprise (white goods), 388–89
  Polfa Enterprise (pharmaceuticals), 423
  Polmo Enterprise (auto parts), 434
  PSP (heavy industry), 24–25, 25–26

Organization and organizational changes *(continued)*
  Salgglas, 218
  Spolana (heavy chemicals), 37
  Tipa (footwear), 110
  Veba Broumov (textiles/cloth), 68
  Wolczanka S.A. (garments), 293–94
  Orkan, 398
  Orosháza Glass Factory, 212
Output
  CS-07 (chocolate/sweets), 95, 96, 101, 103
  CS-13 (plastics), 117–18
  CS-15 (textiles/garments), 57
  Czestochowa Steel Works, 382
  Huta Szkla Hortensja (glass), 335–36
  Kanizsa Brewery Ltd., 239
  Miflex Radio Components Firm S.A., 325
  Motorpal (auto parts), 138–39, 140
  Pafawag Enterprise (railway rolling stock), 272
  Polfa Enterprise (pharmaceuticals), 429
  Polmo Enterprise (auto parts), 435
  PSP (heavy industry), 29, 30
  Spolana (heavy chemicals), 46
  Theta Works (defense), 172
  TVK (heavy chemicals), 180
  Veba Broumov (textiles/cloth), 72
Overemployment
  Motorpal (auto parts), 142
  Spolana (heavy chemicals), 38
Ownership
  changes in, xv
  Elegant Charm (garments), 186
  Polfa Enterprise (pharmaceuticals), 426–27
  Tipa (footwear), 110

Pafawag Enterprise, 267–76
  cost structure, 273, 276
  external shocks, 270–72
  financial indicators, 272–73, 276
  history, 268–69
  inflation, effect of, 271
  inventories, 272, 276
  management, 269–70
  organizational changes, 273

Pafawag Enterprise *(continued)*
  output, 272
  sales, 272
  sectoral setting, 267
  strategic objectives, 274
Pannonglas, 212
Pannonia Brewery Ltd., 232
Pénzintézeti Központ, 165
Pepsico, 345
Petrotech, 157
Pharmaceuticals
  CS-12, 127–35
  EGIS Pharmaceutical Works Ltd., 241–51
  Polfa Enterprise, 419–30
Pilkington Glass, 214, 215
Plastics
  Boryszew-Erg, 409–18
  CS-13, 115–25
  Spolana, 35
PO/5 (engineering/machine tools), 277–89
  cost structure, 284–85, 288
  employees, 281–82
  exports, 283–84
  external shocks, 279–81
  financial indicators, 284–86, 289
  history, 278–79
  liquidity/activity ratios, 289
  management, 282
  organizational structure, 281
  profits, 285
  sales, 283–84
  sectoral setting, 277–78
  strategic objectives, 286–87
  wages, 282
Polar Enterprise, 384–96
  cost structure, 390–91, 395
  credits, 391
  exports, 390
  external shocks, 385–87
  financial indicators, 391, 396
  history, 384–85
  management, 387–88
  organizational structure, 388–89
  pricing, 389–90
  privatization initiative, 392–93
  sectoral setting, 384
  strategic objectives, 393–94

INDEX 455

Polar Enterprise *(continued)*
  taxation, 396
  wages, 391–92
Polfa Enterprise, 419–30
  cost reductions, 424
  distribution system, 425
  exports, 421
  external shocks, 421–22
  financial indicators, 429
  history, 420–21
  management, 423–24
  organizational changes, 423
  ownership changes, 426–27
  payables/receivables (table), 430
  pricing, 425
  production costs, 429
  sectoral setting, 419–20
  strategic objectives, 427–28
  taxation, 425–26, 430
Polish firms
  Boryszew-Erg (plastics), 409–18
  Czestochowa Steel Works, 371–83
  Drops (chocolate/sweets), 344–56
  Huta Szkla Hortensja (glass), 327–43
  Lodzkie Fabryki Mebli (wood products), 357–70
  Miflex (electronics), 315–26
  Mokasyn (footwear), 397–408
  Pafawag Enterprise (engineering), 267–76
  PO/5 (engineering), 277–89
  Polar Enterprise (white goods), 384–96
  Polfa Enterprise (pharmaceuticals), 419–30
  Polmo Enterprise (auto parts), 431–43
  Textilpol (textiles/cloth), 302–14
  Wolczanka (textiles/garments), 290–301
Polish State Reilways, 268, 271
Polmo Enterprise, 431–43
  cost structure, 441
  customers (table), 440
  external shocks, 433–34
  financial data, 441
  history, 432
  inventories, 442
  inventory management, 437
  liquidity/activity ratios, 442
  management, 434–35

Polmo Enterprise *(continued)*
  organizational changes, 434
  output, 435
  profitability, 436–37
  sales, 435–36
  sectoral setting, 431–32
  strategic objectives, 438–39
  taxation, 438, 442
  wages, 435
Portfolio Bank Ltd., 193
Pragodev, 51–52
Pragoinvest, 20
Price liberalization
  CS-03 (electronics), 77
  CS-12 (pharmaceuticals), 130–31
  Motorpal (auto parts), 139–40
  Veba Broumov (textiles/cloth), 64
Price Waterhouse, 340
Pricing
  Czestochowa Steel Works, 374
  Polar Enterprise (white goods), 389–90
  Polfa Enterprise (pharmaceuticals), 425
Privatization
  Bakony Metal and Electrical Appliance Works, 259
  CS-07 (chocolate/sweets), 89
  CS-03 (electronics), 81–82
  CS-12 (pharmaceuticals), 131–33
  CS-15 (textiles/garments), 55
  Drops (chocolate/sweets), 352–54
  EGIS Pharmaceutical Works Ltd., 248–49
  Elegant Charm (garments), 189
  Hungartextile Holding, 193–94
  Huta Szkla Hortensja (glass), 338
  Intercsokoládé Ltd., 225–26
  Kanizsa Brewery Ltd., 233–35
  Lodzkie Fabryki Mebli (wood products), 368
  Motorpal (auto parts), 144
  Polar Enterprise (white goods), 392–93
  PSP (heavy industry), 24–26, 28
  Radion Radio and Electrical Works, 204–5
  Salgglas, 215–16
  Spolana (heavy chemicals), 40
  Theta Works (defense), 169–70
  Tipa (footwear), 105–6

456 INDEX

Privatization *(continued)*
  TVK (heavy chemicals), 178–80
  Veba Broumov (textiles/cloth), 67
  Wolczanka S.A. (garments), 296–99
Production. *See* Output
Production brigades (Huta Szkla Hortensja), 328–29
Productivity (Spolana), 37–38
Product markets, changes in, xiii–xiv
Product mix
  Boryszew-Erg (plastics), 414
  DKG (oil and gas equipment), 156
  EGIS Pharmaceutical Works Ltd., 242
  Elegant Charm (garments), 185, 186–87
  Huta Szkla Hortensja (glass), 328
  Intercsokoládé Ltd., 224
  Kanizsa Brewery Ltd., 232–33
  Lodzkie Fabryki Mebli (wood products), 358, 366
  Mokasyn (footwear), 398–99
  Radion Radio and Electrical Works, 209
  Salgglas, 213–14
  Theta Works (defense), 165–66
  TVK (heavy chemicals), 175–77
Profits and profitability
  Bakony Metal and Electrical Appliance Works, 259
  CS-13 (plastics), 125
  CS-15 (textiles/garments), 57
  Czestochowa Steel Works, 379
  Drops (chocolate/sweets), 356
  Huta Szkla Hortensja (glass), 342
  Intercsokoládé Ltd., 227
  Lodzkie Fabryki Mebli (wood products), 357, 370
  Miflex Radio Components Firm S.A., 319
  Mokasyn (footwear), 408
  Motorpal (auto parts), 148
  PO/5 (engineering/machine tools), 285
  Polmo Enterprise (auto parts), 436–37
  Radion Radio and Electrical Works, 210
  Salgglas, 216
  Spolana (heavy chemicals), 45
  Textilpol, 314
  Theta Works (defense), 172
  Tipa (footwear), 112
  TVK (heavy chemicals), 179

Profits and profitability *(continued)*
  Wolczanka S.A. (garments), 294, 301
  PSP (heavy industry), 16–32
    balance sheet, 31
    competitors, 19
    corporate governance, 25–26
    costs (table), 29
    decision-making process, 26
    employment (table), 28
    exports (table), 29
    financial ratios (table), 30
    foreign trade, 22–23
    history, 18–19
    Krivoi Rog venture, 16, 20–22, 26, 27
    management structure (table), 32
    markets and marketing, 18, 19, 22–23, 28
    organization of, 24–25
    output, 29, 30
    privatization, 24–26, 28
    sectoral setting, 16–18
    strategic planning, 23

Quintie Sweets Industry Ltd, 222

Radion Radio and Electrical Works, 199–211
  assets (table), 211
  cost structure (table), 209
  employment, 204, 211
  financial indicators, 202–3
  history, 199–200
  inventories (table), 209
  labor relations, 205
  management, 204
  privatization, 204–5
  product lines (table), 209
  profits (table), 210
  receivables/payables (table), 211
  research and development, 203
  sales, 200–202, 209
  sectoral setting, 199
  strategic objectives, 206–8
  taxation (table), 210
  training, 204
  undercapitalization, 205–6
  wages, 204, 211
Railway rolling stock (Pafawag Enterprise), 267–76

Reanal, 241
Reorg Ltd., 213
Research and development
  Desta (forklift trucks), 7–8
  Kanizsa Brewery Ltd., 236
  Radion Radio and Electrical Works, 203
  Spolana (heavy chemicals), 41
Restructuring. *See also* Privatization
  Czestochowa Steel Works, 379–80
  Textilpol, 310–12

Saint-Gobain, 214, 215
Salaries. *See* Wages
Sales. *See also* Exports; Markets and marketing; Sales strategy
  Bakony Metal and Electrical Appliance Works, 254–58
  DKG (oil and gas equipment), 156–57
  Drops (chocolate/sweets), 350–51
  EGIS Pharmaceutical Works Ltd., 242–46, 250, 251
  Hungartextile Holding, 195–96
  Intercsokoládé Ltd., 224–25
  Kanizsa Brewery Ltd., 232–33
  Lodzkie Fabryki Mebli (wood products), 359, 367–68
  Pafawag Enterprise (railway rolling stock), 272
  PO/5 (engineering/machine tools), 283–84
  Polmo Enterprise (auto parts), 435–36
  Radion Radio and Electrical Works, 200–202, 209
  Salgglas, 213–15
  Spolana (heavy chemicals), 46
  Theta Works (defense), 166–67, 172
Sales strategy
  CS-07 (chocolate/sweets), 95–96
  CS-03 (electronics), 80
  Huta Szkla Hortensja (glass), 337–38
  Miflex Radio Components Firm S.A., 318–19
  Textilpol, 309–10
  TVK (heavy chemicals), 177
  Wolczanka S.A. (garments), 294–96
Salgglas, 212–21, 252
  cost structure (table), 221

Salgglas *(continued)*
  employment, 218
  exports, 215
  financial indicators, 216–18, 221
  history, 212–13
  industry overview, 212
  inventories, 217, 221
  labor relations, 218–19
  organizational changes, 218
  privatization, 215–16
  product mix, 213–14
  profits, 216
  sales, 213–15
  strategic objectives, 219–20
  Suzuki-project, 214
  tempered glass investment project, 220n. 4
Schweikert, Ludwik, 420
Secotex Textile Dyeing Ltd., 192
Sedzimir Steelworks, 372
SIV, 215
Skoda, 116, 117
Social services
  CS-15 (textiles/garments), 53–54
  Spolana (heavy chemicals), 38
Soiuz Mezhstroiimport, 20
Spolana (heavy chemicals), 33–47
  balance sheet, 44
  bank credits, 39–40
  capital investments, 41–42
  corporate governance, 37
  costs (table), 45
  ecological issues, 42
  employees, 47
  exports, 39, 47
  external shocks, 36–37
  financial indicators, 45
  history, 34–36
  income statement, 44
  liquidity/activity ratios, 46
  management, 40–41
  managment, 37
  markets, 39
  organization, 37
  overemployment at, 38
  privatization of, 40
  production volume (table), 46
  productivity, 37–38

Spolana (heavy chemicals) *(continued)*
profitability ratios, 45
prospects for, 42–43
research and development at, 41
sales (table), 46
sectoral setting of, 33–34
social services provided by, 38
Steel (Czestochowa Steel Works), 371–83
Steierbrau AG, 234
Strategic objectives, xxii-xxiii. *See also* Sales strategy
Bakony Metal and Electrical Appliance Works, 261
Boryszew-Erg (plastics), 415–16
CS-13 (plastics), 122–23
Czestochowa Steel Works, 380–81
Desta (forklift trucks), 13–14
DKG (oil and gas equipment), 162
EGIS Pharmaceutical Works Ltd., 249–50
Elegant Charm (garments), 186–87, 189–90
Hungartextile Holding, 193–94
Intercsokoládé Ltd., 229
Kanizsa Brewery Ltd., 237–38
Miflex Radio Components Firm S.A., 322–23
Pafawag Enterprise (railway rolling stock), 274
PO/5 (engineering/machine tools), 286–87
Polar Enterprise (white goods), 393–94
Polfa Enterprise (pharmaceuticals), 427–28
Polmo Enterprise (auto parts), 438–39
PSP (heavy industry), 23
Radion Radio and Electrical Works, 206–8
Salgglas, 219–20
Subcontracting agreements (Elegant Charm), 185
Suzuki, 214, 252
SWF, 258
SWOT analysis, 66–67
Szerencs Sweets Factory, 223

Taxation, effect of
CS-12 (pharmaceuticals), 134–35
Czestochowa Steel Works, 383

Taxation, effect of *(continued)*
DKG (oil and gas equipment), 158
Drops (chocolate/sweets), 346–47
Huta Szkla Hortensja (glass), 333
Intercsokoládé Ltd., 226–27
Lodzkie Fabryki Mebli (wood products), 364
Miflex Radio Components Firm S.A., 320, 326
Polar Enterprise (white goods), 396
Polfa Enterprise (pharmaceuticals), 425–26, 430
Polmo Enterprise (auto parts), 438, 442
Radion Radio and Electrical Works, 210
Wolczanka S.A. (garments), 299
Technological considerations
CS-03 (electronics), 76
Hungartextile Holding, 196
Motorpal (auto parts), 137–38
Televisions
CS-03, 73–87
Radion Radio and Electrical Works, 199–211
Textiles
CS-15 (garments), 48–57
Elegant Charm (garments), 182–90
Hungartextile Holding (cloth), 191–98
Textilpol (cloth), 302–14
Veba Broumov (cloth), 58–72
Wolczanka S.A. (garments), 290–301
Textilpol, 302–14
costs, 308–9, 313
employment, 304
exports, 303–4, 307–8
external shocks, effect of, 306–9
financial indicators, 313
fixed assets, 304
history, 303
labor relations, 304
liquidity/activity ratios, 314
management, 305–6
profitability ratios, 314
restructuring program, 310–12
sales strategy, 309–10
sectoral setting, 302–3
wages, 304–5
Theta Works, 164–73
cost structure, 173

INDEX 459

Theta Works *(continued)*
  crisis management plan, 168
  financial indicators, 167–68
  future prospects, 171
  history, 164–65
  industry overview, 164
  inventories, 173
  labor/employment, 170–71
  management, 171
  output, 172
  privatization, 169–70
  product mix, 165–66
  profits, 172
  sales, 166–67, 172
Tipa (footwear), 104–14
  annual net profit (table), 112
  balance sheet, 112
  capital investment, 110
  corporate governance, changes in, 110
  external shocks, 108–9
  foreign collaboration, 110
  history, 106–8
  ownership, changes in, 110
  privatization, 105–6
  prospects, 111
  sectoral setting, 104–6
Total Quality Management (at DKG), 156
Tóth, Sándor, 218, 219
TQM. *See* Total Quality Management
Trade unions. *See* Labor relations
Training
  Huta Szkla Hortensja (glass), 330–31
  Radion Radio and Electrical Works, 204
Tridchem, 157
Triola, 51–52
TÜV, 156
TVK (heavy chemicals), 174–81
  cost structure (table), 181
  financial indicators, 177–78, 181
  history, 174–75
  industry overview, 174
  inventories, 181
  output volume (table), 180
  privatization, 178–80
  product mix, 175–77
  profit centers, 179
  rationalization program, 178
  restructuring, 178–79

TVK (heavy chemicals) *(continued)*
  sales strategy, 177

Undercapitalization
  CS-15 (textiles/garments), 54
  Elegant Charm (garments), 184, 185
  Radion Radio and Electrical Works,
    205–6
Unions. *See* Labor relations
Ursus, 432
Vanbrew Ltd., 233

VAZ Automobile Works, 253–57, 261
Veba Broumov (cloth), 58–72
  bidding for privatization shares (table),
    71
  budget constraints, 63
  costs, 72
  and cotton manufacturing techniques,
    61–62
  and currency devaluation, 63
  damask production by, 58–59, 65–66
  domestic market, decline of, 64–65
  employee policy, 69
  external shocks, 62–63
  financial ratios, 72
  history, 62
  human resources, 69
  and international business environment,
    65
  markets, 61, 63–65
  monetary policy, 63
  organizational changes, 68
  output, 72
  price liberalization, effect of, 64
  privatization, 67
  sectoral setting, 59–62
  SWOT analysis used by, 66–67

Wages
  Boryszew-Erg (plastics), 414
  CS-15 (textiles/garments), 49
  Desta (forklift trucks), 10–11
  DKG (oil and gas equipment), 162*n. 1*
  EGIS Pharmaceutical Works Ltd., 247
  Lodzkie Fabryki Mebli (wood products),
    360–61
  PO/5 (engineering/machine tools), 282

Wages *(continued)*
  Polar Enterprise (white goods), 391–92
  Polmo Enterprise (auto parts), 435
  Radion Radio and Electrical Works, 204, 211
  Textilpol, 304–5
  Wolczanka S.A. (garments), 292–93
Warimpex, 215
Warsaw Pact, 164
Weber, 432
Wedel S.A., 345
Western investment, xxiv
White goods (Polar Enterprise), 384–96
Wolczanka S.A. (garments), 290–301
  capital investments, 292
  cost structure (table), 300
  exports, 292
  financial indicators, 300
  history, 291

Wolczanka S.A. (garments) *(continued)*
  liquidity/activity ratios, 301
  management, 293
  market share, 291–92
  organizational structure, 293–94
  privatization, 296–99
  product mix, 291
  profits, 294, 301
  sales strategy, 294–96
  sectoral setting, 290–91
  taxation, effect of, 299
  wages, 292–93
Wood products (Lodzkie Fabryki Mebli), 357–70

X-raying, 198*n. 3*

Zastava, 253
Zavody tezkeho strojirenstvi (ZTM), 3

The Stuart Editions

SHORT FICTION
OF THE
SEVENTEENTH CENTURY

The Stuart Editions
J. Max Patrick, *series editor*

ALREADY PUBLISHED

An Anthology of Jacobean Drama, VOLUME I
   EDITED WITH AN INTRODUCTION, NOTES, AND VARIANTS
   BY RICHARD C. HARRIER

The Complete Poetry of Ben Jonson
   EDITED WITH AN INTRODUCTION, NOTES, AND VARIANTS
   BY WILLIAM B. HUNTER, JR.

Short Fiction of the Seventeenth Century
   SELECTED AND EDITED BY CHARLES C. MISH

The Complete Poetry of Robert Herrick
   EDITED WITH AN INTRODUCTION AND NOTES
   BY J. MAX PATRICK

The Complete English Poetry of John Milton
   ARRANGED IN CHRONOLOGICAL ORDER WITH AN
   INTRODUCTION, NOTES, AND VARIANTS
   BY JOHN T. SHAWCROSS

The Stuart Editions

Short Fiction of the Seventeenth Century

SELECTED AND EDITED
BY
CHARLES C. MISH

New York University Press
1963

This book was first published in 1963 in the
Doubleday Anchor Seventeenth-Century Series.
Library of Congress Catalog Card Number 63–7685
Copyright © 1963 by Doubleday & Company, Inc.
All Rights Reserved
Printed in the United States of America

CONTENTS

Introduction	vii
The Famous and Renowned History of Morindos (1609)	1
Robert Anton: Moriomachia (1613)	43
The Life of Long Meg of Westminster (1620)	79
The Tinker of Turvey (1630)	115
John Reynolds: Don Juan and Marsillia (1635)	193
Bishop Francis Godwin: The Man in the Moon (1638)	235
Aeneas Sylvius (Pius II): Eurialus and Lucretia (1639)	285
Cawwood the Rook (1640)	339
Alexander Hart: Alexto and Angelica (1640)	365
Fortunatus (*ca.* 1700)	423
Notes	453
Bibliography	457

INTRODUCTION

The reader who picks up this volume is about to embark upon a real adventure, for seventeenth-century fiction, in striking contrast to the work of the Elizabethan Age proper, is relatively unknown. In view of the variety of entertaining stories available during the century this general neglect seems strange and rather hard to account for, though perhaps it is the lack of big names among the fiction writers of the period that is to blame. Yet if the seventeenth century has no Sidney or Greene or Lodge it does have a number of interesting and highly readable volumes of fiction which can easily challenge comparison with their sixteenth-century predecessors. The dramatists of the Stuart era certainly thought so, for, like Shakespeare, they borrowed heavily from their story-telling contemporaries, and so too must the general public have thought, to judge from the great number of editions of fiction titles published. Particularly notable is the wide variety of kinds of stories available, ranging in length from the huge romance in the French manner to pithy anecdotes, in tone from the courtly to the everyday, and in style from plain down-to-earth raciness to impossibly high-flown estheticism. Readers in the 1600s had no reason to complain of dearth or dullness.

Perhaps the most striking fact in seventeenth-century fiction is the twofold division into romantic and realistic. The reader always had, theoretically at least, a choice: idealized love and adventure, or crude but entertaining scenes of common life. On the one hand there was the body of romances and tales offering sentimentally refined love, exciting (if incredible) adventure, and bursts of elaborate rhetoric; on the other there was a smaller but still varied group of stories relating the rough and lively doings of middle-class actors in everyday settings. Conscious art naturally lavished its pains chiefly on the romantic fiction of the period, but there was no lack of realistic writers who could catch and hold attention just as well as their more ambitious fellows.

As the century wore on, these two kinds of material came more and more to be aimed each at a specific group of readers, the polite and the vulgar respectively. But the romantic fiction is not all of a piece: the story whose interest lay in its marvellous and fantastic episodes marks itself off from the one whose attraction lay in the courtly grace of the manners and feelings displayed, and, with the passing of time, material once the property of the cultured classes descends to an audience lower in the social scale. Educated readers then—as now—wanted something new, fresh, and different; the middle-class citizen liked things that were tried and true. Hence as decade followed decade the number of titles written especially for the man in the street was swollen by the addition of other stories coming down in the scale of admiration. Greene's *Pandosto* or *Amadis de Gaule* must have been well received by the fashionable when they first appeared, but who would have been reading them in the 1690s except the culturally retarded?

Romantic fiction, to speak of that first, comes in various lengths, ranging from the full-fledged romance, running to several hundred thousand words, to the romantic tale, hardly ever going over fifty thousand. Within the category of romance proper, there are several subdivisions discernible, the chivalric, the sentimental, and the heroic, not to mention their attendants, the anti-romance and the religious romance. Dominating the field at the beginning of the century, the chivalric romance has certain well defined characteristics: it breathes the spirit of the *chansons de geste*, from which it descends; it relates the life history of a great hero, whose story is chronologically unfolded from his birth (sometimes indeed from his very conception) to

Introduction

his death; the staple matter is fighting, for distressed damsels, the Christian faith, and kings and princes in danger; there is little regard for motivation or probability. A number of these romances appeared during the seventeenth century, both older ones like *Valentine and Orson* and the already mentioned *Amadis de Gaule*, along with its rivals, the several members of the *Palmerin* series, and new imitations, like *Evordanus, Prince of Denmark*, and Henry Roberts's *Pheander*. Two of the imitations proved so popular that new editions were demanded every few years throughout the century: these were Richard Johnson's *Seven Champions of Christendom*, and Emanuel Forde's *Parismus, Prince of Bohemia*.

Quite different in form and tone is the romance of sentimental adventure, which made its appearance in English first in 1616 with the publication of Thomas Gainsford's *History of Trebizond*. The prototype of this genre is the *Ethiopian History* of Heliodorus, a late Greek prose romance dating probably from the second century, which was translated into various Western languages in the 1500s —the English version, done by Thomas Underdowne, appeared about 1569—and which was much admired and imitated everywhere. The most obvious influence of Heliodorus lay in the matter of structure; the *Ethiopian History* and its imitations all chose the circular epic form, with its plunge *in medias res* and consequent narration of antecedent action by means of flashback technique. Again, many of Heliodorus's plot devices recur over and over in romantic stories of the Renaissance: oracles, pirates, shipwrecks, disguises, all contribute tellingly if a bit mechanically to the basic plot—to keep hero and heroine apart until the final scene. In spite of these tricks, however, this sort of romance shows more concern with plausibility of motivation and probability in action than the chivalric romance, is relatively more interested in analysis of inward feelings (especially in connection with love), and frequently contains touches of realism. In all respects, these romances are a stage ahead of the chivalric.

The highest development of this sort of romance is seen in the French heroic romance, which began to make its way in England with the publication of a translation of Gomberville's *Polexander* in 1647. In France these romances had a *succès fou*, but relatively few of them got into English; most of the work of Mlle de Scudéry (*Clelia, Artamenes or The Grand Cyrus, Almahide, Ibrahim*) and of La Calprenède (*Cassandra, Cleopatra, Pharamond*) was made available, and there were a few native imitations, such as Boyle's *Parthenissa* and Bulteel's *Birinthea*. But the huge length of these productions—some of them run close to a million words—and possibly too their impossible elegance militated against them. They are difficult to read because the inset tales, in which the antecedent action is narrated, proliferate wildly and there are even inset tales within inset tales, so that one must be most attentive or he loses the thread of the story. The number of named and important characters in each romance is tremendous, and the action, not surprisingly, moves very slowly. The social world depicted is extraordinarily polished, courtly, and noble; it goes about its chief business, the pursuit of love and honor, in an atmosphere drenched with lofty sentiments and tender feelings. To fight nobly and to woo fervently constitute life.

The world of romance was not without its hangers-on, chief of whom were those writers, clerical or lay, who saw in the popularity of these books an opportunity to save souls, or at least to inculcate a religious lesson. The examples of religious romance placed before the English reader in the seventeenth century were practically all translations from the French. The most notable of these was Jean de Cartigny's *Voyage of the Wandering Knight*, first translated by William Goodyear in 1581, and frequently reprinted during the next century. The story is highly allegorized, the action seeming more a parody than a real imitation of chivalric romance, with the hero undergoing adventures much like those in *Pilgrim's Progress*; led by a guide named Folly, he chooses the green and grassy

Introduction

path which leads to the Palace of Felicity, instead of the strait and rocky one which Virtue advised him to follow; almost comes to grief, but luckily repents in time, and is permitted to enter the Palace of Virtue in the end. The most voluminous purveyor of these stories was Jean Camus, Bishop of Belley in France, who turned out a number of pious stories, such as *Diotrephe, or a History of Valentines* (1641), in which allegory is abandoned for out-and-out preaching. The most important English accomplishment in this line before *Pilgrim's Progress* was *The Isle of Man*, by Richard Bernard (1626), a clergyman, of which a good many editions were produced, in England, in Scotland, and even in Boston.

A diametrically opposed reaction to the romance appeared in the so-called anti-romance, which, written by men who apparently found the romantic aspects of the genre far too repugnant to common sense, led ridiculous heroes through mock-heroic and ludicrous adventures. Such is the case with Anton's *Moriomachia*, reprinted below, and also with a later and more highly developed specimen, Samuel Holland's *Don Zara del Fogo* (also called *Wit and Fancy in a Maze*), 1656, which is always quite funny and at times almost brilliant. Charles Sorel's two works in this kind may also be mentioned, *The Extravagant Shepherd*, 1653 (specifically called an anti-romance in its subtitle), and *The Comical History of Francion*, 1655, both translated from the French.

When romance was served up in smaller quantities the result may be called the tale, and of these the seventeenth century had good store too, both in collections and in individually published titles. The best of these tales probably are the reprints of older stories, like the fifteenth-century *Eurialus and Lucretia* by Aeneas Sylvius (Pope Pius II), and the later work of Lodge and Greene. Lodge's *Rosalynde* proved very popular in the seventeenth century, as did too certain of Greene's well-managed tales, *Ciceronis Amor, Pandosto*, Greene's *Never Too Late* (*Francesco's Fortunes*), and *Menaphon*. In general, those tales read like miniature romances of sentimental adventure. Their chief concern, of course, is love, and the course of the development of the tender passion is traced in the usual series of debates, soliloquies, and letters, all conceived in a rather high-minded vein. Frustrated love normally leads to dire sickness unto death, but luckily the plots prefer to end happily. Narrative and speeches alike are couched in a rather elevated style which attempts to mingle good-breeding, refined sentiment, and learned allusion.

Those tales published for the first time during the first half of the century are not as good as the older ones, chiefly because their writers seem less impelled by a desire to tell a story than by a wish to preen their literary style in public. Hence the strained language, bordering on the fantastic, which appears in such confections as Robert Kittowe's *Love's Load-Star* (1600), Hart's *Alexto and Angelica* (1640), and John Reynolds's *Flower of Fidelity* (1650). Reynolds may perhaps be forgiven his departures from the bounds of good taste because he is the author of the collection of thirty tales entitled *The Triumphs of God's Revenge,* which contains perhaps the best stories of the time; they are highly moralized, of course, and the voice of the preacher sounds forth perhaps a little too often, but in spite of this they tell good stories full of rousing crimes and horrors in a fairly straightforward way, and are, all things considered, eminently readable.

There are also other moral tales, ranging from the darkly baroque *Morindos* to the pathetic story of Patient Grisel, the model of wifely obedience. Among these stories are several of a decidedly "folk" character, such as the *History of the Damnable Life and Deserved Death of Dr. John Faustus,* the cautionary tale of *Reynard the Fox* and its close imitation, that of *Cawwood the Rook,* the medieval collection of exempla called the *Gesta Romanorum,* the *Seven Wise Masters* with its imitation, the *Seven Wise Mistresses,* and, one must add, that perennial favorite, Aesop's *Fables,* the latter in several translations. It is likely that these titles, since they appeared regularly in black let-

Introduction xiii

ter text editions, a distinctly old-fashioned, and indeed unfashionable, type face, appealed chiefly to less fashionable readers. They are therefore somewhat allied, in style and appeal, to the material dealing with everyday life or roguery, in which incipient realism makes itself seen.

A realistic or at least an anti-romantic attitude towards men and events is to be found in those short stories of everyday middle-class life called merry tales, characterized by the fact that the theme is ordinarily that of the "tables turned." Designed for the entertainment of a rather coarse-grained audience, they exhibit plots which are fairly rough and tumble, even at times cruel. They seek, professedly, to provoke "honest mirth," which apparently means uproarious, table-thumping laughter of a hearty, boisterous kind. Though there must have been many such stories circulating by word of mouth in the seventeenth century, comparatively few found their way into print. Three such collections, however, exist: Tarlton's *News Out of Purgatory*, first published in 1590 and reprinted in 1630; *The Cobbler of Canterbury*, also 1590, and reprinted at least three times in the next century, the 1630 edition (reproduced below) bearing the new title of *The Tinker of Turvey*; and finally *Westward for Smelts*, 1620. All three are anonymous.

Because their plots turn on the device of the "biter bit," such stories form one class of a kind of literary fare called jestbook material. The other two classes are collections of jokes or similar funny stories, ranging in length from a single exchange of remarks between two speakers to a description of a foolish incident running to a page or a page and a half. Though it is surprising to see how well many of the jokes stand up after three centuries and more, these stories are really too short to offer much of literary interest, and it is in the last class of the jestbook category that the strength of this material lies. This final group is called, rather awkwardly, jest-biographies. Made up of material much like that in the other two classes, these books attempt to organize their narrations of incident around the life of a single well-known individual, of whom they offer a sort of life-story.

Jest-biographies include the stories of such actual historical characters as John Scoggin, Will Summers, Henry VIII's jester, and the dramatist George Peele, as well as those of legendary figures such as Long Meg of Westminster, George a Greene, the famous pinner of Wakefield, and Robin Goodfellow. On the whole these often somewhat crude productions display a good deal more vitality and strength than their upper-class counterparts, and in a few special cases they are surprisingly well done. *Dobson's Dry Bobs*, for instance, a jest-biography, has had many admirers and has been called a worthy predecessor of Defoe; its unknown author had almost all the gifts required of a good novelist. As is the case with the quite similar Deloney, also quite popular in the period, to read these books is to get a first-hand look at seventeenth-century England; they offer some concrete details for a reconstruction of what life was really like in that time at that place.

From material of this sort it is but a step to picaresque stories and the literature of roguery. The anonymous prototype of picaresque fiction, the brilliant and influential sixteenth-century *Lazarillo de Tormes*, was reprinted during the seventeenth century, and the continuation of the story by Juan de Luna was also translated and made available to English readers as *The Pursuit of the History of Lazarillo* in 1622. Other notable examples of the Spanish *picaro* appeared in Mateo Aleman's *The Rogue, or The Life of Guzman de Alfarache*, translated by James Mabbe in 1622, in Carlos Garcia's *The Son of the Rogue*, 1638, and in Quevedo's *The Life and Adventures of Buscon the Witty Spaniard*, 1657. Shortly after this last title appeared there was published the most considerable English book of this sort, Richard Head's *The English Rogue Described, in the Life of Meriton Latroon*, 1665, for which Francis Kirkman provided three successive sequels; the book was reprinted many times and even today is not without its admirers.

Finally there is a body of miscellaneous fiction of various

Introduction

kinds in which the narrative element must share the limelight with the didactic and on occasion yields to it almost entirely. It is not easy to categorize this sort of material, though certainly one or two obvious groupings make themselves seen in the general mass. One such class is utopian fiction, with which may be closely associated the *voyage imaginaire*. The oldest representative of this material is Lucian's *True History*, translated into English in 1634, but pride of place must undoubtedly go to More's own work, which gave the whole genre and the very notion of an ideal commonwealth its common name. The *Utopia* duly made its appearance during the century, first in Ralph Robinson's translation, slightly modernized from its original sixteenth-century dress, and then in Bishop Burnet's version later. The seventeenth century also saw the appearance of some utopias of its own: Bacon's *New Atlantis* in 1626, Joseph Hall's *Discovery of a New World* around 1609, and Francis Godwin's *Man in the Moon,* the last two originally written in Latin but quickly rendered into English for wider circulation. The genre was continued by the translations of Cyrano de Bergerac's *Selenarchia, or The Government of the World in the Moon,* Denis Vairasse's *History of the Sevarites,* and others, leading down to Defoe's *Consolidator, or Memoirs of Sundry Transactions from the World of the Moon* in 1705.

Another group of miscellaneous fiction can be lumped together under the general heading of satire. Lucian again makes his appearance here, as do such native writers as Dekker with his *News from Hell* in 1606 and John Johnson with his *Academy of Love* in 1641 (in which is described, with a good deal of wit, how young ladies and gentlemen learn the rules of amatory behavior proper to a worldly and materialistic society). In most of these books the narrative thread is of the slightest, serving merely to act as a basis for what the writer is really interested in, his criticism of society; in a book like the extremely popular *Visions* by Quevedo, the narrative has faded out almost altogether to give place to invective and railing against the standard targets of satire: venal lawyers, quack doctors, corrupt priests, pedants, fools, lovers, and so on. Somewhere between an amusing story ironically told and a spate of denunciation the spring of fiction runs dry.

Finally we may briefly mention, as the last home of fiction, serious works of admonition which use illustrative anecdotes to point up their precepts. Examples of this sort of book may be found in such works as Thomas Beard's *Theatre of God's Judgments,* at one end of the century, and at the other, in the numerous compilations of Nathaniel Crouch, who, under the pseudonym of Robert Burton, turned out a sizable number of hortatory books with titles like *Wonderful Prodigies of Judgment and Mercy,* 1681; *Unparalleled Varieties,* 1683; and *Female Excellency,* 1688, all of them adorned with many monitory examples.

It will be seen from the above that the seventeenth century had a good deal of fiction, and that of several kinds. It had writers who could tell a story, who could write dialogue, and who were interested in the analysis of feelings. Yet it never took the step of combining all the elements to make the sort of fiction which we have today, or which the eighteenth century had. It has been suggested that if somebody had but thought to graft the seventeenth-century genre known as the prose character—a sort of descriptive sketch of a representative member of a particular class of individuals—on a realistic tale, something like the novel might have emerged. Perhaps so, but for whatever reason the grafting did not take place, and the world had to wait till the next century for the novel. The seventeenth century, however, could hardly have missed what it did not have, and, as things were, it certainly did not lack for entertaining stories entertainingly told.

※　※　※

The stories which follow have been chosen with three things in mind: to give as wide a variety as possible, to offer representative samples of the kinds chosen, and to give examples which were truly popular in their own day.

Larger kinds, like the romance, are necessarily omitted, but it is hoped that the tales selected will not only meet the three requirements above, but also a fourth: to be intrinsically interesting and genuinely entertaining.

A NOTE ON THE TEXTS

Since most readers today find seventeenth-century prose texts in their pure state troublesome to read, the tales which follow have been modernized. Spelling has been normalized, and some attempt has been made to bring punctuation and paragraphing into conformity with present-day practice, though it must be admitted that often enough seventeenth-century constructions are not well adapted to twentieth-century rules. Vocabulary and syntax have not been altered, though occasionally an archaic verb form has fallen victim to respelling. I have silently corrected what seemed to be obvious misprints (e.g. "not" for "now"), have attempted to impose some consistency in the spelling of proper nouns, and have touched up a few mangled foreign words and phrases, but beyond that I have not made any changes. Passages which seemed to be nonsense in the original still stand as possible nonsense.

In each case the particular edition used as the basis for the modernized version is given. I wish to thank the following libraries for their gracious permission to reprint texts in their possession: The Bodleian Library for *Morindos;* the Folger Shakespeare Library for *Long Meg* and *Fortunatus;* the Harvard University Library for *Cawwood the Rook;* the Henry E. Huntington Library for *Alexto and Angelica, Eurialus and Lucretia, The Man in the Moon, The Tinker of Turvey,* and *Moriomachia.* A grant from the University of Maryland Graduate School also provided leisure for some of the reading which went into the selection.

C.C.M.

College Park, Maryland
1962

SHORT FICTION
OF THE
SEVENTEENTH CENTURY

THE
Famous & renowned

Hiſtory of *Morindos* a King of
Spaine; Who maryed with *Miracola* a Spaniſh Witch: and of their ſea-
nen daughters, (*rightly ſurna-
med* Ladies with bleeding
hearts:)*their births,their
liues and their
deaths.*

A Hiſtory moſt wonderfull, ſtrange, and plea-
ſant to the reader.

LONDON
Printed for *H R.* and are to be ſolde at his
Shop in the Poultrie vnder Saint Mildreds
Church. 1609

MORINDOS (1609)

Rivalling the love tale in numerical importance, and perhaps exceeding it in contemporary popularity, is the moral tale, of which *The Famous and Renowned History of Morindos* is an example. A somewhat diffuse category, the genre embraces within its limits both short, pithy, didactic stories like fables and apologues, and longer pieces of fiction which present a narrative of some consequence. Of the latter the two chief divisions are the allegory, earnest and rather depersonalized, and the warmly told stories of strong passions from the dire effects of whose ill-regulated workings obvious lessons may be learned. Of this last kind is the ensuing story.

In *Morindos* we enter an appalling world of evil, one where the dark forces of transcendent wickedness have their abode. Morindos himself is, as the title page tells us, a King of Spain who marries a witch who by him has seven daughters whose strange lives and deaths form the body of the book. The spiritual enormities detailed in their and their mother's stories are prevented from seeming ludicrous to the modern reader, as they easily might, by the intensity of their presentation. The author, whoever he was, has succeeded in producing a real chamber of horrors.

Quite different in style from anything else written in the period, *Morindos* is told with a good deal of narrative strength, the author uniting a truly medieval sense of sin with a baroque feeling for horror. His style conveys his conceptions in an adequately harrowing way, rising at times almost to a burning glow. There is, as will be seen, much vivid and concrete description, lovingly written, of physical detail and of the appearance of persons and settings. Toward the end, the writer's interest or invention flags somewhat, and the stories of the later sisters, disproportionately short, lack the fullness of feeling which characterizes the earlier ones. Perhaps better so; a whole series of tales told with the ferocity of Miracola's own might be too much to bear.

The text which follows is based on the unique copy of the text in the possession of the Bodleian Library.

THE FAMOUS AND RENOWNED HISTORY OF MORINDOS

Chapter 1. How Morindos, a King of Spain, married with Miracola, a witch; and how he was transformed without shape for polluting the temple of God.

When Spain was nursed with the milk of paganism, virtue not known, nor God honored, there lived a people so ripe in sin that the keen edge of shame's sickle lay even ready whetted to reap them down for confusion's harvest; yet the subjects then living were not so wicked as the king vicious: a king we name him, if illustrious title of majesty may grace so pernicious a foe to nature with so royal a style. His birth was fatal, for when the midwife pulled him from the cradle of his conception the earth quaked and heaven rained blood; his parents ominous, the one devoured by wolves, the other burnt to death by thunder; his youth full of unlucky chances, his age tyrannous and mischievous, and all his life subject to black misdeeds. When his parents by heaven's wrath had ended thus their days, he reigned king and wore the imperial diadem, but such a king good men thought never sprung from woman's womb. Morindos, for so we name him, being seated upon the throne of majesty, ruled not in love but by force, making his nobles slaves to his sin and their wives feeders of his lust, for every day in the year he had a several concubine, all young, beautiful, and lovely; nature framed their bodies fair, though sin made their souls black. For both art and riches endeavored to delight his insatiate desires, earth's chiefest pleasures were at his command, and all the lullabies of content rocked him in the cradle of security; thus careless of heaven's wrath he more honored the Devil than he loved God, and what was the vilest to nature he most doted upon. But now after all these pleasures of his wanton youth, the kind embraces of his fair concubines, which like earthly angels made him happy in nature's sports, he wickedly fell enamored upon one of the Devil's black saints, one Madam Miracola, a witch of damnation, now burning in Hell for her black deeds. This Madam Miracola, born of noble parentage, brought up in the deepest arts, skillful in magic charms and incantations, who having spent seven years in that deep mystery of conjuration, seldom sleeping without the society of spirits, fairies, goblins, or nightly shapes, her chiefest study and aim was at principality, to rule sole queen and governor of the kingdom, and no way was there to attain to that imperial seat but by marrying with King Morindos, though not a match fit, he being descended royally, she but nobly. Yet by sorceries, witchcrafts, and magic devices, she obtained her purpose, and in this manner obtained it.

Upon a time when King Morindos, in the height of his revels, whilst some of his fairest concubines danced before him naked in their cambric smocks, the more to enkindle lust's fire, she entered the chamber of their licentious sports, with a masque of wonder, the like never seen in prince's court; for all the masquers, except herself, were infernal spirits, visible but not tangible, all in the shape of young ladies, attired in more changeable silks than the colors of the rainbow, herself in a robe of such richness as it seemed to exceed the glory of the sun for brightness. Her own body she embathed and suppled with a water of such enchantment that what man soever first set eye upon her, either present love or present death had destiny allotted him, for well knew she that no man presumed his presence during this time of pleasure.

This Madam Miracola, assisted by the black states of Hell, by delusions won the King's love, whose inconstant eyes, no sooner fixed their inflecting beams on this killing cockatrice, but all on a sudden fire his love inflamed that nothing could quench it but her love joined to his, which were immediately sealed together. Love, desire, and lust so conspired against his bewitched heart that he presently avoided the chamber of his enticing damsels and she of her deluding spirits. Remaining then but two bodies, two hearts, and two tongues, he began to reveal love's secrecy in this manner. "Madam," quoth he, knowing her to be a long attender in his court, "good or evil fortune hath enchanted me, and now thy present love or hate must either glorify me with earthly happiness or send me wandering to the darksome walks of death, where no society but crawling worms and dead men's bones are resident. Deny me not, therefore, good Madam; I am this country's potentate, I can command both wealth and power, cities, towers and towns; statesmen stoop and humbly kneel unto my foot; royalties, dignities, and all other kingly promotions are at my disposing; unto my pleasure all the land submits; delights are my vassals; both land and sea as subjects strive to make me happy. I am an earthly god; be thou my goddess. Take all these honors; I will attend on thee, I'll be thy subject, thy servant, I will kiss thy foot; deny not my love, for thou hast bewitched my heart, enchanted me, fired me with a quenchless flame, all my body burns and nothing but the sweet dew of thy grant can qualify it. Make me either unfortunate or happy, sweet Madam."

This being breathed from his longing soul, she, far more tractable to love's motions than he, made a full conclusion of a willing acceptance in this sort. "I have a mind, imperious monarch," said she, "soaring up to the battlements of heaven. No base desires nor low-bred thought shall any whit aspire my princely will. I aim at a kingly bed, where majesty sleeps, whose chamber is imperious, guarded with commanding statesmen. Seven weary winters and as many summers have my hopes been climbing up this kingly ladder, and now on the top of Fortune's wheel am I fallen into a prince's bosom. In loving me, great king, thou conquerest Fate, thou subjectest Hell, thou mayest, by my assistance, command legions of the black host to hover over thy palace, and in the twinkling of an eye blast up all thy wicked conspirators. If our minds but once prove equal in the cheer of sovereignty, the earth shall be far too little for thy government; my magic charms shall unbowel the earth, rip up her bosom, ransack her rich treasures for thy use; my magic charms for thee and for thy pleasure shall empty the vast ocean and cram thy kingdom with those riches that man's eye hath not seen since the world's creation; my charms for thy content shall pave thy court with pearls, emeralds and diamonds. Command, great king, and the marble stones that now compass thy palace shall dance and the air like singing cherubins sound us heavenly harmony; contents, delights, pleasures, joys, and all the solaces of heaven and earth shall be thy attendants by investing me thy equal in great majesty." Thus, and in this manner, did she climb the supremacy and tied upon her back the title of a queen.

Being both enchanted thus, and entangled in the snares of desire, they immediately tied Hymen's knot, a band that none sunders but death; the marriage they solemnized the same night, not able to stay the morning's rise, but as black thoughts have black events, so in black manner was this marriage celebrated. It was even at the middle of night, when the screech-owl, rooks, and dormice sleep in foggy mists; it was even at that hour when the ghosts of dead men walk, when murderers dream of villainy, even when the earth had her sable garments on, was this sacred knot united, both being impatient of delay, he burning in lust, she aspiring a kingdom, converted the holy temple to a marriage bed. Be ever black this deed of Hell, and never be it told but with a trembling tongue, for never was night more dark than this. The sable curtains of the air were all as pitch and seemed to hide this polluted sin; the earth cast up such a misty vapor that extinguished both fire and cresset-lights; art could not make one candle's flame, nor any means of brightness to behold each other. So wicked was this enterprise of theirs that both heaven and earth showed fatal prodigies, and everything, that dismal night, grew different from nature: nothing was heard but howling dogs, croaking toads, and hissing snakes, unknown voices bellowed in the court and the polluted temple so vilely stained was compassed about with ghastly spirits, fire-drakes, and walking goblins. But mark now the strangest of all wonders: even at the very instant when the seed of procreation conjoined, even as it were a cry of mandrakes struck the king into a madness, blaspheming heaven till his tongue grew dumb, his eyes blind, his ears deaf, his joints numb, and all his body shapeless, and as a bear new-whelped, like a lump of flesh without fashion, lay clasped in the arms of this new-made queen. But now when the morning came and that the light of heaven summoned all creatures from sleep, the nobles of his court came to his bedside, thinking to give them both a joyful good-morrow, but even as their lips gave way to their tongues' passage, their eyes espied this fearful accident: a judgment that heaven has seldom yet shown, which was a king deaf, dumb, blind, and senseless, but breathing life. Which strange sight struck the nobles into such amaze that without any further speech they forsook the court, confidently thinking it unhappy in harboring so vile a monster as this king was.

Now this new-made queen or damned enchantress, having purchased a kingdom by her black proceedings, was so blinded with the greatness of majesty and so ravished with the brightness of a crown, being now sole queen and governor thereof, made a careless sport of God's judgment, and having in her court none left but parasites and flatterers, such as are commonly the right hands to principalities, made the greatest sinners the most honorable and held the vicious in best regard. The deformed shape of the king, having life but no senses, she caused to be put in a brazen coffin and fed him daily with human blood, which she poured into his mouth through quills of silver. The success hereof you shall hear in the next chapter, and what a strange conception she had after this first night of her marriage.

Chapter 2. How the enchanted queen made the devils a banquet with her husband's body; her three questions to the same devils, and their answers; and of her despairing lamentations in a dark dungeon.

Soon blasted were the hopes of this aspiring queen, and scowling mischance with a bended brow hemmed in their marriage bed; heaven's wrath and Hell's fury laid heavy burdens upon them and, as it were, broke their heartstrings asunder, for Miracola, after she had coffined her deformed husband yet breathing life, melancholy despair and pining grief chiefly attended upon her; discontent, suspicion, and fear were her guardians by day and by night; strange visions, doleful outcries, and unquiet dreams assailed her; wild beasts strayed from the woods and in tame manner made them dens within her court; unlucky birds forsook the air to sit upon her palace, such as night owls and croaking ravens be, sounding forth fatal and harsh harmony. The sun seemed to shine upon her with a scowling face, the moon as ashamed of her soul's damnation in conferring thus with devils as it were drew back behind the pitchy clouds and unwillingly lent light unto the meaner stars; each thing grew contrary to kind, only herself excepted, for she having made an atonement with the princes of the fiery world put her whole confidence in them and only trusted through their assistance to lead Fortune in a string and at her pleasure command kingdoms.

So upon an evening, when the day's bright eye had left heaven's fair palace, and night with her black canopy had compassed in the earth, she betook her to her private chamber, where Medea-like she raised up her old servants, the furies, or rather the spirits of darkness, from their burning beds, such as condemned souls lie flaming upon, who no sooner presented themselves before her but she questioned them in this manner. "I charge you," quoth she, "you enemies to heaven and man, by the band and condition made betwixt you and me sealed with my dearest blood, and by the seven sucking babes that I once offered to you at midnight, and by the hope you have of my soul's purchase at my death's fatal hour, answer me truly to three several questions which here I will presently propound unto you. First, how long my life shall continue; secondly, whether I shall die a queen or not; lastly, the number of my children and their following fortunes." To which propositions, these instruments of mischief immediately condescended to answer, but upon this strange condition following: that as a fee to these black barristers she should deliver up her husband's deformed body and serve it to them in seven several banquets, that both his flesh and blood as a bribe to Hell might be made food for spirits. Which demand to this woman monster seemed but an easy request and therefore like to the viper, which feeds upon her own dam, gave that life and body to the tyranny of Hell, which ought to have been precious in the eye of Heaven, and the dearest jewel of her own heart. These diligent deceivers having no sooner promise of this purchased prize but in a mystical sort, or riddle-like, gave answers to her three former questions in this sort. First, for the continuance of her life, they said she should live till the seven days of the week were forgotten. The second question was whether she should die a queen or not; they answered that neither heaven nor earth, God nor man, should take her kingdom from her. The third and last question was to know the number of her children and their following fortunes; to this they answered that from her body should spring seven branches, whose tops should reach to heaven. These answers to this accursed woman's ears came more joyful than the reports of pardon to a condemned man and more pleasing to her heart than for a Moorish slave from the chained galley to be advanced unto a kingdom. Therefore with a settled trust and assurance of the Spanish crown and government, little mistrusting the sly deceits of these mystical answers, with all convenient speed provided a chamber wherein she might perform her damned condition and deliver up her husband's body to the gluttony of Hell. Therefore ascending to the top of her palace into a marble tower, she caused her husband's body to be brought thither, and after commanded the walls to be hung round about with black mourning cloth, to signify her damned and fatal enterprise. This being done, she purposed to divide the service of her seven banquets into seven several days, and in this manner were they accomplished.

The first day upon a table of black ebony, in two iron plates or platters, she set the two legs of her unhappy husband, which so often in his good days of fortune bestrode the warlike palfrey in the honor of his country. The second day upon the same ebony table she placed his sinewed thighs, in two vessels of lead, whose blue veins signified the force and strength of manhood. The third day she likewise brought to the table his secret parts and bowels, in a vessel of tin or pewter, wherein lay the seed of procreation. The fourth day she furnished the same table, in a charger of brass, with the belly and inward parts of his body, which had so often been cherished with delicious and princely banquets. The fifth day in like manner in a vessel of compounded metal named alchemy she brought to the table his manly breast, which as a tower had many years closed up his heart. The sixth day in a platter of fine silver, she served in the two arms of her husband, which whilst virtue governed held both the scepter of peace and the sword of war. The seventh and last day in a vessel of pure gold, being the dearest and richest service, she brought in his head, which had so often been ornified with an imperial diadem, containing a tongue that could in former times have given thee life or death: all these unnatural services by the hands of a wolvish-natured woman.

Being no sooner finished and the fatal table avoided,

but both heaven and earth, land and sea, as it were gave echoes of terror; Hell itself seemed to tremble and spewed up corrupted savors, and from her fiery furnaces cast abroad such sparkling flames, that even the embroidered vestures beset with goldsmiths' workmanship, so gorgeously beautifying her body, were fired and the golden trammels of her hair burned from her head. Notwithstanding all this, nothing amazed the shameless mind of Miracola, nor any way affrighted her with the terror of heaven's wrath, for the thirst of promotion so bewitched her, ambitious pride so enchanted her, and the desire of a diadem so emboldened her, that thinking both crown and kingdom her assurance forever, by the false promises of Hell, immediately upon this same tower or chamber where she had thus sacrificed her husband's body, she caused certain characters or letters to be engraven upon the marble walls concerning her perpetual happiness.

The first superscription was to this effect following: *Upon this earth Miracola shall live till the seven days of the week be forgotten;* which she thought was forever. The second superscription was: *That neither heaven nor earth, God nor man, should take her kingdom from her.* The third: *That her children like seven branches should reach to heaven.*

These three promises she regarded as oracles and believed that through them her earthly happiness should never end; but suddenly this violent joy turned into an extreme grief, for as she stood contemplating of these never-ceasing delights, there entered invisible into the chamber one of the black potentates of Hell and under every one of these superscriptions engraved these significations. Under the first this: *The seven days of the week be thy seven daughters now breeding in thy womb, who no sooner ripe but rotten, no sooner born but forgotten.* Under the second: *Though neither heaven nor earth, God nor man, will take the kingdom from thee, yet Hell and the Devil shall.* Under the third: *The seven branches whose tops should reach to heaven be the seven deadly sins that shall spring from thy womb, whose bloody enterprises and black deeds shall climb heaven for an eternal judgment.*

These dismal and ominous revelations were no sooner seized upon by the eyes of this accursed queen but all the parts of her body trembled with fear; not a member but the terror thereof distempered. Now fear of God's vengeance by little and little entered into her heart, and the quivering thought of Hell's damnation filled her bosom full of despair. Without all hope of salvation, she enclosed herself in the center of the earth, in a cave where neither light of sun nor the glimmering brightness of the moon might descend, nor any voice of man or other creature could yield her comfort. Thus excluding herself from all worldly solaces, committing the government of her kingdom to sycophants and careless guiders, she wasted away the time of ten months in this dark and solitary dungeon, both day and night making these or such-like woeful lamentations:

"O Nature," quoth she, "thou nurse of every living thing, why didst not thou end me in my first beginning? Why did my mother's womb bring to light this my damned soul? Why did my cradle rock this my body of perdition to so many lullabies? I wish my nurse's pap had yielded nought but venomed poison and that my swathing clothes had been sheets of boiling lead, that both life and body at one instant had been both consumed. But woe is me, I am reserved for an eternal torment; my tongue hath consented to my soul's everlasting damnation and my hand sealed to a band that can never be cancelled till I be cast into Hell's devouring bowels. Fall upon me, thou great frame of heaven and cover me, thunder-claps descend, whirlwinds arise and cast me beyond the bounds of man's imaginations. Thou spirit of red vengeance, transform me to some venomous worm. Make me without soul or feeling, that my torments be not everlasting. Woe upon woe pursues me, for the gaining of a crown and kingdom have I sold and forever lost my dear soul, whom all the treasures both of earth and sea nor the prayers of good men can nevermore redeem. Cursed be mine eyes that trained me to this damned study; banned be my tongue that practised first these incantations; and woe to all my wits and senses that so cursedly gave over themselves to these magic charms and now rave and rage. Be you mad, distraught, and lunatic; dig up the bowels of the earth, and wander far beyond the Antipodes. But, oh, forever weep, weep, thou most miserable soul; howl and lament that grief may split asunder thy sad heart, for such a woeful heart never lived in woman's breast." Thus and in this manner spent she in deep lamentations both minutes, hours, weeks and months, till her womb grew big and the fruit therein ripe and ready to fall.

Chapter 3. How the enchanted queen was delivered of seven daughters at one time; and how she lay in childbed one and twenty years after.

Now betwixt her prodigious and unlucky marriage ten times had the silver moon renewed her brightness and the time of her delivery drew near unto the appointed hour, when in great torments both of soul and body she ascended from her dark habitation, where, for forty weeks her chiefest food was sorrow, grief, and care; but now like unto the owl ashamed of the light, she came abroad and caused provision to be made fitting for her delivery, and although her ladies inwardly hated her life and conversation, yet in charity and Christian love they attended her safety, being conducted to her chamber, where the painful hour of childbearing was to be endured. The pinching throes so tortured her womb, bearing so strange a burden, that she in very grief and agony thereof with her nails tore out her own eyes and would have rent the fruit alive out of her womb, had not the tender care of her ladies prevented her. Thus sightless and comfortless fell she in labor, wherein she continued in great extremity for the space of seven days, making such bitter moan and breathing from her painful heart such doleful groans as would have forced even merciless tigers to pity, and so strange was her delivery that the report thereof might fill large volumes with bitter lamentations. For in seven days she brought forth seven maiden children, everyone as hateful to the world as the seven deadly sins: all at one birth, a thing seldom seen, but that God in justice will show his judgment upon so inhuman a woman.

The first was born upon the Sunday, which we compare unto Pride, as the course of her life hereafter shall declare, which child was called Sola, after the day's name. The second upon the Monday, which we liken unto Envy, according to her life's quality, and bore the name of Lucina. The third upon Tuesday, which we allude unto Wrath, and therefore named Martia. The fourth upon Wednesday, supposed to be Covetousness, which we call Mercuria. The fifth upon Thursday, which we imagine to be Drunkenness, and therefore we name her Jovina. The sixth upon Friday, which we place for Lechery, and give her the name of Venorina. The seventh and last of this ominous brood was born upon the Saturday, which we term to be Sloth and so call her Saturnia.

Thus was the seed of shame brought into the world, at whose births seven black ravens sat croaking directly upon the top of her chamber, and the owlets of mischance with fatal wings fluttered against the crystal windows; each one of them born with teeth in their mouths, whereat the midwife and other her assistants, the ladies there present, were much amazed and with trembling hearts feared to behold so strange a spectacle of nature. But as Fate and Destiny had allotted, they of their own free wills provided for these seven monsters thus born seven several nurses, the wives of seven shepherds, which only had their habitations in woody caves, where they were diligently brought up and not once suffered till their full age to come within the court gates, where we will leave them to Fortune's direction for a time.

The woeful mother of these unfortunate children, being now safely delivered (through her own extreme violence lying sightless in her childbed, the only foe to worldly delights), in the hearing of many standers by breathed forth this pitiful complaint: "Oh, how happy is the silly worm," said she, "that hath neither soul nor understanding, whereby the threatening of everlasting torments may not affright it! The miseries of this world wherein I now deservedly lie are but as delights and sports in regard of them I shall feel when the doomsday of my life is past. I lie now as it were upon a bed of pricking thorns and stung with a thousand serpentine stings; but woe is me, my guilty conscience doubts that for my wilful losing of my soul I shall lie boiling in the red hot cauldron of damnation, more thousands of years than blades of grass grow upon the earth, leaves upon trees, or stars in the crystal firmament; and more, which terrifies my condemned soul, I shall lie there in consuming pain (but never consumed) more millions of years than as if a heap of sand should lie on earth, whose top should reach to heaven and once in every million of years an eagle should fetch away but one sand, yet would those years of torments have an end but mine can never finish, for selling that sweet soul that my dear Saviour's life was shed for. Methinks I hear seven sucking babes knocking at heaven gates for vengeance against me, for giving up their tender bodies as a food for spirits. Methinks I hear seven virgins, all the daughters of mighty potentates, accusing me for enchanting them to a heap of senseless stones. Methinks I hear seven aged men, whose heads were beautified with milk-white pledges of wisdom, all coming as witnesses against me, for sucking away their blood by spirits, in the likeness of asps and adders, and after sacrificing the marrow of their bones to the chief Prince of Darkness, for which my conscience now tells me that heaven's iron hand of vengeance is even ready to strike and that Hell's wrath is inventing new tortures for my soul. And now there is a horrid voice thunders in mine ear that this my ever-stained crime shall be also scourged in my seed, and all my kindred washed from the face of the earth into the unknown vault of forgetful-

History of Morindos

ness." And now in speaking these words, all her joints grew lame and numb, thereby to join in equal misery with her sightless eyes; where we will leave her now, as the picture of calamity, lying in childbed for the space of one and twenty years, and speak of her children's misfortunes, whose lives were as odious to the world as the seven deadly sins.

Chapter 4. Pride's tragedy: The life and death of Sola the proud, the first daughter to the enchanted queen, a history full of dole, woe, and calamity.

The eldest and first child of this viperous queen, born upon a Sunday, bearing the name of Sola, and being the true picture of pride, in life and nature persevering in that deadly sin, for being no sooner grown to the ripeness of age and that the years of discretion had grafted her with understanding, she was by the nobles and ladies of the land brought to the court, in hope that after her mother's decease (by the decree of frowning chance lying then in marvellous calamities) she would prove a gracious and good queen; but it happened far otherwise, for being now on the way of preferment and climbing up the steps of imperial dignity, a kind of commanding pride so bewitched her that she esteemed herself above woman's kind and that nature had framed her of no earthly substance but rather of the pure mold of celestial angels. Her crimson colored cheeks whereon the glory of beauty seemed to shine, her ivory front or forehead where art and nature strove for supremacy, and her bright twinkling eyes within whose pretty balls the god of love seemed to show himself were all, in her proud imaginations, too precious for the sun to shine upon, and herself, with all other parts of her body, the most pure workmanship of nature's experience, she held too angel-like to tread upon the gross earth. Therefore she, the more to advance her great pride, caused a chariot of crystal glass to be made, close framed on all sides to keep both winter's blasts and summer's heat from her delicate body, the which chariot by skillful art was wafted up and down by artificial means devised by man's invention. Her food was the purest restoratives of the earth, both of beasts, birds, fowls, and fishes, and the only quintessence of nourishments to maintain life. Her pleasures were the music and singing voices of young virgins, the daughters of noblemen and knights. Her garments were of the finest Medean silks, woven upon silver looms by Arabian queens. Thus pomp and pride elevating her mind as it were beyond the ambition of Lucifer, who sought to pull God out of heaven, and esteemed no man of that royal birth worthy to match with her in marriage; emperors and kings she accounted but as slaves to Fortune and the only subjects to variable chance. Many high personages enterprised the conquest of her love but reaped the fruits of denial and disgrace, and were not suffered that assuming favor as once to kiss her proud hand. Yet at last three bold adventurous gallants, hearing her thundering fame rumored about the world, attempted to purchase the conquest of this prize that neither emperors nor kings could obtain.

The first was a soldier, whose valor and matchless chivalry upon the wings of fame was carried up and down the earth as far as ever the golden eye of heaven hath showed his glistering brightness. The second was a scholar, whose academic skill in all the seven liberal sciences might challenge in all princes' courts the honors of the golden tongue. The third and last was a merchant, whose travels by sea round about the earth, compassing seven times the equinoctial line, purchased such wealth as builded one of the greatest cities in the world. These three, time's honored champions, coming before this proud lady of the earth, who, sitting then like a goddess upon the tribunal seat of majesty, began their loves' embassage in this manner.

"Divine Sola," said the soldier, "thou miracle of womankind, at whose birth good fortune danced, this body of mine is become thy humble vassal, and now yields all his purchased honors at thy gracious feet. I that by war have foraged kingdoms, unpeopled countries, and made whole fields flowing with blood, will now at thy royal command kiss the sacred plot of ground where thy celestial foot but standeth. I that have dyed the flinty pavements of conquered cities with the purple gore of human carcasses and fed my pampered steeds with the flesh of man am now subjected to thy thrice-glorious person, and challenge to myself no other happiness but one smiling glance from thy angelical eyes. Grant then thy love, thou jewel of nature, and let my soul feed upon the happiness that proceeds from the censure of thy blessed tongue in condescending to my love. Legions of adventurous knights shall fill thy palace with renown and by their knightly prowess fetch conquered kings from all the parts of the world to do obeisance to thy imperial greatness."

"And in loving me, great princess," quoth the scholar, "the unsearched studies of all sciences shall be at thy command: the pleasures of music, the helps of physic, the eloquence of tongues, the secrets of stars, the natures of nations, and moreover the sweet consolation of divine meditations shall elevate thy soul to the shining paradise of unspeakable blessedness. Then make a scholar happy in thy love, sweet Sola, in whose deep understanding lie the secrets both of air, earth, and sea."

"And in loving me, thou paragon of beauty," quoth the merchant, "the far-fetched treasures of rich India, the gold of Arabia, and the unvalued carbuncles of golden Ganges abundantly shall fall into thy lap. I have measured the earth seven times about, and upon the sea spread such a fleet of ships and rich argosies, which like to a topless forest seemed to hide heaven; all these for thee and for thy love shall sail to those nations where no sun shines nor moon gives light, to those kingdoms where one night continues six months, and (their purchase by long travel) those inestimable valued vestures which had wont to beautify the proud queens of Asia: damasks, golden tissues, and robes of silver shall be as common to thy delights as rich scarlets were to the princes of Judea. In loving me thou shalt be attended with more royalties than King Solomon was in all his pomp."

These and such-like were the proffered courtesies of these three gallant gentlemen, every one hoping thereby to obtain the good will of this proud lady, who was as far from kind acceptance of their services as the starved lioness is from mercy when she seizeth upon the innocent lamb; therefore, retaining no other counsellors but pride and ambition, the only nurses of confusion, without any further consideration made them this answer. "That man, high-spirited gentlemen, that in my bed shall set his foot and crop the bud of my virginity, the which I have denied unto kings, shall win the same grace with a severe task or knightly adventure. First to you, thou undaunted knight of war, if thou canst either by policy or manhood, either wit or conquest of thy sword, gain and purchase me a bed that shall be filled with a softer substance than the soft down that grows upon the milk-white swan's back, thou shalt enjoy my love and I will only be thy wife. Likewise to thee, thou scholar-like man of art, if by thy learning or any other deep mystery, thou canst frame me a fountain that shall contain a purer water than that which rains from heaven or that which springs from the conduits of the earth, thou shalt gain my love and I will be only thy wife. Lastly to thee, thou noble adventurous merchant, if thou by any travel either by land or sea canst find me a bread that shall be better than that of wheat, thou shalt have my love and I will only be thy wife." Upon these strict conditions, or rather Herculean labors, these three gallants without any further reply departed each one his several way, striving which of them should accomplish the task proposed unto them. Where we will leave them for a while travelling strange countries, diligently seeking to bring these their strange labors to an end, and speak of the woeful miseries that heaven afflicted this proud lady withal.

Many months passed over the head of this hated woman after their departures, and as she grew in age, so did her pride increase, insomuch that for the maintenance of her vain beauty she had attending upon her a hundred of fair and young wives that once every day with the milk of their breasts filled a cistern of fine gold, with the which every morning she bathed her body, only to make her beautiful fair and white skin more smooth and amiable; and that food which nature gave for the nourishment of young infants, according to God's will, she wickedly abused in the maintenance of pride and in the service of the Devil. This vile course of life she long wandered in, losing herself in the wilderness of black iniquity, till the all-seeing eyes of wrath descended heaven, and in a moment struck this proud creature into such an odious leprosy that neither eye could endure her sight nor nostril abide her corrupting savors. Now that body so finely framed of nature's chiefest mold, that lately would not endure the whistling of the gentle winds, were now more loathsome than the spotted adder; and that clear celestial face, that disdained to entertain the comfortable heat of the warm sun, was now more odious to man's sight than the swelling toad, and all those ladies that had wont to attend upon her forsook her company and fled her chamber as from a den of snakes. They that kept nearest to her were distressed people and vile malefactors, such as were lately delivered from loathsome prisons and deep dungeons, and these, in contempt of heaven's judgment, caused she with sharp razors to flay off the upper skin from her spotted face and leprous body in hope that a new, young, and fresh skin would again grow and that her beauty in a lively manner would again be replenished, and not as now blemished with one stained spot or foul ulcer. All this according to her will was immediately performed, but to small purpose, for the envy of heaven, clothed with red vengeance, had doomed her to a miserable death, for neither art nor nature, by any practice, could ever after cover her hated body with any kind of skin, but that all her flesh continued raw and loathsome and putrefied unto her bones. In this torment, as a judgment of her pride, remained she, desiring death but could not die till the moon had twice twelve times renewed her brightness and that the earth had twice put on her springtime's finery and twice frosty-bearded winter disrobed Dame Nature's gardens. Then, oh then, returned the three wandering lovers, with conquest of their strange adventures, each one hoping to reap the deserts of their true merits.

The soldier whose task was to find a bed filled with a softer substance than the down feathers of swans in this dangerous manner brought he his labor to an end. First, after his departure from this proud lady Sola, he travelled many strange countries, meeting with many strange people, and in searching many strange places he happened into a cave, where lived a satyr of such bigness as man's eye had hardly seen. This satyr lived upon the spoil of travellers, within whose cave lay the signs of such as he had murdered and devoured; the number of the dead bones and skulls which lay heaped there together drove such an admiration into the soldier's heart that for a time his fear so abounded that he stood as it were senseless, but at last being ornified with the bold courage of manhood, he drew forth his short scimitar and with one blow smote off the satyr's head, whilst he lay sleeping upon a bed stuffed with nothing but wind, the which the soldier no sooner perceived but he verily believed his task to be ended, and that a bed stuffed close with wind were far more softer than the down of cygnets. So taking up the same bed and packing it upon his jennet behind him, he arrived as you heard at the palace of this proud lady, whose misfortunes with fatal news no sooner gave him entertainment but he fell into a melancholy despair, and now seeing his long and dangerous travels reaping no better success, as one wearied both of life and good chance, conveyed the said windy bed into a field, up to the top of a high mountain, whereupon he laid his bruised body and was by the said wind immediately carried away forever.

The scholar, whose long travels and deep study, nothing inferior to the soldier, after he had spent two years' practice in framing a fountain that should yield such a water that neither rained from heaven nor sprang from the conduits of the earth, a task as he thought impossible, yet good chance so directed his steps that he arrived in the Isle of Delphos at the Oracle of Apollo, who, after his divine sacrifice, had this pleasing answer revealed to him: The dew of heaven is neither water from the clouds nor water springing from the earth; replenish a fountain therewith and so conquer fate. For indeed he conquered fate, for at his return to the proud lady's court, in hearing of heaven's judgment laid upon her and how that he had consumed two years' labor to no effect, he presently fell lunatic and died.

Lastly the merchant tasted of death's cup as dearly as the others did, for after he had brought a bread far better than the bread of wheat, which is the bread of salvation, the sacred Bible of God which he fetched from the Temple in Jerusalem, but when he saw the end of his hopes rewarded with a vision of calamity, he departed to a desert wilderness, only inhabited with wild beasts, where for want of food he famished himself to death.

Then Sola after she had intelligence of the lives' ruins of those three gallant gentlemen, whom she had so cruelly doomed to miserable travails, and that for her sake they all three lost their lives, she in great despair of eternal happiness breathed her soul into the air, wishing her six sisters by her example to embrace humility.

Chapter 5. Envy's tragedy: The life and death of Lucina, the envious, the second daughter to the enchanted queen.

Lucina, being the second daughter to the enchanted queen, bearing in her breast the burning fire of envy, never differed from that deadly sin all the date of her wretched life; for after the decease of her proud sister, no long time passed on before Julianus, then king of France, took her in marriage, whose nuptial rites these two countries solemnized in most princely manner and the chiefest delights and pleasures belonging to a queen daily attended upon her. All things she could either wish or desire were at her commandment; heaven and earth concluded to make her a happy princess. Only this, content of mind wanted, for nature denied to fructify her body and grace her with the name of a mother. Therefore in wanting children she grew envious to the world and spited those women that heaven had so blessed.

Now in process of time, the king, queen, and the nobility of the land rode a progress into the country more by their presence to win their subjects' love than for their own contents and pleasure; and as in great state and most princely manner they passed by a forest side, where then was situated the castle of an ancient knight and an old servitor to the king's father in the Christian wars, and therefore was entitled one of the Knights of Rhodes, in which castle as the queen passed by a most pleasant and delightful melody of music sounded in her ear. At which not seeing any, she greatly marvelled and demanded the cause of that extraordinary rejoicing; the answer was that upon that day was born to the knight and lady of the castle a man child, who never before that time, for the space of twelve years, was graced with any. "Is this the cause?" said the queen. "Now I see base subjects, in disgrace of the queen's barrenness, will not stick but make thereof a May-game, and to mine own ears give me a dishonorable scandal. As I am now Queen of France this their presumption shall be quittanced with death and short shall be the joy they receive in this child's birth." Thus envy like a conqueror seized upon all the parts of her body, and with the undeserved hate she bore unto this knight and his lady her very heart plotted strange confusions. All the way as she rode along not a word proceeded from her mouth but savored of envy and malice, and not a slumber closed up her eyelids but it begot dreams of hate and fury. All her meditations were of the overthrow of these two guiltless souls, who little mistrusted what deadly plots she devised against their dear lives. Every day to this envious queen seemed a year till their progress ended, which, as ill fortune had allotted, was broken off in this manner.

The commons of Normandy and Picardy made an insurrection against the nobility, and none but the king's presence could allay their tumultuous furies, who with all speed, princely provided with men, money, and munition, took his journey towards them. Whose absence no sooner gave way to the queen's malice but she dispatched a messenger, one of the grooms of the king's chamber, to the betrayed knight and his lady, not yet churched, commanding them by the duty of allegiance to repair unto the court and give attendance in her chamber, till the king's return, only (as she dissembled) the dearest friends to trust unto.

This message of the queen's pleasure being no sooner delivered to the knight and his lady but as dutiful subjects rejoiced that their services in the king's absence could bring unto the queen such high pleasure. Therefore leaving their castle in quiet government, with all convenient speed they repaired to the queen's palace, bearing with them their little child, who at the first were entertained with a friendly regard and their child by the queen's commandment taken from them, and, as she said, put forth to nurse; but such a bloody nursery I think never tender babe endured. Little suspected the good knight and his gentle lady what a baleful banquet was preparing for them, for the envious and angry queen, instead of tender paps to give the infant nourishment, she commanded it to be made food for that womb that gave it first life. So having bloody ministers ready prepared for that tyrannical enterprise according to her wicked meaning, the pretty babe as a service (baked in a pie) was brought to the table of the unhappy parents, whom the queen had then placed in two chairs in her chamber, directly the one against the other, where, after they had satisfied hunger (unknown to them) with the fruit of their own bowels, she locking fast the chamber door, assisted by three or four bloody murderers provided for the same purpose, and bound them both fast in their chairs with hempen cords, bands unfitting for such noble-minded personages, and being now fettered in the gins of confusion, with an envious tongue she uttered forth the rancor of her heart in this manner.

"Marvel not, proud knight," quoth the queen, "nor thou, thou painted minion of beauty, at this your sudden misusage, for till I behold both your hearts lifeless, your eyes sightless, and your tongues speechless, the ravening jaws of fury feeds upon my soul. What hath nature in you grafted more than in me? You, being basely born, have the gifts of children; I, royally descended, am made barren by destiny. And because the seed of procreation prospers in your adulterous beds, you live in all jollity, making rejoicing melody to my disgrace, whilst I, pining in woe, vainly desiring children, cannot obtain them. Therefore know, that I being a queen, having a body young, fair, and likely to conceive, crossed and spited by the cruelties of nature, have protested a secret revenge against you and all such as to my dishonor have their bodies teeming with children, and now you two shall be the beginners of my intended massacre. Therefore know, as the first act to this my black tragedy, you have fed and satisfied hunger with the fruit of your own bowels. So upon thee, thou father of this dead infant, by thine own self here devoured, I will extend such a torment as never tyrant devised, but as thou art a soldier, so soldier-like shalt thou finish up thy days." Whereupon she caused an armor burning red hot from the fire to be brought, and without either mercy or pity, buckled it unto his naked back, where, like unto Hercules putting on the shirt that cruel Nessus sent, he made such pitiful moan as might have enforced tears to fall from a tiger's eye and the very marble stones give signs of laments. But, poor knight, as without cause he endured this dying punishment, so with great patience yielded he up his ghost, in the sight of his beloved lady, who being no less perplexed with the frights of pale death, awaited the fatal hour of the like dying torments, which according to her sorrowful expectation, she was immediately presented withal. For whilst she sat fast bound in her chair, gazing upon the dead broiled body of her husband, this envious queen caused her to be stripped stark naked and to her two tender breasts placed two speckled venomed snakes, almost starved for want of food, which with their poisoned stings sucked her heart's life blood quite through her breasts, during which time of her dying torments, continuing for the space of an hour, these and such-like lamentations she breathed forth.

"O, you dreadful powers of heaven! Why in a mild woman's breast have you placed a tiger's heart? Why have you suffered kind to work against kind, nature against nature, and reason against reason? One woman thus cruelly to betray another? O, where is gentleness become? Whither is mercy fled? One beast will not hurt each other, the vilest worm the earth breeds will by nature pity one another; but here is a woman that hath shamed her sex, distained nature, polluted womankind, an enemy both to heaven and earth. She had made me husbandless and childless and immediately will make me lifeless. O thou celestial tower, where justice sits enthroned, open thy glorious gates to entertain a widow's curse, strike down with a heavy hand, let shame and destruction pursue her to death, let some miracle of her tyranny be the world's mark till doomsday. Some strange confusion finish up her life to appease the souls of three unfortunate wretches, only made miserable through the envy of a malicious queen. And now, thou earth, farewell; thou nurse and mother of my life, adieu. Let three lives in two bodies be in thy bosom entombed, for now I feel death's wrath tearing my heart asunder and the very minute of my life fading, and, gentle death, now art thou welcome. Thus with a groan I close thee in my bosom." And in speaking these words the branches of her life withered.

The envious queen thus triumphing in the victory of their destructions, not any whit relented at the piteous moan of this good lady, but like an untamed panther devised new cruelties against their dead bodies, which she performed in this vile manner. Contrary to good nature and all humanity, she caused a furnace to be heat red hot and therein consumed the substance of these dead bodies into pale ashes, from whence flew sparkling flames of fire like flakes of blood up towards heaven, as it were challenging vengeance at the throne of majesty.

These tyrannical deeds both against life and death were no sooner effected but news came unto her of her princely husband's return from quieting the commons' tumults, whom she purposed with a dissembling countenance of joy to entertain. So attiring herself in her richest ornaments, attended on with a troop of honorable ladies, some mile distant from her blood-stained palace she gratulated the king with a princely welcome home; but, as the angry fates had justly decreed, before the word of welcome could proceed from her mouth, the heavens cast such a dark cloud over the earth, with such a fearful tempest and thunder, that the fruits of the earth flamed and the leaves of trees were scorched to satisfy the angry wrath of heaven. Whereat the king affrighted in mind challenged the queen of some black misdeed by her committed, heavy in the sight of heaven, in being thus offended with the world, but she whose heart blushless sins had hardened grew impatient at his speeches and wished that heaven might make her one of the world's wonders if ever she wrought or consented to any deed of shame, other than what virtue put her in mind to do. This presumptuous wish of hers so displeased the all-seeing powers that immediately the bowels of the earth cleaved and swallowed her up alive into her gaping womb, and directly in the same place where in sinking she gave the world a farewell sprang up a blood-red statue of stone, seeming to have weeping eyes and wringing hands, which to this day there still stands, and is recorded in the French annals to be one of the seven wonders of France.

The king having a conscience touched with remorse and dreading lest the heavy wrath of heaven should for her blood-stained sin light upon the whole country, therefore after he had searched out the whole faction of this black misdeed and put them to execution, as a pilgrim barelegged, bare-footed, clothed in haircloth, he wandered to Jerusalem, and at the Sepulcher of Judea's God craved remission for this his dead queen's offence, by which means he washed away this stained spot from his country's brow, and after spent his days in tranquillity and peace.

Chapter 6. Wrath's tragedy: The life and death of Martia the wrathful, the third daughter to the enchanted queen.

The third sister of this fatal generation might in the right of nature challenge as great supremacy of beauty as the other her two former sisters, and not only an amiable countenance and comely proportion ornified her outward shape, but an excellent gift of art and nature beautified her inward parts, for her mind being replenished with artificial mysteries, so judicial in the tongues of learning, so perfect in eloquence, so curious in needlework, the only exercise of princes, that the world esteemed her one of the Muses' darlings and the very paragon of womankind. In her the whole land's happiness consisted, the only excellent artist of her time, having a supernatural gift in the noble science of limning, wherein she greatly delighted; and the more to make her fame glorious in the world, she with a pencil portrayed in a map or picture the frame of the creation of the world, everything in his right shape, so lively set forth, as both beasts, fowls, and fishes seemed to retain life. The sun, moon, and stars as it were gave a kind of light, so artificially shadowed she their qualities; woods, fields, and forests appeared properly green and flourishing, and the watery sea, gliding through the earth's bosom, glistered like crystal and her swelling billows seemed to rise and fall, that no earthly eye could make a difference betwixt them and the surges of the vast ocean.

This excellent piece of workmanship, being to her heart's content finished, was set to the open view of all eyes, challenged a superiority in that mystery above all others of the time. But now amongst many that came from all parts of the kingdom to behold this rare piece of workmanship, there came one whose skill therein the whole earth admired, the which in former times had been tutor to this princess and first instructed her in the principles of this delightful art. This reverend man, for his milk-white head claimed reverentness, after he had in the presence of many noble personages circumspectly viewed every secret of this rare work and marking every curious shadow how it was laid, lastly found a deformity in the portraiture of man, and to this princess's disgrace (as she took it) found great fault therewith, at which Martia's wrath so enkindled and with such flames fired her whole body, that in presence of all the nobility, with a silver bodkin striking in the golden trammels of her hair, she furiously stabbed the good old man unto the heart, so greatly her wrath prevailed. This bloody and enraged fact by the whole assembly was generally lamented, and by her wrathful hand no sooner done but repented, for wrath being of nature sudden, a little overpassed converts into remorse. So happened it with this lady, for when her eye beheld the purple gore of his lifeless heart panting upon the ground, she strove in revenge thereof to tear out her own eyes, and would have committed that bloody cruelty upon herself had not the standers by prevented her, whereupon in great agony she uttered forth this enraged complaint.

"O, why will not heaven," quoth she, "take my bloodstained life and breathe into his breathless body new air? Or why may not my eyes forsake their hated cells, within his eyes to give a seeing power? O that this breast of mine were now unbowelled and this my wrathful heart torn from my bosom's closet and sacrificed upon that carcass, which my cruel hand hath untimely slain. Be therefore, O thou fatal hand, forever lame, deny to give sustenance to this my vile body, harboring now nothing but cogitations of revenge. Grant this, O Heaven, that from henceforth I may never taste one bit of food in joy, nor walk abroad but in discontent, nor sleep but in frightful fears, nor dream but of melancholy despair, for my sudden hand hath slain the miracle of humanity, within whose head, whilst life lasted, dwelt true wisdom, a tongue tipped with eloquence, and a voice resounding reports of celestial understanding." These and such-like passions uttered she from the fury of her repentant soul, which immediately had broken her heart-strings had not the care of her ladies then there attending conducted her to her chamber, where they with the harmony of music and melody of voices rocked her grieved senses into a silent slumber, in which quiet rest (as they imagined) they left this distressed princess. But far otherwise happeneth still to a troubled mind, for as she lay sighing and sobbing upon her bed, grieving at the blood she so wrathfully spilt, there appeared before her face the ghastly shape of the murdered old man, wan and pale in visage, breathing forth hollow groans, to the deep terror of her soul, and seemed to her affrighted eyes to open the closet of his bleeding breast, as it were thirsting for revenge and desiring blood for blood. This fearful and strange sight so deeply molested her conscience that from that time forward she banished away all thoughts of terrestrial joy and delighted in nothing but her own confusion, so heavy lay the guilt of murder upon her soul, for after that time not any food would she ever take into her body, nor ever after endure the fellowship of people, nor never suffer one small slumber to close up her eyelids, but in great woe and misery overwatched and pined herself to death, to the great discomfort and sorrow of the whole land, who by a general consent entombed both their bodies in one grave and erected thereupon a sumptuous sepulcher, the which to this day standeth in great glory in the city of Paris.

Chapter 7. Avarice her tragedy: Or the life and death of Mercuria the covetous, the fourth daughter to the enchanted queen.

The fourth of these unhappy children, bearing the name of Mercuria the covetous, esteeming the country's content beyond the glories of the court, banishing from herself all princely desires, accounting them the brands of embition and the only spurs of destruction; so making her three former sisters a memorial example of principality's downfall, she purposed to spend her days as a shepherdess in the country, where instead of a royal court she had the sylvan fields and mountains to live in, and in place of her princely attendance she had her flocks of sheep to delight in, whose plentiful increase of wool were as the treasures both of land and sea. Her imperial diadem was her sheephook, her pleasurable music the chirping melody of birds, her guard the pretty watchful cur that with his shrill barking gave notice of ensuing dangers, and the treasons complotted against here were the tyranny of devouring wolves. But such was her sylvan care and country diligence that her flocks sustained small hurt by the bloody rage of this spoiler, by which means in short time her riches grew unvaluable and her treasures without number. But the greedy thirst of her wealth's further increase so bewitched her insatiate desires that her very soul grew sotted with vile covetousness and the smallest loss thereof drew drops of blood from her heart. She feared to trust the air with her money lest the wind should consume it away, nor the earth lest the worms should consume it, nor the sea lest fishes should purloin it, but in a more securer manner (as she thought) she intended to hide it betwixt heaven and earth that both months, weeks, days and hours she might with the sight thereof glut the sight of her thirsty eyes. So having a huge sum of pure gold closed in an iron trunk, the which in a dark gloomy night, the secret concealer of all black deeds, she conveyed and hid in the hollow trunk of an old withered oak, standing betwixt two steepy hills, where the tracking steps of man seldom treadeth. In which hollow tree, almost rotten with age, she secretly hid this rich jewel of her soul, entombing it therein with these speeches: "Lie thou there," quoth she, "my sweet gold, thou great commander of mankind, my desire's content, my earth's happiness, my heart's ravisher. By seeing thee I am ravished with joy and in possessing thee I feed upon the pleasures of the world. What is it not but gold can bring to pass? Gold can purchase kingdoms and betray princes; gold can buy preferment and make men mighty; gold can make the foolish wise and curb authority; gold can win fair ladies and wrong the marriage bed; gold can tempt the chastest and sack virginity; nay, gold can change vice into virtue, falsehood into troth, and vile villainy into pure honesty. Then be thou, sweet gold, my second soul, for in losing thee the world ends with me." In this manner left she this corrupting gold lying in the hollow tree, purposing every day once to feed her eyes with the bewitching sight thereof. But now mark what happened to this covetous woman.

The next morning by the opening of the day's windows, there came unto the same place where this gold lay a poor man, a distressed wretch with a rope in his hand, upon the same tree to end his wearisome life. The reason was that the pitiful cries of his wife and children, complaining for bread at his hands, he not being able to satisfy their wants, came thither to hang himself, and so by that means rid himself from the complaining cries of his poor wife and needy children, but as the good chance of smiling heaven was, in tying the rope about an arm or branch of the same tree, making a noose to put over his head, and in giving the unkind world a doleful adieu, he espied this coffer of gold, at which he stayed from that self-willed murder, and being joyful of so rich a purchase, left the rope there still hanging, and carried the coffer home, to the comfort of his wife and children. Thus you see heaven by good means saved the dear soul of this desperate man and relieved the distressed estate of his almost starved family. Which we leave now in great joy and speak of the woeful calamity tied upon the back of this covetous lady, who immediately after this poor man's departure came unto the aforesaid tree to look upon her gold, whereby her heart might leap at the joyful sight thereof. But no sooner found she her hopes frustrate, her gold gone, and an instrument of death left hanging upon the tree in place thereof, she grew into such a violent despair that without either care of her life's safety or prevention of her soul's damnation, in the same cord she strangled herself. Her body being thus made breathless, exempted from the sight of people, had no other burial but in the ravening maws of hunger-starved fowls, whose strange confusion had never been known but through the voice of her troubled ghost, which walked many years after betwixt those two hills and revealed it to the country inhabitants. Thus was her covetousness scourged for a grievous sin, both by heaven and Hell.

Chapter 8. Gluttony's tragedy: Or the life and death of Jovina the drunkard, the fifth daughter to the enchanted queen.

Jovina, now the subject of our tragic story, and fifth daughter to this enchanted queen, as fate and chance ordained was matched in marriage to the rich Cardinal of Lorraine, whose court for magnificence equalized any prelate's before his time, for every day, up rising and down lying, he had a thousand officers in his palace and provision for the maintenance thereof were the customs of three rich dukedoms. This haughty and proud cardinal was in his life so vicious that he accounted drunkenness a deed of manhood, and he that could best devise new services to pamper up gluttony he advanced to great authority, and his riotous table was accounted the treasury of earth, air, and sea, of beasts, fowls, and fishes. But God owing him a grievous shame, in the middle of his magnificence, when he feasted at one time in the honor of his greatness three Christian kings, to the wonder of them all he was choked with a grape husk happening in a cup of Arabian wine. This his sudden death not only amazed the whole company, but drove such a discontent into the mind of Jovina that she purposed a present revenge upon the whole country, and as the customs of the nation are, that by the death of such an imperious prelate, all the land and revenues fall from the wife, so she to make a spoil thereof made such a funeral banquet as Spain's chronicles to this day speaks of. For no sooner had the earth closed up the cardinal's perfumed body and delivered the same to the fury of consuming worms, but this gluttonous woman by sound of drum and trumpets caused a proclamation to be made throughout all the country of a free banquet for the space of seven days, awarding to him or her that could eat or drink the most a hoop of pure gold to compass in their bellies. The report of this deadly prize of sin being no sooner bruited abroad, but of rioters, spendthrifts, gluttons, and drunkards from all parts arrived such numbers that the walls of Lorraine could hardly contain them. The tables whereat they sat were as nature's storehouse, variably yielding all kind of delicacies, and their pampered wombs as the insatiate gulf of Hell never sufficed. Some there were that had their bellies split asunder by overfilling them; some in the middle of their gluttony choked with superfluities; some by overcharging themselves with wine vomited out their inward parts; and some fell into such deadly sleeps as they never wakened again. And of all these multitudes of people, the tenth man departed not away with life, so consuming a tragedy brought this vile deed of gluttony and drunkenness upon that country.

Now Jovina herself seeing the earth almost strewed over with stifled carcasses began to envy at the powers of heaven, and in contempt thereof drew forth a sharp knife and threw it up toward the air, saying, "I will wound Fate and dismember the Destinies, in crossing thus the glory of my magnificent banquet." But the knife she cast up never more descended, but instead thereof fell down three drops of blood, directly before her upon the table where she sat, which strange and dismal sight struck terror and remorse into her conscience and such a despairing repentance into her cogitations, that from that time forward, as the angry heavens had appointed, she consumed the remnant of her life, which was but short, in bitter lamentations. "Now black vengeance," quoth she, "hath doomed me with a thousand calamities, and the scarlet canopy of destruction is even ready to close in my hated life; in most vile courses have my loathed steps wandered in, and now the reward thereof is shame and confusion. Methinks I hear succorless people calling for that food I so gluttonously have spent; methinks I hear the unpitied widow and the hungry orphan challenging my destruction; methinks I hear the decrepit and aged wretches soliciting heaven for revenge; methinks I hear the pining prisoners in deep dungeons exclaiming against my riotous gluttony; and methinks the troubled earth bellows up revenging echoes against my sin-drowned body." Thus mourned her relenting tongue till her unstanchable womb grew as it were starved with hunger, and then striving to suffice nature, could not, for the pipes of her life's maintenance were clunged[1]* up and by the just powers of mortality had a heavier judgment laid upon her, for that food which heaven and nature ordained for her life's sustenance were converted into a contrary substance, her bread heaven changed into stones, her meat into venomous toads and crawling worms, and her drink into a puddle of poisoned liquor, the stench and savor whereof no nostril could endure. Thus exempted both from heaven's grace and earth's pity, she languished many days, hated of God and man, till the Fatal Sisters finished her wearisome life. This was the heavens' scourge for gluttony and drunkenness, as black a sin and as deadly as any of the seven.

Chapter 9. Lechery's tragedy: Or the life and death of Veneria the lustful, the sixth daughter to the enchanted queen.

Still follows one misfortune upon another's neck, woe upon woe, calamity upon calamity; and this seed so wickedly sown could not choose but be blasted in the bloom. Now to our sad discourses. No sooner had Veneria, the sixth

---

* Arabic numbers throughout the text refer to notes that are arranged by story at the back of the book beginning on p. 453.

daughter of this enchanted queen, yielded up the tender bud of her virginity, changing her maidenhead for a wife's honor, being then conjoined in marriage with the princely King of Bohemia, before one month had consumed thirty days, grew enamored upon a base groom, one of the kitchen scullions, whom in her lustful eye seemed to be a jewel of knightly behavior, though a deformed vassal of humble servitude. Therefore as the temptations of sin had deluded her, careless of her princely husband's honor and regardless of her own reputation, upon a time in her husband's absence, she caused this hated night-owl the scullion to be sent for, touching, as she dissembled, some serious business to be employed in; who, being no sooner privately come into her presence, but revealing the burning heat of her lust, she gave him this unlooked-for entertainment: "Little thinkest thou, good Antonio," quoth she, for so was he named, "what high promotions are heaped upon thy head; for nature in thy first creation ordained thee to enjoy the pleasures of a princely bed. Though envious time now burdens thee with slavery, yet fate and good fortune crowns thee with happiness. Then know, thou jewel of mine eye, that my bosom contains a heart dancing at thy presence, and without the fruition of thy love it will quite consume away. I being a princess am more hapless than the country milkmaid, for she may challenge that same love that fancy leads her to, but I dare not claim the least interest of my pining passions. Be not hard-hearted then, dear Antonio, be as gentle as the clasping vine, hem in my body with thy manly arms, take the pleasures of my honor's sack, feed on content, if content be in my yielding body, for I am impatient of delay. My husband's arms are like unto the twining embraces of serpents, his kisses as the crocodile's, and his bed more loathsome than a den of snakes. O that nature had made me humble as thyself, partner in thy fortunes, and thy second self. Either now yield to my desires, or I vow by him that made both heaven and earth I will pursue thee with a vengeance more terrible than ever man's ireful heart imagined. And conclude on this, that either continual happiness or everlasting misery is put unto thy heart's choice."

Now this poor wretch, unaccustomed to these demands, stood for a time as one new dropped from the clouds, not knowing what to resolve upon, but at last as it were ravished with all celestial blessedness, and seeing time as he thought fit forever to make himself happy by enjoying the delightsome favors of so great a princess, condescended to satisfy the desires of her burning lust, and according to her pleasure with black misdeeds distained the white honors of her marriage bed. Veneria, having thus won him to her wishes, caused his base attires to be stripped off and his body to be clothed in rich vestures, the more to feed lust's gluttony, and appointed him the next night to set foot within her adulterous bed, which in most wicked manner was accomplished. But now mark how shame cannot lie long hid, nor the concealer of sin, dark night, cover this polluted crime; but as confusion's watch-bell sounded these her dishonors abroad, through the faithful duty of the king's chamber-keepers, he had intelligence thereof. So choosing to himself a selected number to effect his revenge, at the middle hour of night, when nothing disquieted the sleeps of human creatures but the gentle blustering of winds and the musical murmurings of running waters, he entered the chamber of this his lustful and adulterous queen, who securely lay then sleeping in the bosom of this base scullion, drove such a rage into the heart of the unquiet king as flesh and blood could hardly endure it. Therefore drawing a short scimitar from his side, he sheathed it in the breast of his wife's minion, whose blood with such fury gushed from his polluted bosom as it wakened the sin-stained queen, who at the first sight of her husband's presence, in her smock all to-besprinkled with the scullion's blood, fell down upon her knees, craving remission for that crime which she so long had thirsted after; but the enraged king to her penitent contrition was as remorseless as the deaf adder, and as far from granting her life as the souls in Hell be from salvation, yet being his second self, a collop of his own flesh and his only marriage choice, he would not defile his clear hands with her detested blood. Therefore as a pining penance for this lustful fact, for this marriage bed so distained, for this nuptial promise broken, for this world's scandal, this married man's dishonor, and for this everlasting spot of disgrace, he inflicted upon her a lingering punishment, which in this manner was immediately effected. First he caused a large coffin to be brought, wherein he put the murdered body of the scullion; then to the same dead body, beginning now to putrefy and stink, he tied the live body of his queen, and so in the coffin closed them up both together, that as she enjoyed his fellowship in life, so might she consume with him being dead, by which means the very worms that bred upon the dead carcass in a manner devoured up her live body. And thus were the sins of lust and adultery scourged with a plague but seldom heard of.

Chapter 10. Sloth's tragedy: Or the life and death of Saturnia the sluggard, the seventh and last daughter of the enchanted queen.

Saturnia, the last but not the unhappiest of these sisters, had the gentlest fortune of them all allotted her, yet in striving to prevent Fate, was taken in her own trap and when she least dreamed on, tasted of the bitter cup of death. The world she accounted the wilderness of iniquity and the very puddle of misery. Therefore, hating the fellowship of mankind, she purposed to forsake all princely glories, courtly delights, and worldly pleasures, and betake her to the solitary life of Diana, and to spend the remnant of her days in some desert wilderness, where no sin abounded. So upon an evening, without company she stole from the court; guided by the pale light of the moon and the twinkling starlight of heaven, she happened into a thick grove of trees, as it were inhabited only by fairies, elves, and the ghosts of dead men. Day and night there seemed all one; the glorious sun as a stranger there showed his face and the voices of human creatures were accounted fatal to be there heard; night-ravens, owlets, bats with leather wings, flying griffins and cockatrices covered quite over these thickets; upon the ground lay red-bellied worms, speckled snakes, hissing adders, venomous toads, loathsome spiders, and sleeping dormice, so that neither heath nor grass was there to be seen, only heaps of brown moss, upon the which she rested her discontented body. Twice twelve months without waking slept she thereupon, only fed by the gentle means of green-capped fairies, in which long sleep her dreams were of the torments of Hell, and the manner of her six sisters' punishments in that damned region.

First in her sleep she beheld her eldest sister, bearing the name of Pride, attired in a garment boiled in molten lead, with a neckercher about her neck of flaming fire and her dainty feet seemed to walk upon red burning coals. Next she beheld her second sister, called Envy, grasping in her hands a pair of fiery stinging snakes, which as it were lay feeding upon her flesh, even ready to burst with the abundance of blood sucked from her bosom. Then she beheld her third sister, called Wrath, wading into a boiling cauldron of fire and brimstone up to the very chin, and in brazen ladles casting the same up and down in great fury. Then fixed she her eye upon her fourth sister, named Covetousness, feeding on melted gold, and every part of her body behung with burning pearls, sapphires, and diamonds, which seemed to sear the very flesh from her bones.

After this she beheld her fifth sister, which was Gluttony, sitting in a flaming chair, at a table of red hot iron, served by devils with broiled toads upon gridirons and drinking down chalices of boiling metals. The next vision was her sixth sister, named Lechery, lying in a bed of smoking sulphur, delivered of a brood of vipers, who with their fiery teeth fed upon her bowels and as it were had her body spread all over with vile leprosy.

These were her fearful dreams and continual apparitions,

History of Morindos 41

in which unquiet sleep she remained without waking till her body grew shapeless, having no proportion, as then made the shelter for toads, frogs, and venomous worms to breed in the excrements of the earth and the deformities of nature. Thus vanished her life away in sleep, being no way able to withstand the severe indignation of heaven.

Chapter 11. Of the enchanted queen's despair, and how she was carried away alive by devils.

After the death of all these seven deadly sisters, now brought to confusion by the black doom of mortality, our tragic story bids us return to the enchanted queen, lying all this while in childbed, sightless and lame, having no feeling in any part of her members, which miracle of misery, after she had intelligence of her seven daughters' tragical ends assuredly believed that then her life was at the last period and the time of fearful death drew near, according to her conditions made to the Devil, who promised she should live till the seven days of the week were forgotten, which she alluded to her seven daughters so named. Now fear, terror, and pining despair assailed her on all sides; now dreaded she every minute her soul's departure to that burning furnace, whose fire is ten times more hot than this earthly fire, and now every small noise she heard she supposed to be the hurrying of devils that came to take possession both of soul and body. Every minute wished she now to be whole years, hours, millions and days endless, time to stand still, or the world to end; now she repented her ambition, her aspiring dignities, and all those desires of a kingdom; now repented she the selling of her soul, her band's sealing with her own blood, and all her agreements with black Hell. Every time the clock struck put her in mind of eternal damnation and how that Hell's gaping mouth stood ready to receive her; cursing the begetters and causers of her creation. Thus in deep remorse of conscience spent she out the tiresome day, the last day of her worldly life, till the cloudy evening with her pitchy mantle approached, the only somparative of gloomy Hell, the which had no sooner shut up the bright eye of heaven but clouds more dark than darkness itself checked the world with motions of pale death. Such tempests of lightning and thunder broke from heaven's crystal portals that it even blasted the beauty of the earth and attired both trees, herbs, and flowers in a mournful livery. This night to all mankind was a night of fear, a night of relentless terror, a night of confused desolation, in which extremity of horror it continued till the midnight's hour, at which instant time, with a clamorous roaring that seemed to shake both heaven and earth, the wrathful powers of black Hell fetched away both her body and soul, the which being done, the heavens cleared, the earth replenished, and after followed a time of plenty, peace and prosperity.

FINIS

MORIO-MACHIA.

Imprinted at London by
Simon Stafford. 1613.

ROBERT ANTON: MORIOMACHIA (1613)

Moriomachia is a parody of chivalric romance, or, to give the work a perhaps more magniloquent title, an "anti-romance," and the first of its kind in English. Like *The Knight of the Burning Pestle*, which its author seems to have in mind often enough, *Moriomachia* is obviously inspired by *Don Quixote*, to which it is indebted both for general conception and particular procedure. Anton parades his hero, a knight amusingly named Tom Pheander (it must be noted that Pheander is the hero of a long romance by Henry Roberts entitled *Pheander, or The Maiden Knight*), through a series of adventures designed to ridicule the romance of chivalry through a *reductio ad absurdum*. Perhaps to appreciate the book's cleverness to the fullest one should have ploughed through a couple of the romances which are being laughed at, but any imaginative reader can probably reconstruct the main features of the genre being mocked simply from what Anton writes.

But if the author's main effort is to satirize the incessant rescues of distressed damsels and the constant earth-shaking clashes of great heroes in combat, which together form so much of the chivalric romance, he is not averse to laughing at other elements in such stories: the strange wonders the hero may encounter, for example, and the presence of supernatural beings in the plot. The pastoral strain comes in for a bit of parody too, while the florid and high-flown style characteristic of the romances is steadily mocked in the most delightful way. That fairies figure so prominently in *Moriomachia* may be the result of Anton's reading of Spenser, of Huon of Bordeaux, and perhaps of Drayton. There is some satire of contemporary London *mores*, together with a few topical allusions, and, in the style, a good deal of *double entendre,* much of it risque. Indeed the chief criticism one can direct against the book is that Anton in attempting too much can not successfully realize the fullest humorous possibilities of his own situations.

Of Robert Anton himself next to nothing, as usual, is known. He took his B.A. at Magdalen College, Cambridge, in 1609–10, and he published one other book, a series of seven poems entitled *The Philosopher's Satyrs,* in 1616. One might have guessed without knowing the date of his degree that *Moriomachia* is a young man's book, so full it is of high spirits and a strong sense of the ridiculous. Yet underneath the foolery there occasionally sounds a harsher note, especially in the section dealing with contemporary London, where the satire leaves the purely literary to become social, as if the general amusement were momentarily replaced with an edged scorn. The tough-mindedness of a real satirist seconds the mockery of the literary parodist.

Moriomachia has been reprinted only once since the original edition of 1613. See G. Becker, "Die erste englische Don Quijotiade," *Archiv für das Studium der neueren Sprachen und Literaturen,* CXXII (1909), 310–322, where a short critical introduction is provided also. The text which follows is based on the Huntington Library copy of the 1613 edition.

MORIOMACHIA

To the most happy and glorious constellation of brotherhood, together with the trinal knot of the most virtuous sisters of the most honorable family of the Howards, Robert Anton sacrificeth this new-born babe of his humble duty, wishing an everlasting motion of happiness both to them, and that honorable house.

❋ ❋ ❋

Moriomachia

Right honorable branches of a fair and spreading family, under whose shades my best fortunes ruminate, I have thought good to unite you all in a whole piece, whom envious time cannot make merchandise in parcels (to conjoin you), which to disjoin were a sin as deep as a lawyer's pate in term time, that sings no song but *De profundis*. I honor that musical consent of fraternity, and hold it not inferior to Pythagoras his harmony; let this modicum of superfluous minutes crave but the privilege of a servingman and wear the cloth of your favor. *Semel in anno ridet Apollo.* Serious hours and grave designs must needs laugh, and amongst them my studies at this time are turned merrygreek.[1] I writ them in dog days, and they must needs bite; but what? not virtue, not honor, not nobility; but error, ignorance, and that pesthouse of the time, foppery. But what I would speak, silence shall be my attorney and plead both for time's reformation and your perpetual happiness.

Your Honors' devoted servant,
Robert Anton

TO THE UNCAPABLE READER

Give place, Ass-crapart,
Start back, Tatifart,*
   Colbrand, be a by-stander:
For here comes to fight
The fairies' fair knight,
   Ycleped Pheander,
To conquer full soon
The man of the moon,
   Sir Archmoriander.
The truth of which battle,
This book well can that tell
   To each understander,
Unless that he be,
As some men are (we see),

* A noisome giant, whom Anus, King of Podolia, beat out of his kingdom.

A goose or a gander.
By which his rare works
He gives secret jerks;
  He one day shall wander,
Though yet he privy lurks
Against the big Turks
  To be a commander.
I mean, thou shalt work nigh
To conquer the Turk high,
  Notorious Pheander,
Until when, let no man,
Of this Knight of the Woman*
  Speak evil or slander.
          W. H.

* For being without a wife, he may be as honest as honorable.

MORIOMACHIA

    About that time of the year when sylvan Pan pipes roundelays and nimble satyrs frisk about the timely palms, old Titan turned swaggerer and revelled in the taverns of the earth so late that he durst not appear to a lantern (fearing the rough examination of a rugged watch and the dogged authority of a common jailer) before the fresh Aurora fetched him forth with a fiery face, and allayed his high color with the cool morning's dew. Then fairy nymphs turned milkmaids and took pleasure in dandling the dug. The Fairy Queen herself at that time disposed to recreation (and to try her huswifery) accompanied her attendant train to their accustomed haunt, which was to a rare and delicate pleasure-fitting meadow, most copious and neatly furnished with divers proper bellowing bulls and many comely courteous gentle cows, where every pretty elf betook her to her several task, to provide milk for ale possets, to welcome home at night their overwearied knights in arms.

    No art in arms gives fairy knights content
    Unless they have their ladies' sweet consent.

The Fairy Queen, not acquainted with such rustic dairy, most unfortunately (but more Cockney-like) by chance happened on a meek and loving bull. She, poor lady, thinking he had been a reasonable creature, made him low curtsey, and fairly entreated him to yield his consent to be quiet and gentle until she had finished her milking. And so takes the teat in her slender hand, which was somewhat too gross for her fine fingers. She, kind madam, drew many a dry draught.

> Good Lady, she did seldom use to milk,
> Or touch such things as were not clad in silk.

The poor understanding beast, proud of his milkmaid, seemed not so much as once to stir, fearing to hinder what she did intend, but stood most loving and kindly to her.

When she began to perceive her own mistake, and withal observing the strange and unusual courtesy of the beast towards her, she pitied his present estate and immediately called a council of her nymphs about her, where all generally yielded their voices and concluded to have him transformed into the habit and shape of a man, but still to retain his brave beastly courage, wherewith he might in time by the assistance of his stars be ranked in eminency with the gallant-seeming courtier, the valorous heir of a gouty usurer, or at least with the farmer's proper gentleman-like son. And for his qualities and manners, having so excellent a tutress, he already was able to keep the company of a mere scholar, a bold bailiff, or a brawny-fisted mechanic; so being provident of his welfare in pursuit of knightly adventures, she suited him in an ass's skin impenetrable, made after the newest fashion, and entitled him Tom Pheander, the Maiden Knight, her champion.

> The ass did wear a biggin[2] being young,
> Which kept his ears from growing overlong.

And for that she would at first let him understand the general dangers of a knight-errant, she put him in a weather-beaten barque with tattered sails, freighting it with a whole firkin³ of valor, and so exposed him to the sea and Fortune, who with the favorable wind of her fan drove him with safety upon the coasts of Morotopia, even at the mouth of a river where grew a goodly vinegar tree, which was very sharply besieged with fat and large overgrown salmons (between whom for this long time hath been mortal war, and waste, by fire and knife), where he so valiantly bestirred himself that he raised the siege and recovered the tree, which he carefully preserves with a garrison of fairies, by reason of the abundance of vinegar it yields, which he found would be very commodious in his Turkish wars, as well to cool his double dags⁴ as also to make sauce to eat the hearts of all such Turks as he should chance to kill.

So travelling up into the country, as he passed through a village, he espied two men threshing out corn in a barn, which struck him into amazement, so that he stood as mute as a politic drunkard to see them beat one against the other with their flails. But taking them to be knights enchanted, he addressed himself towards them and said, "Fair knights, remember yourselves, and call to mind your former estates; resume your noble spirits and be not thus overborne with necromantic spells." One of them looking up said, "Honest man, be gone; for thy idle speeches hinder our work, and our dame will be very angry if our day's task be not finished at night." Quoth the Fairy Champion, "Mistake me not, gentle sirs, for Fortune hath sent me hither to ease and release you both from these magical charms if I may but see or speak with that damned magician." "Marry, sir, my dame and Marian are both within, and Marian is even just now a-charming, and if you will go in and speak with her, you shall." Quoth the Fairy Champion, "With all my heart."

So in he leads him to the milk-house, where Marian was charming butter. As soon as he espied her, he said, "Aha, have I found thee at thy charm, thou foul enchantress? I speak to thee that keepest knights in servile slavery. I'll dissolve your charms and circles, your invocations and incantations," and so takes the charm and cheesefats and throws them about the house. Which Marian seeing, she cried out for help to save her from the madman, when presently one of the servants of the house came with a cudgel and there began a fearful fray.

Why dost thou beat this courteous knight, thou swain? Chud[5] ha' him catch his woodcock wit again.

But Marian, like a wise stickler or moderator, reconciled them with a composition of sour whey, where each drank to other, and so parted loving friends.

Now being in a strange country and altogether unacquainted with the ways and passages or how to bend his course, straggling here and there, the weather being exceeding hot and he extreme thirsty, at length he inquired[a] of harvest people, entreating their directions where he might get drink, who very courteously showed him a plain beaten way, leading to a nobleman's house not far off.

The Fairy Champion put on a bold sharp face, went to the nobleman's house and desired the butler to give him a cup of his giving drink. But the butler, as the custom is, churlishly denied him and bid him be gone, for that he had not any charity, much less commission, to give anything to such an able wandering fellow as he was, bidding him go look for work amongst harvest folks, and take pains for his living.

Whereupon the Fairy Champion, like a valiant sturdy beggar, took the butler by the brains and dashed his heels against the wall, made corks to stop ale bottles of his bones, and threw them into his buttery, for all succeeding butlers that were not boon companions to take example.

He took his brains from forth his head before,
Else sore kibe-heels,[6] perhaps, had made him roar.

[a] After honor.

So he drank up all the beer in the buttery before he could quench his intolerable thirst, for the house was not then so well furnished as at other times, by reason there was no household; for the lord and his lady were gone up to Moropolis to take physic and see the newest fashion at court.

Thus he proceeded on his intended journey, and after he had gone twenty miles or thereabouts, he began to find a fainting in himself and felt his guts shrink together like burnt parchment, yet he took as good courage as necessity useth to drive men to in such a case, and ere long by good hap he espied not far off a very fair new-built house, with many goodly turrets and battlements, and whole clusters of chimneys more than need required for that he could not see any use of those that were needful in regard there was not any tobacco stirring amongst them, which argued there was but little good fellowship. Therefore his heart waxed cold, yet he went and knocked at the gate, but all in vain; for there was not any within to give him answer but only spiders, for all the rats and mice were either gone or else starved with that extreme dearth.

    O Champion fair, what ill did thee befall
    To be deceived? It was no hospital.

It fortuned, as he was thus standing at the gate, a husbandman of a near neighboring village came by and asked the Fairy Champion what he would have there. "Sir," quoth the Fairy Champion, "I am a traveller without money, and altogether without any acquaintance, but only hunger and thirst, and this place afar off promised relief to such wantful travellers as I am." "O zur," quoth the husbandman, "che[7] zee how you ma be dezeived, but come and go along with me, to zuch vittles az old Madge my wife has purvided vor my dinner, and cham[8] zure ye zhall be welcome to hur with all hur heart." "Sir," quoth the Fairy Champion, "I rest much bound to your love and will embrace your kind offer to go along with you."

Moriomachia

> The honest plain countryman in charity mild
> Took up at the gate this poor fatherless childe.

"But I pray sir, tell me: what gentleman owns this fair house where you found me knocking?" Quoth the husbandman, "Zurely, zur, he is no gentleman, vor he is a knight and my londlord too, marry, and now both he and my londlady lie in the zity, a-vollowing a lawing matters, and they zay a has zitch an intercate troubling vowl zute, 'tis a zhame to zee it, and that it is great chance whether a con e'er get out on't or not, vor a has not been here in our country this twelvemonth and more, byrlady, come the time; but I wudd to God a were here vor me, for we miss a great deal of good cheer and dancing and sport at Cursmas, zince my old londlord his vather died. Well, God rest his zoul, for a was the best hondler of a long whip in all our country. Nay, I may tell you, a has not left his mate behind him, and cham sore aveard we zhall ne'er ha zuch another mon as he was, for a wudd be zo yarely up a mornings to vother his zheep himself, as 'twas wondervul; and, Lord, a wudd tell zich a company of old vables, a mon wudd be the better to be in his company. Chee ha heard him zay, that his vather turned him out-a-doors when a was a little boy, to zeek his vortunes, with one poor single groat, all in three hapences, in his purse; but by my vaith chee know not how a got it; but cham zure a died a mizerable rich mon."

"I wonder," quoth the Fairy Champion, "much, that your landlord being no gentleman could come to be a knight." Quoth the husbandman, "Chee ha oftentimes heard him zay, that it cost him well and vavordly vor it, I may tell you."

When the Fairy Champion understood there were more ways than one to attain to a knightship, he held himself in the most fortunatest place of the earth, for in the Fairy Land they only have it by desert. And on the sudden he grew to such an exceeding height of ambition that with all haste he would be gone, and to that purpose took leave of the husbandman, who, as it appeared, was High Constable of the hundred, by reason he went to the parish clerk and caused him to make a pass for the security of Tom Pheander the Fairy Champion in his travels, wherein he charged all the petty constables within the hamlets of his hundred to aid and resist the Fairy Champion against any one whatsoever that should seem to stay, defend, or any way distribute him in his journey, but suffer him to pass quietly without any of their tolerations.

And although the passport was written by the hand of an old woodhen, one would have thought, if hens had had hands, yet the countenance of a magistrate's hand at it bore it out, and made it carry meat in the mouth. So he thanked him for all his good cheer and much kindness, and departed in pursuit of the fortunes he aimed at, which was to be a knight at the least.

When he began to come near the heart of the island, he heard of the rich and flourishing city of Moropolis. Thitherward he repaired with what expedition he could devise, and drawing within sight of it, he met in the way a proper tall trading gentlewoman, set out after the finest fashion of new devices, with a white loose body in a strait black gown, hooped about with the flexible bones of a slender whale; the crown of her cap was so deep in band that it durst not scarce peep out to be seen; her mask came down to the tip of her nose, and her chin tied up with a laced clout, or handkercher, as if she were jaw-fallen.

Her obsequious usher was a little lean fellow with a fair smooth cloak, whose fine thread was not ashamed to show itself to the uttermost; by his side he wore a long sword, which was so quarrelsome that it would draw upon anything it met withal, for the chape[9] was worn out in drawing on the ground, not much unlike a monkey going upright on his hinder legs, drawing his tail after him.

> You do not much in your simile fail:
> For he was an usher unto a wagtail.

This Sir Pandarus was ushering his lump of food and

raiment[b] three miles from the city towards the diseased broken chambers in a brothel, to give meeting with the wise profuse first fruits, or heir, of a rich broker, whose extorting interest, money, did so trouble the use of his memory at the very last hour of his death that he died without bequeathing the least spark of wit to his son, amongst his great patrimony; for he had not the time to remember the least college of poor scholars, nor the meanest hospital of diseased people.

He might have left something, although but little,
To cure his son's diseases in a spital.

This parcel of sin, going towards the place of action, to meet her money-paramour, had an Iceland dog newly shorn, which was going along with her, and being in the fields the dog fetched his courses to and again afar off, so that she was fearful of losing him and with a loud shrill voice she called him by the name of Lion. Which the Fairy Champion hearing, and withal seeing the dog run towards her, he thought she had cried out to save her from the lion, and therefore drew his sword and speedily ran to aid the overpressed virgin, according to the oath and office of an errant knight.

When Tom Pheander espied this dogged lion
He drew his sword, and ran till he was nigh on.

And coming to her, he said, "Fear not, fair sweeting, the outrage of this cruel ravening beast, for I will keep you from any evil whatsoever may betide you, that hereafter historiographers shall, Roman-like, stuff out my valiant acts with the bombast of their perpetual inkhorns."

The dog coming near her began to leap and fawn and licked her hand, which the Fairy Champion seeing, said, "Now do I well perceive that you are a most spotless miraculous maid, for that you are armed with the armor of pure honesty, against the insatiety of this all-devouring cannibal."

[b] For he had no wages.

Pheander showed his judgement was but poor,
To call her maid that was a common —————.

Although he spoke seriously to his own understanding, thinking indeed it had been a lion, yet she, who scorned the name of a maid at those years, thought (as well she might) that he had laughed her to scorn and derided her with scoffs, and therefore with her hand she suddenly dashed him on the lips that the very blood sprang from his teeth, which first he accepted as a token of great favor from her bounteous fist, and with his handkercher sponged the blood from his mouth, which he said he would keep as a perpetual remembrance given by the hand of a fair virtuous virgin. With which speeches she grew so exceeding angry and was so highly incensed against him that she commanded Sir Pandarus to set upon him with his long sword, which he refused to do, being daunted with the fear of having his profession questioned.

A guilty conscience sometimes keeps in awe
That thing which else would not be curbed by law.

The Fairy Champion seeing there were no further adventures fitting the worths of a knight-errant, he quietly departs and addresses himself unto that much renowned city of Moropolis, where he purposed to spend some time about the city to learn a generous carriage of himself. And, for that he would avoid to be deemed an intelligencer to some foreign state, he altogether abandoned ordinaries and taverns, and would not at any time seem to intrude himself into the company of those that understood much, but took a poetical sculler (whose swift Muse borrowed the poet's pretty nag Pegasus to ride post, and coming short of his journey he brought him home pitifully spur-galled)[c], and so crossed the water to visit the bears and puppet plays, the tall Dutchman, the woman tumbler, the dead skin of a strange living fish, the calf with two heads, whose two mouths had devoured more hay than his one stomach

[c] Mariners seldom good horsemen.

could digest, so that it lies yet in his belly as fresh as when he first ate it, without putrefaction, as may be seen. He likewise noted a very strange thing, which was a blind man led through every street of Moropolis by a staff which had eaten so much garlic that he could follow it by the smell. And truly many more great observations he had gotten from amongst the motion-mongers[10] of Nineveh and Babylon, so that now he had sufficient experience to maintain an argument by parrotism after dinner or supper with such ordinary company as use to make great talk of their small travels.

> As their journey by land from Bermuda to Tunis,
> And their voyage by sea o'er the Alps to Venice.

And now having furnished himself with some reasonable store of coin, which he had won at the excellent and most ingenious games of pigeon-holes and trap, he put his fortunes on towards the Morotopian Court, where it pleased the pages of the nobility to do him much favor, and the ladies to grace him with the honor of knightship.

> The lady laid the sword upon his shoulder;
> He arose and swore to beat her foes to powder.

For which he was, anabaptistically, created or nominated (at thirty years of age) Sir Tom Pheander, the Maiden Knight, or Fairy Champion, otherwise The Knight of the Sun, otherwise The Knight of the Burning Pestle. And but that he was most notoriously known to be a mere natural subject, the multiplicity of his names and additions might have brought him in suspicion, to be apprehended for some seducing spy, or at least a knight of the post.[11]

When the Fairy Queen understood by the invisible attendant which she sent with him in his travels of his grace in court with lords, his sometimes desired company of ladies, and the general love and laughter of his jollity and natural conceits from the vulgar,

> He oftentimes showed good pastime of body:
> The whole globe did think him a counterfeit noddy.[12]

She forthwith provided him a rich coat-armor enchanted, which had these properties: that whatsoever he was at any time that put it on his back, should not need to fear any terrible thing whatsoever under the degree of crabtree cudgel, and whensoever he should look in a glass with the helmet on his head, he should be instantly so wise that he should be for that time always opposite to a fool.

This coat-armor was of a singular proof, checkered motley, vert, and argent, parti per pale, ribbed with rows of gules and or, from the very gorget to the skirts. The helmet was of the same, on which was a device of four faces, resembling the four winds. In the midst of those faces were raised little mounts, appearing like noses, on which stood pretty conceited windmills, which in the going made as pleasant a sound as curious falcons' bells. On the crest was advanced the neck, head, and comb of a bloody-crested cock, betokening true valor even after death.

Wit ebbed from his noddle like floods from a rock,
Which made her provide him the comb of a cock.

This complete coat-armor was committed by the Fairy Queen unto the trust and care of Madame Moriana, a fairy lady, to be with all speedy expedition conveyed to her worthy merry champion, the (now) Knight of the Sun.

Madame Moriana seemed to hasten, and with all possible speed dispatched messengers with the greatest expedition that might be, and, lady-like, made a goodly show of that she never purposed, giving the messenger direction to hasten to the Morotopian Court and there inquire after one Sir Archmoriander Duncell dell Cinthia, the Knight of the Moon, her knight, to whom true reason had far engaged her love and due respect, in freeing her from the outrage of Andromago, a monstrous, strong, and terrible little giant, and thus it was:

Madame Moriana, upon a time walking in an evening, as the custom is in Fairy Land, down in a green valley, wherein nature had seated a most pleasant grove, so fit for private recreation and delightful exercise that art itself could not devise a more curious frame; thither she often walked without neglect or missing the least minute of her accustomed hour, who, by her often recourse thither, was espied by Andromago, a mighty, huge, and choleric pygmy giant. He was a full half yard broad betwixt the eyes, and almost eighteen inches by the rule (wanting but the breadth of a superfine wire) from the crown to the heel, and the rest of his body proportionable accordingly.

This monstrous, grim-looking giant, knowing Moriana's usual hours of resort to that grove, ambushed himself in a very great thicket in the middle way, growing on the side of a high cloud-piercing molehill. The fashion of the country is that the nobles and gentry of ancient houses have their arms portrayed in a small escutcheon, which they ever more bear before them to the end they may be known from private persons and that the thronging multitude may give way when they approach near; whereas otherwise they could not have that due respect which belongs to them, in regard it is a warlike nation and subject to insurrections. Therefore for that they may be ever in a readiness upon any domestic war, all go ready armed with masks and mufflers.

Now had Andromago the giant, with his falchion lopped down the great arm of an eglantine tree, where he (Salisbury-plain like) looked through, to see the passing by of Moriana, whom at length he espied coming alone afar off, towards her wonted place of recreation. And drawing near within the apprehension of his eye, he was well assured it was she and knew her by the escutcheon she carried before her, wherein was charged in chief a halfmoon gules in a jagged cloud sable, and the lower, or back, charge was three drops or under a fess argent. This coat she gave, which was the most ancientest in all the Fairy Land, and ever continued hereditary to the heirs female of that house.

When she was come near the thicket, Andromago watched his fit opportunity, and suddenly rushed out like a snake from a hedge, leaping thirty inches by the rod, and caught her in his arms, and with very joy of his prey roared like a bull of eight days old. This hideous yell so affrighted the poor lady that she was ever after troubled with a kind of falling sickness. So leading her along as his prisoner towards a castle he had not far off, which was double-grated with huge iron bars, not much unlike the mighty strong barricadoed windows of a monstrous overgrown mouse-trap, wherein he had imprisoned many ancient tooth-wanting ladies, and fed them with nothing but hard candied sweetmeats, and the sourest juice of the sweetest grape.

It was Sir Archmoriander's good hap to take his way through the Fairy Land homewards from his travels, who had been amongst the barbarous Brasilians, to see the fashion of the country and also to learn the nature of the people; by a most happy chance he met the poor captived lady, led by the hand of this ugly monster, who was near as high as the lady's girdle, which compassed her delicate waist seven times, besides the knot.

The sudden appearance of the giant to Sir Archmoriander (for he had never seen in all his travels and adventures the like creature before) struck him into such a shaking palsy that he could very hardly stand still on his legs,[d] yet he took an indifferent strong heart and addressed himself towards the giant, with a sweet quavering voice, saying "Thou most monstrous and huge diminutive of nature, which hast always been an enemy to ladies, I advise thee surrender thy prisoner into my hands, or else by the light of this martial hand, thou shalt well understand the price of her; for thou hast done her such scurvy paltry wrongs as thy weak state cannot countervail to make her satisfaction; for reason induces my worthy self to weigh both your causes in my upright balance of inequity."

Andromago staring at Sir Archmoriander like a wild goose ready to fly upon, said, "Thou foolish knight, thinkest thou I will so easily part with the thing I have so long stood and waited for? No; I advise thee be gone, or else I

---

[d] He would have been gone.

will wither thy very face and confound thy smelling sense with my breath, for I scorn to stand to thy unequal chandler's weights."

The giant's threats could not discourage Sir Archmoriander one jot more than he was before (although surely the giant's breath was very strong, by reason he was so short-waisted and his two ends were so near neighbors that their friendship were alike and the one did participate the other's strength and savor). But Sir Archmoriander well backed with hope to win the lady's favor and his affection to justice made him look so near to his business in hand, as an old purblind councellor[e] (or rather concealer) whose velvet jerkin is sufficient to make a justice of peace without a commission, that will not suffer the smallest character of a fault to run at random unpunished, but binds it fast in recognizance, to receive either corporal or pecuniary punishment. Even so he considerately bore in mind the execution of some severe justice upon a homicide and with warm courage betook him to his sword, which Andromago perceiving, he likewise provided to defend himself against his adverse assailant.

> The justice's law did so assist his client,
> As Moriander's sword the lady from the giant.

Sir Archmoriander, in the first encounter, had made an end of the fight before they began, but that, being mad with fury, he missed the giant and ran the point of his sword into the ground. Andromago, leering like a sergeant, espied that advantage (seeing him tugging to pull it forth again), omitted no time, but advanced his club, and with one blow pashed Sir Archmoriander's head all into a lump, which ever after looked like a beetle, so that afterwards, when he came to be dressed, the surgeon's opinion was that he was very likely to carry that mark to his grave.

But Sir Archmoriander recovered himself so well as he could, and turned about as swift as a windmill sail in a hot

[e] Purblind men are good husbands, and look near to their business.

summer's day, with strong agility of body and resolution withal, to give a final period to the battle, and most valiantly untrussed his points, put off his doublet, snatched up his breeches by the sides, and with his sword cut off the giant's right hand, so that it only hung by the very bare bone and sinews.

With this blow, Andromago's club fell out of his hand, which Sir Archmoriander suddenly took advantage of by closing with him, and with a nimble strength threw him flat on the earth with as much facility as if the giant had been a child of two years old.

>Sir Moriander cut the giant on the hand
>And hurt his little toe; he could not stand.

The Lady Moriana standing by all the time of the fight, perplexed with an extreme fear of danger, and now seeing a hope of victory attend her champion, she began to take comfort in a pretty medley, between weeping and laughing.

Sir Archmoriander having gotten Andromago under him lay upon him with such a heavy weight and pressed him so sore that till then Andromago felt not Sir Archmoriander's heavy displeasure fall upon him,[1] which caused Andromago to cry out to the lady for pardon, and craved mercy of Sir Archmoriander with a great show of sorrow for the exceeding injurious wrongs offered to the lady and the heavy unsufferable injuries intended against Sir Archmoriander: all which was now fallen upon himself, and the burden did much bruise his conscience.

Upon this submission, with penitency for his faults, Sir Archmoriander most honorably (befitting his worth) cut off his head and set it on his doublet breast (where a button was lost in this fray), wearing it in token of his valor and victory and so set him at liberty to go whither he would.

[1] Archmoriander lay very heavy upon the little giant.

Although the giant would have given a groat,
Yet Moriander vowed to see his naked throat.

Sir Archmoriander having thus freed the Lady Moriana from the outrage of Andromago, he went to comfort her, who was then suddenly fallen into a deep passion of sadness.

"Sweet Madam," quoth he, "you see your dangerous enemy here lie slain; therefore, fair Lady, I much scorn your thoughts should be possessed with any future fear. Let me be the example of your courage, to take a strong heart and valiantly bear up your escutcheon and arms without fear, for under your coat will I fight, whilst I can stand or breathe; for nature hath taught man to be an agent even to brute animals, much more to fair ladies, as for example, the heavy ox he lightens with the goad, the sullen horse he quickens with the spur, and the melancholy dull lady he stirs up to mirth with the prick of witty invention from a good brain."

At these pretty similes, Moriana smiled and bid him kneel down, taking his sword, which was yet bloody with cutting the giant's throat, and laid it on his shoulder, bidding him rise up Sir Archmoriander, otherwise Duncell dell Cinthia, her Knight of the Moon, dubbing him in the order of the escutcheon she bore and entitling him by her half-moon, which bargain he sealed with his lips on the back of her hand[g] with a smacking impression, and kindly said, "Fare you well, sweet Lady," and so departed.

Moriana thus was freed from the giant,
And gave him thanks with tongue which went most pliant.

This well deserved affection from Moriana to Sir Archmoriander possessed him with the armor which of right belonged to the Knight of the Sun, when he, as many gallants use, neglected not the least opportunity that occasion could minister to crack and brag of his mistress's favors most, when, if truth had been known, they least concerned him.

[g] Not on the escutcheon.

Sir Tom Pheander, the Knight of the Sun, had a vision,[h] wherein he had intelligence of a coat-armor that was sent unto him by the Fairy Queen, which coat-armor was likewise showed to him in this dream, whereof he took especial observation for the marks and tokens, so that he could not fail in the challenging of it.

It was likewise told him in this vision that Moriana, a fairy lady, had most treacherously betrayed it into the hands of the Knight of the Moon, who wrongfully detained it from him.

> Sir Pheander had the armor showed in vision,
> Which made him hold Moriander in derision.

This vision put the Knight of the Sun into such a passion of anger that like a foolish madman he tore his hair and vowed a revenge against the Knight of the Moon, which he should be well assured to hear of, and hastens with all speed towards the court, to see whether he could meet with his injurious adversary.

That very morning the Knight of the Moon was ready armed in the Knight of the Sun's armor, and almost upon taking horse to ride abroad for some strange adventures, even at the instant when the Knight of the Sun came to court.

> Archmoriander was armed, I know not how,
> To ride abroad to slay the savage sow.

And meeting the Knight of the Moon, he was well assured (calling his memory to advise and summoning the remembrance of the marks) that it was his armor; therefore he stepped to the Knight of the Moon, and said, "Sir Knight, my simple opinion cannot judge any of your actions less than abominable honest, yet this coat-armor"—and clapped him on the shoulder—"belongs to me. Although you most ignobly detain it from me, yet I am sure 'tis my right, and by cocks and combs, the badge of my honor, I look to have it."

[h] For he was ever a great dreamer of fairy business.

The Knight of the Moon, thinking that he had struck him in earnest, most valiantly blurted out his tongue and bade him come by it how he could. This now likely to grow to a dangerous quarrel, the friends of both parts used their mediations and persuaded them to have the matter put to arbitrament and not fight, or go to law like brabbling fools which arrest one another for moonshine in water; and so with much ado they both yielded to have the matter decided by two indifferent honest men.[1]

So they were both bound, each to other in general acquittances of a hundred pounds apiece, and the Knight of the Moon unarmed himself and delivered the coat-armor and helmet, as he was enjoined, into the custody of the arbitrators then chosen, which were two headboroughs of a hamlet near adjoining to the city Moropolis:

The one had no wit, the other had no land,
But botched up his living by patching with holland.[13]

These headboroughs, being altogether unskilful in deciding controversies of such nature, retained a common lawyer as an umpire to assist them.

The lawyer, when he had seen the coat-armor, took a very great liking to it, insomuch that he purposed to give the two knights satisfaction by money and keep the armor to himself, if it would fit his body; although his conscience told him it belonged but to one, yet he would please both parties to serve his own turn. So putting it on to try the fitness, he felt it give him such a shrewd pinch in the guts, by reason it was too little, that he could never after graze anywhere but on bare commons.

O gaffer lawyer, stay, how do you look?
Sir Pheander will note down your name in his book.

So the lawyer seeing his purpose prevented by misfortune and no benefit like to rise towards himself, he would take no further pains in the business, but left it to the dis-

---

[1] Not too honest, by no means.

cretion of the two headboroughs, who now having the whole and absolute power of determining the cause and withal the coat-armor in their own hands, they made no great haste to beat their heads together about an award, but, like subtle foxes, made good use of the armor for the most part of their whole year, to watch and ward in, and, having learned a trick of the lawyer, fed the two knights with delays till their own turns were served, and in the end, because neither of them could write or read, they returned an *ignoramus*.

When the matter was understood to be so difficult that such understanding men as they were taken to be could not decide the controversy, it was held fit that they should try out their own rights in single combat, by reason both challenged with like proofs and the one would not endure the other to be rival in either's absolute right, where indeed necessity admits no plurality in such a case.

> You say very true, the weather grows hot;
> And two fools at once were too much in one coat.

The day for combat was appointed and the two combatants had warning given them to provide themselves sufficiently for the maintenance of their just claims.

Now does the Knight of the Sun lie ruminating every night, tossing and tumbling in his bed without sleep, bethinking himself, being of a timorous nature, what the issue of this dangerous quarrel may come to, and, oftentimes, heartily wished he had never challenged so worthy a knight for so small a trifle.

On the contrary part, the Knight of the Moon seemed to be very unwilling to expose his body to such an eminent danger, especially against a knight of his own order, but rather could wish him to sleep in peace till he did awake him, which he would not do for a world, but that his knightship's word was so far engaged.

> Alas, poor knights, I much bewail their case,
> To see how meager both look in the face.

Moriomachia

The Knight of the Sun armed himself in a new white armor, which he never tried before, and, for decency's sake, went into his chamber to his looking glass to see how his armor did fit and become him, and finding it to his liking he called his page and asked his opinion. The page answered that the armor did not fit or become him, in his opinion. Quoth the Knight of the Sun, "No, my pretty page? Why, the glass in my chamber tells me it is very proportionable and fit." "Sir, believe not the glass," quoth the page, "for the knavish optic made it to reflect many fair figures on foul faces and they will flatter many and make them seem far better than they are. But, master, content yourself, for you look very well, especially when your beaver is close locked that a man cannot see your face." Which answer pleased the knight so that he rested passing well contented.

But now the time is come and the combatants ready to enter the lists.

Soft, who comes here? I pray can you tell?
The Knight of the Sun; what, can you not smell?[j]

First came in the Knight of the Sun, richly accoutered in a white armor, adorned with a white and azure plume in the crest, with black beaten buckram bases,[14] glistering like the purest black jet, beautified all over with painted devices of suns and stars.

Jack (towering) Daw, that tops the lofty tree,
On a swine's back sits not so upright as he.[k]

On either side were emblems of T P K, figured in escutcheons far more fair than the shelf-clothes in a new grocer's shop. Direct before him, at his saddle pommel, hung a battle-ax which had endured the brunt of many a deep danger, shadowed under the mystery of a burning pestle,

[j] For there was civil wars in his belly, and some ran from the camp.
[k] His black bases glistered like a crow on a hog's back.

flaming out of a common mortar, most artificially wrought in natural colors upon holland.

By his side was clasped a dangerous pair of hangers,[15] wherein was wrought with subtle embroidery of moss and peacock's feathers a landscape of strong grated castles, high-grown woods, and large fields of hemp, in which hung a sword wrought with such cunning that a man could very hardly judge which end should hang downwards. In his hand he carried a proper tall slender lance, so straight as a bent bow (against which the Knight of the Moon did except, fearing to be overreached with a crooked measure), and it was so sharp at the end that it would stick to a coat of steel like a piercing burr.

He was mounted on a brown bay courser, of such a strange understanding that he would apprehend more than himself—could devise to teach him.

> The horse's wit did work, as I suppose,
> Over the tub, and barm dropped from his nose.[1]

For when he but presented his foot to the stirrup, he would stand so gentle as a block, but being up and surely seated, one very whisk of a birch rod would make him fling out his heels like a schoolboy, and run with such swiftness and wonderful speed that the very stuffing of his head would drop out at his nose like turpentine.

The caparisons of his horse were of the same piece that his bases were of, and wrought all over with rich colors of painted needlework, which made a more delightful show than the brave Bucephalus of a Whitsuntide lord in his morris dance. He had such small spurs that a man could very hardly discern the rowels, for they were no bigger than the little forewheels of a small ordinary coach.

> His rowels bore compass, extending so far,
> He looked like a carter, with whip, horse, and car.[m]

---

[1] It was not a brewer's horse, for all that.

[m] His lance, the whip; his spurs, the wheels; the caparisons, the car; and himself the carter.

Before him was carried by strength of man a moral device of wind instruments, figuring a man troubled with the wind-colic, which could neither have ease or take pleasure till he heard the wind break from him with a melodious sound. These instruments in the Fairy Land are called poke-whistles, but here the vulgar most depravingly do give them the plain attribute of bagpipes.

> At length his sullen pipes began to squeak;
> To save his breech, he did alight to leak.[n]

On either side went a squire in the habit of Turks, with red turbans on their heads, wreathed about with white sashes, and truncheons in their hands, betokening banditti, or sturdy highway standers, captived to the mercy of his victorious sword.

He was come into the lists (I mean not of threadbare broadcloth), and had ridden so often about to show himself to the people that it would have tired a horse,[o] before the other combatant came in. But he is not long that comes at last.

Then in came the Knight of the Moon, making no great show, who was likewise in a milk-white armor newly scoured. He bore a plume in his crest, as white as a goose feather, signifying his innocence, for that the Lady Moriana was never had before any justice to be examined how she came by the armor, nor did the messengers that brought it acquaint him that it did belong to the Knight of the Sun. He had parti-colored silk bases of a rich mercer's stuff, but the name I do not well know. His sword and lance were patterned by the Knight of the Sun's. His horse was black and so free-spirited that he rode him without spurs. He came in like a plain ordinary knight[p] without attendants, save only his horse—had rich trappings.

[n] For he cannot hold his water when he hears a bagpipe.
[o] He almost tired his horse before the combat.
[p] I mean not knights that diet in ordinaries.

Sir Moriander's come, grim-looked, as sharp as verjuice,[16]
Without attendants—fie upon this charges.

A brother of their order, hearing of this combat, made his personal appearance with a blue flat cap, wherein stuck a feather bush of all the colors in the rainbow. He had a deep ruff band with wide sets, so great as if the laundress had mistaken the steel and poked it with the band-block. It bore a circumference like the wheel of a brewer's dray cart. He had a long dropping nose, like the pipe of a still, to which his lean chin in courtesy turned backwards to give meeting half way, at the sign of the mouth.

No jesting fool, but a plain-dealing lad,
That speaks his mind, be it good or bad.

At his sudden coming in, the two knights' stomachs began to rise, but not at one another, for they thought he had brought a calf's head and bacon in a charger[q] upon his shoulders, covered with a blue china dish[r] and a bunch[s] of radish, but it fell out otherwise, for he came like a voluntary trumpet, at his own proper costs and charges, to sound the terrible alarm.

He blew alarm, so sweet as any figs,
Which pleased the ears, as Jews love roasted pigs.

So taking his cow-trumpet[t] from about his neck, he sounded a charge, which the two knights hearing, they put on courageously, with as swift speed as their horses could go,[u] to the very shock, where both their horses most unfortunately started off so far that the one could not come near to touch the other with his lance, and running out their full career, the Knight of the Moon, for want of spurs, could not stay his horse, which put him in such a mad standing choler that he forgot to bear up the point of his lance,[v] insomuch that the burr had like to light upon

[q] Ruff band. [r] Blue cap. [s] His feather.
[t] Horn. [u] Not run.
[v] Or picadilla.

the skirts of some of the standers by, and made them cry, Beshrew them that bear burrs.

The Knight of the Sun, premeditating the danger and withal respecting the meanest subject's safety as also his own, most gravely let fall his lance, and took hold of the saddle pommel with one hand and checked in his courser with the other so fiercely and short that he made a sudden stand in less than a quarter of an hour, to the great pleasure and wonderful applause of all the beholders.

In the second course, the Knight of the Moon used his lance for a Jacob's staff, and winking with one eye took the just height of the Knight of the Sun's breast, to which height he most politicly glided his lance, all along on the top of the bar, the whole career to the very shock, where, by great chance, he broke his staff with such a counter-buff that the Knight of the Sun was halfway behind the saddle, before he could catch hold of his horse's mane, which otherwise had kissed his tail to the very ground. But his sure hold so nimbly recovered him that he broke his lance athwart the Knight of the Moon's breast with such fury that the Knight of the Moon was extremely troubled with the passion of the heart; wherewith he was so grieved that the next course he was fully resolved to seal the Knight of the Sun his *quietus est*. And for that purpose he called for a stiff lance, with a full resolve either to break the Knight of the Sun's back or at least to dismount him over his horse's crupper.

The lance was delivered to him, which was a great deal too big for the grasp of his hand, and therefore he put it under his arm and took fast hold with both his hands on the pommel of the saddle, and running his full course he hit the Knight of the Sun against the thumb of his gauntlet, which beat back the lance quite from under his arm, and withal near turned the Knight of the Moon out of his saddle to the ground, but that the buckle of a girth caught hold of his bases and so saved his honor from the dust.

But recovering himself and half mad with fury, he ran his horse about to the same side of the bar where the

Knight of the Sun was, and most cowardly (against the law of legs[w]) set upon the Knight of the Sun with both his armed fists, when the Knight of the Sun had nothing in the world to defend himself but his sword and lance, which he so dearly loved that he carefully preserved it from breaking that course.

In this their last course of tilting, the very dregs[x] of their malice began to appear, and therefore they were resolved to run no more, but to try it out with their single swords at the barriers. So both of them drew, and laid on such heavy load that the very fire itself did not dare to appear from their valiant swords for fear of being quenched with the drops of sweat that fell from their knightships' hide-bound faces.

In this conflict they were both so far spent and tired as ever was hackney horse under prodigal citizen, and the pride of their eager swords, now having their bellies full, were so rebated that neither of them would bite. And therefore, like old overworn servingmen, whose prime of youth was spent in their masters' service, had at last both their coats pulled over their ears and dismissed their masters' service without wages.[y]

The Knights of the Sun and Moon, now being both on foot, made a pause to breathe themselves, staring in opposition one against the other, with full big faces swollen with anger, foaming or slavering at the mouth, like two sucking savage boars, whetting their tushes against a dug.

And on a sudden they closed together, and so fell to wrestling to try their strength of arms, but the Knight of the Moon (being the elder courtier) was too cunning for him in the gripe, and threw him down, but so as both were down together, and the Knight of the Sun undermost, which seemed ominous, portending strange things to come.[z]

[w] Or arms.

[x] Although they were not ale-tubs.

[y] They threw away their swords without scabbards.

[z] Fourteen days soon come about, for the Sun and Moon are in conjunction.

Moriomachia

Why is it so dark? That I can tell soon:
The Knight of the Sun is the Man in the Moon.[aa]

The (Knight of the) Sun and the (Knight of the) Moon, continuing thus in conjunction, caused such an eclipse[bb] as hath seldom been mentioned in any histories of your greatest (almanac) writers, for the interposition of the body of the (Knight of the) Moon did so darken and obscure the light of the (Knight of the) Sun that it made a pitch-black dark day, and wrought such confusions and mistakings on earth, by reason of the darkness, that in Moropolis, where the houses stood thick, one honest citizen could very hardly see another without the help of lantern light.

He was a happy man could keep his wife to himself for fear of losing her, for many wives took other men in their husbands's stead, for want of light. It was so extreme dark that collectors for the poor could not see to distribute the moneys gathered to charitable uses, but were glad to put it up in their own purses and employ it to their own uses till this eclipse was past. The poor constables were glad to take money of malefactors to buy them firelight, to see the peace kept, whereas oftentimes before many of them were forsworn, by reason they could not see to bring in true presentments.

The lawyers could not see their briefs, not to make so much as one motion for his rich oppressing client without three double fees for his motion and torchlight; but for his poor client, if his cause were good, his charge of torchlight was saved by the presence of angels.

And although attorneys swarmed like the grasshoppers in Egypt, yet they kept so close and were so hard to be seen, by reason of this darkness, that a man could very hardly have any one appear, not scarce for ten groats. The fogging solicitor could not see to follow a cause, as in honesty he ought, but neglected the business of him that first retained him and for want of candle-light took fees of the

[aa] The Moon overcame the Sun.
[bb] The eclipse of the Sun.

contrary party, which, after the eclipse was past, came to light, and he called cozening knave for his labor, though sore against his will.

In this dark eclipse, the bankrupt could not see to pay his debts, but his creditors were glad to grope out half a crown in the pound and thank him for it.

The miserable Jewish usurer would not be at charge for so much light as would search the odd corners of his counting-house to find out and deliver up mortgages of land, and old bonds that were formerly paid, but put off the debtors with releases and acquittances, with hope that time might neglect them or cast them aside to be lost; then would he but forswear the payment and all is his own.

The extorting broker, that sucks the very marrow from the bones, worse than the foul disease, for want of candle-light could not see the Devil at his elbow with one paw on his shoulder, ready to tear him in a thousand pieces, for oppressing the poor pawning borrower with threescore in the hundred, and in missing but one hour of his pay-day he should be sure to lose more than thrice the value he borrowed.

Some wicked mothers, after they came home from their revelling cheer and music, for want of candle-light became bawds even to their own daughters.

In this dark eclipse, the peaking pandar sneaked out with his bundle of rotten commodity, which by candle-light made such a fair show that he held it at a pocky dear rate, but the world was grown so cunning that none but young heirs and fools would deal with him in hole-sale, and yet he made shift to retail it out to many gallants by the yard, because they were his common customers.

The tapster could not see to do any man right; it was so exceeding dark in his cellar that he thought the devil had been there, so that he came running up affrighted before his pot was half full.

By reason of this eclipse, the ostler could not give the horse hay, nor see the age in his mouth without a greasy candle in his hand.

O, 'twas a lamentable time with dyers and picture-drawers: for the one could not see by candle-light to put in those true ingredients that would hold color and keep from staining, nor the other by candle-light could not take the true picture of man or woman without great faults.

This dark eclipse was more beneficial to tallow-chandlers than three dark winters before, wherein prentices to the trade took such pains and withal were so careful that many of them were made free,[17] which before were but screalings[18] and ever crawling in the tallow, with their black flat caps like maggots.

And this eclipse did not much hinder haberdashers of small wares, by reason they kept so many lights, for by so much light a man might well discern small wares in many shops.

It was a merry time with carmen, watermen, and porters, for in this eclipse many of them did nothing but drink, domineer, and swagger in ale-houses, but the often going to and fro of the pot made them talk of that which they had nothing to do withal, and many times their obtuse apprehensions would be meddling with the wars betwixt the great Turk and Prester John, how it was likely to end, because they heard their neighbor Goodman Jobson say, they were now grown friends and had put the matter to a bickerment. So that state businesses, which nothing concerned them, and the pot together so stupefied their brains that many of them went reeling out of doors. But if money began to fall out somewhat short before they came to the height of their state matters, then many of them, like a company of foul-mouthed fellows, would swear, curse, and rail, even against those men that set them on work, from whom they had their chiefest means of living.

This dark eclipse was almost the undoing of many bailiffs and sergeants and the impoverishing of marshal's men so much that their mercenary dependences whom they authorize to arrest made men more fearful of their purses than of putting in bail to their actions, by reason their exacting fees, for want of businesses came not in roundly, so that they could not better their apparel but went like renegado Bacchanalians, be dropped all before with grease and ale, whose long continuance begot a glistering substance which made such a cozening show that a man would have thought his preface had been all satin although his doublet was not worth a button and pinned over before,[cc] as if he had been in his swaddling clouts or else born with those clothes on his back.

This dark eclipse proved dismal to the chief miller of a windmill, for he having been abroad amongst his companions carousing was so extremely tippled with drink that he had much ado in the dark to find his mill, although it was but a coit's[19] cast from the ale-house where he got his liquor. At length finding the mill by the noise it made in going, he groped to the stairs to go up, which he could not find, but went under the mill amongst the sacks of wheat that were standing there ready to grind. Amongst these sacks he found good easy elbow-room, and leaning against them fell fast asleep. This malt-sack now among the wheat-sacks was so dead in sleep that indeed he was as senseless as his bed-fellows. The miller's man above in the mill had put up almost the last hopper full of all the wheat that was then ready craned up. Therefore he let down the rope to crane up more, and afterwards came down himself in the dark, like a foolish knave without a candle; so feeling for the sacks of corn, the first that he lighted on was the malt-sack his master, whom he took for a sack of wheat. Then the wicked hangman put the riding device over his master's head, where he felt a handkercher which his master did use to wear with lace and buttons about his neck, after the effeminate fashion,[dd] forsooth, tied with a knot, which his knotty-jointed numbed fingers could not distinguish from the strings of a sack. There he fastened the rope, and away he goes up into his mill to wind up the supposed sack (his master towards heaven

[cc] Not one button on his doublet.
[dd] A caveat for clowns in fashion.

against his will), and having craned him up halfway, he heard the stones of the mill begin to touch each other for want of corn, whereby he was enforced to fasten the wrench of the crane with an iron pin and so let his master hang whilst he went up to put more corn in the hopper, wherein he showed his careful diligence, to look to his master's business, although he were hanged. After the miller's man had filled his hopper, he betook him to his old work, and craned (by favor) his master to the height of his ambition—but pride will have a fall. So he took the supposed sack of corn in, and went to fetch the candle to see to unloose the string, and coming near, he perceived it was his dead master. Then did he wring him by the nose and boxed him about the ears to recall life, but all was in vain. So he stayed his mill, although he durst not stay himself, locked up the door, and put the key in his pocket, fearing his master should follow him to raise the town, and away he ran, and was never heard of to this instant day.

The (Knights of the) Sun and Moon, thus continuing their long conjunction together, made the spectators weary by reason of this eclipse, for it was so dark that those which stood nearest to them could not possibly see any of their valiant deeds, but only they might hear them puff and blow, and therefore it was thought fit to have them parted. So they felt them out, who lay so still, being both over-wearied, as if they had been in a sound sleep.

When they were both up and had breathed themselves awhile, the Knight of the Sun was very earnest to be at the Knight of the Moon again, to try whether he could regain the light which so eclipsed his honor; but he was held back (which made him the more eager) and might not be suffered, because the combat was already adjudged to be lost on the Knight of the Sun's part, and the award given up,[ee] which was:

That the Knight of the Moon should have and enjoy the coat-armor and helmet as his own proper right, without

[ee] As the custom is.

the least trouble or molestation of the Knight of the Sun, and to wear the same, where and when he pleased, according to his discretion. Provided always, that the Knight of the Sun, upon reasonable warning, should have the use of the armor and helmet, so that at any time he could allege some great cause without yielding any reason for the same, but to redeliver the same again to the Knight of the Moon as true and lawful owner, without detaining it by delays any longer than his present use required, upon the forfeiture of his knightship and arms.

So the Knight of the Moon had the coat-armor and helmet delivered to him, wherewith he was immediately armed, and so departed the lists, with a great applause, especially of the younger sort of people,[tt] as victor.

The Knight of the Sun, hearing the award proclaimed, and withal seeing the Knight of the Moon bear away the bell, he stood like a body without a soul, or a man whose heart was fallen into his hose, or indeed like King Belin's armed stake in the fields which archers shoot at.

So this little dangerous combat was ended, which since the battle between Clineasse and Dametasse the like hath not been heard of, save only that of Don Quixote and the barber about Mambrino's enchanted helmet.

Thus endeth the legend of this fearful fight,
'Twixt Pheander the maiden and Moriander the knight,
Which parted between them their indifferent dealings
Did prove them to mean knights, not giants nor screalings.

[tt] Boys.

FINIS

THE
Life of Long Meg
of VVestminster:

Containing the mad merry prankes
shee played in her life time, not onely
in performing sundry Quarrels
with diuers Ruffians about
LONDON:

But also how Valiantly she behaued
her selfe in the Warres of
Bolloingne.

LONDON:
Printed for *Robert Bird,* and are to be sold
at his shop in S*t*. *Laurence lane,* at the
signe of the Bible. 1635.

THE LIFE OF LONG MEG OF WESTMINSTER (1620)

Long Meg of Westminster is a lively and entertaining representative of a group of books, rather few in number, written for popular consumption, which are usually called "jest-biographies." This somewhat opaque term—a translation of the name *Schwankbiographien* conferred on the genre by Ernst Schulz, the author of the first modern study of this and related material—is intended to convey the notion that the several anecdotes or incidents making up the "life" of the protagonist are very close in spirit, content, and general procedure to those making up the ordinary staple of contemporary jestbooks. Theoretically, if one were to take a number of standard jests, most of which for their point turn on a rude discomfiture of somebody or other, arrange them in a roughly chronological order, expand their scope slightly, and then attach them all to a single hero (or heroine), a jest-biography would result. Such a book can, of course, provide no more than a remote simulacrum of a genuine biographical account, but it may, and usually did, offer enough to base at least a rudimentary feeling for character on.

Long Meg follows this pattern quite well. Its eighteen chapters offer as many tableaux in the life of a somewhat boisterous woman (but of course hers were boisterous times), from which certain traits of character emerge: Meg loves to fight but is saved from being a virago by her unexpected but winning wifely submission after she is married; she is extremely good-hearted, being an unwearying defender of the rights of the poor and unfortunate; she is open-handed and generous, and shows a sturdy disrespect for vested authority if it appears to her wrong or corrupt. She is much admired by her own class, and, on the evidence presented, not without reason.

Meg's actual existence as a real person has been both asserted and denied, but though in the nineteenth century the question was hotly debated, notably by the antiquarians Edwin F. Rimbault and Peter Cunningham in the pages of the early volumes of *Notes and Queries*, it remains unresolved. Surely, however, there must have been some living prototype for our heroine, and if she did not actually do everything here recorded of her, the stories which clustered around her name have nothing inherently improbable or inconsistent. From the names of the historical characters who appear in the early chapters of the story it is clear that Meg was active in the early part of the sixteenth century: Doctor Skelton, presumably the poet, died in 1529; Will Summers, Henry VIII's jester and the hero of a similar jest-biography, was installed as court fool around 1525, apparently soon after his arrival in London; Sir Thomas More, who makes his appearance on one occasion, was beheaded in 1535. The last incident in Meg's life takes place in the reign of Queen Mary; perhaps we can date it 1557, the year in which Bishop Bonner was given severe inquisitorial powers by the queen.

Meg was entered on the *Stationers' Register* in 1590 and there are numerous allusions to her in writers of the 1590s and after, but the earliest known edition is one of 1620. (A supposed earlier edition of 1582 has been shown to be spurious.) There are also editions of 1635 and 1636, followed, at a long interval, by chapbook editions in the eighteenth and possibly also early nineteenth centuries. The 1635 edition was reprinted (along with an eighteenth-century chapbook version) by Charles Hindley in v. 2 of his *Old Book-Collector's Miscellany* (London, 1872).

The standard discussion of English jestbooks is Ernst Schulz, *Die englischen Schwankbücher bis herab zu Dobson's Drie Bobs (1607)*, Berlin, 1912; the material therein has been supplemented and corrected in a noteworthy article by F. P. Wilson, "The English Jestbooks of the Sixteenth and Early Seventeenth Centuries," *Huntington Library Quarterly*, II (1939), 121–158. For a summary of what has been said on the question of Long Meg's actual existence the reader is referred to Hingley's introduction.

The text of the present edition is based on the copy of the 1635 edition in the Folger Shakespeare Library.

LONG MEG OF WESTMINSTER

To the Gentlemen Readers

Gentlemen, to please your fantasies many men have made many pleasant gigs, as the jests of Robin Hood and Bevis of Southampton, and such others as serve to procure mirth and drive away melancholy. Now at last, because amongst the three doctors of health Doctor Merryman is not the least, and that longer lives a man of pleasant disposition than a sad saturnist, when I was idle I bethought me of Long Meg of Westminster and her merry pranks, as pleasant as the merriest jest that ever passed the press. A woman she was of late memory and well beloved, spoken on of all and known of many; therefore there is hope of the better acceptance. Gentlemen, Augustus would read over riddles when he had tossed over Virgil's Heroics, and Cicero would oft delirate[1] after his weighty affairs; so I hope you will use Long Meg as a whetstone to mirth after your serious business. And if she have any gross faults, bear with them the more patiently for that she was a woman, and presuming thus far on her behalf I bid you farewell.

THE LIFE AND PRANKS OF LONG MEG OF WESTMINSTER

Chapter 1. Containeth where she was born, how she came up to London, and how she beat the carrier.

In the time of Henry the Eighth of famous memory, there was born of very honest and wealthy parents a maid called for her excess in height Long Meg; for she did not only pass all the rest of her country in the length of her proportion but every limb was so fit to her tallness that she seemed the picture and shape of some tall man cast in a woman's mold. This Meg growing to the age of eighteen would needs come up to London to serve and to learn city fashions; and although her friends persuaded her to the contrary, yet forsooth she had determined and up she would. Wherefore she resolved to come up with a carrier, a neighbor of hers, called Father Willis, and so she did, accompanied with three or four lasses more, who likewise came to London to seek service.

Well, having taken their leave of their friends, forward they go on their journey, and by long travel at last got within the sight of London, which joyed their hearts greatly. But when they drew nigh, her fellow partners waxed sad, which Meg espying cheered them up thus: "What, lasses, in a dump, and we so nigh London? Cheer up your hearts; though we be come from our friends, yet here shall we have good mistresses that will allow us good wages; here at London may we win gold and wear gold, and there are not so many maids before us but we may find husbands as well as the rest. All is not broken stuff the carrier brings, and if it were, what then? That the eye sees not, the heart rues not. Let us do well, and we shall have well."

"Tush, Meg," quoth one of her fellows, "it is not that grieves me, but Father Willis the carrier you know is a hard man, and he asketh more than we have in our purses for letting us ride a little on his pack-saddles." "If that be all," quoth Meg, "fear not. I'll speak the carrier so fair, and if words will not prevail, I'll so rib-roast him with a cudgel as he shall wish he had never been coal-carrier to such shrewd wenches." This somewhat cheered them, and even as they were in this talk, Father Willis overtook them, and seeing they were beyond Islington ready to enter into St. John's Street, he demanded money of them for riding. "What will you have of us?" quoth Meg. "Marry," quoth Father Willis, "ten shillings apiece." "What, what?" answered she, "you are a merry man; ten shillings apiece, 'tis more than we have in our purses. No, Father Willis, you are our countryman and our neighbor, and we are poor wenches and far from our friends; you shall have a gallon of wine, and if ever we come to keep houses of our own here in London, look for amends. In the meantime to make up the bargain you shall have of every one of us a kiss for a favor." At this the carrier stormed and Meg smiled, which made him so mad that he swore if they would not pay him his money he would cudgel ten shillings out of their bones.

"Marry, content," quoth Meg, and she up with her staff and laid him on the shoulders, where she so beswinged the carrier and his man that poor Father Willis desired her for God's sake to hold her hands. "Not I, base knave," quoth she, "unless upon conditions, and that is this, that first thou bestow upon each of us an angel for a handsel[2] to our good luck hereafter in London, and that thou swear not to depart out of this town till thou hast placed us all three with mistresses. Otherwise, as I am a true Lancashire lass, I will so bombast thee, as all carriers shall take example by thee for displeasing a country wench."

The carrier having felt the weight of her arms thought better to give three angels than to have so many lambasts as she would bestow upon him, and therefore not only out with his pouch and gave them the coin, but swore not to depart before he had seen them placed.

Chapter 2. Containing how he placed her in Westminster, and what she did at her placing.

After the carrier had set up his horse and dispatched his lading, he remembered his oath and therefore bethought him how he might place these three maids. With that he called to mind that the mistress at the Eagle in Westminster had spoken divers times to him for a servant. He with his carriage passed over the fields to her house, where he found her sitting and drinking with a Spanish knight called Sir James of Castile, Doctor Skelton, and Will Summers; told her how he had brought up to London three Lancashire lasses and seeing she was oft desirous to have a maid, now she should take her choice which of them she would have.

"Marry," quoth she (being a very merry and a pleasant woman), "Carrier, thou comest in good time, for not only I want a maid, but here be three gentlemen that shall give me their opinions which of them I shall have." With that the maids were bidden come in and she entreated them to give their verdict. Straight as soon as they saw Long Meg they began to smile, and Doctor Skelton in his mad merry vein, blessing himself, began thus:

> Domine, Domine, unde hoc?
> What is she in the gray cassock?
> Methinks she is of a large length,
> Of a tall pitch and a good strength,
> With strong arms and stiff bones:
> This is a wench for the nones.
> Her looks are bonny and blithe,
> She seems neither lither nor lithe
> But young of age,
> And of a merry visage,
> Neither beastly nor bowsy,[3]
> Sleepy nor drowsy,
> But fair-faced, and of a good size.
> Therefore, Hostess, if you be wise,
> Once be ruled by me:
> Take this wench to thee.

> For this is plain,
> She'll do more work than these twain;
> I tell thee, Hostess, I do not mock,
> Take her in the gray cassock.

"What is your opinion?" quoth the Hostess to Sir James of Castile. "Question with her," quoth he, "what she can do, and then I'll give you mine opinion. And yet first, Hostess, ask Will Summers' opinion." Will smiled, and swore that his hostess should not have her but King Harry should buy her. "Why so, Will?" quoth Doctor Skelton. "Because," quoth Will Summers, "that she shall be kept for breed; for if the king would marry her to Long Sanders of the court, they would bring forth none but soldiers."

Well, the hostess demanded what her name was. "Margaret, forsooth," quoth she. "And what work can you do?" "Faith, little, mistress," quoth she, "but handy labor, as to wash and wring, to make clean a house, to brew, bake, or any such drudgery. For my needle, to that I have been little used to." "Thou art," quoth the hostess, "a good lusty wench, and therefore I like thee the better. I have here a great charge, for I keep a victualling house, and divers times there comes in swaggering fellows, that when they have eat and drunk will not pay what they call for; yet if thou take the charge of my drink, I must be answered out of your wages." "Content, Mistress," quoth she, "for while I serve you, if any stale cutter[4] comes in and thinks to pay the shot with swearing, hey, gogs wounds, let me alone: I'll not only (if his clothes be worth it) make him pay ere he pass, but lend him as many bats as his crag[5] will carry, and then throw him out of doors." At this they all smiled. "Nay, Mistress," quoth the carrier, "'tis true, for my poor pilch[6] here is able with a pair of blue shoulders to swear as much." And with that he told them how she had used him at her coming to London. "I cannot think," quoth Sir James of Castile, "that she is so strong." "Try her," quoth Skelton, "for I have heard that Spaniards are of wonderful strength."

Sir James in a bravery would needs make experience, and therefore asked the maid if she durst change a box on the ear with him. "Aye, Sir," quoth she, "that I dare, if my mistress will give me leave." "Yes, Meg," quoth she, "do thy best." And with that it was a question who should stand first. "Marry, that I will, Sir," quoth she, and so stood to abide Sir James his blow, who forcing himself with all his might gave her such a box that she could scarcely stand, yet she stirred no more than a post. Then Sir James he stood, and the hostess willed her not spare her strength. "No," quoth Skelton, "and if she fell him down, I'll give her a pair of new hose and shoes." "Mistress," quoth Meg (and with that she struck up her sleeve), "here is a foul fist, and it hath passed much drudgery, but trust me I think it will give a good blow." And with that she raught at him so strongly that down fell Sir James at her feet. "By my faith," quoth Will Summers, "she strikes a blow like an ox, for she hath struck down an ass." At this they all laughed. Sir James was ashamed and Meg was entertained into service.

Chapter 3. Containing how she used one of the vicars of the church that sung mass, and how she made him pay his score.

It fortuned that not long after she was placed but her mistress liked passing well of her, and Meg proved so good a wench that she was called of everybody Long Meg of Westminster. Much talk went on her; she was in every man's mouth for her tallness and her strength, insomuch that one of the vicars of Westminster, that was a tall lusty lubber and a stout franion,[7] who trusted much of his strength, thought to buckle with her and to give her the overthrow.

Now, sir, his custom was every morning after mass he would come in and call for a pot of ale and a toast, and ever he set it upon the score till it came to a crown or a noble and then he paid. One frosty morning amongst the rest he came with half a dozen of his friends, whom he had made private to his practice, and called for ale. Meg was ready and brought Master Vicar his morning draught. After he and his companions had drunk a while, he said he was come to clear his score, and asked what was on it. "Marry, Master Vicar," quoth Meg, "just five shillings and threepence." "Five shillings and threepence?" quoth he. "Why, I tell thee, foul stallion, I owe but three shillings and a penny, and no more shalt thou have of me. What a cozening quean have you got here, Hostess, that misreckons me at one time but two shillings and twopence? She may well be called Long Meg of Westminster."

"I have referred all to my maid," quoth the hostess, "and I marvel she would deal worse with you than with all the neighbors; but howsoever, shift it between you two."

"The foul ill take me, Mistress," quoth Meg, "if I misreckon the limmer lown[8] one penny; and therefore, Vicar, I tell thee, 'fore thou go out of these doors, I'll make thee pay every farthing, if thy cap be of wool."

"Away, you foul rake-shamed whore," quoth he, "if thou pratest to me, I'll lay thee at my foot." "Marry, there goes the game," quoth Meg; "we'll to it for a pluck or two. I'll give the Vicar the first handsel," and with that she reached the vicar a box on the ear that he reeled again. The vicar stepped to her and together they go by the ears, where between them was many a sore blow. The vicar's head was broken, Meg's clouts were pulled off, and he held her by the hair of the head. The vicar was shaven and so Meg could take no vantage, but at last she pummeled him so that he was clean out of breath, and then Meg (as lusty as she was at the first) took Master Vicar by both the ears and holding his head to a post asked him how much he owed her. "Marry," quoth he, "three shillings and a penny." "Then, knave," quoth she, "must I knock out of your bald pate two shillings and twopence more, and so oftentimes will I wring your head against the wall." And with that she began to sing a fair plainsong between the post and Master Vicar's pate. But he in his triple voice cried out,

"Five shillings and threepence, five shillings and threepence." With that she swore she would not let him go till he did lay down the money, which he did, and for his jest well beaten home to his chamber.

Chapter 4. Containing the merry skirmish that was between her and Sir James of Castile, a Spanish knight, and what was the end of their combat.

There was a great suitor to Meg's mistress, called Sir James of Castile, to win her love; but her affection was set on Doctor Skelton, so that Sir James could get no grant of any favor. Whereupon he swore if he knew who were her paramour, he would run him through with his rapier. The mistress (who had a great delight to be pleasant) made a match between her and Long Meg that she should go dressed in gentlemen's apparel, and with her sword and buckler go and meet Sir James in St. George's Fields; if she beat him, she should for her labor have a new petticoat. "Let me alone," quoth Meg, "the devil take me if I lose a petticoat." And with that her mistress delivered her a suit of white satin, that was one of the guards' that lay at her house. Meg put it on and took her whinyard[9] by her side, and away she went into St. George's Fields to meet Sir James.

Presently after came Sir James, and found his mistress very melancholy, as women have faces that are fit for all fancies. "What ails you, sweetheart?" quoth he. "Tell me, hath any man wronged you? If he hath, be he the proudest champion in London, I'll have him by the ears and teach him to know Sir James of Castile can chastise whom he list." "Now," quoth she, "shall I know if you love me. A squaring long knave in a white satin doublet hath this day monstrously misused me in words, and I have nobody to revenge it, and in a bravery went out of doors and bade the proudest champion I had come into St. George's Fields and quit my wrong if they durst. Now, Sir James, if ever you loved me, learn the knave to know how he hath wronged me and I will grant whatsoever you will request at my hands."

"Marry, that I will," quoth he, "and for that you may see how I will use the knave, go with me, you and Master Doctor Skelton, and be eye-witnesses of my manhood." To this they agreed, and all three went into St. George's Fields, where Long Meg was walking by the windmills.

"Yonder," quoth she, "walks the villain that abused me." "Follow me, Hostess," quoth Sir James, "I'll go to him." As soon as he drew nigh, Meg began to settle herself and so did Sir James, but Meg passed on as though she would have gone by. "Nay, sirrah, stay," quoth Sir James. "You and I part not so; we must have a bout ere we pass, for I am this gentlewoman's champion, and flatly for her sake will have you by the ears." Meg replied not a word, but only out with her sword and to it they went. At the first bout Meg hit him on the hand and hurt him a little, but endangered him divers times and made him give ground, following so hotly that she struck Sir James's weapon out of his hand. Then when she saw him disarmed, she stepped within him, and drawing her poniard swore all the world should not save him. "Oh, save me, Sir," quoth he; "I am a knight, and 'tis but for a woman's matter; spill not my blood." "Wert thou twenty knights," quoth Meg, "and were the king himself here, he should not save thy life, unless thou grant me one thing." "Whatsoever it be," quoth Sir James. "Marry," quoth she, "that is, that this night thou wait on my trencher at supper at this woman's house, and when supper is done, then confess me to be thy better at weapon in any ground in England." "I will do it, Sir," quoth he, "as I am a true knight." With this they departed, and Sir James went home with his hostess sorrowful and ashamed, swearing that his adversary was the stoutest man in England.

Well, supper was provided, and Sir Thomas More and divers other gentlemen bidden thither by Skelton's means to make up the jest, which when Sir James saw invited, he put a good face on the matter and thought to make a slight matter of it, and therefore beforehand told Sir Thomas More what had befallen him: how entering in a quarrel of his hostess's, he fought with a desperate gentleman of the court who had foiled him and given him in charge to wait on his trencher that night. Sir Thomas More answered Sir James that it was no dishonor to be foiled by a gentleman, since Caesar himself was beaten back by their valor.

As thus they were descanting of the valor of Englishmen, in came Meg marching in her man's attire. Even as she entered in at the door, "This, Sir Thomas More," quoth Sir James, "is that English gentleman whose prowess I so highly commend, and to whom in all valor I account myself inferior." "And, Sir," quoth she, pulling off her hat and her hair falling about her ears, "he that so hurt him today is none other but Long Meg of Westminster, and so you are all welcome." At this all the company fell in a great laughing, and Sir James was amazed that a woman should so wap[10] him in a whinyard. Well, he as the rest was fain to laugh at the matter, and all that supper time to wait on her trencher, who had leave of her mistress that she might be master of the feast, where with a good laughter they made good cheer, Sir James playing the proper page, and Meg sitting in her majesty. Thus was Sir James disgraced for his love, and Meg after counted a proper woman.

Chapter 5. Containing the courtesy she used towards soldiers, and other men that carried good minds.

There resorted to the house where Meg was resident all sorts of people, and the more for to see her, insomuch that she was famoused amongst all estates, both rich and poor, but chiefly of them which wanted or were in distress, for whatsoever she got of the rich (as her gettings were great) she bestowed it liberally on them that had need; there was no poor neighbor dwelling nigh whom she would not relieve, and if she had seen one come in that looked like a man and was in distress, if he called for a pot of beer and had no more money in his purse than would pay for his pot, she would straight of her own accord set before him bread and beef, and if the man said he wanted money, "Eat, knave," quoth she, "for they must eat that are hungry, and they must pay that have money." And when he had done she would give him pence in his purse and so let him go. For this cause was she generally loved of all good fellows about the city.

On a day there came a poor soldier to the house that was in great distress, simply attired and worse maimed, and sitting him down, called for a pot of beer, and with that fetched a great sigh. "How now, man," quoth Meg, "what cheer? Faint not, after a dear year comes a cheap, an ounce of care pays not a dram of debt; be merry and fall to some service, for such idle slaves as thou art are moths of the commonwealth that take no other delight but to live off the sweat of other men's brows. Thou art big enough, and God hath done his part in thee. A man proper enough, and now for to live in this distress? If I were a man, by cocks bones I would rather with my sword tear money out of the peasants' throats than live in this want. But see the slavish and base humors of cowards, that for fear live in misery."

"Oh, Meg," quoth he, "you may say what you please, because you are a woman, but divers in the city have known me, and seen the day when I lived like a man. But falling into extreme sickness so lost my service, and now being recovered of my health, because I am poor I cannot get entertainment. And for to pick a pocket, to filch anything out of a house, or to steal a sheet from the hedge or to rob any poor man, woman, or children as they travel, I hold it in scorn and had rather be famished than incur such base discredit. Marry, now that distress wrings me, though I have been true all my life, yet if I had a good sword, and a good horse, perhaps I should be so bold as talk with a purse." "Thou?" quoth Meg. "Trust me, I think thou darest not look on a sword. If thou darest, wilt earn a brace of angels? I will lend thee a sword and buckler; go thy ways into Tuttle Fields and walk there, and when thou seest a servingman, a tall knave with a blue coat and a white satin doublet to pass by, pick some quarrel with him and well beswinge him, and I will beside give thee a new suit of apparel." "It is a match," quoth the fellow, and after he had drunk his pot off, she gave him his tools and sent him packing, and straight slipped on a doublet and a pair of hose and her blue coat, took a sword and buckler, and down to Parliament Stairs, there took boat as though she had crossed the water from Lambeth to the Fields.

She was no sooner on land and walking towards Chelsea, but the fellow spied her and crossed the way and began to give some cross language, whereupon together they went by the ears, Meg loath to hurt was almost put to her shifts, for he being a marvellous tall fellow and one that feared not his flesh laid on such a load that Meg was fain to bid him stay his hand and to discover herself who she was. Then home they went together and straight she gave him a fair suit of apparel, a good sword and money in his purse, and bade him be a true man and get him service, and when that money was spent come to her for more.

Chapter 6. Containing how she used the Baily of Westminster that came into her mistress's house and arrested one of her friends.

On a time it so fell out that a gentleman whom Meg much favored for his courteous and honest conditions was sitting drinking in the house, being a man that was greatly indebted; and his creditor having intelligence where he was went to the Baily and desired him to arrest him. But when he told the Baily where he was he was very loath, yet for that he promised him forty shillings he understood the matter and away he went with his process. And coming into the place where he sat, called for a pot of beer. After he had sat a little, he stepped to the gentleman and arrested him, and desired the rest of the company in the King's name to see the peace kept.

The gentleman at this looked as pale as ashes, and Meg coming in asked, "What's the matter?" "Oh, Meg," quoth he, and fetched a great sigh, "I am arrested and, alas, utterly undone, for if I go to prison I shall have so many actions clapped on my back as I shall never be able to come out." "Arrested?" quoth Meg, "what, in our house? Why, Master Baily, is this a neighborly part, to come into our house and arrest our guests? Well, 'tis done and past, and therefore play the good fellow. Take an angel," quoth she, "and see him not. Here be none that be blabs; hold thy hand, here's the money, man, I'll pay it for the gentleman myself." "No," quoth the Baily, "I cannot do it, for the creditor stands at the door." "Bid him come in," quoth Meg, "and we will see if we can take up the matter." So the creditor came in, but was found very obstinate. Whereupon Meg made no more ado, but rapped him on the pate with a quart pot, and bade him get him out of doors, "for, knave," quoth she, "he can but go to prison, and that is the worst, and there he shall not lie long, if all the friends I have will serve to fetch him out."

The man went away with a good knock, and then the Baily would have been gone with his prisoner. "Nay," quoth Meg, "I'll fetch a fresh pot to drink with my friend, and then fare you well." Presently she came into the parlor again and brings a great rope in her hand, and knitting her brows, "Sir Knave," quoth she, "I'll learn thee whilst thou livest to arrest a man in our house. By gogs blood, you villain, I'll make you a spectacle for all such catchpolls." And with that she fell upon him, and with the help of another maid tied the rope fast about his middle. Then quoth she to the gentleman, "Away, Sir, shift for yourself, take no care; I'll pay the Baily his fees before he and I part." Away slipped the gentleman, as glad as a man might be. Then she dragged the Baily into a backside where was a great pond, and, setting him to one side, she went to the other and bade the Baily either wade through the pond or else she would drag him through. Whereupon the poor Baily was fain up to the chin to go through the water and when he was on the one side, she ran on the other till she made him go through five or six times. Then as soon as he was come out, "Now, Master Baily," quoth she, "I'll pay you your fees," and so up with a holly cudgel and did rib-roast him that he lay for almost dead. When she had done, she bade him beware and always know that their house was a sanctuary for any gentleman, and not a place for bailies and catchpolls.

The poor Baily went thence well beaten and with his amends in his hands, for she was so generally beloved that none durst meddle with her.

Chapter 7. Containing how she used Woolner, the singing man of Windsor, that was the great eater, and how she made him pay for his breakfast.

A company of pleasant gentlemen that thought to be merry with Long Meg went and got one Woolner, a singing man of Windsor, that was a great trencherman and would eat more at once than five or six men. Him they made privy to their conceit and he, being a mad companion, was as willing as the rest, and so they agreed that when the meat stood on the board ready for guests to come to dinner, Woolner should ask what he should pay to break his fast, for that his business was great and he could not tarry till the others came in. So he resolved and went to the house where Meg dwelt. The gentlemen before were come in, and in a room hard by were set at breakfast, looking when Woolner should come in. At last came in Woolner with a great staff in his hand, as though he had been a traveller.

"Ho, Hostess," quoth he, "is there any meat for men?" "Ay, that there is," quoth Meg; "look, man, the table is full. We tarry but for guests, and they will be here presently." "What shall I give you," quoth Woolner, "because I cannot stay, to eat my breakfast?" "Sixpence," quoth

Meg, "eat and spare not whilst thy belly crack." "You shall have it," quoth Woolner. With that he sat him down, and she fetched him drink, having business other where, came not to him almost in an hour's space. In which time Woolner had eaten up all the meat, as much as would have served ten men. With that, taking his staff in his hand, came out, and called for his hostess. "I thank you," quoth he; "here is sixpence, and so fare you well."

"Much good do it you," quoth she, and going in to see what he had eaten, found nothing of all her meat but the bare bones and clean platters. With that she whipped out again, and as he was going out of doors, took him by the cloak and pulled him back. "Friend," quoth she, "you should be sick by your stomach. Need you not a little aqua-vitae? Sirrah, thou hast eaten up all the meat." "Ay, that I have," quoth he, "and if I have pocketed up any crumb but in my belly, I'll give thee ten pound for it." "And shall I have but sixpence for all," quoth she, "there being so much as would have served ten men?" "No," quoth Woolner, "not a farthing more of me, for I agreed with thee for so much, and so much thou hast, and more thou shalt not have." "Then," quoth she, "sit still, and see how honestly I will deal with thee." She went into the larder, and filled all the board again with good meat and at every mess set a pottle[11] of wine, and at the board's end laid a good pikestaff.

"Now, fellow," quoth she, "of three things choose one. Seeing thou hast eaten so much meat for thine own pleasure, eat this for mine, and so drink off all the wine and pay nothing; or else take that staff and have a bout with me for thy breakfast—he that gives the first three venies scape free. Or lastly, fair and orderly pull forth your purse and pay me for my victuals. If you will do none of these three, by Heaven's maker, wert thou a devil (as I think thee little better by thy belly), I would bombast thee till thy bones crack, or mine arms be weary."

"I will do none of them," quoth Woolner; "I have paid you what I promised, and so farewell." "And," quoth she, "you shall have what I promised and so fare you well." With that she shut the parlor door, and with a cudgel began to labor him, insomuch that he cried out, and the gentlemen hearing burst in and in a merry mood told her all and paid for the breakfast, and so made them friends.

Chapter 8. Containing a merry jest how she met a nobleman, and how she used both him and the watch.

It chanced in an evening that Meg would needs be pleasant, and so put on a suit of man's apparel, and with her sword and buckler walked the streets, looking how she might find some means to be merry. The same night it so fell out that a nobleman, being a very wag, would needs go abroad with one man to see fashions. And coming down the Strand, he espied Meg and seeing such a tall fellow swinging up and down, thought to have a cast at him, and came to him. "How now, fellow," quoth he, "whither walkest?" "Marry," quoth Meg, "to St. Nicholas shambles to buy calves' heads." "How much money," quoth the nobleman, "hast in thy purse?" "In faith," quoth Meg, "little enough. Wilt lend me any?" "Ay, marry," quoth the nobleman, and putting his thumb to Meg's mouth said, "There's a tester."[12] Meg with that up with her fist and took him a good box on the ear, and said, "There, Sir Knave, there is a groat again, and now I owe you but twopence." With that the nobleman drew, and his man too, and Meg was as ready as they, and together they go, but Meg housed them both into a chandler's shop. So the constable rose to part the fray, and when he came in and asked what they were, the nobleman told his name, whereat they all put off their caps. "And what is your name?" quoth the constable to Meg. "Mine, Master Constable," quoth she, "is Cuthbert Curry-knave." Upon this the constable commanded to lay hold upon her and to carry her to the Counter.[13] Meg out with her sword and set upon the watch, and behaved herself very resolutely. But the constable called for clubs and then was Meg fain

Long Meg of Westminster 99

to cry out, "Masters, hold your hands; I am Long Meg of Westminster." With that they all stayed, and the nobleman would needs have her, the constable, and all the rest to a tavern, and there ended the fray in a cup of wine.

Chapter 9. Containing how Meg went a-shroving, and as she came home how she fought with the thieves at St. James Corner, and helped Father Willis the carrier to his hundred marks again.

When Shrove Tuesday was come, then maids must abroad with young men for fritters. Meg with two more of her companions and Harry the ostler of the house would needs to Knightsbridge a-shroving, where they had good cheer and paid frankly, for Meg would make every man drink that she saw pass by, and seeing that day came but once a year, she thought to lay it on and spare for no cost. Well, the day slipped away and night came on before they were aware, that they paid what they owed and took their leave to depart.

Father Willis the carrier that brought Meg up to London had been thereaway to take money and had received a hundred marks. And for the next day he must out of town, he would that night needs to Westminster to see Long Meg. He and his men trudge down apace, and as they came just against St. James Corner, there were they met by two tall fellows and rifled of all they had, their money taken from them, and they thrown bound in a ditch. When they had this coin, saith the one, "Now let us be gone." "Nay, by the mass," quoth the other, "we have sped well, and seeing we have so good handsel, we'll have one fling more, whatsoever fall out." As thus they stood talking, they spied Long Meg and her companions. "Yonder are three wenches," quoth he, "will yield us something, and a tall squire that goes with them; lie that we be not spied." As Meg was coming down, she said to the two other maids, "Come, set the better foot afore; 'tis late, and our mistress will think much we tarry so long." "Lord bless us and send us well home," quoth the others, "for this is a dangerous corner. I have heard them say that thieves lie here and rob men as they pass." "Thieves?" quoth Harry. "Fear not thieves as long as I am in your company, for I'll die before you take any wrong."

With that, on they went, and as they passed by where Father Willis lay, he saw them and cried out, "Alas, good gentlemen and gentlewomen, help a poor man that lies bound here, robbed of that he hath." "And there let him lie," quoth Harry, "for I warrant they are thieves that counterfeit themselves bound to have us come to them." "What, man," quoth she, "art afraid? Give me thy staff, for by the grace of God I will go see who it is, and if they be any false knaves, 'tis Shrove Tuesday at night, and I will give them rib-roast for a farewell to flesh." With that she took Harry's staff and forward she went, and when she came at them Father Willis knew her and cried out, "Ah, good Meg, help to unbind me, for I am undone and almost killed." "Why, what art thou?" "I am," quoth he, "Willis the carrier, who brought you up to London." "Alas, poor man," quoth she, and so she unloosed him and questioned with him how the matter fell out. He told her all, that coming to see her he was robbed. She bade him be of good cheer and take no care, for she would do her best towards his losses.

And as they were walking homeward, one of the thieves with a good sword and buckler stepped before and said, "Stand." "Stand?" quoth Meg. "What mean you by that?" "Marry," quoth he, "gentlemen, 'tis hot weather, and you must go lighter home by your gowns and purses." "You look not with the face," quoth Meg, "as though you would hurt women." As thus they were talking together, Harry, Father Willis and his man, ran away and hid themselves, and the two wenches stood quaking for fear and presently put off their gowns and their purses. "Dispatch," quoth one of the thieves, "and off with your gown, and so fare you well." "It shall be done, Sir," quoth she.

As soon as Meg had stripped her into her petticoat and

was light and nimble, she stepped to her staff and, stretching herself, said, "Sirs, this is the matter. You took even now a hundred marks from a poor carrier; now, you rascals, I am come to claim it and I will have it every penny ere I pass, or I will leave my carcass here for a pawn." "She is a good wench, I warrant her," quoth one of the thieves, "and therefore for thy sake take up your gowns and your purses, and farewell, and pray for good fellows." "Nay, your cowardly knaves," quoth she, "we must not part so. I must have a hundred marks out of your flesh, and therefore play me this fair play: you are two to one, lay me down the hundred marks to our gowns and our purses, and they that win all wear all, I or you." "Content," quoth the thieves, "and because thou art so lusty, when we have well beswinged thee we'll turn thee into thy smock and let thee go home naked." "Do your worst," quoth she; "now, lasses, pray for me." With that she buckled with these two sturdy knaves, and hurt the one sore and beat down the other, that they entreated her upon their knees to spare their lives. "I will, villains," quoth she, "upon condition." "Any condition, mistress," quoth they, "whatsoever." "Marry, then," quoth she, "the conditions shall be these:

1. First, that you never hurt woman, nor company that any woman is in;
2. Item, that you hurt no poor man or impotent man;
3. Item, that you rob no children nor innocents;
4. Item, that you rob no packmen nor carriers, for their goods nor money is none of their own;
5. Item, no manner of distressed persons; but of this I grant you exceptions, that for every rich farmer and country chuff[14] that hoard up money and lets the poor want, such spare not, but let them feel your fingers."

"How say you," quoth she, "are you content to agree to these conditions?" "We are," quoth they. "I have no books about me," quoth she, "but because you shall observe your oath firm and without wavering, swear on the skirt of my smock." Although it grieved them to be thus disgraced, yet fear made them grant to anything, and taking her smock, they laid their hands on it and said thus:

> Be we lief or be we loath,
> By the skirt of your smock we will never break our oath.

With that, they kissed her smock and rose up. And Meg she gave the wenches their gowns and their purses and took the hundred marks up under her arm, bade them farewell. The men desiring to know who it was that had so lustily beswinged them, said, "Nay, mistress, for all this sorrow, let us have so much favor at your hands as to tell your name." She smiled and made them this answer:

> If any ask you, who curried your bones,
> Say, Long Meg of Westminster met with you once.

And with that she went away, and they full of grief that a woman had given them a foil.

Chapter 10. Containing how Harry the ostler was pressed, how she used the constable and captain, and how she took press-money to go to Boulogne.

In these days while Meg flourished and was famous through England for her doughty deeds, there fell out great strife between the French king and Henry King of England, whereupon he resolved to levy an army of men, with a mighty fleet to pass into France. Upon which there was a general press through England, and especially about London and Westminster, because the king would leave the borders of his land strong. In this hurly-burly it so fell out that the Constable of Westminster pressed Harry the ostler, that was servant with Long Meg, who, being very loath to go, dealt so with Meg that she began to entreat the constable, and to tell him that he was the only stay of his mistress's house, and if that he were pressed forth his mistress were undone.

All this could not persuade the constable, but Harry must needs go. Whereupon Meg said he should not go.

And so they grew at words till Meg lent the constable a box on the ear. And with that all the street was on an uproar, that the constable was beaten for pressing of a man. The captain hearing this came down himself, and asked who had struck the constable. "Marry," quoth Meg, "that have I, and were it not that I reverence all soldiers and honor captains, I would strike thee too, if thou didst offer to press our man." At this the captain smiled. "Nay, never laugh," quoth Meg, "for I dare do as much as any of thy troop, either advancing my colors, tossing of a pike, or discharging of a piece. For proof," quoth she (and she snatched a caliver[15] out of one's hand that stood by), "see how well I can both charge and discharge," which she performed with such nimbleness and activity that they all wondered at her. "And therefore, captain," quoth she, "press not our man, but if thou wilt needs have one of every house, give me press-money and I will go under thy colors." At this they all laughed, and the captain drew his purse and gave her an angel. Whereupon, according to promise, she made provision for her passage, and went with him to Boulogne.

> Chapter 11. Containing how she beat the Frenchmen from the walls of Boulogne, and behaved herself so valiantly that the King gave her eightpence a day for life.

After the King had passed over the sea and had entered up into France with a strong power, he encamped before Boulogne, and then first won Boulogne and the Oldeman, so that he took the town wholly in possession and placed a garrison in it. The Dauphin of France upon this came down with a great power and lay before Boulogne, and upon one night, taking advantage of the time, he slew one of the sentinels and came to the walls, where he was discovered by the watch, who straight rang alarm. But they in the town, wearied with long waking, were in a dead sleep, so that they made little haste. Meg, being then a laundress in the town and up late at work, stepped up and called up the rest of the women, and with a halberd in her hands came to the walls, upon which some of the French were entered, and there she laid on load and caused her women soldiers to throw down stones and scalding water in such abundance that maugre their teeth she rebated them from the walls before the soldiers in the town were up in arms, and at the issue was one of the foremost with her halberd to follow the chase.

The report of this valiant deed being come to the ears of the King, he for her lifetime gave her eightpence a day.

Chapter 12. Containing the combat she had with a Frenchman before the walls of Boulogne, and what was the issue of the combat.

While the Dauphin's army lay in view before Boulogne, there was a Frenchman that sundry times would as on a bravery come within shot and toss his pike, and so go his way. Long Meg seeing the pride of this Frenchman desired that a drum might be sent, to signify that there was a common soldier, a young stripling, that would at the push of the pike try a veny[16] with their champion. Upon this it was agreed, and a place appointed between both armies where they should meet and fight it out to the death. The day came, the Frenchman all in a jollity came and tossed his pike before the walls. With that Meg was ready and went out and met him, and without any salutations they fell to blows, where there was a long and dangerous combat. But at last Meg overthrew him, and laid him along. When she had done, she pulled out her scimitar and cut off his head, and with that pulling off her burgonet, she let her hair fall about her ears, whereby the Frenchmen perceived she was a woman. And thereupon the English without Boulogne gave a great shout and Meg by a drum sent the Dauphin his soldier's head, and said an Englishwoman sent it him. Whereupon he commended her much, and sent her a hundred crowns for her valor.

Chapter 13. Containing her coming into England, how she was married, and how she behaved herself to her husband.

When the wars were ended in France, Meg came home to her old place of residence to Westminster, where she was married to a proper tall man and a soldier, who used her very well, and she returned him as great obedience, coveting any way that she might to breed his content, which he perceiving loved her passing well. Yet for that he had heard sundry of her exploits that she had done and how mankind she was, on a time he sought to pick a quarrel and fall out with her, and calling her aside unto a back chamber, stripped her into her petticoat and there delivered her one staff and took himself another, and told her that for that he had heard she was so mankind as to beat all she met withal, he would try her manhood and therefore bade her take which cudgel she would. She replied nothing, but held down her head. And with that he laid her on three or four blows. And she in all submission fell down upon her knees, desiring him to hold his hands and to pardon her. "Why," quoth he, "why take you not the stick and strike?" "Husband," quoth she, "whatsoever I have done to others, it behooveth me to be obedient towards you, and never shall it be said, though I can swinge a knave that wrongs me, that Long Meg shall be her husband's master, and therefore use me as you please." At these words they grew friends, and never after fell they at such mortal jar.

Chapter 14. Containing a pleasant jest, how she used the angry miller of Epping in Essex.

Meg going one day with sundry of her neighbors to make merry in Essex, all afoot because the weather was cool and it was a great frost, and none with them but a young stripling of some fourteen years old, for their husbands about business were gone another way, it chanced that they went by Epping Mill, where the miller was looking out, for the wind blew fair and the sails went merrily. The little boy, that was a wag, thought to be merry with the miller, and therefore called to him, "Miller, put out; put out, miller." "What shall I put out, boy?" quoth the miller. "Marry," quoth the boy, "a thief's head and a thief's pair of ears. Put out, miller, put out." At this the miller in great rage came running down and beat the boy. Meg stepped to him and would have stayed his hand, and the miller lent her three or four good bangs over the shoulder. Meg felt it smart and she got within the miller, wrung the stick out of his hand, and beswinged him well. And when she had done, sent the boy up for an empty sack and put the miller in all but the head, and then tying him in the rope wherewith they pulled up sacks, haled him half way and there let him hang. Where the poor miller cried out for help and if his wife had not been coming himself had been almost killed and the mill for want of corn set on fire. Thus Meg plagued the saucy miller of Epping.

Chapter 15. Containing the mad prank she played with a waterman of Lambeth.

Long Meg on a time had occasion to cross the water with a sculler from Westminster. When she was landed, frankly she drew her purse and gave him a groat. As she was going up the stairs, for all she had dealt so liberally with him, he began to hum, which she hearing came back again and questioned which of them all she had behaved herself so ill unto as to deserve a hum at their hands. Every man excused himself and seemed very sorry, for she was well beloved of all the watermen, but at last one said flat, it was he that brought her over. "Then, gentlemen," quoth she, "give me leave to revenge my own wrong." "Do what you will," quoth they. Then she stepped straight to him that brought her over, and with a stretcher beat him while he was not able to stir him; after, by the middle she tied him to the stern of the boat with a great rope, and then taking the sculls herself rowed him over at the boat's arse, and so crossed the water once or twice. And when she had well washed him, she landed him at Westminster, and bade him remember how he misused any honest face, and taking a piece of chalk wrote on the wall hard by the stairs:

> If any man ask who brought this to pass,
> Say it was done by a Lancashire lass.

Chapter 16. Containing how she kept a house at Islington, and what laws she had there to be observed.

After her marriage she kept a house of her own, and lodging and victuals for gentlemen and yeomen, such and so good as there was none better in all Islington, for there then she dwelt. Now for that oftentimes there resorted gentlewomen thither and divers brave courtiers and other men of meaner degree, her house was spoken of. And on a time the constable came to search, and would not be answered what guests she had but needs would be an eyewitness. Whereupon Meg in a great choler started up in her smock, and taking a strong cudgel in her hand opened the door for the constable. "Come in, Master Constable," quoth she, "and let me see your warrant, what suspected persons you seek for in my house. Take heed you go not an inch beyond your text, for if you do, were you a constable of velvet, I will as well beswinge you as ever constable was beswinged since Islington stood. And when you have done, you carry none out of my house tonight, for I will be answerable for all that are resident in my house." Whereupon Master Constable seeing the frowns of Meg's face and the fearful bastinado told her quietly he would take her word and so departed. Meg because she would have a trick above all others in her house, as indeed she surpassed all other victuallers in excess of company, for she refused none of what estate or condition soever, so she hanged up this table in her house, wherein were contained these principles:

1. Imprimis, That what gentleman or yeoman came into

her house, and had any charge about him, and made it privy to her or any of her house, if he lost it by any default she would repay it him ere he passed; but if he did not reveal it, and after said he was robbed, he should have ten bastinadoes with a cudgel and be turned out of doors.

2. Item, Whosoever came in and called for meat and had no money to pay should have a good box on the ear and a cross made upon his back, that he should never be suffered to drink more in the house.

3. Item, That if any good fellow came in and bewailed his case, that he was hungry and wanted money, he should have his belly full of meat on free cost, and money in his purse, according to his calling.

4. Item, That if any ruffler came in and made an alehouse brawl, and when he had done would not manfully go into the field and fight a bout or two with Long Meg, the maids of the house should dry beat him and so thrust him out of doors.

These and many such principles had she set up in her house, that made her house quiet.

Chapter 17. Containing how she used James Dickins, that was called Huffing Dick.

Once it chanced that Meg was making herself ready to go to dinner with certain of her friends at the Bell in Aldersgate Street, amongst the which was Sir James Withrington, an old acquaintance of hers. And in the meantime while she was making herself ready, came in this Huffing Dick, that had made a vow to quarrel with Long Meg, and called for ale. The wench brought him a pot, and he straight in a bravery swore "Gogs wounds, whore, what a pot is this that thou givest me?" and threw it against the wall. The wench began to scold with him for breaking her pot. And he up with his sword, scabbard and all, and beat her so that the girl cried out. And she being above and hearing that noise came running down and asked what is the matter? The poor wench cried and told her all. "Sir," quoth she, very mildly, "what is the reason you break my pots and then beat my servants?" "Why," quoth Dick, "if thou mislikest it, mend it if thou canst." "Marry," quoth she, "I will." And with that reached down a pikestaff and bade him follow.

Out went swearing Dick, all in his huffs with Meg into a close hard by, and together they go, where Meg so beat him that she had almost killed him. "Oh, hold thy hands!" quoth he, "and spare my life." "Then the devil take me," quoth she, "for the king hath granted me a pardon for one man, and hang me if it be not thou, unless thou wilt grant me one condition, and that is this: Thou shalt put my maid's petticoats on and follow me today to dinner with a sword and buckler, and I will be dressed in man's apparel." "Rather kill me," quoth the fellow. "Marry, content," quoth Meg, and began to lay sorer bats upon him.

"Alas," quoth he, "hold your hands, and I will do whatsoever you will have me." Upon this she let him go, and carried him home with her, and dressed him full womanlike. Well-bodied he was, but he had a long beard, to cover which, on his knees he craved he might have a muffler to shadow it. At last she granted it, and having dressed herself in man's attire, took a forest bill[17] on her neck and forward they went down to Smithfield. Everyone that saw the wench carry the sword and buckler laughed, that a multitude of people, of men, women, and boys followed. When they were right against the Bull's Head at the Bars, a crew of cutters that knew Long Meg met her and asked her how she did and what quarrel she had in hand, that herself wore a forest bill and her maid a sword and buckler. "Faith," quoth Meg, "a little broil, and my boy was not at home, and so I took my maid and she forsooth must wear a muffler." And with that she pulled the clout from his face and his black beard was seen. All the crew straight knew him and began to fall into a great laughter, demanding the reason of this strange chance. Meg told them all what had happened, whereupon Dick would not follow any further. "By gogs blood, knave," quoth she, "go to dinner with me, or I will cut off thy legs with my forest bill." So poor Dick was fain to trudge, and in she came and showed Sir James Withrington what a proper page she had got. He and the rest of the guests laughed heartily at the matter, and full mannerly did he wait upon her trencher all dinner time. And when dinner was done, she called him to her and said, "Now, Sirrah, I discharge you my service and cashier you for a brawling knave; yet for that you shall not say you served an ill mistress. Hold, there is forty shillings for thy labor to buy thee a new suit of apparel." Dick took the money, and for very shame went out of London and was never seen within the city after.

Chapter 18. Containing how she was sick and visited by a friar, who enjoined her penance, and what absolution she gave him after for his pains.

In Queen Mary's days, when friars and monks began again to show themselves, it chanced Meg fell sick of a grievous sickness, as such gross bodies are commonly pinched with sorest pains when they once fall into any infirmity, the disease having more matter to work upon in a fat body than a lean. An instance of this principle was Meg, for she lay so mortally sick that the physicians gave her over. Yet at last her critical day came, wherein trial of her health should be had to see whether nature or disease were strongest. Nature had the supremacy and Meg began to amend, insomuch that she could sit upright in her bed.

On a day when she was grown more strong, it chanced that Friar Oliver, who was one of the morrow mass priests, called to remembrance that Meg was sick, whereupon taking his **portice**[18] by his side, he thought to fetch some spending **money** from her and walked to her house, where he came very gravely. And at that instant were divers of her neighbors come to see how she did. As they were talking word was brought to Meg that Friar Oliver was there with his portice and his holy water. "What," quoth she, "after meat, mustard; 'tis no matter, bid him come in," and with that Friar Oliver comes in with "Deus hic" and salutes her and all the rest of the wives, saying he was very sorry to see Meg sick. "But," quoth he, "'tis the visitation of the Lord for the great sins you have committed. For, Meg," quoth he, "you have been counted a lewd woman, a swearer, a ruffler, a fighter, and a brawler, as you may see here in your chamber the signs," and with that he pointed to the swords and bucklers, pikestaffs and halberds that hung there. "These," quoth he, "are tokens of your ill life, and how in your sickness you have not repented you of your former ill life." Many such hard words did Friar Oliver give her, and told her that for her offences she must take the penance of the Church; "otherwise," quoth he, "I must complain to the Ordinary, and so to the Bishop, and compel you to it by injunction."

Meg, who fretted at this sauciness of the friar, because her neighbors were there, forbore him and demanded what her penance might be. "Marry," quoth Friar Oliver, "because you have been a public offender, you must have public penance, and therefore I do enjoin you that presently upon the recovery of your health, the next Sunday at mass you come into the church, and there kneel before the pulpit and declare to the people the vileness of your life. And so shall you then and there before the parish ask God and the world forgiveness."

At this the very fire seemed to sparkle in Meg's eyes for anger, but she concealed it with patience and entreated Friar Oliver to be good unto her and enjoin her some other punishment. The good wives entreated for her, but all in vain; for Friar Oliver swore either she should abide that penance, or else he would complain to Bishop Bonner.

"Why," quoth Meg, "never knew I friar but he was a good fellow. Is there not a shift of descant left for me?" "Faith, no," quoth he, "unless thou bestow five pound for five solemn masses." "Marry, Friar," quoth Meg, "and that shalt thou have straight, rather than I will abide such public shame." With that she called her maid and bade her fetch twenty English crowns, which she gave to the friar, whose heart leaped at the sight of the gold. He soon pocketed it up, and said that he would say five masses himself for her soul's health. And upon this Meg and the friar were agreed.

Well, all seemed to the best, and the company began to be merry. Friar Oliver he was blithe and gamesome with the young wives, and showed fruits of his life in his outward actions, for a more bawdy friar there was not in England, and that knew Meg well enough. But letting that pass, the wives said that they must be gone, for their hour was come. "Why, whither go you?" quoth Meg. "To a churching at Chelsea," quoth they. "Marry, and I will be your man thither," quoth Friar Oliver. The wives were glad of the friar's company and so they took their leaves and left Meg passing melancholy at the knavery of the friar.

Well, revenge broiled in her breast, insomuch that she started up, sick as she was, and dressed herself in man's apparel, and in the afternoon having a good bat in her hand, walked easily into Tuttle Fields to watch the coming home of the friar. Where she had not walked long, but she espied where the gossips came, manned only with the friar. And Meg crossed the leas and met them, and at her first salute greeted the friar and said, "Oliver, I am sent to thee from God, not only to tell thee of thy sins but to enjoin thee penance for the same. First, as concerning thy offences, thou livest not as holy men of the Church should, for thou are a whoremaster, frequenting the company of light and lascivious women, given to covetousness, and sitting all day bibbing at the ale-house when thou shouldst be at thy book, with a thousand more other offences which I cannot rehearse. Therefore hath the Lord sent thee thy choice, whether thou wilt from this place be whipped naked to the Priory in Westminster, or else pay twenty nobles to the poor men's box. One of these resolve upon, for, friar, one thou must do, and shalt do before thou stir." At this Friar Oliver was amazed and could not tell how he should like this sudden greeting, but said, "Who or what art thou?" "No man, Friar," quoth Meg, "but a spirit, sent from God to torment thee." At this the wives were all afraid, and the friar said, "*In nomine Jesus*, avoid, Satan," and would have run his way. "*In nomine Jesus*, stand, Friar," quoth Meg, and with that she reached him such a rap that the friar thought his back had been broken. "Sirrah," quoth she, "dispatch, either choose to be whipped from hence to the Doctor, or else pay down twenty nobles." "Alas," quoth the Friar, "I have not twenty nobles, but here is ten angels in gold, and fourteen shillings in white money. Take that for a satisfaction of mine offences; give it for my sins to the poor."

"Give it me," quoth Meg. As soon as she fingered the money, she told him that seeing he wanted some odd money that his body should pay it, and with that she lighted upon the friar's pilch and beat him so sore that he trusted better to his feet than his hands, and so ran away.

The poor women they were sore aghast, but Meg straight discovered herself. When they saw her face and knew all, their fear was turned to laughter, and away they went to the tavern and spent the friar's fourteen shillings in good cheer. The news of this, as women are good secretaries, came to the ears of all the friars in Westminster, how Friar Oliver was served, which was such a disgrace to him that a long while after he was ashamed to show his face in the streets.

FINIS

THE TINCKER OF TVRVEY,

his merry Pastime in his passing from BILLINSGATE to GRAVES-END.

The Barge being Freighted with Mirth, and Mann'd

With these Persons
- *Trotter the Tincker.*
- *Yerker, a Cobler.*
- *Thumper, a Smith.*
- *Sr. Rowland a Scholler.*
- *Bluster a Sea-man.*

And other Mad-merry fellowes, euery-One of them Telling his Tale : All which Tales are full of Delight to Reade ouer, and full of laughter to be heard.

Euery Tale-Teller being Described in a Neate Character.

The Eight seuerall Orders of Cuckolds, marching here likewise in theyr Horned Rankes.

LONDON.
Printed for NATH: BVTTER, dwelling at St. *Austins* Gate. 1630.

THE TINKER OF TURVEY (1630)

The Tinker of Turvey, a collection of six tales set in a unifying framework—in this case a barge trip from Billingsgate to Gravesend—is a somewhat altered version of a book originally published in 1590 under the title of *The Cobbler of Canterbury*. As the *Cobbler* the book had six stories also, set in the same frame. To make the new version the anonymous redactor dropped the last two tales of the original, told by an old wife and a summoner respectively, and substituted two new tales, those of the tinker himself, which was naturally placed first, and of a seaman. The other four tales were retained unchanged.

As its title hints, *The Cobbler of Canterbury* is a sort of imitation of Chaucer. The company assembled on the barge all agree that Chaucer was the father of English poetry and that he set a mark which many have aimed at but never reached to; after this, the cobbler suggests that all those present tell a tale on their trip in conscious emulation of Chaucer's pilgrims, a proposition enthusiastically accepted. The 1630 version retains this direct reference to Chaucer, the Epistle speaking of following his steps, while the tinker, who now assumes the role of leader formerly held by the cobbler, says that since "most of us are for Canterbury, we will call them Canterbury Tales." And of course the verse descriptions of each of the tale-tellers, inspired undoubtedly by Chaucer's General Prologue, remain in the later version. (The title page re-names them, in good seventeenth-century style, "neat characters.") It speaks a good deal for the general misunderstanding of Chaucer's versification in the Tudor-Stuart period that these ragged octosyllabics could pass current as imitation of the flexible and delicate line which Chaucer employed.

Since the two tales subsequently dropped both dealt with cuckoldry, *The Cobbler of Canterbury* was clearly a collection of merry tales, that is to say, stories with an everyday middle-class setting, realistic attitudes, and broad humor; only the scholar's tale, a romantic love tale, departs from this general type. In the 1630 version, the tinker's own tale, an example of the "biter bit" story, is cut from the proper merry tale cloth, but the other new bit of narration, the seaman's tale of Sir Lionel Aspernoon and the lesson he learns, is a mixture of a somewhat romantic setting with a homely moral which seems more a piece of folk wisdom than anything else. We are hence probably justified in regarding the later version of the book also as a collection of merry tales, though the bawdiness has been noticeably toned down.

Why it was deemed useful to replace the cobbler with a tinker is not clear. No doubt the words "cobbler of Canterbury" would in 1590 have been taken as an allusion to Marlowe and might have thus aided the sale of the book, and no doubt in 1630 such an allusion would have been pointless. Yet the older title served well enough for reprints in 1608 and 1614.

The text which follows is based on the copy of the 1630 *Tinker of Turvey* in the Huntington Library.

THE TINKER OF TURVEY

The Tinker hammers out an epistle to all gentlemen that love Latin, to all strolling tinkers, and to all the brave metal-men that travel on the hoof, with a dog and a doxy at's tail.

Tink, tink, tink, tink, tink, room for a tinker, a rattling metal-man, a hole-stopper, a kettle-drum-beater. Here comes Trotter of Turvey, armed with his budget, bungdagger, new pin and hammer, that has Lattin[1] in his pouch yet never to mend grammar. Many a country have I bestridden, many a town trotted over, in many a dirty fair been drunk, many a tinker's trull have I bum-fiddled and left the knave her walking-mate snoring on an ale-bench. Many a pair of greasy cards have I tossed over at trump, by a toasting sea-coal fire from morning to night, my cur at my feet, my drab by my side; and shall I not now be admitted to gabble in tinkers' rhetoric (tara-ring-tink)? I will please you, though I beat out the bottom of a kettle, for the parish kettle-drum was my intention, and all music came from the hammer.

Is not a tinker a rare fellow then? He is a scholar, and was of Brazen-Nose College in Oxford. An excellent carpenter, for he built Coppersmiths Hall. He is a doctor, too, can cast any water out of a skillet that is crazy, and set him upon his legs again. A soldier's march was taken from the sound of my basin, when I beat an alarum on the bottom of it with my nimble-rapping hammer, which to me is a drumstick.

Be you all then, my brother-strollers and padders on the highway, as jovial as I am. Lives not a merry man longer than a sad? Has not a tinker less care than a Tamburlaine the Great? Is not an hour in honest mirth worth a vintner's hogshead (that has no doings) full of melancholy? Why were taverns painted with red lattices but to tell gallants there's high-colored wine within? And why has a tinker's face a vermilion nose but to show that he loves that alehouse best which washes his cheeks with the strongest nippitaty.[2]

For I, Trotter the Tinker, have been soused over head and ears in the mediterranean sea of metheglin[3] and all other sorts of liquors. As ale? The authentical drink of England. The whole barmy tribe of ale-cunners[4] never laid their lips to the like. The best that ever washed my throat was at an old fat hostess's of mine called Mother Twattlebum, at the sign of a Tinker whipping the cat. Of her ale, the custom was to set before me two little noggins full, and then she bade me take heed how I angered her wasps, for four of them would sting my brains to death. And she said true, for no ale that ever I licked my lips at was like it. Yet I have thrust into my guts dagger-ale, stiletto-ale, pistol-proof-ale, pimlico ale, Mother Bunch's ale, labor-in-vain ale, Darby ale, Ale of Gotham (which makes the men there fools). I have drunk double-lanted[5] ale, and single-lanted, but never gulped down such Hippocrinean liquor in all my life. I asked her who brewed that nectar, whose malt-worm so nibbled at my pericranium, and she said herself, for old Mother Eleanor Rumming was her grand-dam and Skelton her cousin, who wrote fine rhymes in praise of her high and mighty ale.

But now to the tinker's tales, which were told in the barge between Billingsgate and Gravesend, herein following the steps of old Chaucer, the first father of Canterbury Tales. These coming as far short of his as bragget[6] goes beyond the pigs wash or small beer. If I knock any words out of joint, lay the blame on the tinker's hammer, which in mending and stopping one hole, thrusts out the kettle's thin bottom with his thumb and makes two.

Here's a gallimaufry of all sorts: The waiting wench has jests to make her merry, and clowns plain Dunstable doggerel for them to laugh at till their leather buttons fly off. A farmer sitting in's chair and turning a crab in the fire may here pick out a tale to set his chops a-grinning till his belly aches. Old wives that have wedded themselves to Robin Hood, Clim of the Clough, Tom Thumb, Friar and the Boy, and worthy Sir Isenbras, may out of this budget find something to maintain a gossiping: mum then for that.

Fall to and so farewell.

* * *

Sitting in the barge at Billingsgate, expecting when the tide would serve for Gravesend, divers passengers of all sorts resorted thither to go down. At last it began to ebb, and then they cried "Away." When I came to the stairs, though I was resolved to go in a tilt-boat,[7] yet seeing what a crew of mad companions went in the barge, and perceiving by the wind there was no fear of rain, I stepped into the barge and took up my seat amongst the thickest. With that, the bargemen put from the stairs, and having a strong ebb, because much rain water had fallen before, they went the more merrily down. Scarce had we gotten beyond Saint Katherines but a perry[8] of wind blew something loud, so that the watermen hoisted up sails and laid by their oars from labor.

Being thus under sail and going smugly down, it made us all merry, insomuch every one began to chat, some of one thing, some of another, all of mirth, many of knavery. As thus every man was striving to pass away the time pleasantly, a tinker of Turvey, being in the barge, to solace himself rather than any other, set out a throat and fell a-singing, playing very handsomely, first on the bottom of a small kettle with his hammer. His voice, though a bass, was so good, so loud, and so pleasing, that all held their tongues and listened to him.

THE TINKER'S SONG

Here sits a jovial tinker,
Dwells in the Town of Turvey,
I can mend a kettle well,
Though my humors are but scurvy;
    Yet will I sing,
      Tara-ring, tara-ring, boys,
    Room for a jovial tinker,
    I'll stop one hole and make three,
    Is not this a noble tinker?

The music of my kettle,
Brave sound, which forth is sending,
Makes fine girls cry, come, tinker, come,
We ha' many holes lack mending.
    Yet will I cry, &c.

We are the merriest fellows,
That by a trade get moneys,

And when we piece up broken wares,
We are paid by pretty conies.
    Yet will I sing, &c.

From fair to fair we amble,
Our doxies pranking by us,
And have whole chauders⁹ of strong ale,
When any tinkers spy us.
    Yet will I sing, &c.

The marches which each morning
Our hammer-heads are beating,
Make girls think tinkers well can strike,
And long for such a heating.
    Yet will I sing, &c.

The viol, lute, bandora,
The kit, welsh-harp, and cittern,
Make not the wenches so look out
As does a tinker's gittern.
    Yet will I sing, &c.

The basin ever ringing,
When bawds and whores are carted,
Is to my pan, that hellish din,
To hear which fiends have started.
    Yet will I sing, &c.

Here a gust came and stopped this tinker's mouth, but fair weather showing her face presently, "My masters," quoth he, "I have begun our Gravesend voyage with a song to the tune of my kettle. If any man will follow me, let him; if none will, let's pass away the time in telling of tales, and because I think most of us are for Canterbury, we will call them Canterbury Tales." "Agreed," cried all. "Who shall begin?" "Who but the tinker," quoth one, "because 'tis his own motion." Hereupon, lustily first beating his kettle, he settled to begin; but first behold the picture of this tinker.

THE DESCRIPTION OF THE TINKER

It was a sturdy lown,[10]
His black locks dangling down,
Curled and knotty, muzzled beard
To maken country fools afeard;
Grimy face, all smutted o'er,
His tanned hide tough as wild boar;
His broad back leathern pilch[11] did cover,
A greasy bonnet hung his eyes over.
By his side a whinyard[12] hung,
A budget fastened with a thong
And brazen buckle, wherein are
All his tools and tinkery ware,
Like a soldier's knapsack round
Across his shoulder was pie-bound.
That he lapped strong nappy ale
Showed his nose, that ne'er looked pale,
For he crimsoned it so well
It glistened like a carbuncle.
He tobacco eke could snuff,
Whose smoke he out would puff
In clunches'[13] eyes, and if they grumbled,
Them into the mire he tumbled.
Many a purse from many a swain
Had he thrashed on Salisbury-Plain,
With no noise can his tale be drowned,
For he on kettle it does sound.

THE TINKER'S TALE

Of a rich country peddler, being cozened by three and deceiving them again.

Not far from Gotham in Nottinghamshire, in a village dwelt an old rich peddler, that had used to sell wares at most of the fairs round about in those countries. In his house he kept nobody but a good stirring nimble-tongued wench, of some thirty years old, to whom he promised all he had when he died, for looking so well to his house and him. Her name was Gillian.

She, grieving to see the good old peddler every day to harness himself with a hamper and other trumperies tied to his back and in a high pair of clouted startups[14] to trot on foot to so many fairs and markets, counselled him to buy a good strong lusty horse to carry him and his luggage. And so both to ease his body and lengthen his life, for sithence he had money enough, this would not much hurt his estate. He laid careful Gillian on the lips for her learned and physical counsel, and said he would do as she wished him.

The next day, there being a fair where great store of horses were to be sold, the old peddler travels on foot with good store of money in his purse, with intent to come home again with more ease than he went forth, and then to say, "God-a-mercy, horse." Purblind he was, and hardly could he judge either of the color or conditions of a beast, but men wondering to see him busy to buy a prancer that never had bestrid a horse in his life, many offered in good will to help him, lest the cheating horse-coursers and hackney-men should cozen him. And so by their advice he bought a pretty handsome horse for three and twenty nobles.

Three mad colts that had watched the peddler still as he beat his market (the one was a butcher, the other a currier, and the third, one of the gentle craft, a cobbler) laid their heads together, how to get this horse from the old mop-eyed peddler. " 'Tis impossible," said two of the coney-catchers, but the cobbler's wit, being made of reaching leather, told them that the butcher had no more brains than a calf (but not half so good) and that the currier's conceit stunk like new-tanned leather; if they would join with Monsieur Cobbler, he would clap such a patch on the peddler's shoulder that they three would cozen him and share the beast among them. "How?" quoth one. "No more but thus," said the sole-mender, "let us all three part, and be distant one from another some quarter of a mile, in the way that he is to ride, and falling into some by-talk with him, view the horse well and say 'tis a handsome mare. That's all, and maintain it to be a mare, for I know his old foolish peddling conditions, and then see what follows upon this."

They three part, and first the butcher saluting the peddler as he rode inquired how the market went at the fair. "Marry," says the peddler, "all things very dear, and therefore I bought nothing but this beast. What think you my horse cost me?" "Which horse?" says the butcher. "This on which I ride," answered the peddler. "Alas, Father," quoth the other, "you are cozened. This is a mare, a very mare." "A mare," quoth the peddler. "You have good skill in horse flesh," and so rode away laughing aloud at the butcher's simplicity.

Then the peddler overtaking the currier, who stayed of purpose for him on the highway, and spying him come did then set forward. "Bless you, Father," cried the currier, "from whence come you?" "From the fair," quoth the old peddler. "You have a pretty mare under you," says the other. "How? a mare? Put on your spectacles, look better upon it, take your eyes in your hands, and you shall find 'tis a horse," says the old peddler. "So am I, or you an ass," replied the currier. And away spurred the old lad, wondering to see men so out of their wits, but remembering with himself they were Gotham breed, he cared the less, and knew for all his badness of sight he could not be so mistaken.

At last, he spying a third man in the highway before him, and that was the cobbler, whom overtaking, "O Gaffer Peddler," said the cobbler, "this is strange to see you mounted. You have been at the fair; any good doings there? Any fine girls there? Any store of pigs there? How goes leather? What lusty coil keep they there?" "Nay," quoth the peddler, "I looked after no coils, no pigs, no sows, no fine girls, not I; all that I minded was myself and my horse, that I bought there." "Well said, Father; can you jeer your poor friends in your old age?" "Jeer? why?" "Why," says the other, "is't not a jeer to tell me you have bought a horse, when 'tis as plain a mare as you and I are a man?" "What trade art thou?" quoth the peddler. "A cobbler," said he. "So I thought," said the peddler; "hie thee home, set thy coxcomb of an upright last, liquor thy brains better, patch up thy wits, bore a hole or two more in thine eyes, then lift up my horse's tail and with thy nose tell me whether it be a mare or a horse."

The cobbler, being a fellow that would swear anything, rapped out an oath and swore 'twas a mare. "Alas, Father," said he, "why should I swear? What rogues are these to cozen you! To cheat an old man! O fie! As I am true cobbler and an honest man, this beast is a mare, a mere flea-bitten mare, and nothing but a mare." "Swearest then," quoth the peddler, "and is't a mare? Where are mine eyes? But, alas, I am purblind. I now begin to smell that I am ridden like a jade, for two men besides you told me 'tis a mare." "A mare," cried the other, "as I am true cordwainer, body and bones." "If," says the peddler, "it be a mare, I would not ride her for all the cows in Nottinghamshire, for I never bestrid any one beast in my life but a mare, and riding through a market town the stone-horses[15] leaped me as if I had been a mare; one with his forelegs straddled over my shoulders, another gave me three palts[16] on the head, my skull was cracked and I taken up for dead. When I came to myself, I wished I might break my neck when next I backed any mare. And for fear my wish overtake me before I get home, being not far, here, honest cobbler, take my mare, ride her, run her, spur her, and hang her. I know thee when I see thee again, and pay me when thou seest thy time, what thou thinkest she's worth." "Nay," says the cobbler, "come the next market day to Gotham, there I dwell, my name is Yerker (the only cobbler of Gotham), and you shall not lose much by the beast." "A match!" cried the peddler. Away rides the cobbler to his companions who laughing at the old fool's simplicity, and

The Tinker of Turvey

what an ass they had made him, sell the horse and share the money.

The peddler being come home, his maid clapping her hands with admiration to see him, as she said, come creeping home on foot. "What bought you at the fair?" "I bought," said he, "a horse." "A horse," quoth she, "where is he? Is he put to grass already? You have sent him to run on the devil's commons, have you?" "Peace, Gillian," quoth he, "I would have pawned all the pedlary packs that ever I carried; I had bought a pretty horse, paid for a horse, rode him for a horse, but three several men on the highway, one after another, faced me down it was a mare, and I fearing some mischief might fall upon me for cursing myself, as thou knowest, about the other mare, I parted with it to a cobbler of Gotham." "A coxcomb of Gotham like yourself," said she; "some that knew you had but weak eyes have fooled you, out-faced you, and coney-catched you. Would I have been coney-catched so. O that I knew those three cheats; would I could finger this cobbler, I'd cobble him, I'd make him swallow his last!" "Peace, Gillian," said the peddler, "the next market day I shall know whether they be knaves or no, for now I have fleshed them with a horse they will bite at anything. Be thou quiet, and if I fry not in my brain-pan something or other that shall make them swallow a horse-plum, say I'm no peddler. Provide me therefore within these two days a very good dinner, for I shall have friends come to visit me; let me have a breast of veal, a pig, half a dozen of chickens, and a couple of rabbits." She said it should be done.

Now the peddler had two very fair goats in his ground. One of them he takes on the day appointed for the dinner, which he ties to a hedge, leaving it sufficient to feed upon; the other he leads in a cord with him to the market. The goats were of one bigness, one color, and so like one another, it was not possible to distinguish them. The peddler was no sooner come into the market, but the three sharks that lived upon cheating came to him, asked how he did, and how he liked his mare they met him upon. "O," said he, "I found your words true, that I was cozened, and I rid my hands of her." "But why," said one of them, "do you walk up and down the market thus with a goat tied in a string? Can he do any tricks?" "Tricks?" said he. "I would not lose my goat for twenty such mares. To tell you true, my bullies, I look for guests this day; if you will dine with me you shall be welcome. When I have bought my meat, then you shall see what tricks (if you call them tricks) my goat can do."

So the peddler having bought his provision of veal, pig, chickens, rabbits, oranges, spices, and other things, tied them all very handsomely to the goat's back and said, "Sirrah, hie you home to Gillian; bid her dress dinner with all haste and having taken these things from your back, request her to tie you to a hedge, for else I know you will be rambling." The goat runs away as fast as he could, none stopping him as thinking it had been his quality to carry provision, but being got out of the town he ran into a wood and what became of him the peddler never knew.

In the end, after he and our three cheats had drunk together in the market, dinner time drawing nigh, they all four came to the peddler's house. He no sooner stepped within doors, but winking at Gillian asked her if she had done as the goat instructed her; she being as wily as he conceited his meaning and said yes, good cheer was at fire, dinner was ready, and the goat tied to a hedge in the backside was showed them. At which they blessed themselves and secretly conspired to steal the goat from him.

Dinner being set on the board, they all sit down, eat, and welcome, and wondrous merry; whilst their teeth are going their tongues are not idle, but wonder at the strange condition of the peddler's goat. Asking what country goat it was, he told them of Brecknockshire. "You may," said he, "well enough wonder at the conditions of my goat; they are strange ones indeed, and there is a reason they should be strange, for it has cost me above five years his teaching. You will more wonder if I tell you that I dare send him into Waltham with a packet of letters to my friends, and he shall bring the answers, for he never travels in the day time, but all by night. If he goes abroad with me, as oftentimes he does, and spies any peddler of my acquaintance, he will leap, dance, fawn upon him, and lay his horns gently in his lap when he sits down."

They rise from dinner, and having an exceeding desire to get the goat, resolve to steal him, hoping much money might be gathered by showing him in other countries, but the old sole of the cobbler's conscience, being somewhat mended because he had cozened him of his horse, would by no means steal this from him too, "but let us," quoth he "rather all three buy him." They ask his price. "Price?" says the peddler. "He's worth his weight in gold; a lord offered me over fifty pieces for him, but I refused it. I can tomorrow morning have thirty and less I will not take." They three make up the money between them, lead the goat with them, and away they are gone.

Being come home, they show to their wives what a rare outlandish beast they had bought, which they would carry to London first, and so all over England and get a world of money by him. The women called them puppies and fools to believe any such lies as they bragged of. But for trial of the truth, they charged their wives to dress such good cheer as presently they would send by the goat, and so all to be merry. To the market they go, buy excellent meats and send it by the goat, bidding him to tell their wives they must dress it presently, for they and some friends were to come to dinner. The goat having his errand hastens away, hies through the market, then into the fields, and at last, as the other, into a wood, and was never more heard of.

The three wise husbands coming home asked if dinner were ready. "What dinner?" replied their wives. "Did not the goat bring home victuals?" "The goat!" cries one of the women. "The calf's head," said another. "The ass's head," quoth the third, "an ox-head." Upon this the men looked blank, saw they were gulled for bulling the old peddler; one of their wives laughed to see her husband made such a ninny, the other scolded, the third cried for madness. In a short time all the town was in a hubbub; other men's wives clapped their hands at them, their neighbors hissed at them, boys howled. They hid their heads, cursing the peddler and vowing revenge. But the shame of so being fooled, gulled, fetched over, and cheated, they being cheaters themselves, they left their own town and came to London. The butcher took a tobacco shop in Ram-Alley, the currier an ale-house by London Wall, and the cobbler sets patches on old shoes at this hour in Rogue Lane at Westminster. The peddler at every fair was commended, for over-reaching them that outstripped him, and Gillian's wit extolled beyond the wisdom of all the wenches in Gotham.

* * *

The tinker having thus ended, a cobbler in the barge, grumbling that the tinker made a cobbler one of the three cheaters, would needs tell his tale next. So silence being cried, he began to speak. But I think you were best look upon him, and note what a spruce leather-pergo it is.

THE DESCRIPTION OF THE COBBLER

His stature was large and tall,
His limbs well set withal,
Of a strong bone and a broad chest,
He was wide and wildsome in the breast,
His forehead high and a bald pate,
Well I wot he was a mate
That loved well a bonny lass,
For the clown's eyes were as gray as glass,
And oft have I heard my mother say,
The wanton eye is e'er most gray.
He loved well a cup of strong ale,
And his nose was nothing pale,
But his snout and all his face
Was as red as ruby or topaz.

A voice he had clear and loud,
And well he can sing to a crowd.[17]
He was a stout sturdy squire,
And loved eke day good compire;[18]
Drink he would with every man,
In cup, cruse, glass, or can;
And what ever day he got,
He hoarded up in the ale-pot,
That all Canterbury 'gan leer
To talk of this merry cobbler.
Therefore now mark me well,
For thus his tale began to tell.

THE COBBLER'S TALE

Containing the jests that passed between the Prior of Canterbury and a Smith of Saint Austin's.

The Prior of Canterbury had a convent of Friars Augustines that were endued with great livings from the king, and he himself had great revenues, that he lived like a potentate, and he was had in great estimation throughout all the city. Living thus at ease, pampered up with delicates and idleness, the two nurses to lechery, he minded not so much his book but that passing one day through the streets he glanced his eyes to see where he might find some handsome trull that might be his paramour. Many he saw and many he liked, but at last coming by a smith's forge, he spied a proper tall woman meanly attired, after the poverty of her husband, but of such a beautiful visage and fair countenance that she pleased greatly the Prior's eye, that he thought her the fairest in all Canterbury. He returned home that way he went out, because he would have another look at the smith's wife, and as he passed by he gave her a curtsy for his farewell.

Well, home he went to his chamber, and there bethought him of his new love and cast in his mind a thousand ways how he might come to his purpose. At last he sent for the smith to come look upon his horse, who very hastily hied him to the priory, where the Prior welcomed him and entertained him with great courtesy, kissing the nurse, as the old proverb is, for the child's sake, and making much of black Vulcan for fair Venus's sake. The poor smith very carefully looked to the horse and where aught was amiss amended it. The Prior and all his convent gave him great commendations and thanks, and bade him to breakfast, where he had good cheer and store of strong drink, which made the smith passing pleasant. As they sat at breakfast, the Prior told him, sith they had made experience of his skill and that he was cunning about horses, he was content to make him farrier of the Priory. At this the smith was very glad. "Nay, more," quoth the Prior, "because thou shalt have more gains out of the dorter,[19] seeing thy wife is a good cleanly woman, she shall be laundress for me and the whole convent."

The smith hearing this perceived by the weathercock which way the wind blew, shaked the head and began to smile; the Prior demanded of him why he laughed. "Marry, sir," quoth he, "seeing we are at meat, and mirth is good for digestion, I will tell you a merry jest. There was such a poor man as myself, that dwelt (as I do) hard by a Priory, and he had brought up in his house a little lamb which, growing to a sheep, would wander all abroad and returned home safe at night without any hurt. At last this little sheep, being the poor man's treasure, seeing the Priory gate open and the yard full of grass, went in and fed there. The wanton friars that were idle would often sport with the lamb and play withal and pulled off the wool off the back, that it had almost left nothing but the bare pelt, which the poor man espying, kept up his sheep and would not suffer it to go any more abroad. Yet it had gotten such a sweet savor in the Priory yard that as soon as it broke loose it would thither, where the Prior and friars spying it again, consented, and ate it up all. The good man came to ask for his sheep, and they laughing at him, gave him no other amends but the horns. So, my masters, if my wife should be your laundress, I warrant you if I came to inquire for her I might have such fees as the poor man had for his loss. No, no, I am well, I thank you; if myself may serve for a farrier, so it is, but my wife (of all men) shall not have to deal either with Prior or friars."

At this they all laughed, but the Prior not willing to give over the chase thus, made this answer. "Why, smith," quoth he, "thou art a fool. Thou mayest have a proviso for that, for though she wash our clothes, yet she shall neither fetch them nor bring them home, neither shall there ever a friar come at thy house, only the scull of the kitchen, and I hope thou fearest not him." "No," quoth the smith, "they be these breechless yeomen that I stand so much in doubt of, but upon these conditions aforesaid, that she shall neither fetch them nor carry them home, she shall be your laundress." Upon this they agreed, and the smith went to his house and told his wife all. She that was a wily wench thought with herself that whatsoever her husband fished for he should catch a frog, and that dealt he never so warily yet she would make him one of the head men of the parish, as well as his neighbors.

She conjecturing thus with herself, the next morning came the scull early (by that the smith was up and at his work) with foul clothes. "God speed, sir," quoth he. "I have brought your wife the Prior's linen." "Ah, welcome, good fellow," quoth he; "go thy ways up to the chamber to my wife; she is above and I think a-bed." The scull trotted up the stairs and saluted the woman. "Mistress," quoth he, "the Prior hath sent you his clothes and prays you that they may be done on Wednesday next." "They shall be done," quoth she, "with all speed." "And," quoth the scull, "his worship willed me in secret to give you a ring for a token, and to desire you to think that he loves you as heartily as any woman in the world." The poor woman, seeing a gold ring and having never had any before in her life, held herself a proud woman, and bethought her what good gifts she should daily have if she had such a lover as the Prior. Wherefore she returned him this answer by the scull, that she had ever thought well of him, but her husband was a jealous fool and watched her narrowly wheresoever she went, but as far as she might she was at his command.

Home went the scull, and the Prior was risen by that he returned and asked him what news. "What news?" quoth the scull. "Marry, thus, sir: as soon as I came to the door, I found the smith hard at his work, and I saluted him by the time of the day and asked him where his wife was, saying I had brought the Prior's linen. 'Go up the stairs, good fellow,' quoth he, 'for I think my wife is in bed,' and, sir, there indeed I found her, and surely, sir, if you will believe me, methought she lay too lovely in her bed to lie with a smith. So, sir, I gave her your token and told her what you bade me, and she made answer that your worship was the man who she had ever thought well of, but her husband was a jealous fool, yet as far as she could she was at your command."

This satisfied the Prior's expectation, and on Wednesday morning when the scull should go for his clean linen, the Prior compounded with him and gave him a brace of angels to keep his counsel, saying, "Tom" (for so was the scull's name), "thou knowest all flesh is frail, and we are men as well as others, though our profession be more holy. Therefore, Tom, so it is that I have loved the smith's wife a long time, and now may I have opportunity to fill my desires. I will this morning take thy clothes and besmear my face, and with the basket hie for the clean clothes. Only I care for nothing, if thou keep my counsel." "Fear not that, sir," quoth the scull, "but I will be so secret as you can desire." With that the Prior was brief, because he longed to be there, and on with the scull's rags and taking the basket on his neck hasted him very orderly to the smith's house.

By that time day did appear, where he found him hard at work. "Good morrow, sir," quoth the Prior, "I am come for the linen." "Go up the stairs, fellow," quoth the smith; "thou comest very early; my wife is yet in bed." Up trudged the Prior and there he found his paramour in a sweet sleep. The Prior stepped to her and kissed her and with that she awaked, and seeing the scull, "Why, how now, Sir Sauce," quoth she, "can you not speak before you come up? My husband is a wise man to send such companions up into the chamber where I am in bed; 'twere no matter and the match were equal to make him wear the horn for it." "Oh, be content, good love," quoth the Prior, "for know thou that I am not Tom Scull, but the Prior himself that sent thee the ring, who for thy sake is come thus disguised." With that he discovered himself, and she perceived it was he, and blushed. He kissed her and so conjured her that whilst the poor smith was knocking at the smithy he had dubbed him knight of the forked order, and for fear of suspicion putting his linen in the basket away he went, bidding the smith farewell.

Thus the Prior and the smith's wife consented and enjoying their heart's desire; the poor smith loved her not a whit the worse, neither did he suspect anything, for the blind eats many a fly and much water runs by the mill that the miller wots not of. So played it with this smith, for twice a week came the Prior in his scull's apparel to his leman. Thus it continued, till on one morning the Prior was not well, so that he could not go, but Tom Scull after his wonted manner went to carry forth the linen. And as he went by the way, he began to think with himself what a fair woman the smith's wife was and how fain he would be partaker with his master. Hammering this in his head, on he went to the smith's house. "Now, smith," quoth he, "good morrow. Is thy wife up?" "No," quoth the smith, "but she is awake. Go up and carry your linen a God's name." Up came the scull and rushing in at the chamber door, threw down his basket, and seeing the chamber dark that he could not be discovered, slipped to bed and entered commons with the Prior, and with that got him away without saying one word. The smith's wife marvelled at this, and supposed he had heard some rustling and for fear of her husband had gone away so hastily.

Well, within two days after came the Prior again, and after his accustomed manner went up with his basket and saluted her after the old fashion. "I pray you tell me, Master Prior," quoth she, "what meant you the other morning that you came so quiet and slipped away with such silence after you got out of bed?" By this the Prior perceived that the scull had cut a slice on his loaf, and so thought to dissemble the matter. "Faith, sweetheart," quoth he, "I heard a noise, and thought it had been thy husband that had come up." "So I conjectured," quoth the smith's wife, "and therefore after you were come, seeing you were frighted with your own shadow, I laughed heartily." Thus as long as they durst they chatted, but at last the Prior up with his basket and away.

When he came home, in a great chafe he sent for the scull and made inquiry of the matter. The poor fellow, afraid of sore threatenings, confessed the matter and craved pardon, but the Prior forgetting his patience fell upon poor Tom the Scull and beat him so sore that he had almost killed him, and afterwards swearing him on a book, if ever after he went with any clothes he should go no further than the chamber door. The scull agreed to this and confirmed it with a solemn oath, but the remembrance of his sore blows bred in him a mind to revenge.

Whereupon resolving to do any mischief to the Prior that he might, one day he went very orderly to the smith and carried him to the ale-house and there after a long protestation of silence revealed the whole matter unto him, how the Prior every day came in his apparel to his wife, and so made him wear the horns, while he was busy about his hammers. At this the smith fetched a great sigh, "Alas," quoth he, "and am I a cuckold?" "Why not you," quoth the scull, "as well as your betters?" "Indeed," quoth the smith, "and that is all the comfort that I have, that my betters have had as hard hap; for the Abbot of St. Peter's that is a holy man had but one leman and yet she was not content with twenty morsels. And I am a poor smith and a layman, no marvel then if my fortune be as forked as the

The Tinker of Turvey

rest. But by the Holy Rood of Rochester," quoth he, "I will be so revenged on the Prior that after I have taken him he shall hate lechery the worse while he lives." "Ay," quoth the scull, "take heed thou plaguest not me instead of the Prior. To avoid therefore all ensuing danger, if I come tomorrow, thou shalt know me by this token: I will ask thee whether thou hast drunk this morning or no. If thou hearest no such watchword, then know it is the Prior." "So be it," quoth the smith, and upon this they drank their drink and departed.

The next morning the smith was early at his work, and the Prior that longed to be with his leman was as soon awake, and up he got and on with the scull's apparel, and to the smith's house, and after his accustomed manner bade him good morrow and up the stairs. The smith perceiving it was the Prior, because he wanted his watchword, hied up presently after him and took the Prior in bed with his wife. "Why, how now, scull?" quoth he. "Will no worse meat go down with you than my wife? Before you and I part I will learn you how to make Vulcan of me, without you were more like Mars than you be." Whereupon his man and he, two lusty knaves, stepped to him and pulled him out of bed, and thrust him into a great sack, wherein he was wont to put chaff. When he had done, carried him into the street, and laid him down before his door, and then made his wife take a flail in her hand and thresh as hard as she could. But because he perceived her strokes were laid on with favor, himself stood behind her with a great carter's whip and every time she fainted in her blows, he lent her a lash that he fetched the blood through her petticoat. The people that came up marvelled at this antic and asked the smith what he was adoing. "Killing of fleas," quoth the smith, "that I found this morning in my bed, and because my wife is too idle and will not strike home, I stand with my whip to whet her on. Neighbors, therefore give good ear and mark the end, and see when my wife hath beaten them enough and see what foul fleas they be, and by my example learn whensoever you take such great fleas in your wives' bed, to put them to the like punishment."

The people flocked together to see this sport, and although the Prior was almost bruised to death (though for favoring him the smith's wife bore many a lash), yet he durst not cry for fear of further discredit, but lay still and suffered all with patience. At last a multitude of people flocking together, it chanced that upon serious business the Abbot of St. Peter's came by, who seeing such a throng sent one of his men to know what the matter meant. "Oh, may it please your Lordship," quoth the smith, "such a sight as you never saw, wherefore for Christ's sake I ask it that you would take so much pains as to come over the way and see." The Abbot stepped over the channel, and when he came and saw the smith's wife with her flail, and him with his whip, he wondered, and the smith told him as the rest that it was a flea he took in his wife's bed. All this while lay the Prior with a heavy heart, for fear the smith would shake him out of the sack, wishing to abide thrice so much torment so he might escape unknown.

As the Abbot about this matter stood questioning with the smith, the scull, that missed the Prior that passed his hour, thought the smith had played some mad prank with him, went and put on the Prior's apparel and his cowl over his head that he might not be known and went down to the smith's houseward, where seeing a concourse of people he hasted him thither. At last the smith spied him and cried, "Oh, my Lord Abbot, yonder comes the Prior of Saint Austin's; it was one of his fleas." Well knew the smith it was Tom Scull, but his wife supposing it to be the Prior and that he in the sack was the scull that had deceived her, in despite for revenge laid on such blows that she needed no whipping to amend her strokes.

When the Prior came, and after most humble manner had saluted the Abbot, he desired to know the cause of that sight. "Marry," quoth the smith, "Master Prior, I may thank you for this, for a flea of your Priory hath leapt from the dorter to my wife's bed, and finding it there this morning, I put it into a sack and caused my wife to thresh it, and for that both you and Master Abbot and all my neighbors shall see what parlous fleas oft happen into women's beds, I will shake him out before you all." And with that unbound the sack and he threw out the Prior, who being in the scull's apparel was so besmeared and so bloody that he could not be known. "Look here, Master Prior," quoth the smith, "here is the scull of your Priory." "Oh, notable knave," quoth Tom Scull, "to discredit our house. What think you of this, my Lord Abbot? Is this a sufficient punishment or no? considering by this fault he shall give occasion of slander to the whole Priory." "He is," quoth the Abbot, "within the jurisdiction of your censure, and therefore deal with him as you list." "Marry," quoth the scull, "then thus: because it is an open fault, it shall have a more open punishment, for if it be smothered up thus, they will say that I am a favorer of sin." With that he called to certain of his convent, for most of the monks of the Priory were come thither, "how say you, brethren," quoth he, "is it not best that he stand all this forenoon on the pillory and have a paper written on his head containing the whole matter of his offence? And the smith's wife shall stand under him with her flail and the smith with his whip." "And so," quoth the smith, "shall all Canterbury laugh at me that come into the market-place, to prove myself a cuckold. No, Goodman Scull," quoth he, "it shall not be so," and with that he pulled off his cowl and said, "Masters and neighbors, see, here is the scull of the house, and this, beaten in the sack, is the Prior himself, that came to my wife in the scull's apparel."

At this all the people clapped their hands, laughed, and made good game to see how simply the Prior stood, and in what a majesty the scull sat in the Prior's habiliments. At this sight the Abbot abashed, and the friars were ashamed, but the scull nothing amazed began afore all the people to say thus. "My masters," quoth he, "I was once a scholar, though I am now a scull, and then I learned this old saying in Latin, *Caute si non caste,* live charily if not chastely.

Be not so forward in your follies that you discover your faults to the whole world, and especially was this spoken to men of the Church, for, in that they know much and do dehort others from vice, the people look their lives and their learning should agree. But when they offend so grossly as Master Prior through his ill example, to bring a whole house in slander, then are they worthy of double punishment. For we know friars are men, and I warrant you there is a great many in England have done as much to others as he hath to the smith's wife, and yet have escaped without discredit. I hope, my Lord Abbot, if you enter into your own conscience, you can verify as much, and therefore seeing he was so careless of his credit, let him forever after, to avoid perpetual infamy of the house, be banished out of the Priory." To this they all agreed, and the people that heard this collation said Tom Scull was worthy to be Prior, whereupon the Abbot and the friars consenting, and seeing he had good learning, turned away the old Prior and made Tom Scull Prior in his room. Thus was the Prior punished for his lechery, the smith revenged for his cuckoldry, and the scull for his blows stumbled on a good promotion.

At this merry tale of the cobbler, all they in the barge laughed, and said the smith was well revenged. "Yea, but," quoth the cobbler, "so he was made a cuckold, and with a heavy head was the poor smith fain to go to his hammers, being ever after noted for a cuckold through all Canterbury." There sat a smith hard by, who grieved at this, that he should descant thus upon his occupation, and the rather perchance he took pepper in the nose because he was of the same fraternity, if not with a prior, yet with some other good fellow, and therefore in a snuff he began thus to reply. "Why, cobbler," quoth he, "dost thou hold the smith in such derision because he was a cuckold? I tell thee, cobbler, kings have worn the horns, and 'tis a fault that Fortune exempteth from none; yea, the old writers have

The Tinker of Turvey

had it in such question that they have set down divers degrees of cuckolds. There be eight degrees, and that I can prove." At this there was a great laughter, and every man desired him to tell what they were. "That I will," quoth the smith; "they be these:

> THE EIGHT ORDERS OF CUCKOLDS
> 1. An overgrown cuckold
> 2. A cuckold and no cuckold
> 3. A horn-mad cuckold
> 4. A winking cuckold
> 5. An extempore cuckold
> 6. A John-hold-my-staff cuckold
> 7. A cuckold in grain
> 8. An ante-dated cuckold.

These are the colors grinded to draw the cuckolds' faces by. Now behold the faces themselves.

"1. An overgrown cuckold is a gray cuckold, an old ram-headed cuckold, whose horns in their turning are so heavy and crooked, the very tips of them almost run into his eyes. His cornuto-cap has kept his head warm some thirty or forty years (for so long his wife has been an upholsterer and dealt in feather-beds). It was a pretty tit then, the beast has a racking pace still. If all the cuckolds in a parish were to be impaneled upon a jury, this is their foreman. In a voyage to cuckolds-haven, he steers the ship, and lands first, the precedence being given him for the antiquity of his forked crest, as having been a cuckold ever since he entered into the married-men's order.

"2. A Cuckold and no cuckold is he whose wife is handsome, fair, and well-favored, yet very honest, yet this bull-calf fears he has bumps, yet none can see them. He still feels for knobs on his forehead, but finds none. One that thinks better of horns than they do of him. A conceited cuckold.

"3. A horn-mad cuckold is a wild bull, bellowing and

roaring still after his cow as if she had a bree[20] in her tail and ran up and down as mad as he. This cuckold is a mere Tom of Bedlam; if in the shambles a boy cry but 'ptrooh,' he starts, stares, and looks about him, as if his wife were behind him. He sleeps not in quiet, wakes not in quiet, eats nor drinks in quiet. If his wife puts but two fingers daintily into a dish of mince-meat, he swears she makes horns at him. He cannot endure to hear of St. Luke's day, nor of St. Thomas his night, when the Templars and Inns-of-Court men blow their horns under men's windows. A sow-gelder makes him look pale; if he passes by a horner's door, he swoons and must drink aqua-vitae. This is the fool of cuckolds, and most worthy to be laughed at.

"4. A winking cuckold is he that sees a cock-sparrow tread his hen, yet goes away and says nothing. An honest, patient ass that carries his horns as willingly as a tanner's horse carries his master's hides from Leadenhall Market. A mere hum-drum-John-a-droins, who, if he peeps in at keyhole and sees his wife curvetting, goes sneaking away like a dog with his tail between his legs, with this only in his mouth, 'Ah, ha, are you there with your bears?'

"5. An extempore cuckold is no riming cuckold but such a blockhead that his wife on her very wedding day puts him to spell his name in the hornbook. This is a mellow cuckold.

"6. A John-hold-my-staff cuckold has his horns so high they run through his hat. A rascal deer, the basest in the whole herd of cuckolds. A stag in a city, a rhinoceros for his horns in his parish, a pander in his house, a slave everywhere.

"7. A cuckold cried up is a peevish, snappish, quarrelsome ninny-hammer, who so wearies his wife with causeless jealousy, that in the end she gives him cause. He upon the least suspicion runs snuffing up and down, and having found his game (taken the poor whore his wife in the manner), what does he but cry his horns up, arrests his half-sharer (his fellow-commoner), swears he will make him stand in a white sheet (when he had done that already), and for his wife he will firk her soundly. In the end, when all the courts in the civil law have his name, his head, and his horns upon record, then he's quiet, takes his wife again, and every night locks his chamber door with his own shoeing horn.

"8. An ante-dated cuckold is a fruit no sooner ripe but rotten; this is a harmless young codhead, who fools himself into horns: the nightmare rides him the first hour he's married, for the poor credulous Nicodemus, thinking he has a sweet white grape is fallen upon a sour one. No wine is given him at his wedding dinner but bastard, and of that his bride has begun to him in a bowl or two. And at night he may pledge her; if he has no maw, no matter, he's sure of a good cook that can bring up his meat piping-hot to his table. He needs fear no poisoning, for he has two or three tasters.

"Thus," quoth the smith, "you have heard my degrees and their exposition, and because I will be quit with the cobbler for the tale of the smith, give me leave a little and you shall hear a merry jest." But because I will let you know what manner of man he was, before his tale hear his description.

THE DESCRIPTION OF THE SMITH

This smith was a quaint sire,
As merry as bird on briar,
Jocund and gleesome at every sithe[21]
His countenance aye buxom and blithe,
His face full coaly and full black,
Hu'd like unto a collier's sack,
Or as if it had been soil in the mire;
Full of wrinkles was his cheeks with the fire.
Well he could sweat and swink,
And one that aye loved good drink,
For hard by his forge always stood
A stond of ale, nappy and good,
Which made the color of his nose

Like to fire when it glows.
His head great, his brows broad,
Able to bear a great load,
As no man might hold it scorn
On his head to graft a horn.
His coats were fit for the weather,
His pilch made of swine's leather;
So was his breech, and before
A dusty apron he wore,
Wherein not to fail,
Was many a horseshoe nail,
And for to fit him every tide,
Hung a hammer by his side:
Thus attired the smith 'gan say
What befell on a summer's day.

THE SMITH'S TALE

Containing a pleasant jest of a jealous cobbler, and how for all his suspicion he was cunningly made cuckold.

In Romney Marsh by the sea-coast there dwelt a cobbler, a merry fellow, and of his middle age, who was wont on working days to chant it out at his work, and on holidays to bestir his stumps to the churchyard so merrily after a crowd, that he was well beloved of all the country wenches, and noted for the flower of good-fellowship throughout all the parish. This cobbler keeping shop for himself had in house with him an old mother of his, who being as it were his servant, desirous to live more at ease, wished him to take a wife. The cobbler was loath to be persuaded to marriage, and the reason was, for that he feared to be a cuckold. Yet at last he cast his eye on a country lass that was a blithe and bonny wench and the chief of all the maids in old Romney; to her was this jolly cobbler a suitor, and after a little wooing (as women must be got with praises and promises) the cobbler caught her and married they must be in all haste. Which done, they lived pleasantly together, as fools do presently after their wedding.

The Tinker of Turvey

But after the honeymoon was past, she like a good huswife fell to her work, to spin and card and other such deeds of huswifery, as belonged to the profit of her house. The cobbler loved her well and she wanted nothing that might satisfy her humor, only she was charged by her husband not to go abroad a-gossiping with her neighbors, insomuch that either on working days or on holidays, when all the wives in Romney went to be merry, she was fain (as a poor prisoner) to keep home, which although she passed over with silence and patience, so yet seeing his jealousy was without cause, she vowed with herself if ever a friend and opportunity served to her mind to make him wear the horn an inch longer than any of his neighbors. But he kept her short for that, for every day when she was at home, she sat by him in the shop, where he sung like a nightingale, having his eye never off his wife's face, or if she sat within, her mother-in-law, an old jealous woman, bore her company; if she went to fetch water, her mother was at her elbow, whatsoever she did or whithersoever she went, to be brief, her husband or his mother was at one end, which grieved the young woman.

So suspicious and jealous was the cobbler that all Romney talked of his folly, and to vex him as they passed by would say to him, "Ah, neighbor, good morrow. Now that you have gotten a fair wife, we hope to have you one of the brotherhood, and that the cuckoo in April may sit and sing on your house as well as with your poor neighbors." "I fear not that," quoth the cobbler, "let her do her worse, I will give her leave," meaning that he kept such narrow watch over her that he could not be deceived and therefore every day, his wife sitting by him when he was yerking of his shoes, and she at her wheel, then he would chant out this song:

THE COBBLER'S SONG

Whenas the nobility pull down their towers,
Their mansion houses and stately bowers,

And with stone and timber make hospitals free,
Then the cobbler of Romney a cuckold shall be.

When gentlemen leave off their peacockish suits,
And that all their works are charity's fruits,
Tendering the poor which needy they see,
Then the cobbler of Romney a cuckold shall be.

When usurers run up and down with their gold,
And give it to them from whom it was pulled
And colliers' sacks over great you do see,
Then the cobbler, &c.

When Westminster-Hall is quite without benches,
And Southwark Bankside hath no pretty wenches,
When in Smithfield on Fridays no jades you do see,
Then the cobbler, &c.

When maids hate marriage and love to live chaste,
Virgins forsooth till fourscore be past,
And love not that young men their beauty should see,
Then the cobbler, &c.

When wives are not wilfull but needs will obey,
When silent and speechless they sit a whole day,
When gossips do meet and no words will be,
Then the cobbler, &c.

When women's tongues do cease for to wag,
And shoemakers give not their master the bag,
When cuckolds and keepers want horns for their fee,
Then the cobbler, &c.

When tapsters and ale-wives from Berwick to Dover,
Fill third in deal pots till the drink do run over,
When the quart is so full that no froth you can see,
Then the cobbler, &c.

When smiths forswear to drink off strong ale,
And live without liquor while their nose looks pale,
When in vintner's wine no mixture you see,
Then the cobbler, &c.

The Tinker of Turvey

When Dutchmen hate butter, and the Spaniards pride,
When cardinals do want a trull by their side,
When the Pope like Peter humbled you see,
Then the cobbler of Romney a cuckold shall be.

Every day did the cobbler use to sing this song, and there dwelt next unto him a smith that was a tall and a young lusty fellow, proper of personage, of a comely visage, courteous, gentle, and debonair, such a one as this cobbler's wife could have wished to her paramour if time and opportunity would have favored her fancy. And the smith seeing what a smicker[22] wench the cobbler's wife was, and what a jealous fool she had to her husband, sorrowed at the good fortune of the cobbler, that he had so fair a wife, and wished that he could find means to have such a one his friend. Upon this, being near neighbors, and their houses joining together, the smith would oftentimes, when his leisure served him, come to the cobbler's shop and talk with him, where between the smith and the cobbler's wife passed such glances, that he perceiving there was no want but place and opportunity to fulfill their desires.

One day amongst the rest, Fortune so favored this young couple that the cobbler went forth to buy leather and left his wife and his mother in the shop. The old woman not having slept the last night was heavy and fell asleep, and the young woman sat singing at her work. The smith perceiving this laid by his hammers and went to the stall, where he saluted his neighbor and she returned him the like courtesy. At last, seeing the old beldame was sure, he began to reveal unto her how long he had loved her and how he was sorry that she was cumbered with such a one as for his jealousy above all other men deserved to be made a cuckold. Sundry speeches passed between the smith and the cobbler's wife, till at last she rose and gave him her hand that she loved him better than any man in the world, and would, if any occasion would serve, to content him. "Then, sweetheart," quoth he, "do me but this favor. Feign tomorrow some occasion to go to your mother's, and come on the further side of the way, fast by such a door, and then let me alone for opportunity to satisfy both our desires." To this she agreed, and the smith went to his shop. Presently the old woman awaked, the cobbler came home, and all was well.

At night when they were in bed, taking him about the neck, she kissed him and told him that certain of her friends met tomorrow at her mother's, and that she would fain go and see them. "I pray you, good husband," quoth she, "let your mother and I go together. I will not part out of her sight, neither will we make any long tarriance." The husband for shame could not deny this request, but granted it; whereupon the next morning she got her up and on with her holiday apparel and made her as fine as might be. The cobbler seeing his wife so tricked up in her clean linen began to be jealous, and called his mother aside and charged her by that love she bore him not to let his wife part out of her company till she came home again, which she promised with an oath. So away they went, and the cobbler he sat him down and began to sing.

The smith that all this day was not idle had compounded with an old woman by whose house she must pass to favor them with house room, and revealed unto her all the matter: whose wife it was, and how he would have his purpose brought to pass. "By my troth, son," quoth she, "I have heard much talk of that jealous cobbler, and I would do my endeavor to make the ass wear a horn." Upon this they resolved, and she liked well of his policy, and said love had many shifts. At last the smith spied his mistress all in her bravery coming with her mother-in-law, the old wife was ready, and as she passed by the door, threw a great bowl full of bloody water right upon her head, that all her clothes and clean linen was marred, being so bewrayed that she could go no further. "Alas, mistress," quoth the old woman, "I cry you mercy. What have I done? Full sore it was against my will, but for God's sake come into the house and shift you with clean linen. If you have none at home I will lend you of the best that I have." "Go in, daughter," quoth her old mother-in-law, "it is a chance, and against a shrewd turn sometime, no man may be. I'll go home as fast as I can and go fetch you clean linen, the whiles dry you your gown and make all things else ready." "I pray do, good mother," quoth she, and then away goes her mother-in-law and as soon as she was out of doors, the old woman led her into an inward parlor where the smith was, and there these two lovers by this policy made the jealous cobbler wear the horn.

While thus they were solacing themselves, the old wife she came stumbling home, and for haste had like to break her neck over the threshold. Her fall made the cobbler start, and when he saw it was his mother, and that he missed his wife, he was half mad, asked his mother hastily where she was. The old woman, short-winded, was almost out of breath, and for a good space sat puffing and blowing to fetch wind. At last she cried out, "Alas, dear son, such a chance as never was heard of. As we went through old Romney, hard by the church, a woman threw out a bowl of bloody water right upon your wife's head, which hath so bewrayed her linen and her gown that she could go no further, and so I as fast as I could came running home for clean clothes." "Oh, for the Passion of God, mother," quoth he, "hie to her chest, and get her clothes ready, for it may be a fetch to make the poor cobbler a cuckold. A horn, mother, is soon grafted." With that the old woman got all in readiness, and away ran the cobbler and his mother together.

Well, the two lovers out at a little hole kept good watch and ward, that anon they spied where the cobbler and his mother came trudging. In went the wife and sat her down by the fire, where the cobbler found her only sitting with the old woman in her petticoat, drying her gown. As soon as she saw him she wept, and he although he grieved at the mischance, yet for that he spied her in no company, he was satisfied, and wished her to be content, and sent for a pot of beer or two to make her drink. And after he had seen all well and his wife in her clean apparel, setting them a little on the way, home he went again to his shop, and his wife went to her mother's, where an hour or two she passed away the time in chat, and then returned home with her mother-in-law. Thus the cobbler was not suspicious of his wife's being abroad, but took her misfortune for a chance, and the smith every day according to his wonted custom would come and chat with his neighbor the cobbler, and sometime found opportunity to talk with the wife, but never out of the shop.

On a day the cobbler being from home, and the old woman within piecing her hose, the smith came to the shop, and finding her alone began to lay a plot, how to make her husband a cuckold while he held the door. She promised if he would devise it, she would put it in practice, and so agreed, they concluded between themselves and they brought it cunningly to pass thus. It chanced within a fortnight after that as the cobbler and his wife lay in bed, she fell on a great laughter. Her husband demanding the cause, she made him this answer: "I will tell you, husband, a strange thing. So it is, that this other day, when you went to buy leather, my mother and I sat in the shop and she fell fast asleep. Your neighbor the smith, he (as his custom is) came to the window and seeing my mother asleep began to court me with fair words and large promises, and told me that if I would find the means that when you were out I would let him lie with me, he would give me forty shillings. I shaked him off as well as I could, but he would have no nay at all, but threw four angels into my lap, whereupon I took the gold, for methought they were four fair pieces, and promised him that tomorrow you went forth and my mother too, and then he should find me alone in the chamber. Upon this he went away, and left me the gold, and therefore if it please you, tomorrow I think good you should feign yourself to go abroad and my mother too, and then hide you in a chamber hard by, and as soon as he is come in, you may stand at the door and hear all our talk; and when you hear me consent, then break in and take the smith and swinge him well, and, I warrant you, husband, there will divers commodities rise of it, for not only we shall have this gold, and get more for amends, but ever after be rid of such a knave." This motion pleased the cobbler well, and the rather because the smith professed to be his great friend and yet would serve to do him this disgrace. Upon this conclusion they resolved and so fell asleep.

The next day in the afternoon, the cobbler feigned himself to go out and his mother with him, and after coming home at a back door went up into the next chamber and hid themselves. By and by, according to promise, came the smith and went roundly up to the chamber, where he found the cobbler's wife. Wherefore strait shutting the door with a bolt on the inside, he fell to set up plumes on the cobbler's head-piece. The cobbler, he very easily got to the door with a great pole-ax in his hand and began to listen. With that he heard the smith offer fair to his wife. "Nay," quoth she, "I have kept promise with you, for I only promised to let you up into my chamber." "Tush," quoth he, "this is but a cavil," and many words passed between them, the cobbler and his mother standing at the door, with her nay, and his yea, till the cobbler had a new brow-antler grown out of his old horns, and then she answered him, seeing nothing would content him, he should have his pleasure. With that the cobbler was ready to rush in, but that his mother stayed him and bid him hear further. "And dost thou mean good faith?" quoth the smith. "Yea, wherefore else," quoth the cobbler's wife, "came we into this place?" "Why, then," quoth the smith, "hear what I will say to thee: dost thou think though we be here in secret that our faults will not be seen openly, that though thy husband knows not of it, and that it is kept close from the world, that there is not One above that sees all and will revenge it? Yes, vile strumpet as thou art, and for this cause came I to try thee. Thou hast an honest man to thy husband, who loves thee more dearly than himself and works hard to sustain thee that thou shalt not want, and wilt thou in his absence wrong him? Think if ever thou dost, it will come out, and thou shalt be punished with open shame. I am thy husband's dearest friend, with whom I am daily conversant, and dost thou think I could find in my heart to offer him such injury? No, and then art not thou more to blame, that being the wife of his bosom, wilt betray thy husband, who is dearer to thee than all friends? Fie upon thee, vile woman, fare thee well and amend; I will not tell thy husband, unless I spy thee prove light, but I shall never think well of thee while I live."

And with that he opened the chamber door, and the cobbler chopped in and taking the smith by the hand, said, "Neighbor, I thank you for your good counsel. I have heard all the communication that passed between you and my wife, and truly," with that the cobbler wept. "I am heartily glad I have such a trusty friend, to whom in my absence at any time, because my mother is an old woman, I may commit the oversight of my wife. And truly, neighbor," quoth he, "I pray you think never the worse of her, for she told me the whole matter, and appointed me to stand at the door, that when you should have offered her any discourtesy I might have rushed in and have taken you. So that I perceive you are as honest as she, and she as honest as you, and that your meanings were both alike." "I am glad of that," quoth the smith, "that you have so virtuous a wife. I hope I have done the part of a friend to pleasure my neighbor." "You have done so," quoth the cobbler, "and therefore ere we part, we'll drink a quart of wine." So the cobbler bestowed good cheer on the smith and ever after accounted him for his friend, and whensoever he went out of town committed the charge of his wife to the smith, who at all times had free egress and regress to the cobbler's house, without suspicion.

※ ※ ※

This tale of the smith made all the company to laugh and the cobbler he was stark mad for anger, saying that if it had been his case he would have given him wine with a cudgel. "Tush, cobbler," quoth the smith, "never think but our art can surpass yours in such wenching matters, and that the smith can sooner make a cobbler a cuckold, then a cobbler a smith." Upon this they fell to jars, and from words had fallen to blows, if they of the barge had not parted them. So at last they were quiet, and made friends. And then the cobbler he began to entreat that they would go forward in their merry exercise, whereupon a gentleman sitting by, said, "Masters, it is so good to pass away the time, that to continue so honest a sport, I will be the next." And thus therefore I will describe him.

THE DESCRIPTION OF THE GENTLEMAN

His stature was of a middle length,
Well jointed and of a good strength,
Such writes report to us
Was that Trojan Troilus;
For he was of a comely visage,
And his manners of a courteous usage.
His hair in curled locks hung down,
And well I wot the color was nut-brown,
And yet it was full bright and sheen,
Such wore Paris, I ween,
When he sailed to Grecia
To fetch the fair Helena,
His front was of a silver hue,
Powdered thick with veins blue,
His eyes were luminous,
Crystalline and beauteous,
Gray and sparkling like the stars
When the day her light up spars.
His cheeks like the lilies white,
Or as Luna being bright,
And yet comely thereupon,
Was shadowed color vermilion,
That gazers all would suppose,
How the lily and the rose
Did make war each with other;

His surcoat was of satin blue
Like unto a lover true,
His hose were guarded along
With many broad and velvet thong;
His cloak grew large and wide,
And a fair whinyard by his side,
The pommel gilt, and on his head
He had a bonnet colored red.
An alderliefer[23] swain, I ween,
In the barge there was not seen;
And then thus he began to tell
What in Cambridge a scholar befell.

THE GENTLEMAN'S TALE

Containing the contrary fortunes that a scholar of Cambridge had in his loves.

In the University of Cambridge, in Peter's Hostel, there lived a scholar famous for his learning called Rowland, who being placed there by his friends so profited that he grew to be one of the Fellows of the House, being in greatest estimation for the honesty of his life and excellency of his learning. He was a man as well proportioned as he was qualified, and had as well *boni corporis* as he had *bona animi,* and could as well play the wag and the wanton abroad as he could apply his books and study at home. Amorous he was, and one that delighted to feed his eye with every fair face, which after turned to his great prejudice thus.

It fortuned on a day in the summer season that for recreation he walked as far as Cherry Hinton, to eat a mess of cream, where being very pleasant, as he sat jesting with his hostess, there came in a gentleman's daughter in the town, a maid of exceeding beauty, so well proportioned in the lineaments of her face that nature seemed to try in her an experiment of her cunning. This girl, as wise as she was fair, and as wanton as she was witty, came in and questioned with the hostess about some business. Rowland seeing such a nymph come sweeping in thought either Venus or Diana had come in their country weeds to bewitch men's fancies. He cast his eye upon the excellency of her physiognomy with such a piercing look that love entering by the eyes so wrung him at the heart that forsooth fancy her of force he must.

Now my young scholar could do nothing but gaze upon her, for court her he could not, unless he should have begun to woo her with some words of art, or some axioms of philosophy. The young gentlewoman seeing the scholar look so earnestly upon her began to blush and so taking her leave of the hostess went her way. The scholar seeing her gone out of doors thought of the old proverb: Faint heart never won fair lady; and therefore called to her thus. "Fair gentlewoman," quoth he, "you may see we scholars have little manners, that holding the pot in our hands will not make such a saint as you drink. How say you, gentlewoman; will it please you pledge me?" The wily wench hearing such a scholar-like gratulation, seeing by this salute that scholars had read of love more than they could say of love, and though they could tell what was Latin for a fair woman, yet could neither woo her nor win her, turned back again, and with a low curtsey thanked him. He off with his corner cap (for he was a bachelor in arts) and with a glancing look drank to her. She like a wanton pledged him with a smile. Rowland at this taking heart at grass stepped to her and took her by the hand, beginning thus to hold her in chat.

"Your town here, forsooth, of Cherry Hinton hath made me oft play the truant to come hither for cherries, and as mine hostess can tell full many a mess of cream have I eaten in her house, for we scholars are good companions and love to be pleasant, especially if we might have the company of such a fair gentlewoman as yourself. Therefore, mistress, if I chance to come to town to eat a pound of cherries, if I may be so bold, I would trouble you to take part with me, and if I meet you at Cambridge the best wine in the town shall be your welcome."

The wench, that had much ado to keep her countenance, thought to feed him with her fair speeches, till she made him as fat as a fool, and therefore made him this reply. "Truly, sir, indeed many scholars come to Cherry Hinton to eat cherries, but, sir, you are the first man that ever I drank withal, for scholars be so full of their learning and fine terms that country wenches cannot understand them. But I for my part at the first sight like of you so well that, if my leisure serve, whensoever you come and please to send for me, I will as long as I dare bear you company. But now forsooth time calls me away, and I must be gone." "With all my heart," quoth Rowland, "but truly we must not part without a kiss," which she willingly took at his hands and went home, where as soon as she came she revealed all to a young gentleman that lay in her father's house, who was sure to her. They laughing heartily at the scholar's courting resolved to make good sport with him ere they had done.

But Rowland, he that thought every smile was a fancy and every maid that laughed on him loved him, conjectured assuredly by the familiar courtesy of the gentlewoman that she was greatly affectionated towards him, whereupon he began to inquire of his hostess whose daughter she was, of what wealth her father was, what children he had and what dowry the maid was like to have to her portion, as a man resolved the woman was already won because she had given him gracious favors. The hostess, as well as she could, told him all: which done, he paid his shot and went to Cambridge, where he began altogether to muse on the beauty of his mistress and to lay an hundred plots in his head what were best to be done. At last he resolved to send a letter to her to signify his love, or else to go himself and to carry two or three of his fellows with him and so to discourse unto her how he loved her. But at the last he fully determined with himself to write unto her, wherefore taking pen and ink in his hand, wrote a letter to her to this effect.

ROWLAND'S LETTER TO THE FAIR MAID OF CHERRY HINTON

Mistress Marian, Aristotle the great philosopher for all his wit was in love with Hermia, and Socrates the sage could not so far subdue his passions but that he fell in liking with Xantippe. Scholars as they read much of love, so when they once fall in love, there is no hoe with them till they have their love. The finest glass is most brittle, and the best scholars soonest overgone with fancy. For an instance, was not Ovid as deep in love as he was excellent in learning? I bring in these comparisons, Mistress Marian, because the other Sunday being at Cherry Hinton, and seeing your sweet self, I was so overtaken with your beauty and good behavior that ever since the remembrance of your face could never out of my fancy, nor I think, never shall, although I should be drenched in forgetful flood of Lethe. Seeing then my affection is so great, I pray you consider of me and be not unkind, but let me have love for love; and though here in the University you see me simple, yet my parents at home are men of good parentage, and what I want in wealth I shall supply in learning. Ponder with yourself, and read but the lives and answers of the philosophers, and see how they used their wives, with what courtesy; however the women were the most masters and had the sovereignty which they desire. Thus hoping you will consider of my love, desiring you to send me answer, I bid you farewell.

Yours in dust and ashes,
Rowland

When he had thus finished this letter, he thought to show himself somewhat poetical, and thought a letter was not worth a rush unless there were some verses at the latter end, and therefore he affixed as a postscript this amorous ditty.

ROWLAND'S SONG TO HIS MISTRESS

Approach in place, Pierides,
My vein in verse to bend;
Dame Chryseis, which gav'st Homer suck,
Thy tender teats me lend.

Alcmena, thou which Jove didst rock,
In cradle full of joy,
Eke swathe me in those swaddling clouts,
Account me for thy boy.

Yea, Naiades and pretty nymphs,
That on Parnassus dwell,
Lend me your Muse, that I may now
My Mistress' beauty tell.

How that in beauty she doth pass
Venus the Queen of Love,
To whom, if I do gain her grace,
I will be turtle-dove.

Therefore, my dear, conceive my grief
And think how I do love thee,
And in some lines send me relief,
For Time and Truth shall prove me.

Thus hoping pen and paper shall
Thy mind to me short tell,
But love me as I do love thee,
And so, my dear, farewell.

Thus having both finished his letter and his verse, he sent them by a convenient messenger the next Saturday to Cherry Hinton, and that forsooth was his hostess, who very orderly sent for the gentlewoman to her house and delivered the letters to her, with earnest commendations from Sir Rowland. The gentlewoman in outward show seemed to accept them as gratefully as he sent them lovingly, and so hied her home, where presently she called for her new betrothed husband and other gentlemen her friends and revealed unto them how she had received letters from her new lover the scholar. All they flocked about her, to hear what excellent stuff was contained in so learned a man's letter, but when they heard how like a philosophical fool he wrote, they all in a synod peremptorily concluded that the greatest clerks were not the wisest men.

"And I marvel of that," quoth one of the company, "for two reasons: for the one, I have heard this old-said saw, that love makes men orators and affections whetteth on eloquence; secondly, there was none more amorous than Ovid (yet a profound scholar) insomuch that he wrote three books *De arte amandi,* and so did Anacreon, Tibullus, and Propertius." "Yea, but," quoth another, "as they were scholars so were they well brought up in the court and knew as many external matters as they did inward principles. But beware, my masters, when a scholar is once brought up in the universities and hath no other bringing up but plain *ergo* to plod in, nor converseth with none but his books, and then hap to fall in love. Trust me, he will be as ignorant to woo as the ploughman to dispute, thinking that women's fancies are won with figures and their thoughts over-reached with the quiddities of art. But of all that ever I heard write, this setteth down his mind the most simply." "And therefore," quoth Marian, "shall he be answered as foolishly, for I myself will be secretary." "Nay," quoth divers of the gentlemen, "we will put in our verdict with you." "No," quoth she, "try but a woman's wit." "That's knavish enough," quoth one of them. And stepping to her standish[24] she wrote thus.

MARIAN OF CHERRY HINTON TO SIR ROWLAND OF CAMBRIDGE, HEALTH.

Sweet Sir Rowland, I received your letters, wherein I perceive that scholars in love are like to a sow with pig under the apple tree, which either hastily must have a drab or else lose their litter. If I bring in a country comparison, blame me not, in that I am a country wench, and have none but plain country logic. But whatsoever I write, I mean well. Indeed rightly you say that the finest glass is most brittle, and the best scholars soonest pinched with love, which I think to be true, for as soon as ever I saw you, how your eyes waited upon my face as an object of your delight, I took you to be too wise, kind, and amorous. And therefore seeing ever since you have been passionate, it were great pity that you should not have for your pains (even as we use in a homely proverb) a country sackfull of love; and the rather you induce me to think well of you that you bring in the examples of Aristotle and Hermia, and of Socrates and Xantippe, whereby you seem to promise that I shall as they had, enjoy the sovereignty, and that if I be like them in conditions, you will be as suffering as they in patience. Yet will I neither be so proud towards you as Hermia, for she rode Aristotle with a snaffle, like a horse, nor so waspish as Xantippe, for she crowned Socrates with a chamber pot, but between both. And so wishing you hope the best, I bid you farewell.

Yours never, if not ever,
Marian of Cherry Hinton

After she had done her letter, that she might seem to be no whit behind him in any good will, she leaned her head on her hand and in a poetical fury wrote her lover these verses.

MARIAN'S VERSES TO SIR ROWLAND

Fear not, my dear, the storms of love,
   For they are passing sour,
And sometime sweet as honeycomb,
   And all within an hour.

Like to a sunshine summer's day,
    When Phoebus shows amain,
And yet ere night from tawny clouds
    Doth fall a shower of rain.

So whatsoever chance betide,
    Or whatsoever fall,
If father frown, or mother chide,
    Yet you must bear with all.

For why? the cuckoo doth not come
    In April month more sure,
Than I will fix my love on thee
    For ever to endure.

Thus wishing thee to think on me,
    In study or in street,
I bid you heartily farewell,
    Till we in Cambridge meet.

    Having thus ended her song and the letter, she called the convocation of the merry gentlemen and showed them her humor in prose and her vein in verse, asking if she had done it knavishly enough. "Yea," quoth her betrothed husband, "and so exceeding well that you shall stand for four and twenty knaves till Christmas next." "Tush," quoth another, "women's wits are like Sheffield knives, for they are sometimes so keen as they will cut a hair, and sometimes so blunt as they must go to the grindstone." "That is," quoth the second, "when you persuade them to silence or obedience; talk with them but in that doctrine and they are mere dunces."
    Thus they began to descant of women's wit, but the gentlewoman wily enough left them all and went and laid up her letters till Saturday market. Then she went to the hostess and delivered them to her, earnestly entreating her if she saw Sir Rowland to convey that packet to him. The hostess promised her to do it faithfully and effectually, and away to Cambridge she went, where scarce she was set with her butter and her milk but she spied Sir Rowland

come flinging down the market hill in his widesleeved gown and his corner cap. She needed not to call him, for he straight found her out, and she as soon delivered him the packet. Sir Rowland thanked her and away he went to his study to read the contents.

But it was too far to Peter's Hostel, and therefore he called in at a tavern by the way for a pint of wine and there he opened the letter, which when he had read he perceived by the contents she loved him, for he being simple perceived not how she bobbed fool with him. Taking every jest for a sentence, he thought himself the master of all worldly content, and that Fortune could not advance him higher on her wheel than to have so fair a maid to his paramour. Then viewed over her verses and in a sweet passion praised her poetry, commended her wit, saying for stature she was Juno, for beauty Venus, for learning and qualities Pallas. Thus in meditation of his letter and his love sat poor Sir Rowland from eight o'clock till eleven, and then hearing the hostel bell ring to dinner, for fear he should lose his halfpenny chops he put up his letter into his pocket and went his way.

After dinner he fell to his old vein, got alone to be solitary, and then sat ruminating on the good success of his loves, accounting it rather to his profession than his fortune, for he thought none so fair, chaste, nor rich, but a scholar might win with his logic. Thus he passed over day by day, in sending of letters to his love, and divers times resorting thither, but seldom could he speak with her, for that she feigned some excuse; only when she meant to laugh, then she was for his company.

But it fell out, that one Saturday above the rest, Sir Rowland met her in Cambridge and finding her with other of her neighbors, saluted her and would needs welcome her to the town with a pint of wine, which she took very kindly that she might soothe him up still in his vain hope, and forsooth to the tavern she and her companions went with him, where they had good game at our Cambridge wooer. But Marian taking him aside told him that her father and

The Tinker of Turvey

her mother had intelligence of their loves and as far as she could conjecture it was by his hostess; therefore she willed him not to make her privy to his secrets any more, nor to come to Cherry Hinton but when she sent for him, which should be as often as opportunity would serve, hoping, though her father now were not forward, yet in time he would consent, and specially if he saw him Master of Arts. With this the scholar rested satisfied and they drank their wine and departed.

Thus between them passed on all the summer, till the deep of winter, about Christmas, when she on a time and the rest of the gentlemen, desirous to be pleasant, determined to have some sport with the scholar, and so caused Marian to send a letter for him, that he should come that night and speak with her. Which she did, and he, poor soul, no sooner received it but in all haste hied him in the frosty evening to Cherry Hinton, where when he came, he straight spoke with Marian and she wished him to stay in an old barn while her father was at supper and then she would convey him into a back court where he should walk hard under the chamber door, and then when her father was in bed she would let him in. The scholar stood there a while, and Marian came straight and conducted him into a square court, where Rowland rested him till her father should go to bed. The night grew dark, and with that passing cold, so that Rowland waxed weary of his standing and wished that her father were in bed. There stood the poor scholar shaking and trembling in his joints, till it was eleven of the clock; then saw he light at the door and he heard Marian call him.

"Oh, blessed hour," thought he, "that now I shall go both to a good fire and to my love." "Sir Rowland," quoth she, "be still a while; my father and my mother is gone to bed, but my brother and two gentlemen more are up at cards, and they have but a set to play and then they will to their rest." "Alas, sweetheart," quoth he, "I am almost starved for cold, yet the hope that I have to enjoy thy presence doth comfort me, that I take all things with patience." The gentlemen that stood hard by and heard all this laughed at the scholar and up they went again to their chamber to be merry, but still walked poor Rowland, beating his hands about him for cold and expecting still when his lover should call him.

Well, there he traversed his ground still like a peripetician, and only had the sight of the heavens to contemplate till it was above one of the clock, and then came they all down again to laugh, and as soon as he saw the candle at the chink of the door, he began to be comforted and came thither, shaking and beating of his teeth so sore that he could not speak. "Where are you, sweetheart?" quoth she. "Alas, how sorry am I for thy distress. Think that the heart in my belly is as cold for grief as thy joints are with the frost. Fain would I have thee come in, but the losers will not part play and so they sit still. Therefore I hope thou wilt weigh my credit." "Oh, Marian," quoth he, and his teeth jarred one against another that they could scarce understand him. "I am like to perish with cold, yet were it twice as frosty and the night thrice as long, I would walk here rather than procure thy disparagement." "Gramercy, sweet love," quoth she, and with that she bid him be still a while and the gentlemen all fell a-laughing to hear how kind a fool the scholar was, and with what patience he bid penance. "Oh," quoth the one of them, "that is but an experiment of his philosophical principles, for he reads in Tully: *Non oportet sapientem in adversit dolore concidere.*" "Ay," quoth the second, "and Mimus Publius gives him this counsel, *Adversis proba, ut fortunam, cum necesse fuerit. Patienter insultantem feras.*" "You say well," quoth the third, "but let him for me make instance of himself for such axioms; I will rather be a warm fool than so cold a philosopher."

Thus they 'gan descant upon the poor scholar's misery till the clock struck three, and then as they were coming down, they heard a noise at the door, which was this poor Rowland creeping under the shade for warmth, his teeth beating so loud that they might hear them easily up the stairs. All this moved not my young mistress to pity, but increased their laughter. As soon as he heard them come down the stairs, almost dead he called out, "Who is there?" "Oh, sweetheart, it is thy Marian," quoth she. "Then for God's sake," quoth Rowland, "take pity of my life, for I am almost dead. Do but open the door and let me sit here upon the stairs, that I may have some shelter from the cold." "Alas," quoth she, "sweet love, thou shalt and thou wilt, but when the door is opened, it makes such a noise that it wakens the whole house." "Rather," quoth he, "let me suffer death than you be discredited, for if I were to abide the stone of Sisyphus, the wheel of Ixion, the gripe of Prometheus, and the hunger of Tantalus, yet had I rather pocket up all these tortures with patience than bring thy credit within the compass of the least prejudice." At this period she left him and up they went, smiling at the constancy of Rowland.

The gentlemen they were sleepy and went to bed, and Marian, as far as I can conjecture, though it were somewhat before the marriage, that night made trial of her new betrothed husband, where from three she lay with him till six, and then it waxed daylight, and she rose. And remembering her lover went down, opened the door, and found him almost senseless; there wiping her eyes as though she had wept, she persuaded him that she was the most sorrowful woman in the world for his sharp frosty night he had suffered, protesting she was fallen into an ague for fear and grief she had taken to see him in such distress and could by no means redress it. "But, good Rowland," quoth she, "be content; hie thee to Cambridge, and take some hot broths, lest by this means thou fall into a sickness, and then for fear I die." "No," quoth Rowland, and he could scarce speak or go, "fear not me, for the hope of thy after favors will be a sufficient comfort for me," and with that taking his leave, for his cold night's work he had a kiss and so departed.

Well, as weak as he was, home he scrambled, and got to his chamber, and discovered to a friend of his how he was like to perish of an extreme cold he had taken if he did not so much for him as to get him a physician, who straight went and brought him a doctor, that with inward potions and outward oils and unguents so wrought him that he recovered him to his former health, although very hardly, for he was so frozen in his loins and so nipped in his muscles and sinews that if his physician had not been good, he had perished. It was almost a quarter of a year before Rowland was frolic again; in which time Marian, thinking she had lost her lover with a nut, sent him a present of apples to win him again, which he received so gratefully that he valued the worst of them worth a fellowship, eating them with an extraordinary taste that he imagined them as sweet as ambrosia and all for that they came from his Marian.

Thus continued Rowland in his amorous humor until such time as Marian forsooth must be married, and for that it was Advent, there was no asking in the church, but they procured a license the day before. As she and the rest of her friends which were invited to the nuptials were merrily jesting, "Oh, Lord," quoth she, "I had almost forgot myself. Tomorrow must be the wedding, and the bride is yet at Cambridge. Why, gentlemen, it were no bargain if Rowland were not here. Therefore," quoth she, "I will send for him, and lay such a plot that he shall be with us all dinner and yet taste none of our meat." "I pray you," quoth her husband, "let us see your cunning in that." "Alas," quoth one of the gentlemen, "poor Rowland is credulous, and whatsoever Mistress Marian saith, he thinks it is gospel, but if he will be so simple as to think that his last night's work is not a sufficient warning, he is worthy of whatsoever befalls."

Well, upon this Marian sent for him, and come he did in the evening, where, to make my tale short, she made him to walk in his wonted station till one of the clock; then she let him in to a good fire, where he well warmed himself, and she lovingly sat by him, discoursing of the last night's work that he abode so patiently. At last she commanded

The Tinker of Turvey

the maid to lay the cloth, that they might have some quelque chose for a rare supper, which they went busily about, for Rowland said he was very hungry. As the cloth was laid and they ready to sit down, the wench came running in and said that her master was rising, and seeing the light of the fire, was coming into the parlor. "Alas, what shall I do?" quoth Marian. "Hide me somewhere," quoth Rowland, "whiles he be gone to bed." "Come," quoth she, "here stands a new trunk and a large, come, skip into it, and I will for a while rake up the fire and go to bed while the old man be fallen asleep." With that Rowland whipped into the trunk and she locked him in, and straight in a pleasant humor went to her new husband, where she lay all night, and left Rowland safe shut up for starting. Still lay he expecting when she should come, but hearing nothing and extremely weary, for very grief he fell asleep till the next morning.

When the poor scholar awaked and entered into consideration where he was, he began to be half in suspicion that he was mocked and abused. Still he lay patiently till he heard them of the house say, "Good morrow, Mistress Marian, God send you a good day today. The sun shines fair; you shall have a clear day to your wedding." This word went as cold to his heart as a knife, that Marian should be married and he made a fool to suffer such disparagement of his credit. Yet as before he was patient in extremes, and so resolved with content to see the success of his abuse.

Well, to church go the bridegroom and the bride, with all their friends attendants, and married they were with great solemnity. This done, home they come to dinner, and after they were set and placed in the parlor where this trunk stood they fell to their viands, which were very sumptuous, the gentlemen bidding reach down the pig, the capon, goose, swan, turkey, pheasant, bitour venison, and such dainty cates. All this heard Rowland and being passing hungry wished he had a leg of the worst of them in his hand. Still he lay, almost famished and smothered till the tables were taken up and boards shifted, and they fell to dancing. All this heard Rowland, and hearing the music, fell asleep until supper time, and then he awaked and heard how they laid the tables and went to supper, where they were passing pleasant, and the more for that they meant to make sport with Rowland after supper was done, which continued not long, for they made the more haste for that they meant to be merry.

When the cloth was taken up, the bride fetched a great sigh. "What, wife," quoth the bridegroom, "why sigh you? In a dump? Repent you of the match?" "No," quoth she, "but I have a blot in my conscience, and now before you all I mean to reveal it. I was once beloved of a Cambridge scholar who loved me entirely and suffered much for my sake." Then from point to point she recounted unto them the whole discourse of the loves and fortunes passed between Rowland and her, whereat the company had good sport. "A man he was," quoth she, "wise, proper, and well proportioned, and for proof, take this key, open that trunk," quoth she, "and you shall see his picture."

Rowland hearing this armed himself to suffer all, and so the trunk was opened and he rose out like Lazarus from his grave. "Good Lord," quoth the company, "what is this —a spirit? *In nomine Jesus, unde venis?*" "*E purgatorio,*" quoth Rowland, and with that all the people laughed while they could sit. At last when they were weary with laughing Rowland had silence. He boldly said, "Thus I am glad, gentlemen, that my mishap hath made you so merry, and that Mistress Bride hath so large a plainsong to run descant on. *Caveat emptor;* this is but a comedy, but look for a tragedy whensoever it falls." And so he went out of the door sore ashamed that he had such a kindly scoff. The company laughed well, and he patiently went thinking how fortunate a man he should be if he might live to revenge. Rowland at this misfortune had an insight into the world and began to wax wiser, that in short time he began to have as much knowledge in worldly affairs as in his book, and was, for his good behavior and pleasant wit,

The Tinker of Turvey

highly had in estimation, not only amongst scholars but amongst townsmen, that in all the university he was called the gentlemanlike scholar.

Living thus in good credit and yet discontented because Fortune favored him with no opportunity to revenge, it so fell out at length that Marian coming every week to Cambridge espied amongst the scholars one whom she cast her eye on and thought him the properest man in the whole university. Well, she counted it but a glance, and thought as lightly to pass it over, as it slightly entered, but she found love, though he entered in by grant of courtesy, yet he would not be thrust out by force of extremity, insomuch that she could not content herself without but with the sight of her new friend. Which was done so manifestly that the scholar perceived it, and, aiming at the fairest, one Saturday seeing her in the market offered her a quart of wine, which she took gratefully and began to be very familiar with him, insomuch that before they passed, force of love made her so shameless that she was content to yield to his request, so that time and place would serve without the disparagement of her credit.

Upon this they concluded that Master Audrey (for so we will call him) should grow familiar with her husband, and by that means should have a better means to the quieting of his mind. Upon this determination they departed, and he so brought it to pass that he not only was acquainted with her husband but so familiar that he would carry Master Audrey often from Cambridge with him to Cherry Hinton and I hope you do imagine he was no little welcome guest to his wife. Being thus fitted in this in their passions, only watching for place and lingering off the time, at last it was concluded that she should come on a Saturday to Cambridge and feign to stay with a kinswoman of hers that dwelt in the town, and so lie with her all night. This stood for a sentence, and so the next week was decreed.

In the meantime it so fell out that Master Audrey and Sir Rowland being of great acquaintance and such private familiars that nothing was held too secret between them, Master Audrey smothering this joy in himself thought to partake it with his friend, and so as he and Sir Rowland were walking he revealed unto him the love that had passed between him and Marian, and on Saturday was the night when his *posse* should come into *esse,* desiring him to tell him where he might have a house fit for such a purpose. Sir Rowland hearing this smiled, which made Master Audrey to inquire the cause of his laughter, whereupon sitting down upon the grass, he began to recount unto him the whole discourse of his loves with Marian, and what sundry abuses he suffered at her hand, to the great and utter infamy of scholars. M. Audrey hearing this sat a great while in a muse; at last he said, "and will women be crocodiles, to weep rosewater and vinegar at one time, still delay in extremes to love without reason, and hate without cause? Oh, the folly of men to be such to such painted sepulchers, whose painted sheaths hold leaden blades, whose skins are glorious like panthers' but have devouring paunches! By that God that drew that unfortunate female from that fortunate Adam, I hate her as extremely as I loved her earnestly, and I will not only yield thee opportunity to revenge but I'll join issue with thee to perform it to the uttermost."

At this Rowland was tickled with inward joy, and taking Audrey in his arms protested such humble service for that friendly promise as ever should lie in his ability to execute. Thus in this determination of revenge they crossed the fields to Trumpington, and there they ate a mess of cream, whither by chance came one of the proctors, with whom both Rowland and Audrey were very familiar. Him they had in, and made as good cheer as such a simple alehouse could afford, and there in private revealed to him all their practice, desiring his furtherance in the matter. The proctor promised to do what in him lay for the execution of this merry action, and there amongst them they laying and confirming the plot they went all together home to Cambridge, where they passed away the time pleasantly till

The Tinker of Turvey

Saturday came. And then according to promise was Marian there and met with Audrey, who entertained her with all the courtesy that he could, spending the day at the tavern while night came, and then he carried her to the house appointed, such a subaudy domus as was fit for such a purpose, and there they supped.

In the meantime Rowland had sent a letter to her husband in Audrey's name, that his wife being not well was fain to stay at her kinswoman's all night, and desired him to come to her the next morning, and that her father and the rest of the gentlemen would come with him, for that they should see Rowland taken in bed with a pretty wench. This letter in all haste was conveyed to Cherry Hinton to her husband, who reading the contents waxed somewhat jealous, because he had seen very familiar courtesy between Audrey and his wife, and thought scholars were sly fellows and could devise many sophistications to make a man a cuckold. But he concealed his suspicion to himself and showed the letter to his father-in-law and the rest of the gentlemen, who as they sorrowed his wife was not well, so they were all glad to see such a comical fortune of Rowland. Her husband taking every word for his advantage said he would be there by four of the clock to see Rowland taken up. Thus they all agreed and were gone by two of the clock, where we leave them coming to Cambridge, and again to Marian, who after supper sat up late. But Audrey filled her full of wine till she was almost drunk, that she was very heavy and desired to go to bed, which she did, and was no sooner laid but she fell asleep, and Audrey slipping out put out the candle and sent in Rowland and bade him now go to his mistress. He went into the chamber and locked the door, and Master Audrey stole out of the house and went to his chamber, leaving Rowland with his paramour, where I think more for envy of the man than for love of the woman perhaps he dubbed him one of Paris's priesthood. Howsoever it was, she descried not how it was, but both fell asleep.

On the morrow by four of the clock was Marian's husband, her father, and the rest of the gentlemen at Peter's Hostel, where finding the gate open, they went to Master Audrey's chamber, and raised him up, who quickly slipping on his clothes welcomed them, and went with them to find out the proctor, who watching for their coming already was with a dozen masters of art well appointed walking in the courtyard, and presently went his way with them and came to the house where Rowland lay. The proctor knocked and bade open the door. "Who is that?" quoth the good wife. "The proctor," quoth he. "Open the door, and that quickly, or I will beat it down." The goodman came stumbling down in his shirt and the goodwife was so amazed that she could not remember to tell her guests. The proctor came in and by the direction of Audrey went straight up to the chamber. "Who be here?" quoth the proctor. "None, sir," quoth he, "but a stranger and his wife." "Beat it open with a halbert," quoth the proctor, and with that for haste Marian's husband ran against it and the door fell down and he into the chamber.

With that Rowland covered her close and stepping out of the bed in his shirt asked what they meant. "Ah, Sir Rowland," quoth the proctor, "I am sorry I have dis-eased you this morn. I thought full little to have found you here. What is the cause you lie out of the Hostel tonight?" "Truly, sir," quoth he, "I was late abroad this night, making merry with my friends, and so I was fain to take up my lodging here." "How do you, Sir Rowland?" quoth Marian's husband and her father, "I marvel we see you not at Cherry Hinton." "Oh, masters," quoth he, "when there is another comedy to play, look for me, but if you remember, I promised you a tragedy first. When that is studied, I warrant you I will visit you." Poor Marian lying in bed and hearing all this how she was betrayed and had lain with Rowland all night and how her father and her husband were there present thought surely now Rowland to the uttermost would be revenged upon her, so that she fell into a great sweat for fear.

The proctor that had his lesson taught him said, "Well,

Sir Rowland, had it been any other but you that had been taken abroad and in such a suspected house, he should have gone to the toll-booth, but since you have no other company, farewell." Audrey jogged upon Marian's husband, and as they were ready to go out of doors, "tush, master proctor," quoth he, "but I marvel you examine not who it is that lies with him. It may be a pretty wench." "What? is there one lies with him?" "Yea, marry is there, sir," quoth he, and with that stepping to the bed, threw off all the clothes, and there lay his wife in her smock.

> Sancte amen, quoth Rowland, who is here?
> Have you seen such a chance this year?
> What, a woodcock come so soon
> From Cherry Hinton to Cambridge before noon,
> And found a cuckoo's nest?
> Is this, masters, in earnest or in jest?
> That Rowland so early in a morn
> Should make a knave wear the horn.
> What, man, be not aghast,
> For you cannot call back that is past.

At this all the scholars fell a-laughing, and Sir Rowland sat him down in his shirt, and to make the matter up, that it might be a right black sanctus, while they laughed cried "Cuckoo." The gentleman seeing his wife, and the father his daughter, they were in such a maze, that they stood as men senseless. They fell out a-weeping, the scholars a-laughing, the gentlemen a-sighing, and still Rowland kept his wench and cried "Cuckoo!"

At last Rowland began thus. "Why, you my masters and friends of Cherry Hinton, did I not promise you a tragedy, and have I not now brought it to pass? I hope this dame and you all remember my frosty night and how I was brought out of the trunk. Now am not I revenged well, have I not had my penny worth's." "Yes, villain," quoth the gentleman, "and first the whore shall die." And with that drawing out his rapier, he would have killed her, but the proctor stayed him and she protested she knew not how she came there but thought she had been at home in her bed. Upon this all the scholars persuaded the gentleman that Rowland did it by necromancy, and that if she were the honestest woman in the world, magic were able to do as much. Rowland for very pity affirmed it, and so they persuaded him not to wade further in the matter for his own credit, but to clap it up with silence. She wept, and wrung her hands, and her father sat and shed tears, but at last, by persuasion of the proctor and the other scholars, Rowland and he for all this were made friends, his wife and he agreed, as a man persuaded she was faultless and that it was done by necromancy, and so all merrily went to the tavern and drank, they going to the college and he to Cherry Hinton with full resolution never more to let his wife come to Cambridge, for fear of the scholar's art magic.

* * *

This tale made them all heartily laugh, every one commending the policy of the scholars that had invented so good a revenge. The cobbler he marked all very diligently, and swore there was not a more sound history in all the *Legenda Aurea*. Well, it made all the barge merry, yet seeing they began to be all in a dump, one cried, "Who is next?" "Marry, that am I," quoth the scholar, and he began to settle himself, whom I can best describe thus.

THE DESCRIPTION OF THE SCHOLAR

A man he was of a sober look,
Given much unto his book,
For his visage was all pale,
As clerks tellen this tale,
That mickle study makes men lean,
As well as doth a curst quean.
Apollo radiant and sheen
His pattern long had been,
For well skilled was he

In verses and in poetry.
In palmistry he had some lore,
In other arts mickle more,
Mickle could he say at each steven[25]
Of the liberal arts seven,
Of the welkin and the axle-tree
Whereon the heavens turned be,
Of Mercury and Charles' wain
And of the Bears twain;
Calisto and her son conveyed thither,
Which to seamen show the weather;
When Neptune with his mace
Will make smile Amphitrite's face.
Many other matters of sophistry
Could this clerk in secrecy;
He could also speak of love,
Of Paphos and of Venus's Dove,
And perhaps though he were a clerk,
Yet he could skill in the dark,
As well as a man of lay degree,
To dally with a wench in privity.
His attire was all black,
But why do I long clack?
This clerk 'gan report
His story in this sort.

THE SCHOLAR'S TALE

Containing the sundry misfortunes that two Sicilian Lovers had, and how at the end their passionate sorrows came to a pleasing success.

When the King of Tunis was beaten out of his kingdom and sought to enter again by force, Jacomine Pierro and Alexander Bartolo, two noblemen of Sicilia, and both of Palermo, for the good will they bore the king, prepared certain tall barks, and with their aid, maugre his enemies, placed the king again safe in his kingdom. Which done, they returned again to Palermo. This Jacomine Pierro had a son called also Jacomine, and this Alexander had a daughter called Katherine. These two being neighbors, their children fell in love together, insomuch that Jacomine noting the beauty of Katherine, seeing with his eye her outward excellency and hearing with his ears her inward virtues and perfections, entered with such deep insight into her qualities that he resolved in himself she and none but she should be the goddess of his affections. And on the other side, Katherine feeding her eye with the desired object of his person, and with delight pleasing her ear with the general fame that ran through all Sicilia of his courtesy, affability, and valor, determined that none but Jacomine should enjoy the flower of her beauty.

These two lovers being such a sympathy of agreeing passions lived a long while with looks, bashful both to discover the essence of their loves. Yet at last Jacomine taking heart at grass, finding one day fit place and opportunity, discoursed unto her how ever since his years could entertain any amorous thought, the Idea of her beauty and virtues remained imprinted in his heart so deeply that none but she could satisfy the end of his incessant desire, which was no other than the honest and honorable content of marriage. Katherine, who was as willing as he was desirous, told him that upon that condition whensoever their parents should agree, she was ready to be at his command. Thus they wooed and ended, and all in a short space, for that time parting with a kiss. This sweet consent of thoughts continued a long time between these two lovers, insomuch that Jacomine resolved shortly to break the matter to her father, to whom he knew the match would be most pleasing, for that old Jacomine and Alexander loved together as brothers.

Whiles thus these two lovers held their demand in suspense, there fell a deadly jar between the house of the Jacomines and the family of the Bartolos, insomuch that not only all Palermo but almost all Sicilia was in an uproar, for each took arms against other and being men of great parentage, friends took parts and they began to bandy, that they fell to a flat civil dissention. This disagreement between the parents, although it was a heart-break to the two lovers, yet could it not at all disparage their affection, but the greater the mutiny, the deeper was the impression of their minds. But by this means their meeting was hindered; yet Love being a privy searcher of secrets found them out a crevice between two walls, which parted their houses, and there ofttimes they met and parleyed, hoping still some end would grow to this dismal dissention. But as the fire increaseth with the wind, so this jar grew greater by time that the lovers lost all hope ever to have consent of parents, insomuch that wholly in despair of a unity, they concluded to forsake Sicilia and to go into Spain, where they had both friends, and there to remain till their families were accorded.

Upon this resolution, Jacomine provided him a bark, and laid it ready in the haven, and when the wind and weather was fair gave a watchword to Katherine and so got her aboard, hoisted sails, and away they made towards Spain. They were not long gone but they were missed, and by all possible conjectures known to be slipped away together, for divers manifest instances were reported of their loves. The fathers fell both into deep passions, Jacomine having but one son, and Bartolo but one daughter; yea, the grief of their unkind departure did so work in their fathers' minds, that each intended more mischief to other, as it were in revenge, that the broils grew hotter.

But as they dissented, so these two lovers accorded every way, looking for no other haven but the coast of Spain. But Fortune, that delights to sport herself in the variable accidents of love, brought it thus to pass. They had not sailed three days from Sicilia but that there fell a great calm and certain galleys that were rovers under the King of Tunis espied this Sicilian ship and thinking to have some rich prize made out and gave onset, commanding them to yield. The Sicilians, being calm, could not make way from them, but yet although too weak stoutly denied to be boarded, and fought it out to the uttermost, chiefly Jacomine, who was sore wounded. But at last, they of the galleys entered and bestowed the mariners under hatches, and then went to rifle the ship, where they found Katherine all blubbered with tears and almost dead for fear. Her they took for all her pitiful shrieks and cries, conveyed her into the galleys, which Jacomine seeing took so heavily that he was ready to die for grief, but so sore he was hurt that stir he could not but was fain to suffer her to be carried away, whither the mercy of the slaves pleased to transport her. When they had rifled the ship and found nothing but passengers, away they went with fair Katherine, determining with themselves to give her for a present to the King of Tunis, whom they knew did love a fair woman more than half his kingdom, and so fair a creature as Katherine they were sure he never saw before.

Upon this they made sail toward Tunis and when they were arrived, the captain of the galleys causing her to dress her in her richest attire went with her to the King's palace, where when he was admitted to his Highness' presence humbly on his knees he craved pardon as one that contrary to his Majesty's laws had been a rover and a pirate on the seas, but now loathing that course of life was come to submit himself, and having taken that gentlewoman as a prize at sea desired his Majesty to accept her as a present. The King whiles the pirate was telling his tale kept his eye still on the gentlewoman, whose beauty he found such that he thought her some heavenly creature shrouded in some mortal carcase. The King not only thanked the pirate for his present, but gave him free pardon and a letter of marque, with many other rich gifts, so that he returned richly rewarded, and then turning to Katherine, he took her in his arms, kissed her, and gave her such entertainment as in all royalty he could. But nothing could make her cease off from tears, having still her Jacomine in remembrance, which she held for dead, which the King perceiving, commanded that she should be carried to a palace of his, standing fast by the city wall, and there placed and

The Tinker of Turvey

attended upon with all diligence, until she might be comforted and thither when it pleased him he would have recourse.

Seated in that house, there she led a solitary life, washing her cheeks every day with tears for her poor Jacomine, who likewise, wounded as he was, was brought to Tunis and there left in the surgeon's hand, where he was healed. As soon as he might well go, he went as a man forlorn up and down the city, looking everywhere if he might see his Katherine, whereupon he resolved to pass from place to place, and so to end his days in travel if he did not by narrow inquisition find her out. Getting therefore his bag and baggage in a readiness, he was going out of Tunis, and as he passed out of the gates, he cast his eye up to the house where Katherine was, who at that time was looking out of a casement. He espying her and thinking it should be she stood in a maze. Katherine seeing him and thinking him to be her Jacomine was almost ready to fall down in a swoon. Thus stood the two lovers at gaze; at last Jacomine called Katherine. "Jacomine," quoth she, and with that she clapped her fingers on her mouth and made a sign that for that time he should depart.

Back again went Jacomine to his hostess, as merry a man as might be, and there stayed till it was something late in the evening, and then going to the palace sought round about the house and there found a back window into a garden, where they might conveniently talk. He had not stayed there long, but Katherine came to the window and there, after a volley of sighs quenched with tears, they began to discourse their fortunes since their departure. Katherine told unto Jacomine how she was given by the pirates to the King for a present, and how he had placed her there, reserving her for one of his concubines, and that she looked every hour when he would come to deflower her. "Therefore," quoth she, "since we are man and wife, and as we have lived together, even so let us die together, and enjoy thou the chastity of that body whose soul hath been ever thine in all amity. I respect not the King, nor what his tortures can do; therefore at night come hither to this place when it is dark, climb up on the wall and so on this tree, and thou mayst easily come into the casement, which for the same purpose thou shalt find open."

At this motion Jacomine was glad, and so departed, and at the time appointed came, and being made more nimble by love and desire, he leapt up the wall lightly, and so into the tree, and from thence into the casement, where he found his Katherine ready to receive him. Banquet him she could not, lest any might hear, but feast he did with kisses or whatsoever she might afford to his amorous desires, so that in the end to bed they went, and there with pleasure recompensed their former misfortunes.

Love having thus advanced her champion, Fortune envying their happiness meant to have one fling more at them, and brought it to pass that the King that night resolved to have the company of Katherine and therefore after all his lords were at rest took with him his chamberlain and certain of the guard, and went to the place where she lay, coming in by a back gate, having keys for every door, at last opened the chamber where she was and there drawing the curtain to behold his goddess, he saw where she lay with a young man in her arms fast asleep. The King for anger was ready to have killed him, but yet he did qualify his fury with a royal patience, and called his chamberlain and the rest of the guard and showed them this sight, demanding of them if any knew the young man. They all answered no, but supposed he was some stranger. The King straight commanded that certain of his guard should watch them, and as soon as they awaked carry them to prison and let there in the midst of the market-place be erected a great stake, and in the afternoon there let them both be consumed with fire. The guard obeyed the King's commandment, and he went away in great choler and highly discontented.

The King departed, these lovers slept sweetly till the morning, and then they awoke, where presently they heard a rustling of men, that straight told them how the King was there, what had happened, and what he had commanded. Therefore they made them rise and then bound them, and carried them away. The two lovers were no whit dismayed at this news, but embracing and kissing each other, comforted themselves in this, that they should as they lived together so die together, and that their souls nor bodies should never part.

Straight were they carried to prison, and the stake was a-providing, whereupon the rumor of their burning came about the city, that against the hour appointed all the city were gathered together, and forth at last was Jacomine and Katherine brought and bound to the stake back to back. They earnestly desired that they might be bound face to face, but it could not be granted, which grieved them, but they comforted themselves with cheerful words, resolving to suffer death with patience. All the city was gathered together and stood gazing on them and pitying them that so sweet a couple should fall in such fatal extremity, the poor souls ashamed and hanging down their heads, expecting every minute the beginning of their martyrdom.

As thus the fire was ready to be brought, came the Lord High Admiral of Tunis by, and seeing such a concourse demanded the cause. The people told him as much as they knew. He on his foot-cloth came to the stake and looking upon them, seeing them so lovely, asked of them of what country they were. "Of Sicilia, sir," quoth Jacomine. With that the Admiral staring earnestly in his face called to his remembrance the favor of old Jacomine his father. "Of what place in Sicilia, my friend?" quoth he. "Of Palermo." "Thy name?" quoth the Admiral. "Jacomine," quoth he. "Why thou art not," answered the Lord, "the son of Jacomine Pierro?" "Yes," quoth he, "and this the daughter of Alexander Bartolo. And if," quoth Jacomine, "you knew these families, do but so much for us as to speak to the King that we may be bound face to face and so die; for life, that we hold in scorn."

Although the tormentors were appointed to dispatch them by an hour, yet the Lord Admiral charged them not to put any fire to the wood till his return, which they promised, and away galloped the Admiral as a madman through the streets to the King's palace, where when he came he found the King in a great rage discoursing to his lords the villainy of Katherine, that admitted a stranger into her. The Admiral, giving a little way to the King's rage, at last stepped in and on his knee begged the lives of the two lovers, but the King three times denied him. Then said the Admiral, "O Royal Sir, if you put these two strangers to death, you are cruel to yourself, false to the honor of all kings and princes in the world. I know you would not be called an ungrateful man to have ten kingdoms more given you. If you kill this sweet couple, if you part the dear hearts of these two lovers, the sun cannot look upon a man more unthankful, for when you were beaten out of Tunis and got what forces you could of adjacent countries to reinstate you, old Jacomine Pierro, this young man's father, and noble Alexander Bartolo, the young woman's father, both Sicilians and of Palermo, with hazard of their lives and fortunes fought for you and set you up again. And will you now be the murderer of the two old men by taking from them such dear jewels as their children? Look into yourself and see what the fire of love has wrought in you. In them it has been so powerful that to embrace one another freely they forsook country, father, mother, friends, and have run into a thousand dangers, and must fire now be the last, utterly to consume them?"

The King hearing this, sent for them, their pardon in the market-place was proclaimed, people shouted for joy, the lovers were with unspeakable joy brought before the King, and kneeling down to his mercy, he embraced them, kissed her, and made much of him. And charging them to commend him to both their parents, him he knighted and lading a ship with treasure, sent them home, where they were with all gladness welcomed. The two fathers upon this grew friends, the lovers were married and lived in Palermo in the abundance of all happiness.

* * *

This tale of the two Sicilian lovers being ended made all the company as glad to hear how well the lovers sped as before they were sorrowful to consider their tragical misfortunes. A seaman therefore sitting in the company said thus, "My masters, because this gentleman the scholar (who can deliver his mind better than I) hath told his tale of two lovers taken by pirates at sea, I pray give me my turn too, being a creature living by the sea, and let my tale be next." "With all our hearts," they all cried. "My story shall be but short," said the seaman, "because here's a merry gang and many of us." But first look upon the mariner and behold his face.

THE DESCRIPTION OF THE SEAMAN

He was a fellow brown of hue,
Sunburnt in his face he grew,
Well-set, strong of limb and bone,
Yet tight and yare as any one;
Skill he had, the helm to steer,
And o'th'ship's deck to domineer,
Each tacking, little rope and line,
He could find when was no shine
Of sun or moon; in stormiest night
He could trim his sails aright.
His compass conned he at his heart,
And knew what winds blew in each part;
The stars he had as true by name,
As if at font he heard the same,
And with his finger's point could tell
In what house every star did dwell,
As here the Great Bear, that the Small
Such stars are fixed, such shoot and fall
(At least they seemen down to slide)

There does the bright Orion glide,
The Tailor's Yard, and the stars seven,
Is he acquainted with in heaven,
As well as those seven stars (the sign
To tell within is sold good wine).
Shelves, rocks, gulfs, quicksands, could he shun,
And i'th'main ocean his course run,
By his good needle and his card,
Blow grumbling Boreas ne'er so hard.

THE SEAMAN'S TALE

In the University of Oxford, there sometime lived an ancient gentleman, a great scholar, and of great reverence in respect of his age and places of office and honor which he had borne amongst the colleges, his name (for he was in the winter of his life knighted) being Sir Lionel Aspernoone. Lands and livings he had in some shires in England. Three beautiful daughters he had, married to gentlemen of good rank in Cambridgeshire, and but one only son, whose name was Sebastian.

The old knight being struck by sickness and feeling that his weak and weatherbeaten ship of life could not hold out long, prepared himself for a better journey, and to put in at heaven. So that settling his estate, he by his last will and testament appointed his son to be his sole executor and instated him in all his lands as his heir. Yet lying on his death bed, after many other instructions how to bear sail in the troubles of the world, he enjoined him to print in his memory three precepts especially. The first was, when he did marry, he charged him, albeit he should never so much love or dote upon the beauty of his wife, yet never to trust her with his private intentions, nor by any means to reveal any secret of consequence to her. The second was, that if he never was blest with a son of his own, then not to adopt another man's child as one of his begetting, nor at any hand to make him his heir. The third, that he should never put himself into subjection to any man, of what greatness or power soever, that ruled the helm of his country as pleased himself, but rather to trim the sails of his own ship and be a faithful pilot in the navigation of his business by himself.

These precepts being given and the son vowing to perform them, the old knight dies. The son having a mass of wealth, revenues, plate and jewels, and being in the prime of his youth, lusty, brave, and full of spirit, thought it much to lie alone, but to marry some fair gentlewoman, youthful as himself and of good parentage; for her portion he cared not, so he might please his eyes. And because he would tempt any such creature the sooner to come under the lee of wedlock, he with his money got him a knighthood, so that who now but Sir Sebastian Aspernoone? Fate or Fortune, or I know not whether it were the little blind God of Love, brought him to a delicate creature, a young gentlewoman (a squire's daughter), her name Elinora. The wooing voyage was not long, but married they were and our young knight is not more fond of his life than of his dear love.

Long they lived and as long they loved, but that cable at which all married couples lie at anchor with most content was wanting, for in three or four years together they had no children. Hereupon others to their faces much pitying that two such goodly trees should have fair leaves and no fruit, and they themselves lying in their bed as much grieving that they ploughed up a sea which returned them no traffic. In the end they both resolved to take some other man's son, of poor parentage, and to make him his heir, contrary to the commandment which his dying father enjoined him to. A young stripling therefore he took from a poor widow; handsome was the boy in face, well-proportioned in body, and of a good ingenious disposition. His name was Marmaduke, who, as with his supposed father and mother he grew up in years, so he in behavior pleased them the more.

This jovial knight, living at ease, fullness of Fortune, and glutted with all the pleasures of his own country, as hawking, hunting, horse-racing, cock-fighting, and such like, besides seeing plays at London and bringing his wife acquainted with other ladies and gentlewomen and the fine girls of the city, was weary of England and determined with his lady and adopted son to see some other countries. In the lifetime of his father he had been in Italy and could a little speak the language. Italy he called the garden of the world, and thither should his lady go with him to behold the beauties of the brave bona robas there. Money by exchange is to be sent him, rich apparel for him and his wife, with a competent number of followers, are provided; a ship gotten to carry them, and aboard, aboard, hey! cry the mariners, so that in a short time, the wind being fair, with a merry gale they arrive in some part of Tuscany.

The great Duke of Tuscany was a young gentleman and exceedingly given to the pastime of hawking. The report of this English knight and his fair lady coming to the Duke's ear, he was desirous to see them. They are sent for to his court, and come; the Duke in discoursing with Aspernoone (liking him the better because he spoke Italian), conceived so extraordinary an affection towards him, his sweet proportion, behavior, and graces of mind, that in a short time the Duke made him his companion, his play-fellow, his second self, and he so won upon the gallant Italian courtiers, that he lay as dear in their bosoms as in the Duke's.

Hawking he loved as well as the Duke did, and in that pastime he showed himself both expert and noble. Upon a day when our English cavaliero was retired alone into his private chamber, he began to call to mind the favors of this princely Duke, with what a brave gale of wind and in how smooth a sea he sailed in his court, doted on by the Duke, embraced by his courtiers, admired by the Italians, and beloved of all men. Then he considered how blessed he was in Marmaduke his adopted son; he praised his feature, his love, obedience, and humble yet generous carriage towards him. And upon these two thoughts, "Lord," said he, "what a strange man was my father! How was he abused in his judgment! How did his deathbed make him dote! What melancholy, or rather what madness, got up to the top of his brains to read such a Bedlam lecture to me when he was to go out of the world, and I to enjoy all that he left behind him. Why did he most foolishly enjoin me if I had no children of mine own never to make a stranger mine heir? Is not Marmaduke a good boy, an obedient son, a loving youth? And why forsooth must my wise dad forbid me to subject myself to any lord or to fawn upon his humors, who commanded his people and state as best pleased himself? Can any king upon earth so dote upon his favorite as this great Prince of Tuscany does upon me? Does the Duke keep his subjects in awe, and am I not master of his passions? He is the Duke, but his diadem stands on my head. Well, my dead father, I am glad thou art gone because thou wert no wiser. Two of thy lessons I find idle, vain, false, and unnecessary to be listened to. And what's the third? Marry, forsooth, never to trust my wife with a secret. Alas, good old man, let worms make much of thy head, for thy wits were worm-eaten before thou wentst to thy grave. Not trust my wife? Is she not fair? Is she not young? Is she not honest? Does she not lie with me? Does she not love me? Does she not kiss me? Does she not embrace me? Yet I keep any secret from her! Has she not left her country, father, mother, brothers, sisters, aunts, uncles, cousins, and friends to follow me, and shall anything lie in my heart which I will not utter to her? No, no, I must trust her, and I will trust her."

Upon this resolution he left his chamber and went to the Duke's palace, and coming to the perch where stood a great number of brave falcons, he took the fairest secretly away (such a one as the Duke esteemed above all the rest), brought her to a dear friend's house and there left the bird, closely to be kept from the eyes of any man, till he himself either came or sent for it by some good token. This done, he goes to his own lodging, and having falcons there wrings off the neck of one, and bringing it to his lady, said, "Sweetheart, thou knowest the Duke loves me, yet of that fondness of his am I so weary it kills my heart, that I cannot when I would be master of myself and my own man. To get therefore some more liberty I have done a trick to make him fall out with me, and so for a while I shall be at quiet." "What trick?" quoth she. "I have," said he, "killed his best falcon. Look you, here 'tis. I pray thee dress it and we both will eat it, for the Duke's sake, and drink to his health in rich Palermo wine."

"Oh," cried out the lady, "Sir Sebastian, what have you done? You are lost forever. This is a villainy not to be pardoned. Call you this a trick? A trick to break your own neck, to have a stiletto in your guts, or poison in an Italian salad. If the Duke hears of this, thou, silly creature, art but a dead man." "Peace, fool," quoth he, "none in the world knows it but you and I." "Nay," says she, "for my part, cut out my tongue when I prate of it." Well, the falcon is dressed, they both sit down, but she swore not a bit of it should go into her belly. He entreated and entreated her but to taste it. No, if he would hang himself she would not. Hereupon he up with his hand and struck her o'er the face; the blow made her mad, the falcon flew out of the platter, the trenchers one way, table-cloth another, plate at his head, glasses to the ground, and crying for anger swore to be even with him. The next morning (nothing being able for all he could do to please her all night) she went to the Duke and told him how basely her husband had recompensed his favors in killing his best falcon. The Duke, enraged, without hearing him speak condemns him to be hanged and his goods to be confiscated and divided into three parts: the first to his wife, the second to his son, and the third to any one that would be his hangman. He was to die the next day.

The sweet-faced youth his son pondering in his mind the sentence of the Duke made account if his father were hanged it would be better for him. He would to England and live like a gentleman. He was no father of his; all his lands should be his, and hang let him. Nothing stuck in his stomach so much as that any stranger that had a heart to bestride his father's gallows and turn him off should have a third share in the goods as well as he or his mother. To his mother he therefore comes and says, "Mother, is it not better that I play the hangman and with ease dispatch my father, and so gain that third part, which some base Italian rogue will else carry from you and me too?" "Yes, sweet boy," quoth she, "I like thy care; thou art a loving son, and when thy father is under thy fingers, dispatch him as soon as thou canst to put him out of his pain." The gracious stripling went to the Duke, begged the hangman's office, which the Duke between a frown and a smile granted him.

The knight being in prison, ironed, and expecting death, sent privately to his friend that had the falcon, entreating him when he saw him pass by to execution to step to the Duke and entreat him to hear the prisoner speak before he died. This his friend did. Then Sir Sebastian, seeing the villainy of a wife and what misery he was fallen into by being subject to such a prince, remembered his father's counsel and said, "Now, dear father, I see mine own folly and thy wisdom. A wife thou biddest me not trust, nor to warm myself too much in the sunshine of a great man's favor; I have done both and now must lose my honor, my fortunes, and my life. Let thy ghost pardon my disobedience in not following thy counsel; when I am dead I will come to thee and on my knees beg thy pardon."

Being in the midst of this meditation, his officious and most dutiful crackrope son Marmaduke came to the prison with a company of brown bills to guard him, and like an ungrateful, hard-hearted rascal, said thus, "Father, sithence it is the Duke's will you should die, into whose hands can you safelier fall than into mine, your dutiful son's; my intents are honest, loving, and good, not to suffer some rakehelly stranger to share with my mother, your dear lady, in your goods, if any such rascal will undertake to hang you. Now, my dear father, to keep off any such to lay a foul hand upon you, what think you if I (because your goods shall still continue in your name) take that charitable office upon me?" "Oh, my careful son," quoth he, "what father had ever such a forward child? Hadst thou not come thus to comfort me, I had died unwillingly, where now I shall take my leave of the world with a joyful heart, because at my parting I shall last of all receive a kind farewell from thee. Do then thine office," and so kissing him, the boy took a cord and put it about his father's neck, counselling him to die like a gentleman and an Englishman.

Away is the prisoner led with his hands bound and the rope about his neck, and being brought to the gibbet, the ladder he mounts; the young hangman sat straddling on his wooden curtal and bid his father pray, who turning his face to the people told them why he was to die and that his wife's tongue had brought him to his end, his only comfort being that his sweet son would rid him out of the miseries of the world. Some wept to hear him, some were ready to fling stones at the hangman, but were prevented by the prisoner's friend that kept the falcon, for he going to the angry Duke begged on his knees for his friend's life, wept, and offered to be hanged himself if the Englishman were not innocent.

Upon this he was fetched from the gallows, his cord still about his neck, and the carnifex his son attending. Being before the Duke, he falling humbly on the earth acknowledged the infinite favors and high graces received from his Highness, he being unworthy the least, and that he should deserve to be torn in pieces by wild horses should he so spitefully stir up a tempest in the calm bosom of so excellent a prince. What he had done was to try conclusions upon three precepts which his dying father enjoined him to (and so relates them). The falcon untouched and unbruised was presented, the Duke fell about his neck, forgave him, and was ashamed of his rash believing a false woman. The halter was snatched from the father's neck and cast about his cursed son's, the Duke commanding the boy should forthwith be trussed up. But the noble knight begged his pardon, which was at his request granted, and then thus he spoke to him, "O my adopted son, because I have loved thee I cannot hate thee, yet how to bestow thee I know not. Albeit thou gladly wouldst have been my executioner, I will be thy preserver. Yet how am I troubled in my mind. If I save thee, I shall be pointed at for a fool; if I cast thee away, heaven will chide me for spilling thy blood. I will neither be pitiful nor cruel, neither punish thee nor pardon thee; between these two will I go. Take thou this cord bound now about thy neck and instead of my goods which thou didst gape for, be that thy portion. Wear it ever to tell thee thou art a villain, and so never see me more." He went away cursing. The lady took a nunnery and both died miserably, and then the knight lived merrily.

FINIS

THE TRIUMPHS OF GODS REVENGE AGAINST THE CRYING AND EXECRABLE SINNE OF (WILFUL AND PREMEDITATED) MURTHER

With His Miraculous Discoveries, and Severe Punishment thereof.

In Thirty several
TRAGICAL HISTORIES:
(Digested into Six Books) committed in divers Countreys beyond the SEAS.

Never Published or Imprinted in any other Language.

Histories which contain great variety of Mournful and Memorable Accidents, Historical, Moral, and Divine: very necessary to restrain and deterr us from that bloody sin which in these out days makes so ample and large a Progression.

With a TABLE of all the several Letters and Challenges contained in the whole Six Books.

Written by JOHN REYNOLDS.
The Fifth and Last Edition.

London, Printed by A. M. for William Lee, and are to be sold by George Sawbridg . . . and other Booksellers in London and Westminster, 1670.

JOHN REYNOLDS: DON JUAN AND MARSILLIA (1635)

Though in the seventeenth century the Puritan spirit on the whole scorned fiction as a means for promulgating its pious exhortations, there were nevertheless a few notable instances of its working in the narrative medium. One example is *The Triumphs of God's Revenge,* a collection of thirty rather long stories, all very similar in tone and content to "Don Juan and Marsillia," the sixteenth in the collection. Of the author, John Reynolds, we know nothing, beyond what we may glean from reading between the lines of his stories, except that he was a merchant of Essex; of his book we may say that it was truly one of the most popular collections of stories in its age. The first fifteen stories made their appearance in separately published groups of five each in 1621, 1622, and 1623; after a delay of some years, the whole series of thirty came out in 1635 in folio. Subsequently a number of reprints followed down to the year 1736, with the usual earmarks attending on a very popular book: the text acquired copperplate illustrations to each story in 1657, was pirated in 1661, enlarged in 1679 by the addition of ten more tales by another hand, and finally was abridged in 1685. Not surprisingly, the book was read in New England as well as in old England.

Reynolds apparently wrote his book as a counterblast against what he considered the growing wickedness of his times. His titlepage sums up admirably and, in spite of its length, rather succinctly both the content and purpose of his work:

> The Triumphs of God's Revenge, Against the Crying and Execrable Sin of . . . Murder; with His Miraculous Discoveries and Severe Punishment Thereof: In Thirty Several Tragical Histories (Digested into Six Books) Committed in Divers Countries Beyond the Seas. Never Now Published or Imprinted in Any other Language. Histories Which Contain Great Variety of . . . Memorable Accidents, Historical, Amorous, Moral, and Divine, Very Necessary to Restrain and Deter Us from That Bloody Sin, Which, in These Our Days, Makes so Ample and Large a Progression.

The content of the stories is at first somewhat surprising in view of this stated aim: they offer as passionately bloody and desperate a set of deeds and villains as one could hope to find, and somewhat anachronistically breathe the spirit of the "tragical" tales of the 1570s and 1580s. But if the vogue for tales of erotic violence had died out by the time Reynolds wrote, the taste for similar material was kept alive on the stage. Indeed, it is not impossible that the drama, wicked though it may have seemed to him, influenced Reynolds in his writing; his stories are full of intensely dramatic situations and he enjoys developing them scene by scene. The synopses which the author provides for his stories read like abstracts of plays.

In spite of the fact that his presentation at times seems designed to let him (and his readers) eat his cake and have it too, we need not deny Reynolds his genuine sincerity in wishing to preach the consequences of wickedness. He certainly seems truly shocked himself at what he is writing at times, and he even apologizes to the reader for the unpleasant necessity of telling what he has to tell. It is perhaps surprising that he did not attempt to bring the lessons home more forcefully by setting his scene at home instead of abroad—everybody knew that foreigners with Latinized names were usually prone to evil—he may have thought such a succession of purple wickedness localized in England and perpetrated by English men and women would not be accepted as veracious history. Perhaps a touch of the artist came to both temper and reinforce the moralist in Reynolds.

The text which follows is based on a copy of the 1670 edition in the editor's possession.

DON JUAN AND MARSILLIA

BY JOHN REYNOLDS

Idiaques causeth his son Don Juan to marry Marsillia, and then commits adultery and incest with her. She makes her father-in-law Idiaques to poison his own old wife Honoria; and likewise makes her own brother De Perez to kill her chambermaid Mathurina. Don Juan afterwards kills De Perez in a duel; Marsillia hath her brains dashed out by a horse, and her body is afterwards condemned to be burnt. Idiaques is beheaded; his body likewise consumed to ashes, and thrown into the air.

Let malice be never so secretly contrived and the shedding of innocent blood never so wretchedly perpetrated, yet as our conscience is to us a thousand witnesses, so God is to us a thousand consciences, first to bring it to light, and then their authors to deserved punishments for the same, when they least dream or think thereof. For as there is no peace to the wicked, so they shall find no peace or tranquillity here on earth, either with God or his creatures, because if they would conceal it, yet the very fowls of the air, yea, the stones and timbers of their chambers will detect it: for the earth or air will give them no breath nor being, but they shall hang between both, because, by these their foul and deplorable facts, they have made themselves unworthy of either. A powerful example, and a pitiful precedent whereof we shall behold in this ensuing history, where some wretched miscreants and graceless creatures making themselves guilty of those bloody crimes (by the immediate revenge and justice of God) received exemplary and condign punishments for the same. May we read it to God's glory, to the comfort of our hearts, and the instruction of our souls.

In the city of Santarem, which (by tract of time and corruption of speech) some term Saint Aren, and which (after Lisbon) is one of the richest and best people of Portugal, there dwelt a gentleman of some fifty-five years old, nobly descended and of a great estate and means, named Don Sebastian Idiaques, whose wife and lady being aged, of well near fifty years, was termed Dona Honoria: and well she deserved that honorable name, for all sorts of virtues and honors made her youth famous and her age glorious to all Portugal and Spain. They had lived together in the bonds of matrimony almost thirty years, with much honor, content, and felicity, and for the fruits of their affection and marriage they had two sons and four daughters, but God in his pleasure and providence (for some reserved reasons best known to his All-Divine Majesty) took from earth to Heaven all their daughters and one of their sons, so as now they have left them but one son, named Don Juan, a gallant young gentleman, of some twenty-five years old, of disposition brave and generous, who after his first youthful education under his father had his chief breeding under the Duke of Braganza, to whom he was first a page and then a chief gentleman retaining to him: whom, in regard of the death of his brother and sisters, his father called home unto him to be his comfort and consolation, and the prop and stay of his age, as also of the lady his mother, who had formerly acted a great part in grief and a mournful one in sorrow for the death of her children; and indeed Don Juan, this son of theirs, for all regards of courtship was held to be a complete gallant and of the prime cavaliers of Portugal.

As for Idiaques the father, though in all the course and progress of his life, and in all the life and conduction of his actions he betrayed many moral and generous virtues, yet as one discordant string mars the harmony of the best-tuned instrument and the consent of the sweetest melody and music, and as one foul vice is naturally subject and fatally incident to eclipse and drown many rich and fair virtues, so in this his old age, when time had honored him with white hairs, he debauched himself so much and so sottishly sacrificed his irregular affections to heart-killing concupiscence and his exorbitant desires to soul-destroying adultery, that he very often made himself a false and inconstant husband to his wife, and a true, yea, too true a friend to courtesans and strumpets. His virtuous Lady Honoria extremely grieves hereat, that now in his later years he should thus lasciviously forget himself, both towards her and towards God. She useth all persuasions, prayers and tears to dissuade and divert him from it, but seeing that all proves vain, and that he rather proves worse than better thereat, her discretion makes her brook it with as much patience as she can; and therefore she seems not to see or know that whereof, to her grief and discontent, she cannot be ignorant. But here comes an accident which will breed both of them, and their son Don Juan, misery of all sides.

Some six leagues from Santarem was a wonderful fair young gentlewoman being a widow, aged but of twenty-two years, Dona Marsillia, well descended, but by her late deceased husband left but small means, yet she bears out her port bravely and maintains herself highly and gallantly; and indeed she is the prime young lady for beauty in all those parts. Now the base ambassadors and emissaries of Idiaques his beastly and obscene lust (the true vipers and cankers of commonweals) give him notice of her and of her singular beauty, as well foreseeing and knowing that it would be sweet and pleasing news unto him. He visits and courts her, but as young as she is, she puts him off with peremptory refusals, and in virtuous and modest terms checks his age for this his lascivious suit and motion to her. But he is as constant in his affection to her as she is disdainful to him, for his heart is so ensnared and entangled in the fetters of her fresh and delicate beauty, that although she refuse him, yet he will not forsake her; but after many pursuits and visits she, at last well perceiving that he loved her tenderly and dearly, and that he still most importunately frequented her house and company, she as a subtle and cunning young gentlewoman tells him plainly and privately that she will acquaint him with a secret of her heart and a request of her mind and affection, which if he will cause to be performed, she then vows she will forever be at his disposing and command. Idiaques, thinking that she will crave some money of him, or some yearly pension or annuity, he constantly promiseth to grant and perform her request; so she, taking time at advantage, and first swearing him to secrecy, then with many smiles and blushes she tells him that if ever he think to enjoy her love and herself, he must use the means to marry his son Don Juan to her, which being effected, she with much pretended show of piety and affection religiously swears to him that she will never have the power or will to deny him anything, but that his requests shall be to her as so many commands, and (but only for himself) if his son Don Juan be her husband, she with many imprecations and asseverations swears that she will sacrifice her best blood and life rather than distain his bed or offer him the least shadow of any scandal or dishonor whatsoever.

Idiaques wondreth with admiration and admires with wonder at this her strange proposition, the which he finds so knotty and intricate as measuring grace by nature, his judgment by his lust and concupiscence, and his soul by his affections, he knows not what to say or do herein, so he answereth her with more love than wisdom, and for that time leaves her in general terms. He goes home, walks pensively in his garden, and there consults pro and con on this business; fain he would preserve his son's honor and keep the honor of his bed immaculate, but then the sweet roses and lilies of Marsillia's youth and beauty act wonders in his heart and bear down all other reasons and considerations before it. He visits her again and again, but he finds her inviolably constant in her former resolution. All the

Don Juan and Marsillia

favor and courtesy which he can gain from her are a few extorted kisses, which so inflame and set on fire his aged heart and affections, as at last, like a graceless father, he faithfully promiseth her to use his best art and power to procure his son to marry her.

To which end he takes him aside, and in the softest and sweetest terms he can devise, paints out Marsillia's praises and virtues to him in the purest and rarest colors, adding withal, that although she be not exceeding rich, yet that her personage is so exquisite and her perfections so excellent as that she every way meriteth to be wife to a prince. Don Juan (by what fatal fortune, I know not) relisheth this motion of his father, to seek the Lady Marsillia for his wife, with much delight and joy, and far the more and the sooner in regard he, in divers companies, hath formerly heard the fame of her beauty extolled and the glories of her virtues advanced to the sky. So he takes time of his father to consider hereof, and rides over sometimes with him to Saint Estienne to visit her. He finds her wonderful fair and beautiful and wonderful coy, of a very sweet and majestical carriage and of a delicate and curious speech, fit baits to ensnare the heart and to betray the judgment of a more solid understanding than that of Don Juan. She acts her part as wisely as he doth amorously and passionately, for the more she makes show to retire and conceal her affection from him, the more he is provoked to advance and discover his to her, but he cannot be so much enamored of her beauty as she is with the great estate of lands and domains whereunto God and his father have made him heir.

Whiles thus the father privately and the son publicly are seeking to make Marsillia his wife, the old Lady Honoria the mother, by many strong reasons seeks to divert him from her. She hath perfect notice of her husband's long and often frequenting of Marsillia's house and company, and therefore fearing the vanity of his age and doubting the frailty of her youth and chastity, her jealousy and judgment at last finds out and concludes that his familiarity with her is far greater than honor can warrant or honesty allow of. Upon which foundation she in her discontented looks and silence betrays unto her son Don Juan her constant and resolute averseness from him to marry her, the which she peremptorily and religiously forbids him upon her blessing, adding withal that if he marry her there will infallibly more miseries and calamities attend their nuptials than as yet it is possible for him either to know or conceive; the which she prays him to read in her looks and silence, to remember it when he sees her not, and to take it as the truest advice and securest counsel of a dear mother to her only son.

Don Juan ruminates on these speeches and advice of his mother as if there were some deep abstruse mystery or ambiguous oracle contained and hidden therein, the which because he hath equal reason as well to fear that this match of his with Marsillia may prove fatal as to hope and believe that it may prove fortunate, he makes a stand thereat, as vowing to proceed therein with advisement and not with temerity and precipitation, and so forbears for a month or two to visit her.

But the more the son flies off in his affection from Marsillia, the more doth she do the like from his father in requital, whereat he grieves with discontent and she seems to bite her lip with sorrow. Idiaques chargeth his son to tell him from whence this his sudden strangeness and unkindness towards Marsillia proceedeth, the which he answers with a modest excuse as favoring more of discretion than disobedience, but yet wholly concealeth his mother's counsel and advice to him from his father, the which notwithstanding he vehemently suspecteth it proceeds from her and her jealousy. Marsillia is enraged to see herself deprived of Don Juan, whom in her ambitious thoughts, hopes, and wishes, she had already made her husband; and howsoever Idiaques his father seeks to conceal and palliate this business towards her, yet she believes it is his fault and not his son's. She lays it to his charge and, knitting her brows, she conjureth him to tell her from whence his son's unkindness to her proceeds. He tells her he is confident that it is his old mother who hath diverted him from her, whereat she is exceedingly enraged; when seeing this old lecher so open and plain with her, she, soothing him up with many kisses, tells him that this old beldam his wife must first be in Heaven before he can hope to enjoy her, or she his son here on earth, when (being allured and provoked by the treacherous suggestions and bloody temptations of the Devil) she proffers him to visit her and to poison her, which he opposeth and contradicteth; and contrary to all reason and sense, and repugnant to all humanity and Christianity, yea, to nature and grace (as a husband fitter for the Devil than for this good old lady his wife), he undertakes and promiseth her speedily to perform it himself.

Yea, the Devil is now so strong with him and he with the Devil that because he loves Marsillia, therefore he must hate his own dear wife and virtuous Lady Honoria; and because he hates her, therefore he must poison her, a lewd part of a man, a fouler one of a Christian, but a most hellish and bloody one of a husband to his own wife, who ought to be near and dear unto him as being his own flesh and blood, yea, the other half of himself. He cannot content himself to seek to abuse and betray his son, but he must also murder the mother. So wanting the fear of God before his eyes, and replete with as much impiety and cruelty as he was devoid of all grace, he is resolute in this his hellish rage and malice against her, and so to please his young strumpet he will send this good old lady his wife to Heaven in a bloody coffin. So, without thinking of Heaven or Hell, or of God or his soul, he procures strong poison and, acting the part of a Fury of Hell and a member of the Devil, he as a wretched and execrable husband administreth it to her in preserved barbaries, which he saw her usually to love and eat, whereof within three days after she dies, to the extreme grief and sorrow of her son Don Juan, who bitterly wept for this his mother's hasty and unexpected death. But the manner thereof he knows not, and indeed doth no way in the world either doubt or suspect thereof.

His father Idiaques makes a counterfeit show of sorrow and mourning to the world for the death of his wife, but God in his due time will unmask this his wretched hypocrisy and detect and revenge this his execrable and deplorable murder. Now as soon as Marsillia is advertised of the Lady Honoria's death, she, not able to contain her joys, doth infinitely triumph thereat, and within less than two months after her burial, Idiaques and Marsillia work so politicly with Don Juan as he marries Marsillia, although his mother's advice to him in the garden does still run in his mind and thoughts.

And now he brings home his lustful spouse and wife to his lewd and lascivious father's house at Santarem, where (I write with horror and shame) he most beastly and inhumanely very often commits adultery and incest with her, and they act it so close that for the first year or two his son Don Juan hath no news or inkling thereof. And now Marsillia governeth and rules all, yea, her incontinency with her father Idiaques makes her so audacious and impudent as she commands not only his house but himself, and domineers most proudly and imperiously over all his servants. Her waiting-maid Mathurina observes and takes exact and curious notice of her young lady's lustful and unlawful familiarity with her father-in-law Idiaques, the which her mistress understanding, she extremely beats her for the same, and twice whips her stark naked in her chamber and drags her about by her hair, although this poor young gentlewoman with a world of tears and prayers begs her to desist and give over.

God hath many ways and means to set forth his glory in detecting of crimes and punishing of offenders, yea, he is now pleased to make use of this young maiden's discontent and choler against her incensed lady and mistress, for we shall see her pay dear for this cruelty and tyranny of hers towards her. For Mathurina, being a gentlewoman by birth, she takes those blows and severe usage of her lady in so ill part, and lodgeth it so deeply in her heart and memory as she vows her revenge shall requite part of that her cruelty and tyranny towards her. Whereupon, with more haste than discretion, and with more malice than fidelity, she in her hot blood goes to Don Juan, her young master, tells him of this foul business betwixt his young wife and old father, to the disgrace and shame of nature, and makes him see and know his own dishonor in their brutish and beastly adultery and incest.

Don Juan extremely grieves hereat, yea, he is both amazed and astonished at the report of this unnatural crime, as well of his young wife as aged father. He cannot refrain from choler and tears hereat, to see himself thus infinitely abused by her beauty and betrayed by his lust; and if it be a beastly, yea, profane part, for one man and friend to offer it to another, how much more for a father to offer it to his own, yea, to his only son? He expected more goodness from her youth and grace from his age, but as his wife hath hereby infringed her vow and oath of wedlock, so hath his wretched father exceeded and broken those rules and precepts of nature; yea, he is so nettled with the report and inflamed with the consideration and memory hereof, that he abhors her infidelity and in his heart and soul detesteth his inhumanity. So as the knowledge hereof doth so justly incense him against her and exasperate himself against him, that resolving to right his own honor as much as they have blemished and ruined it, and therein their own, he scorns to be an eye-witness, much less an accessary of this his shame and their infamy. So he here enters into a discreet and generous consultation with himself, how to bear himself in this strange and dishonorable accident. When, perceiving and finding that both his wife and father had by this their beastly adultery and incest made themselves forever unworthy of his sight and company, he here forever disdaining henceforth to see her or speak with him, very suddenly, upon a second conference and examination of Mathurina, who stood firmly and virtuously to her former deposition and accusation against them, takes horse and rides away from Santarem to Lisbon, where, providing himself of moneys and other necessaries, he takes post for Spain and there builds up his residence and stay at the Court of Madrid, where we will for a while leave him, to speak of other accidents which fall out in the course of this history.

Idiaques, seeing the sudden departure of his son, and Marsillia of her husband Don Juan, and being both assured that he had some secret notice and intelligence of their lascivious dalliances and affection, he exceedingly grieves and she extremely storms thereat, because they know that this foul scandal will wholly reflect and fall upon them, and now by this his sudden and discontented departure from them will be made notorious and apparent to all the world. But how to remedy it they know not, because he hath neither signified him where he is gone nor when he will return, the which the more betrayeth his small respect and discovereth his implacable displeasure towards them. But as there is no malice and revenge to that of a woman, so Marsillia, assuring herself that it was her maid Mathurina who, to the prejudice and scandal of her honor, had unlocked this mystery to her husband Don Juan, she enters into so furious a rage and so outrageous a fury against her as she provides herself of rods and intends the next morn ere she be stirring out of her bed to wreak her fierce anger and indignation upon her. But this sharp and severe resolution of hers is not so closely carried by her but Mathurina hath perfect notice thereof, and to prevent this intended correction and cruelty of her incensed lady and mistress, she the night before takes horse and so rides home to the town of Saint Saviors to her father, and there from point to point relateth him all which had passed betwixt her lady and herself, and betwixt her husband, herself, and her father-in-law, and that now disdaining any more to serve her, as her body so her tongue is at liberty; for she is not and she will not be sparing to publish her mistress's and her father-in-law's shameful familiarity and adultery together. But this indiscretion and licentious folly of her tongue will cost her far dearer than she thinks of or expecteth.

For her late lady and mistress Marsillia, being now perfectly certified of Mathurina's infidelity and treachery towards her in the point of her dishonor and shame, she (to salve up her reputation and to provide for the same) will not wholly rely upon her own judgment and discretion herein, but resolves to acquaint Don Alonso de Perez, her own only brother, herewith, and to crave his aid and assistance, as also his advice, betwixt whom and herself there was so strict a league and sympathy of affection that, if reports be true, I write it to their shame and mine own sorrow, it exceeded the bounds of nature and honor, and of modesty and chastity; only the presumption hereof is great and pregnant, for if there had not been some extraordinary ties and obligations betwixt them, it is rather to be believed than doubted that for her sake and service he would never have so freely exposed himself to such imminent fears and dangers as we shall immediately see him do; and although of honor and disposition he were brave and generous, yet I believe he would not have undertaken it.

For the reader must understand that to this brother of hers, De Perez, Marsillia speedily acquaints the infidelity and treachery of her maid Mathurina's tongue against her fame and honor, which had so unfortunately occasioned her husband, Don Juan's, discontented departure from her. She protesteth most seriously and deeply to him of her and her father-in-law Idiaques's innocency in this pretended crime and scandal; tells him that Mathurina is the only author and reporter thereof and therefore, till that base and lewd tongue of her be eternally stopped and silenced, she shall never enjoy any true content to her heart or peace to her thoughts and mind, either in this world or this life. When his affection to her makes him to yield such confidence to her speeches, vows, and complaints, that he holds them to be as true as Scripture, yea, and the undoubted oracles of truth and innocency; when to please and satisfy her he bids her be of good cheer and comfort and that he will speedily take such order that Mathurina's scandalous tongue shall not long eclipse her fame, or any further blemish the luster of her reputation; when this base and bloody gentleman, De Perez, to make good this his promise to his execrable sister, he secretly rides over to Saint Saviors and there by night waiting near her father's door, when Mathurina would chance to issue forth, he in a dark night espying her, without any more ceremony or further expostulation, runs her through the body two several times, whereof, poor harmless innocent soul, she falls down dead to his feet without once speaking or crying. So De Perez seeing her dispatched, he presently takes horse, which his man there led by him and posts away to Santarem, being neither seen nor discovered. And thus this bloody villain most deplorably inbrued his guilty hands in the innocent blood of this virtuous young gentlewoman, who never offended him in thought, word, or deed, in all her life; and albeit that her father, Signor Pedro de Castello, makes curious inquiry and research for the murderer of his daughter, yet De Perez, mounted at advantage, hath recovered Santarem in safety. But God will in due time find him out to his shame and confusion; yea, and then when his security and courage little dreams thereof.

As soon as he comes to Santarem, he acquaints his sister Marsillia of his dispatching of Mathurina, who is infinitely glad thereof and extremely thankful to him for the same. And now her malice and revenge looks wholly on her husband Don Juan for offering her this unkind and scandalous indignity of his departure and for tacitly taxing and condemning her of incontinency with his father Idiaques, which her adulterous heart and incestuous soul and conscience doth inwardly confess and acknowledge, though the perfidiousness and hypocrisy of her false tongue do publicly deny it, yea, with her best art and policy, and with her sweetest smiles and kisses, she hath by this time so exasperated this her bloody brother against him that, out of his vanity and folly, he profanely vows unto God and seriously protests and swears unto her, that if he knew where he were, for the vindication of her honor and innocency he would ride to him and fight with him, except he would resolve to give him and her some valuable reparation and honorable satisfaction to the contrary, which he seals and confirms to her with many amorous smiles and lascivious kisses. But as we are commonly never nearer danger than when we think ourselves farthest from it, so God being as secret in his decrees as sacred in his resolutions, we shall shortly see De Perez to verify and confirm it in himself, for as in the heat of this his sottish affection to his sister he is ready to fight with her husband Don Juan, if he knew where he was, lo, the news of his residence in Madrid, when he least thinks thereof, is accidently brought him by a servant of his own, whom he purposely sends to Santarem with these two ensuing letters, the one sent and directed from him to his father, the other to his wife Marsillia. That to his father spake thus:

DON JUAN TO IDIAQUES

Was there no other woman of the whole world for you to abuse but my wife, and was your faith so weak with God, or you so strong with the Devil, that you must therefore make her your strumpet because she was my wife? If nature would not inform you that I am your son, yet you are my father, and it should have taught you to have been more natural to me, more honorable to the world, more respectful to yourself, and more religious to God, and not to have made yourself guilty of these foul crimes of adultery and incest with her, the least whereof is so odious to God and so detestable to men that I want terms, not tears, to express it. For hereby as you have made my shame infinite, so likewise you have made your own infamy eternal, the consideration whereof gives me so much grief and the remembrance sorrow that holding you forever unworthy of my sight and she of my company, I have therefore left Portugal for Spain and forsaken Santarem to live and die here in Madrid. And when hereafter God shall be so merciful to your soul to let you see that the winter of your age makes you fitter for your grave than for my bed, and for your winding-sheet than for my wife, you will then hold this resolution and proceeding of mine towards you as honorable as this your crime to me is unnatural, the which if you henceforth redeem not with an ocean of bitter tears and a world of repentant and religious prayers to God, I rather fear than doubt that His Divine Majesty will make you as miserable as you have made me unfortunate.

Don Juan

His letter to his wife spoke this language:

DON JUAN TO MARSILLIA

What Devil possessed thy heart with lust and thy soul with impiety to make thee violate thy vow which thou gavest me in marriage, by committing those damnable sins of adultery and incest with my natural father? And if the consideration that I was thy husband could not in grace deter thee from it, yet, methinks, the remembrance that he was my father should in nature have made thee both to abhor and detest it. And although my tender affection to thee and filial obedience to him made me expect more goodness from thy youth and grace from his age, yet God is a just judge, and your hearts are true witnesses of these your unnatural crimes and foul ingratitude towards me, which hath cast so great a blemish and scandal on mine honor and dashed my joys with so many untimely afflictions and unmerited sorrows, that I have abandoned Portugal and Santarem for thy sake and betaken myself to live and die in Madrid in Spain for mine; where I will strive to make myself as contented as discontent can make me and so leave this thy enormous crime and the punishment thereof to God, in whom thou mayest be happy but without whom thou wilt assuredly be miserable. And think to what just calamities and miseries thine inordinate lusts and lascivious desires and delights have already deservedly reduced and exposed thee, since henceforth I will no more esteem thee my wife, or myself thy husband, and that God will assuredly look on thee with an eye of indignation, and the world of contempt.

Don Juan

Idiaques having read and perused that letter of his son and Marsillia this of her husband Don Juan, they are therewith so touched in heart with shame and stung in conscience with sorrow for their foul crimes of adultery and incest that they blush each at other, and both of them most bitterly curse the name and memory of Mathurina, who was the first author of this report to him and which so suddenly incensed him and occasioned his departure. So to bear up their reputations to the world and their fames to him, they resolve (without either asking leave or pardon of God) to justify their innocency hereof to him, and so to pursue and solicit his return. To which effect they write and return him by his own servant their two several letters in answer of his: whereof that of Idiaques his father carried this message.

IDIAQUES TO DON JUAN

Thou dost wrong thyself and the truth, God and thy conscience, and thy wife and me, in so basely taxing us of those foul sins of incest and adultery, whereof we are as truly innocent as thou falsely and maliciously deemest us guilty. For I have not abused her nor made her my strumpet, although not God but the Devil, in the slanderous tongue of Mathurina, hath made thee to believe so. For nature hath taught me more grace and goodness nor so little impiety, for that

I know they are sins more odious to God and detestable to the world than either thy sorrows can express or thy anger depaint me. Neither have I made thy shame infinite, or canst thou make my infamy visible, much less eternal, although herein thou show me thy indignation, together with thy disobedience, by leaving Portugal for Spain, and Santarem for Madrid, whereof because thou wilt not make thy duty, I will content myself to make thy discretion judge betwixt us, if thou have not done me more wrong than either thyself and the truth right herein, and offered a scandal likewise to thy wife's honor, who made thy company her chiefest joy, as now she doth thy absence her sharpest misery and affliction. How then can I go to my grave with content, when thou forsakest her bed with malice and my house with disdain? My innocency in thy accusation hath no way irritated or offended God, and, if therefore with tears and prayers thou wilt resolve to ask God, thy wife, and me forgiveness for this thy foul crime and monstrous ingratitude towards us, then mine arms shall be as open as ever they have been to receive and my house to welcome thee, and therein thou shalt make thyself as truly happy as thou falsely and uncharitably thinkest that God will make me miserable.

Idiaques

The answer of his wife Marsillia to him was couched in these terms:

MARSILLIA TO DON JUAN

It is neither lust nor the Devil which can make me infringe or violate my vow given thee in marriage, although thou art as far from the truth as from God to believe it. But how shall I hope that thy tongue will excuse me of these thy pretended foul crimes of adultery and incest when, to my astonishment and grief, I see thou likewise condemnest thy old father to be guilty thereof with me? And if this be any way affection to me, or obedience to him, let all other husbands judge and all sons define and determine. But to return thee truth for thy falsehood: his age expected and deserved more grace, and my youth and virtues more affection and goodness from thee than to have believed those false calumnies and impostures upon the bare report and malicious relation of my handmaid Mathurina, which are now dead with her and are as false as thy rashness and her revenge makes thee believe them true, for it is neither I nor thy father who have any way blemished thine honor or vanquished thy joys, but rather thyself and thy too too unkind and hasty departure from Santarem to Madrid, which, to the prejudice of the truth and of my content and honor, hath occasioned it. For my heart and soul will testify both with me and for me that my affection and constancy is both as spotless, firm, and true to thee as thy jealousy is false towards myself, and therefore as thou leavest my pretended crime, so will I thy real ingratitude both to time and to God, and if yet thou wilt be so wilfully cruel to live from me and consequently not to esteem me thy wife, yet as it is my zeal and duty to beg and pray thee to return to me, so I will make it my integrity and conscience still to hold and love thee for my husband, and so preserving my heart for thee as I do my soul for God, I hope with assurance and confidence that I shall have no cause to fear either his indignation or the world's contempt, in regard I have neither merited the one nor deserved the other.

Marsillia

Upon the writing and contents of these two letters of Idiaques to his son and of Marsillia to her husband Don Juan the reader may please to observe and remember with how much policy and with how little piety they seek to over-veil and deny these their adulteries and incest towards him, thereby to make their actions and themselves appear as innocent as they are guilty both to them and to God. But God, being the author of truth and the father of light, and whose sacred throne and tribunal is environed with more glorious suns than we see glistering stars in the firmament, He will one day unmask this their hypocrisy and bring their foul sins of adultery and incest both to light and punishment. Now as Marsillia is exorbitantly lascivious in her affection to her brother De Perez, and he reciprocally so to her, so with a world of false sighs and tears she shows him her letter and her father-in-law's Idiaques, which they had sent to her husband Don Juan to Madrid, and with many female oaths and asseverations protesteth to him of both their innocencies herein, which her brother believes, yea, her feigned sorrows and false tears had so far trenched and gained upon his credulity that in contemplation and commiseration of her wrongs, he was then so vain and impious as once he thought to have carried these two letters himself into Spain and there to have fought with Don Juan for the reparation of his sister's honor. But at last leaving passion to consult with reason and temerity again to be vanquished and swayed by judgment, first that these letters of theirs should see Spain and then to attend his brother-in-law Don Juan his answer to them, and as he shall therein find him either perverse or flexible to his wife's desires and his father's expectations, he will then accordingly bear himself and his resolutions towards him, and hereon both himself and his sister Marsillia do joyfully determine and conclude.

So Don Juan's own servant returns these two aforesaid letters from Santarem to Madrid to his master, who, breaking up the seals and perusing them, he doth not a little wonder at his wife's impudency and his father's impiety, in so strongly denying these their foul crimes to him. But he is not a little astonished and withal afflicted and grieved when he falls upon that point and branch of his wife's letter which reports the death of her maid Mathurina, for in his heart and conscience he now verily thinks and believes that his wife in her inveterate malice and revenge to her hath caused her to be murdered and sent her to Heaven in a bloody winding-sheet. But, alas, if it be so, how to revoke or remedy it he cannot tell. Once therefore he was minded to have neglected their letters and so to have answered them with perpetual oblivion and a disdainful silence. But then again considering with himself that this might rather increase than extenuate their hopes of his return, he betakes himself to his study, where, taking pen and paper, he neglecting his father traceth his wife this letter in answer of hers, and again sends it her into Portugal by his own servant, which assureth them of his resolution not to return.

DON JUAN TO MARSILLIA

The receipt of thy second letter hath not diminished but confirmed and augmented my confidence of my father's shame and thy infamy in your foul sins of adultery and incest perpetrated against me, and, which is worse, against God, so that I am fully resolved forever to forsake his house and thy company, and to live and die here in Madrid, as grief and disconsolation will permit me. For I prize the unjust apology of thy pretended innocency at so low a rate and value it at so base an esteem as I disdain it for thy sake and thyself for thine own. I do as much grieve as I both doubt and fear thou rejoicest at thy maid Mathurina's death; and as I am ignorant of the manner, so if my father and thyself have been the cause thereof, you have then all the reasons of the world to believe that God (who is as just in his resolutions as sacred in his decrees) will in the end revenge it to his glory, and punish it to your confusion.

Don Juan

This letter of his doth inflame his wife with malice and indignation, for now her father and she see these their lustful and lascivious crimes seated and confirmed in his belief, and his stay in Spain fixed in his anger and eternized in his resolution, when as close as they bear it, yet knowing full well that the world will take notice of it and ere long make it their public scandal and infamy. He is so devoid of grace and she of goodness that to prevent it he wisheth his son in Heaven with his mother and she her old father-in-law in grave with her young maid Mathurina. But these vain hopes of theirs may deceive them, which as yet they two are not so wise to think of nor so cautious or religious to consider, but rather more resembling brute beasts than Christians, they still continue their obscene and incestuous pleasures, the which I take small delight or pleasure to mention in regard of modesty or to repeat in respect of nature and honor.

Here Marsillia again repairs to her brother De Perez as to her oracle and champion; she shows him both these two last letters of her husband to his father and herself, and conjureth his best advice and speediest assistance for the recovering of her honor in that of her husband's affection and company, or else that she were freed from him and he out of this life and this world, that so her scandal and wrongs might die with him and forever be raked up in the dust of his grave and buried with him in eternal oblivion and silence. De Perez in heart and mind is so much his sister's as he is no more himself, when making his affection do homage to her beauty and his judgment and resolution to pay tribute to his affection he prays her to refer this charge and business to the care of his discharge; when giving her many kisses and willing her to read his heart in his eyes, he gives her the good night and the next morning being impatient of all delays he takes one Signor Gasper Lopez, a noble gentleman and a valiant intimate friend of his with him, and relating him his intent to fight with his brother Don Juan and the cause thereof. They undertake this journey of Spain and so arrive at Madrid, where Lopez prays Perez to make him his second in that

Don Juan and Marsillia

duel. De Perez thanks him for this his affection but tells him he will hazard himself but not his friend; so, writing a challenge to Don Juan, he seals it up and requesteth Lopez to deliver it to him and the same night to return him his answer. Lopez accordingly finds out Don Juan in his own chamber and gives it to him in fair and discreet terms, who, wondering it came from his brother-in-law De Perez, but far more to understand that he was now in Madrid, he no way dreaming of a challenge but rather thinking that his wife his sister had sent him thither to him to work her reconciliation and consequently his return to her to Santarem, he hastily breaks up the seals thereof, finds it charged with this language.

DE PEREZ TO DON JUAN

I have seen thy inveterate malice to thy wife my sister in thy false and scandalous letters to her, and Portugal hath read it in thy sudden and choleric departure from her into Spain; wherefore, considering what she is to thee, and I to her, I hold myself bound, both in honor and blood, to make her wrongs and quarrels mine. To which end I have left Santarem to find thee out here in Madrid, purposely to pray thee to meet me tomorrow betwixt six and seven in the morning, at the farthest west end of the Prado, with thy rapier, a confident gentleman of thy friends, and thy surgeon, without a second, where thou shalt find me to attend thy coming and relying upon the equity of my cause and the ingratitude and infamy of thine. I make no doubt but to teach Don Juan what it is for him, without ground or truth, to cast a base aspersion and wrongful blemish upon the luster of his wife and my sister, the Lady Marsillia's honor, whose descent and extraction is as good as thine, and her education and virtues far more sublime and excellent. Thy generosity obligeth thee to the honorable performance hereof, and mine honor reciprocally to perform this obligation.

De Perez

Don Juan having received and perused this challenge of his brother-in-law De Perez and finding his furious resolution to exceed his judgment, he, knowing himself innocent, his cause good, and his courage and valor every way to be superior to the other's, highly disdaining to be out-braved by any nobleman or gentleman breathing in the point of honor and generosity, he with a cheerful countenance returns Lopez to his brother De Perez with this accepting answer.

DON JUAN TO DE PEREZ

My hatred to Marsillia and departure from her was justly occasioned through her treachery and infidelity to me, and therefore my letters to her to that effect are as true as she is false in denying it; notwithstanding, since she is thy sister and my wife, I as much approve of thy affection to her as I condemn thy temerity to me and thy indiscretion to thyself in making her quarrel thine and by forsaking Santarem to fight with me here in Madrid. And because thou shalt see and find that I have as much courage as innocency, I therefore accept of thy challenge and am so far from learning any point of valor of De Perez as to his shame and my glory I hope to teach him, that I have no way cast a false aspersion or blemish on the luster of her reputation, but she on herself; and consequently that I will neither affect her, nor fear thee. For, God lending me life, I will tomorrow break fast with thee at thine own time and place appointed, where my honor and generosity invites me to come, and thine to meet me.

Don Juan

These two inconsiderate gentlemen having thus embarked themselves in the strong resolution of this weak quarrel and rash duel, which earthly honor cannot as justly approve and allow of as divine religion and Christian piety and charity disallow and execrate. Their malice and revenge each to other is so violent and impetuous, that without any thought, either of God or their souls, or of Heaven or Hell, they pass over the night, if not in watchfulness, yet in broken and distracted slumbers, yea, the morn no sooner peeped from Heaven through their windows to their chambers but they leap from their beds to the Prado, where De Perez with his friend Lopez come first on horseback, immediately after them Don Juan in his coach, with a young gentleman his friend, termed Don Richardo de Valdona. So these two duellists, disdaining to be tainted with the least piece of dishonor or shadow of cowardice, they at first sight of each other throw off their doublets, and in their silk stockings and pumps, with their rapiers drawn, they without any further compliment or expostulation approach each other.

But here before they begin to reduce malicious contemplation into bloody action, I hold it fit to inform my reader with a circumstance that now passed between them, wherein doubtless the Providence of God was most conspicuous and apparent. For as by the law and custom both of Spain and Portugal all rapiers should be of one length, yet De Perez curiously casting his vigilant eye upon that of Don Juan, either his fear or his judgment, or both, inform him that that rapier is longer than his, whereat Don Juan grieves far more than De Perez can possibly either rejoice or wonder, for he is so far from any way blemishing his honor with this, or with any other point or shadow of dishonor, as now he gives his rapier to measure, and to write the truth, his is found one inch longer than that of De Perez, when biting his lip for anger he (resembling himself) offers to fight with that either of Lopez or Valdona, which was sufficient reason for one gentleman of honor to give and for another to take. But when he sees that this proffer of his will neither secure De Perez's fear nor confirm his content, then, as a noble and generous gallant he freely exchangeth rapiers with him, gives De Perez the longer, and contents himself to fight with the shorter, whereat De Perez rests satisfied, and well he may, since this action and his receipt thereof doth as much testify Don Juan's glory as his own dishonor and shame; and now they again approach each other to fight.

At their first coming up, Don Juan runs a firm thrust to De Perez's breast, but he, bearing it up with his rapier, runs Don Juan in the cheek towards his right ear, which draws much blood from him, and he in exchange runs De Perez through his shirt sleeve without hurting him. At their second meeting they again close without hurting each other and so part fair without offering any other violence. At their third assault De Perez runs Don Juan through the brawn of his left arm, who in exchange requites him with a deep wound in his right side, from whence issued much blood; and now they breathe to recover wind, and to the judgments of Lopez and Valdona, as also of their surgeons, they hitherto are equal in valor and almost in fortune. So, although these spectators do of both sides earnestly entreat them to desist and give over, yet they cannot, they will not, be so easily or so soon reconciled each to other.

So after a little pausing and breathing, they with courage and resolution fall to it afresh, and at this their fourth encounter De Perez gives Don Juan a deep wound in his left shoulder, and he requites him with another in exchange in the neck; and although by this time their several wounds hath engrained their white shirts with great effusion of their scarlet blood, yet they are so brave, so generous, or rather so inhumane and malicious, that they will not yet give over, as if they meant and resolved rather to make death fear them than they any way to fear death; but their fifth close will prove more fatal, for now, after they had judiciously traversed their ground, thereby to deceive each other of the disadvantage of the sun, whiles De Perez directs a full thrust to Don Juan's breast, he bravely and skilfully warding it, in requital thereof runs him clean through the body, a little below his right pap, when closing nimbly with him and pursuing the point of his good fortunes he whips up his heels and so nails him to the ground, when he had not the strength to beg his life of Don Juan, and God knows he much grieved that it was not then in his power to give it him. For this his last wound being desperately mortal, he presently died thereof, having neither the remembrance to call on God, much less to beg mercy of him for his sinful soul, but as he lived abominably and profanely, so he died miserably and wretchedly.

And although I confess it was too great an honor for him to receive his death from so brave a noble gentleman's hands as Don Juan, yet it is a most singular providence and remarkable punishment of God, that he died by the hands of his own lascivious sister's husband, and which is yet more, by his own sword, as if God had formerly decreed and purposely ordained that the self-same sword should give him his death, wherewith so lately and so cruelly he had bereaved that harmless innocent young gentlewoman Mathurina of her life, although in regard of this his foul and lamentable murder, he with less honor and more infamy every way deserved to have died rather by a halter than a sword. But God's providence is as unsearchable as sacred.

Don Juan having rendered thanks to God for this his victory, he out of his noble courtesy and humanity lends Lopez his coach to transport the dead body of his brother-in-law De Perez into the city, and taking his horse in exchange, he by a private way gets home to his lodging. But this their duel is not so secretly carried but within three hours after, all Madrid rattles thereof, who, knowing the combatants to be both of them noble gentlemen of Portugal, it gives cause of general talk and argument of universal envy and admiration in all Spaniards, especially in the nobler sort of soldiers and courtiers. When the very day after that Don Juan had caused this his brother to be decently buried, Lopez repairs to his chamber to him, and in a fair and friendly manner inquires of him if he please to return any letter of this his friend's death and of his own victory to Santarem, to Don Idiaques his father or the Lady Marsillia his wife, and that his best service herein shall attend and wait on his commands. Don Juan thanks Lopez for this his courtesy, but tells him that for some reserved reasons he will send no letter to either of them, but otherwise wisheth him a prosperous return to Portugal.

So Don Juan remains in Madrid, and Lopez returns for Santarem, and there from point to point relates them the issue of that combat, as the victory of his son Don Juan and the death and burial of De Perez, adding withal that he was so reserved and strange that he would write to neither of them hereof. At the relation and knowledge of this mournful news Idiaques cannot refrain from much sorrow, nor Marsillia from bursting forth into bitter tears and lamentations thereat, for, seeing her dear and only brother thus slain by the hand of her own unkind husband, by losing him she knows she hath lost her right arm, and he being dead she knows not to whom to have recourse, either for counsel or assistance or consolation. And yet as much as he sorrows and she grieves at this disastrous accident, they notwithstanding are yet so far from thinking it a blow from Heaven, or from looking either up to God or down to their own sinful hearts, consciences, and souls for the same, that without making any good use or drawing any divine or profitable moral thereof, they still continue their beastly pleasures and damnable adultery and incest together, as if there were no God to see, nor no deserved torments or misery reserved to punish it. But they and we shall immediately see the contrary.

To the great grief of our hearts and compunction of our souls we have in this history seen wretched Idiaques, by the instigation of the Devil, to poison his wife the Lady Honoria and likewise his daughter-in-law Marsillia to have caused her brother De Perez to have cruelly murdered her waiting-maid in the street, as also by the providence of God Don Juan to have slain the said De Perez in the field;

and our curiosity and expectation shall not go far before we shall see the just revenge and punishments of God condignly to surprise wretched Idiaques and graceless Marsillia for the same. For his divine justice contending with his sacred mercy it hath at last prevailed against these their foul and bloody crimes, so now when they are in the midst, yea, in the height and jollity of all these their foul delights and security, like an unlooked for storm and tempest it will suddenly befall them. Life hath but one way to bring us into this world, but Death hath infinite to take us from it; and what is this but a true argument and reason of God's glory and our misery, of his power and of our frailty and weakness? And therefore because we are as replete of sin as he is of sanctity, and as subject to imperfections as all perfections are both properly co-incident and subject to him, it will be an act of moral wisdom and of religious piety in us rather to glorify than examine his sacred providence, and rather to admire than pry into his divine decrees and resolutions. And because his correction and punishment of all sins, especially of this crying and scarlet sin of murder, is as just as secret, and as inscrutable as just, therefore to draw towards the period of this deplorable history, God is first pleased to exercise and begin his judgment on miserable Marsillia and then to finish it in wretched Idiaques. But his divine majesty is likewise pleased and resolved both to impose and make as great a difference in their punishments as he found a parity and conformity in their crimes.

It is Marsillia's pleasure, or to say more truly, the providence and pleasure of God, that she rides from Santarem to Coimbra to visit a sick gentlewoman her cousin-german, who dwelt there, being only accompanied with her man Andrea on horseback and her footboy Piscator to attend her. And as she comes within a small half-league of that town, having sent away her man Andrea before, and her footboy Piscator being a very little distance behind her, there suddenly starts up a hare between, or close to, her horse's legs, which so amazed her horse, which was as hot and proud as the gentlewoman his mistress whom he bore, as coming off with all four, he throws her to the ground, and kicking her with his hind feet at her fall, he strikes her in the forehead and so dasheth out her brains, God so ordaining that she had not the power to speak a word, much less the grace or happiness to repent her of her horrible sins, adultery, incest, and murder. And thus was the lamentable and fearful end which God gave to this graceless young lady, the which I cannot as yet pass over without annexing and remembering one remarkable point and circumstance therein, in which the justice and mercy of God to both sexes, and all ages and degrees of people, doth miraculously resplend and shine forth, for that very horse which threw and killed her was the very same which she formerly lent to her brother De Perez and whereon he rode to Saint Saviors, when he by her instigation killed her waiting-maid Mathurina. Good God, how just and wonderful are thy decrees! Dear Lord, how immense and sacred is thy justice!

But this is but the forerunner and, as it were, but the entrance into a further progression of this history. For as her footboy Piscator extremely wept and bitterly cried at the sight of this mournful and tragical death of his lady and mistress, God had so decreed and provided that the next that passed by and who were sorrowful spectators thereof were two corregidors (or officers of justice) of the city of Coimbra, riding that way in their coach to take the air, who, in compassion of the deplorable death of this fair unknown young gentlewoman, descend their coach, and having inquired and understood of her sorrowful footboy what she was, they then with much respect and humanity cause her dead corpse to be decently laid in their coach, which they shut, and so mounting their servants' horses they return again to Coimbra. From whence they send her man Andrea in all possible post haste to Santarem to acquaint his master and her father-in-law Don Idiaques with the lamentable death of his daughter-in-law Marsillia, and

Don Juan and Marsillia

to pray him to repair speedily thither to them to take order for her burial.

Andrea is no sooner departed for his master but these two corregidors consult on the fatality of this accident and very profitably consider for themselves that the horse who killed her and all her apparel and jewels, by the custom and royalty of their city, were devolved and forfeited to their jurisdiction; to which effect they cause her rings, chains, and bracelets to be taken from her, and then her pockets likewise to be carefully searched for gold and jewels. So as murder cannot be long concealed or undetected, we may therefore here behold the wonderful providence and singular justice of God, for in one of her pockets they find, folded up in a rich cut-work handkerchief, the last letter which her husband Don Juan had written and sent her from Madrid.

At the sight of this letter one of these corregidors is desirous to have it read publicly, but the other, being more humane and respective to the concealing of ladies' secrets which many times prove that of their honors, he contradicts it, till at last God enlightening their judgments and prompting and inspiring their hearts that the perusal of this letter might, peradventure, import and report something which might tend to his service and conduce to his glory, they fall then on a medium betwixt both their opinions and so, withdrawing themselves to a private chamber, they there secretly o'er-read this letter, wherein with admiration and amazement they understand of the obscene adultery and incest of Idiaques with this his daughter-in-law Marsillia, which was the cause of her husband Don Juan his absence from her in Spain. But at length when they proceed farther therein, and so fall upon these words of Don Juan to her in this his letter, "I do as much grieve as I both doubt and fear thou rejoicest at thy handmaid Mathurina's death; and as I am ignorant of the manner, so if my father and thyself have been the cause thereof, you have then all the reasons of the world to believe that God will in the end punish it to your confusion"; then, led by the spirit of God, they both concur in one opinion: that this their adultery and this murder of Mathurina did not only firmly reflect but equally take hold both on Idiaques and Marsillia, and therefore that this her late deplorable and disastrous end was only a blow from God and the very true forerunner and undoubted harbinger of his own to come. When resolving to seize and imprison Idiaques as soon as he should arrive thither to Coimbra, they hushing up this letter and business in their own bosoms, do then hold it fit to send for Marsillia's footman Piscator to come to them, which he speedily doth. They carefully inquire of him if his dead lady had not sometime a waiting gentlewoman named Mathurina; he answered them yes, and that she was lately murdered in the streets of Saint Saviors, and that her murderers were as yet unknown. They demand of him again whose daughter she was; he informs them that her father is a gentleman who dwells in Saint Saviors, and that his name is Signor Pedro de Castello.

Which being as much as they sought for, putting their servants to watch over this footman that he might not escape to give the least inkling of their demands to his old master Idiaques, they presently send away post to Saint Saviors for Castello, and, in honor to justice, these two corregidors, as Christian magistrates, having put all things in order for the vindication of the truth of these deplorable matters, that very night Idiaques arrives at Coimbra and descends from his coach to the house of one of these corregidors, where the dead body of his daughter Marsillia lay; at whose mournful sight, as soon as his passionate grief and sorrow had caused him to shed and sacrifice many rivulets of tears, when he least dreams or thinks thereof, these two corregidors cause him to be seized on and instantly commit him close prisoner, without acquainting him with the cause hereof; where all that night his guilty heart and conscience, as so many fiends and furies, assuring him that it was for poisoning of his own Lady Honoria. There horror and terror, grief and despair and anguish, do act their several parts upon the theater of his soul.

The next morn Castello, Mathurina's father, likewise arrives at Coimbra, to whom the corregidors communicate this letter of Don Juan to his wife, which he sent her from Spain, wherein they tell him the murder of his daughter Mathurina seems probably and strongly to reflect upon Idiaques and his daughter-in-law Marsillia, when they farther acquainting him with her tragical death, as also with his imprisonment, Castello, with a world of tears and cries, exclaims that undoubtedly they were the authors, if not the actors, of his daughter's lamentable murder, and so very passionately and sorrowfully craves justice of them on Idiaques for the same, which they are as willing to grant and perform as he to desire.

So after dinner, in the public tribunal of justice they send for Idiaques legally and juridically there to appear before them; where this sorrowful father, with much passion and more tears, doth strongly accuse him for the murder committed and perpetrated on his daughter Mathurina, the which Idiaques with many high and stout answers denieth. He allegeth many oily words and sugared and silken phrases to justify and apologize his innocency, which these corregidors, led by the finger of God, hold rather to be far more airy than solid and far more plausible than real or true. So they, still remembering his son Don Juan's letter to his wife Marsillia, do, without regard to his quality or age, adjudge him to the rack. The which Idiaques, fearing infinitely more the murder of his own Lady Honoria than that of Mathurina, endures the tortures and torments thereof with a fortitude and resolution far beyond his strength and age, and with an admirable constancy stands firmly to the denial of this fact and accusation. So seeing the rack taken away and himself from the rack, he is therefore very confident and joyful that his danger is likewise o'erpast and o'erblown.

But these vain hopes of his will yet both deceive and in the end betray him, for as yet his conscience hath not made peace with God. For the griefs and sorrows of this mournful father for this lamentable murder of his daughter have now made him both industrious in this solicitation and religious in this his prosecution against Idiaques towards these corregidors, to whom again he becomes an earnest and yet an humble petitioner, that they will give him eight days time more to fortify his accusation, and that all that time he may still remain prisoner without bail or surety; which they finding reasonable and consonant to all equity and law, they freely grant him. When Castello having God for his counsellor and whom in a small time Idiaques shall find for his judge, calling to mind some words of his deceased daughter touching the suspicion of poisoning her old lady by her husband, to make way for this match for Don Juan, he doth no more accuse him for murdering of his daughter Mathurina, but some two days after, he frames and presents a new indictment and accusation to his judges against him for poisoning his old wife the Lady Honoria. Which these judges admiring and wondering at, they then partly, nay, almost confidently believe that there is some great crime and foul fact in this business against Idiaques, which God will in fine detect and bring to light by the solicitation and industry of this honest poor gentleman Castello. So they admit again of his second indictment against him and by virtue hereof convent him before them at their tribunal of justice.

Idiaques understanding hereof, his guilty conscience now denounceth such thundering peals of fear and amazement to his appalled heart and trembling soul as they will give no peace either to himself or to them, and the Devil, who had ever heretofore promised him his best aid and assistance, now flies from him and leaves him to stand or fall to himself. And here it is that his courage begins to fail him and that his fear and shame is almost resolved and ready to proclaim himself guilty of this his last and worst accusation, the poisoning of his own wife the Lady Honoria. But again the hope of life is yet so sweet to him as the fear of death is displeasing and bitter, and therefore, with a wretched resolution and a miserable confidence, he again artificially endeavoreth to blear the eyes of these his judges with his chiefest eloquence and sweetest oratory; who having given him his full career to speak in his own defense and justification, when they perfectly knew he yet spoke not one valuable word or reason, either to defend or justify himself, then one of these clear-sighted corregidors, in the behalf of both them, returns him this grave reply and pious exhortation.

That as they have not the will to accuse him, so they have not the means or power to excuse him, for being at least accessory to both or either of these murders, of his Lady Honoria or Mathurina; that the sudden death of the first, and the violent and untimely one of the last, the voluntary absence of his son Don Juan in Spain, with his killing of De Perez there, and now the fearful and lamentable end of his daughter-in-law Marsillia, whose body is yet unburied and her blood scarce cold, left a dangerous reflection and a pernicious suspicion on his life and actions, at least of adultery and incest if not of murder (whereof his son Don Juan's letter which he wrote to his wife Marsillia, which they have there to show, is a most strong and pregnant witness) and that the least of these crimes are capable to ruin a greater personage than himself; that he could cast no mist of delusion before God's eyes, though he artificially endeavored and labored to cast a veil before theirs; that the shedding of innocent blood was a crying sin, which despite of sorcery and of Hell would, in God's due time, draw down vengeance to earth from Heaven on their authors; that if he were guilty of his accusation, he had no better plea than confession, nor safer remedy than repentance; that contrition is the true mark of a true servant of God, and though we fall to nature and sin as being men, yet we should rise again to grace and righteousness as being Christians; that to deny our crimes is to augment them and consequently their punishments, both on earth and in Hell; and that he was not a Christian but an infidel who would attempt to save his life with the loss of his soul, with many other religious exhortations concurring and looking that way.

But all this notwithstanding, Idiaques his faith and conscience was yet so strong with Satan, and therefore so weak with God, that he left no excuse, policy, or evasion uninvented to blear the eyes of these corregidors, and so to make his innocency to pass current with them. But his eloquence and asseverations cannot prevail with the solidity of their judgments, for God will not suffer them to be led away with words, nor seduced or deluded with shadows. But from the circumference of circumstances they now fly to the center of truth, and to the author and giver, yea, to the life and soul thereof, God. So they again adjudge him to the rack for his second accusation of murder, as they formerly had done to him for his first.

At the pronouncing of which sentence, if we may judge of his heart by his face, he seemed to be much afflicted, appalled, and daunted, which his judges perceiving, before they expose him to his torments, they in honor to his age and quality, but far more to truth and justice, whom they know to be two daughters of Heaven, they now hold it a point of charity and piety to send him two divines to his prison to work upon his conscience and soul, which they do. And God in the depth of his goodness and the richness of his mercy was so mercifully propitious and indulgent to him that he added such efficacy to their persuasions and power to their exhortations as at the very sight of the rack he with tears in his eyes then there confessed unto them, that he was innocent of Mathurina's murder but guilty of poisoning his own wife the Lady Honoria, for the which he said he most heartily and sorrowfully repented himself. Whereupon his judges and the rest present admiring with wonder and praising God with admiration for the detection of this his foul, bloody, and lamentable crime, they pronounce sentence against him: that for expiation thereof, he at eight of the clock the next morning shall have his head cut off at the place of common execution in that town, when Idiaques, who yet adhered so much to Satan that he could never be divested of his sins before he were first deprived of his sinful life, doth yet still flatter himself with some further hope of life, and so he appeals from the judgment and sentence of this court of Coimbra to that of Santarem, as being native and resident thereof; as also because he committed his murder there, for which they (not his competent judges) adjudged him to death. Whereat although the corregidors of Coimbra for the preservation of the privileges of their court and town do obstinately oppose and vehemently contest it, yet at last well knowing, and being conscious with themselves, that smaller towns and courts in Portugal are bound and subject to depend of the greater, they therefore making a virtue of necessity and contenting themselves to give way to that which they cannot remedy, do ordain that Idiaques should be conveyed and tried at Santarem.

But yet before they suffer him to depart their town, they in honor to justice, in wisdom to themselves, and in reputation to their town and court, do seriously and religiously charge him in the name and fear of God to declare truly to them whether his unburied daughter-in-law Marsillia were not likewise accessory with him in poisoning his wife the Lady Honoria, which at first he strongly denies to them. But then they send away for the two divines who had formerly dealt with him and his conscience in prison, who exhort him to carry a white and candid soul to Heaven and threaten him with the torments of Hell-fire if he do not. When with sighs and tears, he confesseth it to them and that it was he himself who administered that poison to his wife, but that his daughter-in-law Marsillia bought it for him. So these judges, upon the validity of this free and solemn confession, in detestation of this her lamentable crime, do reverently resolve to second and glorify God in his judgments towards her, and therefore they presently condemn her dead body to be burnt that afternoon in their market street, the common place of execution, which accordingly is then and there performed in presence of a great concourse of people, who infinitely rejoice that God so miraculously destroyed the life and their judges the body of so execrable a female monster.

By this time we must allow and imagine that old lecher and new murderer Idiaques, by virtue of his appeal, is brought to his own city of Santarem, and I think either with a ridiculous hope or a profane and impious resolution to see whether God will punish him there with death or the Devil preserve and save him from it. He hath many friends in this court who are both great and powerful, and therefore builds all his hopes of life on this reeling quicksand, this snow, this nothing, that his great estate of money and lands will undoubtedly act wonders with them for his pardon. But still he hopes, because still the Devil deceives him.

He is arrived here at Santarem, where this fair city which might heretofore have proved his delight and glory is now reserved for his shame and appointed and destined for his confusion. They cannot brook the sight, much less the cohabitation and company of such monsters of nature and devils incarnate of men, who glory in making themselves guilty of these foul sins and crying crimes, adultery, incest, murder. So that Idiaques, who hath made himself a principal of this number, and a monster of art in these sins, thinking here in Santarem to find more mercy and pity during his life, shall find less of both of them after his death. For the criminal judges of this court, who reverence and honor justice, because justice doth daily and reciprocally perform the like to them, do confirm the sentence of Coimbra, that the next morning he shall lose his head, but in detestation and execration of these foul and bloody crimes, they add this clause and condition thereto, that both his head and body shall be afterwards burnt, and his ashes thrown in the air, which gives matter of talk and admiration, not only to Santarem, but to all Portugal.

And thus most pensively and disconsolately is Idiaques reconveyed to his prison, where churchmen are sent him by the judges of that court, to direct his soul in her flight and transfiguration from earth to Heaven, whom they find, or at least they make, very humble, mournful, and repentant. According to which sentence he is the next morning brought to the place of execution, which for the greater example and terror to others, and of ignominy to himself, was before his own house, wherein he had acted and perpetrated all his enormous crimes. Where the scaffold is no sooner erected, but there flock an infinite number of people from all parts of the city to be spectators of this last scene of his tragedy. He came to the scaffold, between two friars, in a suit of black taffeta, a gown of black wrought tuft-taffeta, and a great white set ruff, which yet could not be whiter than his broad beard. At his ascent on the scaffold, his grave aspect and presence engendered as much sorrow and pity as his beastly crimes did detestation in the hearts and tongues of the people, to whom, after he had a short time kneeled down and prayed, he made a short speech to this effect.

That although the poisoning of his own wife and his adultery with his son's wife were crimes so odious and execrable as had made him unworthy any longer either to tread on earth or to look up unto Heaven, yet although he deserved no favor of his judges for his body, he humbly repented and begged some of God for his soul; and for the more effectual obtaining thereof, he zealously prayed all those who were present to join their prayers to his. He confessed that it was Marsillia's beauty which first, at the instigation of the Devil, drew him to that adultery with her and this poisoning of his own wife Honoria, whereof from his heart and soul he now affirmed he implored remission of God, of the law, of his son Don Juan, and of all the world, and prayed them all to be more godly and less sinful by his example; and so kneeling down and praying a little while to himself, he rose up, and putting off his gown, ruff, and doublet, which he gave to the executioner, he binding his head and eyes with his handkerchief, bade him do his office, which he presently performed and with one blow of the sword made a perpetual double divorce betwixt his head and his shoulders, his body and his soul;

when presently, according to his sentence, both his head and his body were then and there burnt and consumed to fire, and his ashes thrown into the air.

And this was the deplorable life and death of De Perez, Idiaques, and Marsillia, of whom the spectators, according to their several humors and affections, spoke diversely, all condemning the bloody cruelty of De Perez towards innocent Mathurina and of Idiaques towards his virtuous wife Honoria. Again, some pitied and others execrated Marsillia's youth, beauty, and lust; but both sexes and all degrees of people, as so many lines terminating in one center, magnified the providence and justice of God, in so miraculously and condignly cutting off these monsters of nature and bloody butchers of mankind.

And if the curiosity of the reader will yet farther inquire, what afterwards became of Don Juan, the reports of him are different: for at first I heard that his discontent and grief was so great, yea, so extreme for the death of his parents and wife that he cloistered himself up a Capuchin friar in their monastery at Madrid; so contrariwise I have since credibly been informed that he shortly after these disasters left Spain and still lives in Santarem in Portugal in great honor, welfare, and prosperity. But which of these his resolutions are most inclining and adherent to the truth, it passeth beyond my knowledge, and therefore shall come too short of my affirmation.

FINIS

THE MAN
IN THE
MOONE:
OR,
A DISCOURSE
Of a Voyage thither:

By F.G. B.of H.

To which is added *Nuncius Inanimatus*, written in Latin by the same Author, and now Englished by a Person of Worth.

The Second Edition.

LONDON,
Printed for *Joshua Kirton*, at the Signe of the Kings Arms in St. *Pauls.* Church-yard. 1657

BISHOP FRANCIS GODWIN: THE MAN IN THE MOON (1638)

The fantastic voyage, or *voyage imaginaire,* and the description of utopias frequently go hand in hand. The two genres make an obviously useful combination: the setting of the utopia must be in a strange and remote region on the one hand, and on the other the voyage is more entertaining if it leads to some intrinsically interesting land. Godwin's *Man in the Moon* nicely represents this combination of the two elements, though the relation of the voyage itself here predominates, as indeed it should in the first English account of a trip to the moon. Moreover, as Negley and Patrick show, the success of Godwin's book changed the character of seventeenth-century utopias by reviving this very strain of the fantastic voyage, which dates back as far as Iambulus and Euhemerus.

We do of course hear something of lunar society. Godwin seems chiefly interested in the size of the Lunars, as he calls them, equating superiority in height with moral and physical excellence. He is also interested in the language of the men on the moon, in which musical tones seem to be the chief semantic factor, and in their religion, as one might expect from a bishop. In these and other details, such as the absence of laws on the moon, the fact that theft is unknown, that there is little disease and no fear of death, Godwin's book seems to foreshadow *Gulliver's Travels,* and it is usually believed that Swift read the earlier work.

Godwin was also patently interested in science, or, to use a term perhaps more appropriate to seventeenth-century speculation, in natural philosophy. In his considerations of scientific questions he shows a great resemblance to those men, amateur and professional alike, who made up the later founded Royal Society. Whether his notion that migratory birds spend part of the year in the moon is meant to be taken seriously is dubious, but surely his speculations about the Copernican system and his comments on the low lunar gravity seem more than stabs in the dark. Gonsales's weightlessness en route seems a peculiarly modern touch, though we may not think as well of the assumption that hunger, thirst, and fatigue would be unknown to space travellers. But Gonsales throughout remains the indefatigable observer and speculator, wondering always at the what and the how of each new experience with a philosophical bent and seriousness of mind that render his theories as plausible seeming as they are interesting.

The Man in the Moon was first published anonymously in 1638, in an English translation made by one E. M., usually taken to be Edward Mahon. A second edition followed in 1657, but in the meantime a French version had appeared in 1648, whose influence was such as to make many persons later—Edgar Allan Poe and Jules Verne among them—believe the work to be of French origin. In Swift's lifetime an abbreviated version of the text appeared in the Harleian Miscellany under the title of *A View of St. Helena*. The text has been most recently edited by Grant McColley and published in the Smith College Studies in Modern Languages, Vol. XIX, No. 1, 1937. Besides McColley's excellent introduction, commentary on the book may be found in Marjorie Nicolson's *Voyages to the Moon*, New York, 1948, pp. 71–85, and in Glenn Negley and J. Max Patrick, *The Quest for Utopia*, New York, 1952.

The present text is based on a copy of the 1657 edition in the Huntington Library.

THE MAN IN THE MOON

BY BISHOP FRANCIS GODWIN

To the Ingenious Reader

Thou hast here an essay of fancy, where invention is showed with judgment. It was not the author's intention, I presume, to discourse thee into a belief of each particular circumstance. 'Tis fit thou allow him a liberty of conceit, where thou takest to thyself a liberty of judgment. In substance, thou hast here a new discovery of a new world, which perchance may find little better entertainment in thy opinion than that of Columbus at first in the esteem of all men. Yet his then but poor espial of America betrayed unto knowledge so much as hath since increased into a vast plantation, and the then unknown to be now of as large extent as all other the known world.

That there should be antipodes was once thought as great a paradox as now that the moon should be habitable. But the knowledge of this may seem more properly reserved for this our discovering age, in which our Galileos can by advantage of their spectacles gaze the sun into spots and descry mountains in the moon. But this and more in the ensuing discourse I leave to thy candid censure and the faithful relation of the little eye-witness, our great discoverer.

E. M.

THE MAN IN THE MOON

It is well enough and sufficiently known to all the countries of Andalusia that I, Domingo Gonsales, was born of noble parentage and that in the renowned city of Seville, to wit, in the year 1552, my father's name being Therrando Gonsales (that was near kinsman by the mother's side unto Don Pedro Sanchez, that worthy Count of Almenara), and as for my mother, she was the daughter of the reverend and famous lawyer, Otho Perez de Salaveda, Governor of Barcelona, and Corregidor of Biscaya. Being the youngest of seventeen children they had, I was put to school and intended by them unto the Church. But our Lord, purposing to use my service in matters of far other nature and quality, inspired me with spending some time in the wars.

It was at the time that Don Fernando, the noble and thrice renowned Duke of Alva, was sent into the Low Countries, viz. the year of grace 1568. I then following the current of my foresaid desire, leaving the University of Salamanca, whither my parents had sent me, without giving knowledge unto any of my dearest friends, got me through France unto Antwerp, where in the month of June 1569 I arrived in something poor estate. For having sold my books and bedding, with such other stuff as I had, which happily yielded me some thirty ducats, and borrowed of my father's friends some twenty more, I bought me a little nag, with which I travelled more thriftily than young gentlemen are wont ordinarily to do, until at last arriving within a league of Antwerp, certain of the cursed Guises set upon me and bereaved me of horse, money, and all. Whereupon I was fain, through want and necessity, to enter into the service of Marshal Cossé, a French nobleman, whom I served truly in honorable place, although mine enemies gave it out to my disgrace that I was his horse-keeper's boy. But for that matter I shall refer myself unto the report of the Count Mansfield, Monsieur Tavier, and other men of known worth and estimation, who have often testified unto many of good credit yet living the very truth in that behalf, which indeed is this: that Monsieur Cossé, who about that time had been sent ambassador unto the Duke of Alva, Governor of the Low Countries, he, I say, understanding the nobility of my birth and my late mis-

The Man in the Moon

fortune, thinking it would be no small honor to him to have a Spaniard of that quality about him, furnished me with horse, armor, and whatsoever I wanted, using my service in nothing so much (after once I had learned the French tongue) as writing his letters, because my hand indeed was then very fair. In the time of war, if upon necessity I now and then dressed mine own horse, it ought not to be cast in my teeth, seeing I hold it the part of a gentleman for setting forward the service of his prince to submit himself unto the vilest office.

The first expedition I was in was against the Prince of Orange, at what time the Marshal my friend aforesaid met him making a road into France and putting him to flight chased him even unto the walls of Cambrai. It was my good hap at that time to defeat a horseman of the enemy by killing his horse with my pistol, which falling upon his leg so as he could not stir, he yielded himself to my mercy; but I knowing mine own weakness of body and seeing him a lusty tall fellow thought it my surest way to dispatch him, which having done, I rifled him of a chain, money and other things to the value of two hundred ducats. No sooner was that money in my purse, but I began to resume the remembrance of my nobility, and giving unto Monsieur Cossé the *besa las manos*, I got myself immediately unto the Duke's court, where were divers of my kindred that (now they saw my purse full of good crowns) were ready enough to take knowledge of me. By their means I was received into pay and in process of time obtained a good degree of favor with the Duke, who sometimes would jest a little more broadly at my personage than I could well brook. For although I must acknowledge my stature to be so little as no man there is living I think less, yet inasmuch as it was the work of God, and not mine, he ought not to have made that a means to dishonor a gentleman withal. And those things which have happened unto me may be an example that great and wonderful things may be performed by most unlikely bodies if the mind be good and the blessing of our Lord do second and follow the endeavors of the same.

Well, howsoever the Duke's merriments went against my stomach, I framed myself the best I could to dissemble my discontent, and by such my patience accommodating myself also unto some other his humors, so won his favor as at his departure home into Spain, whither I attended him, the year 1573, by his favor and some other accidents (I will say nothing of my own industry, wherein I was not wanting to myself) I was able to carry home in my purse the value of three hundred crowns. At my return home my parents, that were marvellously displeased with my departure, received me with great joy, and the rather for that they saw I brought with me means to maintain myself without their charge, having a portion sufficient of mine own, so that they needed not to defalc anything from my brethren or sisters for my setting up. But fearing I would spend it as lightly as I got it, they never did leave importuning me till I must needs marry the daughter of a Portuguese, a merchant of Lisbon, a man of great wealth and dealings, called John Figueres. Therein I satisfied their desire, and putting not only my marriage money but also a good part of mine own stock into the hands of my father-in-law, or such as he wished me unto, I lived in good sort, even like a gentleman, with great content for divers years.

At last it fell out that some disagreement happened between me and one Pedro Delgades, a gentleman of my kin, the causes whereof are needless to be related, but so far this dissension grew between us as when no mediation of friends could appease the same, into the field we went together alone with our rapiers, where my chance was to kill him, being a man of great strength and tall stature. But what I wanted of him in strength I supplied with courage, and my nimbleness more than countervailed his stature. This fact being committed in Carmona, I fled with all the speed I could to Lisbon, thinking to lurk with some friend of my father-in-law's till the matter might be compounded and a course taken for a sentence of acquittal by consent of the prosecutors. This matter fell out in the year 1596, even at that time that a certain great count of ours came home from the West Indies in triumphant manner, boasting and sending out his declarations in print of a great victory he had obtained against the English near the Isle of Pines. Whereas the truth is, he got of the English nothing at all in that voyage but blows and a great loss.

Would to God that lying and vanity had been all the faults he had! His covetousness was like to be my utter undoing, although since it hath proved a means of eternizing my name forever with all posterity, I verily hope, and to the unspeakable good of all mortal men that in succeeding ages the world shall have, if at the leastwise it may please God that I do return safe home again into my country to give perfect instructions how those admirable devices, and past all credit of possibility which I have lighted upon, may be imparted unto public use. You shall then see men to fly from place to place in the air; you shall be able, without moving or travelling of any creature, to send messages in an instant many miles off and receive answer again immediately; you shall be able to declare your mind presently unto your friend, being in some private and remote place of a populous city, with a number of such like things; but that which far surpasseth all the rest, you shall have notice of a new world, of many most rare and incredible secrets of nature that all the philosophers of former ages could never so much as dream of. But I must be advised how I be over-liberal in publishing these wonderful mysteries till the sages of our State have considered how far the use of these things may stand with the policy and good government of our country, as also with the Fathers of the Church, how the publication of them may not prove prejudicial to the affairs of the Catholic faith and religion, which I am taught (by those wonders I have seen above any mortal man that hath lived in many ages past) with all my best endeavors to advance, without all respect of temporal good; and so I hope I shall.

But to go forward with my narration, so it was that the bragging captain above named made show of great discontentment for the death of the said Delgades, who was indeed some kin unto him. Howbeit he would have been entreated, so that I would have given him no less than a thousand ducats for his share to have put up his pipes and surceased all suit in his kinsman's behalf. I had by this time, besides a wife, two sons whom I liked not to beggar by satisfying the desire of this covetous braggart and the rest, and therefore constrained of necessity to take another course, I put myself in a cood carrack that went for the East Indies, taking with me the worth of two thousand ducats to traffic withal, being yet able to leave so much more for the estate of my wife and children, whatsoever might become of me and the goods I carried with me.

In the Indies I prospered exceeding well, bestowing my stock in jewels, namely, for the most part in diamonds, emeralds, and great pearl, of which I had such penniworths as my stock being safely returned into Spain (so I heard it was) must needs yield ten for one. But myself upon my way homeward, soon after we had doubled the east of Buena Speranza, fell grievously sick for many days, making account by the same sickness to end my life, as undoubtedly I had done, had we not (even then as we did) recovered the same blessed Isle of St. Helena, the only paradise, I think, that the earth yieldeth. Of the healthfulness of the air there, the fruitfulness of the soil, and the abundance of all manner of things necessary for sustaining the life of man, what should I speak, seeing there is scant a boy in all Spain that hath not heard of the same? I cannot but wonder that our king in his wisdom hath not thought fit to plant a colony and to fortify it, being a place so necessary for refreshing of all travellers out of the Indies, so as it is hardly possible to make a voyage thence without touching there.

It is situate in the altitude of sixteen degrees to the

south and is about three leagues in compass, having no firm land or continent within three hundred leagues, nay not so much as an island within a hundred leagues of the same, so that it may seem a miracle of nature that out of so huge and tempestuous an ocean such a little piece of ground should arise and discover itself. Upon the south side there is a very good harbor, and near unto the same divers edifices built by the Portingales to entertain passengers, amongst the which there is a pretty chapel handsomely beautified with a tower, having a fair bell in the same. Near unto this housing there is a pretty brook of excellent fresh water, divers fair walks made by hand and set along upon both sides with fruit trees, especially oranges, lemons, pomegranates, almonds, and the like, which bear fruit all the year long, as do also the fig trees, vines, pear trees (whereof there are divers sorts), palmettoes, cocoas, olives, plums; also I have seen there such as we call damaxaelas, but few; as for apples I dare say there are none at all. Of garden herbs there is good store, as of parsley, coleworts, rosemary, melons, gourds, lettuce, and the like; corn likewise growing of itself, incredible plenty, as wheat, pease, barley, and almost all kinds of pulse; but chiefly it aboundeth with cattle and fowl, as goats, swine, sheep, and horses, partridges, wild hens, pheasants, pigeons, and wild fowl beyond all credit. Especially there are to be seen about the months of February and March huge flocks of a certain kind of wild swans (of which I shall have cause hereafter to speak more) that like unto our cuckoos and nightingales at a certain season of the year do vanish away and are no more to be seen.

On this blessed island did they set me ashore with a Negro to attend me, where, praised be God, I recovered my health and continued there for the space of one whole year, solacing myself for lack of human society with birds and brute beasts. As for Diego (so was the blackamoor called), he was constrained to live at the west end of the island in a cave, because being always together, victuals would not have fallen out so plenty; if the hunting or fowling of the one had succeeded well, the other would find means to invite him, but if it were scant with both, we were fain both to bestir ourselves. Marry, that fell out very seldom, for that no creatures there do any whit more fear a man than they do a goat or a cow, by reason thereof I found means easily to make tame divers sorts both of birds and beasts, which I did in short time only by muzzling them, so as till they came either unto me or else Diego, they could not feed.

At first I took great pleasure in a kind of partridges, of which I made great use, as also of a tame fox I had. For whensoever I had any occasion to confer with Diego, I would take me one of them, being hungry, and tying a note about his neck, beat him from me, whereupon straight they would away to the cave of Diego, and if they found him not there, still would they beat up and down all the west end of the island till they had hunted him out; yet this kind of conveyance, not being without some inconvenience, needless here to be recited, after a certain space I persuaded Diego (who though he were a fellow of good parts was ever content to be ruled by me) to remove his habitation unto a promontory or cape upon the northwest part of the island, being, though a league off yet within sight of my house and chapel, and then, so long as the weather was fair, we could at all times by signals declare our minds each to other in an instant, either by night or by day, which was a thing I took great pleasure in.

If in the night season I would signify anything to him, I used to set up a light in the tower or place where our bell hung; it is a pretty large room, having a fair window well glazed and the walls within being plastered were exceeding white, by reason thereof, though the light were but small, it gave a great show, as also it would have done much further off, if need had been. This light after I had let stand some half hour, I used to cover; and then if I saw any signal of light again from my companion at the cape, I knew that he waited for my notice, which perceiving, by hiding and showing my light, according to a certain rule

The Man in the Moon

and agreement between us, I certified him at pleasure what I list. The like course I took in the day to advertise him of my pleasure, sometimes by smoke, sometimes by dust, sometimes by a more refined and more effectual way.

But this art containeth more mysteries than are to be set down in few words. Hereafter I will perhaps afford a discourse for it of purpose, assuring myself that it may prove exceedingly profitable unto mankind, being rightly used and well employed, for that which a messenger cannot perform in many days this may dispatch in a piece of an hour. Well, I notwithstanding after a while grew weary of it, as being too painful for me, and betook me again to my winged messengers.

Upon the seashore, especially about the mouth of our river, I found great store of a certain kind of wild swan (before mentioned) feeding almost altogether upon the prey, and (that which is somewhat strange) partly of fish, partly of birds, having (which is also no less strange) one foot with claws, talons, and pounces, like an eagle, and the other whole, like a swan or water-fowl. These birds using to breed there in infinite numbers, I took some thirty or forty young ones of them, and bred them up by hand, partly for my recreation, partly also as having in my head some rudiments of that device which afterward I put in practice. These being strong and able to continue a great flight, I taught them first to come at call afar off, not using any noise but only the show of a white cloth. And surely in them I found it true that is delivered by Plutarch, how that *animalia carnivora*, they are *dociliora quam alterius cuiusvis generis*. It were a wonder to tell what tricks I had taught them by that time they were a quarter old; amongst other things I used them by little and little to fly with burdens wherein I found them able above all credit, and brought them to that pass as that a white sheet being displayed unto them by Diego upon the side of a hill, they would carry from me unto him bread, flesh, or any other thing I list to send and upon the like call return unto me again.

Having prevailed thus far, I began to cast in my head how I might do to join a number of them together in bearing of some great burden, which, if I could bring to pass, I might enable a man to fly and be carried in the air to some certain place safe and without hurt. In this cogitation having much labored my wits and made some trial, I found by experience that if many were put to the bearing of one great burden, by reason it was not possible all of them should rise together just in one instant, the first that raised himself upon his wings finding himself stayed by a weight heavier than he could move or stir, would by and by give over, as also would the second, third, and all the rest. I devised therefore at last a means how each of them might rise carrying but his own proportion of weight only, and it was thus.

I fastened about every one of my gansas a little pulley of cork, and putting a string through it of meet length, I fastened the one end thereof unto a block almost of eight pound weight, unto the other end of the string I tied a poise weighing some two pound, which being done, and causing the signal to be erected, they presently rose all, being four in number, and carried away my block unto the place appointed. This falling out according to my hope and desire, I made proof afterwards, but using the help of two or three birds more, in a lamb, whose happiness I much envied, that he should be the first living creature to take possession of such a device.

At last after divers trials, I was surprised with a great longing to cause myself to be carried in like sort. Diego my Moor was likewise possessed with the same desire, and but that otherwise I loved him well and had need of his help, I should have taken that his ambitious affection in very evil part, for I hold it far more honor to have been the first flying man than to be another Neptune that first adventured to sail upon the sea. Howbeit, not seeming to take notice of the mark he aimed at, I only told him (which also I take to be true) that all my gansas were not of sufficient strength to carry him, being a man, though of no

The Man in the Moon

great stature, yet twice my weight at least. So upon a time having provided all things necessary, I placed myself with all my trinkets upon the top of a rock at the river's mouth and putting myself at full sea upon an engine (the description whereof ensueth) I caused Diego to advance his signal; whereupon my birds presently arose, twenty-five in number, and carried me over lustily to the other rock on the other side, being about a quarter of a league.

The reason why I chose that time and place was that I thought somewhat might perchance fall out in this enterprise contrary to my expectation, in which case I assured myself the worst that could be was but to fall into the water, where being able to swim well I hoped to receive little or no hurt in my fall. But when I was once over in safety, O how did my heart even swell with joy and admiration of mine own invention! How often did I wish myself in the midst of Spain, that speedily I might fill the world with the fame of my glory and renown! Every hour wished I with great longing for the Indian fleet to take me home with them, but they stayed (by what mischance I do not know) three months beyond the accustomed time.

At last they came, being in number three carracks sore weather-beaten, their people being for the most part sick and exceeding weak, so as they were constrained to refresh themselves in our island one whole month.

The captain of our admiral was called Alphonso de Xima, a valiant man, wise, and desirous of renown, and worthy better fortune than afterward befell him. Unto him I opened the device of my gansas, well knowing how impossible it were otherwise to persuade him to take in so many birds into the ship that would be more troublesome (for the niceness of provision to be made for them) than so many men, yet I adjured him by all manner of oaths and persuasions to afford me both true dealing and secrecy. Of the last I doubted not much, as assuring myself he would not dare to impart the device to any other before our King were acquainted with it. Of the first I feared much more, namely lest ambition and the desire of drawing unto himself the honor of such an invention should cause him to make me away; yet I was forced to run the hazard, except I would adventure the loss of my birds, the like whereof for my purpose were not to be had in all Christendom, nor any that I could be sure would ever serve the turn. Well, that doubt in proof fell out to be causeless. The man I think was honest of himself, but had he dealt treacherously with me, I had laid a plot for the discovery of him, as he might easily judge I would, which peradventure somewhat moved him; yet God knows how he might have used me before my arrival in Spain if in the mean course we had not been intercepted, as you shall hear.

Upon Thursday the 21 of June, to wit in the year 1599, we set sail towards Spain, I having allowed me a very convenient cabin for my birds and stowage also for mine engine, which the captain would have had me leave behind me, and it is a marvel I had not, but my good fortune therein saved my life and gave me that which I esteem more than an hundred lives, if I had them, for thus it fell out. After two months' sail, we encountered with a fleet of the English, some ten leagues from the Island of Teneriffe, one of the Canaries, which is famous through the world for a hill upon the same called El Pico, that is to be discerned and kenned upon the sea no less than a hundred leagues off. We had aboard us five times the number of people that they had; we were well provided of munition, and our men in good health; yet seeing them disposed to fight and knowing what infinite riches we carried with us, we thought it a wiser way to fly, if we might, than by encountering a company of dangerous fellows to hazard not only our own lives (which a man of valor in such a case esteemeth not) but the estates of many poor merchants, who I am afraid were utterly undone by miscarriage of that business. Our fleet then consisted of five sail, to wit: three carracks, a bark, and a caravel, that coming from the Isle of St. Thomas had, in an evil hour for him, overtaken us some few days before.

The English had three ships very well appointed, and no sooner spied but they began to play for us, and, changing their course, as we might well perceive, endeavored straightway to bring us under their lee, which they might well do, as the wind stood, especially being light nimble vessels and yare of sail, as for the most part all the English shipping is, whereas ours was heavy, deep laden, foul with the sea. Our captain therefore resolved peradventure wisely enough (but I am sure neither valiantly nor fortunately) to fly, commanding us to disperse ourselves. The caravel by reason of too much haste fell foul upon one of the carracks and bruised her so as one of the English that had undertaken her easily fetched her up and entered her; as for the caravel, she sank immediately in the sight of us all. The bark (for aught I could perceive), no man making after her, escaped unpursued, and another of our carracks after some chase was given over by the English, that making account to find a booty good enough of us, and having us between them and their third companion, made upon us with might and main. Wherefore our captain, that was aboard us, gave direction to run aland upon the isle, the port whereof we could not recover, saying that he hoped to save some of the goods and some of our lives, and the rest he had rather should be lost than commit all to the mercy of the enemy.

When I heard of that resolution, seeing the sea to work high, and knowing all the coast to be full of blind rocks and shoals, so as our vessel might not possibly come near land before it must needs be rent in a thousand pieces, I went unto the captain, showing him the desperateness of the course he intended, wishing him rather to try the mercy of the enemy than so to cast away himself and so many brave men; but he would not hear me by any means. Whereupon discerning it to be high time to shift for myself, first I sought out my box or little casket of stones, and having put it into my sleeve, I then betook me to my gansas, put them upon my engine and myself upon it, trusting (as indeed it happily fell out) that when the ship should split, my birds, although they wanted their signal, of themselves and for safeguard of their own lives (which nature hath taught every living creature to preserve to their power) would make towards the land; which fell out well (I thank God) according to mine expectation. The people of our ship marvelled about what I went, none of them being acquainted with the use of my birds but the captain, for Diego was in the *Rosaria*, the ship that fled away unpursued, as before I told you.

Some half a league we were from the land when our carrack struck upon a rock and split immediately; whereupon I let loose unto my birds the reins, having first placed myself upon the highest of the deck, and with the shock they all arose, carrying me fortunately unto the land, whereof, whether I were well apaid, you need not doubt; but a pitiful sight it was unto me to behold my friends and acquaintance in that miserable distress, of whom notwithstanding many escaped better than they had any reason to hope for. For the English launching out their cockboats, like men of more noble and generous disposition than we are pleased to esteem them, taking compassion upon them, used all the diligence they could to help such as had any means to save themselves from the fury of the waves, and that even with their own danger. Amongst many, they took up our captain, who, as Father Pacio could since tell me, having put himself into his cock with twelve others, was induced to yield himself unto one Captain Rymundo, who carried him together with our pilot along in their voyage with them being bound for the East Indies; but their hard hap was by a breach of the sea near the Cape of Buona Esperanza to be swallowed of the merciless waves, whose fury a little before they had so hardly escaped. The rest of them (as I likewise heard)—and they were in all some twenty-six persons that they took into their ship—they set them aland soon after at Cape Verde.

As for myself, being now ashore in a country inhabited for the most part by Spaniards, I reckoned myself in safety. Howbeit, I quickly found the reckoning I so made mine host had not been acquainted withal, for it was my chance to pitch upon that part of the isle where the hill before mentioned beginneth to rise. And it is inhabited by a savage kind of people that live upon the sides of that hill, the top whereof is always covered with snow and held for the monstrous height and steepness not to be accessible either for man or beast. Howbeit, these savages fearing the Spaniards, between whom and them there is a kind of continual war, hold themselves as near the top of that hill as they can, where they have divers places of good strength, never coming down into the fruitful valleys but to prey upon what they can find there. It was the chance of a company of them to espy me within some hours' space after my landing. They thinking they had lighted upon a booty made towards me with all the speed they could, but not so privily as that I could not perceive their purpose before they came near to me by half a quarter of a league; seeing them come down the side of a hill with great speed directly towards me, divers of them carrying long staves, besides other weapons, which because of their distance from me I might not discern, I thought it high time to bestir me and shift for myself, and by all means to keep myself out of the fingers of such slaves, who, had they caught me, for the hatred they bear to us Spaniards had surely hewed me all to pieces.

The country in that place was bare, without the coverture of any wood, but the mountain before spoken of beginning even there to lift up itself, I espied in the side of the same a white cliff, which I trusted my gansas would take for a signal, and being put off would make all that way, whereby I might quickly be carried so far as those barbarous cullions should not be able to overtake me, before I had recovered the dwelling of some Spaniard or at leastwise might have time to hide myself from them, till that in the night, by help of the stars, I might guide myself towards Las Loeguna, the city of that island, which was about one league off, as I think. Wherefore with all the celerity that might be, I put myself upon mine engine and let loose the reins unto my gansas. It was my good fortune that they took all one way, although not just that way I aimed at. But what then? O reader, *arrige aures,* prepare thyself unto the hearing of the strangest chance that ever happened to any mortal man, and that I know thou wilt not have the grace to believe till thou seest it seconded with iteration of experiments in the like, as many a one, I trust, thou mayest in short time. My gansas, like so many horses that had gotten the bit between their teeth, made, I say, not towards the cliff I aimed at, although I used my wonted means to direct the leader of the flock that way, but with might and main took up towards the top of El Pico, and did never stay till they came there, a place where they say never man came before, being in all estimation at least fifteen leagues in height perpendicularly upward above the ordinary level of the land and sea.

What manner of place I found there I should gladly relate unto you, but that I make haste to matters of far greater importance. There when I was set down, I saw my poor gansas fall to panting and blowing, gaping for breath as if they would all presently have died; wherefore I thought it not good to trouble them a while, forbearing to draw them in (which they never wont to endure without struggling) and little expecting that which followed.

It was now the season that these birds were wont to take their flight away, as our cuckoos and swallows do in Spain, towards the autumn. They, as after I perceived, mindful of their usual voyage, even as I began to settle myself for the taking of them in, as it were with one consent rose up, and having no other place higher to make toward, to my unspeakable fear and amazement struck bolt upright and never did lin[1] towering upward, and still upward, for the space, as I might guess, of one whole hour, toward the end of which time, methought I might perceive them to labor less and less, till at length, O incredible thing! they forbore moving anything at all and yet remained unmoveable as steadfastly as if they had been upon so many perches. The lines slacked; neither I nor the engine moved

The Man in the Moon

at all, but abode still, as having no manner of weight.

I found then by this experience that which no philosopher ever dreamed of, to wit, that those things which we call heavy do not sink towards the center of the earth as their natural place, but as drawn by a secret property of the globe of the earth, or rather something within the same, in like sort as the loadstone draweth iron, being within the compass of the beams attractive.

For though it be true that there they could abide unmoved without the prop or sustenation of any corporal thing other than the air, as easily and quietly as a fish in the middle of the water, yet forcing themselves never so little, it is not possible to imagine with what swiftness and celerity they were carried, and whether it were upward, downward, or sidelong, all was one. Truly I must confess, the horror and amazement of that place was such as if I had not been armed with a true Spanish courage and resolution, I must needs have died there with very fear.

But the next thing that did most trouble me was the swiftness of motion, such as did even almost stop my breath. If I should liken it to an arrow out of a bow, or to a stone cast down from the top of some high tower, it would come far short and short.

Another thing there was exceeding, and more than exceeding, troublesome unto me, and that was the illusions of devils and wicked spirits, who, the first day of my arrival, came about me in great numbers, carrying the shapes and likeness of men and women, wondering at me like so many birds about an owl and speaking divers kinds of languages which I understood not, till at last I did light upon them that spoke very good Spanish, some Dutch, and other some Italian, for all these languages I understood.

And here I saw only a touch of the sun's absence for a little while once, ever after having him in my sight. Now to yield you satisfaction in the other, you shall understand that my gansas, although entangled in my line, might easily find means to seize upon divers kinds of flies and birds, as especially swallows and cuckoos, whereof there were multitudes, as motes in the sun, although, to say the truth, I never saw them to feed anything at all. As for myself, in truth I was much beholding unto those same, whether men or devils I know not, that amongst divers speeches, which I will forbear a while to relate, told me that if I would follow their directions, I should not only be brought safely to my home but also be assured to have the command of all pleasures of that place at all times.

To the which motions not daring to make a flat denial, I prayed a time to think of it, and withal entreated them (though I felt no hunger at all, which may seem strange) to help me with some victuals, lest in the meanwhile I should starve. They did so readily enough and brought me very good flesh and fish of divers sorts well dressed, but that it was exceeding fresh and without any manner of relish of salt.

Wine also I tasted there of divers sorts, as good as any in Spain, and beer, no better in all Antwerp. They wished me then, while I had means, to make my provision, telling me that till the next Thursday they could not help me to any more, if happily then, at what time also they would find means to carry me back and set me safe in Spain, where I would wish to be, so that I would become one of their fraternity and enter into such covenants and profession as they had made to their master and captain, whom they would not name. I answered them gently for the time, telling them I saw little reason not to be very glad of such an offer, praying them to be mindful of me as occasion served.

So for that time I was rid of them, having first furnished my pockets with as much victual as I could thrust in, amongst the which I failed not to afford place for a little *botijo* of good canary wine.

Now shall I declare unto you the quality of the place in which I then was. The clouds I perceived to be all under me, between me and the earth. The stars, by reason it was always day, I saw at all times alike, not shining bright, as upon the earth we are wont to see them in the night time, but of a whitish color, like that of the moon in the daytime with us. And such of them as were to be seen (which were not many) showed far greater than with us, yea (as I should guess) no less than ten times so great. As for the moon being then within two days of the change, she appeared of a huge and fearful quantity.

This also is not to be forgotten, that no stars appeared but on that part of the hemisphere that was next the moon, and the nearer to her, the bigger in quantity they showed. Again I must tell you that whether I lay quiet and rested, or else were carried in the air, I perceived myself still to be always directly between the moon and the earth. Whereby it appeareth, not only that my gansas took none other way than directly toward the moon, but also that when we rested (as at first we did for many hours) either we were insensibly carried (for I perceived no such motion) round about the globe of the earth, or else that (according to the late opinion of Copernicus) the earth is carried about and turneth round perpetually from west to the east, leaving unto the planets only that motion which astronomers call natural, and is not upon the poles of the equinoctial, commonly termed the poles of the world, but upon those of the zodiac, concerning which question I will speak more hereafter when I shall have leisure to call to my remembrance the astronomy that I learned being a young man at Salamanca, but have now almost forgotten.

The air in that place I found quiet, without any motion of wind, and exceeding temperate, neither hot nor cold, as where neither the sunbeams had any subject to reflect upon, neither was yet either the earth or water so near as to affect the air with their natural quality of coldness. As for that imagination of the philosophers, attributing heat together with moistness unto the air, I never esteemed it otherwise than a fancy. Lastly now it is to be remembered that after my departure from the earth, I never felt any appetite of hunger or thirst. Whether the purity of the air, our proper element, not being infected with any vapors of the earth and water, might yield nature sufficient nutriment, or what else might be the cause of it, I cannot tell, but so I found it, although I perceived myself in perfect health of body, having the use of all my limbs and senses, and strength both of body and mind rather beyond and above than anything short of the pitch or wonted vigor. Now let us go on, and on we shall go more than apace.

Not many hours after the departure of that devilish company from me, my gansas began to bestir themselves, still directing their course toward the globe or body of the moon, and they made their way with that incredible swiftness as I think they gained not so little as fifty leagues in every hour. In that passage I noted three things very remarkable: one, that the farther we went, the lesser the globe of the earth appeared to us, whereas still on the contrary side the moon showed herself more and more monstrously huge.

Again, the earth (which ever I held in mine eye) did as it were mask itself with a kind of brightness like another moon, and even as in the moon we discerned certain spots or clouds, as it were, so did I then in the earth. But whereas the form of those spots in the moon continue constantly one and the same, these by little and little did change every hour. The reason thereof I conceive to be this, that whereas the earth, according to her natural motion (for that such a motion she hath, I am now constrained to join in opinion with Copernicus) turneth round upon her own axis every twenty-four hours from the west unto the east, I should at the first see in the middle of the body of this new star a spot like unto a pear that had a morsel bitten out upon the one side of him, after certain hours I should see that spot slide away to the east side. This no doubt was the main of Africa.

Then should I perceive a great shining brightness to occupy that room, during the like time (which was undoubtedly none other than the great Atlantic Ocean). After that succeeded a spot almost of an oval form, even just such as we see America to have in our maps. Then another vast clearness representing the West Ocean, and lastly a medley of spots, like the countries of East Indies. So that it seemed unto me no other than a huge mathematical globe, leisurely turned before me, wherein successively all the countries of our earthly world within the compass of twenty-four hours were represented to my sight. And this was all the means I had now to number the days and take reckoning of time.

Philosophers and mathematicians I would should now confess the wilfulness of their own blindness. They have made the world believe hitherto that the earth hath no motion. And to make that good, they are fain to attribute unto all and every of the celestial bodies two motions, quite contrary each to other, whereof one is from the east to the west, to be performed in twenty-four hours, that they imagine to be forced *per raptum primi mobilis;* the other from the west to the east in several proportions.

O incredible thing, that those same huge bodies of the fixed stars in the highest orb, whereof divers are by themselves confessed to be more than one hundred times as big as the whole earth, should as so many nails in a cartwheel be whirled about in that short space, whereas it is many thousands of years (no less, I trow, they say than thirty thousand) before that orb do finish his course from west to east, which they call the natural motion. Now, whereas to every of these they yield their natural course from west to east, therein they do well. The moon performeth it in twenty-seven days; the sun, Venus, and Mercury in a year or thereabouts; Mars in three years; Jupiter in twelve years; and Saturn in thirty. But to attribute unto these celestial bodies contrary motions at once was a very absurd conceit, and much more, to imagine that same orb, wherein the fixed stars are (whose natural course taketh so many thousand of years) should every twenty-four hours be turned about. I will not go so far as Copernicus, that maketh the sun the center of the earth and unmoveable; neither will I define anything one way or other. Only this I say: allow the earth his motion (which these eyes of mine can testify to be his due) and these absurdities are quite taken away, every one having his single and proper motion only.

But where am I? At the first I promised a history, and I fall into disputes before I am aware. There is yet one accident more befell me worthy of especial remembrance, that during the time of my stay, I saw as it were a kind of cloud of a reddish color growing toward me, which continually growing nearer and nearer, at last I perceived to be nothing else but a huge swarm of locusts. He that readeth the discourses of learned men concerning them, and namely that of John Leo in his description of Africa, how that they are seen in the air many days before they fall upon a country, adding unto that which they deliver this experience of mine, will easily conclude that they cannot come from any other place than the globe of the moon.

But give me leave now at last to pass on my journey quietly, without interruption for eleven or twelve days, during all which time I was carried directly toward the globe or body of the moon with such a violent whirling as cannot be expressed. For I cannot imagine that a bullet out of the mouth of a cannon could make way through the vaporous and muddy air near the earth with that celerity, which is most strange, considering that my gansas moved their wings but even now and then, and sometimes not at all in a quarter of an hour together, only they held them stretched out, so passing on, as we see that eagles and kites sometimes will do for a little space, when (as one speaks, I remember) *cunctabundo volatu pene eodem loco pendula circumtuentur;* and during the time of those pauses I believe they took their naps and times of sleeping, for other (as I might easily note) they had none.

Now for myself, I was so fast knit unto my engine as I durst commit myself to slumbering enough to serve my turn, which I took with as great ease (although I am loath to speak it because it may seem incredible) as if I had been in the best bed of down in all Antwerp.

After eleven days' passage in this violent flight, I perceived that we began to approach near unto another earth, if I may so call it, being the globe or very body of that star which we call the moon.

The first difference that I found between it and our earth was that it showed itself in his natural colors, ever after I was free from the attraction of the earth, whereas with us a thing removed from our eye but a league or two begins to put on that lurid and deadly color of blue.

Then I perceived also that it was covered for the most part with a huge and mighty sea, those parts only being dry land which show unto us here somewhat darker than the rest of her body, that I mean, which the country people call *el hombre de la luna,* the man of the moon. As for that part which shineth so clearly in our eyes, it is even another ocean, yet besprinkled here and there with islands, which for the littleness, so far off we cannot discern. So that same splendor appearing unto us and giving light unto our night appeareth to be nothing else but the reflection of the sunbeams returned unto us out of the water as out of a glass. How ill this agreeth with that which our philosophers teach in the schools I am not ignorant. But, alas, how many of their errors hath time and experience refuted in this our age, with the recital whereof I will not stand to trouble the reader. Amongst many other of their vain surmises, the time and order of my narration putteth me in mind of one which now my experience found most untrue.

Who is there that hath not hitherto believed the uppermost region of the air to be extreme hot, as being next forsooth unto the natural place of the element of fire? O vanities, fancies, dreams! After the time I was once quite free from the attractive beams of that tyrannous loadstone, the earth, I found the air of one and the self-same temper, without winds, without rain, without mists, without clouds, neither hot nor cold, but continually after one and the same tenor, most pleasant, mild, and comfortable, till my arrival in that new world of the moon. As for that region of fire our philosophers talk of, I heard no news of it; mine eyes have sufficiently informed me there can be no such thing.

The earth by turning about had now showed me all her parts twelve times when I finished my course. For when by my reckoning it seemed to be (as indeed it was) Tuesday, the eleventh day of September (at what time the moon, being two days old, was in the twentieth degree of Libra), my gansas stayed their course as it were with one consent, and took their rest for certain hours, after which they took their flight and within less than one hour set me upon the top of a very high hill in that other world, where immediately were presented unto mine eyes many most strange and unwonted sights.

For first I observed that although the globe of the earth showed much bigger there than the moon doth unto us, even to the full trebling of her diameter, yet all manner of things there were of largeness and quantity, ten, twenty, I think I may say thirty times more than ours, their trees at least three times so high as ours, and more than five times the breadth and thickness.

So their herbs, beasts, and birds, although to compare them with ours I know not well how, because I found not anything there, any species either of beast or bird that resembled ours anything at all, except swallows, nightingales, cuckoos, woodcocks, bats, and some kinds of wild fowl, as also of such birds as my gansas, all which (as now I well perceived) spend the time of their absence from us even there in that world; neither do they vary anything at all either in quantity or quality from those of ours here, as being none other than the very same, and that not only *specie* but *numero*. But of these novelties, more hereafter in their due places.

No sooner was I set down upon the ground, but I was surprised with a most ravenous hunger and earnest desire of eating. Wherefore stepping unto the next tree, I fastened thereunto my engine, with my gansas, and in great haste fell to searching of my pockets for the victuals I had reserved as aforesaid, but to great amazement and discomfort, I found instead of partridge and capon, which I thought to have put there, a mingle-mangle of dry leaves, of goat's hair, sheep or goat's dung, moss, and such like trash. As for my canary wine, it was turned to a stinking and filthy kind of liquor, like the urine of some beast. O the illusions of wicked spirits, whose help if I had been fain only to rely upon, you see how I had been served.

Now while I stood musing and wondering at this strange metamorphosis, I heard my gansas upon the sudden to make a great fluttering behind me. And looking back, I espied them to fall greedily upon a certain shrub within the compass of their lines, whose leaves they fed upon most earnestly, where heretofore I had never seen them to eat any manner of green meat whatsoever. Whereupon stepping to the shrub, I put a leaf of it between my teeth. I cannot express the pleasure I found in the taste thereof; such it was, I am sure, as if I had not with great discretion moderated my appetite, I had surely surfeited upon the same. In the meantime it fell out to be a bait that well contented both my birds and me at that time, when we had need of some good refreshing.

Scarcely had I ended this banquet, when upon the sudden I saw myself environed with a kind of people most strange, both for their feature, demeanor, and apparel. Their stature was most diverse, but for the most part, twice the height of ours; their color and countenance most pleasing, and their habit such as I know not how to express. For neither did I see any kind of cloth, silk, or other stuff to resemble the matter of that whereof their clothes were made; neither (which is most strange of all other) can I devise how to describe the color of them, being in a manner all clothed alike. It was neither black, nor white, yellow nor red, green nor blue, nor any color composed of these. But if you ask me what it was, then I must tell you it was a color never seen in our earthly world and therefore neither to be described unto us by any nor to be conceived of one that never saw it. For as it were a hard matter to describe unto a man born blind the difference between blue and green, so can I not bethink myself of any means how to decipher unto you this lunar color, having no affinity with any other that ever I beheld with mine eyes. Only this I can say of it, that it was the most glorious and delightful that can possibly be imagined; neither in truth was there any one thing that more delighted me during my abode in that new world than the beholding of that most pleasing and resplendent color.

It remaineth now that I speak of the demeanor of this people, who presenting themselves unto me upon the sudden, and that in such extraordinary fashion as I have declared, being struck with a great amazement, I crossed myself and cried out, "Jesus Maria!" No sooner was the word Jesus out of my mouth, but young and old fell all down upon their knees (at which I not a little rejoiced), holding up both their hands on high and repeating all certain words which I understood not.

Then presently they all arising, one that was far the tallest of them came unto me and embraced me with great kindness, and giving order (as I partly perceived) unto some of the rest to stay by my birds, he took me by the hand and leading me down toward the foot of the hill brought me to his dwelling, being more than a half a league from the place where I first alighted. It was such a building for beauty and hugeness as all our world cannot show any near comparable to it. Yet such I saw afterwards elsewhere, as this might seem but a cottage in respect of them. There was not a door about the house that was not thirty foot high, and twelve in breadth. The rooms were between forty and fifty foot in height, and so all other proportions answerable. Neither could they well be much less, the master inhabiting them being full twenty-eight high. As for his corporature, I suppose verily that if we had him here in this world to be weighed in the balance, the poise of his body would show itself more ponderous than five-and-twenty, peradventure thirty, of ours.

After I had rested myself with him the value of one of our days, he led me some five leagues off, unto the palace of the prince of the country. The stateliness of the building whereof I will leave unto the second part of this work, as also many other particulars, which will minister more pleasure to the reader than yet I may afford him, being

The Man in the Moon

desirous in this first part to set down no more than what the process of my story concerning my journey doth necessarily draw from me.

This prince, whose stature was much higher than the former, is called (as near as I can by letters declare it, for their sounds are not perfectly to be expressed by our characters) Pylonas, which signifieth in their language *First*, if perhaps it be not rather a denotation of his dignity and authority, as being the prime man in all those parts.

In all those parts, I say. For there is one supreme monarch amongst them, of stature yet much more huge than he, commanding over all that whole orb of that world, having under him twenty-nine other princes of exceeding great power, and every one of them twenty-four others, whereof this Pylonas was one.

The first ancestor of this great monarch came out of the earth (as they deliver) and by marriage with the inheritrix of that huge monarchy obtaining the government, left it unto his posterity, who ever since have held the same, even for the space of forty thousand days or moons, which amounteth unto 3077 years. And his name being Irdonozur, his heirs, unto this day, do all assume unto themselves that name, he, they say, having continued there well near four hundred moons, and having begotten divers children, returned (by what means they declare not) unto the earth again. I doubt not but they may have their fables, as well as we.

And because our histories afford no mention of any earthly man to have ever been in that world before myself, and much less to have returned thence again, I cannot but condemn that tradition for false and fabulous; yet this I must tell you, that learning seemeth to be in great estimation among them, and that they make semblance of detesting all lying and falsehood, which is wont there to be severely punished.

Again, which may yield some countenance unto their historical narrations, many of them live wonderful long, even beyond all credit, to wit, even unto the age as they professed to me of thirty thousand moons, which amounteth unto a thousand years and upwards (so that the ages of three or four men might well reach unto the time of the first Irdonozur), and this is noted generally, that the taller people are of stature, the more excellent they are for all endowments of mind and the longer time they do live.

For whereas (that which before I partly intimated unto you) their stature is most diverse, great numbers of them little exceeding ours, such seldom live above the age of a thousand moons, which is answerable to eighty of our years, and they account them most base creatures, even but a degree before brute beasts, employing them accordingly in all the basest and most servile offices, terming them by a word that signifieth bastard-men, counterfeits, or changelings; so those whom they account genuine, natural, and true Lunars, both in quantity of body and length of life, they have for the most part thirty times as much as we, which proportion agreeth well with the quantity of the day in both worlds, theirs containing almost thirty of ours.

Now when I shall declare unto you the manner of our travel unto the palace of Pylonas, you will say you scarce ever heard anything more strange and incredible. Unto everyone of us there was delivered at our first setting forth two fans of feathers, not much unlike to those that our ladies do carry in Spain to make a cool air unto themselves in the heat of summer. The use of which fans before I declare unto you, I must let you understand that the globe of the moon is not altogether destitute of an attractive power, but it is so far weaker than that of the earth, as if a man do but spring upward with all his force (as dancers do when they show their activity by capering), he shall be able to mount fifty or sixty foot high, and then he is quite beyond all attraction of the moon's earth, falling down no more, so as by the help of these fans, as with wings, they convey themselves in the air in a short space (although not with that swiftness that birds do) even whither they list.

In two hours' space (as I could guess) by the help of

these fans, we were carried through the air those five leagues, being about sixty persons. Being arrived at the palace of Pylonas, after our conductor had gotten audience (which was not presently) and had declared what manner of present he had brought, I was immediately called in unto him by his attendants. By the stateliness of his palace and the reverence done unto him, I soon discerned his greatness, and therefore framed myself to win his favor the best I might. You may remember I told you of a certain little box or casket of jewels, the remainder of those which being brought out of the East Indies I sent from the Isle of St. Helena into Spain. These, before I was carried in unto him, I took out of my pocket in a corner, and, making choice of some of every sort, made them ready to be presented as I should think fit.

I found him sitting in a most magnificent chair of estate, having his wife or queen upon one hand and his eldest son on the other, which were both attended, the one by a troop of ladies and the other of young men, and all along the side of the room stood a great number of goodly personages, whereof scarce anyone was lower of stature than Pylonas, whose age they say is now twenty-one thousand moons. At my first entrance, falling down upon my knees, I thought good to use unto him these words in the Latin tongue: *Propitius sit tibi, Princeps illustrissime, Dominus noster Jesus Christus*, &c. As the people I first met withal, so they, hearing the holy name of our Saviour, they all, I say, king, queen, and all the rest, fell down upon their knees, pronouncing a word or two I understood not. They being risen again, I proceeded thus, *& Maria Salvatoris genetrix, Petrus & Paulus*, &c., and so reckoning up a number of saints, to see if there were any one of them that they honored as their patron; at last reckoning among others St. Martinus, they all bowed their bodies and held up hands in sign of great reverence, the reason whereof I learned to be that Martin in their language signifieth God. Then taking out my jewels prepared for that purpose, I presented unto the king or prince (call him how you please) seven stones of so many several sorts, a diamond, a ruby, an emerald, a sapphire, a topaz, a turquoise, and an opal, which he accepted with great joy and admiration, as having not often seen any such before.

Then I offered unto the queen and prince some other, and was about to have bestowed a number of more upon other there present, but Pylonas forbade them to accept, thinking (as afterwards I learned) that they were all I had, and being willing they should be reserved for Irdonozur his sovereign.

This done, he embraced me with great kindness and began to inquire of me divers things by signs, which I likewise answered by signs as well as I could. But not being able to give him content, he delivered me to a guard of a hundred of his giants (so I may well call them) commanding straitly, first, that I should want nothing that might be fit for me; secondly, that they should not suffer any of the dwarf Lunars (if I may so term them) to come near me; thirdly, that I should with all diligence be instructed in their language; and lastly, that by no means they should impart unto me the knowledge of certain things particularly by him specified (marry, what those particulars were I might never by any means get knowledge).

It may be now you will desire to understand what were the things Pylonas inquired of me. Why, what but these: whence I came, how I arrived there, and by what means, what was my name, what my errand, and such like. To all which I answered the very truth as near as I could.

Being dismissed, I was afforded all manner of necessaries that my heart could wish, so as it seemed unto me I was in a very paradise, the pleasures whereof notwithstanding could not so overcome me, as that the remembrance of my wife and children did not trouble me much. And therefore being willing to foster any small spark of hope of my return, with great diligence I took order for the attendance of my birds (I mean my gansas), whom myself in person tended every day with great carefulness. All which notwithstanding had fallen out to little purpose, had not other men's care

The Man in the Moon

performed that which no endeavor of mine own could. For the time now approached when of necessity all the people of our stature (and so myself among the rest) must needs sleep for some thirteen or fourteen whole days together.

So it cometh to pass there by a secret power and unresistible decree of nature, that when the day beginneth to appear and the moon to be enlightened by the sunbeams (which is at the first quarter of the moon), all such people as exceed not very much our stature inhabiting those parts, they fall into a dead sleep and are not possibly to be wakened till the sun be set and withdrawn out of their sight; even as owls and bats with us cannot endure the light, so we there at the first approach of the day begin to be amazed with it and fall immediately into a slumber which groweth by little and little into a dead sleep, till this light depart from thence again, which is not in fourteen or fifteen days, to wit, until the last quarter.

Methinks now I hear some man to demand what manner of light there is in that world during the absence of the sun. To resolve you for that point, you shall understand that there is a light of two sorts, one of the sun (which I might not endure to behold) and another of the earth. That of the earth was now at the highest, for that when the moon is at the change, then is the earth (unto them in the moon) like a full moon with us, and as the moon increaseth with us, so the light of the earth decreaseth with them. I then found the light there (though the sun were absent) equal unto that with us in the daytime when the sun is covered with clouds, but toward the quarter it little and little diminisheth, yet leaving still a competent light, which is somewhat strange. But much stranger is that which was reported unto me there, how that in the other hemisphere of the moon (I mean contrary to that I happened upon), where during half the moon they see not the sun, and the earth never appeareth unto them, they have notwithstanding a kind of light (not unlike by their description to our moonlight) which it seemeth the propinquity of the stars and other planets (so much nearer unto them than us) affordeth.

Now you shall understand that of the true Lunars there be three degrees. Some beyond the pitch of our stature a good deal, as perhaps ten or twelve foot high, that can endure the day of the moon, when the earth shineth but little, but not endure the beams of both; at such time they must be content to be laid asleep.

Others there are of twenty foot high, or somewhat more, that in ordinary places endure all light both of earth and sun. Marry, there is a certain island, the mysteries whereof none may know whose stature is not at least twenty-seven foot high (I mean of the measure of the standard of Castile). If any other come aland there in the moon's daytime, they fall asleep immediately. This island they call God's Island, or *Insula Martini* in their language; they say it hath a particular governor, who is (as they report) of age sixty-five thousand moons, which amounteth to five thousand of our years; his name is said to be Hiruch, and he commandeth after a sort over Irdonozur himself, especially in that island, out of which he never cometh.

There is another, repairing much thither, they said is half his age and upwards, to wit, about thirty-three thousand moons, or twenty-six hundred of our years, and he commandeth in all things (throughout the whole globe of the moon) concerning matters of religion and the service of God, as absolutely as our Holy Father the Pope doth in any part of Italy. I would fain have seen this man, but I might not be suffered to come near him; his name is Imozes.

Now give me leave to settle myself to a long night's sleep. My attendants take charge of my birds, prepare my lodging, and signify to me by signs how it must be with me. It was about the middle of September, where I perceived the air to grow more clear than ordinary and with the increasing of the light I began to feel myself first dull, then heavy and willing to sleep, although I had not lately been hindered from taking mine ease that way.

The Man in the Moon

I delivered myself at last into the custody of this sister of death, whose prisoner I was for almost a fortnight after. Awaking then, it is not to be believed how fresh, how nimble, how vigorous I found all the faculties both of my body and mind. In good time, therefore, I settled myself immediately to the learning of the language which (a marvellous thing to consider) is one and the same throughout all the regions of the moon, yet so much the less to be wondered at, because I cannot think all the earth of moon to amount to the fortieth part of our inhabited earth; partly because the globe of the moon is much less than that of the earth, and partly because their sea or ocean covereth in estimation three parts of four (if not more), whereas the superficies of our land may be judged equivalent and comparable in measure to that of our seas.

The difficulty of that language is not to be conceived, and the reasons thereof are especially two: first, because it hath no affinity with any other that ever I heard; secondly, because it consisteth not so much of words and letters as of tunes and uncouth sounds that no letters can express. For you have few words but they signify divers and several things, and they are distinguished only by their tunes that are as it were sung in the utterance of them, yea, many words there are consisting of tunes only, so as if they list they will utter their minds by tunes without words. For example, they have an ordinary salutation amongst them, signifying verbatim "Glory be to God alone," which they express (as I take it, for I am no perfect musician) by this tune without any words at all:

Yea, the very names of men they will express in the same sort. When they were disposed to talk of me before my face, so as I should not perceive it, this was *Gonsales:*

By occasion hereof, I discern means of framing a language (and that easy soon to be learned) as copious as any other in the world, consisting of tunes only, whereof my friends may know more at leisure if it please them. This is a great mystery and worthier the searching after than at first sight you would imagine.

Now notwithstanding the difficulty of this language, within two months' space I had attained unto such knowledge of the same as I understood most questions to be demanded of me, and what with signs, what with words, made reasonable shift to utter my mind. Which thing being certified unto Pylonas, he sent for me oftentimes and would be pleased to give me knowledge of many things that my guardians durst not declare unto me. Yet this I will say of them that they never abused me with any untruth that I could perceive, but if I asked a question that they liked not to resolve me in, they would shake their heads and with a Spanish shrug pass over to other talk.

After seven months' space it happened that the great Irdonozur making his progress to a place some two hundred leagues distant from the palace of Pylonas sent for me. The history of that journey and the conference that passed between us shall be related at large in my second book. Only thus much thereof at this time, that he would not admit me into his presence, but talked with me through a window, where I might hear him and he both hear and see me at pleasure. I offered him the remainder of my jewels, which he accepted very thankfully, telling me that he would requite them with gifts of another manner of value.

It was not above a quarter of a moon that I stayed there before I was sent back unto Pylonas again, and so much the sooner because if we had stayed but a day or two longer the sun would have overtaken us before we could have recovered our home.

The gifts he bestowed on me were such as a man would forsake mountains of gold for, and they were all stones, to wit, nine in number, and those of three sorts, whereof one they call poleastis, another machrus, and third ebelus, of each sort three. The first are of the bigness of a hazel nut, very like unto jet, which among many other incredible virtues hath this property, that being once heated in the fire they ever after retain their heat (though without any appearance) until they be quenched with some kind of liquor, whereby they receive no detriment at all, though they be heated and quenched ten thousand times. And their heat is so vehement as they will make red hot any metal that shall come within a foot of them, and being put in a chimney will make a room as warm as if a great fire were kindled in the same.

The machrus (yet far more precious than the other) is of the color of topaz, so shining and resplendent as, though not past the bigness of a bean, yet being placed in the midst of a large church in the nighttime, it maketh it all as light as if a hundred lamps were hanged up round about it.

Can you wish for properties in a stone of greater use than these? Yes, my ebelus will afford you that which I dare say will make you prefer him before these, yea and all the diamonds, sapphires, rubies, and emeralds that our world can yield, were they laid in a heap before you. To say nothing of the color (the lunar, whereof I made mention before, which notwithstanding is so incredibly beautiful as a man should travel a thousand leagues to behold it), the shape is somewhat flat of the breadth of a pistolet[2] and twice the thickness. The one side of this, which is somewhat more orient of color than the other, being clapped to the bare skin of a man in any part of his body, it taketh away from it all weight or ponderousness, whereas turning the other side it addeth force unto the attractive beams of the earth, either in this world or that, and maketh the body to weigh half so much again as it did before. Do you marvel now why I should so overprize this stone? Before you see me on earth again, you shall understand more of the value of this kind and unvaluable gem.

I inquired then amongst them, whether they had not any kind of jewel or other means to make a man invisible, which methought had been a thing of great and extraordinary use. And I could tell that divers of our learned men had written many things to that purpose. They answered that if it were a thing feasible, yet they assured themselves that God would not suffer it to be revealed to us creatures subject to so many imperfections, being a thing so apt to be abused to ill purposes; and that was all I could get of them.

Now after it was known that Irdonozur, the great monarch, had done me this honor, it is strange how much all men respected me more than before. My guardians, which hitherto were very nice in relating anything to me concerning the government of that world, now became somewhat more open, so as I could learn (partly of them, partly of Pylonas) what I shall deliver unto you concerning that matter, whereof I will only give you a taste at this time, referring you unto a more ample discourse in my second part, which at my return into Spain you shall have at large, but not till then, for causes heretofore related.

In a thousand years it is not found that there is either whoremonger amongst them, whereof these reasons are to be yielded: there is no want of any thing necessary for the use of man. Food groweth everywhere without labor, and that of all sorts to be desired. For raiment, housing, or anything else that you may imagine possible for a man to want or desire, it is provided by the command of superiors, though not without labor, yet so little as they do nothing but as it were playing and with pleasure.

Again, their females are all of an absolute beauty, and I know not how it cometh to pass by a secret disposition of nature there that a man having once known a woman never desireth any other. As for murder, it was never heard of amongst them; neither is it a thing almost possible to be committed, for there is no wound to be given which may not be cured. They assured me (and I for my part do believe it) that although a man's head be cut off, yet if any time within the space of three moons it be put together and joined to the carcass again, with the appointment of the juice of a certain herb there growing, it will be joined to-

The Man in the Moon

gether again, so as the party wounded shall become perfectly whole in a few hours.

But the chief cause is that through an excellent disposition of that nature of people there, all, young and old, do hate all manner of vice, and do live in such love, peace, and amity, as it seemeth to be another paradise. True it is that some are better disposed than other, but that they discern immediately at the time of their birth.

And because it is an inviolable decree amongst them, never to put any one to death, perceiving by the stature and some other notes they have, who are likely to be of a wicked or imperfect disposition, they send them away (I know not by what means) into the earth and change them for other children, before they shall have either ability or opportunity to do amiss among them. But first (they say) they are fain to keep them there for a certain space, till that the air of the earth may alter their color to be like unto ours.

And their ordinary vent for them is a certain high hill in the north of America, whose people I can easily believe to be wholly descended of them, partly in regard of their color, partly also in regard of the continual use of tobacco, which the Lunars use exceeding much, as living in a place abounding wonderfully with moisture, as also for the pleasure they take in it, and partly in some other respects, too long now to be rehearsed. Sometimes they mistake their aim and fall upon Christendom, Asia or Africa; marry, that is but seldom. I remember some years since that I read certain stories tending to the confirmation of these things delivered by these Lunars, as especially one chapter of Guil. Neubrigensis, *De reb. angl.*—it is towards the end of his first book, but the chapter I cannot particularly resign. Then see Inigo Mondejar in his description of Nueva Granada, the second book; as also Joseph Desia de Carana in his history of Mexico. If my memory fail me not, you will find that in these which will make my report much the more credible. But for testimonies I care not. May I once have the happiness to return home in safety, I will yield such demonstrations of all I deliver as shall quickly make void all doubt of the truth hereof.

If you will ask me further of the manner of government amongst the Lunars, and how justice is executed? Alas, what need is there of exemplary punishment, where there are no offences committed? They need there no lawyers, for there is never any contention, the seeds thereof, if any begin to sprout, being presently by the wisdom of the next superior pulled up by the roots.

And as little need is there of physicians; they never misdiet themselves, their air is always temperate and pure, neither is there any occasion at all of sickness, as to me it seemed at least, for I could not hear that ever any of them were sick. But the time that nature hath assigned unto them being spent, without any pain at all they die, or rather (I should say) cease to live, as a candle to give light, when that which nourisheth it is consumed.

I was once at the departure of one of them, which I wondered much to behold, for notwithstanding the happy life he led and multitude of friends and children he should forsake, as soon as certainly he understood and perceived his end to approach, he prepared a great feast, and calling about him all those he especially esteemed of, he bids them be merry and rejoice with him, for that the time was come he should now leave the counterfeit pleasures of that world and be made partaker of all true joys and perfect happiness. I wondered not so much at his constancy as the behavior of those his friends. With us in the like case, all seem to mourn, when often some of them do but laugh in their sleeves, or, as one says, under a visard. They all on the other side, young and old, both seemingly and, in my conscience, sincerely did rejoice thereat, so as if any dissembled, it was but their own grief conceived for their own particular loss.

Their bodies being dead putrefy not, and therefore are not buried, but kept in certain rooms ordained for that purpose, so as most of them can show their ancestors' bodies uncorrupt for many generations.

There is never any rain, wind, or change of the air, never either summer or winter, but as it were a perpetual spring, yielding all pleasure, all content, and that free from any annoyance at all.

O my wife and children, what wrong have you done me to bereave me of the happiness of that place! But it maketh no matter, for by this voyage am I sufficiently assured that ere long the race of my mortal life being run, I shall attain a greater happiness elsewhere, and that everlasting.

It was the ninth day of September that I began to ascend from El Pico, twelve days I was upon my voyage and arrived in that region of the moon that they called Simiri, September the 21st following. The twelfth day of May, being Friday, we came unto the court of the great Irdonozur and returned back the seventeenth unto the palace of Pylonas. There I continued till the month of March in the year 1601, at what time I earnestly besought Pylonas, as I had often done before, to give me leave to depart, though with never so great hazard of my life, back into the earth again.

He much dissuaded me, laying before me the danger of the voyage, the misery of that place from whence I came, and the abundant happiness of that I now was in. But the remembrance of my wife and children overweighed all these reasons, and to tell you the truth I was so far forth moved with a desire of that deserved glory that I might purchase at my return as methought I deserved not the name of a Spaniard if I would not hazard twenty lives rather than lose but a little possibility of the same. Wherefore I answered him that my desire of seeing my children was such as I knew I could not live any longer if I were once out of hope of the same. When then he desired one year's stay longer, I told him it was manifest I must depart now or never; my birds began to droop, for want of their wonted migration, three of them were now dead, and if a few more failed, I was forever destitute of all possibility of returning.

With much ado at last he condescended unto my request,

having first acquainted the great Irdonozur with my desire. Then perceiving by the often baiting of my birds a great longing in them to take their flight, I trimmed up mine engine, and took my leave of Pylonas, who for all the courtesy he had done me required of me but one thing, which was, faithfully to promise him that if ever I had means thereunto, I should salute from him Elizabeth, whom he termed the great Queen of England, calling her the most glorious of all women living; and indeed he would often question with me of her, and therein delighted so much, as it seemed he was never satisfied in talking of her. He also delivered unto me a token or present for her of no small value. Though I account her an enemy of Spain, I may not fail of performing this promise as soon as I shall be able so to do.

Upon the twenty-ninth day of March, being Thursday, three days after my awaking from the last moon's light, I fastened myself to mine engine, not forgetting to take with me, besides the jewels Irdonozur had given me (with whose use and virtues Pylonas had acquainted me at large) a small quantity of victual, whereof afterward I had great use, as shall be declared. An infinite multitude of people (and amongst the rest Pylonas himself) being present, after I had given him the last *besa las manos,* I let loose the reins unto my birds, who with great greediness taking wing, quickly carried me out of their sight. It fell out with me as in my first passage; I never felt either hunger or thirst till I arrived in China upon a high mountain, some five leagues from the high and mighty city of Pachin.

This voyage was performed in less than nine days. I heard no news by the way of these airy men which I had seen in my ascending. Nothing stayed my journey any whit at all, whether it was the earnest desire of my birds to return to the earth, where they had missed one season, or that the attraction of the earth so much stronger than that of the moon furthered their labor, so it came to pass, although now I had three birds wanting of those I carried forth with me.

For the first eight days my birds flew before and I with the engine was as it were drawn by them. The ninth day when I began to approach unto the clouds, I perceived myself and mine engine to sink towards the earth and go before them. I was then horribly afraid, lest my birds, not being able to bear our weight, they being so few, should be constrained to precipitate both me and themselves headlong to the earth, wherefore I thought it no less than needful to make use of the ebelus (one of the stones bestowed upon me by Irdonozur), which I clapped to my bare flesh within my hose, and it appeared manifestly thereupon unto me that my birds made their way with much greater ease than before, as being lightened of a great burden. Neither do I think it possible for them to have let me down safely unto the earth without that help.

China is a country so populous, as I think there is hardly a piece of ground to be found in the most barren parts of the same, though but thrice a man's length, which is not most carefully manured. I being yet in the air, some of the country people had espied me, and came running unto me by troops. They seized upon me and would needs by and by carry me unto an officer. I seeing no other remedy yielded myself unto them. But when I assayed to go, I found myself so light that I had much ado, one foot being upon the ground, to set down the other; that was by reason of my ebelus, so applied as it took quite away all weight and ponderousness from my body. Wherefore bethinking myself what was to be done, I feigned a desire of performing the necessity of nature, which by signs being made known unto them (for they understood not a word of any language I could speak), they permitted me to go aside among a few bushes, assuring themselves that for me to escape from them it was impossible. Being there, I remembered the directions Pylonas had given me concerning the use of my stones, and first I took them all together with a few jewels yet remaining of those I had brought out of India, and knit them up in my handkerchief, all except one, the least and worst ebelus.

Him I found means to apply in such sort unto my body as but the half of his side touched my skin, whereby it came to pass that my body then had but half the weight. That being done I drew towards these my guardians, till seeing them come somewhat near together they could not cross my way, I showed them a fair pair of heels. This I did to the end I might recover an opportunity of finding my stones and jewels, which I knew they would rob me of, if I prevented them not.

Being thus lightened, I bid them such a base, as had they been all upon the backs of so many zebras they could never have overtaken me. I directed my course unto a certain thick wood, into which I entered some quarter of a league and then finding a pretty spring (which I took for my mark) hard by it, I thrust my jewels into a little hole made by a want,[3] or some such like creature. Then I took out of my pocket my victuals (to which in all my voyage I had not till then any desire) and refreshed myself therewith, till such time as the people pursuing me had overtaken me, into whose hands I quietly delivered myself.

They led me unto a mean officer, who (understanding that once I had escaped from them that first apprehended me) caused a certain seat to be made of boards, into which they closed me in such sort as only my head was at liberty, and then carried me upon the shoulders of four slaves (like some notorious malefactor) before a man of great authority, whom in their language, as after I learned, they called a mandarin, abiding two days' journey off, to wit, one league distant from the great and famous city of Pachin, or Paquin, by the Chinese called Suntien.

Their language I could no way understand, only this I could discern: that I was for something or other accused with a great deal of vehemence. The substance of this accusation it seems was that I was a magician, as witnessed my strange carriage in the air; that being a stranger, as appeared by my both language and habit, I contrary to the laws of China had entered into the kingdom without warrant, and that probably with no good intent. The mandarin heard them out with a great deal of composed gravity, and being a man of quick apprehension and withal studious of novelties, he answered them that he would take such order with me as the case required, and that my bold attempt should not want its deserved punishment. But having dismissed them, he gave order to his servants that I should be kept in some remote parts of his vast palace and be strictly watched but courteously used. This do I conjecture by what at the present I found and what after followed. For my accommodation was every way better than I could expect; I lodged well, fared well, was attended well, and could not fault anything but my restraint. In this manner did I continue many months, afflicted with nothing so much as with the thought of my gansas, which I knew must be irrecoverably lost, as indeed they were. But in this time, by my own industry and the forwardness of those that accompanied me, I was grown indifferent ready in the ordinary language of that province (for almost every province in China hath its proper language), whereat I discerned they took no small content.

I was at length to take the air, and brought into the spacious garden of that palace, a place of excellent pleasure and delight, as being planted with herbs and flowers of admirable both sweetness and beauty, and almost infinite variety of fruits, both European and others, and all those composed with that rare curiosity that I was ravished with the contemplation of such delightful objects. But I had not here long recreated myself yet the mandarin entered the garden, on that side where I was walking, and being advertised thereof by his servants and wished to kneel down to him (as I after found it to be the usual public reverence to those great officers), I did so, and humbly craved his favor towards a poor stranger that arrived in those parts not by his own destination but by the secret disposal of the heavens. He in a different language (which all the mandarins, as I have since learned, do use) and that, like that of the Lunars, did consist much of tunes, but was by one of his servants interpreted to me; he, I say, wished me to be of good comfort, for that he intended no harm unto me, and so passed on.

The next day was I commanded to come before him, and so conducted into a sumptuous dining room exquisitely painted and adorned. The mandarin having commanded all to avoid the room vouchsafed conference with me in the vulgar language, inquiring first the estate of my country, the power of my prince, the religion and manners of the people. Wherein being satisfied by me, he at last descended to the particulars of my education and studies and what brought me into this remote country. Then did I at large declare unto him the adventure of my life, only omitting here and there what particulars I thought good, forbearing especially any mention of the stones given me by Irdonozur. The strangeness of my story did much amaze him. And finding in all my discourse nothing any way tending to magic (wherein he had hoped by my means to have gained some knowledge), he began to admire the excellency of my wit, applauding me for the happiest man that this world had ever produced, and, wishing me to repose myself after my long narration, he for that time dismissed me.

After this, the mandarin took such delight in me that no day passed wherein he sent not for me. At length he advised me to apparel myself in the habit of the country (which I willingly did), and gave me not only the liberty of his house but took me also abroad with him when he went to Paquin, whereby I had the opportunity by degrees to learn the disposition of the people and the policy of the country, which I shall reserve for my second part. Neither did I by this my attendance on him gain only the knowledge of these things, but the possibility also of being restored to my native soil, and to those dear pledges, which I value above the world, my wife and children. For by often frequenting Paquin, I at length heard of some Fathers of the Society that were become famous for the extraordinary favor by the king vouchsafed them, to

The Man in the Moon 283

whom they had presented some European trifles, as clocks, watches, dials, and the like, which with him passed for exquisite rarities. To them by the mandarin's leave I repaired and was welcomed by them, they much wondering to see a lay Spaniard there, whither they had with so much difficulty obtained leave to arrive.

There did I relate to Father Pantoja and those others of the Society these fore-related adventures, by whose directions I put them in writing, and sent this story of my fortunes to Macao, from thence to be conveyed for Spain, as a forerunner of my return. And the mandarin being very indulgent unto me, I came often unto the Fathers, with whom I consulted about many secrets with them; also did I lay a foundation for my return, the blessed hour whereof I do with patience expect, that by enriching my country with the knowledge of hidden mysteries, I may once reap the glory of my fortunate misfortunes.

FINIS

THE HISTORIE
OF
EURIALUS
AND
LUCRETIA.

Written in Latine by
Eneas Sylvius;

And translated into English
by *Charles Allen*, Gent.

Printed at *London* by *The. Cotes*, for
William Cooke, and are to be sold at his
shop neere *Furnivalls Inne* Gate in
Holborne. 1639.

AENEAS SYLVIUS (PIUS II): EURIALUS AND LUCRETIA (1639)

Eurialus and Lucretia, or to give the story its original title, the *Historia de duobus amantibus Euryalo et Lucretia,* is a tale of two lovers which Aeneas Sylvius of the family of the Piccolomini, who later became Pope Pius II in 1458, composed in his youth (and later apparently regretted). Tremendously popular—indeed embarrassingly so to its creator—the story not only appeared in a surprisingly large number of editions in Latin but was translated into the several important vernaculars as well, duly appearing in English about 1515. Nor was this success confined merely to the book's own era; it continued as a favorite piece of reading matter through the sixteenth century, and even later, with editions of the various translations appearing regularly. In England there were four editions during the 1500s—the last of these, 1596, a euphuistic version by one William Braunche—and one in the seventeenth century when a version by Charles Allen, here reprinted, made its appearance in 1639.

The story, which in all probability owes something to the tale of Troilus and Cressida, is simple, sad, and compelling. To the basically romantic notion of a sweeping and irresistible love fired at first sight it adds as a proviso the basically realistic (and, incidentally, moral) notion that such a love is doomed to be short and tragic; and, perhaps through the influence of its prototype, to a stock situation, stock characters, and routine narrative techniques (the alternating debates of hero and heroine before they yield to their loves, for example), the author has been able to add a good measure of individualization and immediacy through analysis of inner feelings, particularly those of his heroine. That it is Lucretia's story is always made abundantly clear; it is her character that is developed, it is her reactions that we watch with interest, and it is on her that the climax depends. The heroine's readiness to sacrifice without further consideration honor and even life for the sake of her love contrasts strongly with Eurialus's habit of always thinking first of the social consequences of his acts, of his own safety, and in general behaving in a way that is by comparison ungenerous. The story, for all its antique quaintness, remains genuinely moving.

Most remarkable, perhaps, is the quietness with which the story is conducted. Here is no violent behavior or incidental crime or fustian rant; instead, there is a succession of incidents rather ordinary in nature and gaining power more through pathos than through excitement. Allen's translation mirrors this general tone fairly well; though he plays up the language a little at times, he ordinarily maintains a smoothly flowing pace and a pleasantly mild atmosphere, neither straining for emotional effects not attempting high-flown verbal effusions. In spite of the occasional couplets, the aim of which is apparently elegance, the language of the translation keeps to a level happily close to the desired mean.

The best discussion of the story in its proper historical context is to be found in Gustave Reynier, *Le roman sentimental avant l'Astrée*, Paris, 1908, pp. 28–36. The text which follows is taken from a copy of the 1639 edition in the Huntington Library.

AENEAS SYLVIUS PICCOLOMINI: THE HISTORY OF EURIALUS AND LUCRETIA

Aeneas Sylvius to Marianus Sozinus, Health

Sir, Your suit is unproper for my age, but to your own repugnant. For in an argument of love, what can I who am almost forty write, or you who are fifty with convenience hear? It is a thing which delights young spirits and tires upon tender breasts, but old men are as unfit auditors of loves as young men are of morals. Nor is there anything more ugly than age which shall serve Venus with an impotent devotion. Yet shall you find some of these old ones in love, but not reloved, for they are equally contemptible both to maid and matron, nor was woman ever taken but by the flourish of our years. If you shall be taught otherwise, it is but a covert illusion.

But I know that an amorous tractate doth extremely misbecome me, who having passed the meridian of my time do now post to my evening, yet is it not a greater indecency for me to write than for you to solicit me. It is my duty to obey; let it be your care to see what you impose. For as there is the greater ripeness of years in you, so it will be the greater equity in me to subscribe to the laws of friendship, which if your justice fears not to violate by an injunction, my folly shall not doubt to transgress by an obedience. Your good graces to me have been so many, that I cannot dare to deny you, although some looser wantonness were implied in the request. I shall therefore condescend to your petition so often reiterated, nor any longer oppose that which hath been solicited with so much vehemency.

Yet shall I not, as your desire was, feign anything, nor will I there be a poet where I may be a his-

torian. For who is so mad as to make use of a lie who hath a truth can justify him? Because yourself have been amorous and have not yet that fire extinct, it is your pleasure I should compose the history of two lovers.

> This gamesomeness doth hold
> You from being reckoned old.

I shall submit myself to your desires, but will not present you with fiction in so great a variety of truths. For what hath the world so universally common? What city, hamlet, or family is barren of examples? What man arrived to thirty hath not exploited something for love? I ground this conjecture in myself, whom love hath a thousand times engaged, and Heaven hath disengaged a thousand times; in that, happier than Mars whom Vulcan captivated in an iron net and exposed a scorned spectacle to the gods; but I shall rather touch at others' loves than mine own, lest while I stir up the embers of my ancient fire, I discover a spark still living. Yet will I give you the relation of a strange and almost incredible love, with which a noble pair were mutually inflamed, nor will I make use of old and obsolete examples, but discourse of the wanton fires of our own age, which I will demonstrate to you in our own city, not Babylon or Troy, although one of the lovers was born in a northern climate.

And perchance the story may furnish us with this benefit. For since the lady which is our theme, when she had lost her love, breathed out her soul in a mixed passion of sadness and indignation, and the knight was never after the master of any true contentment, it may be a fair advertisement to youth to desist from such vanities. And the tender virgin may be informed by this accident not to lose herself in the pursuit of another. The narration may tutor young gallants, that they address not themselves to this kind of war, where *the gall is so much predominant over the honey, but that renouncing lasciviousness which doth infatuate them, they would rather make virtue their design, which is the only possession that can make its possessor happy. If any man be a stranger to that infinity of miseries which lie concealed in love, let him from hence correct his ignorance.*

Farewell, Sir, and with attention hear that story which I by compulsion write.

THE HISTORY OF EURIALUS AND LUCRETIA

When Sigismund kept his court at Sienna, it fortuned that upon the way to his palace, which was adjoining to St. Martha's Chapel, he encountered four ladies whom feature and nobility, age and habit, had almost made equals, and in the general repute not mortals but goddesses. Had there been but three of them it had been a pardonable error to judge them for those whom fame hath made Paris see in a vision. Sigismund, although old in years, yet young in desires, was much addicted to the courting of ladies, nor did any object beget in him a delight equal to that of an elegant beauty. At this sight alighting from his horse he was entertained in their arms, and turning to his courtiers asked if they had ever beheld such delicate pieces, professing that it was his doubt whether they were human faces, for that their looks were heavenly if not angelical. The ladies fixing their eyes upon the ground, by their modesty gave an addition to their beauty. For the red diffused in the cheeks rendered such a color as the ivory of India distained with vermilion, or the snow of lily married to the purple of a rose.

But among these Lucretia sparkled with greatest luster, a lady not yet twenty married in the family of the Camilli to Menelaus, a rich lord, unworthy to be the jailer of such preciousness, yet worthy to be deceived by his wife and to be taught the note of April.[1] Her stature taller than the rest, her hair thick, which she had not cast back like a virgin but bound up in the rich imprisonment of gold and pearl; her forehead high and of a comely largeness, nor drawn through with a wrinkle; her brows daintily arched with black and few hairs distracted from themselves with a just distance; her eyes lighting with such a splendor that they put out the beholders'; with these she slew and made alive; her straight nose made an equal division between her cheeks; nothing more amiable than these cheeks, nothing more delicious, which with her smile were dimpled. Her mouth small, her lips coral, her teeth crystal, and when she talked it was not so much speech as harmony. What should I speak of her chin or neck, seeing that in the whole frame there was nothing but excellency? Her exterior parts did speak her inward beauty, and so oft as she was seen, so oft was her husband envied. Besides, she was very facetious and spoke like the mother of the Gracchi, or the daughter of Hortensius, and in her discourses modesty and sweetness stood competitors. She made not a show of honesty with a severe brow, but of modesty with a cheerful one; not bold nor timorous, but attempered with a civil bashfulness, she carried a masculine spirit in a feminine breast. Lucretia was the theme of every discourse and the argument upon which Caesar and the whole court employed their oratory. When she turned, the eyes of the spectators turned, as if they had no motion but what they borrowed from her, for her looks were as attractive as the strains of the Thracian lyre and led all in triumph after them.

But Eurialus, a lord of Frankenland, was transported with a desire more violently than any other, a man most fit for love, whether you looked upon his face or fortune. His age two and thirty, and his stature rather comely than tall, his eyes shining and full, and his other parts, graced with a kind of majesty, answered each other with a most exquisite symmetry. The other courtiers were all impoverished by the war, but Eurialus, who was rich both in his own revenue and his prince's favor, saluted every day with a new bravery, his train of followers great, richly apparelled and gallantly mounted, so that he wanted nothing but leisure to awaken that gentle heat of the soul which men call love. Let posterity cease now to admire the tale of Thisbe and Pyramus.

> For they were neighbors and the adjoining wall
> Might easily be their loves' original.

Eurialus is now no more his own master. He no sooner saw but he was set on more with what he saw and his thoughts dwell nowhere but in Lucretia. But he met a reciprocal love, and this is the wonder, that in so great a rarity of perfections and choice of beauties, Eurialus should pitch upon none but Lucretia, and Lucretia fasten upon none but Eurialus, yet at the first either of them being ignorant of the other's flame, either of them thought they were in vain inflamed.

But neither of these had any knowledge of the other, either by the eye or ear: he was of Germany, the lady of Tuscany, and wanting the commerce of language, they discoursed only with their eyes. Lucretia therefore wounded with heavy pain and fed upon with hidden fires, forgetting now that she is a wife, and the memory of husband lives only in her hate. Thus cherishing her wound and carrying the figure of Eurialus deeply imprinted in her breast, she enters into this soliloquy with herself.

"How is it that I now nauseate at my former diet? The embraces of my husband are but hated confinements and his kisses as the arrests of death; the idea of that stranger who stood next Caesar doth ever present itself to my imagination, yet if thou canst, poor Lucretia,

> Out of thy breast which is yet chaste
> Let such notions be effaced.

O, happy if I could, but a sweet violence leads me captive; judgment prompts one thing but desire countermands it with another suggestion. I see what is best by the light of my reason, but pursue the contrary by the instigation of my passion. But what? nothing but a stranger relish my palate? must another world be the boundure of my exorbitancy? But, alas, whom doth not that form take? Certainly it doth me, and I cannot, will not, live if mercy be not the chief ingredient in his constitution. But shall I conform myself to the appetite of a traveller, who when he hath plentifully feasted shall rise and go away without giving thanks?

> But now his worth nor sweetness of aspect
> Do threaten or oblivion or neglect.

Let me therefore dispel these mists of doubts and fears, and confident in the powerful assistance of my own beauty presume him to be my prisoner, as I am his.

"But shall I forsake mother, husband, and country? Why not? She is cruel and he unworthy, and that is my country where I delight to live. But my reputation will suffer. But why should the buzz of fame awe me, since I shall not hear it? They dare do nothing who are so anxiously studious of their credit. Nor am I alone in this kind of love. Helen, Medea, and Ariadne are my precedents, and crimes pass unnoted in the universality of the offenders." Thus disputed the lady with herself and poor Eurialus is melted with an equal fire.

Lucretia had a house adjoining to the court, so that Eurialus could not come to the palace but he received a gentle influence shot by Lucretia from out some window. But so oft as she saw him, so oft did she blush, so that the emperor read her love in those red letters, and passing by her house, he would sometimes pull down Eurialus his hat in his eyes, as if he envied him the fruition of so dainty a spectacle.

Lucretia being alone by herself would resolve to extinguish this new flame, yet his presence ever rekindled it, for his sight was both the fire and the fuel.

> As a dry field, once set on fire,
> If the winds blow it, flameth higher.

Eurialus and Lucretia 295

So did Lucretia burn. True is that opinion of the wise, that chastity is most religiously enshrined in a humble cottage and lust, the inseparable associate of great fortune, inhabiteth the stateliest buildings. Lucretia having now often observed Eurialus and unable to give her passion the check, she sat in counsel with her own thoughts, what cabinet to choose where she might safely lay them up. For

> He doth most torture feel,
> That doth his flame conceal.

She had an old servant, by his name Sosias, by his country a High German. Him she intendeth to assault, not so much trusting the man as his nation.

Caesar was then going through the city with a great train, and when she knew Eurialus was near the house, she called Sosias and commanding him to look down asked if the world would not be posed to produce such another troop of young gallants; their compositions, so strong and yet so lovely, somewhat troubled her faith to believe if they were men of that kind which her native Tuscany bred.

> They are of immortal birth
> And sent from heaven to earth.

"Had fortune drawn me a husband out of this lottery of men, although blind yet could she not have erred; should you have told me thus much of your countrymen, I had given no credit to your relation. But now my eyes come in and confute my unbelief. I suppose that lying northerly they are beholden to the cold for much of their fairness. But know you any of them?" said the lady. He told her many. But Lucretia not willing to be long at Rovers,[2] but to come more speedily to her mark asked if he knew Eurialus of Frankenland. "As myself," said Sosias, "but why make you that question?"

"I shall tell thee," said Lucretia, "and I know my secret will be under seal, for thy goodness bespeaks my confidence. It is he in whom my soul moveth, nor will my thoughts give any truce to my sufferings, until I be made known to him. Let it be your errand to tell him I languish for him. I ask you but this, and for this ask you what you please."

"What is this," said Sosias, "that I hear? Can I act, nay and I think such a villainy? Shall I betray my master and be a knave now I am old, a name I trembled at when I was young? Rather dispossess your breast of so unclean a spirit and follow not the counsels of your deluding hope. Love hath easily the repulse, if you make head against his first sallies, but who by flattering themselves shall give ground to this sweet mischief, they sell their liberty to a most insolent master, and bind themselves to one who will never give them back their indentures. Your fire cannot be hid with so much secrecy but my master will smell the smoke, and then the greatness of the fault may give your expectation assurance what your punishment will be."

"Peace, fool," said Lucretia, "in a heart prepossessed with love there is no room for terror. She fears nothing who fears not death and is resolved to stand the malice of the extremest event."

"But," replied Sosias, "will you sully the splendor of your family, or do you think it an honor to be the first adultress of your house? Nor must you imagine you can sin and securely sin. You have the guard of a thousand eyes about you, besides your husband's two, which have a faculty to discover secrets above that thousand. Your servants are but so many spies, and if you bribe them into a silence, yet may your little dog bark and reveal the fact with his inarticulate dialects. The bed, which was oppressed with your lascivious weight, shall be a plaintiff against you, and the curtains will disclose that lust which they did once conceal so closely. For it is a curse attending high crimes, not to find where they may put affiance. But admit you deceive the diligent observation of espials, yet you cannot be masked from the vindictive eye of heaven, which will penetrate into the most abstruse recesses. In your own bosom shall you carry your own tormenter, and the light of your conscience will ever wait upon the darkness of your sin."

"I confess these truths," said Lucretia, "but by the furious concitation of my spirits I am hurried to their contrary. I see the precipice, yet wittingly do I precipitate. Love and fury have usurped upon me and will not suffer reason to be interested in their possession. Oft have I wrestled but in vain, and therefore conclude to execute love's imperious mandates."

"By these white hairs," said groaning Sosias, "by this loyal breast, by my faithful services, I conjure you to curb this passion, and in that be yourself your self's best physician, for the first degree of cure consisteth in your willingness to be cured."

"Well, Sosias," said Lucretia, "modesty commands me to embrace your counsel. I have but one refuge left: by death to prevent this mischief. Collatine's wife with her dagger vindicated the fact committed, but by a nobler course of justice I will anticipate the commission."

"I shall never permit that," replied Sosias.

"But who," said Lucretia, "can hinder a mind resolved to die? The noble Portia, deprived of all instruments of death, swallowed down burning coals and by fire made a way to follow the ghost of her beloved Brutus."

"Nay," said Sosias, "if you are possessed with so resolute a fury, my studies shall be rather to provide for your life than your reputation. For this fame is but a counterfeit gloss: the worst man may have a very fair one, and the best be published with a harsh comment. I shall therefore assay Eurialus, and express all diligence in the service."

With these words her flame advanced and her wavering mind anchored upon stronger hopes. But his purpose went not with his tongue, for he only intended to extenuate her heat by delays, and put her off with false joys, until either the emperor should leave the city or she her resolution. Lest upon her refusal she might get her death or a new agent, he often feigned to have been with Eurialus and that he thought himself infinitely happy in her love and laid wait for all occasion to have some conference with her. Sometimes he told her he could have no access to him; sometimes upon pretence of business he absented himself from home and so frustrated her sick soul with dilatory evasions.

But that he might have one truth among so many lies, he once gave Eurialus a light intimation: "Oh," said he, "how extremely are you beloved!" Then suddenly withdrew himself, and left the poor gentleman unsatisfied. But certainly Eurialus could give himself no rest; a stealthy fire consuming his veins, which did incinerate his marrow, yet little did he know Sosias and less did he think that he came from Lucretia. So incident is it to man never to have his hopes planted in so high a mounture as his desires. But at last seeing himself to be indeed in love, he severely began thus to call his judgment into question. "Thou knowest, Eurialus, how tyrannical the scepter of love is: a fit of laughter with the penance of many a tear, a minute of joy bought at the dear expense of a month's fear, and a continual dying without a death." But at last instructed with many a trial how vain it was to struggle with his passion, he cried for quarter and yielded, comforting himself with the consideration of the company who before him had fought under the banner of love. He remembers some of the great masters in philosophy admitted in his school, and princes made subject to his empire, denying that assertion which denies,

> That majesty and love
> In the same sphere can move.

"Hercules," said he, "the indubiate seed of the gods, disarmed himself at the command of his mistress, and changing his club for a distaff drew a thread with the same hand with which he drew blood. For it is a passion naturally implanted in all; the airy regiments are galled with this arrow:

> For the turtle's loved, they say,
> Of the green popinjay.

And the cold inhabitants of the water have this fire, boars by whetting their teeth, lions by shaking their manes, and the harts by their bellowings give signals of this fury. Nothing is love-proof, nothing impregnable to love. Why then should I rebelliously oppose a prescript of nature? No, since love is so universal a conqueror, I am content to be his spoil."

Being now confirmed, his query is for some good old woman that might carry a paper to the lady. One at last by the assistance of Nisas, an excellent professor in that science, was procured to convey his letter, which spake thus:

EURIALUS TO LUCRETIA

Lady, these lines should bring you health, if the writer had any, but his health, and the hope of it, have a necessary dependence upon your goodness. Above life I love you, nor can I think you a stranger to this truth, for you might see my love in my tears and hear it in my sighs. Take it graciously if I give you the table of my thoughts. That beauty which hath seated you above comparison hath surprised me and the Venus of your face hath brought me into captivity. I have been ever ignorant of this same love until you taught me the lesson, and although I long contended to defend myself from this servitude, yet were my attempts ever subdued by your splendor and the beams of your eyes, more powerful than those of the sun, mollified me to an obedience. I am therefore your captive and follow the triumphant chariot of your excellencies. You have taken from me the use of repose and repast, nay, myself from myself; you are the subject of my meditations and the center of all my passions. It is you whom I fear and love, hope, and weep for; you have all that I am, so that whilst I am divided from myself, I am undivided in you. You sit upon my life and death; let not your sentence be more cruel than your eyes seem merciful. My letters beg only this favor, to have the honor to speak with you. The grant will be my happiness, but the denial my ruin. Farewell, soul of my being.

* * *

These letters, when his seal had enjoined them secrecy, were by this woman dispatched with all speed to Lucretia, whom she found without any company but that of her thoughts. "Lady," said she, "this missive comes to kiss your hands at the directions of the noblest love in Caesar's court, who humbly begs that you would be but as merciful as you are fair." Lucretia knowing her to be a noted quean was highly offended, not so much at the message as the messenger. "Thou filthy bawd," said she, "what boldness, or madness rather, could counsel you to profane the threshold of a Magnifico's palace and bring with you a little silent bawd, a letter forsooth, to scale the chaste breast of a matron and negotiate the violation of religious wedlock. Were it not that I had my own honor in a higher esteem than your desert, you should bid farewell to all letters and be no longer the devil's footpost. Be gone therefore with your packet, but no matter give me the letters and by their entertainment let your hot gallant be instructed how coldly his suit advanceth." The paper she presently tore in pieces, and spitting upon it (for her teeth watered) threw it upon the ground, where she kicked it up and down, as if the very conceit would not let her hold her heels still. "And thus," said she, "lewd woman, shouldst thou be used. But be gone and show thy love to thyself, in thy care not to meet my husband, who will pay thee my debt with interest."

The bawd might have feared to have miscarried in the action had not her experience taught her that the strong desires of women were inseparable from their strong denials. For the present she asked the lady mercy, and if she had offended begged a pardon for her sin of ignorance, but withal advising her not to commit the greater sin of contempt, she took her leave. So returning to Eurialus, "Happy lover," said she, "take up your passion, and give your sorrow leave to breathe. Time would not give her leave to vie letters with you, but she outvies you with her love. I found her in a great fit of melancholy, but the powerful name of Eurialus conjured her up and the sovereign receipt of your letters, which she often kissed, miraculously restored her to herself." With that she departed, and conscious of the foul play she had shown him resolved to come no more upon that stage.

Soon as the old hag was gone, Lucretia finding the fragments of the letter, set the dislocated parts, and with much questing retrieved the lost words, so that she made a legible copy which a thousand times she read and kissed a thousand times. Then wrapping it up in a fine cloth, she laid it up with her jewels, but prized it above them. And repeating now one word, now another, she drank love in deeply, and determined to write to him. The mind of her letter was this:

> Eurialus: Teach your hopes a lower ambition than to fly at a game which is not feasible. Trouble not yourself to trouble me, but save the charge both of letters and messengers, which imply that you conceit me to be of their trade who sell themselves and are both their own shops and wares. Be disdeceived, Sir; I am not she for whom your error mistook me, nor a woman to be sued to by the mediation of a bawd. Seek to prostitute some other; I will be the mistress only of an honorable love; do with others as your pleasure shall counsel you. Farewell, Sir, and let your requests to me be both advised and noble.

Although this epistle seemed harsh to him, and of a strain different from the bawd's relation, yet it opened a way to their mutual commerce of letters, for he could not but trust her who had adventured to trust him. His ignorance of the Italian was a principal impediment, but love made him so ingenious and so industrious that in a short time he arrived to a competency in the language, so that enabled to be his own secretary he answered to this purpose:

> Lady: It is an act of injustice to be so highly offended with me for that my letters were presented to you by a hand so infamous; for seeing I was a stranger and knew it not, by the law my fact may be excused by my ignorance. That I did send to you, let it be an imputation upon my love, and such a love as harbors nothing but honorable intentions. Let my confidence of your chastity beget in you an assurance of my love, for I detest a woman that is prodigal of her honor, of which being once despoiled she is not the subject of anything which can be the subject of a commendation. Beauty is a good, no less corruptible than lovely, and if it wants modesty it wants too many grains to be current. But she who hath joined chastity to her form hath enrolled herself in the list of the gods. In you, fair lady, is met this admirable union, the sole cause which hath sainted you in his devotion, who would solicit nothing that might prejudice your fame. Deign me only the liberty to speak with you, that my words may give you a full display of that affection which cannot be bounded in the narrow limits of my letter.

This epistle was accompanied with a present, rich for the materials and curious for the work, and thus replied upon by Lucretia:

> Sir: I received your letters and admit of your apology. That you love me is none of my wonders, for you are neither the first nor the only man that hath homaged to my beauty. Many have, and yet do court me, but their travails were frustrated, and do not promise to yourself any better event. To speak with you I

neither can nor will; to find me alone is impossible, unless you could assume the shape of a bird, which is no less impossible. For my lodgings are high, and a guard hath made all the entries inaccessible. I accept your token, and am won to that only by the elegancy of the workmanship. But to let you know I will neither be in your debt, nor take it as a pledge of your love, I return you a ring with a stone in it of such a value that what you sent me was rather sold than given. Farewell.

Eurialus returned this answer:

Excellent Lady: Your mercy hath set a period to your complaints against the bawd, and in that is my joy; but you will not give entertainment to my disesteemed love, and in that is my torment. For although you are beleaguered with a multiplicity of loves, yet none of them dare stand forth to parallel mine. Yet will not you believe this, which infidelity ariseth from your severe refusal of conference; but were that permitted, it would beget faith in you and rectify your opinion of my worth. I could wish to be unmanned into a bird, or rather, if wishes were effectual, to be transformed into a flea, and so not to be excluded by the narrowest crevice.

But, dear Lucretia, why say you you will not speak with him, whose all is yours and whose profession it is to be such a servant as shall anticipate your injunctions by his obedience? Oh, forget that same word I will not, and carry not death in your mouth and life in your looks. Let not that sentence be irrevocable, which pronounced that to love you was but to abuse myself and my time. Abandon this cruelty and turn your style, or conclude to be my murderer, for be confident that to me your breath is more inevitably mortal than another's weapon. Love is the total of my desires, but say, you love, and make me really happy. How that mean present stands in your esteem, I dispute not, seeing your acceptance hath set a price upon it above its first value. Your ring shall never from my finger, which supplies the place of your lips and is kissed for them. Farewell, my delight, and do not envy me those joys which you may confer upon me with such facility.

Having thus often bandied one to another, at last Lucretia took a paper, in which she drew the counterfeit of her mind with these lines.

Eurialus, I could willingly entitle you to what I am, for your worth doth challenge love, and your gallant qualities command it. I speak not how I am surprised with your beauty and extasied with your face so full of loves and Cupids. Yet I dare not love, for were I once entered into those amorous lists I should observe neither measure nor mean. You cannot be here long, and I, if I once come into play, must always be in action. The examples of those so many, forsaken by foreign loves, are my so many advertisements not to prosecute your love. Jason treacherously cozened Medea, by whose alone assistance he finished the adventure of the Golden Fleece; and Theseus whom Ariadne did extricate out of the fatal labyrinth ignobly left that distressed lady in an uninhabited island, the worse labyrinth of the two. I know what an inconveniency it is to embrace a stranger's love, and until I shall be of the forlorn hope will not engage myself in so certain a danger.

You men are of a spirit more confirmed and have a greater command over your passions. But poor impotent women! if they once take this fit of raging, nothing but death can be physic to their frenzy. They are rather out of themselves than in love, and if they meet not a correspondent return of affection, nothing so dreadful as a woman in that fury. When this fire hath once insinuated, we respect neither fame nor fate, and must either enjoy our love or not live. The greatness of the want of what we would have adds degrees to the greatness of our desires, and we expose our breasts to the menaces of destruction, so we may sate the impatient longings of our appetites. But I, who am as nobly married as I was nobly descended, have decreed with myself to barricado all passages and make good the place against the forcible entry of love, and of yours in chief, who being a stranger may give me as unworthy a farewell as Demophoon did to the unfortunate Phyllis. Be therefore over entreated not to solicit my love, and to cancel your own, and if you do love, make demonstration of that truth in desisting from a suit which infers my ruin as its necessary consequent. Farewell.

Eurialus not cooled but heated with these letters called for a pen and contrived this answer.

All happiness to my life Lucretia. You have restored me to health with the dose of your letter, yet was it not all cordial but blended with some gall, which I hope shall be no ingredient in the next. I read it often and kissed it oftener, but it seems to intimate something contrary to your former overtures. It counsels me not to love, because it is not expedient for you to do so, and this you would evince by the instances of some ladies who have been betrayed by strangers, which you have done with such rhetoric that you rather teach me to admire than to forget you, whilst you command me not to love you with eloquence which commands me to love you. The more I read the more my flames advanced to see that delicate conjunction of wit and beauty. To bid me not love is to bid a stream recoil into its first head, and to command a mountain to humble itself to a valley. If Scythia can be without snow, or heaven without motion, then can Eurialus be and his love not be. It is not so easy for men to rake up their flames as you imagine, for what you ascribe to our sex many have imputed to yours.

But I shall not reply upon you, rather answer to your induction, which from the treachery of some few strangers would definitively conclude me false. You have mustered up some few authorities, but I could give you a catalogue of more forlorn souls who have been deserted and ruined by ladies. Troilus deluded by Cressida, Deiphobus undone by Helena.

 And Circe with her charms, her lovers suits
 In skins of swine and hides of other brutes.

But it is bad logic to conclude universally from particular premises, and if for the falsehood of two or three men you shall unjustly quarrel all mankind, by as good a consequence for the perjuries of as few women may I bid defiance to the whole sex. Some other's love may supply us with a better copy after which to write our own: that of Antony and Cleopatra was a love contracted between strangers and yet inviolable.

How many of the Grecians at Troy were taken by those ladies whom they had taken and so powerfully detained by those foreign loves that by a miraculous kind of oblivion they did forget their country before they could forget their mistresses? Dear Lucretia, let these be your precedents, seeing he that now sueth for you will ever love and ever be yours. Nor call me a stranger, for I am a citizen of this place, by a better title than a native, for he was made one by his fortune but I by my choice. No country shall be mine but where you are, for your presence can make me a free denizen of any place. When I go from hence, my return shall be speedy, for my journey into Germany is but to settle my estate that my stay with you may be the longer. I shall easily find pretences to reside here, for Caesar hath many affairs of state in these parts, and I shall so prevail with him that their dispatch may be commended to my care. Sometimes I will be here in some embassage, sometimes upon some other employment. Besides, he must have a deputy in Tuscany, and I dare give myself the promise of that charge. Therefore doubt not, sweet Lucretia, the rather because you and my heart are convertible, and if I can be without one, I can be without the other. At last therefore extend your pity to one,

> Who like snow dissolves away
> Exposed to the sunny ray.

Take my languishment into your noble consideration and at last set a happy period to my misery. Look upon my pale and extenuated body and wonder that my soul removes not out of so ruinous a habitation. Had I killed your father, your ingenious cruelty could not invent more exquisite torments. Ah, my Lucretia, how severe would you be against the profane contemners of your beauty, who thus trample upon your prostrate votaries. No longer continue my sufferings, but receive me into your grace, that I may be, and in that happy, the servant of Lucretia. Farewell.

As a tower which broken within seemeth outwardly impregnable suddenly falleth with the battery of the ram, so did Lucretia fall at this assault. And confident of his loyal integrity, she revealed her dissembled love and unmasked herself in this letter.

Eurialus: I can no longer make good the place against you, nor any longer deny you a place in the breast of Lucretia. You have won the field, and I am yours. I have made myself obnoxious to too many dangers, if I be not secured by your providence and fidelity. Faithfully observe what you have written, for I come now to give you livery and seisin of my love, and if you shall ever surrender this possession you are a villain and a traitor. It is an easy thing to overreach a poor gentlewoman, but the facility of the fact adds to the foulness of it. As yet there is no hurt, and if you think me worthy of a desertion let me know so much before my flame be enraged by the addition of a new violence. And let us not at all begin that which must be concluded with repentance. In all actions the end is principally attended by the agent; I have but little foresight, the true character of my sex, but you are a man and, assuming to yourself a double charge, must be a guardian to us both. I present you with the dedication of myself, and honor your faith, to whose bosom I have let my love for term of life, and not as tenant at will. Farewell, guide of my life and star of my course.

After this, many ejaculations passed between them and never did Eurialus write so ardently but Lucretia answered with an ardency as equal. There was nothing wanting now but conveniency of meeting, which seemed to be joined with a kind of impossibility, the lady being guarded with the observation of so many eyes. Argus kept not a stricter watch over the heifer at the command of the jealous goddess, than Menelaus had set over Lucretia. It is the national sin of Italy to immure and lock up their wives as they do their money, which wise men have thought to be none of the best policies. For women do most violently long after forbidden fruits: what you will, they reject, and your severest prohibitions are their hottest pursuits; had they but the reins in their neck, they would not trip so often. If a woman be not chaste out of her own free and noble inclination, bolts and keepers are but impertinent vanities.

> For who is't can those keepers keep, for them
> Finely to win, is her first stratagem.

Lucretia had a brother, who was of her counsel and the faithful Mercury between herself and Eurialus. He is entrusted with all privacy to receive Eurialus into the house, which he might do, for he lived with Lucretia's mother, whom Lucretia did often visit. The plot was this: that Eurialus being shut up in some closet, after the old lady was gone to her devotions, Lucretia should come into Eurialus, coloring her love with the pretext of a dutiful visit. The term of two days was the time prefixed for this amorous design, which were as so many years to the longing couple, for although to men in fear time hath a winged heel, yet to men in hope it walks with leaden socks. But fortune shined not upon the desires of the lovers, for Lucretia's mother had smelled out the conspiracy, and upon the day assigned she went from home but locked out her son-in-law, who presently carried the sad news to Eurialus, which was no less grievous to Lucretia, who, seeing that the plot was detected, "Well," said she, "since I cannot arrive at my wished port by this passage, I will attempt a new one, nor shall my mother glory that she could stop the eddy of my impetuous affections."

There was one Pandalus, a gentleman allied to her husband. Him she called to the table and made of her counsel, for her mind once enfired was uncapable of rest. She signified to Eurialus by letter that he might confidently impart his counsels to him as a man of experienced fidelity, and the fittest instrument to contrive their meetings. But Eurialus who had observed this Pandalus never to be from Menelaus his side doubted his honesty and suspected some treason. While he is in this demur, he is despatched away to Rome to treat with His Holiness about the coronation of Sigismund, which cast the lovers into an agony, but Caesar's authority must be obeyed. For the space of two months (for so long he was absent), Lucretia confined herself to her chamber and put on mourning weeds, as if he had been departed the world, who was but departed Tuscany. All wondered, but none knew the cause of it, which indeed was the reason why they wondered, for ignorance is the cause of admiration. The whole family thought itself in darkness as if the sun had been eclipsed, for the light of her beauty was commonly overcast with her curtains, and the light of her smiles was never seen.

In this state she continued till she heard news of Eurialus his return, and that Caesar was gone to meet him. Then as if awaked out of sleep, she stripped off her mourning apparel, and resuming her former dress she opened the window and joyously expected him. So soon as Caesar saw her, "O," said he, "Eurialus, no longer deny a truth so evident. This sun was set while you were gone, but you have brought us the morning and the sun is again risen. Love hath no boundures, and it can be concealed no more than the cough." "It is your pleasure, Sir," said Eurialus, "to be merry and to amaze me with riddles. Perchance the noise and neighing of the horses brought her to the window." With that he stole a look, and constellated his eyes with hers; and this was their first parley, but a silent one.

Not many days were passed before Nisus (a trusty servant to Eurialus and a great favorer of the cause) had spied out a victualling house, which being situated on the back side of Menelaus his palace had the prospect of Lucretia's chamber. He quickly had won the victualler to secrecy, and then brought his master thither, where he sat privately expecting when fortune would present herself to his sight, nor was his expectation deceived, for at last she appeared. And Eurialus no sooner saw her but, said he, "how fares the governess of my life? Turn thy aspect hither, and make me happy with its influence." "Art thou there, my dear Eurialus?" said Lucretia. "I have now the happiness to hear thee speak, but this accursed distance envieth me the happiness of thy embraces." "A ladder," said Eurialus, "shall remove that difficulty. Do you but make fast your chamber door, for we have too long procrastinated our joys." "O my Eurialus," said she, "if you tender my safety, be more circumspect. Here is a very suspicious window and a worse neighbor; as for that victualler, a little money will purchase him to betray us both. We will walk in a securer tract, and for the present acquiet ourselves that we have had this liberty of conference." After they had drawn out their discourse to some length, and by a reed mutually interchanged favors, they sadly took their leaves.

Sosias having now sounded their purposes, "In vain," said he to himself, "do I oppose their attempts. If I do not intervene with some device, my lady will be ruined and my mistress defamed. Of these mischiefs it shall be my province to avert one. Let my mistress love; if her love be secret it cannot but be secure. But her passion hath blinded her and put out her providence. If therefore we cannot bridle that, we will labor to muzzle report, and keep the house inviolate from the aspersions of infamy. I have hitherto resisted the commission of this unlawful act, but since I can make head no longer, it shall now be my last care that that be secretly done which I see will be done. For it little differs either not to do or so to do that no man knows the doing. Sensuality is generally implanted in all, nor is he a man whom this fury doth not haunt, and he is most chaste that is most cautious."

Whilst he thus reasons with himself, Lucretia came out of her chamber, to whom having addressed himself, he humbly demanded the reason why she thought his bosom a casket too unworthy for her secrets of love. "I know," said he, "you love Eurialus, and without my privity would love him, but be circumspect whom you make a sharer in your counsels, for you are a servant to him who is the master of your secret. The first degree of wisdom is not at all to love, the second to love closely and to blind the world as your passion hath blinded you. This you cannot do alone without the assistance of a third; my heart hath been proved true to you by the test of time, and the index of a long experience. If you shall please to encharge me with anything, command with all assurance; it shall be my study that your love be not unmasked and your self exposed to punishment, and your husband to obloquy and scorn."

"Honest Sosias," replied Lucretia, "I confess this truth, and confidently repose my trust in you, presuming that my affiance will oblige your fidelity, but you were, methought, somewhat cold in seconding my desires, or rather hot in opposing them. Yet since I see you undertake my cause as a voluntary, I shall entertain your service, nor suspect any treachery, an improvident act of many who have taught others to deceive them by seeming fearful to be deceived. You know that I burn extremely, and therefore cannot burn long, for the violence of a motion is an enemy to its continuance. Eurialus languisheth for love, and I die; and to oppose our passions is to advance them. One meeting would rebate our edge, and rectify our loves to a moderation. Go therefore to Eurialus and inform him that the poverty of our fortune will afford us but one way of access if, four days hence, when our peasants bring the corn home, he will humble himself into the habit of a porter. The gods are his precedents who have masked under more inglorious disguises. Thus dissembling his person and our purpose under a frock, let him carry wheat into the granary. Give him a punctual situation of my chamber, where I shall attend him at the day prefixed, and when courteous opportunity shall leave him alone, let him enter my lodging, where I will be found with no more company than himself brings with him."

Sosias although sensible of the danger, yet apprehensive of a greater, embarks for the action, and finding Eurialus he delivers him those instructions he had in commission from his lady, which although in themselves very weighty, yet they seemed light in the seal of his estimation. He hugs the attempt and addresses himself to the adventure, and complains of nothing but those same four ages, which Sosias had called by the name of four days.

So insensate is the breast of an inamorato, and so desperately is the eye of his judgment seeled up, that his heart takes no impression from the justest cause of terror and the apprehension of a danger was never there. His optics are so irregular that all objects lose the truth of what they are, their ideas being defaced by his abused imagination. What is most inaccessible presenteth a smooth surface in a lover's glass, and the greatness of any undertaking is lessened in his perspective. The anxious watches of a jealous husband are in his valuation as vain as his dreams, which proceeds from the want of fear, which was never

Eurialus and Lucretia

one of Cupid's retinue, and contempt of love, which in his judgment is but a goblin to awe simplicity. Such an invincible rascal is that same blind lad that he can cow the bravest spirit beneath the lowest servitude. Eurialus high in the favor of his prince and fortune, but so high in the impregnable tower of his own judgment that it is not imaginable that he should sink to an humility so base, yet this Eurialus exchanged scarlet with sackcloth and he that grew up in the delicacy of all softness did now harden his shoulders to the patience of a burden. Since our own age hath enabled us to give evidence of a transformation so prodigious, we will not dispute the reality of those famous metamorphoses which were transmitted to posterity by the most delicate of the Roman wits; for although those changes were not natural by the assumption of shapes, yet they were moral by the harmony of conditions, so that where the nobler operations of the discursive parts are drowned in a lethargy of sensuality you must look for such a creature in the History of Beasts, for the inquiry would be ridiculous should you search in the definition of man.

The morning did now leave old Tithonus's bed, to do a courtesy to a younger lover, and the sun rendering all things in their colors could not but give Eurialus a fresh one, who by his own sentence then pronounced himself happy (such corrupt judges are we of felicity) when a child new come from the arch of his cradle would have doomed him miserable, when he was mingled with the contemptible crowd of porters, where he accounted that his glory which is the opposite to glory, to lie obscured and unknown.

Thus our gallant porter jogs on to the house, where he learnedly filleth his sack, and having emptied it in the granary, as being puny[3] in this fraternity came last down. In his way, as his instructions taught him, he gently opened her chamber door, of which, by the description of Sosias, he had a mathematical knowledge; which he as suddenly shut as he had entered privily. There he finds Lucretia alone busy with a needle, in expectation of other employment. Advancing near, "Thou great treasurer of my spirits," said he, "which art president of my life and hopes, I have now found thee alone, out of the danger of any house informers, and shall be initiated in thy chaste embraces, which hath been the summary of my desires. No interposed wall can now eclipse thy beauties, nor the tyranny of distance any longer usurp upon my eyes." Lucretia, although herself the projectress, was astonished at the first encounter, imagining that she saw some spirit, and not Eurialus, and thinking it incredible that so great a man should run so great a hazard, she stood amazed at her own workmanship and her invention almost put her out of her wits.

But Eurialus was a very good woman's doctor and with some kisses well applied restored her to her senses and self. "Poor heart," said she, "art thou he? Art thou my Eurialus?" And having her cheeks double-dyed (for the tincture of a blush was added to their roses), she gave him such an embrace as if she intended a union of souls. His forehead she sweetly pressed with her lips, and, intermingling words with kisses, "Ah," said she, "upon what a doubtful cast has thou played. It shall be to me an indubiate argument of thy loyalty, and I were infidel should I require a second demonstration. Thou hast made an undeceivable experiment of thy love, and my faith shall be found a prize worthy the adventure.

> Fate prosper what we have designed,
> And fan us with auspicious wind.

While I live, not any man but thyself shall by the least color entitle himself to me, no, not my husband, if he may boast that name, who never had my heart, and my hand only which was forced, and therefore not obligatory. Come on, thou extract of my delight and pleasures, cast off this frock and let me see thee as thou art, not personating another in a disguise. Put off the porter, and put on Eurialus." Then uncasing himself of those sordid weeds, he appeared in the luster of an unclouded sun, and by the forwardness of his desires, as well as the bravery of his apparel, he spoke himself to be what she expected.

But now Sosias, who stood sentry, knocked at the door and warned the gentle lovers to provide for their safety, for Menelaus in great haste was coming for something in that chamber. "You must," said he, "play the juggler to cast a mist before his eyes and gull him with some fallacy." Said Lucretia suddenly, "By that bed there is a blind closet, in which are all my jewels of price, of which I value you to be the richest, and will put you up in the same cabinet. You may remember what I have writ to you, if we should be at any time fair to be taken by my husband *dommage faisant*. Go in boldly, the darkness will be your security, so that you neither move nor spit." Eurialus was in some doubt what to do, but finding that time could spare no place for consultation, he resolved upon execution and concluded to take her advice. With that she opened the door, and returned to her needle.

Menelaus and Betus with him are now entered to search for some records appertaining to the state, but not finding them in any of the desks, "they are without question," said Menelaus, "in that closet," and commands Lucretia to bring a light to look there. Eurialus terrified at the word, his blood discomfited in his face made a retreat to his heart. And now beginning to hate Lucretia, he severely declaimed against his own lightness, the alone cause of his present captivity. "I shall now," said he, "be publicly traduced; the loss of my prince's favor is inevitable, and that of my life is too fair a possibility. What power created, or can safety herself rescue me from destruction. O, the simplest of whatever was called man, who have made my own ruin my option. At what intolerable rates are these pleasures of love sold, for the buyer is often the price of his own ware. Yet for love's cause, which like smoke then vanisheth when it is at the highest, we will screw ourselves into the most inextricable straits. I am myself an example of this sad truth, for human reason cannot furnish me with so much thread as will clear me of this labyrinth. If pitying Fate would send me a gracious liberate, love should never make me another *mittimus*.[4] Kind Heavens redeem me hence, and dispense with this youthful error; do not severely measure my ignorances in all their dimensions, but reserve me till repentance hath made an atonement for my delinquencies, for it will be your greater glory that I live a monument of your mercy than die a sacrifice to your justice. It was Lucretia's purpose not to love but to betray, and to bring me like a poor hart into the toil. This day is the period of my life, if the date be not extended by the power of an omnipotent hand. I have often heard of the impostures of women and never had the wit to decline them, but if I come off now, I will bid defiance to all their future stratagems."

Lucretia herself was in as great an agony, distracted with a double fear, both for her lover's safety and her own. But as it happens in unexpected occurrences, the conceit of a woman is more present than that of a man; the suddenness of the danger setting an edge upon her wit, she had instantly contrived a remedy. "Husband," said she, "there is a box in the window, where I remember you used to put some of your records. Let us see if these you now look for be not there." And with that running hastily to the box with a pretense to open it, she thrust it out at the window with such art that they supposed it had been by chance and not her intention. "O, husband," said she, "haste that we suffer not. The box is fallen down; make all speed lest either jewels or writings be lost. For heaven's sake get you down, and in the interim I shall watch that nothing be stolen." See the boldness of the woman; the best eye hath been deluded by their false apparitions. He only was never deceived, whom his wife never attempted to deceive, but he that hath escaped and yet hath been laid at, let him ascribe his felicity to his stars and not to his providence.

Menelaus and Betus, moved with this accident so much concerning them, ran speedily down into the street. The house being built high after the Tuscan manner had many stairs to be descended, which favored Eurialus with time to provide for his better security, who by the counsel of Lucretia took a new covert. Having now gathered up the jewels and writings but not finding those they came for, they returned to search those boxes which were in the closet where Eurialus first took sanctuary. There they met with the papers, and having taken leave of Lucretia they departed. Then did she open the door to her sweet prisoner and invite him forth with the delicate compellations of, "Thou living source of my delights, and summary wherein all my joys are abbreviated and yet not lessened by the contraction, we have now liberty to discharge our minds by conference and to let ourselves loose to the freedom of uncontrolled embraces. Our pleasure will be more endeared and fined by this difficulty of the beginning, which though the perverseness of fortune would have nipped and blasted, yet some favorable power, unwilling to see so loyal a pair abandoned to destruction, kept life in our love by a gentler influence. Here is now neither place nor cause for fear; let me therefore embrace thee, thou armful of roses and lilies. Why dost thou stand? why dost thou doubt? I am thy Lucretia; dost thou abhor her touch?"

Eurialus, his shaking fit having scarce left him, mustered up his spirits and in his arms closely entwined his mistress. "Never," said he, "was I arrested with so terrible an expectation of death. But the greatness of worth makes the sufferings and deservings of thy servants inferior to the acquist; and if things be ratable to their value, then it is a breach of commutative justice that such kisses and embraces should be banished away gratis. And myself (for ingenuity will speak truth) have bought this good at an under rate, having paid nothing for it but the fear of danger. Could I so die as to live again and enjoy thee, a thousand times would I die, to revive and enjoy thee a thousand times. O, the felicity that I am estated in! Do I see a vision, or is my joy a real one? Do I indeed embrace thee, or am I deluded with a phantasm? No, surely, here is no apparition, for this is flesh, not spirit."

Lucretia was arrayed in a very thin pall, which did stick to her so close and without wrinkle, that it rendered her breasts and hips in their true figure and dissembled not her most private motions. Her neck was purely white, and her eyes did flame strongly; but to say white like the snow or flaming like the sun were to dishonor her with the beggarliness of the similitude. A cheerful look, a lively face; the lily and rose are but the obscure types and shadows of those delicate tinctures laid on her cheek by the pencil of nature. Her laughter was free but modest, her breast full, and her paps like two pomegranates did rise up on either side with a gentle and tempting swelling, which as they did beat gave both a signal and a challenge to the encounter.

Eurialus his continency was too weak any longer to abide the trial, and the poor gentleman was not mortified enough to combat so violent a temptation, but having already left his fear he resolved to leave his modesty too, and so boarding the lady, "Now," said he, "let us make ourselves one in each other's reciprocal fruition." She resisted (it seems it is an old fashion), telling him a tale of the great care forsooth she had of her reputation, and that she imagined that his love would be limited within the boundaries of kisses and pretty talking. At that Eurialus smiling assaulted her with this dilemma: "Either it is known," said he, "that I am here, or not. If it be known, who will not suspect the rest? and it will be a simple thing in you to undergo such an imputation and do nothing for it. But if it be unknown, then this likewise shall no man know. It is the earnest of my love, and to want it is to die." "It is a sin," said Lucretia. "Nay," said Eurialus, "it is a sin not to make use of a good thing when you may. To refuse this occasion so freely vouchsafed by yourself, and so diligently labored for by me, were to slight your noble favor and to give the lie to my own endeavors." And with that taking hold of her wrist, he easily overcame her, who did but prevacilate in her resistance and fight with a purpose to be overthrown.

Eurialus and Lucretia 319

Nor did the fruition of her bring any satiety to his appetite, although usually such desires are emptied and evaporated in the enjoying; it did rather add a thirst to his dropsy. But Eurialus having an eye upon his danger, after he had refreshed himself with a banquet took leave of the most unwilling Lucretia, from whom he went unsuspected and unobserved. Being only taken for what he was not, a porter walking homeward, he begins to wonder at himself, being by himself almost put out of his own knowledge, and pensively considers what the event might be if Caesar should meet and know him. "Into what a jealousy," said he to himself, "would this confused habit put him. I should be the common tabletalk, and the best help to discourse; I should never be at quiet till he had extorted from me the mystery of this clownish disguise. But I should be bold to acquaint His Highness with a very little of the truth; he should not know that Menelaus his house was the scene, and that I personated the porter upon that stage, for Caesar is privately my rival and it would prove a matter of dangerous consequence were there but the least whisper abroad that the man had been in the saddle before the master could put his foot in the stirrup. Lucretia must not be discovered; she entertained me, she saved me, and my silence is the least reward I can pay her for her fidelity."

While he thus talked with himself, he espied Palinurus and his trusty Achates, but was at home before they could discover him. Then having doffed his frock, he told them all the passages of his adventure. His passions had so strongly continued their impressions in him that in the relation of his fear and joy he seemed to the spectators really still to fear and really still to joy. "'Fool,' said I to myself, 'to consign my safety to the faith of a woman and adventure my life in so weak a vessel, whose contrary hath been so often commanded by my father that to have perished in the fact had been the merit of my disobedience.' He would discourse to me of their inclinations and manners in so hated a language that he offered violence to my ears, for not any name which implied vice but with him was an epithet worthy that sex. I was thus taught, but I forgot my lesson. If I had been known by any man, sweating under my burden, the dishonor would have been traduced to my posterity, and it would seem an abatement in my coat when my heir should be told that his father bore a sack in his arms. I had been lost to Caesar, who would have thought my levity fitter for a Bedlam than a court. But to interpret favorably for myself, admit my master had passed it for a jest; what if her husband when he was hunting for his papers had started me? The law of Italy is severe enough against the violators of the marriage bed, but the grief of a wronged husband enlargeth itself to a vengeance that will not be limited nor mitigated by law.

> One husband whips th' adulterer dead,
> Another stabs him in his bed.

"But suppose he had spared my life, he would send me to the jail, or which is worse, to Caesar. And grant that I had delivered myself from him, he being disarmed and I having an approved sword secretly by my side, yet there were others with him and the room had weapons to furnish them. Besides in the house were many tall fellows who would presently have shut the doors and then tortured me with such an extremity as would have extinguished the memory of the persecutions. But chance, not cunning, redeemed me from this slaughter-house. Yet why should I call that chance which was the dexterity of Lucretia's wit, and so unjustly rob her the honor of my delivery? Singular is this love, and this lady goes alone. Dear Lucretia, thyself art argument enough to confute my father's invectives, and to vindicate thy whole kind from the imputation of an inconstancy. Why should I doubt then to lay my life in thy fair hands, and dedicate it to the protection of so pure a faith? Had I a thousand necks, I would render them all to thy custody, for thy virtues are fidelity and circumspection, from whence a prudence is derived by which thou knowst how to love and how to

Eurialus and Lucretia

save thy lover. Invention itself could not have contrived a neater trick to divert those importunate searchers, whom thou didst delude with so much art as if thou hadst been born for this end alone, to be recorded the author of so memorable an escape. Thou wert the preserver of my life; be pleased to be the disposer of it, and what it was first thy favor to save, be it now thy grace to accept. I am thy creature, and my breath is from thy benevolence, which in thy service I shall be as ready to lose as thou wert ready to save, for both my life and death are thy prerogative. I am ravished with the speculation of the peculiar rarities of thy wit and beauty, and shall myself be sick, unless I give them another visit.

"When shall I make the second impression of my love upon thy yielding lips, and with my fingers make so many dimples upon thy tender paps? That which thou hast seen, Achates, is not enough to make thee truly say, thou sawest her. There be degrees of activity in her looks, for at a distance they wound and at hand they murder. Hadst thou been with me, thou hadst been struck with a more confounding sight than Tantalus his friend, when that Lydian king, in a pretty frolic, showed him his wife naked. And had I power, my faithful Achates, I would present thee with the like spectacle, for neither can I with all the flourish of rhetoric give you the description of her features, nor canst thou by all the vigor of meditation comprehend the plenitude of my joys. Congratulate therefore with me, and content thyself with this small portion of knowledge, seeing that words are too narrow interpreters to express her many graces, and that my pleasure had something in it more copious and significant than language."

Thus Eurialus talked with Achates, and Lucretia talked as much with herself. Yet was her joy less for want of a partner. Grief, indeed a passion contracting the heart, is lessened by communication, because it is a motion opposite to that contraction. But joy, a passion distending the heart, is augmented by communication, because it is a motion concurring with that distention. But Eurialus must not love alone, for to love Lucretia, and to love without a rival is in the number of impossibles, it being a fortune attending great beauties to have a multitude of flies to court their flames. Baccarus, a knight of Hungary, a man both noble by his birth and by his nearness to Caesar's person, fell extremely in love with her. His hope persuaded that she loved him by an argument drawn from his face, which he knew lovely, but his fear dissuaded the contrary by an argument drawn from her breast, which he thought chaste.

Lucretia, after the manner of the Tuscan ladies, dispensed the smiles of her brows upon the courtiers with so fine an impartiality that, while none of them saw others preferred, every one by a flattering application made himself the man. It is an art, or rather a trick which our ladies practice, whereby to dissemble their love. Baccarus is in a manner dispossessed of the state of his reason, and no counsel can re-establish him in it, until he hath some acquaintance with Lucretia's mind, which was thus attempted.

The gentlewomen of Sienna have a custom to visit Our Lady's Chapel, about a mile from the city. Thither went Lucretia attended with two maids and an old woman. Baccarus followed, with a posy of violets in his hand, very delicately gilded, in whose leaves there was a letter of love with fine subtlety enclosed. And let us stay our wonder at this, since the orator hath avouched that himself saw the Iliads of Homer comprehended in the narrow capacity of a nut-shell. After some humble recommendations, he tendered both himself and violets to Lucretia, and she rejects both. But at the importunity of the Hungarian and by the assistance of the old woman, she was wrought to accept it. "For why, Madam," said she, "should you feign yourself a fear and frame a danger in your imagination to tremble at?" But Lucretia had not long kept it before she gave it one of her maids, who soon after encountering two students was easily over-entreated to part with it, who being

Eurialus and Lucretia

naturally inquisitive had suddenly unveiled the mystery and discovered the paper. Men of this profession have been heretofore principally in the grace of our women, but since Caesar's court came hither, they are but their sport and contempt, for instructed by so fair a precedent as that of Venus and Mars they prefer arms to arts and hold that a pen is not so substantial a weapon as a lance.

The scholars, proud of an opportunity to vindicate themselves of the swordsmen, deliver the letter to Menelaus, and wish him to peruse the tenor of his injuries. Presently the good man was filled with indignation, and the house with noise. Lucretia's innocency pleaded her not guilty, and the narration of the fact and the old woman's evidence did undeniably confirm the plea. Complaint is made to Caesar, and Baccarus convented, who ingenuously confessed a truth so apparent and gave His Majesty an oath never to make new attempts upon her virtue. But he had too much of that heresy, that Jupiter frowns not but smiles upon the perjuries of lovers. This animates him to re-enforce his determination, and the rather because it was forbidden, it being a humor originally traduced, most irregularly to prosecute that which is provided against with the greatest caution and communication.

It was now winter, and Zephyr resigned to a ruder breath; now the women threw snowballs into the streets, and from thence the youth of the city bandied them as fast into their windows. Baccarus will now take an occasion from the winter, as before from the spring; then a violet was his messenger, and now a ball of snow, in which with much cunning he had enclosed a letter, and with no less dexterity directed it into Lucretia's window. Who will not then confess, before the rack be presented him, that there is no bearing of sail which is not of Fortune's trimming, and that she is Lady Regent of all sublunaries.

> One hour of gentle Fate's more prevalent
> Than thy commands to Mars from Venus sent.

There is a wild kind of sect which hath forced this

principle, Fortune hath no interest in wise men. A sort of Stoical wits, who if they were put in Phalaris his bull would not roar but sing. Yet certainly in the managing of the common affair she hath a double stroke, uphill and downhill, to advance a hope and ruin it. She overwhelmed this poor gentleman even when his hopes did almost touch upon the cape of happiness. He was not well advised to enclose his love-letter in a posy of violets, nor at this time to the same purpose to choose no surer convey than a snowball. But had Fortune crowned this device of his with wished success, then had his subtlety and wisdom been extolled by all men above the skies. But see the ill chance; the snowball falling out of Lucretia's hand ran toward the fire, and itself and the seal being dissolved by the heat the letter lay open to view, which Menelaus then in presence presently snatched up, and as greedily perused. The contents occasioned a great combustion, but Baccarus thought it his safer course to trust to a fair pair of heels than to apologies in a fact so evident.

This love of his stood Eurialus in good stead, for the jealous husband taken up in watching Baccarus's steps and actions gave Eurialus fair advantage to put his plots in execution.

>To keep to one's proper use asks mickle pain
>What many seek by love or force to gain.

Between Lucretia's and the adjacent house went a narrow alley; the near posture of the walls afforded an easy ascent into Lucretia's chamber, but this was to be attempted by night only. Menelaus was to go into the country, and to lodge from home. The lovers thought this joyful day long a-coming. He takes his journey; Eurialus changing his habit hies him to the alley. There Menelaus had a stable whereinto Eurialus got by Sosias's directions, and there under the hay took up his lodging. Dromo that was Menelaus's groom in the morning came to the hayloft with his pitchfork, which he struck well nigh into Eurialus's sides and had certainly murdered him had not Sosias by good fortune come that way, who, knowing the danger Eurialus was in, called to Dromo, "Prithee, brother, let me alone to give the horses meat, and in the meanwhile see what good cheer is providing for dinner. Let us be frolic while our lord is away. We live a better life with my lady in his absence; she is merry and freehanded, he peevish, unquiet, covetous, and never pleased. Seest thou not what a miserable house he keeps, how he locks up the victuals from day to day. Wretched caitiff! that seeks by this sordid penury to heap up riches, for is it not the height of foolery to live poor all a man's lifetime to die rich? What a good lady have we that imagining beef and mutton not sufficient feasts us with hollow fowl and denies us not plenty of the rarest wines. Prithee, Dromo, provide good junkets." "Let me alone for that," quoth Dromo; "I have more mind to be in the kitchen than the stable. I brought my master out of town; he gave me not one word all the live-long day, but at evening he bade me tell my lady he should lie abroad all night. I commend thee, Sosias, that abhorrest our master's conditions, and I had long ere now given him the bag if my lady had not retained me by her liberal breakfasts. If you'll agree to it, we'll not sleep a wink tonight; we'll eat and drink till day appear, and waste more in one meal than our master shall have in a whole month."

Eurialus was glad to hear them thus in discourse, yet observed the conditions of servants and imagined that his own in his absence served him with the same sauce. So when Dromo was gone, Eurialus rising up, "What a happy night," quoth he, "Sosias, shall I enjoy by thy courtesy that hast directed me hither, and by an excellent wile kept me from being disclosed. Thou art an honest man, and thy deserts challenge my affection, nor will I prove ungrateful; this good turn shall not go unrewarded."

The appointed hour drew on. Joyful Eurialus, although he had twice escaped narrowly with life, climbs the wall and, the window being open, finds Lucretia by the fire with her junkets about her, expecting his coming. She knowing him to be her sweetheart arose and embraced him. They kiss, and after salutation with wine and dainties refresh their tired spirits. How momentary are our joys! how durable our grief! Eurialus had not had one hour's fruition of content when Sosias brought the sad tidings of Menelaus's return and blasted all their joy. Eurialus is frighted and bethinks himself how to make escape; Lucretia having hid the junkets goes to welcome her husband home.

"Dear husband," quoth she, "thou art welcome. But prithee why stayedst thou so long in the country? Take heed I smell out no piece of waggery. Why dost thou not reside at home? why dost thou excruciate me by thy absence? But prithee, let's sup here, and then we'll go to bed." They were then in the hall where the household used to sit at meals; there she endeavored to stay her husband that Eurialus might more opportunely make escape. But Menelaus had supped abroad and made haste to his bed chamber. Then said Lucretia, "I am nobody in your regard. Why chose you not rather to sup at home with me? I, because you were absent, have neither eaten nor drunk all this day. Some countrymen brought me wine affirming it most neat and terse; my grief would not permit me to taste one drop. Now you be come home, please you, let us go into the cellar, and let us experiment if the wine be suitable to their report." Having thus said, with her right hand she snatched a light and took her husband by the left and so descended the cellar and spun the time out until she thought Eurialus had shifted for himself, and then against her will she went to bed with her husband. Eurialus in the dead of the night returned into the house again.

Next morning Menelaus (whether through provident care or jealousy I wot not) commanded the window to be made up. I verily believe (for our countrymen are shrewd conjecturists and wondrously jealous) that Menelaus suspected the fitting situation of the place, and having none of the best conceits of his wife, was willing to remove the occasion, for though he could not tax her with false play, yet he saw her followed by many suitors, and knew a woman's mind was fickle, having as many changes as a tree leaves, the feminine sex being great lovers of novelty and sated with the fruition, set naught by their own husbands. He therefore tracked the path that all jealous husbands go, who strongly conceit that watchful observation may keep their wives from treading awry. By this means their meeting was debarred, and their intercourse by letters was likewise stopped, for by Menelaus's persuasions the governor put down the vintner, out of whose rooms (situated on the back side of Lucretia's house) Eurialus was wont to talk unto Lucretia and by a reed reach letters to her. They had nothing left them but an interview only, and unspeakable was their grief that were unable to desist yet knew not how to make progression in their amorous negotiation.

Eurialus thus musing what way to take, he remembered Lucretia's counsel concerning Pandalus, a gentleman allied to her husband, and in imitation of learned physicians that in dangerous diseases rather experiment some doubtful dose and perilous potion than desert their patient for incurable, he resolves to assay Pandalus and make trial of a remedy which he had formerly refused. Having called him and being withdrawn into a private room, he thus bespoke him. "Friend, I desire you to sit. I have a weighty business to disclose to you. It requires diligence, trust and secrecy, with all which I acknowledge you are endued. I would long since have intimated the same unto you, had not the tender growth of your acquaintance retarded me. I now both know you and for your approved fidelity love and honor you. But if you were a mere stranger to me, your countrymen's general good report were sufficient, and those friends of mine with whom you be familiar have let me know your rare qualities and what great esteem you merit, by whose insinuations I am informed that you are desirous of my favor, whereof I now deliver you seisin, your merits as much as mine claiming an interchange of our mutual affections. But to the point. There shall not need many words between friends. You are not ignorant what imperious sway love, either virtuous or sensual, bears in the hearts of mortal men; no heart that is not made of adamant but hath felt the force thereof. From this passion I have not read of any man could claim immunity. This frenzy can be no otherwise cured but by the fruition of the party beloved; our times and former ages afford plentiful examples of both sexes, who, prizing love at as high rate as life itself, denied the one, have disdained to retain the other.

"My drift in this relation is to acquaint you with my love and what I would request at your hands. I will not conceal from you what profit will redound hence, because I esteem you as my most intrinsical friend. I love Lucretia, nor am I, my Pandalus, to be blamed, but Fortune, the Lady Regent of this lower world we all adore. I knew not the customs of this city; your women dissemble with their looks what their hearts mean not. Hence grew my error: Lucretia's smiles made me think myself beloved, and can any accuse me for setting my affection on so worthy an object? But finding my hopes beguiled, I not being able to retreat, I left no means unassayed till I won Lucretia to my love. Now our flames have equal vigor, and without your assistance we are both of us undone. Her husband and brother watch her narrowly; the Golden Fleece was not so attended by the restless dragon, or Hell gates by Cerberus as she is. I know your lineage, your nobleness, riches, power. Would I had never known this woman. But who can stand against destiny? Fortune, not my election, made her my mistress.

"In this posture matters now stand. Our love is concealed as yet, but once brought to light will produce some hideous mischief, which I pray heaven avert. Haply I could master my desires by departing this city, which I would do, though to my great grief for your house's sake, if I thought it would do any good. But I know the height of her passion is such she would either follow me or, forced to stay, by her own hands rid her loathed life, which would be an everlasting stain to your family. For the removal of these evils I desired this meeting. To your care I commend the management of this important affair. It lies in you by procuring our congress to assuage our mutual flames. You know the several accesses of the house, what time her husband is away, and know how to introduce me. Your help is needful to beguile her husband's brother that keeps so strict a watch over her. Be diligent and give me inkling at what time her husband is absent. Use some sleight to remove the brother and that he may surrender that charge to yourself alone, which I pray heaven may so fall out. Then by your admission of me by night while all are in a deep slumber all things will sort to a happy conclusion.

"It cannot be unknown to your wisdom what sundry commodities will hence ensue. The honor of your house will be kept untainted; our love concealed, which if it should be known would be an infamy to your family; you shall preserve your kinswoman's life; Menelaus shall be obliged to you for his wife's safety. Of two evils the less is to be chosen. What course soever be taken, there will be danger in it, but this expedient hath the least. Nor would I have you think your pains shall go unrequited. You know my favor with Caesar; you shall obtain whatsoever you will ask. And this I will promise you: you shall be made a Count Palatine to you and your heirs forever. Then bestir yourself. I commend to your care and fidelity Lucretia, myself, our love, our reputation, the honor of your family; they are all in your power. It lies in your hands to ruin all or to preserve all."

Having heard all this, Pandalus smiled, and, pausing a while, "O Eurialus," said he, "all this I knew and wish things had been otherwise, but you have said no more than truth; things are now at that pass that I must of necessity help, or great infamy will light upon our family. Lucretia is so far engaged in love that if I succor not, she will either stab herself or throw herself headlong out at windows; she regards neither her life nor honor. Herself hath disclosed her love to me. I dehorted her, chid her, sought to extinguish the flame, but could not prevail; she regards nothing but you, she thinks on nothing else but you. Calling often to me, she says, "Dost hear, Eurialus?" Love has so changed her that she is not like herself. The whole city had not a chaster, a wiser dame. What a wonderful thing it is that love should bear such rule in human minds. You have hit on the right way of cure.

"I will about this business, nor will I exact any reward at your hands, knowing it is not the part of an honest man to ask any boon where no recompense is deserved. What I do is to remove the scandal threatened our family." "But," quoth Eurialus, "if you do not disdain it, I will procure you the style and dignity of a Count Palatine." "I scorn it not," quoth Pandalus, "but I would not have it by way of bargain, but would have it conferred on me freely and unconditionally. It would have more sorted to my desires to have promoved your wishes and brought you into Lucretia's presence, and you not to have known the author of so good a turn. Farewell." "And fare you well," quoth Eurialus; "set all your wits a-work to bring us together."

Away goes Pandalus, rejoicing with acquisition of so great a man's favor and with the hopes of being made a Count, which dignity the less he seemed to desire, the more he coveted, many men in this being like women, who the more they say nay, the more intensely desire what seemingly they refuse. This man by playing the pandar is honored with an earldom and his posterity ennobled forever after. O Marianus, there are many degrees in nobleness, and if you search the original thereof, in my opinion you will find very few that can rightly boast a lawful propagation. The rich, they commonly are ennobled, but riches and virtue seldom move in one sphere; therefore such nobleness flows from an impure fountain. It is a wonder to see a man grow rich by honest course. All approve that verse,

None ask how wealth's attained but it must be had.

After the bags are well lined, then nobleness is the thing next sought after. I say,

> Virtue alone does make a noble man.

Not many days after, there grew a broil amongst Menelaus's tenants (many whereof being much gone in drink lost their lives), for composing whereof Menelaus's presence was held requisite. Upon this occasion it was concluded that Eurialus about the hour of five in the evening should draw towards the house, and if he heard Pandalus sing should hope the best. Eurialus came at the hour prefixed, and listened attentively for the watchword, but he could hear no music, nor so much as any whispering noise at all. Achates as soon as the appointed hour was past counselled Eurialus to depart, telling him that they meant nothing else but to gull and delude him. It liked not Eurialus to remove, alleging many reasons one after another for a longer stay.

The brother of Menelaus was left behind, whose vigilancy and suspicious scrutiny up and down in every corner hindered Pandalus singing. Quoth Pandalus, "Shall we not go to bed tonight? I can no longer hold open my eyes. I wonder that being in your tender years you should so sympathize with the nature of old men, that deprived of their youthful moisture seldom fall asleep till morning, when it is time for others to rise. It's high time; pray, let's go to rest. I marvel you sit up so late." "Let's go then," quoth Agamemnon, "if you'll needs have it so; yet first let's see that all be sure." So going to the gate he double-locked and bolted it very strong. A huge bar of iron there was which two men were not able to lift, which Agamemnon finding himself unable to wield, "Pandalus," quoth he, "let's make fast the door with this bar, and then we'll go to bed." Eurialus heard these words and whispered with a soft voice, "If they had done with this bar once, then all were done." "Come, come," quoth Pandalus, "what a coil keep you? If it be thieves only you fear, all is cocksure; if enemies, all the ammunition in this house is not able to keep them out. I'll lift no bar tonight; or do it yourself, or it shall be undone for me." "Well, it matters not greatly," quoth Agamemnon, and so went to rest.

Then said Eurialus, "I'll watch here for an hour to see if any will open." Achates was so tired that in his heart he cursed Eurialus for keeping him out of his bed so late. They had not stayed long but at a chink they might perceive Lucretia with a small taper in her hands. Eurialus pressing as near as he could possibly, "Sweetheart Lucretia," quoth he, "all health to you." At first she began to fly, but presently better bethinking herself, she asks who's there. Quoth Eurialus, "I thy Eurialus am here. Open the door, my joy; I have watched here till midnight for thy coming." She knew the voice, yet for more sureness and prevention of any false dissimulation she forbore to open till she heard the byword which they two privily gave each other. Then with much ado she opened the door a little way, and Eurialus made as hard shift to creep in at so strait a passage, and embraced her in his arms. Achates he stood sentinel without doors.

I am not able to say whether it were fear or excess of joy that was the cause, but Lucretia falling into a pale swoon in Eurialus his arms seemed like a lifeless creature; her speech failing and her eyelids being closed up, some warmth remained, and her pulses beat faintly. Eurialus knew not which way to turn him: "If I leave her, I am accessary to her death that left her in so dangerous extremity; if I stay, Agamemnon or one or other of the house will find us and I shall be sure to die. O unfortunate love, more bitter than gall! for thee to how many dangers have I been obnoxious? How many deaths have awaited me for thy sake? Was this a cross that thou keptst for me in store to extinguish my dearest love within my own embraces?" But love overswayed all other respects and nought regarding his own safety he abode with his dear, and being dissolved into tears, oft kissing her speechless corpse, he cried out, "Woe's me! Lucretia, where art thou? Why dost not hear? Why makest thou no answer? Open thy eyes and behold me, and smile on me as thou wast wont. I thy Eurialus am here. O my dear, it is thy Eurialus that embraces thee. O, why dost not return me one, for so many hundred kisses? Is this thy entertainment? Are these the joys thou invitest me to? I conjure thee, arise, look on thy Eurialus; it is I thy Eurialus that am here."

Having ended these exclamations, a cataract of scalding tears he let fall upon her face and temples, whereby as one by strong waters' help resuscitated, seeming like one raised out of a dead lethargy of sleep, and beholding her beloved, "Ah me, Eurialus," said she, "where have I been? Why didst thou not rather suffer me to expire? It is a happy death to die in thy arms. Would heaven I had departed so before thou depart this city." Conferring after this manner, they set forward towards her chamber, where bathing themselves in Venerian delights, "Now," quoth Eurialus, "my toil and danger are changed into joys beyond expression. O summary of all beauty, am I now possessed of thee? It were best dying now whilst this bliss endures, lest intervenient misery again blast our contentments. My happiness is incomparable. But, alas, how swiftly do the hours fly away! O malignant night, what makes thee make such haste? This verily is the shortest night in all the year." This spoke Eurialus, nor was Lucretia behind. They vied kisses, and for amorous phrases were neither in other's debt. At the peep of day our lovers depart asunder.

Caesar having now wrought his peace with Pope Eugenius hastens his journey towards Rome. Lucretia was not without some inkling hereof, for what is it that love perceives not? Thus therefore upon this ground wrote Lucretia to Eurialus.

LUCRETIA TO EURIALUS

Had I power to be angry with thee, it should be now, that being ready to depart canst so cunningly dissemble with me. But my heart is more affectionate to thee than itself, and can by no cause be drawn to conceive displeasure against thee. My dear heart, why didst thou not acquaint me that Caesar will shortly be gone? He prepares for his journey, and I know thou wilt not stay behind. What, I prithee, will become of me? Wretch that I am, what shall I do? Where can I enjoy tranquillity? If thou forsake me, I shall not live two days. I conjure thee by these lines moistened with my tears, by thy hand and faith given unto me, if ever I have deserved aught at thy hands or if ever my acquaintance won thy acceptation, take pity on a forlorn lover. I make no boon that you would still reside here, but that you would make me the companion of your travel. I will some evening give it out that I desire to walk to Bethlehem, attended by one old woman; there let two or three of your train lie in wait that may receive me. It is no hard task to carry one away that is willing to go. Nor think not the attempt will prove your disparagement, for King Priam's son accounted it no disgrace to wed a stolen lady. My husband shall hereby suffer no wrong, for however things go, he shall be sure to lose me. For if you carry me not away, death shall separate me from him. But by your cruelty leave me not to die, who have ever prized you dearer than my own heart.

EURIALUS'S ANSWER

I kept it from thee till this hour, my Lucretia, that thou mightest not torment thyself before the time were come. I know thy nature, and that every light occasion causes thee to fret too too bad. Nor is Caesar to depart hence forever; when we return from Rome our way lies through this city into our native country. Should Caesar make choice of another way, if I do not return to thee, may I never see my own home again, but like Ulysses spend the remnant of my days in foreign peregrination. Give not thyself over to melancholy, my dearest, but cheer up thyself. For the rape you speak of, all the world affords not such a content as that would be to me, but I more value thy honor than my own delight. The confidence you have reposed in me awakens a provident care of your well-doing. You are descended of a right noble house, and your reputation is extolled not at home only but in far remote regions. Should I commit this act, I speak not of mine own, what disgrace would it be to your family? What a heart-break to your mother, what a scandalous rumor throughout all the city. Behold, will they say, Lucretia that was imputed so chaste a dame is turned a whore and run away from her husband. Hitherto you have conserved your credit unstained; this rape would sully your reputation with an indelible disgrace.

But to let pass fame, though she worthily deserve our regard, this way we can never attain the fruition of our love. I depend on Caesar; if I forsake him, my means are too short to maintain thee after thy degree. If on the other side, I follow the court, there's no repose; we daily remove from place to place. Caesar never made so long abode anywhere as he has now at Sienna, enforced through necessity of war. What infamy were it to us both, should I use thee in the camp as a common prostitute? I conjure thee, my Lucretia, upon these grounds alter thy determination; take my advice in good part and regard not thy passion above thy welfare. Haply another lover would have persuaded thee otherwise and been the first that would have counselled thee to make escape, to the end he might abuse thee at his pleasure, never forecasting for the future but greedy to satisfy his present lust; but such a one deserves not the style of a true lover, that prefers the fulfilling of his lust before a care of reputation. I, my dear Lucretia, advise thee for the best. I prithee abide here, and diffide not my return; I will so contrive it that Caesar shall send me agent into these parts and free of all discommodity will compass our mutual fruition. Farewell, live happy, and love thy Eurialus, and wrong me not by thinking my love less fervent than thine own, or that I am willing to depart. O, no more, my sweet. Adieu.

Lucretia acquieted by these persuasions wrote him back word that she would follow his counsel. Few days after, Eurialus set forward with Caesar toward Rome, and shortly after his arrival fell into a fever. Unfortunate man that burning in love was nevertheless seized by aguish inflammations! Love had brought his body low, and his disease brought him even to death's door, insomuch that he was more beholden for life to physicians than nature. Caesar visited him day by day, and was as tender over him as he had been his own child, and commanded to send for all the prime physicians. But a letter sent him from Lucretia, whereby he understood that she was both living and in good health, did him more good than all the doctors' receipts. It drove away his ague, and made him strong enough to walk abroad, insomuch as he was present at Caesar's coronation, and honored with the addition of knighthood.

When Caesar went to Perusium he stayed behind at Rome, as not yet perfectly recovered. From thence he came to Sienna, very feeble and macilent; he might see his Lucretia, but might not confer with her. Letters passed mutually, and the business about her rape is again had in agitation. Here Eurialus stayed three days, but finding it impossible to gain access unto her, he intimated unto her his departure. Their grief at their separation exceeded their joy in their mutual society.

Lucretia stood at the window when Eurialus rode through the street; they cast their blubbered eyes on one another and were so oppressed with sorrow, as they that felt their hearts even violently rent out of their bosoms. Who but a lover like themselves is able to draw the portraiture of their resentments? Laodamia when her husband

Prothesilaus went to the Trojan wars fell into an ecstasy and died at report of her husband's slaughter. Queen Dido slew herself after Aeneas stole away, and Portia would live no longer, her Brutus being dead. Our Lucretia when Eurialus was out of her sight fell down in a swoon, and was by the servants got up and had to bed till she came to herself. But after, suiting herself in mean habit, she was never heard sing, never seen to laugh, nor could never be made merry by all the means that ever could be used.

Thus persevering for some space of time, and living heartless and insusceptible of comfort, in the arms of her weeping mother that in vain sought her consolation, she expired her latest gasp.

Eurialus having lost the sight of Lucretia spoke not one word as he travelled, had Lucretia only in his heart, and his thoughts were whether he should ever be able to return unto her. At last he came to Caesar, keeping his court at Perusium, whom he attended into divers countries. But as he followed Caesar, so Lucretia's ghost pursued him and suffered him not to take any quiet repose.

This faithful lover, understanding that she was dead, struck to the heart with sorrow, he put himself in mourning. At last Caesar made up a match for him, and he espoused a beauteous, chaste, and prudent virgin of princely lineage.

Dear Marianus, you have heard a true narration of the sad catastrophe of a pair of unfortunate lovers. Let the reader hereof by others' harms learn to beware and not be inebriated with the potions of love, which have ever a greater mixture of gall than honey.

Farewell. From Vienna the fifth of the Nones of July, 1444.

FINIS

THE PLEASANT HISTORY OF CAWWOOD the ROOKE.

OR,

The Assembly of Birds, with the severall Speeches which the Birds made to the *Eagle*, in hope to have the Government in his Absence: And lastly, how the Rooke was banished; with the Reason why crafty Fellowes are called Rookes.

As also fit Morralls and Expositions added to every Chapter.

London Printed by *T.C.* for *F. Grove*, and are to be sold at his Shoppe, at the upper-end of Snow-Hill, neere the Sarazens head without New-Gate, 1640.

CAWWOOD THE ROOK (1640)

Cawwood the Rook is an obvious imitation of the much-loved and much-read *Reynard the Fox* (which has been in print steadily, in one form or another, ever since Caxton's 1481 translation), of whose popularity in the seventeenth century it affords additional evidence. The anonymous author of *Cawwood,* however, has not gone beyond the initial situation in his model: the convocation of subjects at their king's court and the accusations levelled at the villain. While in *Reynard* the subsequent action is mainly motivated by the Fox's clever wiles in evading punishment and in duping the king, *Cawwood* is content to hustle the Rook, who is as much victim as evil-doer, off the scene in a rather lame ending which, in an awkward change of direction, moves the story from the realm of moral apologue into that of social satire, where it is uncomfortably out of place. The force of the preceding morals, little enough in all conscience, is further vitiated by the reader's discovery that the whole thing is a sort of joke. How different from Reynard, whose genuine wickedness gives the morality some point! The end hardly crowns the work in this instance.

Nevertheless, the author is not entirely bereft of ability, for he is able to exploit the situation itself entertainingly enough. The sketches of the various birds, each portrait pointed up amusingly by that individual's characteristic speech, are pleasantly done and bear some slight resemblance to that favorite seventeenth-century genre, the "character." It is useless of course to complain that the Eagle's departure seems rather arbitrary and unmotivated or that for a title-character Cawwood has remarkably little to do with the action of his own book. One may wish, however, that the final scene had dealt with the Eagle's return; not only would such a conclusion have been able to enforce the morality, but it could have given us an avian *Measure for Measure*.

First published in 1640, *Cawwood* was reprinted several times, once in 1656, again in 1683, and Esdaile (pp. 28–29) notes two undated editions, the second of which must have appeared around the year 1700. In the early eighteenth century, beginning in 1702, the story was appended to editions of the then current (abridged) version of *Reynard*; at least six editions of the two tales under one pair of covers appeared. The text here presented is based on the Harvard copy of the 1640 edition.

THE PLEASANT HISTORY OF CAWWOOD THE ROOK

Chapter I

In the heat of summer, when the woods were lined with pleasant shade and filled with the cheerful music of the feathered choristers, it happened that the Eagle, the royal king of birds, intending to leave off his government awhile and to live solitary in the deserts of Arabia, made a proclamation to the drawn in this manner: That seeing he purposed for some reasons best known unto himself to retire unto the Arabian desert, and for some few months to leave off all rule and dominion, he therefore tendering the welfare of his subjects, and being careful they might not lack one in his absence to administer justice unto them, thought good to signify his royal will and pleasure, which was that all birds, of what name, color, or degree soever, should repair unto the Wood, called Sylvia, and that there he purposed to choose one amongst them to rule the rest, who could declare himself to be most worthy in merit and desert.

Cawwood the Rook

This proclamation being written and subscribed with *Aquila rex avium,* which is in English, The Eagle King of Birds, it was no sooner made known through all thickets, hedges, and bushy fields where birds do resort, but that presently their hearts were inflamed with ambition, everyone desiring to prove himself worthy of the vice-regency or government, during the retiring of the king. So that in a short time there were come unto the Court of Sylvia Robert the Robin, Mavis the Magpie, Phillip the Sparrow, the Blackbird, Starling, and Jackdaw, with Philomel the Nightingale, Tom Titmouse, Parvis the Wren, Spinck the Finch, Columber the Dove, and Maybird the Cuckoo, with many others which came with prepared speeches to make known their own worth. But now the Eagle, having seated himself on a high cedar tree, began to look down upon the assembly of birds, who sat upon the lower boughs round about him, and by the piercing quickness of his eye, he soon perceived that his cousin, Rapax the Hawk, who was somewhat akin unto him, and Cawwood the Rook were only absent. So that before he would make known his mind unto them, he sent Flywill the Buzzard for his cousin, Rapax the Hawk, and Cawwood the Rook, and withal fearing that the Hawk kept out of the way because he had committed many outrages upon the smaller birds, he sent him a free pardon for all his former offences, bidding Flywill to command him to come away with all speed.

THE MORAL

There is no man hath so mean a conceit of himself but he thinks he deserveth honor and preferment, as may appear by the Wren and the small birds, who all resorted to the Court upon the Eagle's proclamation to make the worthiest vice-regent in his absence. The Hawk and the Rook keeping away from court doth show that a guilty conscience is a self-accuser, and maketh men afraid to come in sight, especially at any public meeting.

Chapter II. How Flywill the Buzzard carried a pardon to Rapax the Hawk, and how the Hawk and the Rook requited him for his pains.

No sooner had Flywill the Buzzard tied the pardon with a string round about his neck, but straight he took wing and flew away to a wood some three miles off, to which he knew the Hawk and the Rook did use to resort, and there accordingly he soon met with them and delivered the pardon to the Hawk, telling him that the King out of his free mercy had sent him a pardon for all his former bloody facts, wishing him to obey the former proclamation and to make all haste that could be to come unto the court. The Hawk took the pardon and, having read it, he gave Flywill the Buzzard many thanks for that he being so short of wing had taken the pains to bring him these good tidings, and so walking aside with Cawwood the Rook, as if they had consulted about going to the Court, the Hawk told the Rook that this Buzzard, albeit he was akin unto him, was a shame and disgrace unto all Hawks, being a coward and not daring to seize on anything but dead carrion or some scattered guts or to take children's bread and butter out of their hands, all which do show the baseness of his breeding and that he never came out of the true nest or aerie of the Hawks, "and therefore, friend Rook, seeing thou hast been accounted a cunning politician in thy days, I would entreat thee to instruct me in some device how we might make him away and yet have no hand in the matter." The Rook scratching his head with one of his claws stood still awhile, till at last turning to the Hawk, he told him that there was a new invention come into his brain how to make away the Buzzard, and set him going with a powder.

After this they returned again unto Flywill the Buzzard, who never suspected what they had contrived against him, but complained unto them that he had gotten a great cold in his head by flying so far in a rainy day, he being only

Cawwood the Rook

used to haunt warrens and there to fly from one old tree to another and so pass away the time. But no sooner had the Rook heard him say that he had gotten a cold, but he presently took hold of the occasion, telling him that there was no better medicine for a cold than warmth, and therefore if he would but tie his head about with a cloth he should find that the rheum would presently void itself and run out of his beak in a great abundance. The Buzzard being full of pain with the headache consented thereunto, so that the Rook very carefully and cunningly tied a clout round about his head and so bid him fly to the next tree. The foolish Buzzard, thinking he could find out the way for all he was blindfolded, took wing and flew directly against the body of a great oak, which beat him back so violently that he came fluttering through the boughs, till at last he caught hold on one of them with his talons, and so having perched himself he thought to sit there till the Hawk and the Rook, his learned physicians, did come unto him; but they flew unto another tree from whence they might behold the Buzzard sitting very demurely by himself. But he had not sat there long, when it happened that one came by with a birding piece, and perceiving so fair a mark, went towards him, and taking his aim gave fire and shot the Buzzard that he came tumbling down stark dead. Which when the Rook and the Hawk perceived, they flew away toward the Court, the Hawk being very glad that his Cousin Buzzard was brought to this end, and so giving the Rook many thanks for inventing this device which had so luckily taken effect, they both flew together to the Court.

THE MORAL

Some are so blindfolded that they cannot discern danger before it come upon them, as may appear by the Buzzard, who sat blindfolded in the tree, till the fowler came by and shot him. The Hawk bringing his Cousin Buzzard to an untimely death showeth that the rich do despise their poor kindred and so do expose them to danger.

Chapter III. How Rapax the Hawk and Cawwood the Rook came to the Court, and how the Eagle declared unto the birds the reason why he called them together.

The Eagle being, as before, mounted upon a cedar, all the birds in a circle sat round about him, making such a charm of several notes, tunes, and ditties, that if you had heard them, you would have sworn you had never heard the like. As they were thus sitting together, in came the Hawk and the Rook with nimble wing, and took their place amongst the other birds. And so the Hawk having made obeisance to the King began in an eloquent speech to amplify the King's mercy, who had not only granted him a free pardon for all his former bloody offences, but also safe protection to come unto that place. But the Eagle cut him off in his speech, saying, "Cousin, I hope my mercy shall find that reward which I expect, which is that you will amend your life, for that is the best way to give me thanks and satisfy the whole Commonwealth of Birds, who else, though they dare not speak yet openly, yet in their hearts they will condemn me of injustice for remitting the bloody murders and slaughters of my subjects which you have daily committed. But I have other matters to declare unto you and therefore I would have you give attention." And so with his scepter, which he held in one of his talons, making a sign unto them for silence, he began his royal speech in this manner.

"My loving subjects, it behooveth a king to be careful of his subjects, even from the highest to the lowest. I therefore do here profess that all my subjects are equally dear unto me, so that my cousin the Hawk is not more dear unto me than the little Wren. It behooveth me therefore that as I have made known my purpose unto you by my proclamation, which is, to leave my Court of Sylvia and fly into the solitary deserts of Arabia, so it is necessary for the establishing of peace and quiet in my absence that I leave

Cawwood the Rook

one to rule and govern over you; and to this end I have called you to this assembly, that whatsoever bird among you can prove himself to be the worthiest, either by parentage, merit, or desert, or any other way, him I will make king in my absence. Therefore let everyone speak boldly in the behalf of themselves, and urge what reasons they can in their own practice."

The birds hearing this began to clap their wings and with chirping and chattering gave a great applause to the Eagle's speech.

THE MORAL

That when a wicked offender receives mercy, either from the king or a magistrate, he cannot show more thankfulness than by amending his life, for so the kingly Eagle told his cousin, Rapax the Hawk. Kings ought to take care of their subjects in their absence, as appeareth by the Eagle's speech to the Commonalty of Birds, whose rejoicing thereat does show how acceptable the gracious speech of a king is to his loving subjects.

HOW PARVIS THE WREN MADE A SPEECH UNTO THE EAGLE

The Wren all this while sat upon thorns, though indeed she were now upon a higher tree than ever she was in her life before, being always wont to creep and peep in the hedge bottom, and therefore it seems that the height of the tree had put high conceits into her head. So that perking up herself, and getting upon a small twig from whence she might be seen of all the company, she began most earnestly to desire the kingly Eagle to make her his substitute. "For," says she, "though I am but a Wren, and of a small body, yet my heart is as big as the best, and for my wit and policy, you may see it in building my nest and the workmanship thereof. And therefore though I am least of birds, yet if you please, I think myself worthy to bear the greatest authority among birds." The Wren would still have gone on, being all heart and tongue, but that the Eagle commanded Robert the Robin to speak next.

THE MORAL

This showeth that men of least desert will put themselves most forward, as is seen by the Wren preferring herself before all other birds, and the reason is because those that have the least worth have the greatest opinion of themselves.

HOW ROBERT THE ROBIN SPOKE TO THE EAGLE

"My Lord the Eagle, I hope Robert the Robin is not unknown unto you, whom men, women, and children do love, honor, and respect. No piece is discharged against me, no snare set for me, so that I fly with safety into houses, butteries, and cellars, because no man will hurt a Robin. The reason why I am beloved is for my courtesy and familiarity towards men, for if I find a dead body in the wood, I and the rest of my fellows do bury it with moss and leaves, and for this I am called the Sexton of the Wood. Besides, I sing in winter, neither can the coldest frosts put me down, when all the other birds like cowards creep into bushes. I therefore having the better heart, and being generally beloved, do know no reason why I may not govern the Commonwealth of Birds in your royal absence."

THE MORAL

It is some argument of worth in ourselves when we are beloved of others, as appears by the speech of Robert the Robin, who urges it as a praise unto himself to be beloved of men.

THE OWL'S SPEECH

The Owl being not in those times afraid of the other birds but esteemed as a grave counsellor, began to speak next; but with such a hollow voice as no man could understand him, yet some of his words were to this purpose. "May it please your royal Eagleship, the Owl was beloved of Pallas, and the Lacedemonians did coin their money with the stamp and picture of an Owl, so much did the Lacedemonians love me." But the birds hearing the Owl speak of the Lacedemonians, they fell all into a confused chirping or laughter, so that the Owl without taking any leave flew away, and ever since that time hath hid his head in an old ivy tree, being ashamed of daylight and shunning the company of the other birds.

THE MORAL

That when men will strive to show learning at unseasonable times, it makes them prove ridiculous, as appears by the Owl, who was laughed at for his learned speech of the Lacedemonians.

THE SPEECH OF PHILOMEL THE NIGHTINGALE

After the Owl was laughed out of countenance, the Nightingale began to delight their ears with her sweet harmonious voice, and no sooner had she framed herself to speak but the birds were ready to give attendance to her speech, which was in this manner. "Most royal Sovereign, if I should declare my sorrows which I record by night, making the thorn my songbook, I know it would move you to compassionate my unjust ravishment; for know that I was daughter to a king and ravished by my sister Progne's husband, called Tereus, and afterward by some strange power we were all changed into birds, Tereus into a Lapwing, my sister Progne into a Swallow, and I Philomel into a Nightingale, who still in lamentable tunes, setting my breast against a thorn, do warble forth my own grief. And seeing every bird hath free liberty to praise herself, I may boldly say that I am the honor of the woods, the darling of the spring, the lovers' joy; for young men and maids will walk out together to hear my notes, and if they hear me before Maybird the Cuckoo they are in good hope they shall enjoy their sweethearts that year. I am called Philomel for my melodious strains; my body is little, my voice is loud, so that one said of me, *Vox et praeterea nihil,* that I was only a voice and nothing else. If therefore my great birth, my former wrongs, or pleasant tunes have any power to declare my merit, I hope the crown and scepter may be worthily resigned unto me, having been sometime a king's daughter and therefore fit to be made queen of the woods."

THE MORAL

Injured virtue is pitied of all men, which made Philomel declare the story of her ravishment, and by the birds giving so diligent attention unto her is showed that a well-delivered speech hath a great power over the mind and affections.

THE CUCKOO'S SPEECH

Maybird the Cuckoo having heard the sweet speech which Philomel had made, thinking he could have made as good himself, for yet he had not sucked so many eggs to make him hoarse, and therefore getting upon a bared bough, he began to wipe his beak and rub it upon the tree, afterwards he fluttered his wings, and at last fetching his breath as if he meant to make a long speech, he began in this manner. "Great King, I am the Cuckoo, Cuckoo,

Cuckoo," and so he could go no further, but still cried "Cuckoo, Cuckoo," whereat all the other birds laughed, and the Cuckoo was much dismayed and since then he will never be seen of the birds but only in May, and for that reason he is called the Maybird.

THE MORAL

This shows that great preparations have small performances, and that those whose brains seem to be in labor with a mountain do at last bring forth a mouse, as may be perceived by Maybird the Cuckoo, who made them believe that she had great matters to speak and at last could say nothing but Cuckoo, Cuckoo, and so was laughed at for her pains.

THE SPEECH OF CORVINO THE CROW

When the Cuckoo had ended with shame as she began with great ostentation, then Corvino the Crow stood up and told them he was a great astrologer, having knowledge in the influence of the stars, the shiftings of the winds, the change of the weather, all which he made known unto men by voice, so that the shepherds are wont to say,

> When the Crow doth cry amain,
> Then you may be sure of rain.

"Besides, my craft and cunning it is such, that I am seldom ensnared and brought to ruin, and therefore I ought for my policy to be preferred. If a horse chance to die, I am presently upon his bones; or if a lamb or sheep be weak, I pick out his eyes, and afterward do fly to some tree and from thence do hear how the shepherds curse me, but yet for all that I thrive the better. If therefore policy or knowledge in affairs may enable one for public government, you may make me your substitute, and deliver the crown unto the Crow, for to him it belongeth, if desert may bear it away."

THE MORAL

Those that have no knowledge will presume many times to be professors of arts, so that every art hath some ignorant fellows who will pretend to have skill therein, as mountebanks will needs be physicians and fellows with a little Latin will needs be scholars, as the Crow, because he cries sometimes before rain, would therefore needs be an astrologer.

THE SPEECH OF MAVIS THE MAGPIE

The Magpie after this began to chatter out his mind, saying he was once a king and so was changed into a pie and therefore he might now again be changed from a pie into a king. "Besides," saith he, "I have been always esteemed as a poet, for I can make verses and chatter them out so fast that you would wonder at it, and I can tell you the Commonwealth of Birds have much delighted in my songs and ditties, being excellent rime with some reason, and therefore I think they have reason to applaud me. And for proof of my skill you shall hear some of my verses."

>Although I am no Jackdaw
>Nor house Crow that crieth caw,
>Yet I am a Magpie,
>That can make sweet melody,
>And sing so in my mother tongue,
>That all birds shall admire my song.

And no sooner had he spoken these verses, but the Magpie seeing the birds laugh at him, he swore they were very good lines and that they had no more wit than Woodcocks or else they would have praised them.

THE MORAL

Because this moral will be offensive to some magpies in the world, I will deliver the moral to two verses out of Persius the poet, entreating of the same matter.

> *Corvos poetas, & poetridas picas,*
> *Cantare credas, Pegaseium melos.*

Crow Poets and poetic pies,
Do think they make sweet melodies.

THE SPEECH OF ANSER THE GOOSE

After this Anser the Goose and Coby the Cock having by chance heard the proclamation as they were standing under a hedge, they came flying thither, but being not able to light upon a tree, the Goose and the Cock stood at the bottom of the tree, which when the Eagle perceived, he came down to them and all the birds sat round about upon the ground. Then the Goose began to speak in this manner. "Albeit I am esteemed a cowardly bird, because when I go under a barn door I stoop down my head, yet I can speak much in my own behalf; for to begin with former times, I, only my gaggling voice, saved the Capitol of Rome from being taken by the enemy, as I know your Eagleship hath read in histories. Besides, if I come unto these times, how could the lawyer's clerk or scrivener make the poor countrymen pay for their law, unless I lent them quills to write their bills and bonds? So that I think the gray goose wing may be as much feared now as in the old time when they headed their arrows with my feathers, for then many times they lost lives and now their lands, while the sheep affords the parchment and I afford the pen with which the prodigal sets his hand to the seal or mortgage of his whole patrimony. Besides, I have a great many two-legged kindred in the world, who yet scorn to acknowledge me, but the world knows them to be Geese. And therefore considering how necessary I am, I hope you will give me pre-eminence above the other birds." After him the Cock spoke as followeth.

COBY THE COCK'S SPEECH

"I am Coby the Cock, or the bird of Mars. I fight single combats and from the cockpit I bear away the bloody victory. I am the country clock, and tell the maids when 'tis time to rise. I call up the laborer to his work and proclaim daylight over the whole world. I am loving to my hens, respected of my dame that keeps me, and fed with the best barley she can get, and in requital I tread her hens lustily and make them lay eggs. To conclude, I am come of a generous kind, being the true emblem of valor, and so necessary that the world could not tell how to do for eggs at Shrovetide if the Cock should fail. And therefore if the matter might be decided by voices, I know the country wives would desire to have me made king, for they do all love a good treading Cock."

THE JACKDAW'S SPEECH

"Though I am last to take boldness to speak, yet I hope you will consider that I am an excellent linguist, and have the knowledge of many languages, so that when we Jackdaws are got together about a steeple, we make a chattering noise like so many Welshmen. Besides, I have some rich treasure which lies hid in the crown of a tree, as namely, beads, tags of points, pewter spoons, and divers other things, which I meant to present unto your Eagleship, for it is my nature to hide whatsoever I find. Besides, for my language, as I said before, I can speak Latin, Greek, Hebrew, French, Italian as easily as my mother tongue, but indeed few can understand me, and therefore I do lose that praise which I deserve. However, I hope you will consider my worthiness and place me as your substitute during the time that your Eagleship shall be absent in the desert of

Arabia. And so ends Jackdaw, praying for your long life, and to give you a taste of my languages, *Levat le roi τὸν βίον foelicissimum.*"

Chapter IV. How the Eagle having heard the birds' several speeches did make a speech to them again, and at last made his cousin, Rapax the Hawk, Vice-regent in his absence.

The Eagle like a wise king having all this while collected the chief matter of their speeches, he began to speak unto them in this manner. "My loving subjects, I have heard what you have spoken in the behalf of yourselves. You, Robert, have pleaded well for yourself, and so have you, Lady Philomel, and all the rest, whose names for brevity sake I omit. But yet you have not showed me any virtues worthy of royal dignity. For in that Philomel was a king's daughter and Mavis the Pie was sometime a king, yet these are but the fictions of poets, and I had rather have you make it appear that your breasts are filled with justice, temperance, magnanimity, mercy, and such other virtues which are required in a king. For to boast of parentage, or gifts of nature, as your fair white feathers, or of art, as languages, learning, and the like, they may be esteemed ornaments to private men; but princes should have power to make them feared and virtue to make them be beloved, but in none of you I find these qualities. And therefore since you have all spoken your minds, I would fain know why my cousin, Rapax the Hawk, hath sat mute all this while."

The Hawk hearing himself named by the Eagle answered thus. "May it please your Highness, I know that my former offences and bloody murders are so odious and hateful in the sight of the birds, that I dare not open my beak to pronounce a syllable in my own behalf. But yet might it please them to remit and forgive my former offences and pardon what is past, I would promise, if so be your Majesty should make me your substitute, to rule over the Commonwealth of Birds with justice, temperance, and equity; instead of killing and slaying them with my talons, I would protect them from the injury of owls and other blood-suckers, who in the winter evenings do pull the small birds out of the bushes and so prey upon them. Then they should spend their days peaceably, sleep securely, sing sweetly, feed plentifully, and live merrily. And besides, as I have power to sway the empire, so I promise to rule over the Commonwealth of Birds with justice and equity, and to give them the better assurance that I will not prove a tyrant, I am willing to have my talons pared off. Therefore if the birds do like of my offer, to show their consent thereunto let them clap their wings." Which was no sooner heard, but the birds on condition that the Hawk's talons should be pared off, they all cried with one voice: *"Fiat rex Rapax;* let the Hawk be King."

THE MORAL

A cunning dissembler will always cover his vice with the death of virtue, as may be seen by the Hawk's speech, who promising to rule with justice amongst them, got so far into the opinion of the birds that they were content to choose him king to avoid farther strife amongst themselves. Take heed therefore of fair speeches, for all their words are mingled with dissimulation.

Chapter V. How Rapax the Hawk had his talons pared off, and how the Eagle had resigned his scepter unto him and made him King of the Birds.

After the birds had consented to the Hawk's speech, the Hawk, because they had no edge tools amongst them, put his talons into the cleft of a tree and so never left pulling till he had pulled them quite off, and yet the hope of sovereignty was so sweet unto him that he felt no pain therein. Being thus unable to hurt, the Eagle rose out of his seat and caused the Hawk to sit therein, and afterward delivered his scepter unto him and put his crown upon his head, and then charged him to remember his promise, which was, to have a care of his subjects and be loving unto them, as also to hear their complaints, to redress their grievances, and to yield them relief. "And this see you perform, as you tender or respect your own life, for if at my return from the Arabian desert I find that you have wronged my subjects, you shall be sure to die for it." The Hawk answered, that he hoped his Majesty should commend him at his return and not find any just cause of punishment, "for though I have been heretofore counted cruel and have plumed upon the carcase of many a small bird, as larks and sparrows and sometimes upon doves, partridges, quails, and the like, yet now your subjects shall find me full of mercy, for indeed I was then enforced to be cruel by necessity." At these words the Eagle took wing, so taking some few birds of note with him he flew away, and when these birds had accompanied him some part of the way, he sent them back again, charging them to be careful to obey the Hawk in all things. And so flew on to the desert of Arabia.

THE MORAL

The nature of man is given to seek honor, which he thinks to be a sufficient reward for all his sufferings, as may appear by the Hawk, who could endure to pluck off his own talons in hope to be made king.

Chapter VI. How the Hawk behaved himself after the departure of the Eagle, and how he requited Cawwood the Rook for teaching him to make away the Buzzard, as is showed in the first chapter.

The Eagle being gone, the Hawk behaved himself very lovingly for the first week, as Nero the first five years of his reign was counted the best of kings, but afterward he proved the worst of tyrants, so the Hawk dissembled his nature for a week or fortnight, but afterward he had a great desire to shed blood and therefore he began to think how he might put Cawwood the Rook to death and requite him for his former kindness in betraying the Buzzard and making him stand blindfolded with a clout about his head till one came by and shot him with a birding piece. Now to bring this to pass, he called many of the little birds together and told them that what cruelty he had formerly committed was by the encouragement of the Rook, who made him believe that, seeing nature had allotted him no other food, it was lawful for him to prey upon all sorts of birds, and that now he was afraid lest he should put into his mind the same bloody principles again, and therefore to avoid suspicion, "My loving subjects," saith he, "if any of you can accuse him of any heinous crime, as I know he is guilty of many, I will grant you a day of hearing against him, that so, if he cannot clear himself, he may suffer the punishment of death, which is due unto his deserts." No sooner had the Hawk spoken these words, but presently they told his Majesty that they had every one cause to complain against him, and therefore if he were once summoned to the Court they would be all ready to accuse him.

THE MORAL

They who employ others in wickedness never love them any longer, until their own purpose is effected, as may appear by the Hawk, who sought the life of the Rook after he had used his invention to make away the Buzzard. So that he which furthers a man's vice is beloved while it is doing, but is hated when 'tis done.

Chapter VII. How Cawwood the Rook was called to the Court to answer for himself, and how all the small birds brought in their accusations against him.

The Hawk began now to make known his bloody nature and therefore sent Corvino the Crow to summon the Rook

Cawwood the Rook

to appear at the Court of Sylvia, who accordingly came at the day appointed, not doubting to receive any injury from the Hawk, being always his friend and therefore not fearing that now being made King he would use his power to his destruction. But it proved far otherwise, for no sooner was Cawwood come unto the Hawk's presence but the Hawk commanded him to stand forth and answer to such matters as should be laid against him, for, says he, "Friend Rook, there are many complaints made against you, and I must do justice as I promised the Eagle at his departure." When the Rook heard this, he began to change color, and his feathers began to stand up on end. "What," thought he, "shall I be betrayed by a traitor?" Yet at last seeing no remedy, he was fain to stand to it, while the birds gathered round about him, being all ready to complain against him, and first Robert the Robin began his indictment.

THE MORAL

Tyrants do always pretend an outward show of justice, as may be seen by the Hawk's speech to Cawwood the Rook, who being afraid thereof does show that a guilty conscience is a thousand witnesses.

Chapter VIII. How Robert the Robin complained against Cawwood the Rook.

"I am glad that we small birds have now free liberty to show our wrongs and grievances which we have received from Cawwood the Rook, who upon a time brought me in danger of my life, for one day as he and I were walking in a field by a hedge side, we chanced to come where there was a turf set up with two sticks and a little hole digged underneath it. I began to ask him what it was. 'Oh,' says he, 'do you not know what this is? Then you have lost many a fair worm, for it is never without one or two, and therefore,' says he, 'if you hop into the bottom of it, you shall find my words true.' 'But,' quoth I, 'is there no danger in it?' 'Oh, no,' says he, 'I'll warrant you for danger.' Whereupon I believing him leapt upon the forked stick, and no sooner was I lighted thereon, but presently the turf fell upon my head so that I was made close prisoner in the pitfall, and there I continued till at last a waggish boy, who had made the pitfall, came and took me out and with great joy carried me to his mother. But she telling him that it was ill luck to hurt a Robin, at last the boy was content only to cut off my tail and let me fly, whereby I escaped the danger that the Rook had brought me into, and therefore I desire that we may have justice on him."

THE SPARROW'S COMPLAINT

"With the same malicious mind, though not in the same manner, Cawwood the Rook brought me in danger and peril of my life. For one frosty morning there being a great many limed straws set on a dunghill, Cawwood the Rook went amongst them and spying me upon the top of a barn, called me down unto him and bid me come to him, for there were a great many wheat ears scattered on the ground. Whereupon I being somewhat hungry, by reason of the cold frosty weather, came flying to him, and no sooner had I begun to peck on one of the ears but straight the end of one of the limed straws caught me by the back and another under the wing, so that I had much ado to get from thence, for when he that watched the straws saw me limed and taken, he came running out to catch me, but then with all the strength I had I made towards a hedge, and having gotten into the bottom thereof escaped the fowler's hands. Thus I was betrayed by Cawwood the Rook, and I think there is no bird but hath some accusation against him."

THE COMPLAINT OF THE WOODCOCK

"May it please you, I was once coming through a wood with this traitor Cawwood the Rook, and as we went,

Cawwood the Rook

there was two or three sticks set just cross the path, with one great bended stick whereon was a noose of hair. And as we came to them I asked the Rook what this meant. 'Why,' says he, 'it is a swing, whereon I am wont many times to stretch myself.' At these words like a Woodcock as I was, I went to take hold of the great stick and thought to have swung upon it, but no sooner had I set my foot upon the bridge but the springe flew up and caught me by one of the legs, so that there I lay upright and looking every hour when the fowler would come to fetch me. And if the hair noose had not broken I had certainly long ere this been roasted and served up to some rich man's table."

The Woodcock had no sooner ended his complaint but there came in a Thrush and a Starling like maimed soldiers hopping upon one leg, and seeing Cawwood the Rook standing at the bar. The Thrush, because she was the better speaker, began to tell their case: how that Cawwood the Rook made them believe that a birding piece was but a pipe which men used to play upon, "whereupon one morning a fowler coming towards us with a piece, we thinking to hear his pipe sat still, so that he taking his aim discharged against us and shot me into the leg, and my brother Starling into the wing. Thus hath the Rook with his craft deceived us many times and many a bird hath he brought to untimely end by his cunning. We beseech the Hawk, therefore, who we hear is left substitute in the Eagle's absence, that he would punish the cruelty of the Rook."

Chapter IX. How Cawwood the Rook would have answered for himself, but that Rapax the Hawk would not suffer him, but condemned him to perpetual banishment.

When Rapax the Hawk had heard these accusations against the Rook, he was very glad thereof. And yet, as it is the nature of cunning treachery, he seemed to pity his calamity and told him he was sorry to hear so many foul matters urged against him. "I have always," says he, "had a good opinion of you, but I see how much we may be deceived. And I wish that some other might give judgment on your crimes and offences, but yet since it hath pleased the Eagle to give me all power and to put the scepter of justice into my talons, there shall no respect of friendship sway me, and therefore you must look for no more mercy at my hands than justice will permit. For albeit you are my friend, yet I must prove myself a loyal subject to the Eagle, who hath put me in trust to see rewards and punishments equally distributed amongst his subjects, and this I take to be the true nature of justice."

At these words the Rook began to prepare himself and would fain have answered the objection of his adversaries, beginning to show that it was not his craft but their folly which brought them into danger. "For," saith he, "if Robert the Robin will needs be peeping into a pitfall, who can help it? Or if the Woodcock will take a springe for a swing, it is not my cunning but their simplicity which brings them into danger, which by escaping they have learned more wit and so ought in justice to give me thanks, for now they know how to avoid the like perils hereafter. Besides all this, you that sit to condemn me ought not to seek my life, but to save me from my enemies, for you know how for your sake I contrived an excellent device to make away Flywill the Buzzard." But at that word the Hawk commanded them to stop his mouth and that with a noose of hair they should forthwith strangle him. When the Rook saw there was no way but death, he began to entreat for mercy, whereupon the Hawk considering better with himself pronounced this sentence against him: "In regard that thou, Cawwood the Rook, hast highly transgressed and offended against the Commonwealth of Birds, by deceiving Phillip the Sparrow, Robert the Robin, and Longbill the Woodcock, I do here banish thee out of the country and send thee to live for ever in the city." Since which time the city hath been always full of rooks. For no sooner was the sentence given but the Parliament of Birds broke up and the Rook flew away to the city, where he

Cawwood the Rook

hath ever since remained, there being divers sorts of Rooks, as for example, your cheating gamester is a Rook, and your fellows that cheat countrymen are Rooks, the tapster that fills not his pot is a Rook, and he that drinks with you and slips away when the reckoning comes to be paid is a Rook. And to conclude, there are so many sorts of Rooks that I cannot reckon them, for sometimes your Rook will be in the shape of a decayed gallant, sometimes in a threadbare cloak waiting at bowling alleys, sometimes in a blue jerkin like a countryman, and sometimes in the market in the shape of a cutpurse. And therefore I would have countrymen buy this book, for though it be *The History of the Rook*, yet it will not cost them so dear as the acquaintance of these city Rooks.

THE MORAL

Crafty fellows, albeit they scape a great while, yet at last are brought to ruin and disgrace, for if they come once to public trial, then all their enemies are ready to accuse them, as appeareth by the Rook, who after all his cunning tricks was at last banished to live in the city, so that your Rook is born in the country and bred in the city, and this is the concluding moral of this chapter.

FINIS

THE TRAGI-COMICALL HISTORY OF ALEXTO AND ANGELICA.

Containing
The progresse of a zealous Candide, and Masculine *Love*.
With a
Various Mutability of a feminine affection.
Together with Loves Iustice thereupon.

Written by *Alex: Hart* Esq.

LONDON:
Printed by *B. A.* and *T. F.* for *Nich: Vavasour*, and are to be sold at his shop in the Inner Temple neere the Church. 1640.

ALEXANDER HART: ALEXTO AND ANGELICA (1640)

Alexto and Angelica, like the much later *Irene Iddesleigh,* is one of that small class of books which, paradoxically, becomes entertaining simply by being so very bad. Presumably wishing to produce a romantic tale in the style of Greene, the author plunges deeply into the world of idealized love and valor to present the familiar spectacle of a violently enamored cavalier making his passionate suit to a lady with the help of conventional settings and vehicles, letters, poems, discussions, tirades. In an apparent effort, however, to refine the style of the story and to thus make it more appealing to a more elegant age, Hart has employed an incredibly high-flown mode of expression which is a paragon of confused floridity and in so doing has caused action to be replaced by a series of set-pieces of empty rhetoric. The author's main interest, indeed, seems to be not the story itself but rather the demonstration of the proper response, learned or polite, to the situations he develops. Unfortunately for the effect, the speeches and letters reproduced are as often awkward as polished, while the amount of learned allusion and outbursts in Latin at especially emotional moments is doggedly pedantic rather than elegant.

The hero—this is perhaps an unconscious autobiographical touch—seems the victim of a too exclusively literary education; he seeks for a bookish precedent, or for advice of a similar nature from his friend, before he can decide what to do, and when he does act, it is always in a way made sacred by literary tradition. That the two young men respond to everything that happens to them by writing letters or poems is indicative of the atmosphere in which the whole story moves: events are incentives merely to proper literary reaction. We may easily agree with the author when in his prefatory statement he calls his tale a "studious" work.

Though it is admittedly an extreme case, this story mirrors the seventeenth-century situation with regard to the romantic tale: no development of the elements of the tale has taken place, save in respect to style. Greene and his contemporaries still remain masters in the field, still read and admired, if we may judge from the number of editions of their tales which were printed. No one arose between 1600 and 1640 to challenge their dominance, and not before the publication in the latter year of Mabbe's translations of some of Cervantes's *Exemplary Novels* was any new note struck in content or treatment. The seventeenth century displayed its originality elsewhere.

The text which follows is based on the Huntington Library copy of the 1640 edition.

THE TRAGI-COMICAL HISTORY OF ALEXTO AND ANGELICA

BY ALEXANDER HART, ESQ.

To the Readers

In precedent times when elocution with poesy joined, invention being their rival, judicious wits with their works were patronized and historical fictions received favor in the royal palace of greatest princes; so hereditarily descending from the poets are in these our times applauded and delightfull to the considerate and true apprehensive reader, they cherishing a young and studious Muse, in future hope of nobler issue, not cropping her by untimely censures ere she display her autumn progenies, for nobleness with vir-

tue mixed gives the true luster of a studious work, when clouded ignorance maligns the best inscription. Therefore presuming on this maxim, I am bold to present unto the world's eye this book, which hath served a prenticeship unseen since it was penned. And now at my coming into England it desires to depart from his fellows and to be set up in print, craving pardon for all his faults, and to be made free by your kind acceptance.

Which shall oblige me yours,
Alex: Hart

THE HISTORY OF ALEXTO AND ANGELICA, OR LOVE'S METAPHOR

In Greece there dwelt many noble men, amongst the which there was one named Alexto, a lord of great account and eminency, who was reverenced and honored of all strangers as well as of his domestic people and those which did inhabit about him, not for the largeness of his patrimony or the greatness of his possessions (though they were such as his neighboring peers could not equalize) but the foundation and original of his extolments sprung from his grave, judicious, and matchless counsels, which so liberally he would extend on all sorts: and also for his charitable alms and benevolences, with which he plentifully would store, succor, and cherish those which were in adversity.

But to our intended discourse. This grave Senator had a son who bearing his name disagreed not from his properties, but punctually had his father's heroic inclinations, which made him as happy as meritorious, and was no less honored of all men than the limits of his deserts did reach unto; whose daily practises were to excel each man in courtesy, but as he was not too much self-conceited, nor too lofty-minded, so were not his thoughts fixed on any base or unworthy object, for they were as magnanimous as he nobly born, which always did aspire unto the height of virtue, and no sooner sought but attained unto. For the comeliness of his portraiture, it was unparalleled, yet had Venus lived in those days, she would have said that her Adonis did exceed him far, who, in my judgment, was not worthy to bear the title of this young Grecian's name.

But now as touching his feature and physiognomy, the colors of this my rural pencil is too sable to him, and figure him in so liberal, lively, and ample sort as the genius of the judicious reader may conceive: and also fearing that in heralding forth his worth, some Demosthenes interrupt me as did Æschines the orator, who being sent from Athens to King Philip of Macedon at his return from the Court to Athens, he much commended and extolled the exquisite beauty of Philip, with his admirable elocution and excessive bearing of drink. The which being related in the audience of Demosthenes, he presently checked Æschines, saying that he made a woman of Philip for his beauty, a babbling sophister for his eloquence, and a sponge for his retaining of liquor.

But now this young Alexto was the only joy and comfort of his aged sire, who having a desire to have his son experienced in martial discipline and also not ignorant for the courting of amorous damosels, he sent him to Athens to be educated in both, and also for his comrade he sent one Sandrico, a man's son of great worth and no less valiant than his own son, for Sandrico's courage was apparently manifested and also proved most eminent.

But in short space these two undaunted spirits were landed at Athens, where not altogether so joyful for their safe arrival as for the good society of each other, to whom they linked their fidelity in a fraternal vow and bound their friendship with such a Gordian knot as the ass was fastened to the Temple of Apollo with.

But after they had spent some few years in Athens, the Thracian emperor began to overrun Greece, which stood in need of the aid, power, and assistance of these two champions, Alexto and Sandrico.

And speedily they were sent for home, for the succor of their aged sires. In which wars they performed exceeding rare deeds of chivalry, whereby they became the only blossoms and mirrors of those times, for still the honor of each day did adorn their crests. But the acting of their exquisite feats, to the no small amazement of each spectator, in which behold how retrograde fortune proved, that these two uncontrolled Greeks became captivated by the arrival and verbal report which the shrill trumpet of fame triumphed through all the army.

Which was of the exquisite feature of the Roman lady Angelica, of whom 'twas said, that if all the goddesses were composed in a union, they could not equalize her; the citation here of each particular of her unparallelized worth would appear too tedious. Only conceive this, that the report which flying fame did demonstrate did still solicit the ears of young Alexto, insomuch that it was deeply rooted in his heart, and the fruit which sprung from thence was his daily squared sighs, whereby he was altogether disabled to negotiate his martial affairs. And thus was he enamored of her whom his eyes were never blessed with the prospect of; yet daily did he surfeit by the excessive quaffing of the nomination of her name, and did as much adore the same as Pygmalion did the senseless portraiture that he carved, on which he so much doted that he made it his bedfellow.

But all this while, we have not treated of the vexation and perplexity which Sandrico sustained—not that he was entangled or captivated—by the amorous report of the terrestrial goddess. But his grief and disability proceeded from the pensiveness which he perceived his friend Alexto to be in.

And as he could not conceive the original from whence it sprung, so would not Alexto relate unto him and divulge the cause of his internal grief, which was apparently descried by his external hue and melancholy gestures, yet poor Sandrico was not so well read in that loving philosophy as to conceive the nature of his unusual passion, for he was more fit for the tents of boisterous Mars than the temples of amorous ladies.

So likewise was Alexto before he was entrapped with the snare of affection. But alas! there is no heart so sovereign good but love can make simple. And so it fell out that one time above the rest, Sandrico came into the tent of his noble friend Alexto, and falling into a deep discourse, at the catastrophe and period of each sentence, Alexto would still close them up with such a sigh that it would seem to rend and cleave in sunder the rafters of his tent.

At which Sandrico laying fast hold upon that occasion, began to importune and request him by all the permanent and unfeigned friendship that so liberally he had and did show on him, that he would not conceal any longer that in obstinacy which might prove his utter ruin, but reveal it unto him, whereby it might be a mitigation of his distress, vowing to participate of the same, and also to lend him the propagation of all his future and faithful endeavors.

Have you beheld how Iris struts whenas her mantle's spread? Or have you marked whenas Sol riseth with his radiant beams, he doth disperse the misty fogs and unsavory vapors, which were obscured in the concavious places of the earth? Even so the true pattern of perfect friendship, which Sandrico spread upon Alexto partly dispersed the sable clouds of that his present calamity. For when birds sing early, it doth betoken a fair day, but when the sunshine garnishes it, it prognosticates a shower; but after a storm comes a calm, so after Alexto had turned over the volumes of numberless sighs, he unfolded his mind unto Sandrico in these words: "O unhappy I! Wars have their ends either hour or death, the Scilian pools by sufficient help may be drawn dry, the Talitian tree in time did wither, the Stoitical flood did drown the usurping tyrant. But Love, O Love! Thou hast no period, neither can I bring thee to a compromise; delay to thee is the unhappy headsman that holding me neither saves nor kills, but leaves me to languish in a burning frozen zone."

Sandrico being attentive, by this understood that an

amorous passion had crept into him and thus began modestly to chide him. "Oh, quench these smothering sparks, lest suffered they grow to a perpetual flame, and like the Amazonian cell, scorch all that doth approach it nigh and at last with Mount Ætna consume itself. But, O my friend, let the buckets of thy undaunted courage draw forth of the noble well of thy understanding so much reason as to quench this unmartial agony.

"Let not thy brave, heroic mind stoop unto so base and lascivious a lure fit for none but panical rustics that never were trained in the Trojan wars, whose whips and prongs are spears and lances; haycocks, shields and targets; and blue bonnets, crests and helmets. I blush at thy thoughts and could take pleasure to deride fancy, were it not in thee, but now I see the poets did well whenas they first feigned Cupid, that disloyal sycophant, to be blind. For had he seen thy worth, he never durst attempt a shaft, as thus rovingly hath light upon thee, the which repulse and send back again in as many pieces about his corpse as there be sands in the Lydian shores; for what's his bolt only headed with a voluntary desire and feathered with a quick consent, which is shot from a bow of idleness? Then rouse up thy disordered senses and remember the soldier's phrase, *Dulcior est Mors quam Amor*.

"Aristotle, Socrates, nay, hadst thou taken lectures from Mercury and studied all thy lifetime for poems to feed the variable incredulity of these insatiable dames, either they would banish thee, as Caesar did Ovid, or condemn thee to die in the height of their displeasure.

"As for beauty, their chiefest pride, it is but time's flower, which, as it is delicate, so it soon withers, for it is like the colors which Phidias drew, which seemed admirable and to the view most excellent, but did vanish and impair at every aerial breath. You know that Venus, the matron of them all, was fair, the sooner to make a wanton; also Helen, the mirror of our Grecian land, but ask Troy of her qualities.

"Therefore whenas you have run through the alphabet

of praising fictions, as in saying, worthiest mistress, my service lies prostrated unto your acceptance, the which if you please to command, I shall think of none other happiness, but in the accomplishment of the same.

"Or shouldst thou figure thy mistress as the poets did Venus to ride in a golden chariot, drawn with silver-breasted doves, or as Juno with golden-plumed peacocks, at the last, whenas they are satisfied by drawing the day of extolments, they will seek to place thee amongst the stars, as Venus did Pythagenes, for a flatterer, a very lofty seat but low in reward, and this is the common course nowadays of our Grecian and Roman damosels. Therefore, use no physic but the consideration of these, which forth of the seriousness of my love to thee I have been emboldened to relate."

After Sandrico had made an end of this discourse, Alexto began to answer him as followeth: "My dearest Sandrico, had Dionysius but ten Platos to tell him truth, he had not erred; Agamemnon wished but ten such as Nestor to vanquish all his enemies at Phrygia and to set our Greeks at liberty; but thou art both a Plato and a Nestor unto me; thy counsels are both true and good. But alas! my heart is filled with such an amorous passion that it admits no attentiveness unto thy friendly advertisements. Yet I must confess I have heard that a woman's love is like the river Tedocheus, which, being tasted, unto some it proves venomous and baneful, but unto others as their daily nutriment, or as the Macedonian image, which unto some champions at the triumph there, it would cast amorous glances, and on others disdainful looks and frowns. And also as on the Saxtenion Mount there was a castle enchanted by the necromancer Bastellotus, wherein he caused to be tortured his fair Polidorca for her cruelty towards him, at the entry of which he had placed a brazen bull, a fierce dragon, and hellish furies: these were guardians whereby none could vanquish nor unloose, but only he which was the mirror of Rome for all perfection, Alcontiodes, and he finished the enchantment.

"Then, O Sandrico, suffer me to try my fortune, which peradventure may prove as these have, and why may not I with Calapassus take a turn in dancing with Jove's daughters in the Pierian green?"

"Tush, tush," said Sandrico, "remember thy own speeches. Wherefore did Bastellotus cause Polidorca to be tortured, but for her cruelty towards him, and may not thy mistress prove as marble-hearted?

"Also, remember how long Lodovicus was enamored of the Lady Dantrissea, and how unfaithful she proved unto him; as also when he died he desired that his heart should be shown unto her, wherein she perceived her own similitude, as transparent as an object is by the sun's reflection in a crystal mirror, yet she regarded it not, but esteemed it ridiculous. But should thy mistress prove so marble-hearted, I would become Santeticus, causing her to be enchanted in that sort, as he did Dantrissea, for being the death of his friend Lodovicus.

"First, he caused her to be placed in a boiling cauldron amongst furies, with the portraiture of his friend Lodovicus in her view, holding his bleeding heart in his hand, whereby she should also gaze on her own dissembling physiognomy, and on Lodovicus' front was engraven in capital letters this motto:

Thy base dissembling face did cause my death,
Thy flattering tongue makes this to bleed on earth;
Torments I did sustain in life for thee:
And now in death thus tortured shalt thou be.

"Secondly, her nutriment was the excrement of toads, adders, and serpents, which was dished in the natural skull of Lodovicus, served her by satyrs which were her attendants, with strange deformed beasts.

"In this sort she still remained, which is too good for all such disloyal sycophants. But, my Alexto, if this amorous conceit do but once creep into thee, I do much dread the success, for thou, that art for beauty like the fair

Roman's paramour, for wisdom like Ulysses, whom Circe could not enchant, for courage like a second Hector.

"Then seeing thou art adorned with all these graces, bequeath not thyself and it unto so foolish a passion, which allows nothing excellent but what it likes, for it shadoweth beggary in Crates, whom Hisparata thought and esteemed rich for his love, but contrariwise, Palperea accounted Croesus a poor fellow because she disliked him. Then yield not thyself to this fancy, which is altogether in extremes and admits no reason, for thou art he from whose mouth flows melody more enchanting than the Sirens'. And in thy lips the Muses make a new Parnassus and thy head contains the subtlety of Aristotle.

"Remember also thou art a warrior whose undaunted courage was never yet quailed by any, neither foreign foe nor home-bred enemy. For the name of noble Alexto is sufficient to vanquish troops of armed men."

After Sandrico had used all the skill he could to persuade his friend Alexto from the entertaining of his new fancy, Alexto began thus to answer him. "My dear Sandrico, as the wounded deer wringeth forth tears, and as the myrtle depressed yieldeth gum, so by the deep impression which I have conceived of fair Angelica's beauty, my sighs lead me captive to pick up a mourner in the time of my own tears. Besides, my Sandrico, the gods should do nature too much wrong, if they should place an adamant heart in a crystal face; therefore twit me no more with Vesta, for Venus is she who can chastise Angelica though she did glory in beauty as Narcissus, who stooping to kiss his own shadow in a brook was immediately drowned therein. Besides, Lucina is a goddess which must be employed, for marriage is honorable, and to live unmatched it were a wrong to nature. The Phoenix, when she is nigh her end, builds her nest with all sweet spices and odoriferous perfumes, as close unto the sun's reflection as she can, whereby at her decease his splendidious and radiant beams should revive a young Phoenix forth of the ashes of the old deceased one.

"But, Sandrico, should either man or woman die without the propagation of issue, their characters and resemblances could not be left behind, but by a dead substance as Dostitetius' was, whose portraiture was carved ere he died by the cunning artist; therefore I say love is divine and marriage honorable, especially to those that are the paragons of this terrestrial paradise.

"Also whenas the Demetrial King esteemed of love, as the barbarian king did of gold which he sent as presents to his enemies, Venus cursed him out of her temple, wherefore he was hated of all and thus hatefully died.

"And when Rossilius would taste no fruit but such as grew in the Gardens of Hesperides, neither then any color content his eyes but such as was stained by the Mauretical fish; that is, he could affect no damosel but she which was accounted the terrestrial goddess of the Thracian land, named Dionela; and because he was loyally affected to her, Venus suffered him to marry her, and whenas she lacked the assistance of Lucina, Diana also came unto her, and at the birth of Dionela's son the goddesses rained pearl, Jupiter gold, Mars trained his warlike legions in the air. This was to signify that where loyal affection is, the gods rejoice triumphantly. Also whenas doves are matched young they never sever but by death, so vines grafted being sprigs, they seldom part but they decay."

Sandrico perceiving that Alexto would still cross him, he thus began again: "I perceive that thy head is not barren of sophistry to prove this thy argument of loving philosophy; but suppose, my friend, that thy autumn showers come too late and cause not thy crop to prove.

"Besides, a woman will say she hath but one heart, as the heavens have but one sun, but none can find how many tricks and false imaginations are observed and shrouded in that one heart of theirs. Then look before you leap, and walk not where no footing can be found, seek not to climb Olympus before you consider the altitude thereof, neither bark with the wolves of Caria against Endymion.

"Settle not too much affection before you know how to be requited, but I perceive that is true which one relates of a certain person which was so ravished in his amorous and fond contemplations that he had the image of his mistress so imprinted in his thoughts that he seemed always to converse with her and perform with her all those actions which lovers use to commit in embracing of their loves, so you, Alexto, grow almost desperate for her whom you have not seen." Alexto perceiving Sandrico spoke unto the purpose, he speedily thus answered him. "Prithee, Sandrico, honor me so much as to bear me company unto Rome, where I will try my fortune with Angelica, and if she prove not so amorous as I am loyal, I will more exclaim of her than Doronus did of our Grecian army." To which request Sandrico consented; perceiving there was no repulsion but Alexto would try his fortune with the Roman lady Angelica, he gave his consent to travel with Alexto. In which journey Alexto began thus to pass away the time.

"Worthiest Sandrico, beauty's arrows are so sharp and the darts that fly from women's eyes so piercing that the choicest armor cannot repulse either of them, no, not the corslet which Vulcan made for the Didonian champion, for it pierceth deeper within the tender breast of an amorous lover than cannon shot in plank; for shot, either it passeth through or sticks, but when love makes battery, if it enters not the defendant, it tears the plaintiff in a thousand pieces. It's also like the Amazonian armor, which being shot at the King of Phrygia, it was repulsed in such sort by magic art that it broke about the ears of Stonatus, who shot it, that it killed him and five hundred of his resolute warriors. Or, it hath resemblance unto the fireballs and thunderbolts which Jove sent at Mars, the one lighting on his helmet and the other glancing on his shield were returned with such fury that the bolts struck Xantussissius (Jove's kinsman) dead and the balls had well nigh fired Jove himself out of his throne. So nothing could extinguish the wild fire which well nigh burnt the castle of Silotus, but the milk and juice of the Stabolian tree.

"So neither will nor can anything assuage the fervent anguish of a loyal lover but the true acceptance of the beloved; for what spoke Apollo, he whose skill in compounds and simples exceeded all men's (for Galen and Hippocrates were not worthy to carry his drugs, whenas an amorous passion crept into him), he said *Hei mihi quod nullis amor est medicabilis herbis;* besides, love, that divine passion, if it be over rash dealt with, it burns dim and dies like the forge of Dedalus. But if it be moderately treated on, it will quickly flame with consent like Arnalian sparkles which smothering lay, but being leisurely blown were soon fired.

"But, my Sandrico, if my fair Angelica would look upon me as the affectionated mother on her smiling infant, or with such an amiable countenance as Doranelia did on Stolotius her constant lover, who rushed into the battle at Phrygia, resolutely resolving there to die or to set at liberty his fair mistress, who after a tedious conflict with expense of blood and the close pursuing of his enemies was almost brought unto the period of life, but casting his decaying eyes about speedily received such strength and fresh courage from the feature of his beauteous love which did so replenish his empty veins that in short time he subdued his haughty foes and brought them to submission; even so an amorous glance from Angelica would revive my drooping heart, which is in a fierce conflict for her sake, and is almost vanquished by death, his deadly enemy.

"But, O Sandrico, do but consider what love is; for as there is no cut to unkindness, so there is no haughty spirit but that the quintessence of love can chastise with celerity.

"For great Alexander stood affrighted at the Amazonian beauties, Hector in the midst of his battle against Alezanto, whenas he saw the Empress Claria he instantly was amazed and sustained the agony of a tertian ague, letting his lance drop from his martial hand, suffering himself to be disarmed, unhelmed, and captivated by his foes."

"I fear," quoth Sandrico, "that this fiction of praising

love will not last long, for the nightingale hath but one May in twelve months, and whereas thou hast surfeited by quaffing the poisoned cup of bitter love, thou shalt find the reward in the bottom thereof to be but the dregs of thy counterfeiting mistress's hate; yield not too much to the impotency thereof, for you know not with how much gall and bitterness the honey of love is tempered with. *Est melle & felle foecundissimus.* Besides, a woman hath as many minds as the alphabet hath letters, for the distinction of their fancies are like the difference of their faces, for Aristes said that his Alderia had two kinds of faces, the one dissembling to please him, the other lasciviously to entertain a friend; also they are merely composed and made of vanity, which makes them prove so light.

"For Phylistis weighing his mistress in the balance of equity found the longer he kept her the lighter she was, and as the marble drops tears against every storm, so a woman will feign weeping upon every slight and light occasion, but that is because they would be thought of as tender nature and constitution as their skins be extolled for whiteness."

All this while Alexto was very attentive and was almost persuaded in the same form to rail against his mistress ere he was arrived at Rome to try her, but by this time you must conceive they are somewhat nigh, and to make short, Alexto thus began to answer him. "I suppose," said he, "that you, Sandrico, was brought forth Minerva-like and not by a woman; for if a woman had been thy mother thou couldst not thus fervently have railed against their sex." "Tush," said Sandrico, "Avicenna said *Hominem posse produci naturaliter ex terra;* if you will not believe a woman was my mother, imagine me to be brought forth of the earth. Besides, I am no scholar unto King Lewis the Sixth, as in learning that sentence which he taught his son, saying, he needs no more Latin but this: *Qui nescit dissimulare nescit vivere;* and though truth gets foes, and flattery friendship, yet I will not soothe thee up in that which I know is baneful. Also I point at no one particular dame, neither include all in general, but I speak of the disloyal and inconstant ones; therefore no virtuous dame will be outrageous but only in reading what I have said and viewing the picture which is here drawn find it to bear resemblance unto themselves, such may dart venom at me that are stung by the worm of conscience.

"But let me say what I will, thou provest regardless thereof, and with Rocardus King of Phristand being by Wolfranius persuaded to be baptized, having one foot in the font, the other out, asked Wolfranius where went the most part of his predecessors that were not baptized. 'To Hell,' said Wolfranius. Instantly Rocardus drew his foot forth of the font, saying, *Rectius est plures quam pauciores sequi.* Extremities and dangers which I relate unto thee of love and what wrong men have sustained, yet thou art the more enamored thereof." By that time Sandrico had made an end of his discourse, they were arrived at Rome at a port named Porta Venetia, the which port was adjoining to the palace of the beauteous Lady Angelica. In which they having arrived, Sandrico for the better satisfaction of his friend and himself began to inquire and demand of the inhabitants what they could inform him concerning the heroical inclination of this Roman goddess, and whether that her feature was transparent unto that which the shrill trumpet of fame had blazed in such an unparallelized sort, whose worth by all relations they found rather to be undervalued than exceeded, at which Alexto's itching ears were still seduced to soft attention, which rapt him in such an ecstasy of pleasure that he could remain silent no longer, but pulling Sandrico by the arm burst forth into this paradoxical speech: "O my Sandrico, he that by the change of Fortune mounteth higher than he should must arm himself with patience to descend lower than he would; as they are not happy which are poor and deformed, so are they not fortunate that are over happily endued with the ornaments of nature and largeness of temporal possessions and patrimonies." Sandrico seeing him so passionate could no longer refrain, but interrupts him in his intended discourse.

"My dear Alexto, over the greatest beauties hangs the greatest ruin. I could wish thee to be wise, for the study of wisdom is the readiest ruin of grief and vexations. The counsel of friends doth assuage and mitigate present perturbations, and also prevents the future ignominy of perilous dangers, but I confess counsel in trouble gives small comfort when help is past cure; besides, where Fortune's beams shine not propitious, diligence doth little avail nor doth it mitigate instant calamities, but, methinks, the cause being your own, do but remove that and of necessity the effect must follow. Then *Medice cura teipsum, tu bene cognoscis morbis artemque medendi;* then seek a speedy remedy lest thy contagious wounds fester thy whole body; but, alas, of all creatures man is the most apt to fall, because being stricken with love, he undertakes the greatest actions. For as I have told thee, do but consider what this fancy is: a map of misery, a world of torments seducing man into a labyrinth of irrevocable tortures." But Alexto interrupting his friend Sandrico made reply: "When the heart is environed with oppression, then the ears are shut up against all good counsel, for perplexed hearts live with tears in their eyes, yet oft die with mirth in their looks; security banisheth dolors, but fear hinders gladness, for grief is a friend to solitariness, foe to sobriety and heir to desperation. But, O Sandrico, what doth it avail if the mind be generous, the body warlike, the joints pliable and active, all the dispositions inclined to heroical and magnanimous actions, if he that taketh arms be unfortunate? But indeed, assidual prosperity is more hurtful and obnoxious than adversity in that the one may be more easily borne than the other forgotten.

"Curtius reports that Darius in his flight drank puddle water polluted with the dead carcasses. He at the drinking thereof reported that he in all his precedent jollity never drunk liquid substance that was more pleasant and delightful unto his palate; the reason was because when he was at the height of fortune he used to drink before he was athirst. So also Artaxerxes, who in a pitched battle was forced to surrender the honor of the day to his enemies, whereby he betook himself to flight, in which he being destitute of corporal sustenance and nutriment could purchase nought to sustain nature but dry figs and brown bread, at the receipt thereof he made a long narration, in which he vowed that such pleasant food did his lips never touch till that instant. Then, my Sandrico, those be but false joys which are not intermixed with tears, perils, and disturbances, for necessity and tribulation are the first steps to honor, thereby a man comes to know himself. Therefore let us derelinquish this discourse and consult how we may become spectators of that superexcellent creature."

Sandrico perceiving that it was to no purpose any longer to discourse with him until he had glutted his longing eyes with the resplendent rariety of Angelica's peerless feature, wherefore he counselled Alexto for to walk into the palace to behold the lady of his affections. Unto this proposition Alexto consented, so both together went there, where no sooner entered but they found this beauteous creature sitting in state adorned with unparallelized habiliments, the splendor of which being accompanied with a saint-like feature gave such a glorious luster, as that it seems unto Alexto that some comet had been beneath the roof. The superexcellent lady was accompanied with divers heroic peers and nobility, which resorted thither because of the jousts and tourneys which were to be performed at a speedy solemnization. But as I said, Alexto's senses being captivated at the sudden unequalized object, he being in this trance began somewhat to rave, breaking forth into extreme passion, crying with a loud voice, "In yonder throne is fixed Ariadne's glittering star, for 'tis no terrestrial dame, nor mortal wight, but an immortal creature and supreme goddess," but ere he could proceed any further Sandrico clapped unto him and pacified his outrages, advising him to lay hold on that occasion and to prostrate himself unto the lady's acceptance, the which he willingly embraced and approaching unto the Lady Angelica, doing her much homage and reverence, as he supposed befitted so high a person, framed his speech unto her in this ensuing form.

"Renowned paragon, you whose illustrious feature needs no silver sockets to adorn and beautify the golden pillars of your unvalued worth, then why should I with metaphorical phrase adorn the feature of your authentic self, which nature cannot parallel? I'll therefore leave the propagation of such praising fictions unto the trifling timers of our age, whose courtship doth in flattery consist, for should I herald your divine presence in such obscure sentence to be illuminated by the luster of your all-conceiving genius, it would not only make my imbecillity the apparenter but conduct me to a labyrinth of fond contemplations; for as an eye in beholding of the sun's reflection twinkleth with the lids, so the rays which shine from the ebon arches of your brows hath not only caused mine eyes to be beauty-blasted but leads me captive unto your royal person, where like the salamander I request my assidual abode." Alexto still running on in this sort of rhetoric, the audience of which did not only drive the noble spectators to a non-plus, but each one seemed to be an orator and to sympathize his comely gestures and court-like behaviors; and as for Sandrico, he through the ecstasy of joy that he received thereat supposed himself to be elevated into the oriental region Palpasus.

But as for Angelica, in her fair face a comely blush with an ashy pale did strive for superiority. But have you beheld when as the silver-fingered morning doth appear, shaking her plumes from whence pearly drops do fall? Or have you seen the blushing of the East, when glittering Phoebus doth begin his course, who lifting up his global front, from Cynthia's glittering palm doth wash his face in Thetis' crystal lap? Even so this goddess did descend her throne, taking Alexto by his warlike palm, bespake after this manner: "Heroic knight, for your gesture speaks your own, had but your oratory the art of persuasion as well as of captivating, I by a thought of fond conceit should imagine myself that which your fiction hath strove to figure me, through the which I with Paulina should adore the shadow of my own feature; if I were as you would make me, your rhetoric had abused my meaning. Then, worthy sir, seek not to praise beauty when desert cannot equal the limit of reason.

"But since Fortune hath conducted you unto our palace, I shall request your stay until our triumphs be ended, and that you depart not without the acknowledgment of your further service and also with my liberty."

Alexto hearing this comfortable speech, thus replied, "Fairest of creatures, he were unworthy to climb the height of prosperity that should voluntarily fall into desperation, and let me be anatomized to less than nothing if I deceive your good opinion."

With these and such like discourses they spent the time until supper was ready to be served, at which she caused Alexto to be placed as her opposite, whereby amorous glances passed on both sides, and as for Sandrico, he was as joyful thereof, as if he were a sharer in his friend's present happiness. But while supper time lasted there began a demand amongst the nobility, which should first enter the lists in the morning, but being they could not decide this controversy between themselves it was proffered to the Lady Angelica to define the same. She having the disposing did command Alexto the first entrance. He no little glad thereof seemed loath, yet willing to accept so great a favor, but he soon perceived a murmuring amongst the nobility and not without just cause that a stranger and foreigner should dispossess them of their right and honor which did appertain unto them; by reason thereof he requested of the lady to be excused and to surrender that favor which she had employed upon him unto some nobler person, whose deserts might exceed his.

The lady entering into consideration with herself did place it, though unwillingly, on the Lord of Montulus, unto the which all the rest willingly did agree, and as for the next places they did accord amongst themselves. By that time they had brought this unto a compromise, supper was ended, where, after some pastimes, bedtime did approach, where each one was conducted, but Alexto and Sandrico were most sumptuously lodged next unto the lady's chamber, to which they were some part of the way conducted by her own person. Then leave being taken and sweet rest bequeathed on both sides, the lady departed and they entered their chamber, the which they found so garnished with unestimable gems and adorned with such gorgeous hangings that it seemed rather to entertain some monarch than their persons, but the door being closed and none resident but themselves, Alexto began to burst forth as thus:

"O fortunate star that thus propitiously hath smiled on me and adorned me with the beams of unestimable favor in suffering this correspondent amity betwixt Lady Angelica and myself! She now have I beheld which is the only phoenix of this terrestrial paradise, and sole mirror for nature's ornaments." Sandrico was stricken dumb and was loath to answer in some space, being in an outrage with himself for his precedent abusing the feminine sex before he had known any just cause thereof, and here, judicious ladies, humbly craves your forgiveness, and so do I being much perplexed with myself that my pen should be enforced to cite his outrageous blasphemies.

And thus he turns unto Alexto: "In Angelica's presence, thou didst seem to exceed Cicero, the most eloquent of all orators; canst thou now in as ample sort figure her comeliness?" Alexto replied that nothing was so easy or performed with such facility, and thus he began:

> Now do I love that never loved before,
> And for requital largely will implore;
> Engaged I am, but to so fair a dame
> Since the Creation nature could not frame:
> First, in her growth she's like the cedar tall,
> Slender as yew, or flourishing laurel;
> Her blush to Phoebus may be equalized;
> This is the dame that hath my heart surprised.

> Her front is like unto the new-fall'n snow,
> Not made for frowns, and wrinkles scorns to show;
> Her eyes exceed rich Caesar's western gems,
> Shining like pearls on th' Angelica's stems,
> For from those eyes shines such resplendent grace,
> As if some sovereign had been in place.
> Her lips are like fair rubies, and within,
> Her teeth, they seemed as if they pearls had been;
> Her neck in view like polished ivory,
> She seems like Venus, or a star in sky.
> There ebbs and flows forth from her silver breasts
> Sacred perfumes, as 'twere the Phoenix' nest's;
> This diadem is not worth less but more
> Than Caesar found beneath the western shore.

"Now, my Sandrico, how likest thou this description? Is it not punctually?" "It is most exquisite," answered Sandrico, and after these and such like speeches sleep did begin to fasten on them both, whereby they resigned the rest of their discourse until the morning that they did awake. Unto which rest we'll leave them, being loath to disturb them any further, and return unto the Lady Angelica, who being in her bed could take no rest, but still her genius conceived an apparition, which seemed to be the portraiture of Alexto's countenance. Thus was she still perplexed, being greedy to be satisfied of his parentage; then did she conceive him to be noble by reason of the rare perfections that she had conceived in him. These things being considered by her, she resolved to conceit nothing of him until she had viewed his feats of arms, which were to be performed on the morn, and with this resolution she betook herself to slumber, but all in vain, because she could not shake off her new conceived fancy. But being she is desirous of rest, we will leave her to enjoy it, wishing her her heart's content, and all other ladies that are in her case, and because silence possessed them all, for this present we will request your patience to the morning.

Which being come, the Lady Angelica was the first that

was awake, for she was most perplexed in mind. Alexto and Sandrico were still secure in a sweet slumber, for Alexto had received so much pleasure overnight at those unestimable favors with the which the lady did adorn him, that he had turned all his precedent despair into hope of a good success. But by this time Angelica had beautified her corpse with her sumptuous and gorgeous vestments. Accompanied with her amiable looks, she went forth of her chamber and descending into the hall, where the nobility did attend and expect her approach, in which she was no sooner entered but salutations being given on both sides, she ascended her chair of state, where we leave her in discourse with the nobility and return unto Alexto, who by this time had a vision, the which gave him to understand that they all were in readiness to enter the lists, only expecting his coming. At the departure of this vision he leaps out of his bed, awaking his friend Sandrico, telling him that they had overslept their time. By the which you must conceive they could have no great discourse, but the time they had for the clothing of them, in which Sandrico thus began: "Noble Alexto, you last night undertook to enter into the lists, as one of the knights of Angelica, in which my prayers shall be that you may return victorious, gaining the honor of the day, and that triumphant glory may adorn thy crest, for by the achieving of this heroic action in the sight of the virtuous lady, it will either procure thee thy heart's content or make thee love's vassal forever, if once condemned to die in the hate of her displeasure, and at thy return if prosperous, we will conclude in what sort to reveal the nature of thy apparent passion unto her soft attention."

By this time they both were ready, and coming down into the hall, the time was at hand of their departure into the lists, each one, doing his duty unto the lady, took their places after the Lord Montulus, who overnight was assigned the first that should enter. So the lady with the rest of her attendants of exquisite beauty descending from their seats and being ready to take places, Angelica requested Alexto to conduct her, the which he was not unwilling to embrace. In the meantime Sandrico went to prepare his horse and martial accoutrements, which were prepared for that exploit. Alexto having placed the lady for her prospect, and doing her reverence, taking his leave, she took a scarf that was most sumptuous to behold, embroidered with pearl and gold, the which she caused to be tied about his arm, wishing his happy success and assidual prosperity, for she seemed much enamored of him, but cautious lest he should conceive anything thereof.

But how much joy Alexto conceived of this unestimable favor, I want the power of expression, therefore resign that to the learned judgments to conceive of. But in this ecstasy Alexto came unto his friend Sandrico, relating to him in brief what had happened between the peerless lady and himself, at the audience whereof Sandrico conceived no small content. But because Alexto would not be accounted prolixious, he mounted his fiery steed, being accompanied with his friend, and by that time the rest were placed, and after reverence done unto the lady, he entered the lists, causing his horse to curvet in that ample sort that he astonished each spectator.

And you must conceive if the lady was enamored of him before, how much more was she now surprised by his matchless actions. But the trumpets warning unto the first encounter, Lord Montulus and Sasetus, a Persian knight, met in such a full career that Sasetus struck Montulus out of his saddle upon the crupper of his horse. But Montulus, loath to pass by without claiming quittance with him, struck so outrageously on the breast of Sasetus that his lance shattered in pieces, and nimbly clapping into the saddle again, meeting so furiously together, dismounted Sasetus, tumbling him and his horse unto the earth. So Montulus passed by, not being further indamaged, but Sasetus seeing himself foiled, especially in the presence of the Lady Angelica, unto whose acceptance his assidual devotions were bent, imagining that it would have been his perpetual disgrace, courageously drew forth his own sword, being on his feet, sheathed it again in his own bowels, uttering these words: "Thus nobly will I die, rather than live dishonorably." This unexpected stratagem proved an astonishment unto each spectator, but especially miraculous unto the ladies; but after some pacification and the cause of this outrage being fully related, it was very well approved of both by the ladies and nobility, whereby the jousts did still proceed which otherwise had dissolved. But had not Montulus been animated and recomforted by Alexto and others, he had surely endangered himself for very anguish and grief that so noble a spirit should fall by his feeble arm. But having recollected himself, he was ready to encounter with the next that made against him.

Alexto as yet was loath to encounter with Montulus until he had overthrown most part of those knights there present, imagining thereby that Montulus should be exceedingly extolled of each spectator, and that the ladies would affirm that he was the choicest of all Europe for kingly knighthood, and whenas Montulus should be adorned with these favors he would instantly entertain to joust with him, being fully assured that having received one amorous glance of favor from his mistress's eye, he should be able to dismount and captivate Montulus and so regain all honor unto himself.

But as he was hammering and contemplating of this matter, his friend Sandrico perceiving no knight prepared for the next encounter, doing reverence unto the ladies, speeded towards Montulus and encountered with him so furiously that he broke his lance upon the helmet of Montulus in such outrageous sort that fire flew forth of his beaver, at which Montulus being much amazed, supposed that Jove had sent a thunderbolt upon his crest, that did so startle him. But meeting both again, Montulus being in the height of his fury, and holding himself perpetually dishonored, gave Sandrico such a recombendibus upon his breast that beat him off one side of his horse, but he speedily recovered himself. Alexto meeting of him embraced him in his arms vowed to be revenged.

But by this time Montulus had recovered himself, and was fitted for the next encounter, the which was entertained by Alexto, who doing reverence unto the ladies, making his pampered courser fly as if he scorned to be controlled and meeting with Montulus in a full career bore him unto the earth with his saddle betwixt his legs, causing his horse to tumble on the other side. But Montulus broke his lance upon the breast of Alexto, who passed on his course still so upright as if that none had encountered with him, the which caused such a general applause, as if he had been some demigod.

But because Alexto should not vaunt long of his prosperous success, some of these knights which were there present and much enraged at his actions set forth together against Alexto, being eight in number, all which he received very nobly, but to their small comforts, for the first two he ran through with his lance, tumbling them from their horses to measure their length on the ground, the third being with him ere he could unsheath his furious sword, he lifted up his martial fist and struck such a ponderous blow upon his crest that he laid him breathless upon the earth, making his brains fly about his horse's heels.

Then drawing his bloody weapon, with which ere any rescue was made he had bereaved three of the other five of life and left the other two sore wounded, the which spectacle caused no little admiration to the beholders. But the ladies being sore affrighted forsook their seats, and Angelica being accompanied with her train entered the lists as Juno among the gods, to nip this early quarrel in the bud, as also fearing further outrage. But Alexto no sooner perceiving her but leapt from his horse, and falling on his knees presenting unto her acceptance his weapon, and uttered these speeches.

"Judicious lady, I have here committed a heinous fact, unbeseeming your presence, and indeed beyond the limits of expression, that speedily requires a just punishment, except your partial censure quit my imbecility in the perpetrating thereof, for like a malefactor I expect a commiserating sentence from your blessed lips."

Angelica seemed to sympathize this his passion and to participate of his grief, and taking him by the hand raised him from the ground and refusing his sword said unto him, "Most valiant knight, your actions merit fame, deserving to be recorded in Hector's register for a perpetual memory, which may survive after ages. I grieve to behold the outrage and uncivil affront that you have sustained in my presence, but every of them have sustained their just deserts from your martial hands for their presumptuous fact." With these and such like words she freed Alexto, requesting that the corpses of the deceased knights should be honorably interred, but especially Sasetus to be entombed in her own chapel with a sumptuous monument over him, the charge of which being committed to certain nobles there extant, she with Alexto and the rest departed into the palace where she entertained them very royally with music and pastimes for the space of three or four days. But Alexto was not content therewith, but still did watch opportunity for a private discourse, but still his intent was frustrate. The Lady Angelica on the other side was as much perplexed for the same opportunity.

But still Alexto's heart did consume, yet was he fixed and constant in the determination, which is the Nepenthe which whoso drinketh of forgetteth all care and grief, for Agrippa reports that nothing in the world sooner remedieth sorrows than constancy. Thus Alexto continues though much perplexed, who was counselled by Sandrico to write a letter unto Angelica, he promising to be the bearer thereof himself, to which Alexto condescended, for Sandrico thus animated Alexto: "Thou knowest," said he, "that ladies delight in praising fictions as hearing their beauties extolled though undeserved, and again poetry is a second nature to make things seem more exquisite than they were first framed by nature; for as the seal leaveth the impression of his form in wax, so the learned poet engraveth his passion so lively in women's hearts that the hearer also is almost transformed into the author." "But should I practise in poesy unto her," quoth Alexto, "I dread of an ill success."

"Tush," said Sandrico, "faint-hearted lawyers are not admitted to put in plea at the bar of love. A cowardly lover without hope shall never gain fair love with good fortune, besides sadness is the punishment of the heart, but hope the medicine of distress, for it is a pleasant passion of the mind which doth not only promise us those things which we most desire, but those things also which we utterly despair of."

"But for all poetry," quoth Alexto, "give me oratory, for it is the spur to arms, for the eloquent oration of Isocrates was the first trumpet that gave Philip an alarm to the Asian wars, which Alexander his son without intermission ended.

"But I must confess unprofitable eloquence is like cypress trees, which are comely in altitude but bear no fruit, and babbling orators are the thieves of time compared to empty vessels, which give a greater sound than those which are full, but a dry thirsty ear must be therewith watered. Eloquence grounded upon reason is able to content and satisfy the hearing."

In this discourse we will leave them and return to speak somewhat of the Lady Angelica, who though she was so superbious yet like a falcon she could stoop to a goodly lure, for she much admired their prolixity from her, which drew her to contemplate with herself what gesture she might have to surprise Alexto, who was her vowed vassal though unbeknown unto her. But at last she calling unto mind his speech unto her at his first approach, which did somewhat mitigate her passion, imagining thereby that he was enamored of her and also hoping that he would make the first assault, of which she was desirous, though modesty was her hindrance. In these contemplations we leave her and return to Alexto, who had penned poetical verses for his lady and mistress, delivering them unto Sandrico for to present unto her, and these are they:

Worthiest of all, could I thee equalize,
To any she that might thee parallize,
In rustic sort then should my rural quill
Herald thy fame, resounding forth it still.
Yet, fairest dame, I deem you'll not disdain
To view these rough-hewn lines whose meaning's plain.
Then by your favor, Lady, I presume
To cast myself beneath your sacred plume.
I homage must if you a goddess were,
But now a frown from your bless'd brow I fear.
To figure you like Venus 'twere unfit,
She was disloyal, beauty-blasted it;
Or say that you resemble Helen's face,
Compared with which 'twould but impart disgrace,
For Troy doth know her qualities so well,
That pens can't write, nor tongues have power to tell;
Yet thus, I'll say, Arabian odors sweet
Distill from your fair cheeks, dear love to greet;
Lady, know this, by knowing which know all:
Your servant proves obedient to your call.

 Now after Sandrico had perused them, he very well esteemed thereof, promising to deliver them, which he performed some two days after, finding a fit opportunity both for time and place, at the receipt whereof the lady knowing from whence they came conceived an inward and unspeakable joy, but dreading to be perceived by Sandrico shrouded this ecstasy beneath the veil of discontent, framing her gesture correspondent unto the stern aspect of her visage, made this answer:

  Dares he presume a goddess to behold,
  Or spot that breast that's beautified with gold?
  Dares he the gods in battle to provoke,
  Or from dark Hell the furies to invoke?
  But what dares he, or dares not for to do,
  That thus doth dare send lines unto our view?

 She willing to proceed but fearing that her sharp answer

would utterly repulse his forwardness and yet loath to seem captivated at first, thus went on: "Sir, I know not how to accept these lines, because I deem them to proceed from presumption and arrogancy, and because I favored his person in the lists he imagines me enamored of him. But his hopes fool him, if so he deems; or have I shown him some other extraordinary favors that he should thus abuse my virtue's meaning? But I perceive he teacheth me to be cautious and circumspect in all my actions, confining my looks upon immovable objects, lest others with himself misdeem them."

Sandrico, perceiving her still to proceed, emboldened himself to interrupt her thus: "Thrice illustrious lady, his perpetual service is offered to your divine person, for at your feet he casts the hope of his world's happiness, uniting the remainder of his life therewith; for he and that little all nature endowed him with lies sole at your disposing.

"Then, seeing you are the first star that ever seduced him to study astronomy, let him not perish by the reflection of your ingratitude, seeing he is loyally affected towards you."

The Lady Angelica, fearing to be entrapped, requested his unwelcome absence, adding that by his lines she perceived no forcing effects; besides, that she had vowed chastity and that a monarch should not cause her infringe her former passed vows to Vesta. But turning aside, she said she must give her conscious tongue the lie, for though a monarch should not, yet Alexto could.

So pulling a gem from her ivory neck, freely presented it to Sandrico, requesting him to pacify his friend and so away she passed and Sandrico returned unto his friend Alexto. But Angelica, seeing she had Alexto at a bay, vowed to keep him off to try his constancy and a while to triumph over him while he was in captivity.

But by this time Sandrico had met with Alexto and relating unto him what answer he received from the beauteous lady, which caused Alexto to fall into a second desperation. But Sandrico showing him her favor recomforted him to send a second epistle.

"My Alexto," said he, "it is natural for women a while to despise that which is offered, but death to them if they be denied of their demands. And he that looketh to have the purest crystal water must dig deep, and he that delighteth in sweet music and madrigals must strain art unto the highest; so he that seeketh to win his love must not spare labor nor fear hazarding his life, for birds are trained with sweet calls but caught with long nets, so lovers are ensnared with fair looks but entangled with disdainful eyes. Then let me be the bearer of another epistle, for he that gathereth roses must be content to prick his fingers, and he that would conquer a woman's affection must not be repulsed by sharp words, and the wisest sort of them are commonly tickled with self-love.

"Come, then, lay hold of my advice, for it is better to prefer the stedfast counsel of advised policy than the rash enterprise of malapert boldness; for as a chameleon hath all colors save white, so a flatterer hath all points save honesty. I wish thee to proceed as if the subject was my own."

"I never found thee otherwise," answered Alexto. "But it is an easy thing for a man being in health to give good counsel to another that is sick, but with such facility the sick man cannot follow it, but I'll write once more ere other exploits I'll try."

THE LETTER

Illustrious Mistress, I never desired to be so good a scholar as to learn to love in Cupid's school, whereby I should attain the courting of beauty with flattering phrases or hypocritical compliments, whose oiled-tongued metaphors so lavish in themselves do warble. But could *the dumb speech of silence* reveal the nature of my apparent passion, or were it engraven in capital letters in my front, whereby the vulgar view of jealous eyes might peruse the secrets of my love, then were this inscription needless, but since not, then equal your inward perfection with your outward excellence, for your apparent beauty hath robbed me of my heart and either I must accuse you of the theft or be accessory to my utter ruin, and for your sake Cupid hath taught me what restless passions are in love. But fearing my laborious pen should prove too sad an orator, I restless rest, until I fully rest,

Yours, or not his own,
Alexto

This he having sealed, enclosed a rich jewel therein, gave it to Sandrico to present unto the lady, the which he most willingly embraced and at a convenient time delivered it her, from whose hands she joyfully kissed the contents ere she had perused the inscription, and well noting each particular, with a modest blush returned this answer, presenting Sandrico an unestimable pearl wherein was carved her portraiture: "Deliver this unto thy friend, whereby ingratitude may not be objected against me; I had rather have a personal appearance than this dumb apparition."

Sandrico understanding her meaning prolonged not time, but with much celerity posted unto Alexto, who expected the sentence of discontent, but, perceiving his friend with such a smiling countenance as the affectionated sire on his studious child, demanded what news.

Sandrico answered he had brought him the loadstone of perfection, and so delivered to him the gem, telling him that he should not omit that occasion but diligently prosecute that proffered opportunity, which was thrown him from the lap of Fortune, which certifying him also where he should find the lady in her bower.

Alexto, now having liberty to gratify Sandrico's diligence, departed with much expedition unto the private walks where he found the lady alone, melodiously playing upon a lute, warbling thereunto an amorous ode, but she no sooner perceiving him come but laid aside her instrument and descending from her bower took him by the hand, being hardly able to dissemble her passion without appearance thereof, for it is their imbecility not to retain their affection long without demonstration unto the affectionated, but she thus began to excuse herself.

"Worthy knight, I little supposed that your ears should have been auditors of my uncivil ode, but let us mount up yonder bower and contemplate a while, for I received two epistles from you, the which being examined, I conceive thereby that an amorous passion hath possessed you, the mitigation of which you affirmed to be resident within the center of my breast, but I know not how to impose the assurance of my affection on any knight because lovers' oaths are like fetters made of glass that glister fair but couple no constraint; besides, love maketh a man that is naturally addicted unto vice to be endued unto virtue, forcing himself to be applied unto all laudable exercises, that thereby he may obtain his love's favor; as also coveting to be skillful in elocution that thereby he may allure her, and to excel in music that by his melody he may entice her, to frame his speech in a perfect phrase that by his learning he may persuade her. So that which is defective in nature, nurture perfecteth and the only original of this virtuous inclination is love."

"Beauteous lady," answered Alexto, "a rolling stone contains no moss and a fickle-headed lover wants no cause of mourning. There are wanton lovers, Lady, I must confess, whose lascivious eyes are like the darts of Cephalus that where it hits, there it deeply wounds. But my meaning is loyal, affection permanent, and both prostrated unto your divine acceptance." "But, noble knight," answered the lady, "young years make their account only of the glittering show of beauty, the mind of a young man is momentary, his affections sick, his love uncertain, and his fancy is fired with every new face, and as young willows bend easily, so green wits are entangled by every new fangle."

"But by your favor, Madam," replied Alexto, "Cupid alloweth none in his court but young that can serve fresh and wise than can talk, faithful to gratify and valiant to revenge their mistress's proffered injuries. And as they that cannot suffer the light of a candle can much worse abide the brightness of the sun, so they that are troubled and damnified by each small trifle would be much amazed to bear the weighty matters which are contained in love.

"For the passionate lover, if he sail, love is his pilot; if he walk, love is his companion; if he sleep, love his pillow: pure love never saw the face of fear, pure love's eyes pierce the darkest corners, and pure love attaineth the greatest dangers. Otherwise, fair Lady, had I not presumed in this abrupt sort to present unto your soft attention the true copy of my perplexed heart, for as mountains that have too much heat of the sun are burnt and valleys having scarcity thereof are barren, but such places as continue in a mean are most fruitful, even so, gracious Lady, pity your distressed servant, who hath no happiness but in the beams of your favor."

Now the Lady Angelica weighing Alexto's grief by the perplexity of her own heart, embraced him in her arms, uttering these words: "Where the knot is loose the string slippeth, and where the water is shallow there no vessel will ride, then here, dear knight, take heart and hand with as true a zeal and perfect love as thy amorous heart can desire to be requited with."

Now was Alexto satisfied, being confirmed thereof by several embracements, in which they spent their time, using the toying sport that lovers commonly commit. But time being at hand of that their present departure, whereby they requested each other that that might be the place of their daily meetings, which was defined to be morning and evening. And so she departed into her chamber and Alexto to find forth Sandrico, being big with joy until he had revealed his proceedings unto his friend, who at the hearing thereof was on a sudden so surprised that he presently burst out as thus:

"Now by the greatest of my name I am possessed with

an ecstasy of joy to see the permanent affections of the loyal lady so well concur and sympathize as rivals to thy best wishes, for now could I bless myself to think that fancy should be so extravagantly predominant over me as to lead me into a labyrinth of fond contemplations that I should urge thy goodness to believe their sex to be implacable, hard-hearted monster that I was. Fair Angelica, thou sole possessor of Europe's choicest rarities, I have uttered blasphemy against thy goodness and the member with which 'twas perpetrated, may never accent drop from thence; nay, may it cease to stir within his roof, unless it be dipped in oil of war by Jove's right hand, whereby with polished phrase, as 'twere from some mercurial wit and by your goodness licensed, then let it warble and with Philomelian notes drown the grove's sweet harmony, may it pierce the skies and make the gods attentive, nay, force their echoes to the applause of feminine loyalty, that the lower world may stand affrighted to the rapture, and if I cannot attain unto this ample manner of blazing virtue, heavenly Angelica, metamorphose me to less than nothing and may your more than saint-like sex conspire to afflict me as you please." Then replied Alexto, "Where's wit and policy, where are the documents you would indoctrinate me with? I cannot choose but smile to think that my tutor is captivated."

"Not captivated, nor in love," said Sandrico, "but my rash abuses unto the sex so undeservedly committed, for which I'll conjure up my wits and raise my genius within the circle of this global head of mine to limn Angelica with poesy as thus:"

TO HIS GENIUS

Mount up, my Genius, aptly seek to raise
A Roman dame unto a goddess' praise;
Limn forth her feature and display her race,
Figure her amply in her active grace;
Call not to aid thee dryads or satyrs,

High-topped nymphs or Jove's time-measuring daughters,
These are too common and so hackneyed they
To poets, abortive brats, therefore not may
Be here corrival in this scene of thine,
Which must be guided by a hand divine.
Invoke the gods, and call the heavens for aid,
Vesta shall homage, Diana be dismayed,
When imitable art shall here make known
This magazine, whose merits enrich her own;
Flame blazon and reciprocally touch
Each lineament of nature and think much
Heavens should now echo unto each shrill voice
That heralds virtue and makes her thy choice.

"Now by my honor," said Alexto, "thou hast invoked thy genius in more than common phrase." "Tush," replied Sandrico, "this is but a flourish, commanding my genius servile to my will, while thus I herald forth her fame."

Uncloud the ebon arches of thy brows,
Wherein two suns are throned, which heaven allows;
The curious spinstry of thy tresses dangle
With radiant pride, thy lovers to entangle;
And from the superficies of thy face
There flow Arabian odors which do grace
The gods which they embrace, as choice perfumes
And silver pride do fan it through their rooms.
Two rows of pointed pearl, thy teeth resemble;
From thy bless'd paps, the nutriment of heaven,
Because such twins and pretty hillocks round
With azure veins on goddess are not found,
The straight proportion of thy slender waist
Invites the gods to be by them embraced.
And thy fair hands might I presume to kiss
No more I'd ask, 'tis too too heav'nly a bliss;
'Cause my o'er-greedy lip I fear would leave
Some deep impression, or itself bereave
Of happiness: I dare no further run,
My unexperienced Muse commands me shun

To flatter any, but keep time and place,
For she is timorous I should disgrace
Her modesty: if from the waist I fall
To treat of lower parts, I hear her call;
Plead then, Angelica, thou art the cause
Makes me thus rude and to forget her laws.

"On my life, thy pardon is gained," said Alexto, "and thy genius hath nobly seconded thy will." Whilst they were thus discoursing and walking towards the palace, Alexto perceiving Angelica coming from the walks, cried out to Sandrico, "O unexpected happiness! From yonder heavenly bower my comet shoots towards me; 'tis my Angelica, let us haste with active willingness to prevent her nimble steps, lest the earth grows too superbious and plains her furrowed front by her saint-like footing on it. Propitious morn betide my heavenly love, their glorious canopies protect thee still."

"I congratulate thy love," answered Angelica, "and no less do my best wishes return to thee and thy noble associate, and with my lips I seal my vow on thine. But prithee tell me, what giddy humor drew you here so soon; I would have stolen on you as unawares to both, but your too curious eyes prevented my intent." "I kiss thy bounty, love, and may it ever flow with such sweet goodness towards me," said Alexto. Then said Sandrico, "It was this pleasant morn, but more especially to gaze upon your place of residence, Alexto being desirous to participate of your odorous breath, lest the gods should surfeit by the gentle winds dispersing of it and so bereave him of his happiness." Angelica vowed that some poetical fury had possessed Sandrico's breast, which Alexto verified, desiring her to witness how well his morning Muse had clothed her excellency. So soon as Angelica had perused the precedent lines of Sandrico's, she merrily answered that if she were not linked in affection to Alexto, she could become amorous of him. "But, love," said she, "opportunity will not smile upon us with conveniency of longer time, lest

Alexto and Angelica

my present miss should prove the unhappy hindrance of our quotidial meetings, but here before thy friend I vow myself as really thine as thy chaste thoughts could wish me, and ere one month's sun should through the zodiac run, Hymen shall celebrate what our plighted faiths engage us to, *Me et te sola mors separabit.*" With that Alexto embracing her in his arms thus answered: "*Hic est verus amor, qui nos conjungit in unum, et ligat æterna mutua corda fide;* and as our laws require, for the ampler gordianizing of the vow, give me an amblet of thy hair, to tie a true love's knot." Angelica answered he that was owner of her and hers should not be denied in his request, and so soon as she had presented him a trace of her hair, she proffered to depart, but Alexto requested her longer stay until he had gratified her bounty.

So tying her hair between them in a true lover's knot, she put it on his wrist, and Alexto sung unto her as followeth:

> Though that my wrist doth wear
> An amblet of thy hair,
> Yet my heart doth bear
> Such correspondency,
>   That of force
>   No remorse
> But thou still must lie.
>
> Incloseted by me
> Thy portraiture must be,
> The hourly bliss I see,
> So amply is it placed
>   That my eye
>   May descry
> By what my heart is graced.
>
> A salamander's urn
> Within whose flames I burn,
> The ashes I return

To thee a sacrifice:
  'Cause my heart,
  Thy nobler part,
Much highly doth it praise.

Here may you see the breast
Of him that cannot rest,
That is with love possessed,
By sighs anatomized;
  Yet must be
  Subject to thee
Thou hast him so surprised.

Commiserate my zeal,
In which I do reveal
(Ere it further steal)
A love reciprocal,
  Which I owe,
  And bestow,
At thy command and call.

Be not marble-hearted,
Ere I am departed
Let my boon be granted:
Repentance comes too late
  At the door:
  I implore,
Since 'tis the will of Fate.

If all this cannot move
Thee to grant him love,
Whenas he doth remove,
Thy tears cannot prevail;
  In thy prime,
  Use thy time,
And fond passion quail.

Were thy love a fleeter,
And a common greeter
Of affections meeter,

Then thou mightst disdain;
  Since not so,
  As you know,
Ease his tortured pain.

Inconstancy to thee,
As chief of his degree
He's vowed for to be,
Be not implacable,
  For of none,
  But thee one,
Is he now pregnable.

If badness by his visit
He did ere solicit,
May he always miss it;
His chaster thoughts doth scorn
  To undo
  Him, or you,
So in Hell's flames to burn.

For all that he requires,
And by his hopes desires,
For to allay his fires,
Is a chaste embracing;
  For you know
  You do owe
Affection's interlacing.

Yet had Hymen but once done
Those rites we will not shun,
Till then I mourn, I burn,
And am afflicted still;
  But O, no,
  'Tis not so,
'Cause I shall have my will.

Peace, war, where'er I be,
The last I'm sure to see,
Because I war in peace for thee,

> Then prayers still be made
>   For us both,
>   That were loath
> Virtue to have betrayed.
>
> When Death shall close mine eye,
> Thy bracelet then shall lie
> As deep enclosed as I;
> Let writers vent their wit;
>   For thy sake,
>   Which I take,
> Death parts not me and it.

After Alexto had thus ended, it pleased Angelica's fancy very much, she making a reiteration of all her precedent protestations unto him, vowing whate'er she perpetrated sprung from that which was enacted in her breast. So with much amorous dalliance as befits lovers to disport time with, they with a very willing unwillingness for that time parted, where we will leave her entering of her palace and Alexto and Sandrico to their accustomed chamber.

You have heard of this their several meetings and how lovingly they accorded together. But Fortune proved herself envious as to mix his present joys with perpetual sorrows, for ere the time was totally expired the Duke of Aragon arrived at the palace, who was very nobly entertained by the lady and her attendants. But to cut off prolixity, he became her suitor and so fervently that nothing could repulse his forwardness.

The lady being mightily perplexed thereat knew not how to demean herself, for fain she would, yet loath she was to condescend, because her vows were passed to Alexto and the worm of conscience turning round did solicit her ears with the sting of memento. Thus betwixt fear and hope, or rather falsehood and dissembling, she remained the most part of a day, but at last considering with herself Alexto was but a lord, the other a duke, who was esteemed a potent monarch, she concluded utterly to renounce Alexto and to entertain the Duke into her favor, and studied with herself how to accomplish it without the impeachment of her honor. At last she resolved not to make a perfect semblance of rejecting him at first, but by degrees requiting his amorous glances with coy and disdainful frowns and to repute his modest embraces lascivious clasps.

With this resolution she went to meet the affectionate Alexto, who expected her presence in the garden, musing at her long delay, but when he perceived her coming, he arose from the bank to meet her, proffering embracement; she refusing it answered that that was childish play and fitter for rurals than these of their degrees, at which Alexto much marvelled, little conceiving her drift and policy therein, yet had he no great cause to admire, because Plato reports that the ferventest mind may be changed between evening and morning; besides, how could truth be expected to lie in falsehood?

But Alexto, rousing his decaying spirits, thus answered: "Lady, is your love like your beauty, both fading like a rose in June? You said a sliding knot is soon loose and that lovers' vows couple no constraint, but like fetters made of glass that glister much but speedily break; your gestures make your words apparent, yet in your vowing you gave me heart and hand." "I mean no otherwise," quoth she, "unto you. If ever I marry, yourself shall be him that shall crown my brows with a laurel wreath." "Why," said Alexto, "the time of our marriage is limited and is almost expired."

With this discourse they spent their time, Alexto urging her still to remember her promise, in so much that Angelica flung forth of the arbor very much discontented, Alexto after her requesting her stay and further conference. She neither returned, answered, nor looked, but shrouding subtlety beneath the mask of anger went her way, leaving Alexto solitary to himself, who stayed not long but went to Sandrico, who was the mitigator of his distress, and no sooner did he meet with him but he thus began.

"To a man in misery life seemeth too long, but to a worldly-minded man living in pleasure life seemeth too short. Pliny reports, a detestable life removeth all merit of honorable burial, for it is a pilgrimage, a shadow of joy, a glass of infirmity, and the perfect pathway to death; for Philip, King Alexander's father, falling upon the sands and seeing there the mark and print of his body, said, 'How little a plot of ground is nature content with!' And the life of man fadeth like a shadow, yet do we covet the whole world."

Sandrico all this while remained astonished, little deeming his lady was the original of this his distemperature, but thus interrupted him: "What unexpected stratagem hath thus perplexed thy mind, condensed your understanding, exiled your judgment, betrayed your spirits to disquiet passions, and leading yourself captive to fond contemplation?" "O my Sandrico," answered Alexto, "the pinnace of my affection is like to sustain shipwreck on the waves of her inconstancy; she begins to disdain me, whom formerly she loved. The world seduceth the eye with variety of objects, the scent with sweet confections, the taste with all delicious dainties, the touch with soft flesh, the body with precious clothings, and all is but the invention of vanity."

"Tush," said Sandrico, "admit she doth forsake thee, as 'tis impossible, never grieve therefore, for that grief is best digested that brings not open shame, but now you have no such cause of mourning. Then cease these brinish tears."

"'Tis true," said Alexto, "Homer so spoke, but what answered Seneca? 'We shall sooner want tears than cause of mourning in this life,' and Gregory said tears crave compassion and submission deserveth forgiveness; but I answer thee as Solon, who, burying his son, wept bitterly being requested to the contrary, 'cause his tears were in vain, 'for that cause I weep the more,' quoth he, 'because I cannot prevail by weeping.'" "Come, come," said Sandrico, "to weep for toyish love thou dost impair thy worth; cease then this, which is the very common emblem of dissimulation.

"For it's common in the eye of a strumpet and like heat-drops in a bright sunshine, and as much to be pitied as the weeping of a crocodile, and peradventure thy mistress dropped angry words to try thy constancy, and might act this with the counterfeit tragedians of Smyrna, who lifting up their bloody hands to the skies and their eyes steadfastly fixed on the earth, cries *Coelum,* meaning the heavens. Come, come, thy lady is loyally affectionated towards thee to my knowledge." Then answered Alexto, "She did disdain me that I should touch her lips and at her departure she gave me not a word but went away in silence. I like not this *muta eloquentia.*" Sandrico then mistrusted the worst, but to hearten on his friend, thus replied: "Perhaps more eyes were present than your own, and that she might fear, or she gave you some private sign by which you might understand her meaning, and peradventure you did not conceive thereof; for Caesar writ unto his captains *per notas,* by marks and notes, lest his letters should be understood by his soldiers, and Tarquin the proud was sent unto by his son Sextus to know what he should do by the Gabians, he brought the messenger into a garden and with his staff *altissima papaverum capita decussit;* the messenger wondered at the stratagem, but Sextus understood his father's mind. So he might give some private note and pass away silent."

Then answered Alexto, "I like not such notes to write as Demetrius did on sand, or as Pythagoras did on glass, nor as Damaratus on wood; therefore what wilt thou advise me to do to answer her dumb gesture?" Sandrico requested him to write some amorous lines unto her in courting sort, and he would present them. Alexto condescended thereunto and writ as ensuing:

> Thy coral lips and rosy cheeks, my dear,
> They were the flame that fired me so near;
> In troth they were, nay more, they are indeed
> The glowing coals that first this fire did breed.
> Thy eyes also doth wound me in such sort
> I feign them not, my sighs may well report;

> Worthiest of all, that seemst so lovely fair,
> Reject me not, nor cause me to despair;
> You are the only motive of my pain,
> Then let me not of cruelty complain,
> But give relief, for little dost thou know
> How much for thee I fettered am in woe:
> Pens cannot write, nor rightly tongues declare
> That fervent love, which to thyself I bear,
> Whereof, alas! my young spirit quaffed so deep,
> That drunk with love my reason falls asleep;
> For I, whom Fortune now hath blinded so,
> Did ne'er till now the art of wooing know:
> Then pity me, for it lies in thy will
> My loathed life either to save or kill;
> Let this suffice, for all the world may see:
> The fault's not mine 'cause thou hast wounded me.

This being done, he delivered it unto Sandrico, who willingly embraced it, promising to present it, and while he is a-seeking of the lady, we meeting with her first will treat with her a while, who remains not much discontented though for a while she seemed so, for she was sorry that she had been so rash with Alexto, yet glad that she had so quickly repulsed his forwardness and instead of being in the arms of Alexto, she was embraced by the Duke of Aragon, from whose lap she had no sooner arose but she met with Sandrico, who presented her the letter, the which she received, but not so friendly as she was wont, and breaking it up perceiving it somewhat large, tore it in pieces, saying she scorned to peruse such tedious epistles, and in rage she flung away ere Sandrico could answer her a word, who was amazed to see such a sudden alteration. Then assuring himself she had forsook Alexto forever and very sorrowful, bearing the doleful tidings in his front, returned unto him, declaring what had happened.

At which Alexto fell into a grievous trance, but being somewhat recovered bursts into this lunatic speech:

Contorted lock of furies I could tear,
Kick Hercules from damned Acheron,
And make the triple-headed bandog roar;
Pluto confront within his jetty throne,
And sink cursed Charon in his ferry boat.
Teach me Narcissus-like, who in a brook,
To kiss himself himself there hath forsook;
Teach me with Dicas still in blood to weep,
And with Philistus waking always sleep;
Let me with dropsy-thirsty Astus drink
The poisoned stuff that ran from Nero's sink,
Or quaff that potion which Agasta made
When he supposed Alphonso was betrayed:
If neither drink nor quaff, then let me sup
My fatal draught from Alexander's cup;
I'll with Philotus to a dungeon hie,
Where I'll remain still in obscurity,
And with Bassacus never more behold
Sol's radiant beams transparent to the gold.
O! that I were a basilisk, that I
Might venom her, or else unvenomed die!
Let me work spite on her, as Antoes did,
Conjuring her still in her tortured bed,
Put m'on a robe that may consume to bone
This flesh of mind, intomb me in that stone
Where Petius lies in the Elysian green,
Who died for love and lives there to be seen;
It is a woman that hath wronged me this,
And cursed me now when I expect a bliss.

Then Sandrico answered, "Fly not with Apollo after Daphne; Diana hath more nymphs as fair and yet not so coy; use love, yet wrestle with Cupid and hold him as a boy. Consider as she is fair, so she is cruel, and as she is well featured, so she is perjured. The curious herbalists measure not their plants by their colors but by their properties; the lapidaries value their stones not by their outward hue but by their secret virtues, for a diamond with a cloud is cast into the goldsmith's dust. Then let lilies wither on the stems, and wear violets both in heart and hand; the one is fair but unsavory, the other black but sweet and virtuous. But have a care lest the impression engender some exorbitant passion in thee. I could repeat many that have been perplexed by the heroical passion of love, but these one or two shall suffice to prevent the enormities that may ensue if you proceed in these frantic fits. For there was one Locustus that had been served in the like manner as the lady serves you, on which he grew frantic and meeting a friend of his requested him to be his second, his friend condescending. Locustus carried him to the Church of St. Mark, at which time the Duke of Venice was resident, who as soon as this dotard saw him, he cried out to his companion, 'see, there is he with whom I have the quarrel; let us set upon him,' pointing to the Duke, and if he had not been resisted by the guard, he had committed the outrage. And the distemperature of Ajax first sprung from love, of whom we read in our Grecian fables." By this and the like discourse he had so well quailed Alexto's passion that he fell into a fine slumber, but presently starts and being again awaked, he began to call to mind the fantasy that had possessed his brain in that his slumber, and thus cried out, "O Sandrico, I have dreamed that Angelica is married!"

"Tush," answered Sandrico, "that I cannot believe, and credit no dreams, for they be fables and commonly fall out by contraries, as they appear; for Hamilcar, General for the Carthaginians, laying siege at Syracusa, an image came to him in his sleep, telling him that he should the next night sup as conqueror in Syracusa, and sup there he did, but as a prisoner and captive by the Syracusans and not as a captain by his Carthaginians. The like did Julius Caesar: the night before he was slain, he dreamt that he was sitting by Jupiter's seat, but suddenly he fell flat with his face on the ground; therefore we must not cocker our genius and flatter ourselves with what we conceive in such illusions."

"But," said Alexto, "me thought there was great triumphs at the solemnization thereof, and that he and divers other nobles were presenting of a masque and dancing. Be it so or not, how shall we come to speech with Angelica?"

"Why," said Sandrico, "pen another epistle, and I vow to thee she shall read it, or I'll engrave it on her breast, and at the back side of the walks thou shalt be placed, and while we are in parley hasten to us, whereby we shall decide it, and not letting of it hang in suspense any longer." Alexto condescended and went to study, whereat we leave him to speak of the Duke of Aragon, who was with the Lady Angelica, and after divers of his courtings, she thus began to answer him: "Renowned Duke, shame and infamy waits at the heels of unbridled desire, for as lust is an enemy to the purse, a foe to the person, a canker to the mind, a corrosive to the conscience, a weakener of the wit, a besotter of the senses, and finally a mortal bane to all the body; so you shall find pleasure in the pathway to perdition and lusting love the loadstone to ruth and ruin."

The Duke protested he meant verily to make her sole owner and governor to him and his, if she would but requite him with her lasting affection. She promised him, so he would utterly renounce all suspicion and, as having no cause given by her, so he would not lay hold on every frivolous occasion whereby jealousy might proceed; "for I will relate a jealous humor and the ill conveniency thereof," said she, and thus she began.

"A jealous man is suspicious ever more, judging the worst; for if his wife be merry, he thinketh her immodest; if sober, sullen; if pleasant, inconstant; if she laugh, it is lewdly; if she look, it is lightly. So he is still casting beyond the moon and watcheth as the crafty cat over the silly mouse; for if the heart be once infected herewith, his sleeps are broken and dreams prove unquiet; the whole night is consumed in slumber, thoughts, and cares; the day in woe, vexation, and misery. Besides, my lord, the jealous man living dies, and dying prolongs out his life in passion worse than death. None looketh on his love but he suspicious says, this is he that would be corrival in my favors; none knocketh at the door but starting up he imagines them to be the messengers of fancy; none talks but they whisper of affection. If she frown she hates him and loves others; if she smile it is because she hath had success in her love; looks she frowardly on any man, she dissembles; if she favors him with a gracious eye, then as a man possessed with a frenzy he crieth out that neither fire in straw nor love in a woman's looks can be concealed. Thus doth he live restless, and maketh love, that is sweet in itself, more bitter than gall. Consider this, my lord, for should you perpetrate the like, it would make a woman wanton, if she were born to chastity."

But by this time Alexto had penned his epistle; therefore we will leave her subtly proceeding in her rhetoric, thereby yoking the Duke unto her servitude, and return unto him, who was reading what he had writ unto Sandrico, and this was it:

> Shall I be stabbed with poniards of disdain,
> Or languish still in my obscurest pain?
> For in my heart thy worth is firmly fixed;
> My groaning sighs with tears are intermixed.
> As spiders' webs hold fast the silly fly,
> Entangled so by thy fair self am I;
> Why planted I heart's-ease, and rue must gather?
> As I did sow, I should have reaped rather:
> This is a paradox beyond relief,
> That I in anguish should prolong my grief.

After Sandrico had perused these lines, without intermission he prosecuted the delivery, knowing the lady frequented the walks in the cool of the day, and thither being come, though unseen, yet they saw the Lady Angelica embraced by the Duke of Aragon, to whom she had newly contracted herself.

Alexto being conveniently placed, Sandrico undaunted proceeded towards her, where she starting up from the Duke's lap demanded the original of his abrupt intrusion.

Sandrico said, "Lady, you must and shall peruse each syllable enclosed here," delivering her the letter, at which the Duke began to storm, but she, having her tricks briefer than her paternoster, soon pacified the Duke, telling him, he was a gentleman sewer to a kinsman of hers, from whom she did not much desire to be solicited; so, craving pardon and his patience, descended the mount and read what was enclosed.

Sandrico demanded her answer. "Why, that I am otherwise provided," quoth she. With that Alexto did approach, vowing not to be so satisfied, at whose coming she did sustain an agony which more tortured her than if grim death had seized each part. Then said Alexto, "Lady, will you falsify your vows?" She replied that she never made any and demanded his witness. "I have none," said Alexto, "but Sandrico and your own conscience. Otherwise, wherefore did you use me so respectively, retaining me into your favor?" "Why, as my servant," she replied, "for that was your first request at your entering of my palace, and so I have counted of you and ever will, if you be resident with me."

"Lady," answered Sandrico, "you are false and disloyal; you are like the mandrake apple, comely in show but baneful in taste, and for your ingratitude you are worse than the serpent, who hath venom to annoy others, but not himself." And then Alexto began: "Lady, is this equity and justice? Oh, no. For justice consists of eight parts: friendship, concord, godliness, humanity, gratefulness, faithfulness, and virtuousness; but you have neither, for it is the badge of virtue, the staff of peace, and the maintenance of honor." "O that I were but some sorcerer as Circe, who altered the shapes of men and women to bears, wolves, lions, asses, apes, and the like, whereby I might make some metamorphosis of thee! If your sex were not worse than ours, wherefore doth serpents engender in your reins and toads in dead men's skulls? And so fare you well," said Angelica.

Alexto seeing himself utterly cast off was desperate, but

Sandrico persuaded him as followeth: "He that bruiseth the olive tree with hard iron fetcheth out no oil but water, and he that pricketh a proud heart with persuasions draweth out nothing but hate and envy; therefore let her go, as better lost than found; for Aristotle reporteth that a virgin's heart is like a cotton tree, whose fruit is so hard in the bud that it soundeth like steel, and being ripe putteth forth nothing but wool."

"Oh," said Alexto, "that I could with Aristotle throw myself into the Euripus, saying *Quia te non capio tu me capies.*"

"Be not wilful," said Sandrico, "to destroy thyself; for many happen to die by chance, whose causes are unknown and obscured; many by infirmity, whose causes are apparent; many by age, whose causes are present; but some die neither by chance, infirmities, nor age, but die for want of grace to live longer."

"Shall I kill her then?" said Alexto. "Oh, no," quoth Sandrico, "how frequent is it, that such men have been frequented with horrible fantasies and imaginations, which come into their heads both sleeping and waking?

"So Thierry, King of Italy, being a Goth by nation, after he had slain Symmachus and Boethius his sons, as Procopius reports, it seemed to him that he saw in the head of a fish served on his table the face of Symmachus in a horrible shape and fashion, knitting of his brows, goggling of his eyes, biting his lip for very anger; the conceit thereof so perplexed the king that he fell sick and died: this is the usual course of murderers." Then replied Alexto, "Thou art a Plato unto me, and I like Dionysius abstain from much tyranny by thy good counsel. Then let her live like the dame in the triumphs of Olympus, for every owl to spend a whoop at. And I'll be warned never to fall into such folly again, and learn that lesson which Socrates taught his scholars, which was *Reminiscere.*

"And nothing sinketh deeper nor cleaveth faster in the mind of a man than those counsels which he learned in his childhood, which I will with Augustine say, *Antide me*

Alexto and Angelica

semen invenes, and well note what I have sustained by a trothless woman. But had I took thy advice, Sandrico, this had not happened, but as cypress trees the more they be watered the more they wither, and the oftener they be lopped the sooner they die, so unbridled youth, the more it is by grave advice counselled, the sooner it falleth to confusion. But if youth blush not at beauty and carry not antidotes of wisdom against flattery, folly will be the next haven he shall harbor in. Experience lets me know so much, for as the strong bitterness of aloe takes away the sweetness of honey, so evil works destroy and take away the praise of good deeds.

"As wine in Plato's opinion is the daughter of verity, so love in Jamblichus' censure is the fruit of idleness; for Sophocles being demanded what harm he would wish to his enemy, he answered that he might love where he were not fancied. I'll therefore describe what love is.

For Love's indeed a fury fetched from Hell,
Making thoughts metaphors where it doth dwell;
With Morpheus' dreams such always are possessed,
Hunting with sighs to keep themselves at rest.
Love's a madness, a restless agony,
Which makes the eyes two fountains never dry;
It is a harsh and uncontrolled desire
Which makes men burn and live in Cupid's fire;
Then why, say I, to burn in Cupid's fire,
When none that's wise needs care for Cupid's ire?
He is a child and fears Diana's rod,
At which he stands as Mars to Venus stood;
But Venus unto Love was ne'er a nurse,
Alas, Love's kept by Fancy, which proves worse;
Fancy breeds Love, Love then breeds doubts and fears,
Engendering thus till it's expressed with tears;
Doubts are as perilous as the quicksand,
And fear makes lovers in amazement stand.
These are the rocks where love's boat's cast away,
Making men live to die with their delay.

But what is Fancy, when it is defined?
Why, Love and Fancy brings men to be shrined.
Her chariot is of a silkworm's head,
The silkworm's silk within serves for her bed;
The wheels whereon this chariot doth run
Are of the motes discovered by the sun;
Her nimble whips the forerib of a spider;
Two gnats do draw and one is the outrider:
This buzzing runs within a lover's brain,
Making their vitals stupefied with pain.

"Cleobulus meeting with his son Ireon solemnizing the ceremony of marriage gave him in his hand a branch of henbane, meaning thereby that the virtuous disposition of a wife is never so perfect but it is interlaced with some froward fancies, but I'll only define what Angelica is, my Sandrico, and so leave her with frantic love.

Catch me a star that falleth from the sky,
Cause an immortal creature for to die,
Drive with a wand back Neptune's flowing seas,
Sail through this center to Antipodes;
Call time again, and hasten future things,
Say nutriment the eastern bird me brings,
Say that Phoebus is fixed in his course,
And from the skies we have but small remorse;
Infuse long life into a breathless creature,
Say that we are made but not by nature,
The winged messenger, stop his career,
And bring a satyr unto human fear;
Say Acheron is light, and Hell's not hell
But a vast Chaos for savages to dwell,
Say Jove ne'er thundered, Mars his sword ne'er drew,
Venus no wanton, these are all as true,
As to find faith in fair Angelica's mind,
Apparent 'tis that such proves never kind;
But them I'll leave unto their own designs,
Desiring fates to turn men's amorous minds.

No sooner had Alexto ended, but on a sudden he was all surprised; each limb was disjointed and sought to separate themselves as strangers to their fellows. But Sandrico cheering him up desired him to be frolic still. "This sudden agony," said he, "prognosticates. Be it bad or ill, welcome the will of Fate; we are both armed to stand the hazard and with each other participate what Fortune shall allot us." But whilst they were thus discoursing, they perceiving Angelica's squire coming from the palace posted to meet them, for so Angelica had cunningly contrived, the time being expired of her appointed marriage to the Duke of Aragon, and, to give a full period to Alexto's further solicitation of her love, sent him a letter to this effect.

Noble Alexto
What antipathy nature could produce in an affectionate way was still thy own, and, not to make thee proud, thine then is mine now. I relent and crave pardon for my arrogancy, for love hath made a changeling of me now, and lent me wings to top the highest plume of amorous conceits thou soarest withal. Within this hour, meet me at the Temple, where Hymen shall marry us; forget, forgive, and believe what thou seest.
                                        Angelica

Alexto at the reading of the letter was very much surprised with an ecstasy of joy, and presently sent his picture unto Angelica, returning this answer: I send myself, because myself will not be absent; and presently after himself with his friend went towards the Temple, and coming somewhat nigh they beheld Angelica with all her train and Hymen leading them towards the Temple. But supposing them to be goddesses, "Look," quoth Sandrico, "if my thoughts prove not strangers to my wish, yon gods are come on purpose with masques and revelling to celebrate thy nuptials."

"I had thought," quoth Alexto, "our marriage should have been privately solemnized, but since it is their wills to have it publicly kept, I'll not contradict it," but coming nearer into the Temple, they beheld Angelica coming towards them arm in arm with the Duke of Aragon as from the marriage. With that, Alexto burst out into a great fury, cried out, "Were my eyes invited witnesses to testify against themselves their master's ruin? What shall I do, Sandrico? Shall I with a poniard give a period to their days of joy, and make their grave serve for their wedding bed?" "Restrain thy fury," said Sandrico; "put off this discontent and let a mask of pleasure veil thy face until they are overpast us."

But Angelica coming near them gave them kind salutation and thus began: "Lords, you are both welcome to revel with us. I doubt not but you wish us joy. Your goodness towards us was never less, but for you, Alexto, I present this favor; wear it for our sake," giving him back his own picture with a wreath of willows about his neck, and so Angelica passed away towards her palace, leaving Alexto in his raging fit. But being somewhat comforted by the good persuasions of Sandrico, Alexto was persuaded to go into the Temple, desiring Sandrico to accompany him, where he might devoutly offer at fair Venus' altar the best of his devotions, and there exasperate his grief in hope her goodness would revenge his wrongs, the which being done, he desired Sandrico to accompany him to the palace, and being resolved not to be any way dismayed. But Fortune frustrated their determination, for before they had gone half the way, they met with an aged palmer of whom they demanded what news at the palace, to whom he bitterly lamenting informed them that the fair Angelica who was made this morn a happy bride, when in her palace she was throned, a buzzing horror did possess her ears, and nothing else was warbled by her tongue but her Alexto, which she so often reiterated, that it caused a present astonishment to the honorable assembly. And in this frantic fit away she ran and the Duke after her, but getting up into the battlements of the palace, then casting herself from the walls, crying out "Into thy arms, I come, Alexto," and so with the fall was battered all in pieces. Then with protestation loud, the Duke vowed to be revenged on Alexto, and is at present in pursuit of him. But no sooner had the pilgrim ended his story, but the Duke presented himself in person, and after divers defiances between Alexto and himself, they encountered each other, in which the Duke receiving his mortal wound, speedily resigned his breath, at which Alexto crying out, "The gods were just, and have at full revenged my injuries. And now Sandrico, let us haste away. There be certain Jews in the west part of India called Espi, who will eat no flesh, drink no wine, nor use the company of any woman, and thither let us go."

Sandrico condescended and so they took their journey, in which we wish them happiness.

FINIS

THE
Comical and Tragical History
OF
FORTUNATUS:

Wherein is contained his Birth, Travels, Adventures, laſt Will and Teſtament to his two Sons, to whom he bequeathed his PURSE and WISHING-CAP: Together with their Lives and Death.

Abbreviated for the Good and Benefit of young Men and Women, whoſe Impatience will not allow them to read the larger Volume. The whole being Illuſtrated with divers Cuts ſuitable to the Hiſtory.

𝕷icens'd and 𝕰nter'd accoᴢding to 𝕺ᴢder.

London, Printed by and for *C. Brown*, and are to be ſold by the Bookſellers of *Pye-corner* and *London-bridge*.

FORTUNATUS (ca. 1700)

Like *Faust, Fortunatus* is a story which first appeared in Germany in the sixteenth century; the edition published at Augsburg in 1509, the earliest known, is now thought to be probably the first appearance in print. But if its origin is German, the story has a rather cosmopolitan setting, for, as Herford remarks, "Almost every country of Europe contributes to its scenery. We hurry to and fro between Cyprus, England, France, Flanders, Venice, Constantinople; we explore the Purgatory of S. Patrick and taste the genial hospitality of Prester John."

Equally varied are the elements which went into the story. To quote Herford again, "Chivalric romances, religious legends, tales of magic are all represented. . . . There are motives from Italian novels and from primitive Teutonic mythology." The character of the book as a whole is markedly folkloristic, with a number of easily recognizable motifs appearing in its pages, the inexhaustible purse, the magic hat, the horn-producing fruit, and so on. At the same time the story has strong touches of realistic detail and is hence in its appeal, and probably origin, clearly middle-class. The purse is, for instance, a middle-class symbol, the hat is used chiefly for comic effect, and there is much emphasis on trade and commerce.

The story was introduced to Englishmen by Dekker's play, *The Pleasant Comedy of Old Fortunatus*. The prose version put in its appearance considerably later and its bibliography is much confused because of undated editions and the existence of several versions. The earliest known dated edition is that of 1676 but at least one other edition probably antedates it. The late appearance of the tale in

English is, however, made up for by the popularity it enjoyed once it was available, a popularity emphasized by the fact that abridgements quickly appeared.

It is one of these abridged versions which has been chosen for reprinting here, as an example of this phenomenon in prose fiction in the late seventeenth century, of which a number of examples appeared. Produced, as the title page puts it, for those whose "impatience will not allow them to read the larger volume," these abridgements present a rather hurried and somewhat unsatisfactory text (unsatisfactory at least to those who have a little more patience). The degree of condensation may vary from reducing the original to a quarter of its original size to the extreme seen in *Valentine and Orson*, where the original 118 chapters have been cut down to about 2500 words. In the present case the abridgement is about one-fifth of the original in length. Often enough cutting makes parts of the text mysterious, if not unintelligible, by dropping out necessary antecedent material, but the main lines of the action are preserved. It must be presumed that these editions were intended for either children or semi-illiterate readers. At any rate, it is only stories popular with the middle class that were so treated.

The best account in English of *Fortunatus* is C. H. Herford, *Studies in the Literary Relations of England and Germany in the Sixteenth Century*, Cambridge, 1886, pp. 203–219; current German scholarship is well represented by Franz Podleiszek, *Anfänge des bürgerlichen Prosaromans in Deutschland*, Leipzig, 1933. The following text, which dates from about the year 1700, is based on the copy in the Folger Shakespeare Library.

THE COMICAL AND TRAGICAL HISTORY OF FORTUNATUS

Chapter 1. Of Fortunatus's parentage and birth in the famous island of Cyprus; how growing up in learning and knowledge, his father by his lavishness was reduced to poverty; and he going to seek his fortune was entertained by the Earl of Flanders in his return from Jerusalem; how the servants envied him for the love their lord bore him; with the stratagem they used to make him secretly withdraw from his service, to the great grief of the Earl.

In the renowned city of Famagosta, in the pleasant island of Cyprus, in times past there dwelt one Theodorius, descended of noble parentage, who left him a great estate, but being brought up to nothing but pleasure, he pursued it so far in all manner of sports and riots that it consumed apace; his friends being grieved hereat thought of no better way to check his proceedings and bring him within bounds of moderation than by matching him to some discreet woman, whose wisdom and good humor might bring him to live soberly and frugally. This being concluded on, contrary to his knowledge, upon diligent search they found one, suitable to what they had proposed, in the city of Nicosia a virtuous young virgin, daughter to a merchant, rich and beautiful, whose name was Gratiana; and proposing it to him, with many reasons and arguments, how much it would be for his good, he resolved to visit her, and liking her comely shape, good features, but above all her modest carriage and witty expressions suiting his humor, after a few months' courtship, they were married in splendid manner, most of the principal men of either city being at the wedding, who gave large gifts, as it is the custom, to the bride and bridegroom. And so for many years they lived in content and great felicity, in which space they had a son, whom they named Fortunatus, at whose christening an old woman, taken to be a prophetess, came in and uttered these words:

> The child is Fortune's darling; he shall share,
> Unsought, those riches which she will prepare;
> To travel he his thoughts full soon will bend;
> Though crossed in some, yet all shall happy end.

This was noted of many but more particularly when the success answered her prediction.

As he grew up, his father, not to be restrained by the tears and entreaties of his wife, squandered away all his patrimony, which much grieved Fortunatus, though he saw no way to redress it. And his father, too late seeing his folly, fell into a deep melancholy, often sighing and shedding tears, which so afflicted his son, that thinking he might have done something that grieved him he came and kneeled before him, entreating to know what caused his afflictions and if he had contributed towards them, he would amend and do any thing that might be pleasing in his sight. But the sorrowful father, sighing, told him he had been very dutiful, which was the greatest comfort he had, yet being afflicted with poverty, which had brought him to be despised by his inferiors, it much afflicted him. Upon this Fortunatus begged leave to rid him of the charge he put him to by suffering him to travel, not doubting, as he said, considering his education, but he should shift for himself, and Fortune might so befriend him and enable him to do for him and his mother, who had been so tender and gave him such liberal education. His father easily consented but his mother not without great reluctancy, but finding there was a necessity for it, with many tender embraces they parted.

Fortunatus having the world to ramble in made to the sea, and at the next haven found a great many armed men landed, which at the first made him start, as supposing it an invasion of the island, but he upon inquiry found it was Baldwin, Earl of Flanders, who had put on shore to refresh him in his return from the wars against the Turks and Saracens in the Holy Land. He took courage, and kneeling before the Earl offered his service, telling him he was put forth to seek his fortune and that he would be very subservient to his commands. The Earl eyeing him and perceiving him a very promising youth, of a comely personage, after a little inquiry into the circumstances of his parentage and former life, he made him his chief servant; and so well he behaved himself that he gained this great lord's entire affection and so departed with him in the galley to the next port, which was the famous city of Venice, built in a marsh in the sea about three leagues from the mainland and defended from the raging of the ocean with mighty banks and monstrous pits; through whole streets run several channels, so that great boats and lighters came with goods and merchandise to the doors of their houses. Fortunatus knew the language of this country, which he had learned from a Venetian in his own, so that meeting with divers merchants there he bought up, by his lord's order, store of jewels and other rich merchandise, which wonderfully pleased him, the which he intended to bestow upon the Duke of Cleves's daughter, to whom he was contracted (before his going to the war) and at his return designed to marry.

And at this marriage being jousts and tournaments, the Earl, to encourage his servants to do well, set up a jewel valued at three hundred crowns to those that should overcome after the nobles and knights had ended their debates. Fortunatus carried the prize from them all, which made them greatly envy him, and the more because a newcomer should have the advantage of their lord's favor; and so they consulted together to find out a contrivance to remove him, which they effected by this stratagem. One Robert, an old servant, came to him as he was reading and told him that their lord being to depart and leave his bride was by reason of her beauty so jealous that he had ordered surgeons to come the next morning, to secure himself of his servants, by gelding them. This so terrified Fortunatus (the man urging he revealed this in good will to him) that without further consideration he besought him to help him make his escape for he would not be so served for his lord's earldom. Robert observing this told him he was loath to part with him, but if he would go, he desired to know where he would reside that when the rest were gelded and his lord's jealousy over, he might return to his service again and very probably escape. But he said he would not return again, whatever betide him, so getting a horse he was led by Robert, who inwardly was pleased and laughed in his sleeve at the fallacy he had put upon him, and being without the gate rode away with all the speed he could, never looking behind him, till he was many miles from the palace.

The Earl at his return missing Fortunatus made great inquiry for him, but the servants utterly denied they knew what was become of him. Then he asked his lady whether she had given him any cause of offence, but she was altogether ignorant of any such thing; so he was forced to content himself, though much against his will, saying, however, that he should at one time or other find it out, and he would severely punish the occasioners of it, which made Robert, who had contrived his flight, much afraid lest he should return and make a discovery of what stratagem had been used to cause his absenting his lord's service.

Chapter 2. How travelling through many countries, he embarked for England and was entertained by a Florentine merchant; who together with all the family being falsely accused of the murder of a knight of the King's court, was with the rest condemned to die; and by what means he only escaped and went for France.

Fortunatus getting away in manner aforesaid was resolved to follow Fortune, and so, coming by divers ways to Calais, he got passage for England, where he fell into the company of two Cyprus merchants and lived with them riotously, spending in wine and upon harlots till his and their stocks was utterly exhausted; and being in a poor condition, void of succor, his mistress, on whom he had spent his pleasure, thrust him out of doors and refused to relieve him. As he wandered about London, he was taken notice of by one Jerinomus Roberti, a Florentine merchant, who examining him found he was of a prompt wit and education and therefore agreed with him to come into his service, which he joyfully accepted, and being acquainted with the customs of merchants was so diligent and so well behaved himself that he got the good esteem, not only of his master, but of all the servants, who entirely loved him.

But soon after, a great calamity befell the family by means of a villain, which cost all but Fortunatus their lives, and he very narrowly escaped. For one Andrew, a young spendthrift Florentine, having been sent by his father to sell a cargo of goods, not only lavished away all the money he had for them, but continued to draw bills upon the old man, with promises of large returns, till he had near ruined him before he had discovered the cheat; at what time being put to his shifts, he left England and went for Bruges, where hearing of an English merchant who lay in irons in a noisome dungeon for forging the King of England's passport he went to visit him. The merchant no sooner knew he came from England but he was exceeding glad, inquiring what news and the welfare of his friends, all which he told him as well as he understood. The merchant said, "You see in what a miserable condition I lie here. If you would return to England and acquaint my friends with it, I make no doubt but they will use their purses and interest at court to release me." To be brief, he promised to do it upon consideration of three hundred crowns, and so took the names of those friends he proposed and money for his passage.

Now among this merchant's friends was Roberti, Fortunatus's master, by which means this wicked Florentine came acquainted with him to his ruin, for having proposed to lay down three hundred crowns for the merchant's ransom, if any others would come in for part security, Andrew at last told him he had found a gentleman of a great estate that would do it, and that he should provide a dinner and he would bring him. This being agreed to, he went to a knight of the court, whom the king had employed to get the richest jewels that might be had to make a present to his sister, who was to be married to the Duke of Burgundy, telling him there was a jeweller of Florence, who hearing of the King's inquiry after rarities was come over with such that the like had never been seen in the nation, and so invited him to come and see them at Roberti's, where he said he lodged, desiring him to bring his own with him that they might compare them. The knight little dreaming of the treachery designed promised so to do, and accordingly came, when after dinner having him into a private chamber he stabbed him, but for what reason we knew not, for he had not brought the jewels with him. Whereupon he took his keys and his signet and ran to his house, delivering them to his wife as a token to give him the jewels, for the King was to send them away. Upon search she could find none, nor were they found for some time after, so that the murderer, frustrated of his expected prize, came to Roberti's again, where the murder was discovered by the dropping of the blood through the ceiling, but he labored to calm their outcries by saying the murdered was a mere cut-throat and designed to have killed him for this money. However, he would rid them of the body, and so taking it on his shoulder, he threw it into a privy and fled by a back-way for fear of being apprehended.

The knight being missing, great inquiry was made. This merchant's house, where they had intelligence he went, was searched, but nothing found till being about to depart one cried, "Come, let's see in the privy; we have not searched that yet," and there, by throwing in a lighted paper, they saw the murdered's heels standing upright. The King being certified of this, the merchant and his servants were examined by tortures, all of them confessing what they knew of the murder but Fortunatus, whom they had kept ignorant of it, he being then abroad. But of the jewels they could tell nothing, so that hereupon they were condemned to be hanged; and of seven only Fortunatus escaped at the gallows, by the others protesting his innocence in the matter. About half a year after, the widow of the knight being advised to think of a young lover and remove her bed into another room, to put her out of her melan-

Fortunatus

choly, putting the latter in practice, found a little cabinet under it, and in it the jewels, which, by the advice of a kinsman, she carried to the King, who for her fidelity gave her the Manor of Woodstock and caused a young knight to marry her, settling a thousand pounds a year upon them during their lives.

Fortunatus having lost his master and happily escaped the gallows grew so fearful of such another bout that he resolved to stay no longer in England, but getting on board soon sailed over to France.

Chapter 3. How travelling from Orleans to Paris he met with Dame Fortune, who gave him a purse of such a virtue that whenever he put his hand into it he drew out ten angels of gold, entailing it upon him and his sons. Of the noble entertainment he had afterwards. How he was imprisoned by Duke Rodolphus and suspected as a robber for his great profuseness; and upon what terms he gained his liberty.

Fortunatus being freed from another danger left the city and resolved to go for Paris, when passing through a great wood and being at a loss which way to go, as he gazed about he saw a comely shape in woman's apparel crossing his way, and coming up to him, he demanded who she was and her business in that desert. "My name," replied she, "is Fortune, and here am I placed by the Great Distributor and Disposer of all things, by whose command I have power to give six things to such as stand in need of them. For but one of them can, by my means, fall to any one man's share; be prudent in your choice, for you may not choose again." He now supposed he had found his good angel, which made him greatly rejoice, and reflecting on his former poverty, he chose riches, saying, "Give me so much that I may never be poor again," so he well knew what power money had in the world, it answering all things, as: make a knave pass for an honest man, a fool for a wit, a dowdy for a beauty, a coward for a valiant man. Upon this she gave him a purse curiously wrought in needlework, with various figures of Providence worked thereon in silk, gold, and pearl, saying, "Take this purse and be thankful for it to Almighty God; for in whatsoever land thou art, put thy hand into it and you shall as often as you do so draw out ten angels of gold of that country's coin." For this he gave her a thousand thanks, leaping for joy, to which she replied, "Direct them to the Divine Giver of all things, for I am but the hand to distribute them as he directs. For," continued she, "I neither see nor have regard to the persons on whom I bestow them, but am always hoodwinked as you see; therefore had wisdom been your petition, she would have taught you better." Upon this Fortunatus, bowing low, begged her pardon. Then she bid him not be proud, but always charitable and courteous to the poor, and then the virtue of the purse should hold to him and his children, and no longer.

Then directing him out of the wood, she vanished from his sight, which made him greatly wonder, and scarcely believe but it was a vision and nothing of reality in it, till coming to an inn he tried the experiment and found it to be otherwise. But his garments were so poor that the host, till he saw his money, scrupled to let him have either victuals or drink; but seeing him draw out gold so fast, he began to be sweet upon him, made him a fire, carried him into the best room, ordering his daughter diligently to attend him, the best in the house being at his service, so that he stayed there all night. And seeing a curious embroidered furniture for a horse, he asked his host to whose horse it belonged. "To none," said he, "at present, for it is left here to be sold." Upon which, resolving to beat it no longer upon the hoof, since he had such means coming in, but to buy a horse, bargained with him for it for fifty angels, and the next morning there being no horse to be got there, he travelled to a village ten miles further, overlooked by a stately castle that stood on a hill. Here he put into an inn, and desired the host to let him know if there were any good horses to be sold. The host told him there was a merchant newly arrived, who had brought three very stately ones out of Barbary, which he designed to sell at the feast that was to be held there upon the Duke of Orleans's wedding, which suddenly was to commence. Upon this he desired to see them; the host seeing him so meanly clad inwardly laughed, knowing the horses were of great price, yet, seeing some money, to humor his guest he went with him, and agreeing, contrary to his expectation, he paid three hundred crowns for them and brought them to the inn. Then he supposed him to be some nobleman in disguise, especially when he asked him for to help him to two servants, he designing to keep them to attend him.

But long they had not passed away the time merrily before Duke Rodolphus, who had bid money for the horses, sent for them at the merchant's price, they having differed before; but when he understood they were sold, he stormed grievously, and sent to know who it was that durst buy them out of his hands. The host told the messenger it was a stranger in plain habit newly come, which he at first did not think was capable of purchasing an ass. Whereupon he sent to apprehend him, suspecting he had committed some robbery; and notwithstanding all his excuses he could make sent him to prison and compelled him ere he could be delivered from the misery he suffered there, to deliver the horses up to him, to pay three hundred crowns as a fine set upon him, and obliged to depart his territories with an oath never to discover what passed between them.

Upon this hard hap, he went to Angers, a considerable city in that province, and there appeared very splendid at the Duke of Saxony's wedding, buying him horses and getting him servants with an extraordinary equipage, so that he passed for a nobleman, taking up the best inn, keeping company, and equally spending with the nobility and gentry of the best rank, who mightily esteemed him.

Chapter 4. How Fortunatus took acquaintance with an Irishman; how they travelled into Ireland, viewed St. Patrick's Purgatory; how they travelled to Rome and other places.

Fortunatus being at the Duke's wedding where were many princes, earls and lords, in the height of their jollity, which was very splendid, divers musicians came in to entertain them, and amongst others, one Leopold, an Irishman. They all said they'd been gentlemen bred and great travellers, but having spent their fortunes, were reduced to that employ, whereupon they gave them plentifully. And an earl asked Leopold if he would be content to live with him and be tutor to his children, but he excused it, saying, "I have left my wife and children many years, and am now desirous to see them, and in order to it am returning to my own country." Fortunatus observing the carriage and behavior of the man, when dinner was ended sent for him and contracted a strict friendship with him, plentifully relieving his necessities, and promised to go with him into Ireland, provided he would travel afterwards.

So passing through France, England, and Scotland, seeing many rarities by the way, they came to Ireland, but Leopold, through his long absence, was unknown to his wife and children till he made them sensible who he was by many tokens they had kept in memory; then they received him with joy. And Fortunatus gave an entertainment to the whole town of Waldrink. After this they went to visit St. Patrick's Purgatory, with other rarities of the country, in which descending too far into the labyrinths they were lost for three days, hearing dismal cries, meeting with strong winds and hot flashes of fire. At last, falling to their prayers, an old man, for the promise of a hundred crowns which the servants offered him in their master's name, who knew the place, went in with his pipe, found and brought them out, when all thought they had been dead or past recovery, and the priests were praying for their souls. For

Fortunatus

which good deed Fortunatus gave the man two hundred crowns, largely presented the abbot and monks that kept the chapel built on the place, and so departed.

Being now again resolved to travel, he persuaded Leopold to go along with him, which he consented to, on condition of leaving his wife and children a competency to live on, which he did, by purchasing thirty pounds a year and leaving them a thousand crowns. So they sailed over to France, and passed through divers countries till they came to Rome, and having sufficiently viewed that ancient city, with the splendor of the bishop's court, they passed from thence to Venice. And, upon notice by a Venetian merchant, of great shows of magnificence to be at Constantinople upon the Emperor's crowning his son in his stead, being weary of the government by reason of his age, they agreed with that merchant to convey them and their equipage thither, which he performed, and coming to that renowned city, one of the fairest in the world, they so dealt with the great officers for money that they had a full sight of the court and all that was rare in it.

This city, by reason of the great concourse, being full of persons of quality of divers nations, they could not hire a house, and therefore were constrained to take up in a public inn, where their host seeing them full of money and being of a thievish nature resolved to have some part with them, so that after they had been there a while, he contrived that their wax tapers, which they burned in the night, might go out, by boring holes to the wick, filling them with water, and stopping them up again. Then came he in at a private door when he knew they were asleep, and took all he could find, which was about fifty crowns. He put his hand but once into the purse, not knowing the virtue of it; yet having cut the strings by which it hung to his girdle, he threw it under the bed and so went out, leaving the doors and windows open.

In the morning when they awaked, they were in a sad taking, not so much for the money they lost as for the purse, whereupon the host hearing them make a noise came up and excused the matter in their being careless of shutting the doors and windows, when so many strangers were in the city. But the servants protested they had shut them. And the host hearing Fortunatus complain more for the purse, where he pretended there was a bill of exchange for a thousand pound, than for the money, the crafty villain, who knew well enough where it was, bid them look about, saying, "Few thieves regarded a purse or bill, for they cannot perhaps receive it," and so helping them to search, he had no sooner removed the bed but, to the great joy of Fortunatus, the purse appeared. Then privately trying and finding it had not lost its virtue though the strings were cut, remembering he had made a vow to give once a year a portion in marriage with a poor virgin of a virtuous life and conversation, he desired his host to seek out such a one, which he did; and on her he bestowed four hundred crowns, disposing of her to an honest young man who was in love with her for her beauty and virtue but declined to marry her for want of riches, lest his father should disinherit him.

The host seeing his liberality resolved to have the other bout at their purse, going in as before, but by his fumbling to find the money Leopold awaked and having his sword drawn by him struck at a venture and gave him such a cut in the neck that he fell with a dismal groan, which waked Fortunatus and his servants, who striking a light found their host weltering in his blood. Whereat Fortunatus was much abashed, remembering the former miseries he underwent on the like occasions, and thinking little to be believed whatever he said in his justification, especially in a strange place. So they laid their heads together and concluded not to stand the test, but ordering two of the servants to convey him privately into a well in the backyard, they paid their reckoning in the morning, pretending urgent business upon reading a letter one of the servants presented his master, they posted away with all speed, and passed through many countries before they thought themselves safe from pursuit.

But at length they arrived at Venice, where Fortunatus bought up a great many rich jewels, embroideries, fringes, etc., and being desirous to see his parents, sailed from thence to Cyprus. Upon his arrival he found his father and mother dead. Through sorrow for their great poverty, which much grieved him, yet that he might not be wanting in what lay in his power he built a stately monument over their graves with this epitaph:

Under this marble lies a noble pair,
Theodorius and Gratiana fair,
Who unto Fortunatus did give birth,
And then exchanged for heavenly joys their earth:
Yet mourn their loss, as I their only son,
With many tears and sighs have often done.

Fortunatus thinking now to settle in his own country built him a noble house at Famagosta, so curiously adorned that the like was not in the island. He made splendid entertainments for the King and Queen, who highly favored him and wondered whence he should be master of so great a treasure, but he kept that as a secret. At last the King advised him to marry in order to keep up a family that was so ancient and had been so honorable in the country, and proposed to him his choice of the three fair daughters of the Lord Nemina. Upon which, having seen and discoursed them, after having consulted Leopold he chose the youngest, named Cassandra, purchasing a lordship to settle for her jointure, because the countess her mother fearing he might spend what he had as his father had done would not be pleased without. The wedding was kept fourteen days with great splendor; the King, Queen, nobles, and all of any note in the island being entertained. Jousts were held for many days, in which himself always carried away the prize. Then he gave very liberal to the poor and gained good report in all places. And the first year of this happy marriage his beauteous Cassandra brought him a son, whom he named Ampedo, and the next year another, whom he named Andolocia, at whose christenings was great feasting and rejoicing, the Queen standing for godmother and the King and the Earl of Nemina for godfathers.

Chapter 5. How Leopold died; and how Fortunatus was bent to travel again, which he did in Egypt, Persia, India, etc., as a merchant, and the various adventures he met withal; how he deceived the Soldan of Egypt, of his wishing cap and returning home died, leaving his riches to his two sons, and soon after died his loving wife.

Fortunatus altering his former resolutions now began to think of travelling into other countries where he had not been (his former being mostly in Europe), and therefore reading of many rarities in other parts of the world, he resolved to have a sight of them; but whilst he was preparing for it, Leopold died. Yet upon the arrival of his wife and children, whom he had sent for, Fortunatus settled them in the country and plentifully provided for them; he likewise buried him in a decent manner, in the chancel of a new church he had built at his own cost. But when he imparted his design of travelling to his dear Cassandra, she was so grieved that she could not contain herself within the bounds of moderation, but bursting into a flood of tears, and hanging about his neck, humbly besought him not to bereave her of the greatest comfort of her life, but, if she had done anything to occasion his withdrawing from her presence, she entreated him to tell her it and she would not only beg pardon but for the future make it her study to avoid doing anything that might offend him. But gently embracing her tender body, he told her she had been the best and lovingest wife to him in the world, but that his fancy led him not to lie idling at home but to accomplish himself in knowledge by seeing strange countries, and that she need not fear but he would always have her in remembrance, and his children, those dear pledges of their nuptial love, would soon bring him back again. Whereupon hearing these and many other reasons that overcame the thoughts of the dangers she objected, her consent, though with some reluctancy, was obtained, upon promise he would return within a year; and so, leaving her, besides his estate, ten thousand crowns in ready money, in a ship he had hired for his own use he departed, resolving to turn merchant as well as traveller.

The first port he touched at was Alexandria in Egypt, where, as the custom was, he immediately went to make a present to the Soldan, which he did in such rich jewels that that mighty prince admired at it, and thereupon entertained him very nobly, sending him in requital very rich merchandise and left him at liberty to traffic in things of Egypt, above the liberty granted to other merchants, inviting him in a short space after to dinner and gave a charge concerning his freedom and entertainment in all places. So that having richly freighted his ship, he sent it by the master to Cyprus, consigned to the use of his wife and children, resolving with ten servants to travel over the land, and so taking his leave of the Soldan, who gave him letters of safe conduct directed to divers princes.

He resolved to pass over the deserts of Arabia and Persia, and so to India, taking Tartary in his way, where he had a view of the Great Cham's court at Cathay, but the people being barbarous and uncivilized in most parts of that country, he soon left it and in his way thence through a vast forest that leads toward India, he slew a monstrous tiger, who had before destroyed many hundreds of people and left the way almost unfrequented by passengers, which was scattered with the skulls and bones of those that had been devoured. This forest took up two days' and two nights' travel, and so passing through many countries, he came to India, where the mighty Emperor Prester John reigned, who, of all those countries, was the only Christian prince, that country being converted to the Christian faith by St. Thomas the Apostle. He has under him sixty-two kings, and is lord of thirty islands, besides a vast country on the continent. Here he met an old hermit, whom he plentifully relieved, and would have had him show him the country, but he told him he was bound under a vow for the Holy Land; yet he gave him an account of the manners and customs of it. So they parted, and though here strangers were forbid to enter the palace without the Emperor's leave, but Fortunatus, knowing that gold was a free passport in all places, soon by that means got admittance and beheld such riches that the like he had never seen, for the walls were plated with fine silver, whereon was engraven the stories of knights and battles of former emperors; some rooms were hung with panthers' skins, casting a fragrant smell; the pillars that supported the roof were cedar, overlaid with gold and embossed with precious stones, as diamonds, rubies, etc. Fortunatus having seen all he could obtained leave of the Emperor to depart with thirty camels laden with the richest goods of the country, having appointed his shipmaster to meet at Alexandria.

The Soldan having notice of his arrival in Egypt sent divers of his officers to meet and welcome him in his name, whom Fortunatus presented with jewels, odors, and spices, and the Soldan with many rarities. So unlading his camels, he shipped all his goods, and remembering his promise to his beloved **Cassandra,** he ordered them to weigh anchor, resolving to sail, but the Soldan desired him to partake of a banquet before he went. After which, he would needs show him his rarities in his jewel-house, which were such as were hardly to be found in the world. But whilst Fortunatus was admiring their richness, the Soldan unlocked a cabinet of gold, and pulled out of it an old hat (to all appearance) saying it was a jewel he esteemed above all the others or anything he had in the world, "for," continued he, "it has that secret virtue in it, given by a great magician long since dead, that put it upon your head and wish to be where you will, you shall be immediately carried thither invisibly." This made Fortunatus wonder, and at the same time inwardly smiled to think, if it were true he should be so weak as to reveal so important a secret to a stranger. And from that moment began to conclude if he had this to join with his purse, they would be the two greatest advantages in the world. Whereupon, having it in his hand, he clapped it on his head, and making to the window, he wished himself on board his ship, and immediately he flew out of the window as swift as lightning, and, to the amazement of the sailors, lighted on the deck without any harm. Immediately he commanded them to make all the sail they could, which they did with such speed that though they were pursued they safely reached the Isle of Cyprus.

The meanwhile the Soldan fretted and stormed exceedingly at his loss occasioned by his folly, and sent to a Venetian merchant to persuade Fortunatus to restore his wishing-hat, which he refused. Then, according to his orders, he complained of the injury done to the King of Cyprus. But he, loving Fortunatus, and siding with him, war was denounced; but whilst the preparations were making, the Soldan of age and grief for his loss died, and his son being given to pleasure those military preparations were laid aside.

Fortunatus having lived long in pleasure and plenty, his two sons being grown to men's estate, he fell sick, and calling them to him bestowed his riches on them, revealing to them the virtues of the purse and wishing-cap, how he came by them, and how the first was only for their lives, so desiring them to live lovingly together and not to part them or ever to discover the virtues of them, but use them by turns. In a most devout manner, recommending his soul into the hands of his maker, he gave up the ghost, and soon after Cassandra, through exceeding grief, falling sick of a fever, died, and both were buried in a stately tomb he had caused to be built in his lifetime in the chancel of the new church he had erected, having left bountifully to the poor and for other charitable uses.

Chapter 6. How Andolocia, the youngest son, got the purse from Ampedo, his brother, and travelled into France, Spain, England, etc. How falling in love with Agrippina, the King's fair daughter, he revealed to her the secrets of his purse; and how she got it from him; whereupon returning to Cyprus he got (by a trick) the wishing-cap.

Fortunatus and his dear consort were no sooner laid in their cold tombs but Andolocia, the youngest son, being of a rambling disposition, incited thereto by the relations he had from his father, agreed with his elder brother, though with much ado to gain his consent, that four coffers should be filled with gold out of the purse, that he should have the wishing-cap and all the visible estate, and he only the purse to bear him company in his travels. So setting forward he came to the Court of France, held then at Paris, the chief city of that kingdom; and here he appeared so splendid in his equipage and so extravagant in his expenses that he was wondered at by all, who took him for some strange prince and rather by reason of his courage, for in the jousts that were made for entertainment he unhorsed divers of the nobility. And by his often being at a poor courtier's house, he fell deeply in love with his beautiful young wife and so doted on her that, finding her coy, he tempted her with a thousand crowns for a night's lodging with her, but she being virtuous refused it and told her husband of his lascivious importunities, who, though he liked not to be a cuckold, longed for the money. And so they laid their heads together how to put a cheat upon him, the gentlewoman for a hundred crowns getting a neighbor's wife to supply her place in the dark, so that when Andolocia thought he had all night embraced the most beautiful creature living, he found by the morning light he had only a common strumpet in his arms. Wherefore vexed at and much ashamed of the trick put upon him, he immediately left the city and travelled for Spain, viewing all the rarities of the country, and at length arrived at Madrid, now the principal place in that kingdom, where the king's court was kept.

There he found them preparing for a war with Portugal, and he, never having seen any armies in the field, resolving to take this opportunity, raised a hundred men and proffered the king his service, who gratefully accepted it and made him a knight, bestowing on him rich presents, and proffered to marry him to the daughter of a marquess, but he refused that, saying he was bent on to travel to see strange lands and as yet was not disposed to marry. The wars ending, wherein he had done wonders, to his high praise and renown, he took leave of that court, and sailed for England, where in like manner he assisted the King in his wars with the Scots, behaving himself so bravely that he was taken notice of above all that fought in the field, breaking through whole squadrons and putting all to rout before him; insomuch that after the battle was over the King took him into especial favor, brought him to court again. And, one day entertaining him at dinner, he was so smitten in love with fair Princess Agrippina, the King's daughter, that he forgot to eat and feasted his eyes only on her, insomuch that great notice was taken of it. And from that time he went in the richest apparel that she might the more esteem him, and was foremost in all the jousts and tournaments. He likewise entertained the Queen and Princess at a splendid dinner, and afterwards the King, giving very liberally to the guards and servants, so that they marvelled how he, having no visible estate, could live at such a rate, and were greatly desirous to know what secret mine he had to carry on this grandeur at such a height.

This, by the advice of the King and Queen, the Princess undertook to discover, which she thought she might the better do because she perceived he was deeply in love with her, and in a little time she showed him such kindness that he was admitted to be in private with her in her chamber, a favor which none before had received. And there being none but they, he thought it was now his time to declare his passion, which he did in such obliging terms that she seemed to be pleased with, only saying, "Your lavish expenses, I fear, will bring us both to poverty, should I marry with you." He told her that could not be, for his treasure during his life was inexhaustible and could not be wasted, spend what he would. "Why, then," says she, "you are certainly the son of some great prince?" "No," said he, "I am not the son of a prince. My father is dead; his estate was equal with mine and never can be more or less." "Well," replied she, "satisfy me in this point and then perhaps I may grant you my favor, for if you love me truly, as you say you do, you will conceal nothing from me. Let me know, I say, from whence you have these great riches." "Ah," said he, "divinest lady, it was my dying father's command not to discover it to any; yet so dearly I love you that I can deny you nothing, no, if my father's ghost should now rise and forbid it, so your Highness will be pleased to promise to keep it secret."

To this she obliged herself, and he, drunk with love, thereupon showed her his purse, told her how it was come by, and all the secrets of it, letting her see it experimentally by pulling out several handfuls of gold, which he presented her with, telling her so he could do all day long and every day as long as he lived. This made her inwardly rejoice, and from that time plotted how to get it, which she effected under the color of a promise he should lie with her before marriage, if he would swear to be true to her when she had rendered up to him her virgin treasure. But, whilst he expected, with a multitude of joy, the fruition of her delicate body, she contrived with her woman to give him drugs in his wine, and so drinking him lustily, he fell fast asleep. Then turning aside his coat, she took his purse and fastened another to his girdle of the same likeness, but different in virtue, so that waking in the morning and finding himself in a chair, he began to wonder what had befallen him. But just as he remembered his assignation with Agrippina, in came her woman, who told him in a sorrowful tone that the fair princess going to bed and keeping awake in expectation of him and he deceiving her, she was risen very angry. This made him very blank and sorrowful, that he had lost an opportunity he should not reasonably expect again, supposing it done by necromancy at the instance of some of his rivals to disappoint him of his joys. And so

Fortunatus

arising, he went to his own house, being ashamed to see the Princess as fearing her reproaches, little dreaming he had lost his treasure.

By this time Agrippina had showed the purse to the King and Queen and told them the virtue of it, whereupon the King would have had it in his keeping, but the Queen told him, seeing the Princess had so fairly ventured for it, she ought to keep it. And now they resolved to put a trick upon Andolocia, whereupon the King sent to tell him he designed to come with the Queen and Princess to dine with him that day. The messenger had no sooner delivered his message and was departed, but he called his steward and bid him immediately provide provision; but he told him in the last two feasts his money was all expended and therefore he must have more. Whereupon Andolocia put his hand readily into his purse, but found nothing; when looking wishfully on it, he perceived it was changed. This made him look blank, not knowing for a time what to say or do; he knew the virtue of it was so rare that those who had it would never part with it by fair means.

And so, pretending his brother was dead, he turned off all his servants, sold his household furniture, and privately getting on shipboard, he sailed for Cyprus, telling his brother Ampedo the lamentable news of the loss of the purse, which greatly grieved him and made him blame Andolocia for his folly and the breach of his father's last commands, yet he relieved his wants plentifully. But he as badly rewarded him, for having gotten what treasure he could, he desired him to lend him his wishing-cap, but he a long time refused it, saying that it should be last reserved when all his money was spent, and he doubted not but when some great prince should come to know of its virtue but to get ten thousand pounds for it, and if he let him have it, he would lose it as foolishly as he had done the purse. To this he said nothing, but one day, desiring to see it, the other brother obliged him so far, when having it in his hand he clapped it on his head, wishing himself at Venice, and he was immediately there, leaving him to repent his folly in the loss of his cap, as he had done his in that of his purse. Being in this rich city, he found out divers Jews who were rich jewellers, and cheapening divers of great value and grasping them fast in his hand, and wishing himself in England, he was immediately carried through the air, to their great admiration, who concluded him to be no less than the Devil, and rejoiced they had taken none of his money, lest he should have come again and fetched away all their other riches.

Chapter 7. How Andolocia came to England, having cheated certain Jews of rich jewels, and counterfeiting a merchant carried away Agrippina with the purse; how she came home, both with that and his wishing-cap; how he, having got goat's horns on his head by eating of certain apples, they were taken off by a hermit; how he caused horns to grow upon Agrippina's head, carried her away, and put her into a nunnery; how he released her from thence, she being to marry the Prince of Cyprus. An account of the death of Andolocia and his brother, with the discovery and punishment of the murderers.

Being in England, he disguised himself in the habit of an Italian merchant, and going to court inquired for the Princess Agrippina. And being brought before her, he laid out his jewels and proffered her them to sale, so that in a little time they agreed. Now that which he looked for was the purse, out of which he supposed she would take the money, for he suspected she had it, and accordingly it succeeded. For going to a coffer and taking it out, she fastened it to her girdle, when he having his wishing-cap on clasped her in his arms, and wishing himself in a wild desert, away they flew together over sea and land, till they came into a vast wilderness in Ireland, and there he set her down, faint and almost breathless, under a tree on which grew very curious apples to see to. Whereupon, casting her eyes upon them, she entreated him to gather some of them to quench her thirst, for she was almost ready to perish with drought. Whereupon he, still loving her, though she had served him such a slippery trick, clapped, unadvisedly, his cap on her head to keep off the scorching sun, as knowing she knew not the virtue of it, and so climbing up, fell to gathering. In the meanwhile she sat pensive and sad, and all on a sudden wishing to God she were out of that desolate place and in her father's court, all on a sudden, contrary to her expectation, she was carried away, leaving Andolocia to fret at his folly and vex himself more than ever.

So wandering up and down, faint and weary, at length he sat down by the brook and fell to eating of his apples, when immediately a grievous pain seized his head, so that he supposed them infectious and began to fear his life; but on the contrary a great pair of goat's horns sprang out of his forehead and then the pain ceased. This made him wonder at himself and stand amazed, but as he was sad and pensive, an old hermit came to him, and seeing him a stranger and in that condition invited him to his cave, and gave him such poor refreshment as he had, which consisted of nuts, wild apples and roots, and his drink proceeded from a pleasant brook hard by. But Andolocia was more solicitous about his horns than anything else, and entreated the hermit that if he knew any way he would use it to cure him, and he would give him ten crowns, which was all the money he had left, for Agrippina had carried away the jewels as well as the hat. But though he promised to cure him, yet he refused his money, telling him he had retired from the world and the vanities of it, and money to him was useless; but going abroad, he brought home six fair apples, two of which Andolocia had no sooner eaten but his horns dropped off, which made him greatly rejoice. So the good old man bidding him give glory to God led him out of the forest and at the edge of it they parted.

Andolocia having some of the hornifying apples and likewise four of the contrary quality began to meditate revenge on Agrippina. And so, coming with all speed for

England, he changed his garb, and got an opportunity to present them to her as fruit growing in the holy garden of Jerusalem, to restore decayed beauty and keep health for several years, make the aged look young, and many other wonders. But she had no sooner eaten two of them, and finding a drowsiness, lying down to sleep and dreaming she was turned into a goat, but awaking she found a strange alteration, and going to her glass and seeing her horns, affrighted, she startled and shrieked out, whereupon her ladies came about her and were as much affrighted at the sight as she. But a grave matron, who had been her nurse, advised them to be silent, to prevent the disgrace that might follow, till physicians were consulted, whose skill might take them away. So she kept close in her chamber, and the old woman was sent to divers doctors, but none of them would undertake it at the penalty she would impose on them, which was two thousand crowns if she revealed the lady's name and they did not cure her. But as she was coming back again very pensive, Andolocia in the garb of a physician met her and told her by her sadness and coming from such a doctor's house he guessed she had some dear friend in danger of life or some other great distress, which if she would accept of his service as a physician, he would not doubt, with the blessing of God, to cure.

The old woman believing him, greatly rejoiced that she had found him so opportunely, and telling him the whole matter, which he very well knew before, conveyed him to the Princess's chamber privately at a back door, where he found her lying on her bed very pensive, but she was comforted when he told her he was come to cure her. So he began to make his application and gave her so little of the apple among the drugs that they only wasted by degrees; then telling her he wanted some costly drugs to make them come off by the roots and so she should be more beautiful than ever, she arose and went to her coffer. In the meanwhile searching about the room, he found his wishing-cap carelessly thrown under the bed, for she knew

Fortunatus

not the virtue of it, but supposed the Devil had carried her backward and forward before. By this time she called him to her to receive the money, and he drawing her toward the window so that he might, as he pretended, the better discern it, drew his hat from under his coat, clapped it on his head, grasped her in his arms, and away he flew with her, purse and all.

This caused great wailing in the court, and made the King and Queen repent she had ever meddled with the purse, verily believing Andolocia was a conjurer. In this airy voyage she was carried into Flanders, and set down in the Forest of Andevia, where presenting himself to her in his true shape, and with a stern countenance reproaching her with treachery and inconstancy, she, bathing her lovely face in tears, fell on her knees and begged his pardon. Whereupon, taking pity of her, at her request he put her into a nunnery, giving the abbess two hundred crowns for her admittance, promising to fetch her so soon as he could find a remedy to take off her horns; and so departed for Cyprus with his hat and purse, the sight of which greatly rejoiced Ampedo, to whom he told all the passage of his travels, and so extolled the beauty of Agrippina that the Prince of Cyprus, enamored on bare report, prevailed with the King his father to send an embassy to desire her in marriage. Whereupon Andolocia was solicited to free her from the nunnery, which he did, taking off her horns and carrying her through the air to London, and then returning again, ambassadors with great presents and the prince's picture were sent. And she, remembering what Andolocia had said of the beauty and virtue of that prince, consented, and so with a noble train of lords and ladies they sailed for Cyprus, where she was royally received and splendidly married, Andolocia making her presents of very rich jewels and winning the chief prize in the jousts, whereupon the Princess, as a signal of her favor, crowned him with a garland of triumph.

This made many of the nobles envy him, especially the Earls of Armandalia and Limehouse vowed his death, who had so much eclipsed their honor, and so setting on him and his six men as he passed through a wood, they and their hundred attendants after a long fight, killing his men took him prisoner, for he had not with him his wishing-cap, and casting him in a dark and loathsome dungeon, set him in the stocks and loaded him with irons to make him confess whence he had those vast riches, which through torment he discovered and gave them his purse, which they having proved thought themselves not safe whilst he was alive, because they knew he could go through the air and so might escape. And they having offered the jailer money to dispatch him and he refusing, the Earl Armandalia strangled him as he sat in the stocks. And Ampedo having in vain sought for his brother and offered great rewards for his discovery, supposing him dead, burned his wishing-cap and soon after, through grief, died. At which time the purse lost its virtue, which made the earls who kept it by turns fall out, one charging the other to have changed it, and the quarrel growing high, Limehouse called the other murderer and letting fall other words, they were both apprehended, and being racked confessed the fact, for which they were broken on the wheel.

FINIS

NOTES

Morindos
   1. shrivelled up

Moriomachia
   1. a boon companion
   2. a child's cap
   3. small cask for liquids (also a measure of capacity)
   4. pistols
   5. I would
   6. chilblains on heels
   7. I
   8. I am
   9. point of scabbard
  10. puppeteers
  11. man who earns living by giving false evidence
  12. simpleton
  13. linen
  14. a plaited skirt reaching from waist to knee
  15. swords
  16. the sour juice of green fruit
  17. became full-fledged journeymen
  18. pygmies
  19. quoit

Long Meg
   1. refresh himself by turning to something new
   2. lucky penny
   3. addicted to drink
   4. bully
   5. neck
   6. leather coat
   7. reckless fellow
   8. scoundrelly rogue

9. short sword
10. beat him with a short sword
11. vessel containing 2 quarts
12. literally, sixpence, but of course a play on words
13. court of justice
14. miser
15. a light musket
16. a bout
17. long-bladed pruning hook
18. breviary

TINKER OF TURVEY
1. Lattin is a mixed metal of yellow color; there is a play of course on the word Latin.
2. good strong ale
3. a spiced variety of mead
4. examiners or inspectors of ale
5. twice adulterated with stale urine
6. a drink made of honey and ale fermented together
7. covered boat
8. beverage made from pears, resembling cider
9. a measure of capacity
10. rogue
11. coat
12. short sword
13. louts'
14. gaiters or leggings
15. stallions
16. blows, strokes
17. fiddle
18. company
19. dormitory
20. gadfly
21. journey (or, fortune on a journey)
22. handsome
23. dearer to all
24. stand for ink and writing materials
25. occasion

MAN IN THE MOON
1. cease

2. small gold coin
3. a mole

EURIALUS AND LUCRETIA
1. The note of April is the cuckoo's song, popularly supposed to indicate that the hearer is a cuckold.
2. to beat around the bush
3. youngest
4. warrant ordering a jailer to take custody of prisoner

A SELECTED BIBLIOGRAPHY

ESDAILE, ARUNDELL. *A List of English Tales and Prose Romances Printed Before 1740.* London, 1912. (The standard bibliography of the field. For the years 1600–1700 a chronological re-arrangement of the material is available: Charles C. Mish, *English Prose Fiction, 1600–1700: A Chronological Checklist.* Charlottesville, Va., 1952.)

BELL, INGLIS F., AND DONALD BAIRD. *The English Novel, 1578–1956: A Checklist of Twentieth-Century Criticisms.* Denver, 1959.

BACKGROUND

DUNLOP, JOHN C. *History of Prose Fiction.* New ed., rev. by Henry Wilson. 2 vols. London, 1888.

WARREN, F. M. *A History of the Novel Previous to the Seventeenth Century.* New York, 1895.

HISTORIES OF ENGLISH FICTION

BAKER, ERNEST A. *The History of the English Novel.* 10 vols. London, 1923–39. (The fullest history of the novel in English, but not very good on early seventeenth-century material. Vol. I: *The Age of Romance: From the Beginnings to the Renaissance;* Vol. II: *The Elizabethan Age and After;* Vol. III: *The Later Romances and the Establishment of Realism.*)

JUSSERAND, J. J. *The English Novel in the Time of Shakespeare.* Rev. ed. London, 1899.

MORGAN, CHARLOTTE E. *The Rise of the Novel of Manners: A Study of English Prose Fiction Between 1600 and 1700.* New York, 1911.

ERNLE, ROWLAND E. PROTHERO, LORD. *The Light Reading of Our Ancestors.* London, 1927.

WRIGHT, LOUIS B. *Middle-Class Culture in Elizabethan England.* Chapel Hill, 1935. (See especially chapters 4, 11, 12.)

MACCARTHY, B. G. *Women Writers: Their Contribution to the English Novel, 1621–1744.* Cork, 1944.

COLLECTIONS

THOMS, W. J., ED. *Early English Prose Romances.* 3 vols. London, 1827–28. (Second ed., enl., 3 vols., London, 1858.)

HOPKINS, ANNETTE B., AND H. S. HUGHES, EDS. *The English Novel Before the Nineteenth Century: Excerpts from Representative Types.* Boston, 1915.

Shorter Novels. Vol. I: *Elizabethan and Jacobean,* ed. G. Saintsbury. London, 1929. Vol. II: *Jacobean and Restoration,* ed. P. Henderson. London, 1930. (Everyman's Library.)

ASHLEY, ROBERT, AND EDWIN H. MOSELEY, EDS. *Elizabethan Fiction.* (Rinehart Editions, 64.) New York, 1953.

WINNY, JAMES, ED. *The Descent of Euphues. Three Elizabethan Romance Stories.* Cambridge, 1957.

PETERSON, SPIRO, ED. *The Counterfeit Lady Unveiled, and Other Criminal Fiction of Seventeenth-Century England.* Garden City, 1961.